A HISTORY

OF PHILOSOPHY

A HISTORY
OF PHILOSOPHY

Third Edition

FRANK THILLY, 1865-1934.

Revised by

LEDGER WOOD

McCosh Professor of Philosophy, Princeton University

HOLT, RINEHART AND WINSTON

NEW YORK · CHICAGO · SAN FRANCISCO
TORONTO · LONDON

Preface to the Third Edition

THE FIRST edition of the late Professor Thilly's *A History of Philosophy* appeared over forty years ago, and an extensively revised edition appeared in 1951. Few books in the fields of philosophy or history have maintained undiminished popularity as texts and usefulness as reference works over so long a period. The remarkable vitality of Professor Thilly's work may be traced to certain features of its original conception and execution.

Perhaps the outstanding characteristic of Professor Thilly's approach to the history of philosophy was the objectivity and impartiality of his historical attitude, which escaped the distorting effect of a dogmatic interpretation of historical development. Professor Thilly allowed the philosophers to speak for themselves and, in the conviction that the later systems in the history of philosophy provide the best criticism of earlier schools, kept his own criticism to a minimum.

Professor Thilly's own two major philosophical commitments were to idealism and rationalism, but he did not allow his own philosophical biases to obtrude in his account of the historical figures with whom he dealt. Indeed, if anything, he was frequently more successful in the presentation of historical theories with which he was in disagreement than of those with which he was in sympathy. Professor Thilly's idealism was closer to the critical idealism of Kant than to the dogmatic idealism of Hegel. He considered mind an indubitable fact whose existence was guaranteed by introspective experience. His idealism was, however, not a subjectivism which denied the external world or reduced it to the status of mere appearance, and his rationalism insisted that experience, or nature, has rational structure and coherence which render it intelligible to man's rational mind. His was not a dogmatic rationalism of the Cartesian variety which posits innate, self-evident truths, but rather a critical rationalism, which considers the basic truths of mathematics and the underlying assumptions of science and philosophy to be indispensable presuppositions of an intelligible world.

A second feature of the book which explains its sustained success is the sense of proportion displayed in the presentation of thinkers in their place in philosophical movements. Without adopting an Hegelian dialectic of the history of philosophy, Thilly discerned an inner logic in historical development. Individual thinkers were integrated to movements, and the movements in their turn formed parts of a larger historical pattern. His recognition of the inner logic of the historical process did not, however, prevent his giving due recognition to the social, political, cultural, and personal or temperamental factors which influence individual philosophers. Thilly's assimilation of philosophers to movements was particularly skillful in his organization of the modern period. Bacon and Hobbes were grouped together as two relatively independent figures who, while not properly part of the British empiricism of Locke, Berkeley, and Hume, prepared the way for it. Descartes and Spinoza were considered together as the founders of continental rationalism, and Leibniz, instead of being included, as was customary, as the third in the triumvirate of rationalists, was introduced after British empiricism as a philosopher of the enlightenment.

A third feature was the clarity and simplicity of Professor Thilly's style. In discussing with me the composition of his history Professor Thilly told me that the book grew out of a study of the history of philosophy written with no intention of publication, but solely for the purpose of clarifying his own understanding of the historical philosophers and their relations to one another. This clarification which Thilly achieved for himself pervades the entire exposition.

Professor Thilly's interest in the history of philosophy was not that of the historical antiquarian who seeks merely to record the achievements of the past, nor was it primarily that of the historian of ideas who merely traces the continuous history of ideas and conceptions. It was that of the philosopher who seeks philosophical illumination in the history of his subject. He thought of the history of philosophy as a repository of philosophical ideas from which the philosopher draws his materials and his insights. He rejected the study of the history of philosophy merely for its own sake, but at the same time deplored the pseudo-originality of those who are ignorant of the philosophical achievements of the past. The study of the history of philosophy, he said in his introduction, "serves as a useful preparation to philosophical speculation, passing, as it does, from the simpler to the more complex and difficult constructions of thought. . . . The man who tries to construct a system of philosophy in absolute independence of the work of his predecessors cannot hope to rise very far beyond the crude theories of the beginnings of civilization." This, Professor Thilly conceived to be the value of this historical study for himself, and this is the value he hoped it would have for his readers. I have tried in both revisions to preserve the objective and impartial attitude of the original, and have retained the basic organization except when modification seemed to be indicated by the altered historical perspective.

The expanded "Introduction" of the third edition emphasizes the relation of the history of philosophy to the social, cultural and historical contexts in which the systems of philosophy arise; the decisive rôle played by the temperament of the individual philosopher in determining the character of his system; and the value of the historical study of philosophy. In Part One on Greek Philosophy, the religious sources of Greek philosophy have been traced, in the light of the work of such histories as Cornford's and Jaeger's, to indicate more clearly how Greek philosophy emerged from Greek religion and the essential differences between philosophy and the religion from which it arose. In the section on Plato (Section 9) the results of recent stylometric investigations concerning the order of the Platonic dialogues have been incorporated and new material on the "Hierarchy of the Sciences," "Cosmology," and the "Doctrine of Immortality" has been included. In the section on Aristotle (Section 10), "The Four Causes" and "Aristotle's Genius and Influence" has been added. In Part Two, the general sections on medieval and scholastic philosophy (especially Sections 17 and 22) have been rewritten in order to provide a more adequate transition from the ancient to the medieval period, and also to afford a preliminary survey of the nature and problems of scholasticism.

Extensive changes and additions have been made in Part Three, on "Modern Philosophy." The chapter on the "Philosophy of the Renaissance," which Professor Thilly placed in Part Two in the context of the decline of Scholasticism, was reoriented and transferred in the revised editions to Part Three, where it serves as a transition to the modern period. The concluding chapters dealing with recent and contemporary philosophy (Chapters XX-XXII) are, with the exception of brief passages drawn from Professor Thilly's text, entirely new. In Chapter XX on "Idealistic Tendencies in Recent Philosophy," new sections on Kierkegaard, Heidegger and Jaspers were added in the second edition and sections on Bosanquet, McTaggart, Croce, Gentile, and Sartre in the present edition. Chapter XXI on "Realistic Tendencies in Recent Philosophy" consists almost entirely of new material prepared for the second edition, to which I have added in the present revision an introductory section on "The Realistic Tradition," and new sections on

Whitehead's cosmology and on the philosophy of George Santayana. Chapter XXII on "Pragmatism, Positivism and Analytical Philosophy" has been considerably expanded in the present revision.

The section on Immanuel Kant, which was considerably expanded in the second edition in order to clarify Kant's philosophical method and to differentiate it more sharply from the methods of empiricism and rationalism, remains unchanged in the third edition. The present edition also retains the comprehensive account of Nietzsche written by Professor Walter Kaufmann (Section 66) which considers Nietzsche in the historical context of German philosophy rather than, as did Professor Thilly's treatment, in the context of contemporary pragmatism. A new section on the "Utilitarianism of Bentham" has been added in the third edition.

The contemporary period is, of course, the most difficult for the historian of philosophy, just as it is for the general historian. The detachment and temporal perspective requisite to the historical enterprise are unattainable, and the historian cannot be confident that his decisions regarding the inclusion and exclusion of contemporary figures and the apportionment of space to contemporary movements will seem justified even for the next decade. He cannot, however, avoid exercising the historian's prerogative of deciding which tendencies and figures of the present are likely to find a place in future histories of philosophy. Professor Thilly was remarkably successful in appraising the contemporary state of philosophy in 1914, and it is hoped that the present revision of his work achieves an equally adequate appraisal of the philosophy of the present.

L. W.

Princeton, New Jersey
October 16, 1956

Acknowledgments

THE ENTHUSIASTIC assistance of colleagues, friends, and members of my family, which I received at every stage in the preparation of the revised edition, made it in a very real sense a cooperative volume. Most of all, I appreciated the constant encouragement of Mrs. Thilly, who felt that I was especially qualified to undertake the revision because of my close personal association with Professor Thilly, an association which began during my undergraduate years at the University of California, and continued while I was a graduate student at Cornell. In the revision of Parts One and Two, on Ancient and Medieval Philosophy, Professor Edward Pols, my former colleague at Princeton, now of Bowdoin College, prepared the new subsections, "The Religious Origins of Greek Philosophy," and "Scholasticism: Its Nature and Problems." My colleague, Professor Walter A. Kaufman, wrote the new section on Nietzsche, which incorporates the interpretation of Nietzsche contained in his highly suggestive volume, *Nietzsche: Philosopher, Psychologist, Antichrist,* published by the Princeton University Press in 1950. My former colleague, Professor Robert M. Scoon, of the Department of Philosophy at Princeton, who used the first edition as a text in his course in the history of ancient and medieval philosophy, made invaluable suggestions for strengthening the sections on ancient philosophy, particularly those on Stoicism and Epicureanism. My wife undertook the arduous task of typing the new material of the second edition, and Mrs. Harley Funk, former secretary of the Princeton philosophy department, spent many tedious hours during the summer of 1950 assembling the manuscript.

In preparing this third edition I have had the same sort of assistance from colleagues, family and friends. I am especially grateful to my present colleague, Professor Gregory Vlastos, who in the light of his experience in using the second edition of the text at Cornell University and later at Princeton University suggested additions to the section on "Plato." The task of assembling and typing the manuscript was ably performed, during the summer of 1956, by Miss Phebe Fleming, secretary of the Princeton philosophy department, and Miss Marjorie Griffin, a student at Ohio Wesleyan University.

The excerpts from my essay, "The Transcendental Method," are included in the chapter on Kant with the kind permission of the Princeton University Press, and the paragraphs on "Recent American Realism" are reproduced from my chapter in *A History of Philosophical Systems,* with the permission of the Philosophical Library. I am also indebted to my former undergraduate research assistant, Mr. Arthur Clements of the Princeton class of 1954, who assisted me in assembling material on French existentialism. In the revision of the concluding chapters on contemporary philosophy I have received helpful suggestions from two of my younger colleagues in the Princeton philosophy department, Mr. Hugo Bedau and Mr. Sylvain Bromberger. In the concluding chapters, I have made use of extensive notes which I assembled in the course of preparation of the articles on "Philosophy" appearing in *The American Yearbook* for the years 1939 to 1945, and the article on "George Santayana" for inclusion in the *Encyclopædia Britannica.*

Contents

PART THREE. MODERN PHILOSOPHY

Introduction

The history of philosophy aims to give a connected account of the different attempts which have been made to solve the problem of existence, or to render intelligible to us our world of experience. It is the story of the development of reasoned human thought from its earliest beginnings down to the present time; not a mere chronological enumeration and exposition of philosophical theories, but a study of these in their relations to one another, the times in which they were produced, and the thinkers by whom they were offered. While every system of thought is more or less dependent on the civilization in which it arises, the character of preceding systems, and the personality of its author, it in turn exercises a potent influence on the conceptions and institutions of its own and succeeding ages. The history of philosophy must endeavor to insert each world-view in its proper setting, to connect it with the intellectual, political, moral, social, and religious factors of its present, past, and future. It must also attempt to trace the line of progress in the history of human speculation, to show how the mental attitude called philosophy arises, how the different problems and the solutions that are offered provoke new questions and answers, and to determine what advance has been made, at each stage.

Philosophy and Temperament. Philosophical systems are not the products of purely intellectual activity occurring in a personal, historical and cultural vacuum; they are instead the achievements of individual philosophical geniuses which reflect not only the temperaments and personalities of their authors but likewise the cultural, historical, and philosophical milieu in which they lived. Every system is the point of convergence of innumerable influences which determine both the doctrinal import and the structural organization of that system. Some of these influences are purely intellectual and philosophical, as is the case when a philosopher consciously or unconsciously incorporates into his philosophy conceptions and doctrines transmitted to him by his philosophical predecessors and modifies them for the sake of logical consistency or to conform to prevailing scientific theories or to satisfy

I

the demands of moral, religious and aesthetic experience. But there is another formative influence of a philosophical system, which the historian of philosophy cannot ignore, and this includes the personality of the philosopher as indicated by his biography and the social and cultural context in which his philosophy arose. To the question: "Why did a certain philosopher develop such and such philosophical doctrines organized into a system having a distinctive structure and organization?" the reply follows either of two lines: the one consists of an enumeration of the personal and cultural factors which produced the system; the other is an examination of the logical, factual, and distinctively philosophical considerations which led the philosopher to adopt his position. These two types of "explanation" of a system are mutually complementary, and both are essential to the understanding of any historical system of philosophy. The historical genesis and personal motivation of a philosophy frequently afford important clues to its philosophical meaning and logical organization.

The purely historical or genetic type of interpretation of a philosophy frequently involves the disentangling of a great complexity of biographical, social, political, and cultural influences. The personal or temperamental factor is of supreme importance in philosophy, since a system of philosophy is the product of the creative thinking of an individual mind and is seldom, if ever, the achievement of any group consciousness; a system of philosophy is perhaps more an individual and personal achievement and less a social product than is a scientific theory or a technological discovery. The biography of a Newton or an Einstein throws little essential light on the understanding of the laws of gravitation or the relativity theory, but the pantheistic naturalism of a Spinoza or the voluntaristic idealism of a Schopenhauer lose much of their significance if divorced from the personalities of their authors. A system of philosophy reflects the personality of its author, and its meaning can only be fully appreciated in this personal context. In this respect, philosophical systems are closer to systems of ethics and religion and the products of artistic, musical, and literary creation than to scientific theories or the products of technology and invention.

That a philosophy reflects and is connected with the personality and temperament of its author is now acknowledged by all except the most extreme of intellectualists. The temperamentalist thesis that "temperament is a factor in all philosophizing" is persuasively defended in the first lecture of William James' *Pragmatism*: "The history of philosophy," says James, "is to a great extent that of a certain clash of human temperaments." [1] The particular dif-

---

[1] *Pragmatism*, p. 6.

ference of the temperament, which in James' view pervades not only philosophy, but literature, art, government, and manners, is a contrast between rationalist or "tender-minded" and empiricist or "tough-minded," between "the lover of facts in all their crude variety" and "the devotee to abstract and eternal principles." [2] The tender-minded are on the whole rationalistic, intellectualistic, idealistic, optimistic, religious, free-willist, monistic, and dogmatical; the tough-minded are empiricist, sensationalistic, materialistic, pessimistic, irreligious, pluralistic, and skeptical. The interpretation of the history of philosophy as a clash between the tender-minded rationalists (Plato, Aristotle, St. Thomas Aquinas, Descartes, Leibniz, and Hegel) and the tough-minded empiricists (Democritus, Hobbes, Bacon, and Hume) is a gross oversimplification: some of the most important figures of the history of philosophy—for example, Spinoza, Locke and Berkeley—straddle this classification by combining some traits which James lists as the tender-minded with others which he lists as the tough-minded. Thus Spinoza qualifies as tender-minded in being intellectualistic and religious, and tough-minded in being materialistic and fatalistic. Berkeley conforms to the tender-minded formula in that he is idealistic, religious, and free-willist, but is tough-minded in his empiricism: as James himself observes, "few of us are tender-foot Bostonians pure and simple, and few are typical Rocky Mountain toughs, in philosophy," yet the antagonism between the two temperamental types "has formed in all ages a part of the philosophical atmosphere of the time." [3]

The term temperament, despite its psychological vagueness and imprecision, serves to focus attention on a diversity of affective, volitional, and imaginative traits of the philosopher's personality which are reflected in his philosophy. The temperamentalist interpretation of the history of philosophy is thus a corrective and an antidote to the traditional dogma that philosophers—and to a lesser degree the rest of mankind—possess an identical and invariant intellect which discloses to each in proportion to his intellectual capacities the absolute truth about reality, untinctured by his personal peculiarities and temperamental preferences. Temperament provides the drive and motivation of a philosophy and determines its general flavor and complexion: a philosophy tends to be naturalistic or idealistic, rationalistic or sensationalistic, optimistic or pessimistic, theistic or atheistic according to the temperamental predilections of the author. This is not to deny that a philosopher's temperamental preferences may be counteracted by the operation of non-

[2] *Op. cit.*, pp. 9 ff.
[3] *Op. cit*, p. 13.

temperamental influences, for example, the impact of an intellectual tradition or the coerciveness of a logical argument, with the consequence that a temperamental idealist finds himself under exceptional circumstances committed to a philosophical naturalism, or a temperamental naturalist to idealism. The sole claim of the temperamentalist interpretation of philosophy is that other factors being invariant, temperament is determinative of philosophical commitments.

Philosophy and the Cultural Milieu. The personal and temperamental factors operative in the thinking of a philosopher are modified, supplemented and perhaps counteracted by numerous social, cultural, and historical influences. The dependence of philosophy upon the general intellectual, cultural, social, and political climate of opinion in which it arises is indubitable; the philosophy of any historical period affords an index of the cultural state of that age or of the immediately preceding age, as there is often a time-lag between culture and its philosophical expression. This philosophical index of culture is perhaps as adequate as any single cultural manifestation, not excepting art, science and technology. The relation between philosophy and the cultural milieu is not, however, only one of dependence of philosophy on cultural environment; philosophy also reacts on the other aspects of culture. A philosophy is both a product of the contemporaneous and preceding cultures and a decisive formative influence on the social and cultural achievements of the ages which follow.

In the analysis of the complex which constitutes the social and cultural setting of a given historical system of philosophy, the following principal ingredients are distinguishable: (1) the actual political constitution of the state in which the philosopher lives and formulates his philosophy, and more particularly the position which the philosopher happens to occupy in the political framework of his time; (2) the general structure of the social and economic framework of the society of which the philosopher is a part, as well as the particular social and economic status of the individual philosopher within that framework; (3) cultural influences of a non-philosophical sort, including the religious, moral, scientific, artistic, and technological features of his own era or of past historical eras, the cultures of which he has assimilated; and finally (4) the influence upon the individual philosopher of the *philosophical* theories of his contemporaries and his immediate and remote historical predecessors. Past and contemporaneous philosophical traditions, movements, and individual systems are as much parts of the total intellectual and cultural environment of the individual philosopher as are his social, political, religious, scientific, and artistic heritages.

The Rôle of Criticism. In dealing with the different systems, we shall allow the authors to present their ideas without extensive criticism on our part. The history of philosophy is, in a large measure, its own best critic; a system is incorporated, transformed, supplemented, or superseded by its successors, its errors and inconsistencies are brought to light, and it is often made the starting-point of new lines of thought. The historian should assume, so far as he can, an impartial and objective attitude in his study, and guard against injecting his own philosophical theories into the discussions. It is, however, impossible to eliminate the personal element altogether: to some extent the historian's preconceptions inevitably shine through his work. They manifest themselves in many ways: in the emphasis which he places on particular philosophies, in his conception of what constitutes progress and decline, even in the amount of space devoted to different thinkers. All this is unavoidable. Each philosopher, however, should be permitted to tell his own story without being interrupted by constant objections before he has had the opportunity of stating his case completely, and we should not criticize a system solely in the light of present achievement, that is, measure it by present standards to its detriment. Compared with modern theories, the early Greek world-views seem naïve, childish, and crude, and it would be no great mark of intelligence to ridicule them; whereas, considered in the context of their times, as the first efforts of a people to understand the world, they may well stand out as epoch-making events. A system of thought must be judged in the light of its own aims and historical setting, by comparison with the systems immediately preceding and following it, by its antecedents and results, by the development to which it leads.

Our method of study will, therefore, be both historical and critical. The guiding principles of this critical-historical method are: (1) The attempt should be made to understand each philosophical system in its integrity, that is to say, the philosophical historian should for the time being enter sympathetically into the doctrinal insights of each system, and seek to grasp the system as a structural whole. (2) The attempt should be made to formulate the logically basic assumptions of the system—not merely those which are explicitly promulgated by the philosopher, and which are often relatively unimportant, but more especially the implicit or tacit presuppositions of the system. The discernment of the tacit assumptions of a philosophy is no mere routine performance, but is an exacting task requiring philosophical discernment and penetration. Assistance in this task is frequently gained from a study of later philosophers in the same movement or tradition. For example, Hume succeeded in making explicit the basic assumptions of empiricism which were only implicit or at best vaguely adumbrated in the empiricism of Locke, and, again, Leibniz discerned more clearly than his predecessor, Descartes, the basic tenets of rationalism. (3) Each system should be subjected to rigorous philosophical criticism, *first,* of an *internal* sort calculated to reveal fundamental inconsistencies either between the different assumptions of the system, whether implicit or explicit, or between the assumptions and the alleged implications of these assumptions and *secondly,* of an *external* sort which discloses the limitations and inadequacies of a given system when it is judged by the standards of a richer and more profound philosophy or by reference to phases of human knowledge and experience to which it fails to do justice. Such criticism should not, however, be allowed to intrude into and interfere with the exposition of the system: the system should be understood before it is subjected to criticism either of an internal or external sort. Philosophy in one of its very important aspects is criticism of past systems.

The Value of the History of Philosophy. The value of the study of the history of philosophy should be apparent to everyone. Intelligent persons are interested in the fundamental problems of existence, and in the answers which the human race has sought to find for them at the various stages of civilization. Besides, such a study helps men to understand their own age and other times; it throws light on the ethical, religious, political, legal, and economic conceptions of the past and the present by revealing the underlying principles which they presuppose. It likewise serves as a useful preparation for philosophical speculation: passing, as it does, from the simpler to the more complex and difficult constructions of thought, it reviews the philosophical experience of the race and trains the mind in abstract thinking.

The study of past theories is, further, an indispensable aid in working out one's own views of the world and of life. This is because philosophy, to a far greater extent than other forms of creative activity, presupposes a thorough historical orientation. The scientist can successfully pursue his original researches, provided he has at his disposal only an essential grasp of the *present* state of knowledge in his chosen field of investigation; a creative artist having a very limited acquaintance with the general history of art may, nevertheless, achieve greatness in his art; but the man who tries to construct a system of philosophy in absolute independence of the work of his predecessors cannot hope to rise very far beyond the crude theories of the beginnings of civilization. The history of philosophy, when properly understood, is a great repository of the philosophical insights of the past which provides materials indispensable to the constructive philosopher.

But though the creative philosopher derives much from a study of the history of his subject, philosophy would soon become a barren and futile pursuit were each generation of philosophers to derive its materials and its data solely from the study of the history of philosophy. The creative philosopher must enrich traditional conceptions and insights derived from the history of philosophy with new concepts suggested by science, art, literature, politics, morals and other phases of contemporary culture. The philosopher, since he has at his disposal no distinctive set of "philosophical data" comparable to scientific data afforded the scientist by the employment of the experimental method, derives his materials on the one hand from other contemporary disciplines, and on the other from the history of philosophy. Thus the history of philosophy affords not only a summary of the past achievements of philosophers, but the indispensable materials for future philosophic enquiry.

Primary and Secondary Sources. The sources of our study will be: (1) *Primary sources:* the works of the philosophers themselves or the fragments of their writings, when only the latter are extant. (2) In the absence of either of these, we have to depend for our knowledge of their teachings on the most trustworthy and accurate accounts of them by others. Among the sources which will help us here are expositions of the lives and doctrines of particular philosophers, general and special treatises on the history of philosophy, criticisms of certain teachings, and references to them in various books. Such *secondary sources* are indispensable where the primary sources have disappeared and may even be of value when the primary sources are available. The historian of philosophy will also appeal to whatever fields of research give him an understanding of the spirit of the times under examination: to the history of all human activities, such as science, literature, art, morals, education, politics, and religion.

Scope and Periods. A universal history of philosophy would include the philosophies of all peoples. Not all peoples, however, have produced real systems of thought, and the speculations of only a few can be said to have had a history. Many do not rise beyond the mythological stage. Even the theories of Oriental peoples, the Hindus, Egyptians, and Chinese, consist, in the main, of mythological and ethical doctrines, and are rarely complete systems of thought: they are pervaded with poetry and faith. We shall, therefore, limit ourselves to a study of the Western countries, and begin with the philosophy of the ancient Greeks, on whose culture our own civilization, in large part, rests. We shall follow the customary classification of historical periods and divide our field into Ancient Philosophy, Medieval or Christian Philosophy, and Modern Philosophy.

Works on the History of Philosophy: W. Windelband, *A History of Philosophy,* trans. by J. H. Tufts, 2nd ed., 1901; W. Turner, *History of Philosophy,* 1903; H. E. Cushman, *A Beginner's History of Philosophy,* 1920; C. C. J. Webb, *A History of Philosophy,* 1915; A. Weber, *History of Philosophy* (trans. by F. Thilly), with *Philosophy since 1800,* by R. B. Perry, 1925; A. K. Rogers, *A Student's History of Philosophy,* 1926; G. Boas, *The Major Traditions of European Philosophy,* 1929; T. G. Duval, *Great Thinkers,* 1937; S. G. Martin, G. H. Clark, F. P. Clarke and C. I. Ruddick, *A History of Philosophy,* 1941; B. Russell, *A History of Western Philosophy,* 1945; F. Copleston, *A History of Philosophy,* 1947; W. P. Montague, *Great Visions of Philosophy,* 1950; V. Ferm, ed., *A History of Philosophical Systems,* 1950; R. A. Tsanoff, *The Great Philosophers,* 1953; B. A. G. Fuller, *A History of Philosophy,* 3rd ed., rev. by S. M. McMurrin, 1955; C. Brinton, *Ideas and Men: The Story of Western Thought,* 1950; S. P. Lamprecht, *Our Philosophical Traditions: A Brief History of Philosophy in Western Civilization,* 1955.

More advanced works: F. Ueberweg, *History of Philosophy,* 3 vols., trans. by G. S. Morris, 1905; J. E. Erdmann, *A History of Philosophy,* 3 vols., trans. by W. S. Hough, 1910; P. Janet and G. Séailles, *Histoire de la philosophie: Les problèmes et les écoles,* 14th ed., 1928; *Supplément Période Contemporaine,* 1929; P. Masson-Oursel, *La philosophie comparée,* 1923, 2nd ed., 1931; A. O. Lovejoy, *The Great Chain of Being,* 1936; E. Bréhier, *Histoire de la philosophie,* 5th ed., 1938; N. P. Stallknecht and R. S. Brumbaugh, *The Spirit of Western Philosophy,* 1950; W. T. Jones, *A History of Western Philosophy,* 1952; G. Lehmann, *Geschichte der Philosophie,* 2 vols., 1953.

Histories of special subjects: Logic and Theory of Knowledge: R. Adamson, *Short History of Logic,* 1911; L. W. Keeler, *The Problem of Error from Plato to Kant,* 1934; Esthetics: B. Bosanquet, *History of Aesthetics,* 1892. Ethics: J. Martineau, *Types of Ethical Theory,* 2nd ed., 1886; H. Sidgwick, *Outlines of the History of Ethics,* 1892; J. Watson, *Hedonistic Theories from Aristippus to Spencer,* 1895; F. Paulsen, *System of Ethics,* ed. and trans. by F. Thilly (contains survey of history of ethics, pp. 33-215), 1899; A. K. Rogers, *Short History of Ethics,* 1911, and *Morals in Review,* 1927; R. A. Tsanoff, *The Moral Ideals of Our Civilization,* 1942. Politics: F. Pollock, *History of the Science of Politics,* 1883; W. A. Dunning, *History of Political Theories,* 1902-23; C. H. McIlwain, *The Growth of Political Thought in the West,* 1932; G. H. Sabine, *A History of Political Theory,* 1937; C. M. Andrews, *Famous Utopias,* 1937; H. Cairns, *Legal Philosophies from Plato to Hegel,* 1949. Science: H. F. Osborn, *From the Greeks to Darwin,* 1894; E. Dodd, *Pioneers of Evolution from Thales to Huxley,* 1897; W. Libby, *An Introduction to the History of Science,* 1917; F. A. Lange, *History of Materialism,* 3 vols., trans. by E. C. Thomas, 1925; G. Sarton, *Introduction to the History of Science,* Vol. II, 1927; B. Ginsburg, *The Adventure of Science,* 1930; C. Singer, *A Short History of Science,* 1941; L. Thorndike, *History of Magic and the Experimental Sciences,* 1941; W. C. Dampier, *A History of Science and Its Relation with Philosophy and Religion,* 3rd ed., 1942; M. P. Rousseau, *Histoire de la Science,* 1945; E. T. Bell, *The Development of Mathematics,* 2nd ed., 1945.

Dictionaries of philosophy: D. D. Runes, ed., *Dictionary of Philosophy,* 1942; A. Lalande, *Vocabulaire technique et critique de philosophie,* 5th ed., 1947.

Selections from the writings of philosophers: T. V. Smith, ed., *Philosophers Speak for Themselves,* 1935; I. Erdman and H. W. Schneider, *Landmarks for Beginners in Philosophy,* 1941; W. Sellars and J. Hospers, *Readings in Ethical Theory,* 1952.

PART ONE

Greek Philosophy

1
Philosophy of Nature

1. Origin and Development of Early Greek Thought

History of Greek Philosophy. Few of the ancient peoples advanced far beyond the mythological stage, and perhaps none of them can be said to have developed a genuine philosophy except the Greeks. It is for this reason that we begin our account with them. They not only laid the foundations upon which all subsequent systems of Western thought have been reared, but formulated nearly all the problems and suggested nearly all the answers with which European civilization occupied itself for two thousand years. Their philosophy is one of the best examples that any people has furnished of the evolution of human thinking from simple mythological beginnings to complex and comprehensive systems. The spirit of independence and the love of truth which animated their thinkers have never been surpassed and rarely equaled. For these reasons the study of Greek philosophy ought to be an attractive and valuable discipline to the student interested in higher speculative thought.

By the history of Greek philosophy we mean the intellectual movement which originated and developed in the Hellenic world. We shall include in it, however, not only the systems of the Greeks themselves, but also those which exhibit the essential features of Greek thinking and which are manifestly the products of Hellenic civilization, whether they flourish at Athens, Rome, Alexandria, or in Asia Minor.

Environment. The people whose philosophy we are to study inhabited the mountain peninsula of Greece, a territory whose natural characteristics were favorable to the development of a strong and active race, and whose many harbors, while encouraging navigation and commerce, furnished an outlet for emigration over the islands to the lands beyond. Greek colonies were

11

established in an unbroken chain from the mainland to the coasts of Asia Minor and, eventually, to Egypt, Sicily, southern Italy, and the Pillars of Hercules; without losing touch with the mother country, these colonies enjoyed the benefits which active contact with peoples of different customs, traditions, and institutions is apt to bring. The wonderful economic progress resulting from such conditions, the development of commerce, industry, and trade, the rise of cities, the accumulation of wealth, and the increasing division of labor exercised a profound influence on the social, political, intellectual, and religious life of the entire Greek world and opened the way to a new and richer civilization. This physical and human environment helped to stimulate both intellect and will; it gave men a broader outlook upon life and the world, quickened the spirit of criticism and reflection, led to the development of unique personalities, and made possible a varied progress along all lines of human thought and action. To a people naturally endowed with keen and quick intelligence, a burning thirst for knowledge, a fine sense of beauty, and practical energy and ambition, it supplied the materials upon which to try its powers and talents; and enabled it to make rapid progress in the field of politics, religion, morals, literature, and philosophy.

Politics. The political fortunes of the Hellenic city-states, on the mainland and in the colonies, exhibit certain common characteristics: we find everywhere an evolution from patriarchal monarchy through aristocracy to democracy. The society described by the Homeric epics is a caste society and the form of government a patriarchal monarchy. The acquisition of wealth and culture by the few leads to the establishment of aristocratic forms of government and, as time goes on, to the rise of oligarchies. With changing social conditions, a citizen class (the Demos) arises and begins to dispute the leadership of the privileged class. The transition from aristocracy to democracy, during the seventh and sixth centuries B.C., is accomplished through the efforts of bold and ambitious men who wrest the power from the lords and establish "tyrannies" throughout the Hellenic world. In the end, the people themselves assume the reins of government, and tyranny gives way to democracy.

Literature. We may view these changing social and political conditions as the result of the awakening of the Greek consciousness. The new movement is both a symptom and a cause of enlightenment: it is the outward sign of growing reflection and criticism of the traditional; it issues in a protest against the old institutions and in a demand for reform. The history of Greek literature before the sixth century B.C. reveals the development of a spirit of reflection and criticism similar to that expressing itself in political life. The Homeric cheerfulness and objectivity, reflecting the naïveté of childhood, gradually disappear; the poets become less optimistic, more critical and subjective. Even in Homer we find occasional moral reflections on the behavior of men, the foolishness of mortals, the misery and transitoriness of life, and the wickedness of injustice. In Hesiod the note of criticism and pessimism grows louder; his *Works and Days* is a moral handbook that attacks the foibles of the age and offers moral maxims and practical rules of life, praising the homespun virtues and lamenting the decline of the good old days. In mournful and satiric strain, poets of the seventh century (Alcaeus, Simonides, Archilochus) decry the rise of the *tyrannis* and deplore the weakness of men, urging them, however, to bear their lot bravely and to leave the outcome to the gods. The didactic and pessimistic spirit is still more marked in the poetry of the sixth century; the political fortunes of the people are made the subject of comment, and the new order of things is condemned, often with great bitterness. To this period belong the fable-writer Aesop and the so-called *gnomic* poets (Solon, Phocylides, Theognis), whose wise maxims embodying ethical reflections may be characterized as an embryonic moral philosophy. The individual is beginning to analyze and criticize life—not merely living it. He is pondering its meaning and is no longer content to give voice to the traditional concepts and ideals of his race, but is prompted to set forth his own personal ethical, political, and religious thoughts and yearnings. Eventually this spirit of inquiry and discontent, which results from larger and more complex experiences, culminates in a philosophical study of human conduct in the form of theories of ethics and politics.

Religious Origins of Greek Philosophy. The religious life of the Greeks is of peculiar importance for a study of the history of their philosophy; but the relations between religion and philosophy in the Greek world are as complicated as they are intimate. The interplay between Greek religion and philosophy is complicated by the fact that Greek religion has two major aspects: (1) In its first aspect, it is the anthropomorphic religion of the gods of Olympus, made familiar by the Homeric epics in which the gods exhibit, although on a most majestic scale, human passions and a concern for the affairs of men. (2) The second aspect of Greek religion, which becomes prominent in the religious revival of the sixth century, B.C., is associated with the so-called mystery cults. Greek religion in its anthropomorphic aspect undergoes a long and refining development from the earliest times until the culmination of Greek civilization in the fifth and fourth centuries B.C., and this development is intricately related to that of philosophy.

The development of the concept of Zeus, who is supreme among the gods, well illustrates the interpenetration of philosophic and religious ideas. In Homer, Zeus is, like the other gods, subject to fate, but some centuries later, in the dramas of Aeschylus, fate itself has come to be identified with the supreme will of Zeus. The religion of the Olympian gods has influenced philosophy, only to be influenced in turn by conceptions developed independently by philosophy. The Homeric conception of the gods as subject to fate may have contributed to the attitude of mind that produced the first Greek philosophy: the so-called Milesian natural philosophy of the sixth century B.C. Unquestionably the subsequent development of the Milesian philosophy, together with the philosophies of Pythagoras, Parmenides, and Heraclitus, which were influenced by the new and quite different religiosity of the sixth century, furnished an intellectual background for the monotheistic tendency we find in the Zeus of Aeschylus. These and many other diverse influences mingle in the philosophic monotheism of Plato and Aristotle in the fourth century B.C.

When philosophy became clearly differentiated from other elements of Greek intellectual life, the religious spirit of a certain period is frequently expressed as much in its philosophy as in the utterance of cult or myth. Indeed, Greek religion, because it lacked a highly organized and specialized form, often expressed its theology in art, poetry, and philosophy. Typical of the interpenetration of all these diverse aspects of Greek culture is the fusion of poetry and the religion of the Olympian gods in the Homeric poems.

Speculation about the gods becomes more intellectualized in Hesiod, the second in the procession of Greek poets. His *Theogony,* which has been placed in the eighth century B.C., is representative of a group of epic poems in which the attempt is made for the first time to account for the phenomena of the world in terms of the divine beings, of the traditional mythology. Indeed, such works in so far as they deal with the structure of the universe present a *cosmology;* in their concern with the nature of the gods they contain a *theology;* and in offering accounts of the origin of the world and of the gods they provide a *cosmogony* and *theogony.* According to Hesiod, even the gods came into being. In his cosmogony and theogony, he declares that even Chaos or empty space, which existed before all other things, itself came into being. After Chaos, Heaven and Earth came to be; and Eros, or Love—himself coeval with Heaven and Earth—then brought about their union. From this union there issued in turn a whole series of unions engendered by the power of Eros in which the natural forces of the world receive a poetic and mythological explanation. Darkness and Night together generate Day, and the Earth, fructified by Heaven, gives birth to the rivers. The Titans are the progeny of the marriage of Heaven and Earth, and they are eventually superseded by the more orderly powers represented by Zeus and the other Olympians. Aristotle speaks of Hesiod and those like him as early and primitive theologians, and contrasts their method with that of the first philosophers, pointing out that the writers of the theogonies promulgated doctrines and attempted explanations in mythical form, while the first philosophers proceeded by methods of strict proof. The theogonies, though not properly philosophy, prepared the ground for it. They represent an advance toward rational explanation in comparison with the purely mythological approach of Homer: the Eros of Hesiod, which governs the generation and relationships of the gods, is an advance beyond the mythological conception of fate of Homer in the direction of the doctrine of natural law. Hesiod's conception of Eros contains the germ of the conception of a single natural principle which is characteristic of the later philosophers. But in general the early theogonies attempt to explain the origin of things, not in a scientific and logical manner, but in that of the poetic imagination and the popular mythology.

The revival of religious feeling that quickened the Greek mind toward the end of the sixth century owed much to the so-called mystery cults. Although the Homeric poems largely ignore them, the Greeks venerated, side by side with the Olympian gods, local gods representing elemental forces important to those engaged in a struggle with the soil. Indeed, these gods often enjoyed a greater ritualistic significance than did the gods of the aristocratic myths, and they often retained their old character even after the names of Olympians became attached to them. These gods now came into their own. A form of worship native to the countryside made its way into the cities, and the worship of these new gods was often encouraged as a demagogic measure by the tyrants of the time. Dionysus, a Thracian god of barbaric aspect, whose worship was brought to Athens after a period of naturalization in the Greek countryside, received a ready welcome from the priesthood of Apollo; and Demeter, a goddess of the native countryside, was also quickly assimilated to the Olympians. The worship of Dionysus was at the heart of the cult-aspect of the religious renaissance; like Demeter, whose worship centered at Eleusis, he was associated with the revivification of the earth in spring, symbolized by the resurrection after death, or return of the god after his disappearance. In Attica, Dionysus was also worshiped as the God of the vine, and Demeter as the goddess of the grain. Cults like those of Dionysus, varying from place to place, but alike in having at their

center rituals called mysteries, by means of which the initiated were thought
to achieve unity with the god, became widespread throughout the Greek
world. In addition to the esoteric worship involving the mysteries (the Latin
form of the Greek term for mysteries later becomes our word "sacrament"),
there was also a public and official form of this worship. In the case of the
Dionysiac cults the esoteric rites were often orgiastic in character, but were
modified as they met with civic acceptance; indeed, as is well known, the
festivities associated with the public worship of Dionysus had much to do
with the evolution of Attic drama. The cults devoted to Dionysus underwent
a further modification by their merger with religious cults associated with
the name of Orpheus. The Orphic movement is less barbaric than were its
Dionysiac antecedents, and contains an ethical element in its striving for
immortality through identification with the god; indeed, many of the cults
associated with Orpheus substituted an ascetic regimen for the orgiastic rites
of many of the mystery cults. The Orphic movement represents a refinement
of the worship of Dionysus; the figure of Orpheus has been described as a
tamed and clothed Dionysus.

Most of the influences of the sixth-century religious revival which are
traceable in philosophy are Orphic in origin. Among these influences is the
Orphic doctrine of the soul, especially in the modified form which the
Orphic religion took in the Pythagorean brotherhood. The Orphic cults
believed in the transmigration of the soul, which was thought to be immortal,
and to have undergone a primal fall from a blessed state, to which in its
successive reincarnations it strives to return. The religious revival of the sixth
century, particularly in its Orphic expression, affords a favorable background
for the development of the religiously oriented philosophies of the Pythagorean school, of Parmenides, and of Heraclitus.

Survey of Greek Philosophy. Greek philosophy begins with an inquiry into
the essence of the objective world. From external nature it gradually turns
its eye inward, on man himself. The shifting of interest from nature to man
leads to the study of the human mind and of human conduct: of logic,
ethics, psychology, politics, and poetics. Of these studies, attention is centered
more particularly on ethics, and the chief question for philosophy now
becomes: What is the highest good, what is the end and aim of life? In the
course of this investigation the study of metaphysics and of human knowledge becomes indispensable. Finally, the problem of God and man's relation
to him, the theological problem, is pushed into the foreground, and Greek
philosophy ends, as it began, in religion.

(1) The first great problem, that of external nature, was taken up in the pre-Sophistic period, which extends from about 585 to the middle of the fifth century B.C. The scene of the philosophy of this period is the colonial world; it flourishes in Ionia, southern Italy and Sicily. The earliest Greek philosophy is naturalistic: its attention is directed to nature; it is mostly hylozoistic: it conceives nature as animated or alive; it is ontological: it inquires into the essence of things; it is mainly monistic: it seeks to explain its phenomena by means of a single principle; it is dogmatic: it naïvely presupposes the competence of the human mind to solve the world-problem.

The philosophers of the naturalistic period were concerned with two interdependent problems regarding external nature. The first was the problem of substance: What is the basic substance—or substances—of which the natural objects are constituted and from which they originate? The second was the problem of change: What is the nature of the process by which the basic substance—or substances—changes into the familiar objects of sense? Among the earliest nature philosophers of the Milesian school—Thales, Anaximander and Anaximenes—and among the Pythagoreans the two problems are scarcely distinguishable, but even here we can detect some differentiation between the question of *what* the basic stuff of things consists of and *how* the basic stuff changes into things. The problem of change emerges in a radical form in Heraclitus and in the Eleatic school, of which Parmenides is the chief exponent. The question for them is not so much *how* the change takes place but *whether* there is any change at all. For Heraclitus, change is ultimate and permanence a mere sensory appearance. For Parmenides, the permanent is fundamental and change a mere appearance. For these philosophers, the problem of substance is relegated to a secondary position. Later, in the naturalistic period, in the philosophies of Empedocles and Anaxagoras, the problems of substance and change both receive attention. The entire period is naturalistic in its almost exclusive concern with external nature. The humanistic problems of knowledge and conduct are discussed only incidentally, as in the distinction between reason and sense implicit in the theories of Heraclitus and Parmenides, in the crude ethical views of the Pythagoreans, and in the hedonistic ethics of Democritus.

(2) The second phase of the development of Greek philosophy, the period of the Sophists and Socrates, turns away from ontological and cosmological speculations regarding the constitution and origin of the external world and devotes its attention almost exclusively to the problems of man—to human knowledge and conduct.

The Sophistic movement, which belongs to the fifth century, is a phase of transition. It shows a growing distrust of the power of the human mind to solve the world-problem and a corresponding lack of faith in traditional conceptions and institutions. This movement is skeptical, radical, revolutionary, indifferent or antagonistic to metaphysical speculation; in calling attention to the problem of man, however, it makes necessary a more thorough examination of the problem of knowledge and the problem of conduct, and ushers in the Socratic period. Athens is the home of this new enlightenment and of the great schools of philosophy growing out of it.

The Socratic period, which extends from 430 to 320 B.C., is a period of reconstruction. Socrates defends knowledge against the assaults of skepticism, and shows how truth may be reached by the employment of a logical method. He also paves the way for a science of ethics by his efforts to define the meaning of the good.

(3) The systematic period of the two great philosophers of antiquity, Plato and Aristotle, is characterized by a concern for all the problems of philosophy—the metaphysical problems concerning reality and the humanistic problems relating to man's knowledge, conduct and place in the world-order. Plato and Aristotle build upon the foundations laid by the master, Socrates, and construct rational theories of knowledge (logic), conduct (ethics), and the state (politics). They likewise work out comprehensive systems of speculative thought (metaphysics), and interpret the universe in terms of mind, or reason. We may, therefore, characterize this philosophy as critical: it investigates the principles of knowledge; as rationalistic: it accepts the competence of reason in the search after truth; as humanistic: it studies man; as spiritualistic or idealistic: it makes mind an important if not the chief factor in the explanation of reality. It is dualistic in that it also recognizes matter as a factor in reality, though secondary to mind.

(4) The last period, the ethico-religious, which extends from 320 B.C. to 529 A.D., when the Emperor Justinian closed the schools of the philosophers, is called the post-Aristotelian. The scene is laid in Athens, Alexandria, and Rome. Two phases may be noted, an ethical and a theological one. (a) The paramount question for both Zeno, the Stoic, and Epicurus, the hedonist, is the problem of conduct: What is the aim of rational human endeavor, the highest good? The Epicureans find the answer in a life of pleasure; the Stoics in a life of virtue. Both schools are interested in logic and metaphysics: the former, because such knowledge will destroy superstition and ignorance and contribute to happiness; the latter, because it will teach man his duty as a part of a rational universe. The Epicureans are materialists and mecha-

nists; according to the Stoics, the universe is the expression of divine reason. (b) The theological movement, which took its rise in Alexandria, resulted from the contact of Greek philosophy with Oriental religions. In Neoplatonism, its most developed form, it seeks to explain the world as an emanation from a transcendent God who is both the source and the goal of all being.

Works on Greek Philosophy

General histories: J. Marshall, *History of Greek Philosophy,* 1891; W. Windelband, *History of Ancient Philosophy,* 1899; E. Zeller, *Outlines of History of Greek Philosophy,* trans. by Alleyne and Abbot, 1931; A. W. Benn, *Philosophy of Greece,* 2 vols., 1898; J. Burnet, *History of Greek Philosophy,* 1914; R. Adamson, *Development of Greek Philosophy,* 1908; A. W. Benn, *History of Ancient Philosophy,* 1912, and *The Greek Philosophers,* 2nd ed., 1914; B. A. G. Fuller, *History of Greek Philosophy,* rev. ed., 1945; R. B. Appleton, *The Elements of Greek Philosophy from Thales to Aristotle,* 1922; F. P. Boswell, *A Primer of Greek Thought,* 1923; M. E. J. Taylor, *Greek Philosophy, an Introduction,* 1924; W. T. Stace, *A Critical History of Greek Philosophy,* 1928; J. M. Warbeke, *The Searching Mind of Greece,* 1930; A. H. Armstrong, *An Introduction to Ancient Philosophy,* 1947.

More advanced histories: E. Zeller, *Philosophy of the Greeks,* 9 vols., trans. by Alleyne and others, 1881-88; T. Gomperz, *Greek Thinkers,* 4 vols., trans. by Magnus and Berry, 1912; M. Wundt, *Geschichte der griechischen Ethik,* 2 vols., 1908; H. Leisegang, *Hellenistische Philosophie von Aristoteles bis Plotin,* 1923; G. Sortais, *Histoire de la philosophie ancienne,* 1912; R. Hönigswald, *Die Philosophie des Altertums: problemgeschichtliche und systematische Untersuchung,* 1924; E. Howald, *Die Anfänge der europäischen Philosophie,* 1925; L. Robin, *Greek Thought,* 1928; C. Werner, *La philosophie grècque,* 1938; W. Jaeger, *Paideia,* Vol. I, 1939, Vol. II, 1943; E. Cassirer, *Logos, Dike, Kosmos in der Entwicklung der griechischen Philosophie,* 1941; A. Cresson, *La philosophie antique,* 1947.

Special works: H. O. Taylor, *Ancient Ideals,* 1900; J. P. Mahaffy, *Survey of Greek Civilization,* 1896, and *What Have the Greeks Done for Modern Civilization,* 1909; H. B. Cotterill, *Ancient Greece,* 1913; C. H. Moore, *The Religious Thought of the Greeks, from Homer to the Triumph of Christianity,* 1916; R. W. Livingstone, *The Mission of Greece,* 1928; A. Messer, *Geschichte der Philosophie im Altertum und Mittelalter,* 1923; H. Gomperz, *Die Lebensauffassung der griechischen Philosophen und das Ideal der inneren Freiheit,* 1927; L. Robin, *La pensée hellénique des origines à Epicure,* 1942; F. M. Cornford, *Before and After Socrates,* 1932; L. W. Keeler, *The Problem of Error from Plato to Kant,* 1934; H. Frankfort, ed., *The Intellectual Adventure of Ancient Man,* 1948; W. R. V. Brade, *From Plotinus to St. Thomas Aquinas,* 1926; P. E. More, *Hellenistic Philosophies,* 1923; A. O. Lovejoy, *The Great Chain of Being,* 1936; T. G. Duvall, *Greek Thinkers,* 1937. Religion: F. M. Cornford, *From Religion to Philosophy,* 1912; E. Caird, *Evolution of Theology in the Greek Philosophers,* 1904; E. Rohde, *Psyche,* trans., 1925; J. Adam, *The Religious Teachers of Greece,* 1904-06; E. R. Bevan, *Later Greek Religion,* 1927. Logic and Theory of Knowledge: J. I. Beare, *Greek Theories of Elementary Cognition,* 1906; E. Kapp, *Greek Foundations of Traditional Logic,* 1942. Psychology, Ethics, and Esthetics: J. H. Hyslop, *The Ethics of the Greek Philosophers,*

Socrates, Plato and Aristotle, 1903; M. W. Bundy, *The Theory of Imagination in Classical and Medieval Thought*, 1927; H. D. Oakley, *Greek Ethical Thought*, 1925; J. Walter, *Die Geschichte der Aesthetik im Altertum*, 1893; C. S. Baldwin, *Ancient Rhetoric and Poetic*, 1924. Science: T. L. Heath, *History of Greek Mathematics*, 2 vols., 1921; L. Robin, *Greek Thought and the Origins of the Scientific Spirit*, 1928; F. M. Cornford, *The Laws of Motion in Ancient Thought*, 1931; J. Croissant, *Matière et changement dans la physique ionienne*, 1944; W. H. S. Jones, *Philosophy and Medicine in Ancient Greece*, 1946; J. F. Callahan, *Four Views of Time in Ancient Philosophy*, 1948.

Collections of fragments, English translations of fragments, etc.: H. Diels, *Fragmente der Vorsokratiker*, 1934-38; K. Freeman, *The Pre-Socratic Philosophers, A Companion to Diels, "Fragmente der Vorsokratiker,"* 1946; T. V. Smith, *Philosophers Speak for Themselves*, 1935; A. Fairbanks, *First Philosophers of Greece*, 1898; C. M. Bakewell, *Source Book in Ancient Philosophy*, rev. ed., 1939; M. C. Nahm, *Selections from Early Greek Philosophy*, 3rd ed., 1947; K. Freeman, *Ancilla to the Pre-Socratic Philosophers*. 1948. (A complete translation of the fragments in Diels', *Fragmente der Vorsokratiker*.) Consult Aristotle's *Metaphysics*, Bk. I. See also H. Jackson, *Texts to Illustrate the History of Philosophy from Thales to Aristotle*, 1901.

2. DEVELOPMENT OF PRE-SOPHISTIC PHILOSOPHY

The speculative impulse first finds genuine expression in the Ionian physicists, the Pythagoreans, Heraclitus, the Eleatics, Empedocles, the Atomists and Anaxagoras, who attempt to explain phenomena by natural causes and without appeal to mythical beings. The development of pre-Sophistic philosophy displays a remarkably logical pattern: the period has a structural organization in which each problem emerges naturally from earlier problems and the various possible solutions are explored in almost systematic fashion. There is, perhaps, no other period in the history of philosophy during which the historical sequence of problems and solutions so nearly coincides with the order dictated by the principle of logical organization. As we have already indicated, the first problem to which these early philosophers addressed themselves was the problem of substance, and the substance selected as basic by each of the Milesian philosophers was a *concrete* substance. They ask the question: What is the basal stuff of which the world is composed? and answer in terms of such concrete objects of sense perception as water, air or a hypothetical undifferentiated mass from which sense objects are derived. By means of a single principle (monism) they endeavor to account for the qualities of different bodies and their changes which are transformations of the primal stuff. Observation shows that substances are changed into other substances (water, for example, becomes steam or vapor) and, by a similar process, the original element must have been transmuted into the different substances found in our present world of experience.

The problem of change is not entirely ignored by the Milesian philosophers; but it has not yet emerged as distinct from the problem of substance. The fact of change itself is explained by the view—tacitly assumed by all the early Greek thinkers—that reality is alive: the original substance bears within itself the cause of motion and change (hylozoism).

The individual philosophers, although they are all hylozoists in supposing that the cause of change and motion animates the primitive substance and is not a separate principle, differ among themselves in their description of *how* things arise from the primordial stuff. Thus Thales naïvely assumes that the first principle, water, simply *becomes* other things—that things are produced by the transformation of water. In Anaximander, however, there are suggestions of the more sophisticated view that things are somehow separated from the Boundless in which they originally existed in mixture or fusion. Anaximenes described the emergence of the variety of things from the primary substance, air, as due to processes of *condensation* and *rarefaction.* The early Greek thinkers thus brought three principal solutions to the problem of how the numerous derived things proceed from the original primary substance: (1) by *sheer transformation* of one thing into another, without any further attempt to describe the exact character of the transformation; this is presumably the attitude adopted by Thales; (2) by the *separation* of things from the primary substance which was a homogeneous mixture or fusion of them; this view is tacit in Anaximander and explicit in Heraclitus; (3) by *condensation* and *rarefaction;* this is the view held by Anaximenes, for whom air, when condensed, becomes water and when expanded becomes fire.

The problem of substance is also the primary concern of the Pythagoreans, who advance an abstract number-theory: numbers are the primary causes of things. They fix their attention not so much upon a concrete, sense-perceived substance, as upon the relations existing between things, the order, uniformity, or harmony in the world. Since this may be expressed in numbers, they make entities of numbers.

The problem of change assumes central importance in Heraclitus and the Eleatics who are divided on the issue of the existence or nonexistence of change, but the problem of substance remains for them also. Heraclitus resembles the Ionians in assuming an animated substance (fire) as the principle, but consciously singles out the fact of change, or becoming, as the significant thing: the world, according to him, is in constant change; everything is in a state of flux; there is no real permanence in things. He also brings out, more clearly than did his predecessors, the idea that there is a reason in the world controlling its happenings. The Eleatics, too, turn their attention to the notion of change, but reject it as absolutely inconceivable. It is unthinkable that an element, like fire, should ever become anything else; a thing cannot become something other than itself. Whatever is, must remain what it is; permanence, not change, is the significant characteristic of reality.

The radical issue between Heraclitus and the Eleatics constituted a challenge to Empedocles and Anaxagoras, who sought a compromise between the philosophy of change and the philosophy of permanence. Empedocles and Anaxagoras agree with the Eleatics that absolute change is impossible, that nothing can become anything else, in the literal sense of the term. Nothing can come from nothing; nothing can go into nothing; and nothing can change into anything absolutely different. Nevertheless—and in this they agree with Heraclitus—things do change. The change, however, is only relative, not absolute. There are permanent elements or particles which are combined to form bodies: this is origin. The parts of the bodies are separated: this is decay. Nothing can really change, originate or disappear in the absolute sense; but the permanent, unchangeable elements of the world can and do change their relations to one another. Empedocles and Anaxagoras make a significant departure from the hylozoism and animism which characterized most of their predecessors. The causes of motion and change, instead of residing in and animating the original substance or substances, tend to become separated from the elements. The Love and Hate of Empedocles and the Mind of Anaxagoras are such separate moving principles. The elementary substances of which all things are composed are, according to Empedocles and Anaxagoras, qualitatively differentiated; the view which they share is, accordingly, designated qualitative atomism, to distinguish it from the quantitative atomism of Leucippus and Democritus. The quantitative atomists accept the new conception of unchanging elements and changing relations, but differ from Empedocles and Anaxagoras in other respects: whereas the latter assume elements and separate moving forces, Leucippus and Democritus presuppose numberless minute indivisible particles of matter, called atoms, and conceive motion as inherent in the atoms themselves.

In the three sections which follow we shall consider: (1) the problem of substance with reference to (a) the theories of concrete substance of Thales,

Anaximander and Anaximenes, and (b) the abstract number-theory of Pythagoras; (2) the problem of change in terms of the issue between (a) the philosophy of change of Heraclitus, and (b) the philosophy of being of the Eleatic school; and (3) the problems of substance and change as they appear in (a) the qualitative atomism of Empedocles and Anaxagoras, and (b) the quantitative atomism of Leucippus and Democritus. The Sophists assume a negative attitude towards all these theories, declaring the attempts to solve the world-problem to be futile, on the ground that certain knowledge in this field is out of the question.

Works on pre-Socratic Philosophy:

J. Burnet, *Early Greek Philosophy*, 4th ed., 1930; W. A. Heidel, *Study of the Concept of Nature Among Pre-Socratics;* K. Goebel, *Die vorsokratische Philosophie*, 1910; E. Zeller, *A History of Greek Philosophy from the Earliest Period to the Time of Socrates*, 1881; J. I. Beare, *Greek Theories of Elementary Cognition*, 1906; N. Hartmann, *Über das Seinsproblem in der griechischen Philosophie vor Plato*, 1908; A. W. Benn, *Early Greek Philosophy*, 1908; J. Burnet, *Greek Philosophy: Part I, Thales to Plato*, 1914; G. Kafka, *Die Vorsokratiker*, 1921; E. Howald, *Die Anfänge der europäischen Philosophie*, 1925; R. M. Scoon, *Greek Philosophy before Plato*, 1928; R. K. Hack, *God in Greek Philosophy to the Time of Socrates*, 1931; P. Guerin, *L'idée de justice dans la conception de l'univers chez les premiers philosophes grecs*, 1934; M. T. McClure, *The Early Philosophers of Greece*, 1935; H. F. Cherniss, *Aristotle's Criticism of Pre-Socratic Philosophy*, 1935; W. Capelle, *Die Vorsokratiker*, 1935; J. Croissant, *Matière et changement dans la physique ionienne*, 1944; O. A. Gigon, *Der Ursprung der griechischen Philosophie, von Hesiod bis Parmenides*, 1945; W. Jaeger, *The Theology of the Early Greek Philosophers*, 1947. Fragments and translations of fragments: H. Diels, *Die Fragmente der Vorsokratiker* (Greek and German), 1934-38; K. Freeman, *Ancilla to the Pre-Socratic Philosophers*, 1948; C. M. Bakewell, *Source Book in Ancient Philosophy*, rev. ed., 1939; M. C. Nahm, *Selections from Early Greek Philosophy*, 3rd ed., 1947; A. Fairbanks, *The First Philosophers of Greece*, 1898.

3. THE PROBLEM OF SUBSTANCE

Thales. Thales' importance lies in his having put the philosophical question squarely and in having answered it without reference to mythical beings.

Thales was born in Miletus, a colony of Greece, about 624 B.C., and died between 554 and 548 B.C. He was noted as a statesman, mathematician, and astronomer, and as the first philosopher of Greece. It is said that he predicted the eclipse which occurred May 28, 585. All the writers who give lists of the Seven Wise Men of Greece include his name. Thales probably never wrote anything; at any rate we possess no work of his, since the book *Nautical Astrology,* which has been ascribed to him, is spurious. Our knowledge of his teaching is, therefore, limited to secondary sources.

He declared water to be the original stuff, basing his conclusion, perhaps, on the fact that nourishment, heat, seed, which are essential to life, contain moisture. In selecting water as his primary substance, Thales may have been influenced by the myth of Oceanos and Tethys. This suggestion has some plausibility in view of the emergence of Greek philosophy from Greek mythology and religion. Water has the capacity of assuming solid, liquid and vaporous forms and thus seems to be in process of transformation before one's eyes; water evaporates in the heat of the sun and this is readily interpreted in Thales' view as the transformation of water into fire; water comes down again in the form of rain and is absorbed into the ground—this could be regarded as the transformation of water into earth; and finally, water is necessary to life. John Burnet, in examining the reasons for Thales' selection of water, discounts the biological ones, suggesting that they are products of a later age. Out of water everything comes; he does not tell us how, most likely because the transformation of one substance into another was accepted by him as a fact of experience, and was not a problem for him at all. He evidently looked upon nature as alive, as moving, acting, changing, as did all the early Greek philosophers—so at least Aristotle tells us. If we may believe Hippolytus, all things, according to Thales, not only come from water, but return to water. Perhaps he conceived it as a kind of slime, which would explain most satisfactorily both solids and liquids and the origin of living beings. Our knowledge of Thales' philosophy is largely conjectural; the views attributed to him by Aristotle are reducible to three: (1) all things are full of gods; (2) the earth is a flat disc floating on water; and (3) water is the material cause of all things.

Anaximander. Anaximander reasoned thus: The essence or principle of things is not water, as Thales supposes—for water itself must be explained—but the Boundless or Infinite, conceived as an eternal, imperishable substance out of which all things are made and to which all things return. By this he most likely meant a boundless, space-filling, animate mass, the nature of which he did not define specifically, because he regarded all qualities as derived from it. Among a number of conflicting interpretations of Anaximander's Boundless enumerated by Burnet are:[1] (1) that the Boundless is a *mixture* from which things arise by separation—an interpretation which rests on a somewhat questionable passage in Aristotle which contrasts Anaxagoras' first principle with the mixture of Empedocles and Anaximander; (2) that the Boundless is an indefinite, indeterminate and qualitatively *un-*

---

[1] Burnet, *Early Greek Philosophy,* p. 59.

differentiated matter—an anticipation of Aristotle's "indeterminate potential matter"; (3) that the Boundless is something intermediate between the observable elements, for example, between air and water or air and fire. The second interpretation, despite its vagueness—perhaps even because of it—has considerable plausibility; perhaps, as Burnet suggests, a reconciliation of these views is possible. The Boundless is infinite, or rather indefinite in extent, he naïvely infers, otherwise it would be consumed in the creation of things.

From this great mass of undifferentiated matter different substances are separated in consequence of its eternal motion; first the hot and then the cold, the hot surrounding the cold as a sphere of flame. The heat of the flame turns the cold into moisture, and then into air, which expands and breaks up the sphere of fire into wheel-shaped rings. The rings have openings like the holes of a flute, through which the fire streams, and these are the heavenly bodies, which the air, surrounding them, forces to move around the earth. The sun is the most remote body in the heavens, next comes the moon, and then the fixed stars and the planets. The earth, which is in the center of the system, is a cylindrical body. This conception of the earth as a cylinder, unsupported by anything but held in equilibrium by other bodies, conveys perhaps a dim recognition that there is no absolute up and down in the world.[2] Indeed, Anaximander's cosmology—despite its many fanciful details—foreshadows some features of the universe of modern astronomy.

The first living beings arose out of the moist element. In the course of time some of these creatures came out of the water upon the drier parts of the and adapted themselves to their new surroundings. Man, like every other animal, as in the beginning a fish. Anaximander's speculations on the origin of living creatures—like his cosmological speculations—have an astonishingly modern flavor. Everything must return again to the primal mass whence it sprang, only to be produced anew *ad infinitum*. This is the doctrine of the alternation of worlds prevalent in early thought. According to Anaximander's doctrine of cyclical recurrence, innumerable worlds presumably succeed one another in time but are not coexistent. The creation of things is injustice in the sense that, by becoming what they are, they rob the infinite, and justice demands their return the infinite. There is thus an eternal, cyclical recurrence of the processes of eration from and return to the primordial substance. (This cosmological hypothesis may very well be the original source of the modern cyclical theory of history, the view that history repeats itself in different cultural media—though, to be sure, with a difference.)

[2] Burnet, *op. cit.*, p. 73.

Anaximander was born in Miletus, in 611 B.C., and died in 547 or 546 B.C. He is mentioned as a pupil of Thales, and we may assume that, as a fellow-townsman, he was acquainted with the latter's views. We know that he was interested in astronomy, geography, and cosmology, that he made maps of the earth and of the heavens, and that he introduced the sundial into Greece. His treatise *On Nature,* of which only fragments remain, was, so far as we know, the first philosophical book written in Greece and the first prose work in the Greek language.

Anaximander's thinking represents an advance over that of Thales, first, in its attempt to explain as a derivative the element (water) which Thales sets up as a principle, and, secondly, in its attempt to describe the stages of the process of becoming. Anaximander likewise seems to have had some notion of the indestructibility of matter. His refusal to ascribe quality to the Boundless shows a tendency towards a more abstract mode of thought than we find in his predecessor's concrete, sense-perceived substance.

This is not to suggest that Anaximander's Boundless is abstract infinitude; it is a concrete indeterminate substance, but the tendency towards abstraction is manifest in his thinking. We must not make the mistake—a mistake encouraged by Hegel—of interpreting the Boundless in abstract or logical terms: it is not the mathematicians' abstract infinity; it is an infinite, concrete mass. As Zeller put it, "The Boundless is predicate, not subject." Although concrete and not abstract, the Boundless differs from the particular things observable by the senses. The adoption of a principle of explanation different from an observable element like water is an advance in philosophical sophistication. Anaximander's original biological doctrines are mentioned as perhaps the earliest formulation of the theory of evolution, while his theory of the spheres plays an important part in the subsequent history of astronomy.

Anaximenes. Anaximenes (588-524 B.C.), another citizen of Miletus, is supposed to have been a pupil of Anaximander. He wrote a prose work in the Ionic dialect, of which only a small fragment is left.

According to Anaximenes, the first principle of things, or underlying substance, is one and infinite, as his teacher had held, but it is not indeterminate: it is air, vapor, or mist. Perhaps one of the reasons for selecting air as the first principle is that it is dry and cold and thus intermediate between fire, the warm and dry element, and water, the cold and moist element. Moreover, air is the principle of life in our bodies: deprived of breath, the organism dies. As air or breath is the life-giving element in man, so is it the principle of the universe. The world is represented by Anaximenes as breathing. As man's soul, which is air, holds him together, so breath or air surrounds and sustains the whole world. The cosmic air is animate and extends infinitely through space.

Anaximenes' chief advance beyond his predecessor is his doctrine of rarefaction and condensation to explain the emergence of the observable elements from the primary substance. From air all things arise by the processes of rarefaction and condensation: When it is rarefied, air becomes fire; when condensed, it becomes, in turn, wind, cloud, water, earth and stone. Anaximenes' doctrine of condensation and rarefaction as explaining the emergence of "elements" from the primary substance is significant as an advance toward a truly scientific mode of explanation: Condensation and rarefaction are purely quantitative notions—the former an increase, the latter a decrease in the amount of matter occupying a given volume. Thus his theory is a long stride in the direction of the reduction of qualitative difference to quantitative terms which is so clearly enunciated in the atomism of Democritus. Or, to express Anaximenes' advance somewhat differently: he sought to effect the reduction of all change to motion. All changes are produced by motion, and motion is eternal.

Later followers of the Milesian school are: Hippo (fifth century B.C.), Idaeus, and Diogenes of Apollonia (440-425 B.C.).

Pythagoras and His School. The thinkers whom we have just considered were interested in the problem of the essence of things: What, they asked, is the stuff of which the world is composed? They regarded it as a concrete substance, either determinate like water or air, or as an indeterminate substance from which such elements are differentiated. We come now to a school of philosophers, the Pythagoreans, who were concerned less with substance than with the question of the form and relations of things. As mathematicians, they were interested in quantitative relations, which are measurable, and began to speculate upon the problem of the uniformity or regularity in the world, attempting to explain this fact by making an entity of number, and setting it up as the principle of all being.

The founder of the school was Pythagoras. Many fantastic stories are told of this man, particularly by writers coming centuries after his time. He is said to have traveled extensively and to have derived his ideas from the countries through which he passed, but these accounts are untrustworthy. He was born in Samos, between 580 and 570 B.C., and emigrated to the Greek colonies in southern Italy about the year 529. It is stated that his opposition to the tyranny of Polycrates and his loyalty to the aristocratic party caused him to leave his home. He settled in Crotona and founded an association, the purpose of which is described as ethical, religious, and political. His ideal was to develop among his followers the political virtues, to teach them to act for the good of the State, to subordinate themselves to the whole. In order to realize this end, he emphasized the need for moral training: The individual should learn to control himself, to subdue his passions, to harmonize his soul; he should have respect for authority, for the authority of his elders, his teachers, and the State. The Pythagorean brotherhood seems to have been a practical training-school for citizenship, in which the ideals of the master were put to the test. Its members cultivated the virtue of friendship, and practiced the habit of self-examination with a view to improving their character. They formed a community, living together as a large family, taking their meals in common, wearing the same kind of dress, and applying themselves to the arts and crafts, as well as to the study of music, medicine, and, particularly, mathematics. It was customary for members to pass through a novitiate, the watchword being: first to hear, then to know. It is probable that the society was, originally, a form of the great popular religious revival which took place in Greece at this time, and which had as its aim the purification of life and the participation of the entire people in worship, particularly in that form of it exemplified in the so-called mysteries. In the teachings of these mysteries, the future destiny of the soul was made dependent on man's conduct during his earthly life, and rules were laid down for the governance of his conduct. The Pythagorean society is credited with having extended the usefulness of this religious movement, which was spreading among the lower classes, by adapting it to the needs of the more educated and aristocratic classes. The political tendencies of the Pythagorean brotherhood brought it into conflict with the political authorities of many cities in which it gained adherents, and ultimately provoked serious persecution of the society. Presumably in consequence of these disturbances, Pythagoras himself was forced to seek refuge in Metapontum, where he died about 500 B.C., while many of his followers were driven from Italy and found a home in Greece. These misfortunes put an end to the Pythagorean brotherhood, though disciples of the master continued to teach and develop his doctrines for hundreds of years. Pythagoreanism was taught by Philolaus at Thebes toward the end of the fifth century B.C., and at a still later period Pythagorean doctrines were propounded by the statesman, Archytus of Tarentum.

Pythagoras himself left no writings, and we can ascribe to him with assurance only the ethical, political, and religious teachings which have been mentioned; it is likely, however, that he is also the originator of the number theory which forms the central idea in the doctrines of the school that bears his name and to which we shall now turn. The system, as it has come down to us, was worked out by Philolaus, in the second half of the fifth century B.C., and was continued by other members of the school (Archytas, Lysis) into the fourth century.

J. Burnet, "Pythagoras," in Hastings' *Encyclopedia of Religion and Ethics,* 1908-21; K. S. Guthrie, *Pythagoras,* 1919; K. von Fritz, *Pythagorean Politics in Southern Italy,* 1940.

The Pythagorean number-theory. The Pythagoreans are impressed by the fact of form and relation in the world; they find measure, order, proportion, and uniform recurrence, which can be expressed in numbers. Without number, they reason, there can be no such relations and uniformities, no order, no law; hence number must lie at the basis of everything. Numbers must be the true realities, the grounds of things, and everything else an expression of numbers.

Numbers are, for the Pythagoreans, the principles of things—not as being the stuff or substance of things in the Milesian sense—but rather as constituting their formal or relational structure. Things are the copies or imitations of numbers. The later distinction between matter and form, which is central to the Platonic and Aristotelian systems of metaphysics, was foreshadowed by the Pythagorean distinction between numbers and things. The Pythagoreans made entities of numbers, just as many persons today make entities of the laws of nature, speaking of them as though they were the causes of whatever happens. In their delight over the discovery that there is a numerical relation, for example, between the length of the string and the pitch of the tone, they called number, which is only a symbol or expression of the relation, the cause of the relation, and placed number behind phenomena as their basal principle and ground.

Now if number is the essence of things, then whatever is true of number will be true of things. The Pythagoreans, therefore, devoted themselves to the study of the countless peculiarities discoverable in numbers, and ascribed these to the universe at large. Numbers are distinguished as odd and even— the odd cannot be divided by two, the even can—to this extent, the former are limited, the latter unlimited. The odd and the even, the finite and the infinite, the limited and the unlimited, constitute the essence of number and of reality. Nature itself is a union of opposites, of the odd and the even, the limited and unlimited. A table of ten such opposites is offered: limited and unlimited; odd and even; one and many; right and left; male and female; rest and motion; straight and crooked; light and darkness; good and bad; square and rectangle. The Pythagorean doctrine of the dualism of the limited and the unlimited and their harmony is no doubt traceable back to Anaximander and Anaximenes. The doctrine of the conflict of opposites was foreshadowed by Anaximander; and the concept of the unlimited was shared by Anaximander and Anaximenes.[3] The Pythagoreans regarded the unlimited as prior to the limited: individual things arise through the limitation of the unlimited space by the imposition of forms on space.

The corporeal world is also numerical, being based on the unit. The point is one, the line two, the figure three, the solid four. Again, earth is a cube; fire, a tetrahedron; air, an octohedron; water, an icosahedron, and so on. That is to say, the lines and surfaces of bodies were conceived as entities

[3] Cf. Burnet, *op. cit.*, pp. 106 ff.

having an independent existence; for there can be no bodies without lines
and surfaces, whereas lines and surfaces can be thought without bodies. The
spatial forms are the causes of bodies, and since these forms can be expressed
by numbers, the latter are the ultimate causes. Arithmetical distinctions are
thus carried over into the physical world. The Pythagoreans were led by this
transfer to the doctrine of an unlimited space or void which contrasts with
the limited bodies in space.[4] The influence of the Pythagorean number-
mysticism on physics and astronomy has been appreciable; the theories of
Kepler, for example, display marked Pythagorean and neo-Pythagorean
influences.[5]

The historical significance of the Pythagorean number-mysticism resides
in the fact that, despite its absurd and fantastic correlation of numbers with
things, it represents an unusually obstinate attempt to discover the abiding
order and lawfulness in things and to formulate this order in the abstract
conceptual terms of numbers and numerical relations. It is certainly one of
the main historical sources of the conception of a mathematically expressible
natural law which is at the very core of modern science and philosophy.

Astronomy. The Pythagorean school also gave its attention to the study
of astronomy and produced a number of noted astronomers. In the center of
the universe, which is spherical in form, they placed the central fire; around
it the planets revolve, turned by means of transparent moving spheres to
which they are attached. The opposition between the limited and the unlimited which dominates the Pythagorean metaphysics also appears in
astronomy, in the dualism between the stellar system with its relative fixity
and uniformity, and the terrestrial regions which lack the order of the other
world. This sharp separation of the two astronomical regions was incorporated into the later systems of Greek astronomy of Plato and Aristotle, and
was not seriously challenged until the modern period. The fixed stars are
fastened to the highest arch of heaven, which revolves around the central fire
in the course of 36,000 years; below this follow, in concentric spheres, Saturn,
Jupiter, Mars, Mercury, Venus, the sun, moon, and earth. But since ten is
the perfect number, there must be ten heavenly bodies; hence, the Pythagoreans place between the earth and the central fire a counter-earth, which
screens the earth from the rays of the central fire. The earth and counter-
earth daily revolve around the central fire in such a way that the earth
always turns the same face to the counter-earth and the central fire, and for

---

[4] Cf. Windelband, *History of Philosophy*, trans. by J. H. Tufts, p. 46.
[5] Cf. E. A. Burtt, *Metaphysical Foundations of Modern Physical Science*, pp. 49 ff.

this reason we, living on the opposite side of the earth, do not see the central fire. The sun, which encircles the central fire once in the course of the year, reflects the light of this body. The movement of the spheres represents an octave and is, therefore, a harmony; every sphere produces its own tones, and the harmony of the spheres results from their combination.

Fantastic as these astronomical notions may seem, they paved the way for the construction of the heliocentric theory, which was propounded by Aristarchus of Samos about 280 B.C. In the course of time, the counter-earth and central fire were given up, and Hicetas and Ecphantus taught the axial rotation of the earth. Heraclides found reason to reject the view that all the planets revolve around the earth in concentric spheres, and connected their movements with the movement of the sun. Aristarchus concluded from the larger size of the sun that it did not revolve around the earth and made the earth move round the sun.[6]

T. L. Heath, *Aristarchus of Samos, the Ancient Copernicus*, 1913.

Ethics. The Pythagorean philosophy includes ethics—an ethics which is rooted in number-mysticism. The Pythagoreans applied to non-corporeal things an interpretation which parallels that given for corporeal things: Love, friendship, justice, virtue, health, etc., are based on numbers—love and friendship being expressed by the number eight, because love and friendship are harmony, and the octave is harmony. In a famous simile, Pythagoras is said to have likened life to a public game, and to have distinguished three classes of people corresponding to the buyers and sellers—the vendors who have no interest in the game except the opportunity for profits; the participants in the game who are seeking praise and honor; and the observers, whose aim is neither gain nor honor but wisdom.

4. THE PROBLEM OF CHANGE

Permanence and Change. The Ionian physicists were interested in the substantial nature of things, the Pythagoreans in quantitative relations, order, harmony and number. The next problem to attract attention was the problem of change or becoming. The first philosophers spoke of the process of change, transformation, origin and decay, in a naïve objective way; it was not a problem for them at all. They did not stop to speculate about the notion of change, but made use of it, in their explanations, without reflection. They described how everything emerged from their assumed primal unity and

[6] See T. Gomperz, *Greek Thinkers*, Vol. I, p. 121.

how everything returned to it; how, for example, air became clouds, clouds water, water earth, and how all these substances could be transformed back again into the original substratum. Implicit in all these theories of the transformation of substance was the assumption that nothing could absolutely originate or be lost: it is the same principle that appears now as water, now as cloud, and now as earth. It was only natural that some thinker should isolate the phenomenon of change, growth, origin and decay, and make the concept of change central to his system. This is what Heraclitus did. He is deeply impressed with the fact of change in the world, and asserts that change constitutes the very life of the universe, that nothing is really permanent, that permanence is an illusion, and that, though things may appear to remain stable, they are actually in an endless process of becoming, in a state of constant flux. The Eleatics take the opposite view and deny the very possibility of change or becoming. To them it is unthinkable that reality should change, that a thing should really and truly become something else; they declare that change is illusory, a mere sense appearance, and that being is permanent and eternal.

Heraclitus. The fundamental thought in the teaching of Heraclitus is, as we have already seen, that the universe is in a state of ceaseless change. "One cannot step twice into the same river," for other and yet other waters are ever flowing on.

Heraclitus (535-475 B.C.) was born in Ephesus, the son of a noble family. He remained an uncompromising aristocrat all his life, displaying an extreme contempt for democracy. He was serious, critical, and pessimistic, independent in his opinion of men, dogmatic, proud, and inclined to find fault. He speaks disparagingly of Hesiod, Pythagoras, Xenophanes, and even of Homer, and prides himself on being self-taught. "Polymathy," he says, "does not train the mind; if it did, it would have made Hesiod and Pythagoras and Xenophanes wise." His style is obscure, possibly intentionally so— indeed, he came to be called "the Obscure." Nevertheless, he was a forceful writer, full of wise and original sayings, and given to oracular utterances, which he made no attempt to support by proof. Only fragments of his work, which is supposed to have borne the customary title *On Nature,* remain, and it appears to have been divided into three parts: physical, ethical, political. The *Letters* frequently ascribed to him are spurious.

G. T. W. Patrick, *The Fragments of the Works of Heraclitus on Nature,* 1889; I. Bywater, *Fragments of Heraclitus,* 1877; H. Diels, *Heraclitus Ephesius,* 1901.

Fire and the universal flux. To signalize the notion of incessant activity, Heraclitus chooses as his first principle the most mobile substance he knows, something that never seems to come to rest, the ever-living fire—sometimes called by him vapor or breath—which is regarded by him as the vital principle in the organism and the essence of the soul. According to some interpreters, the fire-principle is merely a concrete physical symbol for ceaseless activity, or process, not itself a substance, but the very denial of all substance. It is, however, very unlikely that Heraclitus reasoned the thing out to so fine a point; it sufficed for him to have a principle that changes incessantly, undergoing continual qualitative transformation; and fire satisfies this demand. The fire of Heraclitus is not the abiding substratum of his predecessors; it is that which is constantly being transformed into other things.

Fire changes into water and then into earth, and the earth changes back again into water and fire, "for the way upward and the way downward are one." "All things are exchanged for fire, and fire for all things; as wares are exchanged for gold and gold for wares." Things seem to be permanent because we do not perceive the incessant movements in them, and because what they lose in one way they gain in another. Even the sun is new every day, kindled at its rising and quenched at its setting.

Opposites and their union. The primal unity itself is in constant motion and change; its creation is destruction, its destruction creation. When it passes into something else, e.g., from fire into water, the fire is lost in a new form of existence. Everything is changed into its opposite and everything, therefore, is a union of opposite qualities. There are no persistent qualities and hence nothing remains permanent by virtue of its qualities. Everything both is and is not; the universal process is a transition from one condition to its opposite and, in this sense, everything unites opposites within itself. Such opposition alone makes the world possible. Harmony in music, for example, results from the combination of high notes and low notes, i.e., from a union of opposites.

The world is ruled by strife: "War is the father of all and the king of all." If it were not for strife or opposition, the world would stagnate and die. "Even a potion dissolves into its ingredients when it is not stirred." The oppositions and contradictions are united, and harmony is the result. Indeed, there could be no such order without movement or change with its inherent opposition and contradiction. Ultimately, the oppositions will all be reconciled in the universal principle; the world will return to the original state of fire, which is also reason, and the process will begin anew. In this sense, good and bad are the same. "Life and death, waking and sleeping, and youth and old age, are the same; for the latter change and are the former, and the former change back to the latter." For God all things are fair and good and just, for God orders things as they ought to be, perfects all things in the harmony of the whole; but men mistakenly suppose some to be unjust and others just. Harmony is the union of opposites and at the same time the law governing the process of change. The law must not be construed as something over and above the process: the process and its law are one.

Harmony and the law of reason. The cosmic process, therefore, is not haphazard or arbitrary, but in accordance with "fixed measure"; or, as we should say today, governed by law. "This one order of things neither any one of the gods nor of men has made, but it always was, is, and ever shall be, an ever-living fire, kindling according to fixed measure and extinguished according to fixed measure." Heraclitus sometimes speaks of the order of things as the work of Fate or Justice, and thereby introduces into his philosophy of change the idea of necessity. In the midst of all change and contradiction, the only thing that persists or remains the same is the inexorable law that underlies all movement and change and opposition; it is the reason in things, the *logos*. The first principle is, therefore, a rational principle; it is alive and endowed with reason. "This alone is wise," says Heraclitus, "to understand the intelligence by which all things are steered through all things." Whether he conceived it as conscious intelligence, or as an impersonal rationality we cannot say with absolute certainty; in its influence on later philosophy the *logos* doctrine is interpreted in both ways, but perhaps the latter interpretation is the more frequent.

Psychology and ethics. On this theory of the universe, Heraclitus bases his psychology and ethics. Man's soul is a part of the universal fire and nourished by it. We breathe it, and receive it through our senses. The driest and warmest soul is the best soul, most like the cosmic fire-soul. Sense knowledge is inferior to reason; the eyes and ears are bad witnesses. Perception without reflection does not reveal to us the hidden truth, which is discernible only by reason.

The controlling element in man is the soul which is akin to divine reasoning. Man, in his moral conduct, must subordinate himself to the universal reason, to the law that pervades all things. "It is necessary for those who speak with intelligence to hold fast to the universal element in all things, as a city holds fast to the law, and much more strongly. For all human laws are nourished by one which is divine." To be ethical is to live a rational life, to obey the dictates of reason, which is the same for us all, the same for the whole world. Yet, "though reason is common, most people live as though they had an understanding peculiar to themselves." Morality means respect for law, self-discipline, control of the passions; to be moral is to govern oneself by rational principles. The following excerpts from his writings illustrate the lofty idealism of Heraclitus' ethics: "The people ought to fight for their law as for a wall." "Character is a man's guardian divinity." "Wantonness must be quenched more than a conflagration." "It is hard to contend with passion; for whatever it desires to get it buys at the cost of the soul." "To me one man is ten thousand if he be the best."

Heraclitus had a low opinion of the masses who "follow the bards and employ the crowd as their teacher, not knowing that many are bad and few good," and "eat their fill like cattle." Life is a sorry game at best: "Lifetime is a child playing at draughts; the kingdom is a child's." "Man, like a light in the night, is kindled and put out." For the popular religion, too, he had nothing but contempt: "They purify themselves with blood, as if one who had stepped into the mud were to wash it off with mud. If any one of men should observe him doing so, he would think he was insane. And to these images they pray, just as if one were to converse with men's houses, for they know not what gods and heroes are."[7]

The Eleatic School. Heraclitus is impressed with the phenomenon of change and motion; the Eleatics insist that change and motion are unthinkable, that the principle of things must be permanent, unmoved, and neverchanging. The school takes its name from the town of Elea, in southern Italy, the home of its real founder, Parmenides. We distinguish three phases in this philosophy: (1) Xenophanes, who may be regarded as the precursor of the Eleatic philosophy, since he presents its fundamental insight in theological form. He, however, is scarcely to be credited with founding the Eleatic school because, although he advanced the thesis of the permanence of God, he retained the changing world alongside the permanent God. (2) Parmenides is the true founder of the philosophy of permanence since he develops the doctrine of permanence into a complete system of ontology. (3) Zeno and Melissus are the defenders of the doctrine: they are the dialecticians of the school. The former attempts to prove the Eleatic theses by showing the absurdity of their opposites, while the latter offers positive proofs in support of the theories.

Y. Freudenthal, *Über die Theologie des Xenophanes*, 1886; H. Diels, *Parmenides*, 1899; K. Reinhardt, *Parmenides und die Geschichte der griechischen Philosophie*, 1916.

[7] Translations from Fairbanks, *First Philosophers of Greece*.

Xenophanes. In Xenophanes we discern the first trace of skepticism in Greek thought: certain knowledge about the gods and nature of things is impossible. But he asserted that we are at liberty to advance theological conjectures, and he believed that these speculations might approach the truth. Xenophanes is thus a speculative theologian rather than a philosopher. Like Pythagoras, he came under the influence of the popular religious movement of the sixth century. He attacks the prevailing polytheism with its anthropomorphism, and proclaims the unity and unchangeableness of God. "But mortals think that the gods are born as they are, and have perceptions like theirs, and voice and form." "Yes, and if oxen or lions had hands, and could paint with their hands and produce works of art as men do, horses would paint the forms of the gods like horses and oxen like oxen. Each would represent them with bodies according to the form of each." "So the Ethiopians make their gods black and snub-nosed; the Thracians give theirs red hair and blue eyes." [8] God is one, unlike mortals in body or in mind; without toil he governs all things by the thought of his mind. He abides in one place and does not move at all; he sees all over, thinks all over, and hears all over, that is, in all his parts. God is eternal—without beginning and without end. He is unlimited in the sense that there is nothing beside him, but limited in the sense that he is a sphere, a perfect form, and not a formless infinite. He is immovable as a whole, for motion is inconsistent with the unity of being— but there is motion or change in his parts.

Xenophanes (570-480 B.C.), poet, skeptic, and theologian, emigrated from Colophon in Asia Minor to southern Italy where, as a rhapsodist, he wandered from place to place. He was a satyric poet rather than a philosopher; he criticized Greek manners and beliefs—his chief polemic was against anthropomorphism and polytheism in religion. His religious attitude is skeptical—but his skepticism is a temper of mind and an attitude rather than a definitely formulated and reasoned philosophical skepticism. He presumably wrote little and only a few fragments of his works are extant.

Xenophanes is a pantheist, conceiving God as the eternal principle of the universe, as the One and All in which everything is: God, in other words, is the world; he is not a pure spirit, but the whole of animate nature. In Xenophanes' pantheistic identification of God and the world the emphasis is on the world, not on God; he is interested in reducing God to the level of the forces of nature, rather than in elevating the world to the level of the divine. Xenophanes never resolved the incompatibility between the unmoved One and the sensible world of constant change, and this opposition in his pantheism was a challenge to his successors. Xenophanes thus accepts the

[8] Trans. by Burnet, *op. cit.,* p. 115.

hylozoism of the early Greeks by conceiving nature as animate. If he believed in the gods of polytheism at all he regarded them as parts of the world, as natural phenomena; the God of his own theology is a divinity animating the world.

Xenophanes, although he formulated no broad ontological or cosmological hypotheses, did offer some natural scientific theories. From the evidence of shells and imprints of sea products in stone, he infers that all things that come into being and grow, including man, arose from earth and water. At one time the earth was mingled with the sea, but in the course of time it freed itself from moisture, and one day it will sink back into the sea, become mud again, and the race will have to begin anew. The sun and the stars he regards as fiery clouds, which are extinguished and rekindled daily; he makes the interesting suggestion that when the stars come above the uninhabited regions they are extinguished.

Parmenides' ontology. Parmenides was the metaphysician of the Eleatic school. He challenged Heraclitus' teaching that everything changes, that fire becomes water, and water earth, and earth fire, that things first are and then are not. How is this possible, he asks, how can a thing both be and not be? How can anyone think such a contradiction, how can a thing change its qualities, how can one quality become another quality? To say that it can, is to say that something is and something is not, that something can come from nothing, and that something can become nothing. Or, to employ another line of argument: if being has *become,* it must either have come from non-being or from being. If from non-being, it has come from nothing, which is impossible; if from being, then it has come from itself, which is equivalent to saying that it is identical with itself, and thus has always been.

It is evident, then, that from being only being can come, that nothing can become something else, that whatever is always has been and always will be, that everything remains what it is. Hence, there can be only one eternal, underived, unchangeable being. Since it is all alike and there cannot be anything in it but being, it must be continuous and indivisible. There can be no break in it, for if the break is real, it is itself being and so being is continuous after all; whereas if the break is not real, it is non-being, and again being is continuous. Further, it must be immovable, for there is no nonbeing (empty space) for it to move in. Moreover, being and thought are one, for what cannot be thought, cannot be; and what cannot be, i.e., non-being, cannot be thought. That is, thought and being are identical; whatever is thought has being. Thus Parmenides may be characterized as a rational or dialectical idealist. Parmenides may also have believed that being and thought are one in the sense that reality is endowed with mind; but there is scarcely sufficient evidence to warrant ascribing to him this mentalistic type of idealism.

Being or reality is a homogeneous, continuous, indeterminate mass—which the esthetic imagination of our philosopher pictures as a sphere—endowed with reason, eternal and immutable. All change is inconceivable, and, therefore, the world of sense is an illusion. To regard as true what we perceive by the senses is to confuse being with non-being. Parmenides shows a firm belief in reason: reality is conformable to reason and what is contradictory to thought cannot be real.

Besides the doctrine of "truth" which we have just outlined, Parmenides offers a doctrine of "illusion," based on sense perception, according to which there are both being and non-being, and hence motion and change. The world is the result of the mingling of two principles, the warm and light element and the cold and dark element. Organic beings arose from slime. The thought of man depends on the mixture of the elements in his body, the warm element perceiving the warmth and light in the world; the other, its opposite.

Parmenides shows us in his "true" teaching that logical thought compels us to conceive the world as a unity, as unchangeable and immovable. Sense perception, on the other hand, reveals to us a world of plurality and change: this is the world of appearance and opinion. How it is possible for such a world to exist, or how it is possible to perceive such a world, he does not tell us. The distinction between thought and illusion, which had considerable plausibility in the Heraclitean philosophy where the illusion of permanence was explained by the constant proportion maintained at each stage in the process of change, is discordant with the Parmenidean scheme. What place is there for error and illusion in a homogeneous continuous being? Perhaps the chief lesson to be learned from Parmenides is the negative one that to entify and hypostatize the objects of abstract thought and language is to obliterate the qualitative differences of the world of sense. Russell, in *A History of Western Philosophy,* has suggested that Parmenides was a victim of the linguistic fallacy of arguing from language to reality. Of Parmenides' reasoning he says:

Parmenides' reasoning is the first example in philosophy of an argument from thought and language to the world at large. It cannot, of course, be accepted as valid, but it is worthwhile to see what truth it contains. . . . The whole argument shows how easy it is to draw metaphysical conclusions from language, and how the only way to avoid fallacious arguments of this kind is to push the logical and psychological study of language further than has been done by most metaphysicians.

Zeno's dialectic. Zeno (*ca.* 490-430 B.C.), a statesman of Elea and pupil of Parmenides, attempted to prove the Eleatic doctrine by pointing out the absurdity of its opposite. He argued that, if we assume plurality and motion, we involve ourselves in contradictions; such notions are self-contradictory, hence it is impossible to accept them. His refutation of plurality is this: If the whole of being is a plurality, it is made up of many parts, and this whole can be proved to be both infinitely small and infinitely great: infinitely small because it consists of infinitely small parts (any part, no matter how small, can always be further subdivided), and the sum of such parts will itself be infinitely small; infinitely great, because to any finite part we can always add an infinite number of other parts (beyond any totality of beings no matter how large, there are always more beings) and the whole will be infinitely great. It is absurd to say that one and the same whole is both infinitely small and infinitely great, and hence we must reject completely the initial assumption of a plurality. Motion and space are impossible for similar reasons. If we say that all being is in space, we must assume that this space is in a space, and so on *ad infinitum.* Similarly, let us assume that a body is moving through space. In order to pass through a certain space, it must first have moved through half of that space; in order to have passed through this half, it must first have gone through half of this half, and so on *ad infinitum.* In short, the body can really never get anywhere; and motion is impossible.

Paradoxes of motion. Zeno advanced four famous proofs of the impossibility of motion—commonly referred to as Zeno's Paradoxes of Motion—which are reproduced by Aristotle.[9] Of these arguments, the first demonstrates the impossibility of moving from a position to a goal because of the necessity of passing through the infinite number of points between the starting point and the goal. The second, the paradox of Achilles and the tortoise, demonstrates the impossibility of passing a moving goal: Achilles—despite his greater speed—cannot reach the tortoise for, while Achilles is moving from his initial starting point to the tortoise's initial starting point, the tortoise has moved a certain distance beyond and the same holds for all subsequent intervals. The third argument—the paradox of the moving arrow—demonstrates that the arrow apparently moving to its target is at any given

[9] *Physics,* VI, 9, 239b.

instant in a definite position in space—i.e., it is at rest or has zero motion, but no summation of zeros can yield motion. All three of these arguments rest on the questionable supposition that space and time consist of discrete instants and points respectively.[10] Zeno also advances a fourth argument, which appeals to the relativity of observed motions: The variable and conflicting testimony of the senses, depending upon whether a moving object is observed from a position at rest or in motion at various speeds, undermines the very possibility of motion as such. This argument, though it differs in its presuppositions from the other three, is perhaps of equal interest. Zeno's paradoxes can, to be sure, be resolved, but only in the context of mathematical, physical or philosophical theories of the continuum and of reality.

Melissus of Samos, a successful admiral, attempted a proof of the Eleatic doctrine. With Parmenides, he asserted that being is one. Moreover, being cannot have originated, for that would mean that there was a non-being before there was being; and from non-being being cannot come. Being is thus infinite in time, or eternal. Melissus asserted that being is also infinite in space; his doctrine of the spatial infinitude of being is not only at variance with Parmenides' teaching that being is a finite sphere, but with the general tendency of Greek thought to repudiate the infinite as meaningless and unthinkable. There is, according to Melissus, no empty space or non-being, hence motion, which requires space, is impossible. If there is neither multiplicity nor motion, there can be neither separation nor combination, and no change. Hence, the senses deceive us in presenting motion and change.

5. QUALITATIVE THEORIES

Solution of the Riddle of Change. The old nature philosophers had all implicitly assumed that nothing can arise or disappear, that absolute creation or destruction is impossible. They did not, however, bring this thought to consciousness. They accepted it without criticism. It was implicit rather than explicit in their minds. The Eleatic thinkers became fully conscious of the axiom. They did not merely tacitly presuppose it in their reasonings, but deliberately asserted it as an absolute principle of thought and rigorously applied it. Nothing can arise or disappear, and nothing can change into anything else; no quality can become another quality, for that would mean the

[10] Cf. Windelband, *History of Philosophy,* trans. by J. H. Tufts, pp. 42 ff.

disappearance of a quality on the one hand, and the creation of a quality on the other. Reality is permanent and unchangeable, change a fiction for which the senses are responsible.

Still, things *seem* to persist, and things *seem* to change. How is it possible for things to persist and yet to change? How can we escape from this impasse? Philosophy could not leave the matter thus. The riddle of permanence and change had to be solved, the static and the dynamic views of the world had to be reconciled in some way. The successors of Heraclitus and Parmenides attempted such a reconciliation.

In general, the solution of the riddle proceeded along these lines: *absolute* change, they say, is impossible; so far the Eleatics are right. It is impossible for a thing to come from nothing, to become nothing, and to change absolutely. And yet we have the right to speak of origin and decay, growth and change, in a *relative* sense. There are *beings* or particles of reality that are permanent, original, imperishable, underived, and these cannot change into anything else: they are what they are and must remain so, just as the Eleatic school maintains. These beings, or particles of reality, however, can be combined and separated, and when combined they form bodies that can again be resolved into their elements. The original bits of reality cannot be created or destroyed or change their nature, but they can change their relations in respect to each other, and this is what is meant by change. In other words, absolute change of the elements is impossible, but relative change is quite possible. Origin means combination, decay separation; change is an alteration of the mutual relations of elements.

Empedocles, Anaxagoras, and the atomists give the same general answer to the problem proposed by Heraclitus and Parmenides. They agree that absolute change is impossible, but that there is relative change. They differ, however, in their answers to the following questions: (1) What is the nature of the particles of reality of which the world is composed? (2) What causes these particles to combine and separate? According to Empedocles and Anaxagoras, the elements have definite qualities; according to the quantitative atomists, they are without quality. Empedocles asserts that there are four qualitative elements: earth, air, fire, water; Anaxagoras, that there are countless numbers of such elements. According to Empedocles, two mythical beings, Love and Hate, cause the elements to unite and divide; according to Anaxagoras, a mind outside the elements initiates motion. The quantitative atomists, Leucippus and Democritus, assert that motion is inherent in the elements themselves.

Empedocles. For Empedocles, there is neither origin nor decay in the strict sense of the word, but only mingling and separation. "For it cannot be that aught can arise from what in no way is, and it is impossible and unheard of that what *is* should perish; for it always will *be,* wherever one may keep putting it." [11] There are four elements, or "roots of things," each having its specific nature: earth, air, fire, water; they are underived, unchangeable, and indestructible. Bodies are formed by the coming together of these elements, and destroyed by their dissolution. The influence of one body on another is explained as the passing of effusions from the one into the pores of the other, into which they fit.

Empedocles was born in Agrigentum, southern Sicily, 495 B.C., the son of a wealthy and public-spirited family. He was for a long time the leader of the democracy of his native city, and it is said of him that he declined the kingship. He died, probably as an exile, in the Peloponnesus, 435 B.C. The story that he committed suicide by leaping into the crater of Mt. Aetna is legendary. Empedocles was not only a statesman and orator, but a religious teacher, physician, poet, and philosopher. Many stories are told of the miracles he worked, and it is not unlikely that he himself believed in his powers of magic. We possess fragments of two poems, the one cosmological, *On Nature,* the other religious, bearing the title *Purifications.* See *Fragments of Empedocles,* trans. into English verse by W. E. Leonard, 1908.

What causes the elements to unite and divide? Empedocles explains change by assuming two mythical forces, Love and Strife, or Hate, in addition to the four elements and controlling their union and division. Empedocles did not deny that the two motive forces—which we might call attraction and repulsion—may exist together, the former causing bodies to be formed and the latter causing them to be destroyed. Originally, all the elements were mingled together in the form of a sphere in which Love reigned supreme and from which Hate was excluded. But gradually Strife, gaining the upper hand, entered and scattered the elements. At this intermediate stage, when the elements are partially separated, things exist; but with the ultimate triumph of Hate the elements are completely separated from one another and there are no longer individual bodies of any kind. At this point, the process is reversed and Love again enters and gradually re-establishes the original homogeneous mixture; and then the process of disintegration will begin anew, and so on in periodic change. In the two extreme states—of complete union and complete separation—there are no individual bodies; the stage of individual bodies, as exemplified by the present state of the world, is an intermediate state of partial mixture and partial separation.

[11] Trans. by Burnet, *op. cit.,* p. 221.

In the process of formation of the present state of the cosmos, air or ether first separated, forming the arch of the heavens; fire came next, forming the sphere of stars beneath; water was pressed from the earth by rotating motion, and seas were formed; and the evaporation of the water by the fire of heaven produced the lower atmosphere. Organic life arose from the earth: first plants, then different parts of animals, arms, eyes and heads. These parts were combined, haphazard, producing all kinds of shapeless lumps and monsters—creatures with double faces, offspring of oxen with human faces, children of men with oxen's heads—which separated again until, after many trials, such forms were produced as were fit to live; and these are perpetuated by generation.

Man is composed of the four elements, which accounts for his ability to know each of them: like is known by like; it is by earth that we see earth; and by water, water; and by air, glorious air; and so on. Sense perception is explained by the action of bodies on the sense organs. For example, in vision, particles of fire and water pass from the object seen to the eye, where they are met by similar particles passing through the pores of the eye, under the influence of the attraction of the particles from without. By the contact of these bodies, near the surface of the eye, images are produced. Only such particles, however, affect the eye as fit into its pores. In hearing, air rushes into the ear and there produces sound; in taste and smell, particles enter the nose and mouth. The heart is the seat of intelligence.

Empedocles, in the hylozoistic fashion of the early Greek philosophers of nature, ascribes psychic life to all things: "All things have power of thought." In his religious work he teaches the fall of man and the transmigration of souls, doctrines which seem to connect him with the great Orphic sect that influenced all Hellas.

Anaxagoras. The problem for Anaxagoras, as for Empedocles, was to explain the phenomenon of change. He accepted the Eleatic notion that absolute change is impossible, that no quality can become another quality, that reality must be permanent and unchangeable in its fundamental essence: "Nothing comes into being or passes away." He did not, however, deny the fact of change. There is relative change; things do come into existence and pass away in the sense of the mingling and separation of elements. The number of elements, in his opinion, must be more than the four proposed by Empedocles; for a world so rich and full of qualities as ours cannot be explained by so few. Besides, earth, air, fire, and water are not elements at all; they are mixtures of other substances. Anaxagoras, therefore, assumed, as his ultimates, an infinite number of substances of specific quality, "having all sorts of forms and colors and tastes," particles of flesh, hair, blood, bone, silver, gold, and so on. Such extremely small, but not indivisible, corpuscles are uncaused and changeless, for "how could flesh come from that which is not flesh?" Their quantity as well as their quality is constant, nothing can be added or taken away, or altered in quality. He was led to this view by the following reflections: The body is made of skin, bones, blood, flesh, etc., differing in lightness and darkness, in heat and cold, softness and hardness, and so on. It is nourished by food, hence food must contain portions of such substances as make up the body and, since food draws its ingredients from earth, water, air, and the sun, the latter must furnish the substances composing food. Hence, the so-called simple elements of Empedocles are in reality the most complex things of all; they are veritable reservoirs of extremely small particles of matter of all kinds. They must contain all the substances to be found in the organic body, otherwise how could we account for the presence of skin, bone, and blood in the body?

Anaxagoras (500-428 B.C.) was born in Clazomenae, in Asia Minor, took up his abode at Athens, and became the friend of the great statesman Pericles, who aimed to make his city the intellectual as well as political center of Hellas. Faced with the charge of atheism, brought against him by the enemies of his patron, he left Athens after a residence of thirty years (464-434), and settled at Lampsacus, where he died. He was a noted mathematician and astronomer, as well as philosopher. We have important fragments of his work *On Nature,* which was written in clear and simple prose.

F. Breier, *Die Philosophie des Anaxagoras,* 1840; M. Heinze, *Über den* νοῦς *des Anaxagoras,* 1890.

In the original state of the universe, before the formation of worlds, infinitely small particles of matter—which our philosopher called germs or seeds (spermata) and which Aristotle, in his account of Anaxagoras, designated homogeneous parts or *homoiomere*—were all mingled together in a confused mass, filling the entire universe, and not separated from one another by empty spaces. The original mass is a mixture of an infinite number of infinitely small seeds. The world, as it exists now, is the result of the mingling and separation of the particles composing this mass. But how were the seeds separated from the chaos in which they lay scattered, and united into a cosmos or world-order? By mechanical means, or motion, by change of place. The seeds, however, are neither endowed with life, as the hylozoists hold, nor are they moved by Love and Hate. What, then, caused them to move? Anaxagoras finds the clue to his answer in the rotation of the heavenly bodies observed by us. A rapid and forcible whirling motion, produced at a certain point in the mass, separated the germs; this motion extended farther and farther, bringing like particles together, and will continue to spread until the original chaotic mixture is completely disentangled. The first rotation caused the separation of the dense from the rare, the warm from the cold, the bright from the dark, the dry from the moist. "The dense, the moist, the cold, the dark, collected where the earth now is; the rare, the warm, the dry, the bright, departed toward the farther part of the ether." The process of separation continued and led to the formation of the heavenly bodies, which are solid masses hurled from the earth by the force of the rotation, and to the formation of different bodies on the earth. The heat of the sun gradually dried up the moist earth; and from the seeds filling the air which were deposited in the earth-slime by the falling rain, organic bodies arose. To these organic bodies Anaxagoras ascribed souls in order to explain their movements.

The entire complex world-process, as it now appears, is accordingly the result of a long series of movements, which followed necessarily from the original rotation. And what caused that? To account for the initial motion, Anaxagoras has recourse to an intelligent principle, a mind or *nous*, a world-ordering spirit, which he conceives as an absolutely simple and homogeneous substance—not mixed with other elements or seeds, but absolutely separate and distinct from them—that has power over matter. *Nous* is a spontaneous active being, the free source of all movement and life in the world: it knows all things past, present, and future, it arranges all things and is the cause of all things. It rules over all that has life. The *nous* is a teleological or purposive principle, and this teleological point of view precluded either a plurality of successive or contemporaneous worlds; the ordering mind forms only the one unique and most perfect world. In Anaxagoras we encounter for the first time the linking of teleology with the uniqueness and perfection of the world-order. If the world-scheme is the product of a purposive mind, there can be no cyclical recurrence such as Empedocles asserted.

Interpreters of Anaxagoras differ as to whether mind or *nous* was pure spirit, or an exceedingly fine matter, or something not entirely material and not entirely immaterial. Although he sometimes expresses himself awkwardly on this point, calling mind the most rarefied of all things and thus suggesting that it is a kind of matter, it is presumably a distinct principle in that it never mingles with anything else. We may accordingly describe his position as a vague dualism, a dualism not yet sharply defined. Mind initiated the world-process, but it also seems to be present in the world, in organic forms, even in minerals—indeed, wherever it is needed to account for movements not otherwise explicable. It exists in the surrounding mass, in the things that were separated, and in things that are being separated. To use modern terms, it is both transcendent and immanent; theism and pantheism are not sharply separated in the system. Aristotle is quite right in criticizing Anaxagoras for invoking mind only when mechanical explanation fails: "Anaxagoras uses mind as a device by which to construct the universe, and when he is at a loss for the cause why anything necessarily is, then he drags it in, but in other cases he assigns any other cause rather than mind for what comes into being." [12] The fact is, Anaxagoras endeavored to explain everything by mechanical principles, and had recourse to mind as the intelligent cause of motion only as a last resort. Nevertheless, by virtue of his introduction of mind as an explanatory principle in his philosophy, he has become one of the founders of philosophical idealism.

6. QUANTITATIVE THEORIES

The Atomism of Democritus. Empedocles and Anaxagoras paved the way for the natural-scientific view of the universe, which, under the name of the atomic theory, has remained influential in science to this day. The teachings of Empedocles and Anaxagoras needed revision in several important respects, and this they received at the hands of the atomists Leucippus and Democritus.

The atomists agree with their predecessors in the acceptance of original and changeless particles of reality, but they deny them the qualitative properties ascribed to them by Empedocles and Anaxagoras, and reject the view that they are moved from without by Love and Hate or by a mind. Earth, air, fire and water are not the "roots of all things" as Empedocles claimed, nor are there numberless "seeds" of different qualities, as Anaxagoras supposed. Such things are not real elements, but are themselves composed of simpler units, invisible, impenetrable, indivisible spatial entities, or atoms, which differ from one another in form, weight, and size; and these units or atoms have their own inherent motion.

The significant differences between the qualitative theory of Anaxagoras and the atomic theory of Democritus which superseded it are these: (1) Anaxagoras posited an unlimited number of qualitatively differing elements, while Democritus assumed an infinite number of atoms, differing from one another solely in quantitative respects such as shape, size, etc. (2) The ele-

[12] Trans. by Fairbanks, *op. cit.*

ments of Anaxagoras admitted of indefinite subdivision into smaller and smaller particles, whereas the atoms of Democritus were simple and physically indivisible, for that in terms of which everything else is explained must be ultimate and incapable of being split into parts *ad infinitum*. (3) Anaxagoras says nothing about empty space and presumably believed that reality is everywhere qualitative; Democritus, on the other hand, insisted on the reality of empty space as a condition of the motion of the atoms. (4) Anaxagoras explained motion by reference to mind—a principle apart from the moving elements; Democritus considered motion an intrinsic property of the atoms. (5) Finally, the mind of Anaxagoras is a purposive or teleological principle; the atoms of Democritus are subject to mechanical law.

The founders of the school of atomists are Leucippus and Democritus. Of Leucippus we know almost nothing; his very existence has been doubted by some, while others, with Aristotle, regard him as the real originator of the atomic system.[13] The latter view is probably the correct one. He is said to have come from Miletus, to have studied under Zeno at Elea, and to have established the school at Abdera which his pupil Democritus made famous. His writings, which were few, were, so it is reported, incorporated in the works of his disciple.

Democritus was born about 460 B.C. in the commercial city of Abdera, situated on the coast of Thrace, and died 370. He traveled extensively, wrote many books on physics, metaphysics, ethics, and history, and ranked high as a mathematician.

Comparatively few fragments of his writings have come down to us, and we cannot always decide with certainty what belongs to him and what to Leucippus. We may, however, with the help of the materials at hand, form a very adequate notion of the atomic theory, even though the question of its authorship must be left in doubt.

A. Brieger, *Die Urbewegung der Atome*, 1884; F. Lortzing, *Über die ethischen Fragmente Demokrits*, 1873; P. G. Natorp, *Die Ethika des Demokritos*, 1893.

Metaphysics and Cosmology. The atomists agree with the Eleatics that absolute change is impossible; reality is, in its essence, permanent, indestructible, unchangeable. At the same time, it cannot be denied that change is going on, that things are in constant motion. Now, motion and change would be unthinkable without empty space, or the void which Parmenides had called non-being. Hence, the atomists insist, non-being, or empty space, exists. They have the audacity to assert that the non-being of Parmenides actually exists—that it is the empty space in which the atoms move. This does not mean that empty space is real in the sense of being corporeal, but that it possesses its own kind of reality. Bodies are no more real than space; a thing can be real without being a body. The atoms and the empty space in which

---

[13] Cf. Burnet, *op. cit.*

they move are the sole realities for the atomists: everything is either plenum or void. Being, or the full, and non-being, or the void, are equally real. That is, the real is not one continuous, undivided, immovable being, as the Eleatics held, but a plurality, an infinite number of beings, separated from one another by empty space.

Each of these beings is indivisible, impenetrable, and simple, an atom. The atom is not a mathematical point, or a center of force, as some moderns conceive it, but has extension; since it is extended, it is not a mathematically indivisible point, but a physically indivisible particle, i.e., it cannot be physically split or divided into parts. All atoms are alike in quality; they are neither earth, air, fire, or water, nor are they germs of specific kinds. They are simply very small, compact, physical units, differing in shape, size, weight, arrangement and position. They are underived, indestructible, unchangeable. What they are, they always have been and ever shall be. In other words, atoms are the one indivisible being of Parmenides broken up into small bits that cannot be further divided, and each atom possesses the eternity and unchangeability and indivisibility which Parmenides ascribed to his single being.

These atoms, which are separated from one another by empty spaces, are the building stones of reality from which the different objects are formed, as comedies and tragedies are composed of the same letters of the alphabet, combined and recombined in different ways. All bodies are combinations of atoms and spaces: origin means union; destruction, separation. Bodies differ because the atoms constituting them differ in the ways already mentioned. They act on one another by direct contact only, through pressure and impact, or by means of emanations moving from one body and striking another—any action at a distance being excluded by the atomistic hypothesis. What causes atoms to unite and separate is the motion inherent in them. The motion of the atoms is governed by inexorable mechanical law: "Nothing happens without a ground, but everything for a reason and necessarily." The inherent motion of the atoms is uncaused like the atoms themselves; they have never been at rest, but have been in motion from the beginning. Space cannot be the cause of motion; and hence motion must be regarded as an inherent property of each atom. Owing to the many different shapes of atoms, some having hooks, others eyes, or grooves, or humps, or depressions, they interlace and hook together. The solidity and rigidity of physical objects consisting of larger groupings of atoms are due to this interlocking.

Cosmic evolution is explained as follows: The cosmos consists of number-less atoms of various shapes, sizes and motions, impinging on one another from different directions and forming, as a result of their impact a vortex. This vortex motion brings together atoms of similar shape and size and thereby generates composite things such as fire, air, earth and water. The whirling motion extends farther and farther, and multitudes of worlds are produced in this way, each system having a center and forming a sphere. Some systems have neither sun nor moon, while others have planets larger and greater in number than those of our system. The earth is one of the bodies thus created. From the moist earth, or slime, life arose. Fiery atoms, which are distributed over the entire living organism, account for the heat of living bodies; and are especially abundant in the human soul.

Psychology and Theory of Knowledge. The soul is composed of the finest, roundest, most nimble, and fiery atoms, which are scattered over the entire body—there being always one soul-atom between two other atoms—and which produce the movements of the body. Certain organs of the body are the seat of particular mental functions: the brain, of thought; the heart, of anger; the liver, of desire. The resistance of every object, whether alive or not, to the pressure of surrounding forces is explained by the presence in it of such a soul. We inhale and exhale soul-atoms, and life exists only so long as this process continues. At death, the soul-atoms are scattered; when the vessel of the soul is shattered, the soul spills out. We have here the crude beginnings of a physiological psychology on a materialistic basis.

Sense perception is explained as a change produced in the soul by the action of emanations, or images, or idols resembling the perceived body. All bodies project images which are transmitted through the intervening air and finally impinge on the organs of sense. Images thrown off by an object modify the arrangement of the particles next to the object; these in turn modify the object immediately adjoining it and so on, until the emanations reach the sense organs and the atoms constituting the soul. If the images or effluxes proceeding from objects interfere with each other in the process of trans-mission, illusion results. If they proceed without interference—if they make a direct hit on the organs of sense and finally on the soul—true knowledge ensues. The like perceives the like, that is, perception is possible only when the images emanating from a body are like those projected by the sense organ. By means of such images, which emanate from objects everywhere, Democritus explains dreams, prophetic visions, and the belief in gods.

The sensible qualities (color, sound, taste, smell, etc.) which we attribute to the different bodies are not in the things themselves, but merely effects of combinations of atoms on our sense organs. Atoms, as such, have no qualities other than those we have already mentioned, impenetrability, shape, and size. Hence, sense perception does not yield a true knowledge of things; it indicates merely how things affect us. The Greek atomists antici- pated the distinction, which we shall encounter in modern philosophy, between primary qualities (impenetrability, shape, etc.) and secondary quali- ties (color, sound, smell, etc.). We cannot *see* atoms as they are; we can, however, *think* them. Sense perception is obscure knowledge; thought, which transcends our sense perceptions and appearances, and reaches the atom, is the only genuine knowledge. Democritus is a rationalist, as, indeed, all the early Greek philosophers are. Rational thought is not, however, independent of sense perception; indeed reason, "the genuine way of knowing," begins where sense perception ends. The senses reveal only the gross aspects of ob- jects; and "when the investigation must be carried into that which is still finer," the reason must transcend sense knowledge. Reason is the highest function of the soul—indeed, for Democritus soul and reason are the same thing.

Theology and Ethics. Gods also exist and are composed of atoms; the gods are mortal like men—though longer-lived. The gods are more powerful than men and possess reason of a high order. They are knowable by men in dreams and perhaps in other ways, but they do not interfere in the affairs of men and hence they need not be feared or propitiated. Like all other things, the gods are subject to the impersonal law of the motion of the atoms.

The superiority of reason to sense which we have noted in Democritus' epistemology is extended to the sphere of ethics: The end of all conduct is well-being, by which he means not the pleasures of sense alone but rather the satisfaction which accompanies the exercise of the rational faculties. In the ethical fragments attributed to Democritus, we can trace the outlines of a refined hedonistic ethics. The association of materialism and hedonism, encountered here for the first time, no doubt reflects a natural affinity between these two doctrines; pleasure has a quantitative and palpable character which harmonizes well with the materialistic and naturalistic philosophy. The true end of life, says Democritus, is happiness, which he describes as an inner state of satisfaction or pleasure, depending on the tranquillity, har- mony, fearlessness of the soul. This inner happiness does not depend on wealth or material goods, nor on the pleasures of the body—for these are brief, productive of pains, and require repetition—but on moderation in pleasure and symmetry of life. The less we desire, the less apt are we to be disappointed. The best way to achieve the goal is to exercise one's mental powers, through reflection and the contemplation of beautiful acts.

All virtues are valuable in so far as they contribute to happiness, the highest good; chief among them are justice and benevolence. Envy, jealousy and bitterness of mind create discord and are harmful to everybody. We should do right, not from fear of punishment, but from a sense of duty. To be good, one must not merely refrain from doing wrong—one must not even desire to do wrong. "You can tell the man who rings true from the man who rings false, not by his deeds alone, but also by his desires." "The right-minded man, ever inclined to righteous and lawful deeds, is joyous day and night, and strong, and free from care." We ought to serve the state because "a well-administered state is our greatest safeguard." "When the state is in a healthy condition, all things prosper; when it is corrupt, all things go to ruin."[14]

---

[14] Translations taken from Bakewell, *Source Book in Ancient Philosophy.*

II
Problems of Knowledge and Conduct

7. The Age of the Sophists

Progress of Thought. Philosophy had made great progress since the days of the theogonies and cosmogonies. The old conceptions of the world and of life had been profoundly transformed under its influence. The extent of the transformation is plainly shown by the contrast between the naïve theory of a universe full of gods and occult mythical forms and the machine-theory of the atomists. The spirit of free inquiry, however, was not confined to the philosophers' schools, but, as was inevitable, permeated other fields of thought. There, too, new conceptions were gradually displacing the old. We may note the change in the dramatic poetry of Aeschylus (525-456 B.C.), Sophocles (496-405 B.C.), and Euripides (480-406 B.C.); their views concerning life and religion are deepened and broadened by criticism and reflection. We see it in the writings of the historians and the geographers: the old legendary tales and superstitions, which had formerly found such ready acceptance, are discredited, and Herodotus (b. 480) paves the way for a critical study of history, of which Thucydides (b. 471) is the finest classical representative. In medicine, the old fantastic ideas and practices are abandoned by the leaders of the craft; the need of a knowlege of nature and of man is felt, and the physical theories of the philosophers, many of whom were themselves physicians, are applied in the art of healing. The name of Hippocrates (b. 460) stands out as a landmark of the progress made by Greece in the direction of a scientific study of medicine. The investigations of the physicians came to be of great value to students of philosophy, by showing the importance of observation and experience.[1]

[1] Cf. T. Gomperz, *Greek Thinkers*, Vol. I.

We now reach a period in the history of Greek philosophy in which the construction of great systems of thought temporarily ceases. Some thinkers simply continue to develop the teachings of the existing schools, others seek, in eclectic fashion, to combine the doctrines of the earlier philosophers with those of later masters; some turn their attention to the natural-scientific investigations which were being pursued by the schools of medicine, others are interested in the study of the mental disciplines forming the basis of morals, law, and politics. The zeal for investigation was intense and extended to all sorts of problems, including questions concerning the origin and purpose of the state, the principles of conduct, religion, art, and education. Highly specialized manuals were produced in abundance; rules were formulated for every form of human activity, from the cooking of food to the creation of works of art, from taking a walk to carrying on war. In all these endeavors philosophy was a leavening influence. The spirit of independent reflection and criticism, so characteristic of the beginnings of philosophy in Greece, had invaded every field of study, and was preparing the way for another and greater era of speculative thought. But the human mind had to follow many false paths and lose itself in many blind alleys before the culmination was reached. We shall attempt to describe the fortunes of philosophy during the second half of the fifth century B.C., a century of great significance for the history of Greece and civilization in general.

Greek Enlightenment. We have observed in the political, moral, religious, and philosophical development of the Hellenic people a growing tendency toward freedom and individualism. The critical attitude toward life and human institutions had already made itself felt in their early poetry, faintly in Homer, with increasing force in Hesiod and the poets of the seventh and sixth centuries B.C. These men meditated upon the manners and customs of their times, upon the social and political institutions, upon the religious ideas and practices, upon the origin, nature, and behavior of the gods. They developed a purer concept of deity, and, in their theogonies and cosmogonies, prepared the way for the coming of philosophy. In the philosophies of the sixth century, the tendency to independent thinking appears almost full-fledged. During this century and the first half of the fifth, natural science and nature philosophy are the order of the day; the inquiring mind turns outward to the world of physical things. An effort is made to understand the meaning of the cosmos; system after system is offered to solve the riddle of the universe. The chief object of interest is the world and its ways; man's place in nature is determined by the conclusions reached in metaphysics.

The political, economic, and intellectual experiences of the Greek people during the fifth century were highly favorable to the development of the spirit of enlightenment which characterized their philosophers. The Persian wars (500-449 B.C.) had left Athens the mistress of the sea and a world-power, as well as the commercial, intellectual, and artistic center of Greece. Poets, artists, teachers, and philosophers now entered her gates and helped to entertain and instruct her wealthy citizens; magnificent buildings and statues adorned the city, and the theaters rang with the plaudits of a self-satisfied people. When we call to mind the illustrious men who dwelt within the city-walls during the second half of the fifth century—Pericles, Anaxagoras, Thucydides, Phidias, Sophocles, Euripides, Aristophanes, Hippocrates, Socrates—we can well understand the proud claim of the great funeral oration delivered by Pericles, that Athens was the school for Greece.

The great economic changes and the establishment of democratic institutions fostered by the new order of things, gave a further impetus to independent thought and action, and with these came the desire for power and for the things that bring power: wealth, fame, culture, efficiency, and success. The traditional views of religion, morality, politics, philosophy, science, and art were subjected to criticism. The old foundations were examined and in many cases torn up. The spirit that denies was abroad in the land. The demand for instruction in the new subjects of study grew strong. Public life offered a splendid field for men skilled in persuading and convincing the people, and preparation in the arts of rhetoric, oratory, and dialectics became a practical necessity.

The age we have been describing was an age of enlightenment (*Aufklärung*), strikingly parallel to the eighteenth-century enlightenment of the modern era. The attitude of mind engendered could not fail to encourage the growth of individualism. The individual began to cut loose from the authority of the group, to strike out for himself, to think his own thoughts and to work out his own salvation, independently of the old traditions. Although this critical habit of thought made an invaluable contribution to the development of Greek culture, it assumed an exaggerated form in some quarters and culminated in mere quibbling and hair-splitting; in others, it tended to degenerate into intellectual and ethical subjectivism and relativism: What I happen to think true, *is* true; what I happen to believe right, *is* right. One man's opinion is as good as another's; one man's way of acting is as good as another's. It is not surprising, under the circumstances, that *no* man's opinion should have been esteemed very highly, that skepticism should have flourished in the theoretical sphere, and that the gospel of self-interest should have been preached in the field of practice. An often quoted passage from Thucydides, though it perhaps exaggerates, throws some light upon a degenerate phase of the new movement:

The common meaning of words was turned about at men's pleasure; the most reckless bravado was deemed the most desirable friend; a man of prudence and moderation was styled a coward; a man who listened to reason was a good-for-nothing simpleton. People were trusted exactly in proportion to their violence and unscrupulousness, and no one was so popular as the successful conspirator, except perhaps one who had been clever enough to outwit him at his own trade, but any one who honestly attempted to remove the causes of such treacheries was considered a traitor to his party. As for oaths, no one imagined they were to be kept a moment longer than occasion required; it was in fact an added pleasure to destroy your enemy if you had managed to catch him through his trusting to your word.[2]

Aristophanes, in his comedies, also shows us the seamy side of the new civilization. According to him, says Benn,

the ancient discipline had in time become very much relaxed. The rich were idle and extravagant; the poor mutinous; young men were growing more and more insolent to their elders; religion was derided; all classes were animated by a common desire to make money and to spend it on sensual enjoyment.[3]

This was one side of the picture, the picture of the free-thinking, individualistic, wealth-seeking child of the age. On the other side we see the conservative, the representative of the good old times, who opposes the new thought, the new education, the new virtues, or rather the new vices, because intellectual pursuits seemed to him to lead "to irreligion and immorality, to make young people quite unlike their grandfathers, and [to be] somehow connected with loose company and a fast life."[4]

The Sophists. The new movement was represented by the Sophists. The term Sophist originally meant a wise and skillful man, but in the time we are describing it came to be applied to the professional teachers who traveled about, giving instruction for pay in the art of thinking and speaking, and preparing young men for political life. The name Sophist, however, gradually became a term of reproach, partly because the Sophists took pay, partly owing to the radicalism of some of the later Sophists, which scandalized the conservative element. The Sophists devoted themselves to their chosen task with feverish zeal. "If you associate with me," Protagoras is represented by

[2] *History of the Peloponnesian War,* Bk. III, 82.
[3] Benn, *The Greek Philosophers,* Vol. I, p. 74.
[4] Benn, *op. cit.,* p. 93.

Plato as having said to a young man, "on the very day you will return a better man than you came." And when Socrates asks how he is going to bring this about, he answers: "If he comes to me, he will learn that which he comes to learn. And this is prudence in affairs, private as well as public; he will learn to order his house in the best manner, and he will be able to speak and act for the best in the affairs of the state." In order to fit himself for a career, it was necessary for a young man to perfect himself in dialectics, grammar, rhetoric, and oratory. Such subjects the Sophists began to study with narrowly practical ends in view, but they unwittingly broke the soil for new fields of theoretical investigation. They also turned their attention to moral and political questions, and thereby gave a strong impetus to a more systematic and thorough treatment of ethics and the theory of the state. As the moral earnestness of the times declined and was superseded by the desire to succeed at all costs, some of the later Sophists, in their anxiety to make their pupils efficient, often went to extremes. The object of their instruction now became to teach their pupils how to vanquish an opponent by fair means or foul, to make the worse appear the better cause, to confound him with all sorts of logical fallacies—indeed, the terms "sophism" and "sophistry" now denote such fallacious reasoning—and to render him ridiculous.

Theory of knowledge. The sophistic age was not primarily one of a moral and religious reformation—this is a mistaken view which has arisen through exaggerating its similarity to the eighteenth-century Enlightenment. On the contrary, sophistry is, in the first instance, a protest against the paradoxical conclusions of the nature philosophers or cosmologists.[5] The Sophists' attention was directed to the problem of knowledge by the diversity of opinions found among the Greek nature philosophers; the conclusion they reached was that the lack of agreement among their predecessors was due to a limitation of the human faculty of thought, which was incapable of grappling with the problems which the cosmologists had propounded. In other words, the critical spirit of the age, which had, in a large measure, been fostered by philosophy, began to react upon philosophy itself and led to a temporary depreciation of metaphysical speculation. Thought weighs itself in the balance and finds itself wanting; philosophy becomes self-critical. No two philosophers, it is argued, seem to agree in their answers to the question of the essence of reality. One makes it water, another air, another fire, another earth, and yet another all of them together; one declares change to be impossible, another says there is nothing but change. Now, if there is no change,

[5] Cf. Burnet, *Greek Philosophy,* Part I, *Thales to Plato,* p. 109.

there can be no knowledge: we cannot predicate anything of anything, for how can the one be the many? If everything changes, there can be no knowledge either; for where nothing persists, how can we predicate anything of anything? And if we can know things only so far as they affect our senses, as some philosophers maintain, again we cannot know, for then the nature of things eludes our grasp. The upshot of it all is, we cannot solve the riddle of the universe. The truth begins to dawn on the Sophist that the mind of man is an important factor in the process of knowing. Thinkers before him had assumed the competence of human reason to attain truth; with all their critical acumen they had forgotten to criticize the intellect itself. The Sophist now turns the light on the knowing subject and concludes that knowledge depends upon the particular knower, that what seems true to him *is* true for him, that there is no objective truth, but only subjective opinion. "Man is the measure of all things," so Protagoras taught. Protagoras' relativistic doctrine of man the measure (*homo mensura*) is a repudiation of the paradoxical conclusions of the philosophers—especially Parmenides and Zeno—in favor of the common sense judgments of the individual man. "Man," as referred to in Protagoras' formula, is not man generically, *genus homo,* but the individual man. The individual is a law unto himself in matters of knowledge. The opinions of individuals which are often opposed to one another may, according to this formula, *all* be true: "Nothing is one thing rather than another"; two opposite statements may both be true—each relative to the subjective make-up of the individual enunciating the statement. It is, accordingly, the business of the Sophist not to demonstrate *the* truth, but to persuade people to embrace one of two opposing statements rather than the other. Even though Protagoras insists that two mutually contradictory statements might be equally true, he concedes that one might be "better" than another—by which he presumably means that one is more normal or natural than the other: the vision of the normal eye is more reliable than that of the jaundiced eye. In appealing to the normal, Protagoras is guilty of reinstating a standard of truth after having denied all standards.[6]

Whereas Protagoras solved the problem raised by the conflict of opinions by asserting that they are *all* true—though some among them are more normal than others—Gorgias took the extreme position that *none* of them are true. In his work entitled *On Nature or the Nonexistent,* he sets forth a completely negativistic philosophy in three statements: (1) there is nothing; (2) even if there were something we could not know it; and (3) even

---

[6] Cf. Burnet, *op. cit.,* p. 116.

if it existed and we could know it we could not communicate this knowledge to others. The sophistic theory of knowledge is for the most part negative and skeptical, but it does, at least for some of its exponents, have its positive side also. The dialectical arguments employed by the Sophists, though they were designed to confute their adversaries rather than to establish true knowledge, by their cleverness and ingenuity paved the way for the dialectic of Plato and the logic of Aristotle. Another positive contribution of the Sophists consists in a recognition of the pragmatic aspects of knowledge. Absolute theoretic truth, they urged, is unattainable, but the relative knowledge achieved by the individual has a practical bearing on the conduct of the ordinary affairs of life. In their emphasis on the applicability and workableness of truths, relative to the individual, the Sophists formulated a position which has been revived in recent times under the name of pragmatism.

Ethics. The subjectivism and relativism which characterize the sophistic theory of knowledge appear in their ethical views also. From theoretical skepticism the step is not far to ethical skepticism, to the view that man is a law unto himself in matters of conduct. If knowledge is impossible, then knowledge of right and wrong is impossible, there is no universal right and wrong and conscience is a mere subjective affair. The ethical arguments of sophistry parallel the epistemological ones: just as the conflicting cosmological speculations of the nature philosophers led the Sophists to question the possibility of theoretical knowledge, so the diversity of customs, morals and traditions of various nations lead them to question the validity of any absolute, objective standards of conduct and social action. These extreme ethical implications were not drawn by the older Sophists, such as Protagoras (b. *ca.* 490 B.C.) and Gorgias. Protagoras' social and political philosophy is neither radical nor revolutionary; to be sure, he insisted that all established institutions, including law and morality, were merely conventional, but he recognized at the same time their necessity—in other words, that certain legal and moral rules *must* be adhered to, *if* there is to be any social and moral order at all. The moral and social conventions raise man above the level of the brute and transform him into a social animal. Gorgias, too, in spite of his radical skepticism in the sphere of knowledge, shared Protagoras' conservatism in morals. A more negative approach to morality and the law was current among the young radical set which included Polus, Thrasymachus, Callicles, and Euthydemus, who are spokesmen in Plato's dialogues; but even they did not adopt a complete ethical nihilism. For them morality is mere convention; it represents the will of those who have the power to enforce their demands on their fellows. The rules of morals are contrary to "nature." The Sophists were largely responsible for drawing a distinction between "nature" and "convention," which played a dominant part in the subsequent development of Greek thought. By reference to this distinction they asked: Are moral standards and rules of conduct grounded in the very nature and constitution of things, or are they the product of convention and arbitrary agreement among men? The Sophists thought the latter to be the case. According to some, laws were made by the weak, the majority, in order to restrain the strong, the "best," to hinder the fittest from getting their due: the laws, therefore, violate the principle of natural justice. Natural right is the right of the stronger. According to others, the laws are a species of class legislation; they are made by the few, the strong, the privileged, in order to promote their own interests. It is to the advantage of the strong individual to impose laws on others so that he can the more profitably break them. Two versions of the Sophistic doctrine that law and justice are conventional devices for the promotion of group interests are expressed in the following quotations from Plato's dialogues.

The makers of the laws, says Callicles in the Platonic dialogue *Gorgias,* are the majority who are weak; and they make laws and distribute praises and censures with a view to themselves and their own interests; and they terrify the stronger sort of men, and those who are able to get the better of them, in order that *they* may not get the better of them; and they say that dishonesty is shameful and unjust; meaning by the word injustice the desire of a man to have more than his neighbors; for knowing their own inferiority, I suspect that they are too glad of equality. And therefore the endeavor to have more than the many, is conventionally said to be shameful and unjust, and is called injustice, whereas nature herself intimates that it is just for the better to have more than the worse, the more powerful than the weaker; and in many ways she shows, among men as well as among animals, and indeed among whole cities and races, that justice consists in the superior ruling over and having more than the inferior. For on what principle of justice did Xerxes invade Hellas, or his father the Scythians? (not to speak of numberless other examples). Nay, but these are the men who act according to nature; yes, by heaven, and according to the law of nature: not, perhaps, according to that artificial law, which we invent and impose upon our fellows, of whom we take the best and the strongest from their youth upwards, and tame them like young lions,—charming them with the sound of the voice, and saying to them, that with equality they must be content, and that the equal is the honorable and the just. But if there were a man who had sufficient force, he would shake off and break through, and escape from all this; he would trample underfoot all our formulas and spells and charms and all our laws which are against nature: the slave would rise in rebellion and be lord over us, and the light of natural justice would shine forth.

Thrasymachus develops much the same theme with a different emphasis in the *Republic:*

The just is always a loser in comparison with the unjust. First of all, in private contracts: wherever the unjust is the partner of the just you will find that when the partnership is dissolved, the unjust man has always more and the just less. Secondly, in their dealings with the state: when there is an income-tax, the just man will pay more and the unjust less on the same amount of income; and when there is anything to be received the one gains nothing and the other much. Observe also what happens when they take an office; there is the just man neglecting his affairs and perhaps suffering other losses, and getting nothing out of the public, because he is just; moreover he is hated by his friends and acquaintances for refusing to serve them in unlawful ways. But all this is reversed in the case of the unjust man. I am speaking as before of injustice on the large scale in which the advantage of the unjust is most apparent; and my meaning will be most clearly seen if we turn to that highest form of injustice in which the criminal is the happiest of men, and the sufferers or those who refuse to do injustice are the most miserable,—that is to say tyranny, which by fraud and force takes away the property of others, not little by little but wholesale; comprehending in one, things sacred as well as profane, private and public; for which acts of wrong, if he were detected perpetrating any of them singly, he would be punished and incur great disgrace,—they who do such wrong in particular cases are called robbers of temples, and man-stealers and burglars and swindlers and thieves. But when a man besides taking away the money of the citizens has made slaves of them, then, instead of these names of reproach, he is termed happy and blessed, not only by the citizens, but by all who have heard of the consummation of injustice. For mankind censure injustice, fearing that they may be the victims of it, and not because they shrink from committing it. And thus, as I have shown, Socrates, injustice, when on a sufficient scale, has more strength and freedom and mastery than justice; and, as I said at first, justice is the interest of the stronger, whereas injustice is a man's own profit and interest.[7]

The ethical position expressed in the above quotations is not entirely negativistic or nihilistic; in the ethical, as in the intellectual sphere, many Sophists tended to develop a positive theory in conflict with their dominant skepticism. To say that justice is the interest of the stronger, that justice prevails when a strong individual asserts his power without consideration for others, is not to deny all meaning to the ethical concept of justice. Justice, in the ethical sphere, like truth in the intellectual, has a pragmatic significance.

---

[7] B. Jowett trans. of *Gorgias* in *Dialogues of Plato*, pp. 483 ff., of *Republic*, pp. 343 ff. (marginal pagination).

The significance of sophistry. Owing to the hostile criticisms of Plato and Aristotle, as well as to the nihilistic teachings of some of the younger Sophists, the importance of the sophistic movement in the history of thought was long misjudged. It is only since Hegel and Grote attempted to give a fairer estimate of these thinkers that justice has been done them. There was good and there was evil in their teachings. Reflection and criticism are indispensable to sounder conceptions in philosophy, religion, morals, politics, and in all fields of human endeavor. The appeal to reason was commendable in itself, but the fault lay in the inability of sophistry to use the instrument of reason in anything like a constructive way. The Sophists brought philosophy down from heaven to the dwellings of men, as Cicero said, and turned the attention from external nature to man himself; for them the proper study of mankind was man. But they failed to recognize the universal element in man; they did not see the forest for the trees, they did not see *man* for men. Sophistry exaggerated the differences in human judgments and ignored the agreements; it also laid too much stress on the illusoriness of the senses. In emphasizing the accidental, subjective, and purely personal elements in human knowledge and conduct, the Sophists failed to do justice to the objective elements consisting of the truths and principles which are accepted by all.

Nevertheless, their criticisms of knowledge made necessary a profounder study of the problem of knowledge. The older speculators had naïvely and dogmatically assumed the competence of the mind to reach truth; in denying the possibility of sure and universal knowledge, the Sophists forced philosophy to examine the thinking process itself and opened the way for a theory of knowledge. In employing all sorts of logical fallacies and sophisms, they made necessary a study of the correct laws of thought and hastened the birth of logic.

The same thing may be said of moral knowledge and practice. The appeal to the individual conscience was sound: from mere blind, unintelligent following of custom, morality was raised to the stage of reflective personal choice. When, however, the appeal became an appeal to mere subjective opinion and self-interest, it struck a false note. Independence of thought easily degenerates into intellectual and moral anarchy; individualism, into pure selfishness. Yet in this field, again, sophistry rendered a service: radical criticism of the common notions of right and wrong, of public and private justice, made necessary a profounder study of ethics and politics—a study that was soon to bear wonderful fruit.

The great value of the entire sophistic movement consisted in this: it awakened thought and challenged philosophy, religion, customs, morals, and the institutions based on them, to justify themselves to reason. In denying the possibility of knowledge, the Sophists made it necessary for knowledge to justify itself: they compelled philosophy to seek a criterion of knowledge. In attacking the traditional morality, they compelled morality to defend itself against skepticism and nihilism, and to find a rational principle of right and wrong. In attacking the traditional religious beliefs, they pressed upon thinkers the need of developing more consistent and purer conceptions of God; and in criticizing the state and its laws, they made inevitable the development of a philosophic theory of the state. They forced philosophy to build upon more solid foundations, to go back to first principles: What is knowledge, what is truth? What is right, what is the good? What is the true conception of God? What are the meaning and purpose of the state and of human institutions? These problems finally forced the thinkers of Greece to reconsider, in new perspectives, the old question, which had been temporarily obscured, but which no great culture can long ignore: What is the nature of the world and man's place in nature?

G. Murray, *Euripides and His Age,* 2nd ed., 1946; W. J. Oates and E. G. O'Niel, eds., *Complete Greek Drama,* 2 vols., 1938; F. R. B. Godolphin, *The Greek Historians,* 2 vols., 1942; articles on "Sophists" and "Protagoras" in Hastings' *Encyclopedia of Religion and Ethics.*

8. Socrates and the Socratic Schools

We have described the philosophical and ethical situation, as it began to shape itself toward the end of the fifth century b.c. A thinker was needed to bring order into the intellectual and moral chaos of the age, to sift the true from the false, the essential from the accidental, to set men right and to help them to see things in their right relations—a moderator who might hold an even balance between the ultra-conservatives and the ultra-liberals. Such a thinker appeared in Socrates, one of the greatest figures in the history of thought, the intellectual father of a line of philosophers whose ideas and ideals dominated Western civilization for two thousand years, and continue to influence speculation to this day.

Socrates was born in Athens in 469 b.c. He was the son of poor parents, his father being a sculptor, his mother a midwife. How he acquired an education we do not know, but his love of knowledge evidently created opportunities for intellectual growth in this cultured city. He took up the occupation of his father, but soon felt "a divine vocation to examine himself by questioning other men." It was his custom to engage in converse with all sorts and conditions of men and women, on the streets, in the market-place, in the gymnasia, discussing the most diverse topics: war, politics, marriage, friend-ship, love, housekeeping, the arts and trades, poetry, religion, science, and, particularly, moral matters. Nothing human was foreign to him. Life with all its interests became the subject of his inquiries, and only the physical side of the world left him cold; he declared that he could learn nothing from trees and stones. He was subtle and keen, quick to discover the fallacies in an argument and skillful in steering the conversation to the very heart of the matter. Though kindly and gentle in disposition, and brim-ming over with good humor, he delighted in exposing the quacks and humbugs of his time and pricking their empty bubbles with his wit and logic.

Socrates exemplified in his conduct the virtues which he taught: he was a man of remarkable self-control, magnanimous, noble, frugal, and capable of great endurance; and his wants were few. He gave ample proof, during his life of seventy years, of physical and moral courage, in war and in the performance of his political duties. His bearing at his trial furnishes an impressive picture of moral dignity, firmness, and con-sistency; he did what he thought was right, without fear or favor, and died as beauti-fully as he had lived, with charity for all and malice toward none; condemned by his own people, on false charges of atheism and of corrupting the youth, to drink the poison hemlock (399 B.C.). His respect for authority and his loyalty to the state he proved by obeying the laws himself and insisting that others obey them. When, after his condemna-tion, friends arranged a plan of escape, he refused to profit by it, on the ground that he had enjoyed the benefits of the laws during his whole life and could not, in his old age, prove disloyal to his benefactors.

In personal appearance Socrates was not prepossessing. He was short, stocky, and stout, blear-eyed and snub-nosed; he had a large mouth and thick lips, and was careless in his dress, clumsy and uncouth. In his physical appearance he resembled a Satyr, and he was likened by Alcibiades, in Plato's *Symposium*, to the busts of Silenus. But all these peculiarities were forgotten when he began to speak, so great were his personal charm and the effect of his brilliant conversation.

Xenophon, *Memorabilia*, in *Works of Xenophon*, Vol. III, trans. by H. G. Dakyns, 1890-97; Plato's *Dialogues*, especially *Protagoras, Apology, Crito, Phaedo, Symposium, Theaetetus*, trans. by Jowett, 3rd ed., 1892; Aristotle, *Metaphysics* (I, 6; XIII, 4), trans. in Bohn Library, also by W. D. Ross; Aristotle, *Ethics*, trans. by J. E. C. Welldon, 1892; E. Zeller, *Socrates and the Socratic Schools*, trans. by O. J. Reichel, 1885; J. T. Forbes, *Socrates*, 1905; A. E. Taylor, *Varia Socratica*, 1911; R. Cross, *Socrates, the Man and His Mission*, 1914; R. P. Millet, *Socrate et la pensée moderne*, 1920; F. M. Cornford, *Before and After Socrates*, 1932; G. Bastide, *Le moment historique de Socrate*, 1939; A. E. Chaignet, *La vie de Socrate*, 1868; A. Fouillée, *La philosophie de Socrate*, 1873; E. Pfleiderer, *Sokrates, Plato und ihre Schüler*, 1896; M. M. Dawson, *The Ethics of Soc-rates*, 1924; A. K. Rogers, *The Socratic Problem*, 1933; A. D. Winspear and T. Silver-berg, *Who Was Socrates?*, 1939.

Socrates is a unique figure in the history of philosophy. He wrote noth-ing, yet he was a genuine thinker who, through his disciple Plato, has exerted an incalculable influence on the entire development of Western philosophy. The Platonic dialogues represent a fusion of the thought of the teacher and his disciple, and the problem of distinguishing the doctrines actually advanced by the "real" historical Socrates from Platonic doctrines of which Socrates was only the mouthpiece, is an insoluble one. Russell has aptly remarked that "there are many men concerning whom it is certain that very little is known, and other men concerning whom it is certain that a great deal is known; but in the case of Socrates the uncertainty is as to whether we know very little or a great deal."[8] The independent evidence we have for distinguishing the historical Socrates from Plato's idealized version is very inadequate. Aristophanes in *The Clouds* gives us a caricature of Socrates, but we can glean very little of his philosophy from this source. Xenophon, in his *Memorabilia,* gives us a sympathetic but extremely prosaic account of Socrates and his philosophy; his sober and literal statement may serve as a useful corrective of Plato's idealization of Socrates. Xenophon, however, was a military man with no particular philosophic competence, and his judgment cannot be entirely trusted in philosophical matters; Russell's comment on Xenophon is pertinent: "A stupid man's report of what a clever man says is never accurate. . . . I would rather be reported by my bitterest enemy among philosophers than by a friend innocent of philosophy."[9] For our reconstruction of the Socratic philosophy we must rely almost exclusively on the Platonic dialogues, and the decision as to which doctrines are really Socratic and which Platonic must remain largely conjectural. A few interpreters have gone to the extreme of reducing the actual Socratic teachings to a minimum by considering Socrates' philosophy as merely a stage in Plato's philosophical development; others have gone to the opposite extreme of crediting Socrates with the Platonic theory of forms or ideas. The correct view probably lies somewhere between these extremes; we can undoubtedly credit Socrates with the invention of the philosophical method of conceptual analysis and definition exemplified in the Platonic dialogues, and with the application of this method in the definition of ethical concepts.

The Socratic Problem. Socrates' chief concern was to meet the challenge of sophistry, which, in undermining knowledge, threatened the foundations of morality and the state. He looked upon philosophical reflection as the most timely and practical of tasks, for if skepticism was to be the last word of the age, there would be little hope of escaping the nihilistic implications

[8] *A History of Western Philosophy,* p. 82.
[9] *Op. cit.,* p. 83.

of the fashionable views of life. He saw clearly that the prevailing ethical and political fallacies sprang from a total misconception of the meaning of truth, and that the problem of knowledge was the key to the entire situation. It was in this conviction, and with an optimistic faith in the power of human reason to meet the practical difficulties of his times, that he entered upon his mission. The aim which he set himself was not to construct a system of philosophy, but to arouse in men the love of truth and virtue, to help them to think right in order that they might live right. His purpose was practical rather than speculative; he was interested in the correct method of acquiring knowledge rather than in a theory of such a method, or methodology. He did not offer a theory at all, but practiced a method, lived it, and, by his example, taught others to follow it.

In order to reach truth, so his thought ran, we must not trust every chance opinion that enters our heads. Confused, vague, and empty thoughts fill our minds; we have a lot of undigested opinions which we have never examined, a lot of prejudices which we have accepted on faith, and of which we do not understand the meaning; we make a lot of arbitrary assertions for which we have no warrant. In fact, we have no genuine knowledge at all, no real convictions; we have built our intellectual house on sand, and the whole edifice will collapse unless we reconstruct its foundations. Our most urgent task is to make our ideas clear, to understand the real meaning of terms, to define correctly the notions we employ, to know exactly what we are talking about. Then, too, we should have reasons for our views, prove our assertions, *think*, not guess, put our theories to the test of verification by the facts, and modify and correct them accordingly. The Sophists say there is no truth and that knowledge is unattainable; men differ from one another, opinion is set against opinion, and one opinion is as good as another. This, says Socrates, is a dangerous mistake. It is true that there is a diversity of thought; but it is our duty to discover whether beneath the clash of opinions there may not be a fundamental agreement, some common ground on which all can stand, some principle to which all can subscribe. To evolve such universal judgments was the purpose of the Socratic method, which Socrates employed in his discussions, and which is an ingenious form of cross-examination. He pretended not to know any more about the subject under discussion than the other participants; indeed, he often professed to know less than they (the Socratic irony). Yet they soon felt that he was master of the situation, that he was making them contradict themselves, and all the while deftly guiding their thought into his own channels. "You are accustomed to ask most of your questions when you know very well how they stand," complained one of his listeners. Before one's very eyes, the confused and amorphous notions of the disputants gradually take shape, growing progressively clear and distinct, and finally standing out like beautiful statues. Socrates had not learned the art of sculpture for nothing.

The Socratic Method. In discussing a subject, Socrates generally sets out from the popular and hastily formed opinions of his company. These he tests by means of illustrations taken from everyday life, showing, wherever necessary, that they are not well-founded, and that they are in need of modification and correction. He helps those taking part in the dialogue to form for themselves the correct opinion, by suggesting relevant instances, and does not rest content until the truth has developed step by step. A well-known example from Xenophon will make clear the essential features of the Socratic method. By skillful questioning, Socrates gets a young man named Euthydemus to confess his ambition to become a great politician and statesman. Socrates then suggests to him that in order to pursue his ambition, he must, naturally, hope to become a just man himself. The young man thinks he is that already.

But, says Socrates, there must be certain acts which are the proper products of justice, as of other functions or skills. No doubt. Then of course you can tell us what those acts and products are? Of course I can, and the products of injustice as well. Very good; then suppose we write down in two opposite columns what acts are products of justice and what of injustice. I agree, says Euthydemus. Well now, what of falsehood? In which column shall we put it? Why, of course in the unjust column. And cheating? In the same column. And stealing? In it too. And enslaving? Yes. Not one of these can go to the just column? Why, that would be an unheard-of thing. Well but, says Socrates, suppose a general has to deal with some enemy of his country that has done it great wrong; if he conquer and enslave this enemy, is that wrong? Certainly not. If he carries off the enemy's goods or cheats him in his strategy, what about these acts? Oh, of course they are quite right. But I thought you were talking about deceiving or ill-treating friends. Then in some cases we shall have to put these very same acts in both columns? I suppose so.

Well, now, suppose we confine ourselves to friends. Imagine a general with an army under him discouraged and disorganized. Suppose he tells them that reserves are coming up, and by cheating them into this belief, he saves them from their discouragement, and enables them to win a victory. What about this cheating of one's friends? Why, I suppose we shall have to put this too on the just side. Or suppose a lad needs medicine, but refuses to take it, and his father cheats him into the belief that it is something nice, and getting him to take it, saves his life; what about that cheat? That will have to go to the just side too. Or suppose you find a friend in desperate frenzy, and steal his sword from him for fear he should kill himself; what do you say to that theft? That will have to go there too. But I thought you said there must be no cheating of friends? Well, I must take it all back, if you please. Very good. But now there is another point I should like to ask you. Whether you think the man more unjust who is a voluntary violator of justice, or he who is an involuntary violator of it. Upon my word, Socrates, I no longer have any confidence in my answers. For the whole thing has turned out to be exactly the contrary of what I previously imagined.[10]

In this way, by a process of induction, Socrates evolves definitions. With the help of examples, a provisional definition is formed; this is tested by other examples, and broadened or narrowed to meet the requirements until a satisfactory definition is finally reached. What Francis Bacon later called "negative instances," that is, cases which contradict the traditional definition offered, play an important rôle in the process. The aim is always to discover the essential characteristics of the subject to be defined, to reach clear and distinct notions, or concepts. At times, Socrates tests the statements made by going back at once to first principles, by criticizing statements in the light of basic definitions assumed to be correct. Here the method is deductive. You say, for example, that this man is a better citizen than that one. Your assertion, however, is a mere subjective opinion, having no value whatever unless you can give reasons for it by reference to an acceptable definition. The question as to whether the man under discussion is a good citizen can be decided only if you know what a good citizen is, only if you have defined your terms with precision.

Whenever any person contradicted him on any point who had nothing definite to say, and who perhaps asserted, without proof, that some person whom he mentioned, was wiser or better skilled in political affairs, or possessed of greater courage, or worthier in some such respect (than some other whom Socrates had mentioned), he would recall the whole argument, in some such way as the following, to the primary proposition: Do you say that he whom you commend, is *a better citizen* than he whom I commend? I do say so. Why should we not then consider, in the first place, what is the duty of *a good citizen?* Let us do so. Would not he then be superior in the management of the public money who should make the State richer? Undoubtedly. And he in war who should make it victorious over its enemies? Assuredly. And in an embassy he who should make friends of foes? Doubtless. And he in addressing the people who should check dissension and inspire them with unanimity? I think so. When the discussion was thus brought back to fundamental principles, the truth was made evident to those who had opposed him.

When he himself went through any subject in argument, he proceeded upon propositions of which the truth was generally acknowledged, thinking that a

[10] Xenophon, *Memorabilia,* Book IV, ch. 2, trans. by Marshall, *Greek Philosophy.*

sure foundation was thus formed for his reasoning. Accordingly, whenever he
spoke, he, of all men that I have known, most readily prevailed on his hearers
to assent to his arguments; and he used to say that Homer had attributed to
Ulysses the character of a sure orator, as being able to form his reasoning on
points acknowledged by all mankind.[11]

Knowledge, then, is possible after all, but only if we pursue the proper
method; we must define our terms correctly, and we must carry our reasoning
back to first principles. Knowledge is concerned with the general and typical,
not with the particular and accidental. This the Sophists failed to understand, and Socrates sets them right. In one important respect, however, he
agreed with the Sophists: He shared with them the belief in the futility of
cosmological and metaphysical speculations. "Indeed, in contrast to others,
he set his face against all discussions of such high matters as the nature of
the universe; how the 'cosmos,' as the savants phrase it, came into being;
or by what forces the celestial phenomena arise. To trouble one's brain about
such matters was, he argued, to play the fool." His interests were ethical and
practical, and he did not see what was to come of such speculations.

The student of human learning, he said, expects to make something of his
studies for the benefit of himself or others, as he likes. Do these explorers into
the divine operations hope that when they have discovered by what forces the
various phenomena occur, they will create winds and waters at will and fruitful
seasons? Will they manipulate these and the like to suit their needs? . . . He
himself never wearied of discussing human topics. What is piety? what is im-
piety? What is the beautiful? what the ugly? What the noble? what the base?
What is meant by just and unjust? What by sobriety and madness, what by
courage and cowardice? What is a State? What is a statesman? What is a ruler
over men? What is a ruling character? and other like problems, the knowledge
of which, as he put it, conferred a patent of nobility on the possessor, whereas
those who lacked the knowledge might deservedly be stigmatized as slaves.[12]

In emphasizing the importance of the Socratic method, we must remember
that Socrates was no methodologist; he did not himself explicitly describe
his method of philosophical inquiry—Aristotle was the first to set himself
this methodological task. Socrates did, however, put a method into practice,
and his own thinking so well exemplifies a pattern of philosophical procedure that it is difficult to believe that he was entirely unaware of its character and its principal steps. The method which Socrates employed in his
philosophical analyses has five readily distinguishable characteristics:

[11] Xenophon, *op. cit.,* IV, ch. 6, pp. 12 ff., trans. by J. S. Watson in Bohn Library
edition.
[12] Xenophon, *op. cit.,* I, ch. 1, pp. 11 ff., trans. by Dakyns; see also IV, ch. 7.

(1) The method is *skeptical;* it begins with Socrates' real or professed ignorance of the truth of the matter under discussion. This is the Socratic irony which seemed to some of his listeners an insincere pretense, but which was undoubtedly an expression of Socrates' genuine intellectual humility. This skepticism Socrates shared with the Sophists and, in his adoption of it, he may very well have been influenced by them. But whereas the sophistic skepticism was definitive and final, the Socratic is tentative and provisional; Socrates' doubt and assumed ignorance, like the initial doubt of Descartes, is an indispensable first step in the pursuit of knowledge. (2) It is *conversational;* it employs the dialogue not only as a didactic device, but as a technique for the actual discovery of truth. In the firm conviction that, despite the diversity of opinions amongst men, there are truths upon which all men can agree, Socrates proceeds to unfold such truths by discussion or question and answer. Beginning with a popular or hastily formed conception proposed by one of the members of the company or taken from the poets or some other traditional source, Socrates subjects this notion to severe criticism, as a result of which a more adequate conception emerges. His method, in this aspect, is often described as the maieutic method; it is the art of intellectual midwifery, which brings other men's ideas to birth. (3) It is *conceptual* or *definitional,* in that it sets as the goal of knowledge the acquisition of correct definitions of concepts, such as the ethical concepts of justice, piety, wisdom, courage and the like. Socrates tacitly assumes that truth is embodied in correct definitions—an assumption which is scarcely tenable; precise definitions are no doubt indispensable to knowledge, but definitions alone cannot constitute knowledge. (4) The Socratic method is *empirical* or *inductive,* in that proposed definitions are criticized by reference to particular instances; Socrates tests definition by recourse to common experience and to general usages.

But (5) the method is also *deductive,* in that a given definition is tested by drawing out its implications, by deducing its consequences. The definitional method of Socrates is a real contribution to the logic of philosophical enquiry: it inspired the dialectical method of Plato and exerted a not inconsiderable influence on the logic of Aristotle.[13]

The Socratic Ethics. Socrates' faith in knowledge, in clear and reasoned thinking, is strong—so strong that he sees in it the cure of all our ills. He

[13] A suggestive description of the method is given by Windelband in *A History of Philosophy,* pp. 96 ff., and an appraisal of its value and limitations by Russell in *A History of Western Philosophy,* pp. 92 ff.

applies his method to all human problems, particularly to the problems of morality, and seeks to find a rational basis for conduct. The radical thinkers, as we saw, looked upon the ethical ideas and practices of their times as mere conventions; after all, might makes right. The conservatives regarded them as self-evident: rules of conduct are not things about which one can reason; they have to be obeyed. Socrates endeavors to understand the meaning of morality, to discover a rational principle of right and wrong, a criterion by which to decide moral issues. The questions uppermost in his mind are: How shall I order my life? What is the rational way of living? How ought a reasoning being, a human being, to act? The Sophists cannot be right in saying that man is the measure of all things in the sense that whatever pleases *me,* the *particular* me, is right for me; that there is no universal good. There must be more to the matter than that; there must be some principle, or standard, or good, which all rational creatures recognize and accept when they come to think the problem through. What is *the* good, what is the good for the sake of which all else is good, the highest good?

Knowledge is the highest good, so Socrates answers. The central thesis of the Socratic ethics is contained in the formula: "Knowledge is virtue." Right thinking is essential to right action. In order to steer a ship or rule a state, a man must have knowledge of the construction and function of the ship, or of the nature and purpose of the state. Similarly, unless a man knows what virtue is, unless he knows the meaning of self-control and courage and justice and piety and their opposites, he cannot be virtuous; but, knowing what virtue is, he will be virtuous. Knowledge is both the necessary and the sufficient condition of virtue: without knowledge virtue is impossible, and its possession insures virtuous action. "No man is voluntarily bad or involuntarily good." "No man voluntarily pursues evil or that which he thinks to be evil. To prefer evil to good is not in human nature; and when a man is compelled to choose between two evils, no one will choose the greater when he may have the less." The objection is raised that "we see the better and approve of it and pursue the evil." Socrates would have denied that we can truly know the good and yet refuse to choose it. With him knowledge of right and wrong was not a mere theoretical opinion, but a firm practical conviction, a matter not only of the intellect, but of the will.

Socrates deduces a number of other implications from his identification of knowledge and virtue. Since virtue is knowledge it follows also that virtue is one: Knowledge is a unity, an organized system of truth and hence the several virtues are merely so many different forms of virtue as such.

Furthermore, virtue is not only good in itself; it is to a man's interest. The tendency of all honorable and useful actions is to make life painless and pleasant; hence the honorable is also the useful and good. Virtue and true happiness are identical; no one can be happy who is not temperate and brave and wise and just.

I do nothing, says Socrates in the *Apology,* but go about persuading you all, old and young alike, not to take thought for your persons or properties, but first and chiefly to care about the greatest improvement of the soul. I tell you that virtue is not given by money, but that from virtue comes money and every other good of man, public as well as private.

And the last words which he speaks at his trial are these:

Still I have a favor to ask of them [my condemners and accusers]. When my sons are grown up, I would ask you, oh my friends, to punish them; and I would have you trouble them as I have troubled you if they seem to care about riches or about anything, more than about virtue; or if they pretend to be something when they are really nothing—then reprove them, as I have reproved you, for not caring about that for which they ought to care, and thinking that they are something when they are really nothing. And if you do this, both I and my sons will have received justice at your hands.

The Socratic Schools. Socrates, as we have already pointed out, did not construct a system of metaphysics nor did he offer a theory of knowledge or of conduct. It remained for his pupils to build upon the foundations laid by the master. Some made the logical problems suggested by his method the subject of their study, others turned their attention to the questions implicit in his ethical techniques, and attempted to work out theories of ethics. The Megarian school, founded by Euclides (450-374 B.C.), combined the Socratic teaching that virtue is knowledge with the Eleatic doctrine of the unity of being: the notion of the good constitutes the eternal essence of things; nothing else—neither matter, motion, nor the changing world of sense—has real being. Hence, there can be but one virtue, and hence, also, external goods can have no value. The successors of Euclides exaggerated the dialectical phase of his teaching, and, in the tradition of Zeno, the Eleatic, and the Sophists, delighted in all kinds of subtleties and hair splitting (eristic).

The Socratic ethics was many-sided, and its different aspects were often in conflict with one another. Each of those conflicting aspects was exaggerated by his followers. The two principal ethical schools, each basing itself on certain phases of Socrates' teachings, were the Cyrenaic, founded by Aristippus (b. *ca.* 435) at Cyrene, and the Cynic, established by Antisthenes (d. 366) at the gymnasium of Cynosarges in Athens. The Cyrenaics seized upon

Socrates' enthusiastic portrayal of the joy and satisfaction to be derived from intellectual pursuits. The *summum bonum,* or highest good, became for them the attainment of the greatest amount of pleasure and the avoidance of pain. The Cyrenaic doctrine was a pure quantitative hedonism: it did not distinguish higher pleasures from lower, but advocated the pursuit of those pleasures which are most intense, whether of the body or the soul. Crude hedonism contains within itself the germ of pessimism: the attainment of a preponderance of pleasure over pain seems impossible, and the exclusive pursuit of pleasures leads to boredom and frustration. Hegesius, the pessimist of the school, observed that the man is fortunate who attains even a painless state; that for most men, life is a preponderance of pain over pleasure. Under these circumstances, suicide appears to be the only way out and he thus became "the urger to suicide."

The Cynics exaggerated the Socratic thesis that virtue, which is identical with knowledge, is something worth while for its own sake, apart from any rewards in the form of pleasure. It is accordingly man's duty to be virtuous and to seek independence of all wants. The emphasis on independence and freedom from want is an exaltation of traits exemplified by Socrates—his personal independence and indifference to the opinions of others. The ethics of virtue and duty led its exponents to extremes of discipline, restraint, self-renunciation and complete independence of possessions—in other words to asceticism. It also led to a rejection of the artificialities of civilization and to the advocacy of a return to a state of nature. Diogenes of Sinope was the practicing exponent of this radical aspect of Cynicism.

The two Socratic schools of ethics, despite their opposition, had one important element in common. They both sought the salvation of the individual, the one in pleasure, the other in the renunciation of pleasure. The two schools exerted parallel influences at a later period of Greek philosophy: the Cyrenaic doctrine of pleasure as the highest good was adopted and modified by the Epicureans, while the Cynic teaching, which rejected the pleasure theory and advocated the doctrine of virtue for virtue's sake, was developed by the Stoics.[14]

G. Grote, *Plato and the Other Companions of Socrates,* 4 vols., 1888; J. Watson, *Hedonistic Theories from Aristippus to Spencer,* 1895; P. E. Moore, *Hellenistic Philosophies,* ch. I, 1923.

[14] See D. R. Dudley, *History of Cynicism.*

III

The Age of the Great Systems

9. PLATO

Plato and His Problem. None of the Socratic schools succeeded in constructing a comprehensive and integrated system of thought along lines indicated by the philosophical method and humanistic insights of Socrates. Yet the achievements of the great master provided a challenge to such an undertaking. The problems suggested by him had to be thought out to the end; they were intimately connected with one another and with the problem of the ultimate nature of being, and they could not receive an adequate answer unless studied in their interrelations and as parts of the larger ontological question. The problems of the meaning of human life, human knowledge, human conduct, and human institutions depended, for their complete answer, on the solution of the problem of the meaning of reality. It was Plato, the greatest pupil of Socrates, who set himself to this task. He developed not only a theory of knowledge, a theory of conduct, and a theory of the state, but crowned his work with a theory of the universe.

Plato's system incorporates and transforms the doctrines of his predecessors. Plato shares the skepticism of the Sophists regarding knowledge of sense appearances, and agrees with Socrates that genuine knowledge is always by concepts. He accepts Heraclitus' doctrine that the world is in constant change, but restricts its application to the world of sensuous appearances. With the Eleatics, he agrees that the real world is unchangeable, but substitutes for Parmenides' unchanging being his world of eternal ideas. With the atomists, he agrees that reality is manifold, but replaces a plurality of atoms by a plurality of forms or ideas. With Anaxagoras, he assumes that mind is a dynamic factor in the world, and finally he agrees with nearly all Greek philosophers that reality is basically rational. His system is the mature fruit of the history of Greek philosophy down to his time.

73

Plato was born in 427 B.C., the son of noble parents. According to tradition he first studied music, poetry, painting, and philosophy with other masters and became a pupil of Socrates in 407, remaining with him until the latter's death (399), when he accompanied the sorrowing Socratics to Megara. He is said to have traveled in Egypt and Asia Minor, to have visited Italy and the Pythagoreans (388), and to have lived for a time at the court of Dionysius I, the tyrant of Syracuse, who became his enemy and sold him into slavery as a prisoner of war; but all of these stories have been denied. He founded a school in the groves of Academus, the *Academy,* where he taught mathematics and the different branches of philosophy, by means of connected lectures and the dialogue. The story goes that he interrupted his work on two occasions (367 and 361), by further visits to Syracuse, presumably in the hope of assisting in the realization of his ideal State, and that he was disappointed in this hope. His death occurred in 347 B.C.

Plato was a poet and mystic, as well as a philosopher and dialectician; he combined, in a rare degree, great powers of logical analysis and abstract thought with flights of poetic imagination and deep mystical feeling. His character was noble; he was an aristocrat by birth and by temperament, an uncompromising idealist, hostile to everything base and vulgar.

It seems likely that all of Plato's works have come down to us. Of the writings transmitted under his name (35 *Dialogues,* 13 *Letters*), most of the *Letters* and all of the *Definitions* are considered to be spurious, although it seems likely that several of the *Letters,* including the philosophically important *Seventh Letter,* are genuine.

Attempts have been made by many scholars to arrange the dialogues in chronological order. One method of ordering them employs the criterion of relative maturity of philosophical doctrine, but this method has produced very different orderings by different scholars. A method which has in recent years proven very useful is the ordering of the dialogues in accordance with stylometric considerations, adopting as a standard the style and vocabulary of the *Laws,* which is universally accepted as the latest of the dialogues. Sir David Ross, after summarizing the results of these stylistic and linguistic investigations, suggests the following probable order of the Platonic dialogues: (1) First Period (before 389-388): *Charmides, Laches, Enthyphro, Hippias Major,* and *Meno;* (2) Second Period (between 389-388 and 367-366): *Cratylus* (date doubtful), *Symposium* (385 or later), *Phaedo, Republic, Phaedrus, Parmenides, Theaetetus* (369 or later); (3) Third Period (between 367-366 and 361-360): *Sophistes, Politicus;* (4) Fourth Period (after 361-360): *Timaeus, Critias, Philebus, Seventh Letter* (353-352), *Laws. (Plato's Theory of Ideas,* ch. 1. This list does not include those of the earlier dialogues which throw little or no light on Plato's theory of ideas: the *Apology, Crito, Lysis, Protagoras, Gorgias,* and *Euthydemus.*)

Among the thirty-five dialogues the following are now generally rejected as spurious: *Alcibiades* I and *Alcibiades* II, *Epinomis, Anteras, Hippachus, Theages, Minos, Cleitophro, Io,* and *Menexenus.* Many scholars have questioned the genuineness of *Hippias Major.*

Bibliography

Translations and Commentaries: *The Dialogues of Plato,* trans. by B. Jowett, 3rd ed., 5 vols., 1892; Jowett trans. of *The Dialogues of Plato* with an Introduction by R. Demos, 2 vols., 1937; *Thirteen Epistles,* trans. by L. A. Post, 1925; A. E. Taylor, *Plato: Timae-*

and Critias, 1929, and The Laws of Plato, 1934; J. Howard, The Platonic Epistles, 1932; F. M. Cornford, Plato and Parmenides, 1939; Plato's Cosmology, 1937; Plato's Theory of Knowledge, 1935; G. R. Morrow, Studies in the Platonic Epistles, 1935; A. E. Taylor, Commentary on Plato's Timaeus, 1928; R. Hackforth, Plato's Examination of Pleasure: A Translation of the Philebus, 1945, and Plato's Phaedrus, 1952; Republic, trans. by F. M. Cornford, 1942; J. B. Skemp, Plato's Statesman, 1952; R. S. Bluck, Plato's Phaedo, 1955.

G. Grote, Plato, 1865; E. Zeller, Plato and the Older Academy, trans. by S. F. Alleyne and A. Goodwin, 1888; B. Bosanquet, A Companion to Plato's "Republic," 1895; D. G. Ritchie, Plato, 1902; T. Gomperz, Greek Thinkers, vols. II and III, 1905; J. A. Stewart, The Myths of Plato, 1905; W. Lutolawski, Origin and Growth of Plato's Logic, 1905; E. Barker, Political Theory of Plato and Aristotle, 1906; J. A. Stewart, Plato's Doctrine of Ideas, 1909; R. L. Nettleship, Lectures on the "Republic" of Plato, 1914; J. Burnet, The Socratic Doctrine of the Soul, 1916; P. E. More, Platonism, 1917, and The Religion of Plato, 1921; E. Barker, Greek Political Theory: Plato and His Predecessors, 1918; E. Rohde, Psyche, 1894, 1925; A. E. Taylor, Plato: The Man and His Work, 1926; A. E. Taylor, Platonism and Its Influence, 1927; G. Santayana, Platonism and the Spiritual Life, 1927; J. Burnet, Platonism, 1928; G. C. Field, Plato and His Contemporaries: A Study in Fourth-Century Life and Thought, 1930; F. M. Cornford, Before and After Socrates, 1932; C. Ritter, The Essence of Plato's Philosophy, trans. by A. Allan, 1933; P. Shorey, What Plato Said, 1933, and Platonism Ancient and Modern, 1938; F. H. Anderson, The Argument of Plato, 1934; R. L. Nettleship, Theory of Education in Plato's "Republic," 1935; F. M. Cornford, Plato's Theory of Knowledge, 1935; G. M. A. Grube, Plato's Thought, 1935; L. Robin, Platon, 1935; W. F. R. Hardie, Study in Plato, 1936; R. Demos, The Philosophy of Plato, 1939; J. Stenzel, Plato's Method of Dialectic, 1940; P. Leon, Plato, 1940; R. Robinson, Plato's Early Dialectic, 1941, 2nd ed., 1953; F. Solmsen, Plato's Theology, 1942; W. Jaeger, Paideia, vol. III (The Conflict of Cultural Ideals in the Age of Plato), 1945; A. Koyré, Discovering Plato, 1945; H. F. Cherniss, Aristotle's Criticism of Plato and the Academy, 1944, and The Riddle of the Early Academy, 1945; J. Wild, Plato's Theory of Man, 1946; R. S. Bluck, Plato's Life and Thought, 1949; W. D. Ross, Plato's Theory of Ideas, 1951.

Socrates had practiced the art or method of evolving truth in the form of the dialogue. Plato in his writings not only employs, with wonderful artistic effect, this method of pursuing truth, but he also speculates on the method. He formulates a theory of method—dialectic, or logic—in which he describes the art of forming and combining concepts. In his account of the logical operations by means of which truth is reached, we have the beginnings of a theory of knowledge and of formal logic. Plato is not content, however, with describing how true concepts and judgments may be obtained; his chief object is to obtain them, to know reality in all its phases—physical, mental, and moral—to comprehend it in its unity and completeness. Indeed, it is plain to him that the problem of knowledge cannot be solved without an understanding of the nature of the world. Thus, in the spirit of the teachings of the great thinker whose philosophical method served as his ideal, he developed a universal system of philosophy. Although Plato did not explicitly divide philosophy into: (1) logic, or dialectic (including theory of knowledge); (2) metaphysics (including physics and psychology); and (3) ethics (including politics), such a division is implicit in his work and we shall, therefore, be guided by this order in our exposition of his thought. We shall begin with logic, or dialectic.

Dialectic and Theory of Knowledge. Plato clearly understood the great importance of the problem of knowledge in the philosophy of his day, and that a thinker's concept of its nature and origin largely determines his attitude toward the engrossing questions of the age. If we rely solely on sense perception and opinion, Plato argued, then the Sophists are quite right in their contention that there can be no genuine knowledge. Sense perception does not reveal the true reality of things, but gives us mere appearance. Yet opinion may be true or false; even when it is proved true, it rests on persuasion or feeling and hence has no value whatever. As mere opinion it is not knowledge, since, even when it happens to be true, it cannot justify itself. Genuine knowledge, on the other hand, which is based on reason, can authenticate itself. The great majority of men think without knowing why they think as they do. Ordinary virtue rests on sense perception and opinion; it is not conscious of its principles. Men do not know why they act as they do; they act instinctively, according to impulse, custom or habit, like ants, bees, and wasps; they act selfishly, for pleasure and profit, hence the masses are a great unconscious Sophist. The Sophist is guilty of confusion between appearance and reality, between the pleasant and the good.

The advance from sense perception and opinion to genuine knowledge cannot be accomplished unless we have a desire for or love of truth, the *eros,* which is aroused by the contemplation of beautiful ideas and which leads to the contemplation of truth. The love of truth impels us to dialectic; it impels us to rise beyond sense perception to conceptual knowledge of the idea, from the particular to the universal. The dialectical method consists, first, in the comprehension of scattered particulars into one idea, and second, in the division of the idea into species, that is, in the processes of generalization and classification. In this way alone can there be clear and consistent thinking; we pass from concept to concept, upward and downward, generalizing and particularizing, combining and dividing, synthesizing and analyzing, carving out concepts as a sculptor carves a beautiful figure out of a block of marble. Dialectic is this art of thinking in concepts; concepts, and not sensations or images, constitute the essential objects of thought. We cannot, for example, call a man just or unjust unless we have a notion, or concept, of justice, unless we *know* what justice is; such knowledge alone enables us to determine whether a man is just or unjust.

But, Plato warns us, the concept or idea—of justice, for example—does not have its origin in experience; we do not derive it by abstraction from particular cases of justice. These are merely the means of clarifying and making explicit the concept of justice which already existed obscurely and implicitly in the soul. In the process of developing the meanings and implications of an idea such as justice, we achieve a system of new and absolutely certain knowledge. Man is, therefore, indeed the measure of all things, of all truth, in the sense that universal concepts, ideas, and principles lie imbedded in his soul and form the starting-point of all his knowledge.

Experience, then, is not the source of our concepts, for nothing in experience, in the world of sense, exactly corresponds to the concepts of truth, beauty, goodness. No particular object is absolutely beautiful or good, yet we approach the sense world with ideals or standards of the true, the beautiful and the good. In addition to these value-concepts, Plato also came to regard mathematical concepts and certain logical notions, or categories, such as being and non-being, identity and difference, unity and plurality, as inborn, or a priori.

Conceptual knowledge, then, is the only genuine knowledge: that was the teaching of Socrates which Plato adopted as the starting-point for his inquiries. The question, however, arises: What guarantee have we of its truth? Plato's answer is based on the metaphysical teachings of certain of his predecessors, especially Parmenides. Knowledge is the correspondence of thought and reality, or being; knowledge must have an object. If the concept is to have any value as knowledge, something real must correspond to it—there must, for instance, be pure, absolute beauty corresponding to the concept of beauty—realities must exist corresponding to all our universal ideas. In other words, such ideas cannot be mere passing thoughts in men's minds. The truths of mathematics, the ideals of beauty, truth, and goodness, must be real, must have an existence independent of our knowledge of them. If the objects of our ideas were not real, our knowledge would not be genuine knowledge. Thus conceptual knowledge presupposes the reality of corresponding ideal or abstract objects.

The same result is reached in another way. Truth is the knowledge of reality, of being as such, of that which is. The world perceived by our senses is not the true world; it is a changing, fleeting world, one thing today, something else tomorrow. Heraclitus correctly described the world of sense but this world is, according to Plato, mere appearance, illusion. True being is something permanent, unchangeable, eternal—it has the characteristics of Parmenides' being. In order to have genuine knowledge, we must know the permanent and unchangeable essence of things. Thought alone, conceptual thought, can grasp eternal and changeless being; it knows that which is, that which persists, that which remains one and the same in all change and diversity, namely the essential *forms* of things.

Plato's theory of knowledge is summarized in the famous figure of the divided line at the end of Book VI of the *Republic*. A vertical straight line is divided into four segments, each of which represents a level of knowledge; each of the four types of knowledge has its peculiar object and appropriate method of inquiry. (1) The lowest segment represents conjecture, a kind of sensuous knowledge conversant with images, shadows, reflections, dreams, etc. A mirage seen on a desert would no doubt be an example of what Plato calls conjecture. Conjectural knowledge is mere guesswork and is at best probable, but even this low grade of cognition affords some clue to the character of the physical object which it distortedly reflects. (2) The second segment of the divided line represents belief, the knowledge of sensible objects, whether material objects such as trees, mountains, rivers, etc., or human artifacts such as houses, tables, works of handicraft, etc. The source of belief is sense perception and, although it is more reliable than conjecture, it likewise is only probable knowledge. In the *Theaetetus*, Plato examines critically the identification of knowledge with perception—a doctrine which he attributes to the Sophist Protagoras.[1] Conjecture and belief are grouped together by Plato under the heading "opinion," which embraces all sense-derived knowledge. (3) The third segment of the line represents discursive intellect, or the understanding which occupies itself not with sensuous particulars but with mathematical entities such as numbers, lines, planes, triangles and other arithmetical and geometrical objects. This form of knowledge is hypothetical in that it proceeds deductively from definitions and unproved assumptions. Plato clearly anticipated the modern postulational interpretation of mathematics when he suggested that mathematics rests on assumptions or suppositions rather than on self-evident principles or axioms. Mathematical knowledge is also characterized by its use of sensuous imagery, such as the diagrams used in geometrical proof, or the symbolization of numbers by means of collections of objects or dots. The sensuous imagery employed in this type of knowledge functions only sym-

---

[1] Cf. Russell's chapter on "Knowledge and Perception in Plato," in *A History of Western Philosophy*, pp. 149 ff.

bolically to assist the intellect in its thought processes; the figures in a geometrical diagram are symbols of the ideal circles and triangles with which the proof is concerned. (4) The highest segment of the line represents rational insight, the objects of which are the forms or ideas; the method by which such knowledge is achieved is dialectic. Dialectic considers the forms, not as isolated essences, but as constituting a systematic unity—as related to the form of the Good. Dialectical knowledge rests on categorical first principles, not on hypotheses, and is able to dispense entirely with sensible figures. Each level of knowledge, symbolized in the figure of the divided line, has not only the characteristic method but its characteristic objects.

Hierarchy of the Sciences. Plato's hierarchy of the sciences, presented in *Republic,* Book VII, in connection with his theory of higher education, conveys a clear picture of the nature, objects and special significance of each of the abstract sciences, beginning with arithmetic and concluding with dialectic. (1) Arithmetic he describes as the abstract science of number and of numerical relations; its theoretical value consists in the fact that it liberates the intellect from sense and thereby promotes abstract thought. Arithmetic by its exact, quantitative methods also resolves apparent contradictions in sense perception. Although Plato is primarily concerned with arithmetic as a pure or abstract mathematical science, he calls attention to its applicability, to its employment in computation in the practical arts. (2) After arithmetic, he mentions plane and solid geometry, the sciences of figures in two and three dimensions. Again, though his primary concern is theoretical, with the ability of abstract geometry to draw the mind toward the eternal forms, he does not ignore the application of geometry to warfare, architecture, land measurement, etc. (3) Astronomy, by which he means the science of solid bodies in motion, is the next science in the hierarchy. Plato makes it clear that for him astronomy is not the descriptive science of the motion of the heavenly bodies, but the study of the principles governing such motion—to use modern terms, he has in mind celestial mechanics or astrophysics, and not descriptive astronomy. The chief value of such knowledge is that it directs the mind to the law and harmony of celestial motion and thus paves the way for the dialectical study of the harmony of the eternal forms; but Plato does not entirely ignore its practical application in the art of navigation. (4) Harmonics is the study of the motions of bodies which produce harmonious sound. Like astronomy, it directs the mind to ideal harmony. Harmonics, in Plato's scheme, is the science of the principles of har-

mony, which are, to be sure, exemplified in music—music is applied harmonics—but the two are by no means the same. (5) Dialectic is the coping
stone of the sciences, the systematic unity of the earlier sciences of the hierarchy; it is concerned with the forms in their organic unity. In its theoretic
aspect, dialectic is the completion and fulfillment of scientific inquiry; on
its practical side it serves as a guide in morals and statecraft, and in the other
humanistic pursuits.

Plato's theory of knowledge contains throughout a reference to the *objects*
of the several sciences and levels of knowledge. Clearly, for him epistemology or theory of knowledge cannot be divorced from metaphysics or
theory of reality. Plato found it necessary to appeal to metaphysics, to his
world-view, in order to validate knowledge. Sense knowledge—the kind in
which the Sophists believed—presents to us the passing, changing, particular, and accidental. Sense knowledge cannot therefore be genuine knowledge; for it does not reveal the truth or get at the heart of reality. Conceptual knowledge is conversant with the universal, changeless, and essential elements in things and is, consequently, the only true knowledge. Philosophy has for its aim knowledge of the universal, unchangeable, and
eternal reality behind the particular and transitory appearances of sense.

Doctrine of Ideas. The idea, or concept, as we have seen, comprehends or
holds together the essential qualities common to many particulars; the
essence of things consists in their universal forms. The doctrine of universal
essences is difficult to grasp; we are more apt to consider such generic ideas
as mental processes only. If particulars alone exist, there is nothing corresponding to the idea or type outside the mind. "I see a horse, but 'horseness'
I do not see," as Antisthenes is reported to have said. Plato did not share this
view; according to him, the ideas or forms are not mere thoughts in the
minds of men or even in the mind of God—indeed, the divine thought is
itself directed toward them. He conceives them as existing in and for themselves, as having the character of substantiality. They are substances, real or
substantial forms, the original, eternal transcendent archetypes of things,
existing prior to things and apart from them, and thus uninfluenced by the
changes to which they are subject. The particular objects which we perceive
are imperfect copies or reflections of the eternal patterns. Particulars may
come and go, but the idea or form goes on forever. Men may come and men
may go, but the man-type is eternal. There are many objects or copies, but
there is only one idea of a class of things. The variety and diversity of independent forms, or ideas, is endless, nothing being too lowly or insignificant

to have its idea. There are ideas of things, relations, qualities, actions, and values; ideas of tables and beds and chairs; of smallness, greatness, likeness; of colors, odors, and tones; of health, rest, and motion; of beauty, truth, and goodness.

The ideas or archetypes, though numberless, are not disorganized and chaotic; they constitute a well-ordered world, or rational cosmos. The ideal order forms an interrelated, connected organic unity; the ideas are arranged in logical order, and subsumed under the highest idea, the idea of the Good, which is the source of all the rest. This idea is supreme; beyond it there is no other. The truly real and the truly good are identical; the idea of the Good is the *logos,* the cosmic purpose. Unity, therefore, includes plurality; in the intelligible or ideal world there is no unity without plurality, and no plurality without unity. Plato's emphasis on unity in the diversity and multiplicity shows the influence of Parmenides. The universe is conceived by Plato as a logical system of ideas, an organic unity, governed by a universal purpose, the idea of the Good, and it is, therefore, a rational, significant whole. The meaning of the Good cannot be grasped by the senses, for they perceive only the imperfect and fleeting reflections of the Good, but can never rise to a vision of it as a perfect and abiding whole. It is the function of philosophy, by the exercise of the reason, to understand the inner order and connections of the universe, and to conceive its essence by logical thought.

Plato's theory of ideas is his most original philosophical achievement. Although the way was prepared for the ideal-theory by the Pythagorean number-mysticism, the eternal being of Parmenides, the Heraclitean logos-doctrine, the qualitative atomism of Anaxagoras, and most of all by the Socratic doctrine of concepts, the theory of universals as a fully articulated metaphysical position must be credited entirely to Plato. The essentials of the theory are so clearly delineated in the Platonic dialogues that we may without risk of over-simplification summarize it in a few definite statements: (1) Forms or ideas, defined as the objects corresponding to abstract concepts are real entities; the Platonic form is simply the reification or entification of the Socratic concept—endowed with the properties of the Eleatic being. (2) There is a great variety of forms, including the forms of classes of things—house, dog, man, etc.; of qualities—whiteness, roundness; of relations—equality, resemblance, etc.; of values—goodness, beauty, etc. (3) The forms belong to a realm of abstract entities, a "heaven of ideas," separable from concrete particulars in space and time. The separation of the forms and their exemplifications is commonly referred to as *the* Platonic dualism.

(4) The forms are superior to particulars in degree of reality and value; the forms are the realities of which particulars are mere appearances. The form is a model or archetype of which the particular is a copy. (5) The forms are non-mental and subsist independently of any knowing mind; they are not "ideas" residing in the minds of men nor even in God's mind. The suggestion that a form is merely "a thought in our minds," a name for a group of particulars having a common predicate, is seriously entertained but presumably rejected by Plato, on the ground that a name is insignificant unless there is "a common nature" to which it refers. Their mode of being is unique; they are neither mental nor physical, but are none the less real. (6) Since they are non-temporal, as well as non-spatial, they are eternal and immutable. (7) The forms are logically interrelated and constitute a hierarchy,[2] in which the higher forms "communicate" with lower or subordinate forms. The supreme form in the hierarchy is the form of the Good. (8) The forms are apprehended by reason, not by sense—though sense may provide the occasion and the stimulus for the apprehension of the form which it embodies. (9) Finally, the relation between a particular and the form which it exemplifies is called "participation"; all particulars with a common predicate participate in the corresponding form. A particular may participate simultaneously in a plurality of forms, and when it undergoes change it participates successively in different forms. The doctrine of participation presents serious difficulties for the theory of forms—difficulties of which Plato was fully cognizant.[3]

The philosophical position summed up in the above statements, commonly referred to as Platonic realism, has had its exponents from the time of Plato to the present. Its period of greatest influence, however, was during the Middle Ages.

Philosophy of Nature. We turn now to the relation of Plato's ideal world to the *so-called* real world. As has been said before, the particular objects in nature are copies of ideas. How is this to be interpreted? How can the pure, perfect, and changeless principles be responsible for the incomplete and ever-changing world of sense? To answer this, Plato invokes another principle, which is diametrically opposed to the ideas, and to which sensuous existence owes its imperfections. This second principle, which Aristotle calls the Platonic "matter," is the basis of the phenomenal world; as such it provides the raw material upon which the forms are somehow impressed. Matter is per-

---

[2] Cf. *Sophist*, 259b (this pagination is given in margin of Jowett trans.)
[3] Cf. *Parmenides*, 156a ff.

ishable, imperfect, and unreal, it is non-being; whatever reality, form, or beauty the *perceived* world has, it owes to ideas. Some interpreters of Plato conceive this Platonic "matter" as space; others as a formless, space-filling mass. Plato needs something besides the idea to account for our world of sense, or nature, which is not a mere illusion of the senses, but a level of reality lower than the changeless ideal realm. This substratum, untouched by the ideal principle, must be conceived as devoid of all qualities—formless, indefinable, imperceptible. Nature owes its existence to the interplay of the ideal world and non-being or matter; as a ray of light, in passing through a prism, is broken into many rays, so the idea is broken into many objects by matter. The formless something is non-being, not in the sense of being non-existent, but in the sense of having a lower order of existence: the term non-being expresses a judgment of value. The sensible world partakes of a measure of reality or being, in so far as it takes on form. Plato does not define very precisely the nature of the relation between the two realms; but it is plain that the ideas are somehow responsible for all the reality things possess. Things owe their being to the presence in them of ideas; they participate in ideas. At the same time, non-being, the substratum, is responsible for the diversity and imperfection of the many different objects embodying the same idea. There are, then, two principles, of which the idea is the true reality, the thing of greatest value, that to which everything owes its form and essence, the principle of law and order in the universe; while the other element, matter, is secondary, a dull, irrational, recalcitrant force, the unwilling slave of the idea, which somehow, though imperfectly, takes on the impress of the idea. Matter in relation to the idea is both friend and foe, an auxiliary and an obstruction, the ground of physical and moral evil, of change and imperfection. Since the world of ideas is the source of goodness, the non-ideal must be responsible for evil. If we had to label this part of the system, we should call it *dualism:* the idea is the paramount principle of things, and matter an inferior and secondary principle; but neither is reducible to the other.

Cosmology. Plato attempts to explain the origin of nature in his *Timaeus,* a work that reminds one of the early pre-Socratic philosophies, since it is devoted to cosmological speculations. His cosmology is permeated with many mythical elements and often contradicts his other teachings, but he claims for it nothing more than probability. Like a human artist or workman, the Demiurge or Creator fashions the world after the pattern of the ideal world; guided by the idea of the Good, he forms as perfect a universe as it is possible for him to form, hampered, as he is, by the principle of matter. The Demiurge is not really a creator, but an architect; the two principles, the ideal and the material, are already in existence; they are not created by the Demiurge. The function of the Demiurge is to impose the forms on a pre-existent material or receptacle. The world so generated is composed of the four material elements: earth, air, fire, water, and an animating soul, the world-soul. This world-soul is compounded of the indivisible and the divisible, of identity and change, and is thus able both to know the ideal and perceive the corporeal. It has its own original motion, which is the cause of all motion; in moving itself it also moves bodies; it is diffused throughout the world and is the cause of all beauty, order, and harmony. The world-soul is an intermediary between the world of ideas and the world of phenomena; it is the cause of all law, mathematical relations, harmony, order, uniformity, life, mind, and knowledge. It moves according to fixed laws, and is the cause of the motion and distribution of matter in the heavenly spheres. Besides the world-soul, the Demiurge created souls or gods for the planets—which he arranged according to the Pythagorean system of harmony—and rational human souls, leaving it to the lower gods to create animals and the irrational part of the human soul. Everything has been made for man, plants to nourish him, animal-bodies to serve as habitations for fallen souls. We have, accordingly, in Plato's cosmology many gods—to none of whom he definitely ascribes personality—the total world of ideas, including the idea of the Good, the Demiurge, the world-soul, the planetary souls, and the gods of popular religion.

Plato's cosmology is a teleological world-view clothed in mythical garb, an attempt to explain reality as a purposeful, well-ordered, cosmos, and the world as an intelligence, guided by reason and directed toward an ethical goal. Purposes or final causes are the real causes of the world, the physical causes being merely cooperative ones. Whatever is good, rational and purposeful in the universe is due to reason; whatever is evil, irrational, and purposeless is ultimately traceable to matter.

Plato's cosmology may be considered an attempt to differentiate the "causes" or creative factors productive of the actual world. His account is expressed in mythological language as a "story of creation," but it was not intended as a literal description of creation as a temporal process, but rather as an analysis of the constitutive factors of the actual world; what he seems to be saying is that the real or actual world contains various features which may be understood by considering them *as if* they had been produced by a creative process. The four factors in creation enumerated in the *Timaeus* are: (1) The *Demiurge* or God, the active and dynamic cause of the world. The Demiurge is, as we have already seen, a world architect and not a world creator, since he molded a pre-existent matter and did not create the world out of nothing. The Demiurge is the source and principle of all power, energy and activity in nature and in mind. Though not a personal divinity, God is the source of the goodness of the world and is not responsible for its evil. (2) The *pattern* as archetype of the world. The Demiurge, in the creation of the world, was guided by an eternal and pre-existent model which resided in the world of forms. This pattern is the source of the ideal elements in existence, of the order, the lawfulness and the regularity of natural processes. (3) The *receptacle*. This principle provides the locus and matrix of creation; it is the source of the indeterminacy, the brute factuality, the disorder and the evil of the world. (4) The form of the *Good*. This principle functions in Plato's cosmology as the source of the purposiveness of things, of the teleological and valuational aspects of nature and mind.[4] The entire natural order, including physical things as well as minds, is a product of creation in which features derived from all four factors are fused; the world-soul, which animates the entire physical world as the individual soul animates its body, is among the products of creation.

The historical influence of Plato's cosmological speculations is enormous. We shall encounter it in Aristotle's physical and theological theories (the four factors of creation correspond very closely to the four causes of Aristotle's analysis: (1) the efficient, (2) the formal, (3) the material and (4) final), in the Neoplatonic theory of creation, and, as modified by the Hebrew account of creation, it dominates the idea of Creation in scholastic philosophy. With the possible exception of Plato's theory of forms, no other Platonic doctrine has exerted a longer or more continuous influence.

Psychology. Plato in his theory of knowledge distinguished two kinds of knowledge: (1) opinion, dependent on sense perception; and (2) genuine knowledge, or science. The counterpart of this dualism of knowledge is apparent in Plato's psychology. In sensation and opinion, the soul is dependent on the body, but the soul, in so far as it beholds the world of ideas, is pure reason. The body is an impediment to knowledge, from which the soul must free itself in order to behold truth in its purity. The copies of the pure ideas, as they exist in the phenomenal world, merely incite the rational soul to think; sensation occasions and provokes the apprehension of ideas, but

---

[4] A systematic reconstruction of Plato's thought in terms of the four creative factors is presented in R. Demos, *The Philosophy of Plato,* Part I.

does not produce it. The soul must somehow possess an apprehension of ideas prior to its contact with the world of experience. Plato teaches that the soul has viewed such ideas before and has forgotten them. The imperfect copies of ideas in the world of sense suggest to the soul its past, remind it of what it has seen before. Thus all knowledge is reminiscence (*anamnesis*) and all learning is a reawakening. Plato appeals to such reminiscence to establish the doctrine of the soul's pre-existence. The myth of the charioteer in the *Phaedrus* conveys the insight that the soul must have existed prior to its union with the body; the human soul, then, is, in part, pure reason, and this rational part is its most characteristic aspect. When the soul enters a body, there is added to it a mortal and irrational part, which fits it for existence in the sense world. The irrational part is further divided into the spirited part, by which Plato means the nobler impulses (anger, ambition, love of power) situated in the heart, and desire, by which he means the lower appetites or passions, placed by him in the liver, the part with which the soul loves and hungers and thirsts. The union with the body is a hindrance to the *intellectual* aspirations of the soul, the presence of impulses and desires is a hindrance to the ethical supremacy of reason, which, as Plato shows in his ethics, reason itself must seek to overcome.

Plato's psychology is dualistic in its separation of the soul into a higher, rational, and a lower, irrational part, but since the irrational is further divided into the spirited and the appetitive, his division of the soul is in fact tripartite. (1) The *rational* faculty is, as we have seen, primarily an intellectual one, but Plato seems to include within it such traits of character as gentleness, humility and reverence, which, though not purely intellectual, are associated with a philosophic disposition. (2) The *spirited faculty* is an executive faculty somewhat resembling the will, but it is misleading to equate it with the will as the faculty of decision and free choice. This latter concept of the will, which is a product of medieval thought, is of Hebraic and Christian, rather than Platonic origin. It is extremely doubtful—though this is a matter of controversy—whether Plato ever envisaged freedom of choice and of will. The spirited faculty resembles the will only in being dynamic and executive. Plato embraces within the spirited faculty such emotions, sentiments and traits of character as ambition, anger, resentment and righteous indignation. (3) The appetitive faculty corresponds very closely to the term "desire" in modern psychology. Among the bodily appetites listed by Plato are desire for pleasure, desire for wealth, desire for food, shelter and other bodily satisfactions. Pleasure is not exclusively appetitive; there is a kind of pleasure accompanying the exercise of each of the faculties of the soul: the pleasures of reason are enjoyed by those who exercise the rational faculty in mathematics, science and dialectic; the pleasures of honor and fame accompany successful pursuit of ambition for political, social and military advancement; the pleasures of sense are associated with the satisfaction of the bodily appetites. The order of superiority of pleasures is the one in which we have listed them. The criterion of the ordering is the judgment of the competent critic who is acquainted with all three types, for the judgment of the libertine or the man of ambition are biased and unreliable. Plato's psychology of pleasure and pain is characterized by great subtlety and sophistication. He observed that, though pleasure and pain are both positive feelings, there is a neutral state between pleasure and pain which appears pleasurable in contrast to a preceding pain, or painful in contrast to an earlier pleasure. He was perhaps the first to enunciate a doctrine of psychological relativity.

Plato's tripartite division of the soul is a form of faculty psychology—a forerunner of the faculty psychologies of scholasticism. The soul functions through its faculties, which are to some extent separate and distinct principles. The separation of the faculties rests on the principle of contradiction, the principle that one and the same thing cannot produce opposite effects at one and the same time. By appealing to this principle Plato argues that the reason and the appetites are distinct faculties; the soul may be pulled in opposite directions by the two, as when reason restrains thirst when only poisonous drink is obtainable, or the spirited faculty rebels against morbid bodily appetites. The observable conflict between the faculties within the soul of each one of us is conclusive evidence of their distinctness. But Plato's separation of the faculties is not so extreme as to preclude their interplay and cooperation. The spirited faculty is frequently the ally of reason in the control of the appetites, and even our natural desires may be in conformity with reason: for example, a moderate desire for food and drink. The soul, despite the plurality and separation of its faculties, possesses a unity and indivisibility.

Doctrine of Immortality. Plato ascribes immortality to the soul and in several of his dialogues offers arguments for immortality. The most characteristic of these is the argument from the soul's knowledge of forms: a soul that has contemplated the pure, eternal ideas must, in part at least, be like these ideas, pure and eternal; for only like can know like. He also makes use of the doctrine of reminiscence to prove the pre-existence, and also presumably the continued existence, of the soul after the death of the body. This argument infers the pre-existence of the soul from its possession of interpretative principles and axiomatic truths which have not been acquired in this life. Since these principles are part of the native endowment of the soul, they must be recollections of eternal verities apprehended in an earlier state and recalled on the occasion of sense experience. The argument from reminiscence is formulated in the *Phaedo* (where it appears as the second argument) and in the *Phaedrus,* and its epistemological basis is strikingly demonstrated by Socrates' questioning of the slave boy in the dialogue *Meno:* by a series of questions Socrates is able to elicit from the boy the proof of a geometrical theorem of which he was previously ignorant. How can this be explained except on the assumption that geometrical knowledge is latent in the soul at birth and was somehow acquired in a pre-existent state?

Besides the two epistemological arguments for immortality, Plato advances a variety of metaphysical proofs, of which two are especially prominent: the argument from the unity and simplicity of the soul and the argument from the vitality of the soul. The soul is by nature simple and indivisible; it can, therefore, neither be produced by composition nor be destroyed by disintegration—whatever is simple cannot be decomposed (the third argument of the *Phaedo*). The soul is a principle of life or spontaneity; it would be a contradiction to suppose that the principle of life should die—life cannot become death; hence the soul is immortal (the fourth argument of the *Phaedo*). The argument from the vitality of the soul reflects a survival in Plato's thought of animistic conceptions and is closely allied with a cosmological argument that the souls or spirits, as the ultimate sources of motion in the world, must be eternal. The soul as the source of motion is self-moving, initiating its activity from within; consequently its motion, as well as its life, is perpetual and eternal. Plato finally advances a number of valuational and moral arguments, which ascribe immortality to the soul on the ground of its supreme worth and the demands of justice. The main value-argument is that the superior dignity and value of the soul attest to its survival over the crass body which, indeed, persists for a considerable time. This is reinforced by considerations of justice: the world as a moral, rational and just order demands a future life of rewards and punishments for the rectification of the imperfections of this life. An interesting variation of the moral argument is found in the *Republic,* Book X: everything is destroyed by its peculiar or connatural evil; the worst vices, injustice, intemperance and ignorance are the peculiar evils of the soul; yet they do not destroy the vicious soul, hence the soul is indestructible. None of these arguments—epistemological, metaphysical or valuational—is perhaps convincing when taken alone; together they constitute an impressive array. However carefully we may search the subsequent philosophical literature on immortality, it will be difficult to find any argument advanced which has not been clearly foreshadowed by Plato.

The question now arises: How does the pure rational soul happen to unite with a body? At this point, Plato again has recourse to mythical explanation, combining conceptions suggested by his theory of knowledge and by empirical psychology, with Orphic and Pythagorean mysticism. The pure, rational soul, which was created by the Demiurge, once inhabited a star, but having become possessed with a desire for the world of sense, was enclosed in a material body as in a prison. Should it ever succeed in overcoming the lower side of its nature, it will return to its star, otherwise it will sink lower and lower, entering in succession the bodies of different animals (the doctrine of metempsychosis or transmigration of souls). Had the soul resisted desire in its celestial life, it would have continued to enjoy a transcendent existence, and to occupy itself with the contemplation of ideas. Since it has failed in this, it is condemned to pass through a stage of purification.

An important phase of Plato's psychology is the doctrine of eros. Just as sense perception awakens in the soul the remembrance of pure ideas, of truths apprehended in a pre-existent state, so the perception of sensuous beauty, which excites sense love, also revives in the soul the memory of ideal beauty contemplated in its former existence. These recollections of truth and beauty inspire a yearning for the higher life associated with the world of pure ideas. Thus sensuous love and the yearning for the beautiful and the good derive from one and the same basic impulse. The sensuous impulse which seeks the continued existence of the species is, in its higher manifestations, the craving for fame, the urge to create science, art, and human institutions. In yearning for eternal values, the soul yearns for immortality. Indeed, these impulses are construed as evidence of the immortality of the soul, for what the soul passionately aspires to must be attainable.

Ethics. The question of greatest moment to Socrates related to the morally good: What is the nature or meaning of the good, what is a good life, and how can we justify such a life to reason? How should a rational being act, what ought to be his controlling principle? Having raised the problem, Socrates gave his answer; though he did not offer a complete and systematic philosophy of life, he laid the foundations for such a system of moral philosophy. Plato takes up the problem and seeks to solve it in the light of his comprehensive world-view. As we said before, the question of the meaning and worth of life and human institutions he regards as involved in the larger question of the nature and meaning of the world and of man. His ethics, like his theory of knowledge, is based on his metaphysics.

The universe is basically a rational universe, a spiritual system. Objects of sense, the material phenomena around us, are mere fleeting shadows of eternal and never-changing ideas; such objects, since they are transitory and ephemeral, have no absolute worth, for only that which endures is real and has value. Reason, which alone is conversant with the highest good, has absolute worth. Hence the rational part of man is the true part, and man's ideal must be to cultivate his reason, the immortal side of his soul. The body and the senses are alien to the soul; indeed, the body is the prison house of the soul, a fetter, deliverance from which is the final goal of the spirit. "Wherefore we ought to fly away from earth as quickly as we can, and to fly away is to become like God." The release of the soul from the body and the contemplation of the beautiful world of ideas—that is the ultimate end of life.

Although release from the body is its ultimate destiny, the soul, with its reason, its spirited part, and its appetites, is meanwhile enclosed in its dungeon and has its problems to solve. The rational part is wise and has to exercise forethought on behalf of the entire soul: hence, its essential function is to command. The individual is *wise* in whom reason rules over the other impulses of the soul, knowing what is advantageous for the whole inner economy and for each member of it. The function of the spirited part is to be the subject and the ally of reason. After the two principles have been trained and educated, and brought into unison, they exercise control over the bodily appetites. Reason takes counsel, the spirited faculty fights the battles of reason, obeys it, and gives effect to its counsels by its bravery. An individual, therefore, is *brave* when the spirited part holds fast, through pain and pleasure, to the instructions of reason as to what is to be feared and what is not. He is *temperate* when spirit and appetite yield to reason and submit to its authority. Temperance, or self-control, is mastery over certain kinds of pleasures and desires. When these three inward principles are in tune, each doing its proper work, the man is *just*. The just and honorable course is that which a man pursues in this frame of mind; he has achieved the ethical attitude when he is wise and brave and temperate, when he has brought harmony into his soul. Such a man would not repudiate a deposit, commit sacrilege or theft, be false to friends, a traitor to his country, or commit similar misdeeds. Justice is the supreme virtue, and any soul in which it dwells is incapable of any sort of wrongdoing.

The ethical ideal, therefore, is a well-ordered soul, one in which the higher functions rule the lower, one which exercises the virtues of wisdom, courage, self-control, and justice. A life of reason, or of virtue, is the highest good. Happiness attends such a life, and the just man is after all the happy man. Pleasure, although it is not an end in itself, accompanies the gratification of desire and the more reasonable the desire, the more pleasurable its gratification.[5]

We have already referred to another aspect of Plato's ethical teaching which lays strong emphasis on the rational element in the soul, while regarding the irrational aspect as something not merely to be subordinated, but to be subdued and cast out. This part of his teaching differs from the usual Greek conception; it is ascetic in its tone, and foreshadows the doctrine of *contemptus mundi* which we shall encounter in primitive Christianity: the world we perceive is but a passing show: "The glory of the world passeth away, and the lust thereof." That which alone endures, for Plato, is reason, truth; all else is vanity. Matter is imperfection, a dead weight on the soul; to be free from this clog and to lose oneself in the contemplation of beautiful ideas, or to see God, as the Christians put it, is a consummation devoutly to be wished. This ascetic tendency of the Platonic philosophy culminates in mysticism.

Politics. Plato's theory of the state, which is set forth in the *Republic,* is based on his ethics. Since virtue is the highest good, and the individual cannot attain the good in isolation, but only in society, the mission of the state is to promote virtue and happiness; the purpose of its constitution and its laws is to bring about conditions which will enable as many men as possible to become good; that is, to secure the general welfare. Social life is a means to the perfection of individuals, not an end in itself. To be sure, the individual must subordinate his private interests to the public welfare, but that is only because his own true good is bound up with the social weal. If all men were rational and virtuous, there would be no need of laws and a state: a completely virtuous man is governed by reason, and not by external law. Few, however, are perfect; hence laws are necessary to the realization of our true good. The state thus owes its origin to the imperfections of human nature. The state should be organized like the universe at large and the individual virtuous soul; that is, reason should be in the ascendency.

There are as many classes in society as there are functions of the soul, and the harmonious relations of these classes to each other correspond to

[5] Cf. *Republic,* Bk. IX, 581 ff.

those obtaining in a healthy soul. Those who have philosophical insight embody reason and ought to be the ruling class; the members of the warrior class possess the spirited element: their task is defense; the agriculturists, artisans, and merchants represent the lower appetites, and have as their function the production of material goods. Among the nations of his time, Plato regarded the Phenicians as dominated by the lower appetites, the barbarous people of the North as exemplifying the spirited element, the Greeks as representing reason. Justice is realized in a state in which each class, the industrial, military, and guardian, does its own work and attends to its own business without meddling in the tasks of the other classes. A state is temperate and brave and wise in consequence of certain affections and conditions of these same classes. A state is master of itself when the desires of the vulgar many are controlled by the desires and the wisdom of the few, when the governors and the governed are unanimous on the question as to who ought to govern. Every individual ought to have some occupation in the state, the one to which his natural capacity is best adapted. Justice is to have and do what is suited to one's capabilities and place in society; to mind one's business and not be meddlesome.

The ideal society forms a complete unity, one large family; hence, Plato opposes private property and monogamous marriage, and recommends, for the two upper castes, who are to be supported by the workers, communism and the common possession of wives and children. Among his other recommendations are eugenic supervision of marriages and births, exposure of weak children, compulsory state education, education of women for war and government, censorship of works of art and literature. Plato did not have a high opinion of art, regarding it as an imitation of the world of sense, which is itself a mere copy of the true essences of things; art, therefore, is an imitation of an imitation. Despite his disparagement of art, however, Plato thought that it could be made to contribute to moral culture.

The state is an educational institution, the instrument of civilization, and as such it must have its foundation in the highest kind of knowledge attainable, that is, philosophy.

Unless it happen either that philosophers acquire the kingly power in states, or that those who are now called kings and potentates be imbued with a sufficient measure of genuine philosophy, that is to say, unless political power and philosophy be united in the same person . . . there will be no deliverance for cities nor yet for the human race.[6]

[6] *Republic,* Bk. V, 473.

The state shall undertake the education of the children of the higher classes, following a definite plan of instruction, which shall be the same for the citizens of both sexes during the first twenty years of life, and shall include: the narration of myths, selected with a view to their ethical influence; gymnastics, which develops not only the body but the spirited faculty of the soul; reading and writing; poetry and music, which arouse the sense of beauty, harmony, and proportion and encourage philosophical thought; mathematics, which tends to draw the mind from the concrete and the sensuous to the abstract and the real. A selection of the superior individuals shall be made from the ranks of the young men at twenty, and these shall study the different subjects of their childhood in their interrelations and learn to survey them as a whole. Those who, at the age of thirty, show the greatest ability in their studies, in military affairs, and in their other activities will study dialectic for five years. Then they will be put to the test of holding military commands and subordinate civic offices. At the age of fifty, those who have shown themselves worthy will devote themselves to the study of philosophy, until their turn comes to administer the higher offices for their country's sake.

Plato's *Republic* is the depiction of a perfect state, the dream of a society embodying the principles of justice. It is frequently spoken of as utopian, and indeed, Plato himself acknowledges that his ideal state can never be fully realized in any actual society; the most that can be hoped for is an approximation to the utopian ideal. But the unrealizability of the ideal state does not, in Plato's opinion, detract from its worth as a guide in the organization and administration of actual societies. Furthermore, we must remember that it was conceived by Plato as a small city-state, that many of his "ideals" where actual realities in the Sparta of his day. Thus the charge of utopian impracticality so frequently leveled against Plato's ideal state is not entirely justified. In his later work, the *Laws,* Plato greatly modifies his political theory by abandoning certain of the idealistic and rationalistic features of his earlier scheme. A good state should have, besides reason or insight, freedom and friendship. All citizens should be free and have a share in the government; they are to be landowners, while all trade and commerce should be given over to serfs and foreigners. The family is restored to its natural position. Knowledge is not everything: there are other motives of virtuous conduct, e.g., pleasure and friendship, pain, and hate. Virtue, however, remains the ideal, and the education of the moral will be a primary goal of the state. The concern for the moral foundation of political and social institutions characterizes Plato's entire political philosophy.

Plato's Historical Position. Plato's philosophy is rationalistic in the sense that it holds a rational knowledge of the universe to be possible, as well as in the sense that the source of knowledge lies in reason and not in sense perception. Experience, however, plays an indispensable rôle in knowledge; our a priori ideas are aroused and suggested by experience. His philosophy is realistic in that it affirms the existence of extra-mental realities—the forms or ideas; idealistic, in that this world of forms is conceived as an ideal realm transcending the particular things in space and time; phenomenalistic, in that the sense world is reduced to the status of phenomena or appearances of the real world. In its refusal to equate reality with the physical world, Plato's philosophy is radically anti-materialistic. It is pantheistic in the sense that all phenomena are looked upon as manifestations of an intelligible world-order, and also in that it introduces an all-pervading world-soul. It is theistic in its acceptance of a Demiurge, a creative principle which imposes the forms on the plastic receptacle. It teaches transcendency in that its ideal world is above the world of actual experience: the pure ideas seem to shun the contamination of the material element. It is immanent, in that the world-soul is diffused through all space. It is anti-mechanistic and teleological in that it seeks the ultimate explanation of the world in final causes or purposes, all of which are embraced under a universal purpose: the idea of the Good. It is dualistic in its adoption of two principles of explanation, the ideal and the material. It is fundamentally valuational in that the final cause of the whole world is the idea of the Good which embraces ethical, esthetic, and logical values. Its ethical theory is anti-hedonistic, intuitionistic, and idealistic, a version of the self-realization theory. Its political theory combines aristocratic with socialistic and communistic elements. The Platonic system, by combining apparently incompatible doctrines into the unity of a great creative synthesis, escapes the radical incoherence and inconsistency of philosophical eclecticism.

The deep influence of this system on later Greek thought and on Christian philosophy and theology is easily understood. It is a world-view with a remarkable scope; it attempts to rationalize nearly every field of human interest and endeavor. For Christianity, when it sought to make its message intelligible and reasonable to the educated Roman world, Plato's philosophy became a treasure house of thought. Its idealism, its teleology, its conception of a system of ideas as archetypes and patterns of the actual world, its dualisms, its mysticism, its exaltation of reason and contempt for the world of sense, its ethically rooted state, its proofs for the immortality of the soul, its doctrine of the fall of man—all these teachings, and many more besides, were highly congenial to those who wished to justify the new faith to reason. We shall have occasion, later on, to point out how much Christian theology owed to the Greeks, and how profoundly the greatest thinker of the early Church, St. Augustine, was influenced by Plato. What a vital force his idealism has remained in the philosophy of the entire European world, down to the present, will be evident at every step.

The Platonic School. The Academy established by Plato was continued by his pupils after his death. The school at first followed the Pythagorean doctrines which Plato had adopted during his old age, and identified ideas with numbers. It also emphasized ethical studies. This phase of the school is called the Older Academy: its scholars or heads were Plato's nephew, Speusippus (347-339), Xenocrates (339-314), Polemo (314-270), and Crates (270-247). Other members of the Old Academy were: Heraclides of Pontus, Philippus of Opus, Hestiaeus of Perinthus, and Eudoxus of Cnidus. Crates' successor Arcesilaus (247-241) introduced skepticism into the Academy and founded the Second or Middle Academy, which remained true to the teachings of Arcesilaus until Carneades became head of the school (*ca.* 156), and founded the Third or New Academy.

10. ARISTOTLE

Aristotle's Problems. Plato was the first Greek thinker to construct an idealistic philosophy on a comprehensive scale. His system, however, presented difficulties and inconsistencies which had to be considered and, if possible, overcome. The early Platonic school did little to develop the thought of its founder; it did what schools generally do, it transmitted his doctrines very largely as they had been received. It was left to Aristotle, a pupil of independent mind, to reconstruct the system, to develop it in what seemed to him a more consistent and scientific manner. First of all, the problem of transcendent ideas had to be reconsidered: Plato seemed to place the eternal forms, as Aristotle calls them, beyond the stars, to separate them from the actual world of experience, and to degrade the latter to mere appearance. Then there was the conception of the secondary element, the Platonic matter, which needed to be defined more precisely in order to become a satisfactory principle of explanation. The gulf between form and matter had to be bridged somehow: How could the remote and changeless ideas place their impress upon a lifeless and irrational substratum? Other difficulties presented themselves. How shall we account for the progressively changing forms of things; how for the existence of individual immortal souls and their presence in human bodies? The Demiurge and the world-soul are makeshifts; the recourse to mythology and the popular religion a confession of ignorance. The radical dualism of ideas and things remains, and infects every phase of the system; so, at least, it seemed to Plato's pupil.

Aristotle retains the changeless eternal forms, the idealistic principles of the teacher, but rejects their transcendency. He brings them down from heaven to earth, so to speak. Forms are not *apart from* things, but *inherent* in them; they are not transcendent, but immanent. Matter is not to be equated to non-being but is a dynamic being; form and matter are not separate, but eternally together: matter combines with the form to constitute individual things, each individual moves and changes, grows, or evolves under the control and direction of its form. The world of sense, the phenomenal order, is not a mere imitation or shadow of the real world; it *is* the real world, form and matter in one, and the true object of science. Because he conceives the domain of science in this realistic fashion, Aristotle feels at home in science, he studies it sympathetically, his theories always keep in close touch with it, and he encourages the natural sciences.

Aristotle was born 384 B.C., in Stagira, the son of Nicomachus, the court physician of Philip of Macedon. At the age of seventeen he entered Plato's Academy, where he remained for twenty years as student and teacher. After the death of Plato (347), he journeyed to Assos, in Mysia, thence to Mitylene, and is said to have returned to Athens to open a school of rhetoric. In 342 he was called by King Philip to direct the education of his son Alexander, afterwards called the Great. Seven years later he came back to Athens, this time to establish a school in the gymnasium dedicated to the Lycean Apollo, from which the school received its historic name, the Lyceum. It has also been called the *Peripatetic School,* because of Aristotle's habit of walking while giving instruction. He taught by means of lectures and the dialogue. After the sudden death of Alexander in 323, the philosopher was accused of sacrilege by the anti-Macedonian party at Athens and compelled to flee to Euboea, where he died 322 B.C.

Aristotle was a man of noble character, realizing in his personality the Greek ideal of measure and harmony taught in his system of ethics. His love of truth was strong, his judgment sober, impartial, and acute; he was a master of dialectic, a lover of detail, a great reader, a close observer, and a specialist. His literary style was like his thinking, sober, scientific, familiar, free from embellishment and flights of fancy, even dry. One seldom feels the glow of his personality in his works; it is only on rare occasions that he gives expression to his emotions. In these respects, he was unlike his great teacher Plato. In perusing his works we seem to be in the presence of calm impersonal reason.

He is one of the greatest figures in the history of thought, a universal genius. He wrote on a large number of topics: logic, rhetoric, poetics, physics, botany, zoology, psychology, ethics, economics, politics, and metaphysics.

A large collection of writings attributed to Aristotle has come down to us, most of them genuine. Many of his books, however, seem to have been lost. Andronicus, who published an edition of his works between 60 and 50 B.C., places the number of books—chapters, we should say—written by Aristotle at 1000. Of the works published by him for wider circles of readers, only fragments remain; the material that has been preserved represents his lectures to his pupils and was not intended for publication.

The extant writings can be arranged in the following groups: (1) Logic (called by the followers of Aristotle the *Organon,* the organ or instrument for acquiring knowledge). The *Organon* includes: *Categories,* largely genuine, though mutilated and added to by later hands; *De Interpretatione,* an elementary work, the authenticity of which has been questioned, but which is now generally accepted as genuine; the *Prior* and the *Posterior Analytics,* containing Aristotle's account of the syllogism, of definition and demonstration are unquestionably genuine; *Topics* (nine books concerned largely with dialectical reasoning concerning general opinions). *Sophistic Fallacies* is the last book of the *Topics.*

(2) Natural Sciences. *Physics* (eight books); *On the Heavens* (four books); *Origin and Decay* (two books); *Meteorology* (four books); *Cosmology* (spurious); *Botany* (spurious); *History of Animals* (ten books); *On the Parts of Animals* (four books); *On the Progression of Animals; On the Origin of Animals* (five books); *On the Locomotion of Animals* (spurious).

(3) Psychology. *On the Soul* (three books, treating of sensation, memory, imagination, thought); a group of smaller treatises, collectively known as *Parva Naturalia,* including *De Memoria et Reminiscentia, On Dreams,* etc.

(4) Metaphysics. A series of fourteen books, dealing mainly with first principles, were placed, in the collection of Andronicus, immediately after the writings on physics, and bore the heading *ta meta ta physica,* or writings coming after the writings on physics, simply to indicate their position in the collection. This is the origin of the term metaphysics: Aristotle himself never used it, but called such discussions of first principles "First Philosophy." These fourteen books were not intended by Aristotle as a single work. Book II is a later compilation not originally cast in this form by Aristotle, and the first eight chapters of Book X and the first half of Book XI are a rearrangement of Aristotelian extracts.

(5) Ethics. *Nicomachean Ethics* (ten books; additions from the *Eudemian Ethics* have been made in Books V-VII); *Eudemian Ethics* (a revision of the former by Eudemas: only Books I-III and VI are preserved); *Magna Moralia,* the Greater Ethics (a compilation of the two preceding).

(6) Politics. *Politics* (eight books, apparently incomplete); *On the Constitution of Athens* (discovered 1890). The work on economics attributed to Aristotle is not authentic.

(7) Rhetoric. *Rhetoric to Theodectes* (based on Aristotle's teachings, but not his work); *Rhetoric to Alexander* (spurious); *Rhetoric* (three books, the third of which is of doubtful authenticity). The *Poetics* in its extant form is only part of a work in two books. It is concerned with literature in its three principal forms of the epic, tragedy, and comedy.

Bibliography

Translations of Aristotle's *Works,* appearing under the editorship of J. A. Smith and W. D. Ross, 1910–31. E. Wallace, *Psychology,* 1882; W. D. Ross, *Aristotle: Selections,* 1927; R. P. McKeon, ed., *The Basic Work of Aristotle,* 1941; *Introduction to Aristotle,* ed. by R. P. McKeon (contains translations of *Posterior Analytics, De Anima,* and *Nicomachean Ethics*), 1927; S. H. Butcher, *Aristotle's Theory of Poetry and Fine Art* (contains trans. of *Poetics*), 1895; P. Wheelwright, ed. and trans., *Aristotle: From Natural Science, Psychology, The Nicomachean Ethics,* 1935.

E. Zeller, *Aristotle and the Earlier Peripatetics,* 2 vols., 1897; E. Barker, *Political Thought of Plato and Aristotle,* 1906; A. E. Taylor, *Aristotle,* 2nd ed., 1919; E. Wallace, *Outlines of the Philosophy of Aristotle,* 3rd ed., 1908; A. Grant, *Aristotle,* 1874; G. Grote; *Aristotle,* 2 vols., 1883; D. P. Chase, *Ethics of Aristotle,* 1890; T. Davidson, *Aristotle and Ancient Educational Ideals,* 1892; T. E. Lones, *Aristotle's Researches in Natural Science,* 1912; H. Siebeck, *Aristoteles,* 1899; F. C. Brentano, *Aristoteles und seine Weltanschauung,* 1911; C. Piat, *Aristote,* 2nd ed., 1912; T. Gomperz, *Greek Thinkers,* vol. IV, 1912; W. D. Ross, *Aristotle,* 1923; J. L. Stocks, *Aristotelianism,* 1925; W. Jaeger, *Aristoteles,* 2nd ed., 1948; G. Kafka, *Aristoteles,* 1922; C. Lalo, *Aristote,* 1922; H. F. Cherniss, *Aristotle's Criticisms of Pre-Socratic Philosophy,* 1935; J. M. Le Blond, *Logique et methode chez Aristote,* 1939; N. Hartmann, *Aristoteles und das Problem des Begriffs,* 1939; L. Robin, *Aristote,* 1944; A. Mansion, *Introduction à la physique aristotélicienne* (deuxième èdition), 1945.

Philosophy and the Sciences. Aristotle accepts the organic and teleological presuppositions of his teacher: the universe is an ideal world, an organic whole of interrelated parts, a system of eternal and unchangeable ideas or forms. These are the ultimate essences and causes of things, the directing forces or purposes that make them what they are. Ideas are not, however, detached from the world we perceive, but part and parcel of it, immanent in it; they give it form and life. Our world of experience is not an untrustworthy appearance, but is a reality, for us to study and understand. Experience is the basis of knowledge. Starting from experience we rise to the science of ultimate principles. This conception of reality is in harmony with Aristotle's respect for the concrete and particular, accounts for his interest in natural science, and determines his method. Genuine knowledge, however, does not consist in mere acquaintance with facts, but in knowing their reasons or causes, and why they cannot be otherwise than as they are. Philosophy, or science in the broad sense, embraces all such reasoned knowledge. It includes mathematics and the special sciences. The science or philosophy which studies the ultimate or first causes of things is called by Aristotle the first philosophy; we call it metaphysics. Metaphysics is concerned with being *qua* being; the different sciences, with certain parts or phases of being; physics, for example, with being in so far as it is subject to change and motion. The special sciences or philosophies are named second philosophies. Aristotle's differentiation of knowledge into special branches or "sciences" has persisted to this day. We are so accustomed to thinking of physics, chemistry, biology and the rest as distinct spheres of knowledge, separate from each other and from philosophy, that it is difficult to conceive of the state of knowledge before this separation took place. Previous to the transformation wrought by Aristotle, all knowledge, whether concerned with nature, man or God, was embraced in philosophy—philosophy being the love of wisdom in all its forms.

The classification of the sciences proposed by Aristotle possesses great merit and is not without its significance even at the present day, despite the enormous progress of science since his time. He arranged the sciences as follows: (1) Logic, which elaborates the method of inquiry employed in all the other sciences. (2) Theoretical sciences, which are concerned with pure, abstract knowledge. The theoretical sciences enumerated by Aristotle are: mathematics, physics, biology and psychology, and first philosophy, or what is now known as metaphysics. (3) Practical sciences, in which knowledge is pursued as a means to conduct rather than as an end in itself. The practical sciences are ethics and politics. (4) The productive sciences, in which knowledge is subordinated to artistic creation. Aristotle's *Poetics* is an investigation of this sphere; it is a part of what is now called esthetics.

Aristotle's classification of the sciences is so thoroughly logical that there is no reason to depart widely from it in the exposition of his philosophy. We may, to be sure, omit mathematics, because Aristotle made no original contribution to this subject, but was satisfied to appropriate the results of his contemporaries. We are also justified in disregarding much of the detailed exposition of his physics and biology, both because many of his theories in these departments of knowledge are now antiquated, and because of the slight philosophical worth of many of his conclusions. With these relatively minor deviations, we shall keep his scheme of the sciences intact.

Logic. The creation of the science of logic is in a certain respect Aristotle's most amazing achievement. There is no parallel case in the whole history of man's intellectual pursuits in which a single thinker has brought to completion a new science. There were, it is true, some anticipations of logical doctrines in the dialectical arguments of Zeno, the subtleties of the Sophists, the Socratic method of definition of concepts, and the Platonic dialectic. But no one has ever denied that Aristotle is the true founder of logic in the sense of a scientific treatment of the valid forms of reasoning, the first to work it out in detail and to make it a special discipline. Logic as formulated by Aristotle has dominated, to an almost unbelievable extent, the thought of later times. There have been only two major revolts against the traditional logic in modern times. The first was led by Francis Bacon in his advocacy of the inductive method; and the second is the one carried on at the present time by the mathematical logicians. With these two exceptions, the Aristotelian logic has held undisputed sway over man's thinking for over two thousand years. The function of logic is to describe the method of attaining knowledge. Aristotle considers it an important instrument for the acquisition of genuine knowledge, and holds that we should not proceed to the study of the first philosophy, of the science of the essence of things, until we have familiarized ourselves with the principles of logical thought. Logic, accordingly, is a preliminary—or, to use the more technical expression, propaedeutic—science; it is an elaboration of the method employed in the pursuit of all knowledge and is therefore antecedent to all special inquiries. In this sense it may be described as "the science of sciences." It is not merely one among other sciences, on a par with physics, biology, and politics; it is the indispensable preparation for all science. Aristotle regarded his logic as a tool or instrument of scientific research to be applied in every sphere of knowledge. Let us attempt here a description of the broad features of his logic.

Its theme is the analysis of the form and content of thought, of the processes by which we reach knowledge; it is the science of correct thinking. The Aristotelian logic defines with precision the prerequisite of genuine scientific knowledge. Scientific truth is characterized by strict necessity; it is, in his own words, "something which cannot be other than it is." In order to establish a scientific proposition, it is not sufficient to show that such and such has been found to be the case; it must be proved that it could not possibly be otherwise. An arithmetical proposition such as "two plus three equals five" is the archetype of all scientific truth; it is literally inconceivable that it should be false. On the other hand, the statement that swans are white or that fire produces heat, might conceivably prove untrue; these are accidental or contingent judgments, and must be excluded from the domain of science. Thinking consists in reasoning, or scientific demonstration, in deriving the particular from the universal, the conditioned from its causes. Inferences are composed of *judgments* which, when expressed in language, are called *propositions;* judgments are made up of *concepts,* which are expressed in *terms.*

Concepts do not receive exhaustive treatment in Aristotle's logic; he does, however, deal with them in connection with terms and their definition and also when he discusses the highest concepts or categories. Aristotle's primary concern is with the logic of judgments or propositions. He discusses the nature and different kinds of judgments, the various relations in which they stand to one another, and the different kinds of demonstration.

Aristotle treats at great length the nature of demonstration—the process of elaborating the derivative propositions from the original truths. His demonstration or deduction always takes the form of a syllogism or series of syllogisms. He was the first to discover in the syllogism a basal form in which all thought moves, and to give it a name. The syllogism is a discourse in which from certain presuppositions (premises) something new (the conclusion) necessarily follows. It consists of two premises (called major and minor) and a conclusion. Thus in the stock syllogism, "All men are mortal; Socrates is a man; hence Socrates is mortal," "all men are mortal" is the major premise, "Socrates is a man" the minor premise, which makes possible the conclusion, "Socrates is a mortal." In the syllogism the particular is derived from the universal; it is thus a form of deductive reasoning—indeed, for Aristotle the syllogism is the form to which all deduction is reducible. Valid or scientific demonstration is, therefore, always in the form of the syllogism: it is syllogistic and deductive. In order to be true, the conclusion must follow necessarily from the premises. And the premises themselves must be universal and necessary, hence they, too, must be proved, i.e., grounded on other premises. The goal of knowledge is complete demonstration. The ideal science in Aristotle's day was mathematics, and the use of mathematics as a model explains the important rôle deduction plays in his logic. His aim was to attain in other sciences the demonstrative certainty of mathematics. This is possible only in a series of syllogisms in which conclusions depend on premises which, in turn, are the conclusions of other premises, and so on. But the process cannot go on forever; we must finally reach propositions or principles which cannot be proved deductively, but which, nevertheless, have absolute certainty. The system of scientific knowledge thus rests on certain axioms or basic truths which neither admit of nor require proof. They are the basis of all truth, and as such are indemonstrable. "A basic truth," says Aristotle, "is one which has no proposition prior to it." The axioms are thus the first links in the long chain of our reasoning. The basic truths are known by intuition, e.g., by the immediate and direct insight of the reason. Intuition is the apprehension of the universal element in the particular. Since intuition departs from the apprehension of the particular, Aristotle refers to the process as one of induction. "We get to know the primary premises by induction," he says. For example, reason assures us that the whole is greater than any of its parts. The examination of even one instance of a principle may be sufficient to assure us of its universal truth. Other examples of such direct or intuitively self-evident principles are the axioms of mathematics and the principle of contradiction. Each particular science has such principles of its own, and there are, besides, universal principles common to all the sciences, the principles of the first philosophy, or metaphysics.

The basal axioms or principles are inherent in reason itself, the highest part of the soul; they are direct intuitions of reason. Intuition is the essential element in induction, the process in which thought rises from sense perception, or the perception of individual things, to general concepts, or the knowledge of universals. Human reason has the power of discerning the forms in their particular exemplifications. Such forms constitute the essences of things, they are real; at the same time they are principles of reason. Thus they are both forms of thought and forms of reality. It is one of Aristotle's basic ideas that thought and being coincide; truth is the essential coincidence of thought with being. The basic truths are potential in the mind, but experience is necessary to make reason aware of them, to bring them to consciousness. Aristotle thus reaffirms in more precise and less metaphorical terms the insight of Plato's theory of reminiscence that rational knowledge is implicit in the mind and is made explicit by experience. Our knowledge always begins with sense perception, and rises from particular facts to universal concepts, from "that which is the better known to us" to "that which is the better known and more certain in itself." Universals are the last things we reach in our thinking, but are first in nature: they are the first principles of reality.

Induction is a preparation for deduction. The ideal of science must always be to derive particulars from universals, to furnish demonstration or necessary proof; this cannot be done until induction has done its work, until experience has aroused the knowledge of the universal lying dormant in our reason. Aristotle, by assigning to experience and reason their different functions in knowledge, reconciles empiricism and rationalism. Knowledge is impossible without experience; but truths derived from experience alone would not be certain—they would yield probability only—hence they must also have a rational or a priori basis. To sum up Aristotle's logic: genuine scientific knowledge is a body of necessary truths, some of which are basic and guaranteed by intuition; the rest are syllogistically deduced.

Logic concerns itself with the thought-forms, with the molds to which our thinking must conform if it is to achieve certain truth. Obviously, thought is directed toward some object or other, for thought which is not thought of something is mere empty nothing. The transition from logic, or theory of knowledge, to metaphysics, or theory of being, is thus a natural and inevitable one.

The famous Aristotelian theory of the categories, while included among his logical doctrines, is also a part of his metaphysics. The categories are the fundamental and indivisible concepts of thought; they are at the same time basic features of the real. It is impossible to think of any real and existent thing except as subsumed under one or more of the categories. Anything taken at random belongs under substance, or quality, or quantity, or relation, or one of the other categories in the list. Thus "white" is a species of quality; "here" of place; "yesterday" of time, etc. The categories are different kinds of being, and not mere subjective concepts.

Substance, which is the first on Aristotle's list, is pre-eminent among the categories. By substance, in the primary sense, he means "that which is neither predicable of a subject nor present in a subject." This is Aristotle's somewhat abstruse way of saying that a substance is something ultimate and independent of all other things, while the latter must depend upon substance. Only the individual conforms to the requirements of substance thus defined; mortality may be predicated of the individual man, e.g., of Socrates, but it is meaningless to predicate Socrates of anything else.

By the categories, then, Aristotle means the most fundamental and universal predicates which can be affirmed of anything. He enumerates ten, sometimes only eight, such categories. We can say of a thing *what* it is (man: substance), *how* it is constituted (white: quality), *how large* it is (two yards long: quantity), *how related* (greater, double: relation), *where* it is (in the Lyceum: space), *when* it is (yesterday: time), *what posture* it assumes (lies, sits: position), the *condition* it is in (armed: state), what it *does* (burns: activity), and what it *suffers* (is burned: passivity). All this means that the objects of our experience exist in time and place, can be measured and counted, are related to other things, act and are acted on, have essential and accidental qualities. The categories are not mere forms of thought or language, but are also predicates of reality. A particular, perceivable substance is the bearer of all these categories, that of which they can all be predicated. Hence, the category of substance is the all-important one, and the others exist only in so far as they can be predicated of substance. Science, therefore, deals with the category of being, or essence, or substance, i.e., with the essential constitution of things, and thus the transition is made from logic to metaphysics.

Metaphysics. Substance, which was formally and abstractly defined in the logic, acquires a fullness and richness of meaning in Aristotle's metaphysics or first philosophy; it is, indeed, its key concept. Metaphysics in the Aristotelian sense is definable as a science which investigates the nature of being *qua* being, that is, of substance.

The Aristotelian notion of substance is formulated in sharp contrast to the Platonic. For Plato, substance was the universal, the type or form which he assumed to reside in a world apart, the eternal and transcendent world of ideas. Aristotle rejects this account of substance, and adopts its extreme antithesis: substance, for Aristotle, is the concrete individual. In criticizing the Platonic theory of ideas, he offers seven arguments, which group themselves in such a way that there are virtually only two main criticisms of Plato. The first criticism is that the ideas, although they are intended to explain the nature of things, are not adequate to do so. This thesis is developed in four special arguments: (1) the ideas are mere abstractions and as such cannot account for the existence of concrete things; (2) they are static and eternal, and are thus unable to explain the motion and change of concrete things; (3) ideas are posterior rather than prior to particular things, and cannot therefore be used to explain them; in short, ideas are copies of things, not their causes; (4) the ideas are unnecessary reduplications of things and not explanations of them. The second broad criticism of the ideal theory is that the relation between things and ideas is inexplicable. This criticism is expanded into the following three arguments: (1) nothing is explained by saying that things are the "copies of" or "participate in" ideas; to say that the individual man participates in the ideal man adds nothing to our understanding of the individual; (2) the alleged relation between the ideas and the corresponding things leads to an infinite regress for, between the individual man and the type-man there exists an ideal relation which must itself be related both to the individual and to the type. This criticism is commonly referred to as the "third man" argument, since, in addition to the individual man (the "first man") and the type-man (the "second man"), it introduces "a third man" (the relation between the individual man and the type-man). A continuation of the argument requires a fourth and a fifth man and thus leads to an infinite regress; (3) the theory of ideas completely separates the essence or form of a thing from the thing itself, but such a separation is at variance with the unity of the particular as observed by the mind.

The problem of metaphysics is the discovery of ultimate principles of reality. How shall we explain the world, what is its essence? Aristotle's positive solution to this problem is allied both to the naturalistic or materialistic theory of the atomists, and to the ideal theory of Plato. Democritus and his school had explained the world by moving material atoms, Plato by transcendent ideas which somehow influence formless matter. Aristotle rejects both answers, and seeks to mediate between them. The idea or form cannot be a self-existent essence, apart from matter, as Plato maintains; there can be no form without matter. Nor can the changing reality perceived by us be explained by mere purposeless matter in motion, as the materialists hold; there can be no matter without directing purpose or form. Plato regarded the objects of concrete experience as mere incomplete copies of the universal idea, as accidents, and the form as the substance; Aristotle, on the other hand, regards the particular objects or individual beings as real substances. But the essence or true nature of the particular concrete being is constituted by its *form,* by the essential qualities of the class to which it belongs; so that after all, the form or idea is for him, too, the most essential element.

There is, according to Aristotle, a plurality of individual substances; his metaphysical position is pluralism rather than monism. Moreover, the substances arrange themselves in an ascending scale, the limits of which are indeterminate matter at the bottom and God or pure form at the top; the whole array of substances—individual physical objects, plants, animals, and men—lies between these two extremes. Every individual substance is an admixture of matter and form. By form Aristotle understands the universal aspect of a thing, the essential unity shared by all things of the same type; matter, on the other hand, is that which confers particularity and uniqueness; matter and form are inseparable aspects of the individual thing. On this point, Aristotle differs radically from Plato, who asserted the separation of the form from the thing; Aristotle strongly insists that the universal and the particular are fused into the complete unity of the individual. The individual object changes or grows; all that is perceived is changeable. It assumes now these qualities, now those, it is now seed, now sapling, now tree, now fruit. How shall we explain this process of becoming? There must be something underlying change, something that persists in the change, something to which the different qualities pertain. This particularizing and individuating principle is matter; as conceived by Aristotle it is not the self-sufficient substance of the early materialistic philosophers; it is matter which is inseparable from its form, coexistent with it. Thus, when we say an object changes its form, we do not mean that the form itself changes or becomes different: no form, as such, can change into another form. Matter assumes different forms, a series of forms, one form following another; the form it first had does not change into another form, but a new form fashions the matter. The different forms have always existed, they do not suddenly come into being. Neither matter nor forms arise or disappear; they are the eternal principles of things. In order to explain change or growth, we must assume a substratum (matter) that persists and changes, and qualities (forms) which, though never changing, are responsible for the rich and growing world around us.

Closely allied to the antithesis between form and matter is that between potentiality and actuality. Whereas form and matter are inseparable yet distinguishable aspects of a single substance, potentiality and actuality are stages in the development of a substance—the potential being an earlier and the actual a later stage. Aristotle himself defines the distinction by means of particular instances: as the acorn is to the oak, the materials of the building to the completed structure, sleeping to waking, the eye shut to the eye seeing, so is potentiality to actuality. The potential is that which lies latent within a thing; the actual is the completed thing. The distinction is clearly relative, i.e., the same thing may in relation to one thing be actual, in relation to something else merely potential. For example, the oak is the actuality of the acorn, but the potentiality of an oak table. In the ascending series from potentiality to actuality there is a progressive realization of a greater preponderance of form over matter. Thus the two distinctions between form and matter, and between actuality and potentiality, though not identical, are closely parallel. When a thing has reached its growth, it has realized its meaning, its purpose, or form: the form is its true being, its realization or completion. Its possibilities have been realized, that which was potential in it has become actual. Matter has taken on form. The acorn which later becomes an oak is a potential oak; the oak is the realization of this potentiality, it is the form made manifest, real, actual. Aristotle, therefore, calls matter the principle of potentiality, and form the principle of reality, or actuality. Only primary or formless matter, however, which we can think, but which does not exist as such, is mere potentiality; concrete matter always has form and is, in a sense, actual. But it is a mere potentiality as regards some other form or actuality: the seed is matter for the oak; the marble matter for the statue. In order, then, to explain our world of change, we must assume form and matter. Every form is, like the Platonic idea, eternal, but instead of being *outside of* matter, it is *in* matter: forms and matter have always coexisted; they are coeternal principles of things. Form realizes itself in the thing; it causes the thing to move and to realize an end or purpose. The cooperation of form and matter which is discernible in the processes of nature is even more clearly illustrated in the creative activity of man. An artist in producing a work of art has an idea or plan in his mind; he acts on matter through the motion of his hands, being governed in his action by his plan, and so realizes a purpose. The developmental process described in terms of the antithesis of potential and actual, of form and matter, is governed by causes.

The Four Causes. The causal concept is much wider in its application for Aristotle than for modern science: it designates any condition requisite to the occurrence of something. Aristotle recognizes four principles operative in any process, four varieties of cause: (1) the *material cause,* by which he understands the crude and relatively undifferentiated stuff, that *from which* the thing in question is made. It was this type of cause which was introduced by the Milesian nature philosophers in their attempts to explain the world by means of water, air, or some other material substratum. Aristotle illustrates the material cause by the formless bronze from which the sculptor plans to fashion his statue. (2) The *formal cause* is the pattern or structure which is to become embodied in the thing when it is fully realized; it is that *which the thing* essentially *is.* The formal cause of a statue is the general plan or idea of the statue as conceived by the sculptor; it is the Aristotelian counterpart of the Platonic form. (3) The *efficient* or *moving cause* is the active agent which produces the thing as its effect, it is that *through which* the thing is produced. This type of cause corresponds closely to cause in the modern scientific sense. The efficient cause of the statue includes the chisels and other instruments used by the sculptor in his work. (4) The *final cause* is the end or purpose toward which the process is directed; it is that *for the sake of which* a thing is made. In sculpturing, it is the fully realized and completed statue.

We must not make the mistake of supposing that each individual thing has only one type of cause; everything, whether it be a natural object, a living plant or animal, or a manufactured article is explicable by means of all four types of cause. The four causes can be much more readily discriminated in a fabricated article or an artistic production, but Aristotle insists that they can also be distinguished in natural processes and in the growth of living organisms. The discovery of one type of cause in no way precludes the discovery of one of the other types. The four causes which are so readily distinguishable in the creative activities of man are at work in nature, particularly in the organic world; the only difference is that in nature the artist and his product are not separate, but one; the artist is in his work, so to speak. The form or plan and the end or purpose coincide: the purpose of the or-

ganism is the realization of its form, and the form or idea is also the cause
of the motion, so that, after all, we have only two essential causes—form and
matter—which constitute one indivisible whole, distinguishable only by
thought.

Forms are purposive forces which realize themselves in the world of
matter. Every organism becomes what it is through the action of an idea or
purpose. There is a directing principle at work in the seed that makes it impossible for the seed to become anything but a plant or animal of the same
species as that from which it came. Since forms are unchangeable, species are
immutable, though individuals arise and pass away.

If this is so, if form controls matter, which is potential form, how does it
happen that nature so often fails of its mark; that it is so often incomplete,
imperfect, and deformed? Aristotle lays the failures in nature to the imperfection of matter: matter is no longer mere possibility, but something which
offers resistance to the form, has power of its own; to its recalcitrancy are
due the plurality and diversity of individuals expressing a type, the differences existing between male and female, as well as all the monstrosities and
deformities in the world.

Motion or change is explained as the union of form and matter. The idea
or form is what causes motion in matter; the idea is the mover, matter the
thing moved. Motion is the realization of the potentialities of a thing.
How is this brought about by the mere presence of the idea? Matter strives
to realize the form, it is aroused to action by the presence of the form, it has
a desire for the form, and, since form and matter are eternal, motion is
eternal.

Theology. Aristotle's metaphysics culminates in a theology: the eternal motion on the part of matter which has just been described presupposes, according to him, an eternal *unmoved mover,* something that causes motion, without itself moving. A given motion in the universe is produced by some other
motion, this motion by a third motion and so on, and since an infinite regress
is impossible, it is necessary that there should be, as the first cause of the
series of motions, an unmoved mover or God. If the first cause of motion
were itself in motion it would have to be moved by something else that
moves, and so on *ad infinitum,* and this would leave motion unexplained.
Somewhere, motion must begin without being caused by something that
moves. Hence, there must be an eternal unmoved first mover, who is the
final ground of all vital forces in nature.

Aristotle's argument from motion to the unmoved cause of motion is per haps the first complete formulation of what has come to be known as the cosmological argument for God's existence. The production of motion by that which is unchangeable and devoid of motion is a metaphysical enigma which Aristotle seeks to resolve by the suggestion that God induces motion in other things in a fashion similar to that in which a fixed ideal or object of desire moves the human will to act. "The object of desire and the object of thought," he says, "move in this way; they move without being moved." God acts on the world, not by literally moving it, but as a beautiful picture or an ideal acts on the soul. Expressed in other words, God is the *final cause* of all that occurs; he is the highest purpose or highest good of the world. All beings in the world, plants, animals, men, desire the realization of their essence because of this highest good, or God; his existence is the cause of their desire. Hence God is the unifying and directing principle of the world, the goal towards which all things strive, the principle which accounts for all order, beauty, and life in the universe.

God is *pure form* unadulterated by matter; since the first cause is unmoved, it must be form without matter, pure form, for where there is matter, there is motion and change. God thus constitutes the one exception to the principle that matter and form are inseparable. Some of Aristotle's critics regard this as a renunciation of the central thesis of his philosophy, and a return to Platonism. Has not the Platonic dualism between the world of forms and the world of things been revived in a new guise? It must be admitted that this objection has considerable cogency. God is complete *actuality,* i.e., he is the end or goal toward which all things are striving. Yet there is in him no potentiality. He enjoys the unique distinction among substances of being the fulfillment of all and at the same time the potency of none. He is substance *par excellence,* indeed, in a significant sense of the word he may be said to be the only substance. Finally, God is *thought-thinking-thought*. Thought alone of all human activities is ascribable to God. It is the highest function of man, the one trait of man which is truly divine. Man's reason is conceived as a spark of the divine reason. But what is the object of God's thought? Obviously the only worthy object is God himself; it is in this sense that God is describable as thought-thinking-thought. In Aristotle's own words, ". . . it must be itself that thought thinks; and its thinking is a thinking on thinking." God's thought obviously differs in its character from that of man. The latter is discursive, that is, proceeds in step-by-step fashion from premise to conclusion; God's thought is entirely intuitive, that is, it grasps its object by a single flash of insight. God can scarcely be said to syllogize; whatever he knows he knows all at once.

The Aristotelian view of God as reflective thought—reflective in the literal sense of turning back upon itself—has been subjected to considerable ridicule, and not without some justification. Is it not unintelligible that God should play the dual rôle of the subject and the object of knowledge? Is not self-knowledge of a literal and direct sort an utter impossibility, even for God? And even though it were admitted to be possible, could it have any real significance? Such thought would be thought *in vacuo,* thought so pure as to be empty. A God whose thought has no object but its own activity of thought may be likened to a mirror which reflects another mirror and hence reflects nothing. The inadequacies of the Aristotelian conception of God are too patent to require further consideration. God's activity consists in thought, in the contemplation of the essence of things, in the vision of beautiful forms. He has no impressions, no sensations, no appetites, no will in the sense of desire, no feelings in the sense of passions; he is pure intelligence. While our intellect is discursive, our knowledge piecemeal, moving along step-by-step, God's thinking is intuitive: he sees all things at once and sees them whole. He is free from pain and passion, and is supremely happy. He is everything that a *philosopher* longs to be.

Let us conclude this exposition of Aristotle's theology with a brief formula which incorporates its salient features. Reality, as conceived by Aristotle, is a plurality of individual substances, each of which is a fusion of form and matter; these substances are ordered in a continuous series according to the predominance of form over matter; the supreme substance is pure form or God.

Physics. Aristotle's physics, the science of bodies and motion, is characterized by its antagonism to the atomistic and mechanistic theory of Democritus. He rejects the attempt to explain all processes in the corporeal world quantitatively in terms of changes in the local relations of atoms. Matter is interpreted by him more dynamically than by Democritus, who tended to conceive it as passive and inert; indeed, he sometimes endows it with the qualities which hylozoism had ascribed to it. Empty space is denied along with atoms; and space is defined as the limit between a surrounded and a surrounding body. Whatever is not bounded by another body, is not in space; thus there is no space beyond the fixed stars, because there are no bodies to limit them. Where there are no more bodies, space ceases to exist. There can be no infinite space; the world is finite; and it does not move as a whole, but only its parts suffer change. Since space cannot be conceived without motion and God does not move, God is not in space.

By motion Aristotle means all kinds of change; in the context of his teleo-logical theory he defines motion as "the realization of the possible," and enumerates four kinds of motion: substantial (origin and decay); quantita-tive (change in the size of a body by addition and subtraction); qualitative (transformation of one thing into another); and local (change of place). The elements, of which there are according to Aristotle four or, in some enumerations five, can be transformed into one another; and the mixture of substances gives rise to a new substance. Qualities are not mere subjec-tive effects of quantitative changes, as the atomists held, but real qualities of the things themselves. Changes in quality cannot, therefore, be explained mechanically, as mere changes in the local arrangement of atoms; there are absolute qualitative changes in matter.

All these conceptions are fundamentally opposed to the theories of natural science as they had been worked out by the atomists. For Aristotle, nature is dynamic rather than passive, teleological and not mechanical, qualitative rather than quantitative. Convinced of the truth of his metaphysical presup-positions, Aristotle often settles questions in science by declaring certain occurrences impossible because they are inconceivable—that is, inconceivable within the framework of his metaphysics. Judged from the point of view of the mechanism which prevailed in modern science until very recent years and which still has some scientific adherents, Aristotle's conceptions repre-sent a decidedly backward step in the progress of thought; but recent devel-opments in sub-atomic physics have tended to reinstate his dynamic or "energetic" interpretation of nature, and there are scientific thinkers who would even find some confirmation of his teleological interpretation of nature.

The universe is eternal, subject neither to origin nor decay. The earth is in the center. Around it, in concentric layers, are water, air, fire. Then come the celestial spheres, which are composed of ether and some of which carry the planets, the sun, and the moon. Last comes the outermost sphere of the fixed stars. In order to explain the motion of the planets, Aristotle intro-duced a large number of counter-spheres or "backward-moving" spheres. God encompasses the outermost sphere of the fixed stars and causes it to move; the motion of this sphere influences the movements of the other spheres. Aristotle, however, departs from this explanation in that he also assigns to each sphere a spirit which initiates its motion.

Biology. Aristotle may be called the founder of systematic and comparative zoology. His biology, like his physics, is opposed to the purely quantitative, mechanical, causal conception of nature; he subordinates it to the qualitative, dynamic, and teleological interpretation. There are forces in nature which initiate and direct movements; the form is dynamic and purposive and, as we have seen, it is the soul of the organic body. The body is an *organon* or instrument; instruments are intended for use, presuppose a user, a soul; the soul is that which moves the body and determines its structure; it is the principle of life. Aristotle's biological theory, in so far as it posits in the organism an animating and directing vital principle, may be described as vitalism. Man has hands because he has a mind. Body and soul constitute an indivisible unity, but soul is the controlling, guiding principle; that is, the whole is prior to the parts, and the immanent purpose of the whole is prior to its realization in the parts; we cannot understand the parts except in relation to the whole.

Wherever there is life—and there are traces of life all through nature, even in inorganic nature—there is soul. Different grades or degrees of soul exist, corresponding to different forms of life. No soul can exist without a body, and no soul without its specific body: a human soul could not dwell in the body of a horse. The organic world forms an ascending scale of bodies, from the lowest to the highest; and a graduated series of souls, from the plant soul, which governs the functions of nutrition, growth, and reproduction, to the human soul, which possesses additional and higher powers.

Psychology. Man is the microcosm and the final goal of nature, distinguished from all other living beings by the possession of reason. The soul of man resembles the plant soul in that it controls the lower vital functions, and the animal soul in the possession of faculties of perception, the so-called common sense, imagination, memory, pleasure and pain, desire and aversion. Sense perception is a change produced in the soul by things perceived, through the mediation of the sense-organs. The different senses inform the soul of the qualities of things; the common sense, whose organ is the heart, is the meeting place of all the senses; by means of it we combine the qualities furnished by the special senses and obtain the total picture of an object. It also gives us a clear picture of qualities—such as number, size, shape, motion, and rest—which are common to all the senses. The common sense also forms generic images, composite images, and has the powers of retention or memory and associative thinking. The feelings of pleasure and pain are referred to perception; pleasure arises when functions are furthered, pain when they are impeded. These feelings arouse desire and aversion, which alone cause the body to move. Desire arises only on the presentation of a desirable object, one considered by the soul as good. Desire accompanied by deliberation is called rational will.

The human soul possesses, beside the foregoing functions, the power of conceptual thought, the faculty of thinking the universal and necessary essences of things; as the soul by perception apprehends sensible objects, so, by reason, it beholds concepts. Reason is, potentially, whatever the soul can conceive or think; conceptual thought is actualized reason. How does reason come to think concepts? In answering this question, Aristotle distinguishes active or creative reason and passive reason. Creative reason is pure actuality; its concepts are actualized by it, the essences are directly cognized—here thought and its object are one; it resembles Plato's pure soul which contemplates the world of ideas. In passive reason concepts are merely potential; passive reason is the matter on which creative reason, the form, acts; the concepts which are potential in passive reason are made real or actual by creative reason. Just as, in the growth of a particular organism, a complete form or idea exists which the particular organism will realize in its material, so, in the reasoning process, a form must exist potentially in the passive reason. Aristotle's general philosophical distinction between form and matter when applied to the mental world seems to require him to distinguish between the formal and material phases of reason, between active and passive, actual and potential reason: the concepts which are potential in passive reason are actual in creative reason.

Perception, imagination, and memory are connected with the body and perish with it; passive reason since it operates in the medium of sensuous images—such images are the occasion for the arousal of concepts in passive reason—is likewise perishable. Creative reason, however, is not tainted by sense; it presumably exists prior to both the body and the sensuous soul; it is absolutely immaterial, imperishable, not bound to a body, and therefore immortal. The active reason is a spark of the divine mind coming to the soul from without; it does not arise in the course of the soul's development, as do the other psychic functions. Since it is not an individual reason, personal immortality has no meaning in relation to it; some interpreters of Aristotle even identify it with the universal reason or the mind of God.

Ethics. Aristotle's metaphysics and psychology form the basis of his theory of ethics, which is the first comprehensive scientific theory of morality. It is an attempt to give a definitive answer to the Socratic question of the highest good. All human action has some end in view. This end may be the means to a higher end, this to a still higher, and so on; but finally we must reach a supreme end or purpose, an ultimate principle or good, for the sake of which every other good is to be sought. What is this highest good? The goodness of a thing consists in the realization of its specific nature; the end or purpose of every creature is to realize or make manifest its peculiar essence, that which distinguishes it from every other creature. This for man is not mere bodily existence or sensuous feeling, the exercise of vegetable and animal functions, but a life of reason. Hence, the highest good for man is the complete and habitual exercise of the functions which make him a human being. This is what Aristotle means by the term *eudaemonia,* which has been translated by our word "happiness," and there is no objection to this word so long as it is not interpreted to mean pleasure. Pleasure, according to Aristotle, accompanies virtuous activity as a secondary effect and is thus included in the highest good, but not identical with it.

The soul, however, does not consist of reason alone; it has an irrational as well as a rational part—the irrational part includes feeling, desires, appetites. With these latter reason should cooperate; in order to realize its purpose, the different parts of the soul must act in the right way, the body must function properly, and the total individual must possess adequate economic goods— neither a slave nor a child can attain the ethical goal, and poverty, sickness, and misfortune may interfere with its attainment. A virtuous soul is a well-ordered soul, one in which the right relation exists between reason, feeling, and desire. The perfect action of reason as such constitutes intellectual efficiency or "dianoetic" virtue, the virtue of wisdom or insight; the perfect action of the emotional-impulsive functions of the soul is called "moral" virtue, which embraces temperance, courage, liberality, etc. There are "moral" virtues for all spheres of action; they consist in assuming a rational attitude toward bodily appetites, toward fear, danger, anger, the desire for economic goods, fame, and so on. The question arises: In what does this attitude consist? Aristotle replies: In seeking the mean between two extremes; virtue is a kind of moderation in that it aims at the mean—the mean between excess and deficiency. Courage, for example, is a mean between foolhardiness and cowardice; liberality, between extravagance and avarice; modesty, between bashfulness and shamelessness. Aristotle does not claim that the principle of the mean is universal in its applicability; he frequently abandons it in his discussions as being inapplicable in many cases—some actions and feelings such as malevolence, shamelessness, envy, adultery, theft, and murder, are bad in themselves and not merely in excess or deficiency. The mean is not the same for every individual, and under all circumstances; it is "relative to ourselves," and "determined by reason, or as a right-minded man would determine it."

It is not, however, a matter of subjective opinion or arbitrary choice; what moral conduct is, is decided by the right-minded man: the virtuous man is the standard and measure of things; he judges everything correctly, and the truth is manifest to him in every case. Two other points are to be remembered: Moral conduct does not consist in an isolated action, but in an expression of a stable character or disposition of the will. Moreover, it is voluntary action, consciously purposive action, freely chosen action: "Virtue, as well as the evil, lies in our power." Aristotle includes all these ideas in the following definition: "Virtue is a disposition, or habit, involving deliberate purpose or choice, consisting in a mean that is relative to ourselves, the mean being determined by reason, or as a prudent man would determine it." [7]

The highest good for man, then, is self-realization. This is not, however, to be interpreted as a selfish individualism. A man realizes his true self when he loves and gratifies the supreme part of his being, that is, the rational part, when he is moved by a motive of nobleness, when he promotes the interests of others and serves his country. One has but to read Aristotle's books on friendship and justice in his *Nicomachean Ethics* in order to appreciate the exalted altruistic spirit of his teaching. "The virtuous man will act often in the interest of his friends and of his country, and, if need be, will even die for them. He will surrender money, honor, and all the goods for which the world contends, reserving only nobleness for himself, as he would rather enjoy an intense pleasure for a short time than a moderate pleasure long, and would rather live one year nobly than many years indifferently, and would rather perform one noble and lofty action than many poor actions. This is true of one who lays down his life for another; he chooses great nobleness for his own." [8] The virtuous man is a lover of self in the sense that he assigns to himself a preponderant share of noble conduct. Man is a social being and disposed to live with others; he needs somebody to do good to. "A virtuous friend is naturally desirable to a virtuous man, for that which is naturally good is good and pleasant in itself to the virtuous man"; that is, loving goodness for its own sake, he is bound to love a virtuous friend; in this sense, his friend is a second self (an *alter ego*) to the virtuous man.

Justice is a virtue implying a relation to others, for it promotes the interests of another, whether he be a ruler or simply a fellow-citizen. Justice is

[7] *Nicomachean Ethics*, Bk. II, ch. 6. This and subsequent quotations are taken from the Welldon trans.

[8] *Op. cit.*, Bk. IX, ch. 8.

taken in two senses, lawfulness and fairness. Laws pronounce upon all subjects with a view to the interest of the community as a whole, or of those who are its best or leading citizens, whether in virtue or in some other respect. All the virtues, then, are included in the concept of justice; the only difference between virtue and justice lies in the varying contexts in which they are considered: That which considered in relation to one's neighbor is justice, is, as a state of character, virtue.[9] The term justice is also used in the more restricted sense of giving each man his due (distributive justice).

Nor is the happiness-theory to be understood in the hedonistic sense, as a pleasure-theory. Pleasure is the necessary and immediate consequence of virtuous activity, but not the end of life. Pleasure is the completion of activity: it is something added, just as youthful beauty is added to youthful power. Pleasure is a concomitant of action, and "the activity will be most pleasant when it is most perfect, and it will be most perfect when it is the activity of the part being in sound condition and acting upon the most excellent of the objects that fall within its domain."[10] It is reasonable to aim at pleasure, since it perfects life in each of us. Pleasure and life are bound together and do not admit of separation; pleasure is impossible without activity and every activity is perfected by pleasure. According to Aristotle, the things which are honorable and pleasant to the virtuous man are really honorable and pleasant. The fact that people who have never tasted a pure and liberal pleasure have recourse to the pleasures of the body does not prove that bodily pleasures are preferable; only the judgment of the truly virtuous and honorable man is to be relied upon in ethical matters.

The highest happiness is speculative activity, an activity which takes the form of contemplation. The life of contemplation is the highest, the most continuous, the most pleasant, the most self-sufficient, the most intrinsically worth-while way of life. Such a life may seem too exalted for a mere human being, and, indeed, man will enjoy such a life not in virtue of his humanity, but in virtue of some divine element in him.

If then the reason is divine in comparison with the rest of man's nature, the life which accords with reason will be divine in comparison with human life in general. Nor is it right to follow the advice of people who say that the thoughts of men should not be too high for humanity or the thoughts of humanity too high for mortality; for a man, as far as in him lies, should seek immortality and do all that is in his power to live in accordance with the highest part of his nature.[11]

[9] Cf. *op. cit.*, Bk. V, ch. 1.
[10] *Op. cit.*, Bk. X, ch. 4.
[11] *Op. cit.*, Bk. X, ch. 7.

Aristotle rejects the Socratic maxim that knowledge is virtue, in the sense that knowledge of the nature of virtue is sufficient to insure virtuous action; we must, according to Aristotle, in addition to a knowledge of virtue, endeavor to possess and exercise it. Theories may be strong enough to stimulate youths already liberally minded, but they alone will not suffice to incite the mass of men to chivalrous action. Moral action is fostered by a moral society, and it is difficult for one to receive from his early days a right inclination to virtue unless he is brought up under virtuous laws. Laws are also required to teach us the duties of life when we have come to man's estate, for most people are moved by necessity and fear of punishment rather than by reason and the love of nobleness. The state should seek to provide a social environment conducive to the morality of its citizens and should, when necessary, employ punishment and other legal devices to enforce morality. Thus, anyone who wishes to elevate the people must acquaint himself with the principles of legislation. In order, therefore, that his philosophy of human life be as complete as possible, Aristotle examines the subject of politics. Ethics and politics are never divorced by him: the moral ends of man are promoted by legal and political means.

Politics. Man is a social being, who can realize his true self only in society and the state. Families and small communities are prior in time to the state; but the state, as the goal of the evolution of human life, is prior in worth and significance to its component societies, in conformity with the Aristotelian principle that the whole is prior to its parts. Social life is the goal or end of human existence, but this doctrine does not commit Aristotle to the complete subjugation of the individual to society and the state. The aim of the state is to produce good citizens. Aristotle presents a reconciliation of the view that the individual is the end of life, and the view that society is the end; society is composed of individuals, and its purpose is to enable the individual citizens to live a virtuous and happy life. Aristotle was perhaps even more successful than Plato in steering a middle course between "statism" and individualism.

The constitution of the state must be adapted to the character and requirements of its people. It is just when it confers equal rights on the people in so far as they are equal, and unequal rights in so far as they are unequal. Citizens differ in personal capability, in property qualifications, in birth and freedom, and justice demands that they be treated according to these differences.

There are good constitutions and bad ones; the monarchy, the aristocracy, and the polity—a form in which the citizens are nearly equal—being good forms, and the tyranny, oligarchy, and democracy bad. As the best state for his own time, Aristotle advocates a city-state in which only those are citizens whose education and position in life qualify them for active participation in government, that is, an aristocracy. He justifies slavery on the ground that it is a natural institution: it is just that foreigners, who alone composed the slave-class in Greece, should not, being inferior to the Greeks, enjoy the same rights as they.

Aristotle's Genius and Influence. Aristotle's claim to the title "master of those who know" can easily be substantiated. He occupies an unique position in philosophy by whatever standard we may judge him, *breadth of learning, originality,* or *influence.* Superlatives cannot be avoided in estimating his importance in these respects. In its scope, Aristotle's philosophy is perhaps the most comprehensive synthesis of knowledge ever achieved by the mind of man. No other thinker, ancient, medieval, or modern—with the possible exception of the German philosopher Hegel—has incorporated into his system so great a bulk of knowledge. Aristotle's philosophy embraces the whole range of sciences: logic and mathematics; physics, biology and psychology; ethics, politics, and esthetics, as well as metaphysics. The Aristotelian philosophy is more than a mere encyclopedia of facts, it is an original and creative synthesis. It is this trait which differentiates a truly great philosophy from mere eclecticism. The genius of Aristotle lies in his ability to fuse an enormous amount of knowledge into a unified whole. He achieved this unification by means of certain integrating concepts: substance, matter and form, actuality and potentiality, etc. He exerted an almost incalculable influence on all subsequent philosophy. He forged the fundamental concepts and elaborated a terminology for philosophy which has been incorporated into all speculations from his day to the present. His influence was greatest during the Middle Ages, but it is also apparent in the greatest systems of the modern period, including those of Descartes, Leibniz, and Hegel.

Post-Aristotelian Philosophy. The philosophy of Aristotle was continued by his pupils, many of whom showed independence of thought. Theophrastus (d. 287 B.C.), his successor as the head of the school, wrote a work on botany and a history of the doctrines of the "physicists." Eudemus is known by his history of mathematics and astronomy; Aristoxenus, by his studies in the theory of music; Dicaearchus, by his geography and politics; Strato, successor of Theophrastus in the school from 287-269 B.C., devoted himself to the philosophy of nature. After Lyco, who succeeded Strato (269-225), the Peripatetic School lost its importance, and the writings of the master were neglected. In the first century B.C., the school turned its attention to text-criticism and interpretation, a task which was begun by Tyrannio and Andronicus of Rhodes, and carried on for many centuries. To this movement we owe the preservation and transmission of the Aristotelian writings.

The history of Greek philosophy after Aristotle is a story of continuous decline. During this period there appeared no great and original systems; thinkers were for the most part satisfied to repeat the opinions of the great classical philosophers, Plato and Aristotle. The age is characterized by (1) individualism, (2) eclecticism, (3) concern with ethical problems. Individualism was rampant in this period of social and intellectual chaos; the individual had no concern except for his own personal welfare, and philosophy was cultivated solely for the light it might throw on the fate and destiny of the individual man. Eclecticism took the place of creative philosophical activity, the philosophers of the time were satisfied to appropriate the insights of their predecessors and to patch them together as best they could. Ethical interests were paramount. Men had little faith in abstract metaphysical inquiries; they occupied themselves with problems about reality only when these seemed to be directly relevant to the conduct of life. Theoretical knowledge was subordinated to practical concerns.

IV
The Ethical Period

11. THE OUTLOOK

The vital question for Socrates had been the ethical problem: he conceived it as his mission to set his age right in matters of morals as well as in matters of truth. His interest in the problem of knowledge derived from his conviction that clear thinking is essential to right action, and that it is possible to discover ethical principles acceptable to all reasonable men. With the Socratic schools, too, ethical questions were uppermost—although the Megarians also showed a fondness for dialectical discussions—and Plato's earlier writings breathe the ethical spirit of his master. Even in his developed system, the founder of the Academy never lost sight of the highest good; his entire philosophy constituted a rational basis for his ethical idealism. It is true that Aristotle, in his concept of God, exalted theoretical activity; but he, too, regarded ethical self-realization as the noblest end of man. After the death of Plato and Aristotle, their schools for the most part adhered to the teachings of the founders and made little further progress in the development of thought, merely drawing upon the intellectual legacy which had been bequeathed to them. The Cyrenaics and the Cynics continued to preach the opposing ethical doctrines of hedonism and asceticism respectively; and, influenced by the Cynic Diogenes of Sinope, the Megarian Stilpo turned his attention to ethical problems.

The social conditions which had assisted in the birth of the Socratic movement did not disappear with the death of its founder. The general moral tone of the times did not improve, the pursuit of enjoyment and gain was not checked, nor was faith in the popular religion strengthened. The long and frequent wars between the Greek city-states broke the power of one after the other, and left Hellas an easy prey to the Macedonian conqueror. The Peloponnesian War (431-404 B.C.) ended in the complete overthrow of the political hegemony of Athens; the Corinthian War (395-387) broke Corinth; the Theban War (379-362) brought Sparta to defeat. After a long and stubborn struggle, Philip of Macedon defeated the allied Athenians and Thebans at the battle of Chaeronea (338) and became the master of Greece. Alexander the Great conquered the Persians, and his generals after his death (323) divided a large part of the world among themselves. From the hands of the Macedonians Greece was delivered into the hands of a new world-power: in 146 B.C. Greece became a Roman province.

Under the conditions we have described, it was inevitable that the ethical problem should again become paramount in many thoughtful minds. In the midst of the breakdown of the old institutions and the general demoralization of public and private life, the problem of the meaning of life acquired a new urgency. When the state lost its independence and civic duty degenerated into mere compliance, the question of how he might save himself forced itself upon the intelligent individual. How shall the weary soul find rest? This is the old and ever new problem which human beings put to themselves when life becomes too complex and difficult for them, and they are confronted with the danger of being lost in the confusion. It is the problem of value, the problem of the highest good: What is the thing of most worth in the world, how shall a man shape his life, what is there left for him to strive for? Then as now, different answers were given to these questions by different groups of thinkers. According to one school, the Epicureans, the highest good or ideal is pleasure; hedonism is the only goal worth striving for, everything else has value only in so far as it brings pleasure, only in so far as it is a means to happiness. In the storm and stress of existence, it is the part of wisdom to keep the mind unruffled and to move through the world with the greatest possible advantage to oneself. According to another school, the Stoics, the thing of most worth is not happiness, but character, virtue, self-discipline, duty, the subordination of particular interests to universal ends.

The teachings of the Epicureans and Stoics had a wider and more popular appeal than the great classical systems of Plato and Aristotle; but, like the classical systems, they sensed the need of offering a rational basis for ethical conceptions, of justifying them to reason, and of relating them to metaphysical theories. They were based on the belief that the moral question could not find a satisfactory answer without a knowledge of the very nature of things, that we cannot tell how man ought to act in the world unless we know its meaning. Man's conduct will depend on the kind of universe he is living in; his theory of life will be determined by his theory of the world, his ethics by his metaphysics. With all their insistence on the practical, these schools never lost the Greek love of speculation.

In order to realize the highest good, then, it is necessary to have a knowledge of the meaning of the universe, to know the truth. Hence the questions arise: What is truth? What is the criterion of truth and what is its origin? How can we know when we have attained the truth? Logic answers these questions for us; it furnishes us with a standard or criterion of knowledge, and enables us to distinguish truth from error. The Epicureans and the Stoics, therefore, grounded their philosophy of life on logic as well as on metaphysics; their systems include inquiries in the fields of (1) logic or theory of knowledge, (2) metaphysics or theory of the universe, and (3) ethics or theory of conduct. Their primary interest was in ethical problems, but logic and metaphysics afforded them an indispensable background for ethical inquiry.

The Epicureans based their conception of the good on the mechanistic materialism of Democritus, according to which the universe is the result of the interaction of countless material atoms, without purpose or intelligence to guide them. Man is one of the many combinations of jostling particles of matter, formed, in the ever-changing flow of existence, after many trials and failures; he will last his little day, only to be scattered again into the great atomic whirl whence he came. Hence, while he lives, let him live untroubled by superstitious fears of the now and the hereafter; let him enjoy the few short moments of life as best he may, conducting himself so as to get as much happiness out of the game as it will yield. The Stoic philosophers, on the other hand, regarded the universe as a beautiful, good, and well-ordered cosmos, held together and ruled by an intelligent principle or purpose; for them it was a living God. It is the duty of man to play his part in this great rational whole, to subordinate himself to the universal harmony, to subject his will to law and reason, to help realize the will of God. And all this he should do, not for the sake of his own narrow personal advantage, nor for the sake of pleasure, but for the sake of the perfection of the whole. There is no happiness possible for the Stoic except that which he can obtain through obedience to the reason or law of the universe.

12. EPICUREANISM

The thinker with whose name hedonistic ethics became most intimately linked in antiquity was Epicurus. His metaphysical theory is reproduced almost entirely from the system of Democritus, which we have already

studied. The essential features of his ethical doctrine had also been anticipated by Democritus, as well as by the Cyrenaic school. The historical
formula descriptive of Epicureanism is a refined version of the Cyrenaic
hedonism, set in the context of a modified form of the mechanistic and
materialistic atomism of Democritus.

Epicurus was born on the island of Samos in 341 B.C., of Athenian parents. Through
his teacher Nausiphanes he became acquainted with the writings of Democritus and
with the skeptical doctrines of Pyrrho. After teaching in various Greek cities, he founded
a school at Athens (306), where he lived quietly until his death (270), surrounded by
an admiring group of pupils and friends, among whom were many women. No philosopher, perhaps, has been more unjustly reviled and misunderstood than this amiable
and cheerful man whose very name has become a term of reproach.

Epicurus was a fertile writer, who published many works (one *On Nature*, consisting
of thirty-seven books), of which only fragments remain. He summarized his system in
forty-four propositions (a kind of catechism), the gist of which is given in Book X of
the *Opinions* of Diogenes Laertius.[1] His successors made very little change in his system,
their work consisting largely in reproducing his thought. His philosophy began to win
many converts from the first century B.C. on. The most famous of his followers was the
Roman poet Lucretius (94-54), who gave an exposition of the materialistic philosophy
in his poem, *On the Nature of Things* (*De rerum natura*),[2] and made it popular with
many poets and literary men of the Augustan age. Of Epicurus' writings we possess
three letters (two of which are held to be authentic), and several fragments. The
Herculanean fragments are largely from his work *On Nature*.

C. Bailey, *Epicurus, the Extant Remains*, 1925. W. J. Oates, ed., *The Stoic and
Epicurean Philosophers*, 1940, contains translations of the complete extant remains of
Epicurus and Lucretius.

W. Wallace, *Epicureanism*, 1880; R. D. Hicks, *Stoic and Epicurean*, 1910; A. E.
Taylor, *Epicurus*, 1911; W. Pater, *Marius the Epicurean*, 2 vols., 1910, reprinted in
Modern Library, 1920; E. Zeller, *The Stoics, Epicureans and Sceptics*, 1892; A. E.
Taylor, *Epicurus*, 1910; P. H. and E. A. de Lacy, *Philademus On Methods of Infer-
ence: A Study of Ancient Empiricism*, 1941; H. A. J. Munro, *Lucretius' "De Rerum
Natura*,*" 3 vols., 1905-10; J. Masson, *Atomic Theory of Lucretius*, 1884, and *Lucretius,
Epicurean and Poet*, 1907-09; G. Santayana, *Three Philosophical Poets*, 1910 (ch. 2,
pp. 19-73); C. Bailey, *The Greek Atomists and Epicurus*, 1928.

Ethical Orientation. The aim of philosophy, according to Epicurus, is for
man to lead a happy life. Sciences which do not contribute to this purpose,
like music, geometry, arithmetic, and astronomy, are valueless. Some knowledge of logic or theory of knowledge is necessary to furnish us with a criterion of knowledge. We require physics, or a metaphysical theory of the uni-

---

[1] *Lives and Opinions of Eminent Philosophers,* trans. by R. D. Hicks, 1925.
[2] Translated by H. A. J. Munro, also by C. Bailey. See also essay on Lucretius in
G. Santayana, *Three Philosophical Poets*.

verse, in order to understand the natural causes of things; such knowledge is useful, since it frees us from the fear of gods, natural phenomena, and death. The study of human nature will teach us what to desire and what to avoid. The main thing, however, is that we understand that all things are produced by natural rather than supernatural causes. We may, therefore, divide the Epicurean philosophy into logic or canonic, metaphysics, and ethics.

Logic and Epistemology. The logical—or rather epistemological—problem is that of determining how propositions should be constituted in order to be true. What is the test—the *canonic,* as Epicurus called it in his work entitled *Canon*—or criterion of their truth? It must be based on sense perception; what we hear and see and smell and taste is real, "just as real, just as evident as pain." Without sensations, we could have no knowledge at all. Illusions are not deceptions of the senses, but of judgment; they arise when sensations, which are copies of objects, are falsely interpreted or referred to the wrong objects. The causes of illusion are many and include such factors as disturbances in the sense organs, and distortions of the copies of objects on their way to the organs. Erroneous judgments of sense can, however, be corrected by repeating the observation and appealing to the experiences of others. The Epicureans achieved an elaborate theory of knowledge and truth in terms of sense experience; they were pioneers of the empirical tradition in epistemology.

General ideas or images have the same kind of certainty as the sensations from which they are derived, but there are no abstract qualities corresponding to such ideas, no independent essences as asserted by Plato and Aristotle; the only realities corresponding to an idea are the particular concrete objects of the class of which the general idea is a mark or a sign. The Epicureans are thus the forerunners of medieval nominalism as well as of modern empiricism.

In addition to sensations and ideas, we also form opinions and hypotheses. In order to be true, these must be directly confirmed or verified by sense perceptions, or at least suggested by sense observations and not contradicted by them. Thus we form ideas of hypothetical and unsensed realities, such as atoms; we do so by analogy with our common experiences, and assign to them only such qualities as our sense perception reveals. The Epicurean theory of verification anticipates in a remarkable degree many of the characteristic doctrines of contemporary logical positivism.

In the theoretical field, then, sensation is the criterion of truth; we know what we perceive; and we imagine, and have a right to imagine, that the things we do not perceive are like the things which we do perceive. Epicurus rests his entire proof of the trustworthiness of sensations on the Democritean theory of sense perception. It is not the objects themselves which are directly perceived but copies of them, produced by the influence of objects on the sense organ. His theory of truth stands or falls with his theory of sensation.

Metaphysics. Our senses show us nothing but material bodies, but if bodies alone existed, there would be nothing in which they could be contained or through which they could move; hence, in addition to bodies there must be empty space, "intangible nature," or non-being. Since nothing can be created or destroyed in an absolute sense, the origin, growth, change, and disappearance of bodies can only be explained as the combination and separation of indestructible elements. These elements are exceedingly small particles of matter, imperceptible, physically indivisible, indestructible, and unchangeable. Atoms are absolutely full, i.e., there are no empty spaces within them, although, as we have seen, there is empty space between them. Moreover, they are absolutely hard and impenetrable, they cannot be broken or cut, and it is by virtue of this property that they are called atoms. Atoms have, in addition to the qualities already enumerated, size, shape, and weight in which they differ one from another, and they are in a continual state of motion. Differences in bodies are explained by differences in the size, shape, weight, and relation of atoms; the number of diverse shapes is, according to Epicurus, limited. Since there is an infinite number of atoms there must be infinite space to hold them, i.e., an infinite universe.

On account of their weight, atoms move downward in vertical lines, at equal rates of speed. But if they simply moved downward in this way, we should have nothing but a constant rain of atoms and no world. We must, therefore, imagine that they have the power to swerve just the least bit from the vertical. Epicurus endows his atoms with spontaneity, partly to explain the physical world, partly to make possible free will in man. Unless the atoms of which man is made be endowed with the power of free action, freedom of the will would be impossible. Epicurus regards the notion of freedom as less disturbing to man's peace of mind than blind fate or inexorable necessity.

Living beings are explained by the same principles which operate in the physical world. Living organisms originally arose from the earth; at first monsters were produced, shapes not adapted to their surroundings, but these could not survive and were later succeeded by organisms better adapted to their environment. The heavenly bodies are accounted for in the same natural way; they are not the creations of gods nor are they endowed with souls, for such cannot exist outside of living forms.

The Epicureans assert that there are gods, but not gods such as men in their fear and ignorance ordinarily conceive. That they exist is proved by the common belief in them—the idea of divinity is a natural idea, and it is necessary to assume a cause for this idea in us. But the gods did not create this world; why should supremely happy beings feel the need to create a world? Besides, whence could they have derived the idea of such a world? Finally, how could such perfect beings make so imperfect a world? The gods dwell in the *intermundia;* they have the shape of men, only they are more beautiful. They are of both sexes, require food, and even speak the Greek language. They have no concern for the affairs of men nor do they interfere in the course of the world, but live peaceful, blessed lives, free from care and trouble.

The Epicurean metaphysics is thus, in its essentials, a restatement of the atomistic and mechanistic materialism of Democritus; with Democritean atomism it shares the following tenets: (1) The universe consists of an infinite number of discrete atoms—each of which is absolutely hard and does not admit of physical division—which differ one from another in shape and size. These atoms are uncreated and indestructible. (2) The atoms are endowed with an inherent, uniform downward motion and motion is as real and indestructible as matter itself. (3) The motion of the atoms takes place in infinite space. But to this consistently elaborated materialism and mechanism of Democritus, Epicurus adds another proposition which, as we have seen, nullifies the "pure" mechanistic theory: the atoms are endowed with the capacity to deviate spontaneously from the straight, vertical line of fall. The "swerve" of the atoms introduces an element of contingency into the scheme and this one modification of the original atomism invalidates the entire mechanistic theory. The motive for introducing chance and contingency was to provide for the possibility of human freedom, which seemed to Epicurus a prerequisite of moral activity. Moreover, the Epicureans introduced a theological element into their system by asserting the existence of gods whom they conceived in strictly materialistic terms as aloof beings residing in the *intermundia,* devoting themselves to the Epicurean pursuit of the life of pleasure and unconcerned with human affairs.

Psychology. The soul, like all other things, is material, otherwise it could do nothing and suffer nothing. It is composed of extremely fine, minute, round, and, therefore, nimble, atoms; fire, air, breath, and a still more refined and mobile matter enter into the constitution of the soul. It is diffused over the whole body and whatever sensation the body has, it owes entirely to the presence of the soul. There is a directing or rational part, seated in the breast, whose will and inclination the rest of the soul obeys. The soul is mortal; when the body is dissolved, the soul is dissolved into its elements and loses its powers. When we are convinced that consciousness ceases with death, death loses its terrors for us; there is nothing to fear in a life to come, for death ends all. In the words of Lucretius, "Death therefore to us is nothing, concerns us not a jot, since the nature of the mind is proved to be mortal." [3]

Sense perception is explained, after the manner of Democritus, by idols or images or thin film-like forms, which emanate from the objects around us and impinge on the sense organs. Illusions, hallucinations, dreams, and similar states are produced by images of objects which no longer exist, or by images which adhere to one another, or in other perfectly natural ways. Will is explained thus: an image of walking, let us say, presents itself to the rational part of the mind; the force of this image is communicated to the rest of the soul, which is spread over the whole body, and finally the force of the soul strikes the body, and the body moves.

Ethics. Man's nature is bent upon pleasure; all animals from the moment of their birth seek pleasure and avoid pain by a natural instinct. Pleasure, therefore, is the goal at which we all aim, and, indeed, ought to aim: happiness is the highest good. Every pleasure, as such, is good, every pain bad. But we should exercise prudence in the choice of our pleasures. If one pleasure lasted as long as another and were just as intense, one would be just as good as another. If the things which give the debauched man pleasure could give him peace of mind, no one could blame him for leading a life of debauchery. But this is not the case. Not every pleasure is worthy of being chosen, not every pain ought to be avoided. Some pleasures are followed by pains or by loss of pleasures; many pains are followed by pleasures, and are, therefore, better than some pleasures. Moreover, pleasures differ in intensity. Mental pleasures are greater than the pleasures of the body, mental pains worse than physical pains; for while the flesh is sensible only to present pleasure and affliction, the soul recalls past and anticipates future pleasures and pains. Not only is mental enjoyment greater than physical, but physical enjoyment is not possible without mental. Hence Epicurus declares

[3] *On the Nature of Things*, Bk. III (Bailey trans.).

that it is the part of wisdom to choose the joys of intellectual life. The reason for this is plain. We are afraid of the catastrophes of nature, of the wrath of the gods, of death and the hereafter; we worry over the past, present, and future. So long as we do this, we cannot be happy. To rid ourselves of our fears, we should seek to understand the natural causes of things, that is, study philosophy.

We can obtain pleasures by satisfying a desire or by having no desire. Pleasure accompanying the satisfaction of a desire, like hunger, is not pure, but a mixture of pleasure and pain; pure pleasure ensues when a desire has been satisfied and disappears, when we no longer desire. Freedom from pain is the highest measure of pleasure; it cannot be intensified, hence desire that aims beyond this state is immoderate.

In order to be free from trouble and fear, we should know the causes of things, and in the light of this knowledge decide what pleasures to follow and which to avoid. We should, in other words, be prudent. And if we are prudent, we will be virtuous, we will obey the rules of morality, for no one can be happy without living prudently, honorably, and justly. Virtue, then, or morality, is not an end in itself, but, like the art of healing, is a means to enhanced pleasure, happiness or repose of spirit. We praise it and exercise it for its utility. Epicurean happiness cannot be realized by a life of sensual indulgence and debauchery. Epicurus extolled the same virtues as did Plato and Aristotle and the Stoics—wisdom, courage, temperance, and justice—but for different reasons. Although a hedonist, Epicurus achieved one of the most noble and elevated ethical positions of all times. The starting point and foundation of his ethical system is the postulate that pleasure is the sole good and pain the sole evil; but upon this foundation he erects a very moderate and refined theory. Epicureanism in ordinary parlance has come to connote licentiousness and self-indulgence, but this was far from having been the intention of its founder. Although the pleasure-theory of Epicurus is not a doctrine of sensuality, it is easy to understand how it came to be so interpreted by many of his followers, who used it to justify their own desires for a life of luxury and sensuous enjoyment. If pleasure is the highest good for each individual, then whatever gives him pleasure is good. If he prefers the life of the senses to the higher pleasures, if he can rid his mind of superstitious fears and attain repose of spirit without leading an intellectual life, without philosophy, who can gainsay him? "The quantity of pleasure being equal, push-pin is as good as poetry"—to use Bentham's phrase. Epicurus preferred poetry and science and the life of virtue, and so did Atticus and Horace and Lucretius. The truth is, the Epicurean philosophy is essentially a doctrine of enlightened self-interest; the individual is asked to make his own happiness the goal of all his strivings, and such a theory of life may be used to justify a selfish disregard of others.

Social and Political Philosophy. The social philosophy of the Epicureans accounts for the origin of society by a social contract: social life is based on the principle of self-interest; individuals join together in groups for self-protection. Justice and right, in that they owe their origin to a social contract, are merely conventional: there is no such thing as absolute justice, and so-called natural rights are rules of conduct on which men agree because of their utility. All laws and institutions are just only in so far as they make for the security of the individual, that is, in so far as they are useful. We are just because it is to our advantage to be just. There is nothing inherently evil in injustice; only the consequences of injustice are evil. We should avoid injustice in order not to fall into the hands of the authorities or to live in constant fear of punishment. Since participation in public life does not contribute to happiness, the wise man will avoid it as much as possible. Certain rules of action have been found by experience to be necessary wherever men live together in society, and this accounts for such universal laws as prevail in all societies; but laws also differ from country to country according to conditions. The Epicurean social and political philosophy, which bases justice and right on expediency and utility rather than on reason and the structure of reality, is in sharp contrast to the Platonic and Aristotelian theories; indeed, it is a regression to the type of theory represented by the Sophists. The Stoic philosophy of society is, as we shall see, an absolutistic and metaphysically rooted theory in the main tradition of Greek philosophy.

The Epicurean ethics and social philosophy may be summed up as follows: (1) A state of pleasant calm or repose of mind is preferable to the violent pleasures accompanying the physical appetites and passions; this attitude of calm is the Epicurean counterpart of the Stoic apathy. (2) The intellectual pleasures, though they do not differ qualitatively from bodily pleasures, are superior to them on account of their greater duration and freedom from pain. (3) Epicurus exhorted prudence in the pursuit of the life of pleasure; the prudent hedonist looks beyond the pleasures of the present moment in his concern for the pleasures of a lifetime; it is often necessary to sacrifice an immediate pleasure for the sake of a greater future pleasure, or even to endure a present pain to avoid a greater pain in the future. Epicurus also emphasized the pleasures of anticipation and recollection, and thus advocated what has been called the cult of memory. (4) He extolled the idealistic virtues of justice, courage and temperance, but, consistent with his basic hedonism, valued these virtues not as ends in themselves, but merely for their contribution to the life of pleasure. Finally, (5) Epicurus did not ignore the ethical significance of social and political life; but here again, in the interests of consistency with his underlying hedonism, he reduced the social virtues to enlightened self-interest, and approved legal and political institutions in so far as they contribute to the security of the individual.

13. STOICISM

Zeno and His School. The Stoic conceptions of the world and of life are opposed to the naturalistic, hedonistic and egoistic philosophy of the Epicureans. Stoicism is thus much closer than Epicureanism to the philosophy taught by Socrates, Plato, and Aristotle. After the death of the great leaders, the essential elements of their theory of life were presented in popular form by the Stoics, a school founded by Zeno at Athens around 300 B.C. It had many followers in Greece and Rome, and continued its existence far into Christian times. Zeno shows the influence of the Cynics and Megarians, as well as of Plato and Aristotle. He frees Cynic ethics from its narrowness and places it on a logical and metaphysical foundation; he makes use of Platonic and Aristotelian notions in modified form, but refuses to conceive form and matter as different in kind, thus reverting to the hylozoism of Heraclitus. The historical formula which describes Stoicism is this: The metaphysical theories of Heraclitus—particularly the logos doctrine—are used as a foundation for an ethics, which, though derived from Cynicism, shows the moderating influence of Plato and Aristotle.

Zeno (336-264 B.C.) was born in Citium, Cyprus, a Greek city with a large foreign, perhaps Semitic, population. He came to Athens in 314, and studied under Crates the Cynic, Stilpo the Megarian, and Polemon of the Academy, all of whom influenced his teachings. In 294 he opened a school in the Stoa Poikile (the painted corridor or porch), from which the doctrines represented by him received their name. Zeno was esteemed for his upright character, the simplicity of his life, his affability, and moral earnestness.

Zeno was followed in the leadership of the Stoic school by his pupil Cleanthes (264-232 B.C.), who does not seem to have possessed the qualities needed to meet the attacks of the Epicureans and Skeptics. Next came Chrysippus of Soli, Cilicia (232-204), a man of great ability, who clearly defined the teachings of the school, gave unity to the system, and defended it against the Skeptics. Among the pupils of Chrysippus were Zeno of Tarsus, Diogenes of Babylon, and Antipater of Tarsus. Stoicism, as developed by Chrysippus, found favor in Rome during the Republic, Panaetius (180-110) being one of its first Roman adherents of note. During the Empire it divided into two sections, the one popular, represented by Musonius Rufus (first century A.D.), Seneca (3-65 A.D.), Epictetus (first century), and the Emperor Marcus Aurelius (121-180); the other scientific, whose sole aim was to preserve intact and interpret the old doctrine. Corinthus and Herocles, whose work on *Ethics* is a relatively recent discovery, belong to this branch. We shall present the Stoic philosophy as it was worked out in the course of the development of the Greek school, limiting ourselves to its most important phases.

Of the old Stoa (304-205 B.C.) and Middle Stoa (down to the Roman Empire) we have no primary sources except the *Hymn of Cleanthes* and numerous quotations in later works. Thus we have to depend for our knowledge of Stoic teachings on secondary sources, especially Diogenes Laertius, Stobaeus, Cicero, Plutarch, Simplicius, and Sextus Empiricus; from these we may learn the spirit of this philosophy, though we are unable to distinguish with certainty the respective contributions of the leaders. Of the later Roman Stoa we have numerous Greek and Latin writings. In addition to the collections of fragments already mentioned, consult: J. von Arnim's collection, 3 vols.; Pearson, *Fragments of Zeno and Cleanthes;* Diels, *Doxographi Graeci.*

Translations of Epictetus: *Discourses* (with Encheiridion and fragments), by Long, Higginson; of Marcus Aurelius: *Meditations,* by Long. English translations of extant writings of Epictetus and Marcus Aurelius are contained in W. J. Oates, *The Stoic and Epicurean Philosophers,* 1940; see also G. H. Clark (ed.), *Selections from Hellenistic Philosophy,* 1940; A. C. Pearson, *The Fragments of Zeno and Cleanthes,* 1891; E. Zeller, *The Stoics, Epicureans and Sceptics,* 1880; W. L. Davidson, *The Stoic Creed,* 1907; R. D. Hicks, *Stoic and Epicurean,* 1910; E. V. Arnold, *Roman Stoicism,* 1911; F. W. Bussell, *Marcus Aurelius and the Later Stoics,* 1910; G. Murray, *The Stoic Philosophy,* 1915; E. Bréhier, *Chrysippe,* 1910; E. R. Bevan, *Stoics and Sceptics,* 1913; R. M. Wenley, *Stoicism and Its Influence,* 1927; P. E. More, *Hellenistic Philosophies,* 1923.

Logic and Theory of Knowledge. The goal of the Stoic philosophy is to find a rational basis for ethics. The Stoics agree with the Epicureans that we cannot understand the meaning of the good unless we have a criterion of truth and a theory of the universe, that is, unless we study logic and metaphysics. The Stoics compared philosophy to a field, of which logic is the fence, physics the soil, and ethics the fruit.

We begin with logic, which is the science of thoughts and discourses, i.e., of concepts, judgments, and inferences, as well as of their expression in language. The Stoics included grammar in logic, and became the founders of our traditional science of grammar. We shall limit ourselves to the so-called dialectical part, which deals with the theory of knowledge and discusses two main problems: What is the origin of knowledge, or how do we reach truth? and, What is the criterion of knowledge?

Our knowledge is gained through perception. There are no innate ideas, as Plato held; the soul is at birth an empty tablet, a *tabula rasa,* which receives the impressions of things, as a wax tablet receives the impression of the stamp. Chrysippus speaks of sensation as a modification of consciousness. Impressions persist and form memory-images, which, when combined, constitute experience. From sensations and images general ideas are formed and these, when based on common experiences, are called common notions (*notitiae communes*). They are the same in all persons, and not subject to illusion or error. Scientific concepts, however, are produced consciously and methodically, as the result of voluntary reflection.

Sense perception is the basis of all our knowledge. The mind has the faculty of forming general ideas and concepts of a large number of particular cases which are alike, and of forming universal judgments. This faculty which is called reason is a faculty both of thought and speech and is, in essence, identical with the universal reason which pervades the world. The human mind can know the world-order because human reason and the world-reason are in essence identical. Concepts, if they are to be true, must agree with the rational order of things. The Stoics posited objective rationality in the world and yet opposed the Platonic doctrine of ideas. They held that only particular objects have real existence and regarded universals as subjective abstractions.

Our knowledge, therefore, rests on perceptions and on the general ideas and concepts derived from them. A sense image is true when it is an exact copy of the sense object. A concept is true when it agrees with the qualities pervading similar things. Percepts and concepts may, however, be false; it is evident that many of our percepts and ideas are entirely delusive and do not yield truth. How can we distinguish the true from the false? What shall be our criterion? How can we tell whether there really is anything corresponding to our ideas? How do we know that they are not merely the creations of our own fancy? All our knowledge is based on perception. In order to be true, a percept must be accompanied by the consciousness or immediate conviction that there is a real object corresponding to it with which it agrees. Man is entitled to his conviction of truth when he has satisfied himself that his sense organ is in normal condition, that the percept is clear and distinct, and that repeated observations by himself and others verify his first impression. A sensation that carries such conviction with it is called by Zeno "a conceptual impression," or, as some translate it, "the apprehending presentation."

The criterion of knowledge, then, is the self-evidence of the impression or concept, the conviction that there is a reality corresponding to it. Some of our concepts compel such a feeling, some of them do not. Merely subjective or imaginary ideas are not accompanied by this consciousness; we need not give our assent to such ideas, or pronounce judgment where conviction is absent, hence we ourselves are responsible for error whenever we give assent to a judgment lacking this element of conviction. Intellectual judgment implies an act of free will. No reasonable man, however, can refuse assent to a "conceptual impression" which is clearly presented to consciousness.

Knowledge of truth is not the exclusive possession of science or philosophy. All men share in knowledge through their general ideas. But such common notions do not carry conviction with them, as does genuine knowledge, which is acquired by reasoning. Science is an organized body of true judgments, in which one proposition is deduced from another by logical necessity. The faculty of drawing correct inferences is, accordingly, another means of reaching truth, and dialectic an essential qualification of the Stoic sage. The Stoics consequently gave considerable attention to formal logic, particularly to the doctrine of the syllogism, which they regarded as its most important phase; indeed, they made some minor additions to the Aristotelian logic of the syllogism and revised Aristotle's table of categories.

The main purpose of the Stoic logic was to show that the mind cannot create knowledge out of itself, that the source of all our knowledge is perception, and that this furnishes the materials of knowledge. The Stoics did not, however, deny the activity of thought; indeed, they insisted that knowledge is advanced by reflection on experience, by organizing the raw material into concepts, by forming judgments concerning it, by passing inferentially from that which is directly given to the remote in time and place.

Metaphysics. The Stoic metaphysics may be described as a materialistic version of the Aristotelian metaphysics; it is Aristotelianism translated into the more primitive idiom of Pre-Socratic nature-philosophy. The Stoics agree with Aristotle that everything that exists results from two principles, a principle that acts, moves, and forms, and a principle that is acted on, moved, and formed. They agree with him also that these two things are not separate entities—although they may be distinguished in thought, but united in one reality. They differ from him, however, in their notion of the nature of the principles. For them nothing is real unless it either acts or is acted upon; and since only bodies are active and passive, form or force and matter are both corporeal. These, however, differ in the degree of their corporeality; force consists of a finer kind of stuff, while matter, as such, is coarse, formless, and immovable. The two are inseparable, as we have said; there is no force without matter and no matter without force: matter is everywhere permeated with force. Everything in the world, including the human soul and God, is corporeal. Even qualities are corporeal; they consist of a pneumatic substance which is a mixture of fire and air. It is these qualities which make each particular object what it is. Fire and air are active elements, the principles of life and mind; water and earth are passive elements, utterly inert and lifeless, like clay in the hands of the potter. The pneumatic substance pervades every particle of matter; it does not merely fill the spaces between the particles. It is present in the smallest piece of reality and is continuous throughout the universe. Each particular thing has qualities which distinguish it from every other thing, and which are due to the material forms permeating them.

Only forces have causality, and causes can act only on bodies. But the effect is always incorporeal; a cause produces a *state* in another body, a movement or a change, which is neither a body nor a quality of a body. Causal action and force are here identified; causal action can be exercised only on a body; the effect which results, however, is not a cause or force, but a mere accidental state of the body. If the effect were a body, the force would have produced another body, which is impossible. Relations, too, are incorporeal. But the active principle, it must be remembered, is alive and intelligent; in this respect, the Stoics approximate the Aristotelian conception of God as pure form. Their sensationalistic and materialistic point of view, however, does not permit them to conceive it as pure form or thought. The Stoic metaphysics is a partial reversion from the Platonic-Aristotelian philosophy to the hylozoism of an earlier stage in the development of Greek thought; it combines, in somewhat anomalous fashion, materialism with rationalistic pantheism. The forces in the universe form one all-pervasive force or fire—as Heraclitus had taught—and the ultimate principle is the rational, active soul of the world. The principle must be *one* because the universe is a unity, because all its parts are in harmony; it is conceived as fire because heat produces everything, moves everything, and is a giver of life. Most important of all, the animating principle of things is *reason*—intelligent, purposeful, and good. The universe is a *cosmos*—a beautiful, well-ordered, good and perfect whole. The rational principle is related to the world as the human soul is related to its body. All life and movement have their source in the logos: it is god; it contains the germs or seeds (spermata) of life; in it the whole cosmos lies potential as the plant in the seed. The Stoic metaphysics, in positing a rational principle pervading the cosmos, is pure pantheism, and the argument from the harmoniously ordered cosmos to its source in the rational principle is an anticipation of the later teleological argument for God's existence.

The universal reason or soul pervades the whole world, just as the human soul pervades the body. But just as the governing part of the soul is situated in a particular part of the body, so the ruling part of the world-soul, the Deity, or Zeus, is seated at the outermost circle of the world, whence its influence spreads through the world. The two aspects of God form a single godhead, though one of them assumes the form of the world, while the other retains its original shape. God, the father of all things, the perfect and blessed being, has prevision and will, is a lover of man, benevolent, cares for everything, punishes the wicked and rewards the good. In these respects the Stoic god is like the god of theism. But there is a difference. He is not, when considered in his entirety, a free personality, a free creator of the world, but, as we have seen, the substance from which everything proceeds with the necessity of a process of nature. The Stoics assign will and forethought to him, but they likewise identify him with necessary law. Neither the pantheistic nor the theistic aspect of the Stoic theology is consistently carried out. As in many modern systems, pantheism and theism dwell together in the Stoic system. It is, however, unquestionably true that pantheistic aspect prevails over the theistic in the Stoic theology.

Cosmology. The Stoics offer a detailed description of the evolution of the world from the original divine fire. Air, water, and earth arise from fire; fire, which is the divine or active principle, however, always permeates the lower elements, earth and water, which are presumably condensed forms of fire; in other words, when fire has lost its force, the lower forms of matter remain as a waste-product. The divine element itself can be differentiated into forms of varying degrees of purity, acting in inorganic nature as blind causality, in the vegetable kingdom as a blind but purposive natural force, in animals as a purposive impulse guided by ideas, in man as rational conscious purpose. Natural objects are explained as combinations of the four elements; their differences, partly as differences in mixture, partly as differences in the formative action of the divine fire. The universe is a perfect sphere floating in empty space, held together and animated by its soul. It arose in time and will, in the great conflagration, return to fire, to the pure life and rationality whence it came, only to pass through the same cycle again and again, world without end. But every recurring world will resemble its predecessors in every detail—the theory of cyclic recurrence—for each is produced by the same law. Everything is absolutely determined, even the human will; the universe forms an unbroken causal chain in which nothing happens by chance, but everything follows necessarily from the one first cause or mover.

Man is free in the sense that he can assent to what fate decrees, but, whether he assents or not, he must obey. Yet, in so far as the law or reason of the world, and the necessity associated with it, are dependent on the will of God, everything accords with divine providence; whatever evolves from the original principle is in accordance with it. In this sense, Fate and Providence are not opposed: fate or law is the will of God.

The question now arises: If everything is a manifestation of God, how shall we explain the existence of evil in the world? The Stoics adopted two solutions of the problem of evil: (1) the so-called negative solution, which denies the very existence of evil: the world is good and perfect, and what we call evils are only relative evils, which, like shadows in a picture or discords in music, contribute to the beauty and perfection of the whole; (2) the so-called positive solution, which consists in regarding evil, e.g., disease, as the necessary and inevitable consequence of natural processes or as a necessary means of realizing the good. They also argued that, since physical evil cannot affect human character, which alone has intrinsic value, it is not really evil. As for moral evil, it is impossible to have virtue without its opposite—indeed, virtue grows strong in combating vice. The truth is that the universe, when viewed in cosmic perspective, is a beautiful, good, and perfect whole, in which every part has its own proper place and purpose, and no part, when considered in relation to the whole, is ugly or evil.

Psychology. Man is composed of body and soul; the soul is a material substance, a spark of the divine fire. Its ruling part, which is situated in the heart, exercises all the psychic functions: perception, judgment, inference, feeling, and will; it becomes rational, in the course of time, acquiring the power of conceptual thought. Man is free in so far as he has logical thought; he is not merely governed by images and impulses, like the brute, but deliberates and chooses only such acts as gain the assent of reason. A man is free when he acts in accordance with reason, that is, in obedience to the eternal laws of nature. There is, then, no conflict between what the wise man wishes to do and what reason or nature commands. The philosopher who is in possession of the complete system of truths is as free as God himself. The Stoic conception of freedom is one of rational self-determination; free acts are those which are in conformity with a man's rational nature and, ultimately, with the rational nature of the universe. The freedom of conformity to rational law is very different from the Epicurean freedom of chance or causal indeterminacy.

There is no single Stoic doctrine of immortality. According to some members of the school, all souls continue to exist until the end of the world; according to others, only the wise and virtuous souls persist. The Stoic doctrine of cyclical recurrence implies that all souls necessarily reappear with the re-creation of the universe.

The entire Stoic philosophy is humanistically oriented; the doctrines of man's rational nature as a reflection of the cosmic reason, of man's freedom as conformity to nature, and of human immortality are of crucial significance to Stoicism. Indeed, we would not seriously misrepresent the Stoic position were we to say that man is the end or purpose of nature, or of God —provided we do not lose sight of the complementary principle that the ends or goals of man are prescribed by the rationality at the core of the universe.

Ethics. The ethical philosophy of the Stoics is closely integrated with their psychological and metaphysical theories as set forth in the foregoing pages. They conceived the universe not as a mechanical-causal series, but as an organized rational system, a beautiful well-ordered whole, in which every part has its function to perform with respect to the whole, and in which all things work together for the common good. The cosmos was for them a harmonious unity with a ruling purpose, a living, intelligent God. Man is a part of the universal order, a spark of the divine fire, a small universe (microcosm) reflecting the great universe (macrocosm). Hence it behooves him to act in harmony with the purpose of the universe, to seek to fit his own purposes into the larger design envisaged by the divine purpose, to reach the highest possible measure of perfection. In order to do this, he must put his own soul in order; reason should rule in him as reason rules the world. He ought to subordinate his will to the will of the world, submit to the law of the universe, take his place in the great order, and strive to do consciously, intelligently, and voluntarily that which it is his office to do as a part of the cosmos. To live according to nature, is, for a human being, to act in conformity with reason, the logos. This is the full meaning of the Stoic injunction that we live according to nature. For the Stoic ethics, virtue is the highest good and the highest happiness, for only a virtuous life can be a happy life. To live thus is to realize one's self, and to realize one's true self is to serve the purposes of universal reason and to work for universal ends. The Stoic ethical ideal implies a universal society of rational beings with the same rights; for reason is the same in all, and all are parts of the same world-soul.

The same conclusions may be reached by a consideration of the natural impulses of man; for, according to the Stoics, the universal logos expresses itself in the lower instincts no less than in human reason. Every being strives to preserve itself; self-preservation, not pleasure, is the goal of impulse, and pleasure is merely a concomitant of the successful realization of impulse. Yet individual self-preservation is not the only goal, for there is inherent in all living creatures an instinct to preserve the species, a desire for something beyond themselves. With the development of reason man comes to regard his rational nature as his true self, and finds satisfaction in the perfection of reason and the promotion of rational purposes everywhere. What he loves in himself he cannot but love in others. Theoretical speculation is not, for Stoicism, an end in itself; reason is valued highly only because it reveals to us our duty. Virtue is the only good and vice the only evil, all else is indifferent. According to the Stoic ideal, health, life, honor, wealth, rank, power, friendship, success are not in themselves good; nor are death, disease, disgrace, poverty, humble birth in themselves evil. Neither pleasure nor happiness is an absolute good; either may result from action but neither should be made an end. The attainment of such things as pleasure and happiness is not in our power; though the attitude we adopt toward them is in our control. Their value depends on what use we make of them, on their bearing upon our character; in themselves they are nothing. Virtue alone is intrinsically worthwhile, and it alone can make man truly happy.

A truly virtuous act is one that is consciously directed toward the highest purpose or end, and is performed with conscious knowledge of moral principles. Thus, virtuous conduct implies complete and certain knowledge of the good and a conscious purpose, on the part of the doer, to realize the supreme good. To act unconsciously and without knowledge is not virtue. If we look at the matter in this way, virtue is *one,* for here everything depends on the disposition, on the good will: a man either has it or he has it not; there is no middle ground; he is either a wise man or a fool. In this sense, where one virtue is, all others are. The virtues are expressions of one and the same disposition and, therefore, inseparably connected with one another.

The doctrine of the unity of virtue is the typically Stoic view which Chrysippus alone among the Stoics did not accept. He held that virtue is not natural in man, but is acquired by practice and through instruction. Inasmuch as virtue implies complete knowledge, only a mature man can possess it. The assumption underlying this view is that a man will act according to his judgment, that he will naturally strive for what appears good to him, and avoid what is evil. Hence, evil conduct is the result of wrong judgment, or false opinion: the Stoics sometimes regard evil as the cause, sometimes as the effect, of the passions or immoderate impulses. There are four such passions: pleasure, desire, grief, and fear. A false judgment of a present good arouses—or is aroused by—pleasure; of a future good, desire; of a present evil, grief or pain; of a future evil, fear. All these passions and their many variations are diseases of the soul which it is our business, not merely to moderate, but to eradicate, since they are irrational, exaggerated feelings—the result of false opinion. Apathy or freedom from passion is, accordingly, the Stoic ideal. To attain it, complete knowledge is necessary and such knowledge is connected with strength of will or character. To be free from passion means to be brave and temperate, and it lies within the power of the individual himself to decide whether he will obey the moral law or not. The will of man is, in this sense, free. It has been said that the Stoics in their metaphysics teach determinism, and in their ethics free will; but the moral freedom postulated by the Stoics is not really incompatible with the metaphysics of determinism.

Politics. As we have already shown, the ethics of the Stoics is not egoistic. Man has not only the impulse of self-preservation, but also a social impulse, which leads him to an ever-widening group life. The promptings of this social instinct are made fully conscious and are reinforced by rational thought; reason teaches that we are members of a cosmic society of rational beings toward whom we have duties dictated by justice and benevolence. This society is a kind of universal State, in which there is but one law— natural law—and one right—natural right, because there is but one universal reason. In this universal State, morality is the sole standard of discrimina- tion between citizens; here gods and sages are the privileged individuals, whom, however, everyone is free to join. All men are related, all are brothers, children of the same father; they have the same origin and des- tiny; the same universal reason speaks in them all; they stand under one law and are citizens of one state; even our enemies are entitled to our help and pardon. Reason demands that we place the universal welfare above our own particular interests, that we sacrifice ourselves for it if need be; for in realizing the universal good we are fulfilling our true mission and preserving our true selves. This is the Stoic cosmopolitanism.

Unlike the Epicureans, who held themselves aloof from public affairs, the Stoics recommended participation in political affairs: it is the duty of every man to take part in social and political life in the same spirit in which he behaves as a citizen of the world, to labor for the welfare of his own people and his own State. But they could never become narrow chauvinists for their nationalism was broadened by a humanitarianism that embraced the entire world. The laws of the particular states must be rooted in the universal law and justice of the universal State; natural right is the basis of the positive law. Friendship and marriage were highly prized by the Stoics as, indeed, were all forms of social life in which the individual might learn to subordinate himself to a universal ideal.

Religion. True religion and philosophy are one, according to the Stoics. They were defenders of the popular religion and regarded the universal recognition which it received from mankind as a proof of its truth. Religion was, in their eyes, a necessary support of morality. They objected, however, to the superstitious and anthropological elements in popular religion and offered an allegorical interpretation of them—perhaps the first systematic attempt which had been made in this direction.

Piety is the knowledge and worship of the gods: it consists in forming an adequate conception of them and imitating their perfection. Submission to the universal will, or resignation, constitutes the true essence of religion.

Résumé of Greek Ethics. Common to nearly all the Greek theories of morality is the ideal of order, harmony, symmetry: man should subject himself to the rule of reason, control himself, keep measure in all things. Materialists and idealists agree, also, on the importance of intelligence: right action depends on correct thinking. Nor do the opposing schools differ regarding the kind of conduct conducive to a good life. The fundamental virtues—wisdom, self-control, courage, and justice—are recommended by the refined hedonists and their opponents alike: they are at one in asserting that by living a life of virtue, by being wise, moderate, brave, and just, man attains happiness, repose of spirit, peace of mind. They differ in that the hedonists enjoin virtue for the sake of happiness, while the ethical idealists regard a well-ordered, beautiful soul as good in itself, as something worthy of attainment even if it does not bring happiness. All prize kindness to fellow men, friendship, benevolence, brotherhood; and both Stoics and Epicureans widened the circle of sympathy to include all mankind. Epicurus tended, at least in theory, to base social action on self-interest: we cannot be happy unless we are at peace with our fellow man. The Stoics, on the other hand, made love of neighbor a good in itself: my fellow man is not a mere means to my happiness, but, so far as I am concerned, an end in himself.

In the value which it placed on man as such, the ethical philosophy of Stoicism even transcended that of Plato and Aristotle. Both of these had defended slavery in some form, and both were influenced by national prejudices; both looked upon "barbarians" as inferior peoples and upon slavery as a natural and just institution. The ideal of universal brotherhood and equality was not theirs. They preached justice and equal rights for all full-fledged and equal citizens of the State, and held that the State was made for peace and not for conquest. But the citizens they had in mind were always free and intelligent Hellenes. It was not until the loss of Greek independence and the conquest of the so-called barbarians by Alexander that the idea of universal brotherhood and equal rights for all rational human beings began to dawn on some minds; and this ideal was preached by the Stoics. The solidarity of the human race became a central thought in their system. The notion of the dignity of man developed: the idea that all rational beings are children of the same father and citizens of the world, having the same rights and the same duties, subject to the same law, the same truth, and the same reason. The value of a man depends not on his wealth, rank, or class, but on his moral worth, on his good will. "Virtue despises no one, neither Greek nor barbarian, man nor woman, rich nor poor, freeman nor slave, wise nor ignorant, whole nor sick." [4] Character is the supreme possession of man, which no one can give and no one can take away.

14. SKEPTICISM AND ECLECTICISM

The Skeptical School. The philosophical movements we have been discussing, though chiefly concerned with the ethical problem, offer comprehensive systems of metaphysics and attempt to prove the competence of human reason to reach truth. In this respect they follow in the footsteps of the great thinkers after Socrates, who had defended knowledge against the attacks of skepticism and had restored the faith of thought in itself. But the time seemed ripe once more for a period of negation. Contemporaneously with Stoicism and Epicureanism, as a kind of shadow to their dogmatism, there appeared a new philosophy of doubt. It was preached by Pyrrho of Elis and called Pyrrhonism, a name which has become a synonym for skepticism.

Pyrrho (365-270 B.C.), who studied Democritus in his youth with a pupil of the great Atomist and became acquainted with the Elean-Megarian teachings, did not write anything himself; but his views were set down by Timon of Phlius (320-230), of whose satires only fragments remain. After Timon the skeptical school was absorbed by the Platonic Academy, and did not emerge again as an independent movement until the Academy purged itself of skepticism. Arcesilaus (315-241) was the first of the leaders

[4] Denis, *Histoire des théories et des idées morales.*

of the Academy to give up the traditional doctrine and to devote himself to the criticism of Stoicism and Epicureanism, which he regarded as pseudo-philosophies. He trained his pupils in dialectic, or the art of proving and disproving every thesis. He advocated suspension of judgment with respect to metaphysical problems. The greatest skeptic in the Academy was Carneades (213-129) who, like his predecessor, wrote nothing; he was followed by Clitomachus (d. 110), Philo of Larissa (d. 80), and Antiochus of Ascalon (d. 68).

The Academy—called Middle Academy during the skeptical period—purged itself of skepticism under the leadership of Philo of Larissa and Antiochus; skepticism again became an independent movement under Aenesidemus, at the beginning of the Christian era, and was later represented by Sextus Empiricus (active from 180-210 A.D.). Aenesidemus wrote a work on Pyrrhonism, fragments of which are preserved by Sextus, and Sextus Empiricus wrote *Against the Mathematicians* and *Pyrrhonic Hypotyposes.*

Sextus Empiricus, *Against the Mathematicians,* in *Works,* trans. by R. G. Bury, 3 vols., 1933-36.

M. M. Patrick, *Sextus Empiricus and the Greek Sceptics,* 1899; N. Nicoll, *The Greek Sceptics,* 1869; V. C. L. Brochard, *Les sceptiques grecs,* 1923; M. M. Patrick, *The Greek Sceptics,* 1929; L. Robin, *Pyrrhon et le scepticisme grec,* 1944.

Doctrines of the School. The thought common to this school is that we cannot know the nature of things. Our senses tell us only how things *appear* to us, not what they are in themselves. If sensation is the source of all our knowledge, how can we know whether objects agree with sensations or not, since we never get outside our sensations? Moreover, our thoughts and sensations conflict, and we have no criterion here for distinguishing the true from the false (Pyrrho). The Epicureans regard every sensation as a criterion of truth; the Stoics say it is only the sensation carrying conviction with it that commands our assent; but neither criterion is a safe one. Sensation deceives us constantly; percepts that have nothing corresponding to them may be just as clear, distinct and self-evident as true ones—an argument advanced by Arcesilaus. We cannot tell whether a sensation is a true copy of the real object, because we never have the object with which to compare it. Besides, says Carneades, we cannot assent to an idea, we can assent only to a judgment, and judgment is a form of thinking, and in need of a criterion. He also declares that we cannot prove anything; for to do so we must either assume the premise from which the truth follows, which is begging the question, or we must try to prove the premise by basing it on other premises. If we adopt the latter procedure, we never reach a stopping place, and thus our conclusion can never be established with certainty.

If we cannot know anything, we ought to suspend judgment, that is, assume nothing at all. All we can say is that we have such and such states of consciousness, that an object *appears* white or black, not that it *is* white or black—and this is sufficient for all practical purposes (Pyrrho). Certainty of knowledge in moral matters is also out of the question, and we can save ourselves much unhappiness if we suspend judgment and cease striving for ideals. Peace of mind will be the result of such an attitude of moral indifference and resignation. Carneades holds that, although we have no criterion for knowing with certainty the nature of things, we do have sufficient assurance, e.g., the clearness and vividness of a percept, to guide us in our practical behavior. There are, in his opinion, various degrees of probability; and thus it is not necessary to suspend judgment entirely. The wise man will assent to an idea according to its degree of probability; he will, however, always remember that even the highest degree of probability does not guarantee truth. This attitude of Carneades fostered eclecticism, a common-sense philosophy which combines truths from various sources without seeking a unified system of certain knowledge.

Carneades attacks the system of the Stoics, endeavoring to bring out its contradictions, and to show the futility of all knowledge. He repudiates their teleological argument for the existence of God on the ground that the world is not rational, beautiful, and good; even if it were, it would not prove that a god made it. Their conception of God or the world-soul is criticized on the ground that if he has sensation or feeling, he is changeable, and that a changeable god cannot be eternal. If, on the other hand, he is unchangeable, he is a rigid, lifeless being. Again, if God is corporeal, he is changeable and perishable; if he is incorporeal, he has neither sensation nor feeling. If he is good, he is determined by the moral law, hence not supreme; if he is not good, he is inferior to men. The idea of God is full of contradictions; our reason cannot grasp him; and knowledge of him is, therefore, impossible.

Philo of Larissa declares that, though the Stoic criterion of truth is not adequate, it does not follow that knowledge is impossible. He does not believe that either Arcesilaus or Carneades ever intended to deny the possibility of knowledge. Antiochus abandons skepticism for eclecticism.

Later Skeptics. The skeptical view is worked out in greater detail by the later skeptics, Aenesidemus and Sextus. Among the reasons given by Aenesidemus for the uncertainty of knowledge are these: The same objects seem different to different beings, to different persons, to the same person, to different senses, to the same sense at different times and under different conditions of the subject and the environment. Every sensation is conditioned by subjective and objective factors, and is therefore never the same on two different occasions. Proofs are brought by him against the possibility of proof, against the notion of cause and effect, and against the arguments for the existence of God.

The skeptical movement was not without influence on the history of philosophy. It tended to weaken the extreme dogmatism of some of the schools and induced philosophers to modify their views to meet the attack of the skeptics. By pointing out the contradictions in and among various systems, it caused thinkers to soften their differences and to emphasize their agreements, and encouraged them to select from each system what appealed to their common sense. In this way the philosophical movement called eclecticism took its rise.

Eclecticism. Eclecticism was also encouraged by the growing intellectual intercourse between Greek scholars and the Romans. The Romans had no genius for philosophy; they lacked speculative power and paid little attention to theories of the world and of life. It was not until Macedonia was conquered by Rome in 168 B.C. and Greece became a Roman province (146), that interest arose in philosophical reflection. Greek teachers came to Rome, young Romans attended the philosophical schools in Greece, and Greek philosophy began to be regarded as an indispensable part of higher culture. The Roman thinkers, however, never produced any independent systems of thought; they were eclectics, taking from different systems what most appealed to them. Even when they accepted a system, they modified it to suit their taste. They had no patience with subtleties, sophistries, and paradoxes, and avoided the hair-splittings and fine distinctions in which the Greeks reveled; nor were they fond of controversies and disputations. They were not profound thinkers, but were governed by common sense: "They sought and found in philosophy," as Denis [5] says, "nothing but a rule of conduct and a means of government."

Eclecticism made its way into nearly all the schools, into the Academy, the Lyceum, and the Stoa; the Epicureans alone remained true to their creed. We mention among its representatives: Antiochus, of the Newer Academy; Panaetius (180-110 B.C.), Posidonius (d. 91 B.C.), of the Middle Stoa; Cicero (106-43 B.C.); Sextius (b. 70 B.C.); L. Annaeus Cornutus (first century A.D.); L. Annaeus Seneca (3-65 A.D.); and C. Musonius Rufus (first century A.D.).

Histoire des théories et des idées morales.

V
The Religious Period

15. JEWISH-GREEK PHILOSOPHY

Philosophy and Religion. We have passed in review the different philosophical movements which succeeded the great systems of Plato and Aristotle, and come now to a period in history when philosophy seeks refuge in
religion. Epicureanism, interpreting the world as a machine, advises its followers to turn the world to their use and to derive as much happiness from it
as possible. The Stoics, conceiving nature as a teleological system, find
it wise to subordinate themselves to the universal will and to assist in realizing the purpose of the whole. Skepticism, refusing to give any answer whatever to the problem of the nature of the universe, advises the abandonment
of all philosophy and recommends, as a guide in practical matters, the following of nature, custom, and probability. Eclecticism, finally, adopts what
seems good in all the theories that have been offered, and endeavors to piece
together a satisfactory world-view from the materials at hand.

These philosophies, however, did not satisfy all types of mind. Some temperaments found it impossible to look upon the world as a mechanical interplay of atoms and to cease from troubling about God. They were unable, by
silencing their yearnings and resigning themselves to the universal will, to
find both peace and power "within their own pure hearts." Nor did they,
with the skeptics, succeed in rooting out the desire for certain knowledge
of God; they refused to surrender themselves to the fate of blindness and
longed not only to know but to see God. Zeller characterizes the period we
have reached in the following words:

The feeling of estrangement from God, the yearning for a higher revelation,
is characteristic of the last centuries of the old world. This yearning expresses
nothing less than the consciousness of the decline of the classical peoples and
their culture, and the premonition of the approaching new era; it brought to

145

life not only Christianity, but, even before its advent, pagan and Jewish Alexandrianism and its kindred phenomena.[1]

This attitude gave rise to a philosophy strongly tinctured with religious mysticism; and Greek thought, gathering together the achievements of its intellectual history, ended, as it began, in religion. The religious movement was encouraged by the contact of Greek speculation with the Egyptian, Chaldaean, and, particularly, Jewish religions. The cosmopolitan city of Alexandria, in Egypt, furnished the favorable physical medium for bringing the diverse forces together. We may distinguish three currents in this religious philosophy: (1) an attempt to combine an Oriental religion, Judaism, with Greek speculation: Jewish-Greek philosophy; (2) an attempt to construct a world-religion upon Pythagorean doctrines: Neopythagoreanism; (3) an attempt to make a religious philosophy of the Platonic teaching: Neoplatonism. Common to all these theologies, or theosophies, are the concept of God as a transcendent being, the dualism of God and world, the idea of revealed and mystical knowledge of God, asceticism and world-denial, the belief in intermediary beings, demons, and angels. Some of these elements, such as monotheism, dualism, revelation and prophecy, angelology, were characteristic of the Jewish religion as it appeared at the time we have reached, and it therefore readily lent itself to a form of syncretism, an amalgamation with certain Greek systems of thought. All the systems represent a union of Hellenistic and Oriental culture: in Neoplatonism the Greek element predominates, in the Jewish-Greek philosophy Orientalism is strongest.

Beginnings of Jewish-Greek Philosophy. Alexandria, which was founded by Alexander the Great in 333 B.C., became, under the rule of the descendants of his general Ptolemy (323-181), the leading commercial and intellectual city of the world and the chief meeting place of Hellenic and Oriental civilization. Here a great scientific museum with its celebrated library of 700,000 volumes was established under Ptolemy II (285-247), which attracted poets, men of science, and philosophers from every region of the classical world. Among them were the poets Callimachus, Theocritus, and Apollonius of Rhodes; Euclid the mathematician; the astronomers Apollonius of Perga, Arystillus, Timocharus, and Ptolemy, the author of the *Almagest* and the geocentric or Ptolemaic theory of the heavens; and the geographer Eratosthenes. Here, under Ptolemy II, the sacred Jewish Scriptures were translated into Greek (the Septuagint) for the benefit of the large Jewish population

[1] Zeller, *The Philosophy of the Greeks,* Part III, Vol. II.

which had forgotten its mother tongue. The Greek influence on Jewish thought was, however, not limited to Alexandria, but extended to Palestine itself, as we know from the efforts made by King Antiochus IV to hellenize the Jews and from the encouragement he received among the educated classes of Jerusalem.

The first direct trace of the union of Jewish and Greek ideas is found in a treatise by a Peripatetic Jew named Aristobulus (about 150 B.C.), who wrote a commentary on the Pentateuch. He tried to show a harmony between the teachings of the Old Testament and the Greek philosophers, and asserted that the Greeks—Orpheus, Homer, Hesiod, Pythagoras, and Plato— had drawn upon the Jewish Scriptures for their knowledge. In support of his position he appealed to a number of verses in the Greek poets, which were afterward proved to be forgeries. He also attempted to get rid of the anthropomorphism in the Scriptures by means of allegorical interpretations after the fashion of the Stoics, and sought to reconcile the Scriptures with Hellenic thought. He conceived God as a transcendent, invisible being, whom no mortal soul ever beheld because he is visible only to pure intelligence. The world-soul of the Stoics is, he claimed, not God himself, but one aspect of God, the divine power that governs all things. The influence of Aristotle and the Stoics is plainly noticeable in these views, and traces of Greek philosophy are found in other Jewish writings, e.g., in the work called *Wisdom of Solomon,* in the *Book of Maccabees,* the *Sibylline Oracles,* and *Wisdom of Sirach.*

Philo. These tendencies culminate in the system of Philo (30 B.C.-50 A.D.), an Alexandrian Jew of priestly family. He wrote historical, political, ethical, and exegetical works, of which many are extant. According to Philo, Judaism is the sum-total of human wisdom. One and the same reason speaks in the Greek philosophers Pythagoras and Plato, and in the inspired teachings of Moses and the Prophets; to prove this, Philo read Greek philosophy, especially Platonism and Stoicism, into the Scriptures by means of the allegorical method which was in common use at Alexandria. Adam stands for spirit or mind, Eve for sensuality, Jacob for asceticism, and so on.

The Works of Philo, trans. in *Loeb Library,* 1939; Translation of *Works* by C. D. Yonge, 4 vols., 1855-1900; J. Drummond, *Philo-Judaeus,* 2 vols., 1888; F. Conybeare, ed. and trans., *Philo on the Contemplative Life,* 1895; H. Lewy, *Selections from Philo,* 1947; E. R. Goodenough, *An Introduction to Philo,* 1940; H. A. Kennedy, *Philo's Contribution to Religion,* 1919; H. Wolfson, *Philo,* 2 vols., 1947; T. H. Billings, *The Platonism of Philo Judaeus,* 1919.

The fundamental concept in the system of Philo is the idea of God. God is an absolutely transcendent being, so far above us that we cannot comprehend him or define him; he is the ineffable one, the greatest good, who is above both knowledge and virtue. We know *that* he is, not *what* he is; we are immediately certain of his existence, knowing him through our highest reason or pure intelligence. His existence can, however, also be proved. He is the ground and source of everything; everything is contained in him. He is absolute power, absolute perfection, absolute goodness, absolute blessedness, and pure mind, intelligence, or reason. God is too exalted to come in contact with impure matter. In order to explain his action on the world, Philo makes use of the Jewish notions of angels and demons, and of the Greek conceptions of the world-soul and ideas to mediate between God and the world. Sometimes he describes these powers as properties of God, as ideas or thoughts of God, as parts of the universal power or reason, sometimes as messengers or servants of God, as souls, angels, or demons—thinking now in terms of Greek philosophy, now in terms of the Jewish religion. All such powers he combines into one, the Logos, the Divine Reason or Wisdom. We conceive the Logos through the logos in ourselves, which is a second faculty of knowledge, different from pure intelligence. The Logos is the container or place of all ideas, the power of all powers, the highest of the angels, the first-born son of God, the image of God, the second God, the God-man, the heavenly Adam. In fact, Philo's Logos is the Stoic world-soul, the molder of the world, the pattern of the universe, or the Platonic world of ideas, made into a being intermediate between God and the world. Sometimes he speaks of this principle as a radiation of the divine light, a conception which anticipates to some extent the emanation-theory of Plotinus. Whether or not the Logos is to be conceived as a person, is left uncertain.

The Logos is the wisdom and power and goodness of God substantialized, or conceived as an entity distinct from him. In order that it may have something to act upon, another principle is introduced: quality-less matter, or a mass occupying space, of which God is the cause. From this chaotic mass, and using the Logos as his organ, God fashioned the world of visible things, which are the images or copies of ideas. We know the sensible images of the Logos, or the world of sense, through sense perception, which is a third faculty of knowledge in man. Philo, adhering to the Jewish conception of creation, held that the world had a beginning in time, but no end; time and space were created when the world was created. Since the Logos is perfect and good the defects and evils of the world must owe their origin to matter.

Man, the most important piece of creation, is the microcosm which, like the universe, is composed both of soul and matter. Pure thought, however, constitutes man's chief essence. The body and the irrational part of the soul belong to the world of matter; the ruling part consists of desire, courage, and reason (logos). The incorporeal mind or pure intelligence is added to the soul from above, making man an image of God. The body is the source of evil in man; the incorporation of the soul is a fall: by its union with the body the soul becomes predisposed to evil. If a fallen soul fails to free itself from sense, it enters other mortal bodies. Although, according to Philo, human intelligence is in constant connection with the divine mind, it is nevertheless free to declare for or against God, free to lose itself in sensuality or to rise above it; how this is possible, we are not told. Man should deliver himself from his body, the evil principle in him, eradicate his passions and all sensuality by theoretical contemplation (asceticism). But we cannot do this unaided, for we are too weak, too sinful; we need divine help. God must illuminate us, penetrate our souls. "The sun of consciousness must set." In this state of ecstasy we immediately apprehend God, plunge ourselves into the pure source of being, literally see God (mysticism). In the philosophy of Philo, the doctrines of asceticism and mysticism are combined in a way which later, especially during the Middle Ages, established itself as a familiar pattern.

16. Neoplatonism

Pythagorean Sources of Neoplatonism. The school, founded by Pythagoras in the sixth century B.C. led a precarious and intermittent existence during the classical period of Greek philosophy. In its mystical and ethical aspects, the Pythagorean philosophy intermingled with Platonism and enjoyed a resurgence in the congenial climate of opinion of the religious period. Pythagoras' original teaching had emphasized the ethical, political, and religious implications of his number-mysticism; it had aimed at an ethical-religious reform. After his death, the practical phases of his doctrine survived, particularly in Italy, but the school, as a philosophical organization, died in the fourth century. Plato, in his old age, absorbed the number-theory and the religious mysticism of the Pythagoreans, and his immediate successors in his school emphasized these latter-day teachings of the master. With the rise of Aristotelianism and the later Greek systems, the Academy abandoned Pythagoreanism as its official creed. The Pythagorean secret societies with their mysteries, continued to lead a precarious existence until they

were revitalized by the religious upsurge which took possession of the
Roman world in the first century B.C., and the spirit of the times encouraged them to devote themselves once more to philosophy. The leaders in
this movement, however, did not go back to the Pythagoreanism of the
early days; they took the doctrine as it appeared in Platonism, and combined
it, in the eclectic fashion of the age, with other Greek theories. Pythagoras
came to be regarded as the source of divinely revealed knowledge. Whatever
the Neopythagoreans accepted as truth, and whatever appealed to them in
the writings of Plato, Aristotle, and the Stoics, they naïvely ascribed to the
great teacher whose personality and work had been surrounded with the
nimbus of mystery.

Among the Neopythagoreans may be mentioned the name of P. Nigidius
Figulus, Sotion, the pupil of Sextius, Apollonius of Tyana, Moderatus, of
the first century A.D., and Nicomachus and Philostratus of the second century. Apollonius declared Pythagoras to be the world-savior, while Philostratus gives this title to Apollonius himself. The Neopythagorean movement also influenced many Platonists: Plutarch of Chaeronea (50-125),
Maximus of Tyre, Apuleius (born between 126 and 132), the physician
Galen (second century), Celsus, Numenius, and others.

Philostratus, *Life of Apollonius of Tyrana,* trans. by F. C. Conybeare, 1912.

Neoplatonism. The attempts to construct a religious philosophy on the basis
of Greek thought culminate in Neoplatonism. Plato's system becomes the
framework for a religious world-view, or theosophy, which utilizes whatever
seems valuable in the other theories, especially in Peripatetic and Stoic speculation, in an independent manner. God is conceived as the source and goal
of everything; from him everything comes, to him all things return; he is
the alpha and omega, the beginning, middle, and end. Communion with
God or absorption in God, therefore, is the real object of all our strivings,
and religion the heart-beat of the universe.

A number of stages may be distinguished in the school: (1) The Alex-
andrian-Roman school, to which belong: Ammonius Saccas (175-242 A.D.),
the founder, who left no writings; Plotinus (204-269), who develops the
system; and Porphyry (232-304), his pupil. (2) The Syrian school, represented by Iamblichus (d. 330). (3) The Athenian school, of which Plutarch
the younger (350-433) and Proclus (411-485) are the chief figures.

On Neoplatonism see E. R. Dodds, *Select Passages Illustrative of Neoplatonism,* 1924;
P. E. More, *Hellenistic Philosophies,* 1923; T. Whittaker, *The Neoplatonists,* 2nd ed.,
1928; R. Klibansky, *The Continuity of the Platonic Tradition,* 1939.

Plotinus. Plotinus (204-269) was born in Lycopolis, Egypt, and studied philosophy under Ammonius Saccas in Alexandria for eleven years. In 243 he went to Rome, where he established a school; but he did not put his philosophy in writing until he was fifty years old. After his death (269), his pupil Porphyry revised and published his manuscripts, with a biography of his teacher, arranging them in six Enneads, or series of nine writings each. This work has come down to us.

Translations of Plotinus' *Enneads* by S. Mackenna, 1917-30; G. H. Turnbull, *The Essence of Plotinus*, 1934; translations also in G. H. Clark, *Selections from Hellenistic Philosophy*, 1940; B. A. G. Fuller, *The Problem of Evil in Plotinus*, 1912; W. R. Inge, *The Philosophy of Plotinus*, 2 vols., 3rd ed., 1948; E. Bréhier, *La philosophie de Plotin*, 1928; A. H. Armstrong, *The Architecture of the Intelligible Universe in the Philosophy of Plotinus*, 1940; B. Switalski, *Plotinus and the Ethics of St. Augustine*, 1946.

God the source of all being. God is the source of all existence, of all oppositions and differences, of mind and body, form and matter, but is himself devoid of all plurality and diversity, and absolutely one. He is the One who in his infinity contains everything; he is the first causeless cause from which everything is produced, from which everything emanates; for plurality always presupposes unity; unity is prior to all being and beyond all being. His transcendence is such that whatever we say of him merely limits him; hence we cannot attribute to him beauty or goodness, or thought or will, for all such attributes are limitations and, in reality, imperfections. We cannot say what he is, but only what he is not. We cannot define him as being, for being is thinkable, and what is thinkable implies subject and object, and is, therefore, a limitation. He is higher than beauty, truth, goodness, consciousness, and will, for all these depend on him. We cannot conceive him as thinking, because this implies a thinker and a thought; even a self-conscious being, who thinks himself, divides into subject and object. To say that God thinks and wills is to limit him by what he thinks and wills, and, therefore, to rob him of his absolute independence.

Although the world proceeds from God, he did not create it, for creation implies consciousness and will, i.e., limitation. God did not decide to create a world, nor is the world an evolution from God, for God is the most perfect. The universe is an emanation from God, an inevitable overflow of his infinite power or actuality. Plotinus employs several metaphors to suggest the meaning of emanation. God is a spring from which the stream flows without exhausting its infinite source; or, God is the sun from which the light radiates without loss to the sun. He uses these metaphors to convey the absolute power and independence of the first principle. The cause does not pass over into, or lose itself in, its effect; the effect does not limit the cause;

the effect is non-essential so far as God is concerned. The world depends on God, but he does not depend on the world. God, like the parent in organic reproduction, continues the same after the birth of his offspring.

The farther we are from the sun, the source of light, the nearer we are to darkness (matter). Creation is a fall from the perfect to the imperfect, and the farther down we go in the scale of being, the greater the imperfection, plurality, change, and separation we find. Every later stage is the necessary effect of the preceding one—its copy, its shadow, its accident. But every later stage also strives for the higher, turns back to its source, finds its purpose or goal in that from which its being is derived.

Three stages of being. Three principal stages may be distinguished in the process of emanation: (1) pure thought or mind, (2) soul, and (3) matter. In the first stage, God's being divides into thought and ideas, that is, God thinks thoughts, he contemplates the pure ideal cosmos. Thought and its ideas, subject and object, are, however, one at this stage, not separate in time or space: in the divine mind the thinker and his thoughts are one and the same. This is as it should be if God's thinking is to be perfect truth, for truth implies the oneness of thought and its object. God thinks his own thoughts, which flow from his very essence: in the divine mind the activity of thought—the thinker—and the thought are one and the same, not separate. His thought is not discursive, passing from idea to idea, from premise to conclusion, but intuitive, static, as it were, contemplating the system of ideas as a whole, and all at once. There are many ideas—as many as there are particular things in the phenomenal world—and they differ from one another; but they form a unified system, as with Plato. The absolute unity of God, the first principle, is reflected in this *system* of many different ideas.

For each particular object in the sense world, there is an idea in the mind of God. The world of pure thought is spaceless and timeless; it is a perfect, eternal and harmonious intelligible world which provides the pattern or model of the phenomenal world. The ideas are not merely patterns; they are also efficient causes; every stage in the process of emanation is, as we have seen, the cause of the succeeding one.

The soul, the second stage of the divine emanation, proceeds from pure thought; wherever there are ideas or purposes, they must seek to realize themselves, to produce something. It is the effect, image, or copy of pure thought, and—like every effect or copy—less perfect than the original. It is supersensuous and intelligible; it is active and has ideas; it possesses the power of thought, though, being discursive, in less complete form than pure thought, it is self-conscious, though transcending perception and memory. There are two phases of the soul: in the first it is turned in the direction of pure thought; in the second, it is turned in the direction of the world of sense; in the former, it acts as thought and contemplates pure ideas; in the latter, it is impelled to bring order into matter and has desire. The first phase Plotinus calls the world-soul, the second phase he calls nature. Sometimes he speaks as if there were two world-souls: the second, constituting the unconscious soul of corporeal existence, emanates from the first—the conscious soul. As conscious soul, having ideas, contemplating the mind, it is indivisible; as soul with the desire to animate the objects of the phenomenal world, it is capable of division.

The soul cannot realize its desire to exercise its powers, to act and to form, unless it has something to act on; thus it produces matter—the third and lowest level of emanation. Matter, as such, has neither form, quality, power nor unity; it is absolute impotence and privation, the principle of evil. It is farthest removed from God; it is darkness. We can form no image of it; all we can do is to assume it as the necessary substratum behind the phenomena of changing qualities, as that which persists in our passing world of sense. Upon this matter, the efficient powers or souls which are contained in the world-soul and are identical with its ideas, act, fashioning it into a sensuous image or copy of the intelligible world contained in the divine intelligence. These particular powers or souls which impress themselves upon matter, thereby producing particular sensible objects in space and in time, are themselves all comprehended in the indivisible world-soul, and as such neither exist in space nor are spread out. The spatial arrangement of objects is due solely to matter; the beauty, order, and unity of the phenomenal universe are due to the world-soul, which harks back to God.

Plotinus conceives the emanation of the world from the world-soul as a necessary consequence of its nature, not as a process that has begun in time— in response, say, to an act of will. The emanation of the world-soul from pure thought, the creation of matter, the differentiation of matter into bodies, constitute one continuous process, which abstract thought can analyze into phases, but which are one eternal and indivisible act. With Aristotle, Plotinus teaches the eternity of the universe. At the same time, he tells us that matter can receive its forms only successively, and that the world-soul creates time in order that it may operate. He likewise accepts the Stoic doctrine of periodical recurrence. How these views are to be reconciled, he does not indicate: the general thought he seeks to impress is that the world has always been and always will be, and that the world of sense, as a whole, is eternal, though its parts change.

The human soul. The soul of man is a part of the world-soul, and as such is supersensuous and free. Originally, before its incarnation, it contemplated the eternal *nous* in mystical intuition, it pointed toward God and knew the good; but then it turned its gaze toward earth and body, and so fell. This fall is in part the necessary consequence of the world-soul's desire to fashion matter, partly the result of an irresistible impulse for a life of sense on the part of the particular soul itself. In this way the soul has lost its original freedom, for its freedom consists in turning in the other direction, away from sensuality, in accordance with its higher nature. If it fails to do this, that is, if it remains steeped in the bodily life, it becomes attached after death to another human, animal, or plant body, according to the degree of its guilt. The part of the soul which radiates into the material body, however, is not the real self, but merely a shadow of it, the irrational, animal part of the soul, the seat of the appetites and of sense perception, the source of sin and even of virtue. The true self consists of thought and logos; it can realize its mission only by turning from the sensuous life to thought, and, through it, to God. But this return to God is possible in this earthly life only on rare occasions.

Mysticism. In order to reach the goal of union with God, the ordinary virtues will not suffice. Moderation of impulses is not enough; the soul must purge itself of all sensuality, free itself from the contamination of the body. There is, however, a still higher stage to be reached than purification, which is only a preparation for theoretical contemplation, or the immediate intuition of ideas; theory is superior to practice, because it brings us nearer to the vision of God. The highest stage, however, union with God, cannot be realized even by thought of this exalted kind; it is possible only in a state of ecstasy, in which the soul transcends its own thought, loses itself in the soul of God, becomes one with God. This is the mystical return to God.

This system is a combination of Greek philosophy and Oriental religion. It is theistic in teaching a transcendent God, pantheistic in conceiving everything, down to the lowest matter, as an emanation of God. It is religious idealism, for the final goal of the soul is to find rest in the mind of God; and, though this is beyond attainment in this life, man should prepare for it by keeping his mind on God, by freeing himself from the shackles of sense.

Plotinus does not reject polytheism; gods, too, are manifestations of the divine. He also believes in the existence of good and evil demons in the sub-lunary regions, and in the possibility of psychic action in the distance: the entire universe being spiritual, it seems but natural that spirits should act upon one another sympathetically. Many of his successors exaggerated these superstitions, defended the popular polytheism, attacked the Christian religion, and reveled in magic and theurgy.

Later Neoplatonism. Porphyry of Tyre (232-304), a pupil of Plotinus, published the writings of his teacher with an account of his life. His object was to give an exposition of the philosophy of Plotinus rather than to develop it. He lays greater emphasis than the master on asceticism and the popular religion as means of purification, and hence accepts all kinds of superstitious beliefs and practices, such as demonology, prophecy, idolatry, magic, and theurgy. He also wrote a biography of Pythagoras, commentaries on some of Plato's and Aristotle's works, an *Introduction to the Categories* (of Aristotle), an *Outline* (of the philosophy of Plotinus), a *Letter to Anebo on Demons,* and fifteen books *Against the Christians.* The *Introduction,* which played an important rôle in the philosophy of the Middle Ages, the *Outline* (in Latin translation), the biographies of Plotinus and Pythagoras, the *Letter,* and the fragments of a short commentary, are still extant.

Iamblichus (d. *ca.* 330) of the Syrian school, a follower of Neopythagoreanism as well as of Neoplatonism, made use of philosophy largely as a defense and proof of his polytheistic religion. Superstition plays a still greater rôle in his doctrines than in those of Porphyry. Among his writings are: *On the Life of Pythagoras, Exhortation to Philosophy,* and commentaries on Plato and Aristotle.

Among the followers of Iamblichus were Julian the Apostate (Emperor from 361-363), who attempted to restore the old religion; Theodorus of Asine; Themistius, an excellent commentator of Plato and Aristotle; Macrobius; Olympiodorus; and Hypatia, an able expositor of the works of Plato and Aristotle, who was put to death by the Christians in Alexandria (415). One of her pupils was Synesius, who later became a Christian bishop.

Iamblichus, *The Egyptian Mysteries,* trans. by A. Wilder, 1915, and Porphyry, *Life of Pythagoras,* trans. by T. Taylor, 1818 (3rd ed., 1918).

Closing of the School at Athens. Neoplatonism was revived in the fifth century by Proclus (410-485), the head of the Academy at Athens. He was succeeded by Marius, Isidorus, and Damascius. In 529 the school at Athens was closed by an edict of the Emperor Justinian, and the history of Greek phi-

losophy came to an official end. After this time, some good commentaries on
the writings of Plato and Aristotle were published by Simplicius, the younger
Olympiodorus, Boethius, the author of the well-known *Consolations,* and
Philoponus. The works of Boethius, as well as his translations of Aristotelian
writings and of Porphyry's *Introduction,* contributed largely to the knowledge of Greek philosophy in the early Middle Ages.

Boethius (480-524), author of the celebrated *Consolation of Philosophy,*
is the best known figure of the final period of Greek philosophy. He attained
high political office under Theodoric, but his political career came to a
sudden end when he was accused of conspiracy against Theodoric and was
imprisoned; during his imprisonment he wrote the *Consolation,* which takes
its place along with Marcus Aurelius' *Meditations* and Thomas à Kempis'
Imitation of Christ among the great documents in which religious, ethical,
and philosophical ideas are applied in the personal life of their authors.
The religious and philosophical ideas to which the *Consolation* appeals are:
the governance of the world by a Divine Providence, which, however, is
not incompatible with the freedom of the individual man, and the acceptance
of human suffering in the knowledge that Divine Providence insures that
the good shall be ultimately triumphant.

The life span of Greek philosophy which began in the sixth century B.C.
extends into the early years of the sixth century A.D. Greek Platonism during
its final religious period made a desperate attempt to maintain itself in
competition with the new Christian world-view but Greek philosophy at
this period had lost its vitality. Its efforts to resuscitate the old polytheism
and to save the old civilization were in vain; it had outlived its usefulness.
The future belonged to the Christianity against which Greek philosophy
in its final phase was engaged in a bitter contest; and, by a strange irony
of fate, the Christian religion, in its attempt to conquer the intellectual
world, made an ally of the philosophy of the Greeks.

Proclus, *Elements of Theology,* trans. by E. R. Dodds, 1933; L. J. Rosán, *The Philosophy of Proclus,* 1949. W. J. Sedgfield, ed., *King Alfred's Version of the Consolations
of Boethius* (in modern English), 1900; L. Cooper, *A Consolation of Boethius,* 1928;
H. R. Patch, *Tradition of Boethius,* 1936; K. Dürr, *The Propositional Logic of Boethius,*
1953.

PART TWO

Medieval Philosophy

a form of Christianity which has been called Hellenistic Christianity, and which is exemplified by St. Paul. The new religion sought to set forth its dogmas in forms adapted both to the emotions of the common man and the intelligence of the educated, and to differentiate itself from the pagan and Jewish doctrines prevalent in the ancient world. In the writings of St. Paul—particularly in his Epistle to the Hebrews—and in the Gospel according to St. John, two features of patristic philosophy may already be discerned: first, the exaltation of the person of Jesus Christ, the incarnate and unique Son of God; and second, the interpretation of the person of Christ in terms of the philosophic concepts then dominant in the Hellenistic world.

The Christian apprehension of the nature of the person of Jesus Christ received no definitive form until it merged with philosophic speculation. As expressed in St. Paul's writings, it contains only the germ of the later doctrine of the Trinity and of the union of the human and divine natures in Christ. Moreover, that the Pauline doctrine also contained anticipations of formulae other than those finally accepted is well attested by the controversies prior to the Council of Nicaea. The doctrine of the Trinity, on which the whole theology of Western Christianity is ultimately based, was not given a definitive form until the Council of Nicaea in 325. It was not established as a secure and accepted basis for the new Church until the Trinitarian disputes involved in the controversy between the Arians and the followers of Athanasius had been settled by the Council of Constantinople in 381, and until the further disputes regarding the relation between the divine and the human nature in Christ were ended, at least for the West, by the Council of Chalcedon in 451. Prior to these developments there was considerable theological controversy, employing the philosophic terminology then current in the Hellenistic world. This terminology is largely Platonic and Christian philosophizing in the ante-Nicene period, and belongs for the most part in the Neoplatonic tradition deriving from Philo. Stoic and Aristotelian elements are also present in early Christian thought, but the Neoplatonic elements are dominant. Indeed, the Christian philosophy of this period at times gives the impression that the Christian elements, in being assimilated to Hellenistic philosophy, lose many of their distinctive and unique features, whereas the Hellenistic elements undergo little transformation in the process. This is true of most ante-Nicene philosophy, which had its stronghold in Eastern and Greek centers. It is true above all of Origen (d. 254), who succeeded Clement as head of the Christian school in Alexandria.

The Council of Nicaea (325) turned away from Neoplatonism when it devised a formula for the Christian conception of Jesus Christ which described him as the Son of God, and as being at the same time himself truly God incarnate. For Christian Neoplatonism had tended by its principle of emanation to make the *Logos,* identified with Christ, a kind of secondary deity, intermediate between a transcendent God and the world of sensible things. Indeed, the Nicene definition was devised in specific repudiation of the heresy of Arius, presbyter of Alexandria, whose philosophical predecessors were Philo, Origen and the Neoplatonists. In the course of the proceedings of the Council, the earlier deposition of Arius by an Alexandrian synod was confirmed and his teachings were anathematized. The Nicene definition established the meaning of the faith which Christians were to hold, and its defenders had recourse less to philosophical or theological speculation than to Scripture as they understood it.

It was Athanasius who, in the course of controversies with the Arians which continued for many years, gave the Nicene formula a more philosophical character. He had been present at Nicaea as a deacon, and in 328 succeeded Alexander as bishop in the episcopate of Alexandria. Athanasius completed the Nicene definition in such a way as to include the third member of the Trinity—the Holy Spirit—and achieved a definition which became the starting point of a genuinely philosophical doctrine. By doing this he set the stage for St. Augustine's formulation of a truly Christian philosophy, which made use of Hellenistic and classical Greek phraseology without being subservient to it.

Although the fourth century was a turbulent one, both in the doctrinal life of the new Church and in the political life of the Empire, it was a time in which the Empire remained for the most part intact. But at the very end of the century, the outlook began to change. The year 395 in which Theodosius died is indeed often cited as the last year in which the whole of the Roman Empire was under a reasonably effective and unified rule. Thereafter, with the accession of his two sons, Honorius and Arcadius, East and West go their separate ways. In the West, which was the theater for the development of medieval Christian philosophy, there existed no effective rule except that supplied by one or the other commander of the Germanic invaders. In 392, just three years before his death, Theodosius proclaimed the Christian religion—which in its orthodox form had been so ardently defended and so subtly expounded by the indefatigible Athanasius in the years after Nicaea—as the official religion of his realm. In the chaotic fifth century this religion remained the only organized bearer of the rich Graeco-Roman heritage of the Western Empire, and became the seminal power through which the classical tradition, now transformed into a mature and self-aware Christian dogma, was passed on to the northern invaders. Patristic philosophy, which combined Christian elements with those derived from the Graeco-Roman philosophical tradition, provided the materials of the medieval synthesis achieved during the Scholastic Period and thereby determined the complexion of Western European civilization of the Middle Ages.

The Scholastic Period. After the establishment of the fundamental doctrines and the triumph of Christianity as an organized Church, there began a period of philosophical construction devoted to the elaboration of a philosophy in which the subject-matter and guiding principles were determined by dogma. This Christian philosophy, which constitutes the largest part of the philosophy of the Middle Ages, had for its aim the exposition, systematization, and demonstration of the Christian dogmas and the construction of a theory of the world and of life on a Christian basis. The thinkers who performed this service were called schoolmen and their systems scholastic philosophy. Scholastic philosophy derived its doctrinal commitments from Christian dogmas as formulated by the Church Fathers, but cast these in a philosophical mold which bore the stamp of the methods and concepts of Greek philosophy.

Although the schoolmen drew upon Greek philosophy for the solution of the problems confronting them, their attitude of mind was not that of the ancient thinkers. The aim of the Greek philosophers had been to give a rational explanation of the universe, independent of the popular religion, and they approached the task in a more or less scientific spirit—often even in a spirit antagonistic to the prevailing creed. The schoolmen, on the other hand, accepted the truths of Christianity as beyond dispute; these formed the point of departure and regulative principles of their speculation; and these they sought to render intelligible and reasonable. To accomplish this, they had recourse to such systems of Greek thought as best suited their purpose; with them, philosophy was placed in the service of religion; it became the handmaiden of theology (*ancilla theologiae*).

Within the limits set by Christian dogma, the mind was left free to exercise its skill; so long as it did not conflict with established truths, human reason could interpret the world as it pleased. In the course of time, however, the intellect began to free itself from its theological bondage and to seek satisfaction outside the circumscribed domain; the scholastic attitude and method proved unsatisfactory, and attempts were made to construct philosophical systems on a basis independent of Christian dogma. The entire rationalistic movement of scholasticism was also attacked from another side: the dogmas and the whole ecclesiastical system were criticized and the inner religious life transformed by appealing to the Bible and the individual conscience. The reform of Christianity in its theoretical and practical aspects culminated in the two preludes to the modern era: the Renaissance and the Reformation.

18. The Beginnings of Christianity

Early Christianity. During the last period of Hellenic speculation a new religion, which possessed many elements to recommend it to the times, was making converts in the Roman world. This religion, which had sprung from the soil of Judaism, preached the gospel of a Father-God who is merciful and just and loves all his children alike, and promised the redemption of mankind through Jesus Christ, his Son. It taught that no man was too lowly to be saved, that there was hope for all, that Christ would come again to establish his kingdom, first on earth and then in heaven, but, whether on earth or in heaven, it would be a kingdom of righteousness and love. It taught that, on the judgment day, the wicked, rich and powerful though they might be, would be confounded, and the pure in heart, however poor and lowly, would enter into glory. In promising deliverance from the sinful world and a future life of blessedness, Christianity struck a popular chord and satisfied a longing of the age. The conditions of deliverance were not made dependent on external and accidental goods, but on a virtuous life, repentance, and love of God and man. The Pharisaic conception of the literal interpretation of the Laws is transformed by the founder of Christianity into the doctrine of the righteousness of the spirit. Men should act from love and reverence for God and not from fear; purity of heart is of more avail, in the sight of God, than external observance of levitical rules and practices, the inner spirit of greater worth than outward forms. There is but one way to achieve salvation, and that is to rid oneself of evil passions, of envy, anger, hatred, and revenge; to forgive even those that hate us, for it is better to suffer wrong than to do wrong. Love and forgiveness take the place of hate and revenge. Every man shall love his neighbor as himself, and every human being is his neighbor.

Christianity and Classical Culture. With its spiritual monotheism, its doctrine of a life to come, its gospel of love, and the example of the suffering Christ, the new religion appealed to the Roman world-kingdom. As the number of its converts increased among the cultured classes, it could not ignore the philosophical conceptions rooted in the civilization in which it had to make its way. Indeed, Christianity, as it appeared in Palestine, owed its origin, in part at least, to this Graeco-Roman civilization; Judaism had not been able to resist the ethical, political, social, religious, and intellectual influences which pervaded the great Roman Empire, and the Christian revolt was in part a product of these influences. The new world-religion arrived when the times were ripe for its appearance. Among the factors which contributed to its appearance and spread were the existence of a universal empire; the growing spirit of cosmopolitanism and brotherhood, which Stoicism had done so much to inculcate; the prevalence of the concept of a spiritual deity as taught by the philosophers; the wide-spread acceptance of the doctrines of immortality of the popular Greek mysteries and Oriental religions; and the influence of the Jewish ideal of a personal God, which succeeded in awakening the religious spirit where the abstract notions of the metaphysicians had failed. Christianity was, in a large measure, a child of its age, a child of Judaism and Hellenic-Roman civilization. Nor did the influence of the age cease with the emergence of the new religion into the world; in addressing itself to Greeks and Romans, Christianity gradually assimilated the culture of the world to which it brought its tidings. Had the Jewish-Christian section of the new religion, which regarded itself as a phase of Judaism, triumphed, it is not unlikely that Christianity would have been buried beneath the walls of Jerusalem.

In order to deliver its message effectively, Christianity had to solve a number of challenging problems. It had to justify its faith to reason, to defend itself against the attacks of the publicists and philosophers who in time came to take notice of it. It was necessary for its leaders to meet their opponents on their own ground, to make use of the philosophical conceptions familiar to them, to fight them with their own intellectual weapons—their own philosophy. Such defenders of the faith, or Apologists, appeared when they were needed. But it was also necessary to define the new creed, to formulate articles of faith, to establish a body of doctrine or dogmas. Here, again, minds trained in philosophy were of service in giving rational expression to the traditional beliefs of the Christian communities; and once more Greek thought exercised a significant influence on Christianity. The dogmas were officially defined by the great councils of the Church. The victorious creed became the orthodox creed, and its protagonists became the Fathers of the Church; the Christian philosophy they formulated is Patristic philosophy.

Christianity as a Creed. The Christian creed emerged from the interplay of the new faith and classical philosophy. It should be pointed out that the

Church had organized itself in institutional forms drawn from contemporary secular society: the bishop, for instance, exercised functions analogous to those of the officers of the municipality. It had given the episcopal system a means of unified action in the form of synods of bishops, and it had based the system on an authoritative apostolic tradition, in which the position of the episcopate of Rome was already central. It had culled a canon of sacred Scripture from the mass of writings associated with the founders of the Church; and, finally, it had formulated its faith, rather than its philosophy, in brief summaries or creeds. The importance of the creed, or rule of faith (*regula fidei*), which was professed by believers at baptism, can hardly be overestimated. It embodied doctrines to which the believer must cleave, however difficult he might find it to give them a philosophical form, should a private speculative bent cause him to make the attempt. Such a creed, in a form from which the Apostles' Creed as we know it is derived, was already a tradition in the third century in the Church at Rome. It expressed faith in One God, and in his only Son, Jesus Christ, who was made Man by being born of the Holy Ghost and the Virgin Mary; and it promised, in the doctrine of the resurrection of the flesh, eternal life to the whole man.

The Church's view of salvation maintained the infinite worth of the individual human soul, and carried with it a sense of universal brotherhood in Christ, under the rule of love. The commonwealth, taken as an ultimate standard for the behavior of man to man, was thereby challenged, and with it the idea of reason that lay at the heart of the classical conception of ethics. It is not strange, therefore, that a very complex kind of anti-secularism should have arisen at an early date. This tendency had already found expression in St. Paul, for whom the wisdom of this world was mere foolishness; and later in Justin the Martyr—whose point of view on these matters is that of a second-century convert from Platonism—and in Tertullian's attack on all the values and pretensions of the Empire. It culminates, finally, in St. Augustine's distinction between the earthly city and the City of God—a distinction which arose from reflections provoked by the sack of Rome in 410.

Our main contention is that the Christians achieved, in virtue of their faith, an independence from the premises and scheme of values of the classical world, and that they were therefore able to confront the heritage of Rome and Greece with a sense of assurance. In the third century, which we have chosen because it marks an important turning point, Tertullian was perfectly aware of the rôle played by faith in the achievement of a new attitude toward the state, history, and nature. His condemnation of reason, in its classical sense, as a source of error, confusion, and heresy, was extreme and is expressed in this characteristic pronouncement: "The Son of God was born. I am not ashamed of it because it is shameful; the Son of God died, it is credible for the very reason that it is silly; and, having been buried, He rose again, it is certain because it is impossible." [2] This is a polemical overstatement of the Christian position, but it suggests to us that in the third century, from the point of view of Christianity as a faith, classicism was bankrupt both in epistemology and ethics.

The assurance characteristic of Christianity as a faith and an institution does not extend to Christianity as a body of philosophical speculation; the Christian effort to give religion an expression in terms of the prevailing philosophies of the age was, at least in the third century, in a much less happy condition than the Church taken as a whole, as an institution and a faith. The speculative effort initiated by the Apologists of the second century underwent its most trying test in its battle with the first great Christian heresy, that of the Gnostics. Its exponents in the third century, at the time of Tertullian, are Clement and Origen of the Catechetical School of Alexandria. Clement of Alexandria (d. 216) was the first head of the school; he was followed by Origen (185-254), who is perhaps the most important figure illustrating the relationship between Christianity and philosophy in the third century. We can, however, form no clear idea of the temper of the time if we forget that this is also the century of Plotinus (204-289), who gave Neoplatonism the definitive form we have already studied; for the tendencies of his philosophy dominate the *philosophical* tone of the age, and are especially evident in the work of Origen, who attended for a time the school of Ammonius Saccas, the founder of Neoplatonism and teacher of Plotinus.

19. The Development of Christian Theology

Early Theology. The new religion was compelled to define its doctrines and to construct a Christian theology declaring its attitude toward the prevailing Jewish and Hellenistic theological traditions. A main source of Christian dogmatic theology is the writings of St. Paul. The Epistles ascribed to him betray the influence of the so-called *Wisdom of Solomon*—a work doubtless known to Paul—in which Christ is identified with God's power and wisdom, the Logos. The historical elements of Christianity are interpreted in the light of the Greek Logos-doctrine; religious and philosophical elements are welded together in a way to emphasize the religious aspect. The Logos is a person, the Son of a Living Father, not a cold philosophical abstraction.

[2] *De Carne Christi*, trans. by Cochrane in *Christianity and Classical Culture*, p. 223.

The Gnostics. The Gnostics were theologians of the second century who sought to rationalize the new religion; to transform faith into knowledge (*gnosis*). They speculated upon their faith, and sought a harmony of faith and knowledge, religion and science.

Gnosticism is an embryonic scholasticism, crude and fantastic though it is. The Christian Philonists, as we might call them, asserted that their doctrines had been transmitted by Jesus to such of his followers as were able to receive them, and that they constituted the secret or esoteric doctrine of the educated Christian. They taught that Christianity was an entirely new and divine doctrine, Judaism a corrupt form of religion, the revelation of an inferior being, and paganism the work of evil spirits. The Jewish God, or Demiurge, they regarded as a false God, opposed to the kingdom of light, the abode of the highest spirits, and to the true God. Christ, one of the highest spirits, entered a human body in order to free the spirits of light imprisoned in matter by the Demiurge. Those able to comprehend the genuine teachings of Christ become gnostics, or "pneumatic beings," and are eventually delivered from their material bondage—asceticism being one of the means of escape; those who cannot free themselves from sensuous matter perish with it, while the literalists or "psychic beings" go to the heaven of the Demiurge. The world is the result of a fall; matter is the principle of evil. The exoteric doctrine is contained in the Christian creed; the esoteric doctrine is a secret tradition transmitted to the Gnostics.

Chief among the Gnostics are: Cerinthus, Saturninus, and Valentine. The system of Marcion, who formed a church at Rome in 144, and accepted as canonical the Gospel of St. Luke and ten Pauline Epistles, contains teachings resembling Gnosticism; but since it emphasizes faith instead of knowledge, it cannot be assigned to this sect.

E. de Faye, *Gnostiques et Gnosticism,* 2nd ed., 1925; E. K. Rand, *Founders of the Middle Ages,* 1928.

It is evident that the Gnostics were not equal to their task: instead of a genuinely philosophical system, they offered only a "semi-Christian mythology." Besides, their doctrines were in conflict with the prevailing concepts of the teaching of Jesus; their repudiation of the Old Testament, their distinction between an esoteric and exoteric Christianity, their conception of Jesus as a man whose body is used by a heavenly Christ, a creature far beneath God and even beneath the angels, their belief in specially endowed natures or pneumatic beings, and their allegorical interpretations antagonized the Apologists and other conservative leaders of Christianity, and were denounced as heresies. At the same time, the gnostic movement exercised a considerable influence on the new religion and its theology and gave an impetus to the philosophical formulation of the faith by Christian theology. Some of the fundamental ideas of Gnosticism, deriving from Greek philosophy, found their way into the works of the early writers of the Church, and became formative factors in the evolution of the dogma.

The Apologists. The Apologists shared with the Gnostics their general aim of rendering the new religion intelligible; they appealed to philosophy in their defense of the faith against the heathen as well as against the fantastic interpretations of Gnosticism. For them, Christianity was both philosophy and revelation; its truths were of supernatural origin and absolutely certain, but they were *rational* truths, even though they could be comprehended only by a divinely inspired mind. In the words of Harnack:

> The conviction common to them all may be summed up as follows: Christianity is philosophy, because it has a rational content, because it gives a satisfactory and universally intelligible answer to the questions which all true philosophers have endeavored to answer; but it is not philosophy, indeed it is the direct opposite of philosophy . . . in so far as it is revealed truth and, hence, has a supernatural, divine origin, upon which alone the truth and certainty of its teaching ultimately rests.[3]

The Apologists were acquainted with the literature and philosophy of their times and addressed themselves to the educated classes. Indeed, many of the early leaders of the Church were men who, after their conversion, took up the cudgels for the new religion and sought to win favor for it among the literate and educated. This explains why the philosophical element generally predominates in their writings and why the purely religious aspect is so often relegated to the background.

Among the leaders in this field are: Justin the Martyr (d. 166), Tatian, Athenagoras, Theophilus, Irenaeus (b. 120-130), Hippolytus, Minucius Felix (second century), Tertullian (160-240), Cyprian (200-258), Clement of Alexandria (d. 216), and Origen (185-254). The movement culminated in the catechetical schools, perhaps the first of which was established in Alexandria in 180 by Pantaenus, formerly a Stoic philosopher. The object of these schools was not only to defend the new religion and demonstrate its reasonableness, but to reduce the teaching to systematic form for the benefit of the clergy, whose duty it became to instruct the pagan and Jewish proselytes in the principles of the Christian religion. Origen, the greatest leader of the Alex-

[3] *Outlines of History of Dogma,* trans. by Mitchell, p. 121.

andrian school, worked out a comprehensive Christian theology in which, as has been noted, the influence of Neoplatonism, which had its home at Alexandria, is evident.

Collections of the writings of the Fathers (Latin and Greek) edited by Migne, 1840; de Gerhardt and others, 1875; new edition, *Corpus Scriptorum Ecclesiasticorum Latinorum* by the Vienna Academy (since 1866); Collection of the Greek Fathers of the first three centuries by the Prussian Academy (since 1897); English trans. in *The Ante-Nicene Christian Library,* ed. by Roberts and Donaldson, and in *Library of Nicene and Post-Nicene Fathers,* ed. by Schaff and Wace.

E. R. Goodenough, *The Theology of Justin Martyr,* 1923.

Teachings of the Apologists. The fundamental thought in the writings of the Apologists is this: The world, though perishable, exhibits traces of reason and order, and points to one eternal, unchangeable, good and just First Cause, the source of all life and being. This principle transcends all life and being: the sublimity, power, wisdom, goodness, and grace of God are beyond all human notions, beyond all description. Yet the First Cause of all creation must be rational; reason must always have been potential in him as a part of his inner nature; and to the presence of reason, or the Logos, in God, are due the order and purpose in the universe. In other words, reason and goodness lie at the root of the world, and God is the eternal and abiding principle in all change.

By an act of free will God emits the Logos: the Logos proceeds from him as the light proceeds from the sun. As the light emitted from the sun does not separate from the sun, so the divine reason does not separate from God in the procession; by generating the reason which is, indeed, inseparable from him, God clearly does not lose his reason; the Logos remains with the Creator, subsists within the source whence it sprang. At the same time, the Logos is conceived as another personality—identical with God in essence, but numerically distinct from him—a second God who is coeternal with God. The Logos became man in Jesus Christ, Christ being the Logos incarnate, "the word made flesh." The Holy Ghost is another emanation from God, and is also conceived as an entity.

We encounter in these concepts the personification of divine reason with which we have become familiar in the Greek philosophy of religion. Reason is the instrument by which the world is fashioned and through which God indirectly acts on the world. The transcendency of God is proclaimed, and yet the attempt is also made to maintain the independence of the Logos. The Logos is conceived to be eternally with God or coeternal with him, potential, identical with him in his very nature; and, at the same time, the

Father is said, by Irenaeus, for example, to be the source of the being and activity of the Logos, and hence the Logos would seem to be a creature subordinated to the Father. Moreover, the Logos becomes a person by God's will; there was thus a time when he was not, and this again implies that he is a creature. Origen undertakes to solve this difficulty by combining both ideas in teaching that the Logos is eternally created. The act of creation is not an act in time, but is an eternal and continuing process (*semel et simul*); the Son is eternally and continuously created by the Father.

The creation of the world is interpreted in accordance with Greek ideas. God is the cause and purpose of all things; from him they come and to him they return. The Logos is the pattern, or archetype, of all created beings; everything is created in the image of reason and by the power of reason or divine intelligence. The Creator fashioned the world from formless matter, which he had created out of nothing, in conformity with a pattern or rational plan subsisting in his mind. This rationalistic system of thought is, for the Apologists, a personal entity, which, as an active cause, forms, preserves, and controls everything. According to the majority of the Apologists, creation is an act in time; according to Origen, God creates eternally, and creatures have always existed. The universe is for him, as it was for Aristotle, eternal, but the world now existing has had a beginning and will pass away, to be replaced by other and different worlds.

Creation is an expression of God's love and goodness and is for the benefit of man. But although the world was made for the sake of man, the goal of man resides not in this world, but in the hereafter. Other-worldliness, flight from the world, the withdrawal of the soul from the world of sense to God, is the highest good. The resurrection of the body and the soul is taught in some form by all the Apologists; sometimes both soul and body are regarded as mortal by nature, but capable of having immortality bestowed on them as an act of divine grace, in accordance with the soul's work (St. Justin); sometimes man is held to possess, in addition to body and soul, a higher spirit which is inherently immortal and through which both body and soul participate in immortality (Tatian). This spirit, as distinguished from the soul, is said by some Apologists to be conferred by God upon those souls which control their passions.

Another teaching common to the Apologists is that of free will and the fall of man. God created spirits with the capacity to distinguish between good and evil, and the freedom to choose between them. Some of these spirits chose, in disobedience to God, to turn toward the flesh and away from him; as a punishment for this sin, they fell to a lower level of life—a life in carnal bodies. Man, by leading a Christian life, may regain his lost estate through divine grace and the revealed truth of the Logos. On the day of judgment, after a sojourn in Hades or Purgatory, the just will enter eternal life and the unjust will be forever rejected. Origen alone believed in the final redemption of all. The theme running through the teaching of the Apologists is that, in sinning, the first man or a heavenly spirit, as the case may be, brought sin into the world, for which mankind is suffering, but that there is hope for ultimate redemption if man will only turn away from the things of sense and seek to be reunited with God.

The fundamental article of faith declares that the human race is redeemed by Jesus Christ, the Son of God, that the Son of God came to deliver man from sin. This simple proposition gave rise to a number of problems which Christian theologians debated for centuries, and which were officially settled only after long and bitter controversies. The proposition contained three important notions: God, Jesus Christ, and man. How shall we conceive God the Father, the Son of God, and human nature in the scheme of salvation? How are these beings related to one another: the Father and the Son, or Logos; the Son and the man Jesus; and God and man?

The Logos Doctrine. The Logos doctrine, which appears so prominently in early Christian theology, did not penetrate into the rank and file of the early Church. The simple-minded Christian of the first centuries, living in a polytheistic community, believed in the Father, Son, and Holy Ghost without interpreting his faith metaphysically; for him Jesus the man was somehow the Son of God, and the Holy Ghost was a second supernatural being; the metaphysical nature and relation of the Son of God and the Holy Ghost to one another and to God, he did not attempt to fathom. The intellectual leaders of the Church, in their endeavors to defend the faith against Gnostics and pagan philosophers, were carried farther and farther into the speculations of the Greek schools, until they finally hellenized the Gospels. It was inevitable that the Logos doctrine should meet with serious opposition in many quarters and that efforts be made to reach a less metaphysical interpretation of the fundamentals of the faith. Many sects arose which sought to express the teachings of Christianity in a form intelligible to those unfamiliar with theological speculations. The doctrine which had the largest following among Christian groups from 130 to 300 was Modalism, which appeared as Patripassianism in the Western Roman world and as Sabellianism in the East. According to the former, God assumed flesh, became man, and suffered in the flesh—hence the designation Patripassianism;

according to the latter, God manifests himself in three successive ways or powers, as Father, Son, and Holy Ghost. In either case, the three persons are one and the same God in different forms or modes (modalism).

But these loosely conceived views did not prevail against the Logos theology; by the end of the third century the philosophical theology had triumphed, and, in the words of Harnack, "even read its articles into the creed." The influence of Origen prevailed; his successors made the faith so philosophical that it became unintelligible to laymen. The purely cosmological and philosophical elements were emphasized at the expense of the idea of salvation; in some formulations of the doctrine, the name of Christ was not even mentioned. The Neoplatonism of Origen's system threatened to swamp Christianity.

The question of the relation of the Logos to God, or of the Son to the father, formed the subject of a great controversy at the Council of Nicaea, in 325, between the Arians, the followers of Arius, and the anti-Arians, of whom Athanasius afterwards became the leader. According to Arius, Christ is a creature of God, endowed with free will, which God foresaw he would use for good; he therefore conferred on him the dignity of a God at his creation. According to Athanasius, the Son, as the principle of salvation, is begotten, not made, by the Father; he is coeternal with the Father, of one substance with the Father, sharing fully in the nature of the Father, without loss to the Father and without ceasing to be a distinct person. In the historical Jesus, the Logos-God, or the Son, was united, in essence, with a human body, in a complete incarnation. The Holy Ghost is a third being; the one Godhead is a trinity, consisting of three persons identical in substance.

The anti-Arians were victorious at the Council; the Arian doctrines were condemned and Arius and his followers excommunicated. The words "begotten, not made, being of one substance with the Father," were inserted in the creed which has come to be called the Nicene creed. Both parties to the controversy had sought support for their views in the Neoplatonic philosophy of Origen; and the orthodox interpretation, no less than the defeated theory, is based on the Logos doctrine. An unsuccessful attempt was later made to effect a compromise between Arianism and Athanasianism by declaring God and Christ to be, not of the *same* substance (*homoousios*), but of *like* nature (*homoiousios*), and failure to agree on this point led to a division between the Roman and Greek churches.

4 Cf. Harnack, *Outlines of History of the Dogma*, pp. 193 ff.

Another question which stirred up controversy was the problem of the relation of the man Jesus to the Logos-God, the Christological problem. Many answers were offered and many factions formed in support of different theories. The interpretation that Christ had two natures, "each perfect in itself and each distinct from the other, yet perfectly united in one person, who was at once both God and Man," was accepted by the Synod of Chalcedon, in 451, and became the orthodox dogma.

After the establishment of the dogma at Nicaea, Christian philosophy was studied chiefly in the school of Origen at Alexandria. The orthodox doctrines were adopted, in the main, and such teachings in Origen's system as conflicted with them were rejected. Among the representatives of the school who assisted in the work of reconstruction were Gregory of Nyssa (d. 394), Basil the Great (d. 379), and Gregory of Nazianzen (d. 390). Neoplatonism, as taught by Plotinus, also had a large following; among its leaders were: Bishop Synesius, Bishop Nemesius, Aeneas of Gaza, Zacharias Scholasticus, and Johannes Grammaticus (Johannes Philoponus), all of the sixth century. The Neoplatonic work, falsely attributed to Dionysius the Areopagite, appeared at the end of the fifth century.

Free Will and Original Sin. A third question demanded an official answer: What is the place of man in the scheme of salvation? According to one view, which was widespread, the whole human race had been corrupted by the sin of the first man or a fallen angel; and divine help, in some form or other, was needed to redeem mankind. The fundamental article of faith that Christ had come down from heaven for our salvation seemed to favor such an interpretation: if it was necessary to deliver man from sin, then evidently he could not save himself, he was a slave to sin and by nature a sinner (the doctrine of original sin), or had become a sinner in some way; in either case he was not free to save himself. This conception received support from the Manichaeans, a numerous sect accepting the teachings of the Persian Mani (d. 277), who read Persian dualism and Gnosticism into the Scriptures and combined Christianity with the doctrines of Zoroaster. They taught that the principle of light in man was under bondage to matter, the principle of darkness, and that the soul could be purified and enabled to return to the kingdom of light whence it came, only by asceticism, by abstention from meat, wine, marriage, property, and labor. But it was possible to read quite a different view into the article of faith: Christ came to save man from sin. Sin implies guilt, guilt implies responsibility on the part of the guilty person; only a being who is free to choose between right and wrong can be a sinner. Hence, if man sinned, he must have been free. The same conclusion was reached in another way: God is absolutely good and just, and cannot, therefore, be responsible for sin; man himself must be the author of sin, and hence, free.

Pelagius, a monk, came to Rome in the year 400, with a doctrine opposed to the notion of original sin: God is a good and just God, and everything created by him is good; hence, human nature cannot be radically evil. Adam was free to sin or not to sin; his sensuous nature, which is evil, prevailed, and he chose sin. Sin, however, cannot be transmitted from generation to generation, because every man has free will: sin implies freedom. Freedom has its source in an original act of divine grace; it is the first gift bestowed by a good God; hence man can, without outside help, resist sin and will the good. Although Adam's sin was not transmitted, the example of his sin was baneful, and the imitation of his bad example has become a habit which is difficult to overcome, and which explains man's fall. But the churchman asks: If man is not enslaved by sin, if his freedom of choice has not been destroyed, what part can divine grace and the Christian religion play in his redemption? The Pelagians reply that, by an act of divine grace, knowledge is revealed to man in Scripture, in the teachings and example of Jesus, and in the doctrines of the Church—knowledge which assists the human will in choosing the good, for example, the knowledge that baptism and faith in Jesus Christ are necessary to salvation. God, being omniscient, knows exactly what choices men are going to make in their lives—how they will use their power of freedom—and determines beforehand the rewards and punishments which shall be meted out to them (the doctrine of predestination).

K. Lake, ed., *The Apostolic Fathers*, Vol. I (Loeb Classical Library), 1913.

F. J. Hort, *Six Lectures on the Anti-Nicene Fathers*, 1895; W. Fairweather, *Origen and Greek Patristic Theology*, 1901; C. Bigg, *Christian Platonists of Alexandria*, 2nd ed., 1913; R. B. Tollinton, *Clement of Alexandria*, 1914, and *Alexandrian Teachings Concerning the Universe*, 1932; R. Cadion, *Origen and Greek Patristic Theology*, 1928; E. Faye, *Origen and His Work*, 1929; W. B. Warfield, *Studies in Tertullian and Augustine*, 1930.

The Nicene Creed. The development of Christian theology which culminates in Augustine does not derive its power primarily from speculations of the kind we have found in Origen, but from the doctrine of the Church expressed in the creeds, especially in the creed promulgated at Nicaea.

The spirit of the Nicaean achievement is best conveyed by describing the work of Athanasius. In his writings the problem of the relation between faith and reason is not presented in terms of a sharp contrast between that which is accepted on authority, and that which is rationally intelligible. The doctrine of the Trinity is indeed a mystery, the logical explanation of which is fraught with difficulties; but its reality, its workings and power in the world around us, are self-evident to the believer. It is a first principle on which all explanation must ultimately rest, and it is the source of the intelligibility of all other things. The categories that had hitherto seemed adequate and self-evident to the Greek mind now lose their persuasiveness, or at least their ultimacy, and nature no longer seems intelligible unless interpreted by categories of a higher sort. Although the doctrine of the Trinity stems from a religious insight or prejudice, it is also a defensible rational position. God is conceived as the source of all existence; both form and matter are viewed as dependent on a free creative act—the source of both Being (God the Father) and Order (God the Son). Athanasius, being primarily concerned with the significance of Christ, left the question of the third member of the Trinity to those who came after him. The doctrine of the coinherence of God the Father and God the Son, and of their common eternality, means that the Son is not to be conceived as a secondary demiurgic power, and that the dependence of all reality on the Father is not to be conceived as a necessitated emanation. If the objection be made that the doctrine of the Trinity—the basic premise—is unintelligible, Athanasius' reply is that it is intelligible in the highest religious sense, though not in a narrow rationalistic sense.

Just as the universe in its entirety depends on and derives its intelligibility from the Trinity, so do man and his history. A freely creating God bestows freedom, even to err, on human nature which, once fallen, can only be restored if God himself literally becomes man. According to Athanasius, Scripture held that Christ was always God the Son, the Word and Wisdom of the Father, and that he became man as the son of Mary, remaining at the same time wholly God and wholly man, both in his suffering and in his miracles. Other men are potential sharers in this Incarnation; the possibility of redemption is held out to them, as unified personal existences.

A. Harnack, *History of Dogma*, 7 vols., 1894-1899, *What Is Christianity?*, trans. by T. B. Saunders, 2nd ed., 1901, and *The Mission and Expansion of Christianity*, trans. by J. Moffatt, 2 vols., 1908; E. Bevan, *Hellenism and Christianity*, 1921; G. P. Fisher, *History of Christian Doctrine*, reprint, 1922; A. C. McGiffert, *The God of Early Christians*, 1924, and *A History of Christian Thought*, 2 vols., 1932-33; W. R. Holliday, *The Pagan Background of Early Christianity*, 1925; R. Jolivet, *Essai sur les rapports entre la pensée grècque et la pensée chrétienne*, 1931; S. J. Case, *Makers of Christianity*, 1934; K. S. Latourette, *The First Five Centuries*, 1937, and *A History of Christianity*, 1953; C. N. Cochrane, *Christianity and Classical Culture*, 1944; H. A. Wolfson, *The Philosophy of the Church Fathers*, Vol. I, 1956.

20. St. Augustine

St. Augustine was the greatest constructive thinker and the most influential teacher of the early Christian Church. In his system the most important theological and philosophical problems of his age are discussed, and a Christian world-view is developed which represents the culmination of patristic thought and becomes the guide of Christian philosophy for centuries to come. Augustine achieved a philosophy which, although not thoroughly systematic, touches on all the basic philosophical problems. St. Augustine was greatly indebted to classicism and availed himself of classical terminology —sometimes Platonic, sometimes Aristotelian—but the dominant factor in his philosophy is the Christian faith of Athanasius and Ambrose which he applies to ethics, epistemology, metaphysics, and the philosophy of history. At the heart of his philosophy is the doctrine of the Trinity, which in his monumental work, *On the Trinity,* he treats as the inexhaustible principle, accepted on faith, which sheds intelligibility on the whole of reality. In view of the significance of St. Augustine's views for medieval philosophy, as well as for the Christian theology of the Reformation and the modern period, we shall give a systematic exposition of the various aspects of his philosophy.

Aurelius Augustinus was born in Tagaste, North Africa, in 353, of a pagan father and a Christian mother, Monica, who exercised a profound influence on her son. He became a teacher of rhetoric, first in his native city, later at Milan (384-386), and devoted himself to a study of theological and philosophical questions, which carried him from Manichaeism to skepticism, and which left him unsatisfied. In 386 he began to read some of the writings of Plato and the Neoplatonists, which gave stability to his thought. At the same time, he came under the influence of the eloquent St. Ambrose, Bishop of Milan. After his conversion in 387 he returned to Tagaste, where, for three years (388-391), he lived according to monastic rules, and was ordained to the priesthood. In 396 he was raised to the bishopric of Hippo, in Africa, which he held until his death in 430, devoting his great gifts to the development and propagation of Catholic doctrine.

Among the works of St. Augustine are: *De libero arbitrio; De vera religione; De praedestinatione et gratia; De trinitate; De civitate Dei; Confessiones; Retractiones;* and *Letters.*

English translations: *Works,* ed. by Dods, 15 vols., 1871-77; *Letters of St. Augustine,* by W. J. Simpson, 1919; *Selected Letters,* by J. H. Baxter, 1931; *Basic Writings of St. Augustine,* ed. by W. J. Oates, 1950; R. H. Barrow, *Introduction to St. Augustine: The City of God,* 1950.

J. McCabe, *St. Augustine and His Age,* 1902; Boissier, *La fin du paganisme,* 2 vols., 7th ed., 1913; J. N. Figgis, *The Political Aspects of St. Augustine's "City of God,"* 1921; W. P. Tolley, *The Idea of God in the Philosophy of St. Augustine,* 1930; E. Gilson, *Introduction à l'étude de St. Augustin,* 1931; J. Healey, *St. Augustine's City of God,*

1934; H. Pope, *St. Augustine of Hippo,* 1937; J. Ritter, *Mundus Intelligibilis* (St. Augustine's Ontology), 1937; H. I. Marrou, *St. Augustin et la fin de la culture antique,* 1938; E. Chapman, *St. Augustine's Philosophy of Beauty,* 1939; V. J. Bourke, *Augustine's Quest of Wisdom,* 1944; M. C. D'Arcy and others, *A Monument to St. Augustine,* 1930, 1945.

Theory of Knowledge. Characteristic of the spirit of the entire Christian age is the Augustinian view that the only knowledge worth having is the knowledge of God and self. All other knowledge, such as the sciences of logic, metaphysics, and ethics, has value only in so far as it contributes to the knowledge of God. It is our duty to understand what we firmly believe, to see the rational basis of our faith. "Understand in order that you may believe, believe in order that you may understand. Some things we do not believe unless we understand them; others we do not understand unless we believe." Intelligence is needed for understanding what faith believes; faith, for believing what intelligence understands. "Faith seeks, understanding finds. . . . And yet again, understanding still seeks Him whom it finds . . ."[5] The function of this pursuit is insight or wisdom (*sapientia*), the highest function of reason when it is directed toward the creative principle. All intelligibility, including that attainable by the scientific intelligence (*scientia*), depends on this divine, creative principle.[6] The *ratio scientiae* seeks to find the elements, or principles of nature, by an analysis of what is given from the outside. On the other hand, the *ratio sapientiae* turns inward, finding there both God and the soul. Just as the One God is thought of as a Trinity of existence, order, and motion, so the substantial unity of the soul, a reflection of the Trinity, exhibits existence, knowledge, and will. To find the one is therefore to find the other also: the self which Augustine finds, and of which he thinks he achieves a knowledge more reliable than that which he has of external nature, is both a product of and an aid toward the search for God which he undertakes under the stimulus of the doctrine of the Trinity. Furthermore, the self has an intelligibility similar to that of the Trinity; justification or explanation of the self, or soul, is not, therefore, to be found in the world of nature.

Augustine's dictum, "Believe in order that you may understand," (*crede ut intelligas*) differs both from Tertullian's repudiation of reason and from the extreme dualism which opposes faith and reason. Reason must first decide whether a revelation has actually occurred; when it has been decided that a revelation is authentic, faith affirms it and reason seeks to understand and interpret it. We cannot, however, expect to understand everything we

[5] *On the Trinity,* XII, 14.　　　[6] *Ibid.*

believe, but must be prepared to accept the truths of faith solely on the authority of the Church, which is the representative of God on earth.

I know that I exist; my thinking and existence are indubitable certainties, and I know that there is eternal and immutable truth. My very doubts prove that I am conscious of truth, and the fact that I call a judgment true or false points to the existence of a world of truth. Augustine here conceives truth, after the Platonic fashion, as having real existence, and regards the knowledge of it as native to the human mind. Sometimes he speaks as if the mind of man literally intuited the divine ideas; at other times he says that God created them in us. In either case, truth is objective, not a mere subjective product of the human mind; it is independent and coercive; whether you and I apprehend it or not, it exists and has always existed. The source of this eternal and changeless world of truth is God; indeed, the divine mind is the abode of the Platonic ideas, forms, archetypes, or essences; in addition to the universal ideas, it contains the ideas of particular things.

Theology. Dominant in Augustine's theology is the Neoplatonic conception of the absoluteness and majesty of God and the insignificance of his creatures, considered apart from him. God is an eternal, transcendent being, all-powerful, all-good, all-wise; absolute unity, absolute intelligence, and absolute will; that is, absolute spirit. He is absolutely free, but his decisions are as unchangeable as his nature; he is absolutely holy and cannot will evil. In him willing and doing are one: what he wills is done without the help of any intermediate being or Logos. In his intelligence are all ideas or forms of things; which means that he proceeded rationally in creating the world and that everything owes its form to him. Augustine accepts the Athanasian doctrine of the Trinity, but the illustrations by which he elucidates it are tainted with Sabellianism (Patripassianism).

God created the world out of nothing; it is not a necessary evolution of his own being, as the pantheistic Neoplatonists held, for this transcends the nature of his creatures. His creation is a continuous creation (*creatio continua*), for unless it were sustained by God the world would dissolve; it is absolutely and continuously dependent on him. We cannot say that the world was created in time or in space, for before God created the world there was neither time nor space; in creating, he created time and space; he himself is timeless and without space. Yet, God's creation is not an eternal creation; the world has a beginning; creatures are finite, changeable and perishable. God also created matter; it is not older than the form, though prior to it in nature; that is, we have to presuppose matter logically as the basis of the form. God's omnipotence requires that every conceivable thing, even the most insignificant, exist in the universe.

The Problem of Evil. In order to maintain the divine omnipotence, St. Augustine is driven to the position that God is the cause of everything; in order to maintain his goodness, he has to exclude evil from the world or to explain it away. The whole of creation is an expression of God's goodness; in creating the universe he was prompted by his infinite love, but—St. Augustine hastens to add, for fear of depriving the Deity of absolute power—he was not bound to create, his love inclined him but did not compel him; creation was an act of his free will. Existence of every kind is, therefore, good; we should judge its value in relation to the divine will, not from the standpoint of human utility. If God has created and predetermined everything and is at the same time an absolutely good being, he has willed everything for the best interest of his creatures, and even so-called evil must be good in its way. Like the shadows in a picture, which contribute to the beauty of the whole, evil is indispensable to the goodness of the world. Evil is not good, but it is good that evil is. Or, evil is conceived as a defect, as a privation of essence (*privatio substantiae*), as an omission of the good; according to the privative theory of evil, evil is the negation or the privation of good. Good is possible without evil, but evil is not possible without the good; for everything is good, at least in so far as it has any being at all. Privation of good is evil because it means an absence of something nature ought to have. All kinds of evil, including moral evil, are brought under the concept of privation. Moral evil cannot mar the beauty of universal creation, since it springs from the will of man or of fallen angels; it is the result of an evil or defective will, which is nothing positive, but merely represents a privation of good (*privatio boni*). The worst evil is *privatio Dei,* the turning away from God, or the highest good, to the perishable world.

The problem of evil, as it presented itself to St. Augustine, is essentially theological: How is it possible to reconcile the goodness and omnipotence of God with the existence of evil in the world created by him? The problem exists only for the optimist, for one who believes in the ultimate goodness of the universe. God could have omitted evil altogether from the scheme of things, but he preferred to use it as a means of serving the good; the glory of the universe is enhanced by the presence of evil. He foresaw, for example, that man would turn from the good to sin; he permitted it and predetermined his punishment. In order to save God's goodness along with his omnipotence, Augustine employs several devices characteristic of the theological optimist: (1) he ascribes to evil a relative status; evil is necessary to the good; (2) he defines evil as a privation of the good; (3) he shifts the responsibility for it to man. At one time or another he adopted each of these mutually complementary solutions of the problem of evil.

Psychology. Man, the highest creature in nature, is a union of soul and body. This union is not the result of sin; the body is not the prison house of the soul; it is not inherently evil. The soul is a simple immaterial or spiritual substance, entirely distinct in essence from the body, but at the same time its life principle, directing and forming the body; but how it acts on the body is a mystery. Sensation is a mental, not a physical process.

Augustine rejects the doctrine of the soul's pre-existence. How the souls arose, he leaves unsettled. He finds it hard to decide in favor of either of the two prevalent views of his day: (1) God creates a new soul for every child that is born (*creationism*); or (2) souls are generated from the souls of parents at the same time and in much the same manner as their bodies are produced by their parents' bodies (*traducianism*).

Although the soul has a beginning in time, it does not die. Augustine proves its immortality by the usual arguments of his age, all of which stem from Plato. Although the soul is immortal in the sense of continuing to exist after bodily death, it is not necessarily immortal in the sense of realizing eternal blessedness. The eternal blessedness of the soul in God cannot be demonstrated: our expectation of it is an act of faith.

Ethics. The supreme goal of human conduct is a religious, mystical ideal—the mind's union with God in the vision of God. Such union cannot take place in an imperfect world, but only in a future life, which is the true life. Our earthly life is but a pilgrimage to God; in comparison with eternal blessedness, it is not life, but death. Augustine exemplifies the pessimism characteristic of early Christianity with respect to the visible universe, and buoyant optimism so far as the hereafter is concerned: *contemptus mundi* on the one hand, and *amor Dei* on the other. His dualism between the good God and the evil world is, however, somewhat mitigated by his theory of evil which, as we have already seen, acknowledges no absolute evil.

In his account of the virtues, he also suggests a way in which the ethical dualism between the highest other-worldly good and our day-to-day morality may be bridged. By love we are united with God; hence love is the su-

preme virtue, the source of all the other virtues. Temperance or self-control
is love of God as opposed to love of the world; fortitude is the overcoming
of pain and suffering by love; justice is the service of God; and wisdom is
the power of right choice guided by love of God. Love of God is the
basis of true love of self and of others. It alone makes the so-called pagan
virtues genuine virtues; unless inspired and prompted by this love, they
are nothing but "splendid vices."

The love of God is the work of divine grace acting within man's soul, a
mystical process taking place through the sacraments of the Church under
the influence of God's power. Faith, hope, and charity are interdependent
and are all essential to conversion. "Without (love) faith profits nothing;
and in its absence, hope cannot exist. . . . There is no love without hope,
no hope without love, and neither love nor hope without faith." [7]

In this teaching lies the possibility of a more positive attitude toward
earthly life and human institutions than seemed possible under the ideals
of primitive Christianity. The early Christians had assumed a negative attitude toward human institutions such as marriage, the affairs of state, war,
the administration of justice, and commercial pursuits. But with the development of an organized Church and the Christianization of the Roman
Empire, greater cognizance was taken of the worldly pursuits of man; this
resulted in an oscillation between world-denial and world-affirmation. Augustine wavers between the ascetic ideal and the worldly idea, and his attitude is characteristic of medieval moralists. He recognizes the right of property; he disagrees with the communistic teachings of the old Fathers that
all have an equal right to property, that property is based on injustice, that
wealth is a "damnable usurpation" (Ambrose). He also regards rich and
poor alike as capable of salvation. Nevertheless, he looks upon the possession
of private property as a hindrance to the soul, and places a higher value upon
poverty. Let us, therefore, abstain from the possession of private property,
he says, or if we cannot do that, let us abstain from the love of possession.
The same dualism confronts us in his estimate of marriage and celibacy:
marriage is conceived as a sacrament, and yet the unmarried state is the
higher. His conception of the State reveals the same dualistic tendency. The
earthly State is based on self-love and even contempt of God (*contemptus
Dei*); the City of God is achieved by love of God and contempt of self. The
temporal State is, indeed, an ethical community whose mission it is to promote the reign of justice, and to achieve happiness. The goal of the State

[7] *Enchiridion,* trans. by J. F. Shaw. The quotations are contained in Edman and
Schneider, *Landmarks for Beginners in Philosophy,* p. 203.

is relative, while that of the Church is absolute; and consequently, the State is subordinate to the Church. The authority of the Church is infallible, since it is the visible appearance of the kingdom of God.

In short, St. Augustine envisaged a twofold ideal: The highest good or perfection is a transcendent good, which even the Christian is unable to realize in the flesh because he remains under the sway of carnal concupiscence; this perfection consists in the love of God, in the absolutely good will. A relative perfection, however, a kind of holiness, may be reached by the performance of external works: thus venial sins may be wiped out by prayer, fasting, alms. Yet the supreme and true goal is, after all, asceticism, renunciation of the world, withdrawal from social life, imitation of Christ. The monastic life remains, for St. Augustine, the closest approximation to the Christian ideal.

Idealism is the most prominent feature of his ethical teaching. The highest values in the universe are not to be found in the material aspect of existence, but in the spirit; the highest part of man is not his body, not his sensuous-impulsive nature, but his spirit.

Freedom of the Will. St. Augustine opposes the Pelagian theory of the will. Man, in the person of Adam, was free to sin or not to sin; God not only created man free, but also endowed him with supernatural gifts of grace: immortality, holiness, justice, freedom from rebellious desire. But Adam chose to disobey God and thereby not only lost the divine gifts, but corrupted the entire human race, so that it has become a "mass of perdition." The first man transmitted his sinful nature, and the punishment necessarily connected with it, to his offspring, for he represented the whole human race. And now it is impossible for man not to sin (*non posse non peccare*): he went into sin free and came out unfree. Adam's sin is not merely the beginning and example of sin, it is original, hereditary sin. As a result, the entire human race stands condemned, and no one will be saved from merited punishment except by the mercy and freely bestowed grace of God. God alone can reform corrupted man. He does not select the recipients of his grace according to their good works—indeed, the works of sinful man cannot be good in the true sense of the term. Only those whom God has elected as beneficiaries of his grace can perform good works: "The human will does not achieve grace by an act of freedom, but rather achieves freedom by grace." God can so change the human soul that it will regain the love of the good which it possessed before Adam fell. The knowledge and love of the highest good, or God, restores to man the power to do good works, the power to turn away from the life of sense, the will to emancipate himself from the flesh. Love of the good is synonymous with freedom; only the *good* will is free.

Underlying this entire teaching is the conviction that unless a man has a notion of the good, unless he knows what is truly good and loves it, he is lost. Some men possess a good will, others lack it. Augustine's problem is to account for its appearance in some persons and not in others. His explanation is that, in the last analysis, a good will is a free gift of God.

Why God should have chosen some for eternal happiness and others for eternal punishment is a mystery; but there is no injustice in his choice, since man has by original sin forfeited any claim he may have had to salvation. Yet, is not predestination identical with fatalism; does it not mean that God has determined beforehand who shall be saved and who destroyed, and that his choice is purely arbitrary? Predestination is the eternal resolve of God to confer eternal life on this man or that by the infallible means of grace. Predestination implies God's foreknowledge of man's choice, but Augustine thinks that such foreknowledge is in no way prejudicial to man's freedom. Man was free to choose eternal life, he did not choose it; God knew that he would not and decided beforehand whom to save and whom not. Again we encounter an example of Augustine's conception of the absolute power of God. He is unwilling to limit divine freedom in the slightest degree: God can do as he pleases with man, and he has settled from all eternity what is going to happen to every individual. Man, in the person of Adam, has had his chance; he abused the privilege. God knew he would abuse it; but since man was under no compulsion to do wrong, no individual has a right to complain if he is not among the elect. Nevertheless, if a man truly loves God, if he has the good will, he will be redeemed.

Philosophy of History. In his influential work, *The City of God,* St. Augustine presented a Christian interpretation of history which, by virtue of its scope and its attempt to subsume world history under a pervasive formula, can properly be called a universal philosophy of history. It became the prototype of such modern—though radically different—philosophical interpretations of history as those offered by Rousseau, Hegel, Comte, Nietzsche, Marx and Spengler. The Augustinian philosophy of history considers the temporal and historical process in the context of the eternal nature and purpose of God, and seeks a vindication of the ways of God in dealing with men. Augustine realized that a philosophical interpretation of history must be based on an adequate conception of time. "Eternity and time," he says, "are rightly distinguished by this, that time does not exist without some movement and transition, while in eternity there is no change." [8] Change and time are thus inseparably joined, and the supposition that the world was created in a pre-existent time is patently absurd: "the world was made, not in time, but simultaneously with time." [9] God by an eternal act created both the world and time, and in the original creative act God envisaged under the form of eternity the entire succession of temporal and historical events which was destined to unfold in time. God "beholds all things with absolute unchangeableness," and in such a way that all things which shall emerge in time, including the entire course of human history, are "by Him comprehended in his stable eternal presence." [10] The cause of creation is the goodness of God, and consequently all created things which emerge in time contribute to the goodness of the created universe: "no nature at all is evil, and this is a name for nothing but the want of good." [11]

Human history as interpreted by Augustine is a perpetual conflict between two kingdoms: the earthly kingdom and the heavenly kingdom; the former has been formed by the love of self and the contempt of God; the latter by the love of God and the contempt of self. The kingdom of earth is dominated by self-seeking, glory, pride, vanity, debauchery, and corruption; it is the domain of war, political intrigue, and social injustice. The kingdom of heaven is the realm of love and peace, of the social virtues and, above all, it is dedicated to the glorification of God. Although the earthly city is manifested in the state, it is not identified with it for the state is, according to Augustine, a necessary institution, and may at times even be a noble institution promoting the interests of the higher kingdom.

The essential features of the Augustinian philosophy of history are: (1) The conviction that the entire historical process is a purposive or teleological whole, the parts of which, down to the most minute detail, contribute to the goodness and perfection of the whole; (2) The belief that the historical process moves in a direction which was predestined and foreordained by God in such a way as to bring about the ultimate redemption of some men and the destruction of others. The whole of history was predestined and foreordained by God, but this does not in his opinion preclude the free will of individual men.

[8] *The City of God*, X, 6. Translated in *Landmarks for Beginners in Philosophy*, 1941, ed. by I. Erdman and H. W. Schneider, p. 212.
[9] *Loc. cit.*
[10] *Op. cit.*, X, 21.
[11] *Op. cit.*, X, 22.

VII
The Formative Period
of Scholasticism

21. The Spirit of Medieval Philosophy

The Rise of Medieval Culture. Patristic philosophy reached its climax in the system of Augustine, which was the last great product of classical-Christian civilization and a heritage bequeathed by dying antiquity to its barbarian successors. The century which had given birth to this system also witnessed the downfall of the Western Roman Empire and the rise to political power of the young and vigorous peoples of the North. The Visigoths took possession of Gaul and Spain, the Vandals overran Africa, and the Ostrogoths placed themselves on the throne of the Caesars in 476. The task of the age was to amalgamate Roman-Christian culture with the beliefs and institutions of the Germanic peoples, a task which required a thousand years to complete. During this period, a new civilization slowly developed, and a new political, social, intellectual, and religious order arose. How thoroughgoing was the process of transformation is demonstrated by the evolution of new languages, new states, new customs and laws, new religions, new cultural and institutional forms of every kind; the old civilization disappeared in the great melting-pot of European races. The completion of the process marks the beginning of the modern era.

It is not surprising that medieval civilization developed slowly; the traditions and institutions of the past could be only gradually assimilated. Life does not change all at once for a people, nor can that people ever be completely transformed. Before becoming the bearers of the civilization offered by Roman Christianity, the barbarous tribes had many lessons to learn; they were obliged to assimilate the new culture into their primitive cultural pattern. Nor is it surprising that the higher culture of the old world should

186

have fallen into neglect and that the field of philosophy, which the Christians had in part appropriated and cultivated, should have lain fallow for many centuries. It was no time for the construction of metaphysical and theological systems; the age was confronted with serious practical problems in every department of human activity. The very elements and instruments of knowledge had first to be acquired before they could be employed for the assimilation of the highest achievements of a cultivated race.

The immediate problems were educational. The learned literature of the period from Augustine down to the ninth century was largely restricted to textbooks on the liberal arts and to compendia of Christian dogmatics. The seven liberal arts consisted of grammar, rhetoric, and dialectic, which constitute the *trivium* or linguistic studies, and arithmetic, music, geometry, and astronomy, constituting the *quadrivium* or scientific studies.

Philosophy, tethered as it was to Christian theology, did little more than preserve the traditions of the past. In the more cultivated Eastern Empire interest in theological questions was widespread, but it expressed itself in fruitless dogmatic controversies and in the production of encyclopedic manuals or systematized collections of the dogmas, such as that of John of Damascus (around 700). In the West, scientific, logical and philosophical textbooks and commentaries were written by Martianus Capella (around 430), Boethius (480-525), and Cassiodorus (477-570), while the Venerable Bede (674-735) achieved a great reputation for learning by compiling compendia remarkable only for their meagerness of original thought. For several centuries there were two practically distinct literary traditions, the pure classical and the hybrid classical-Christian. The pure classical philosophy, which adhered to Stoicism, Neopythagoreanism, and Neoplatonism, was cultivated by the highly educated Greeks and Romans who had nothing but contempt for the hybrid tradition.

Beginnings of Learning. With the conversion of the educated classes to Christianity in the Roman Empire, and the development of the ecclesiastical organization, the Christian clergy had gradually assumed the intellectual leadership which formerly resided in the philosophers' schools, and had become the custodians of learning; nearly all the great writers in the East and West belonged to the clergy. However, with the ascendency of the Germanic races at the beginning of the Middle Ages the torch of knowledge flickered and dimmed, and the Christian clergy, recruited now for the most part from the sons of barbarians, found neither pleasure nor honor in the cultivation of Greek philosophy, literature, and art. The seventh and eighth centuries constitute perhaps the darkest period of our Western European civilization, a period of boundless ignorance and brutality, in which the literary and artistic achievements of the classical past seemed destined to be lost in the general ruin. During this age, the monasteries became the refuge not only of the persecuted and oppressed, but of the despised and neglected liberal arts. In them, what had survived of literature, science, and art was preserved and cultivated; manuscripts were copied and the love of higher spiritual ideals kept alive. The monasteries also established schools and gave instruction, meager and barren though it was. A more hopeful epoch began when Charlemagne, in order to encourage education, called scholars to his realm and founded schools in which the seven liberal arts were taught. Among these scholars were Paul, the Deacon, historian of the Lombards, Einhard, Angilbert, and, greatest of all, the Anglo-Saxon Alcuin (735-804), a pupil of the monastic school at York. It was he who became the Emperor's chief adviser in matters of education, and who, at his monastic school at Tours, succeeded in arousing a lively interest in philosophical questions. Alcuin himself wrote textbooks on grammar, rhetoric, and dialectic—the *trivium*—and a work on psychology which shows the influence of Platonic-Augustinian conceptions.

No work of any importance to the history of thought appeared, however, until the middle of the ninth century, when John Scotus Erigena (or Eriugena) published a book which was a development of patristic philosophy, and the forerunner of a new era in the history of Christian thinking. To this main period of the Middle Ages, the period of scholasticism, we shall now turn.

The Spirit of the Age. During the Middle Ages, the words authority, obedience, and subordination form important terms in the vocabulary of life. In politics, religion, morals, education, philosophy, science, literature, and art—in every sphere of human activity—the influence of organized Christianity is supreme. As the representative of God on earth and the source of revealed truth, the Church becomes the guardian of education, the censor of morals, the court of last resort in intellectual and spiritual affairs, indeed the organ of civilization and the bearer of the keys to heaven. Since the Church receives the truth directly from God, what need is there of searching for it; what need of philosophy except as the handmaiden of theology? Human reason is limited to systematizing and rendering intelligible the revealed truths or dogmas of the Christian religion. The individual is subordinate to the Church in his religious beliefs and practices, the Church stands between him and his God; on all the important matters of life and death, the shadow of the cross is cast. There is no salvation for the individual outside the great City of God, which watches over him from the cradle to the grave and even gives him his passport to heaven. Education, too, is a function of the ecclesiastic hierarchy, for who should keep God's truth but those through whom it is revealed; and who should exercise the censorship over human conduct but the supreme earthly authorities on matters pertaining to right and justice? The Church likewise holds herself superior to the State and seeks to apply her theory in practice, as witness her conflicts with the German Emperors; as the sun is to the moon, so is the Church to the State. The ambition of Pope Innocent III (1198-1216), under whom ecclesiastical power reached its climax, was to be the master of the world. The State itself in time assumes the same absolute authority over the people previously claimed by the church: kings rule by divine right and their subjects are divinely enjoined to obey. Within the body politic the individual finds himself under a restraint and a discipline which embrace all his social, political, and economic activities: for the great mass of people, obedience was the law of life—obedience to the ruler, obedience to a lord, obedience to the guild, obedience to the master, obedience to the head of the family. In every phase of life the individual submits to the authority of the group. Authority and tradition are superior to public opinion and the individual conscience; faith, superior to reason; the corporation, superior to the person; and the caste, superior to the man.

The Purpose of Scholasticism. The philosophical thought of this period mirrors the spirit of the times in assigning to tradition and authority a leading rôle: scholars swear by the church, by Augustine, Plato or Aristotle, by their monastic orders or their schools. Accepting on faith the truth of the Church doctrines, and yet feeling a strong urge for philosophical speculation, they endeavor to harmonize the two by reading the Christian faith into their philosophies, or their philosophies into the Christian faith. The faith is, however, the beginning and the end of their labors, theology the crown of all knowledge, the royal science. Even when knowledge is dumb, when reason stumbles, the truths of religion are still believed—all the more firmly by some—because of their mystery. Speculative philosophy, when it conflicts with theology, is either cast aside as futile or, in accordance with the principle of a two-fold truth, which distinguishes truth of reason and truth of faith, is assigned to another domain of truth.

Patristic philosophy had faced the task of developing and formulating the articles of faith and organizing them into a rational system; the process of fermentation is virtually at an end when scholasticism appears upon the scene, thus confronted with a fixed body of established doctrine. It is likewise confronted with an organized hierarchy, ready and able to defend with the weapons of church and state the established truths against all dissenters. The problem now is to elaborate a system of thought which will square with the dogmas, and thus harmonize philosophy and faith. The schoolmen, like the Greek philosophers before them, aim at a rational explanation of things; unlike them, they approach the task with a definite preconception of the goal. Certain fundamental truths are already known; the scheme of salvation is itself a universally accepted fact: the task of the philosopher is to interpret it, to connect it with the rest of our knowledge and thereby to render it intelligible.

The assumption of the medieval thinker is either that the truths of religion are rational, reason and faith agree, and there can be no conflict between divine revelation and human thinking; or that, even though some truths of religion may transcend human reason, they are nonetheless guaranteed by faith, which is an independent source of knowledge. Within these assumptions a number of alternative procedures are possible: the thinker may, accepting the Christian world-view on faith, seek to prove it with the help of some existing system of philosophy; or he may develop his own system of philosophy in harmony with Christian principles; or he may give his attention to problems that have no direct connection with theology. In any case, however, the dogma will be the regulative principle: the schoolman will not knowingly accept as true a proposition contradicting an essential article of faith, unless he can offer some explanation of the conflict—such as the doctrine of two-fold truth—which leaves the truth of the dogma unimpaired. He may, in some way, satisfy himself that both propositions are true even though contradictory, but he will under no circumstances reject the dogma.

Characteristics of Scholasticism. The purpose of scholasticism determines its method: in so far as it consists in the demonstration of propositions already accepted, it will largely employ deduction. The nature of these propositions, and the need of proving them, account for several other characteristics of scholastic philosophy. The chief concern of the schoolman is the transcendent world, the world of God, the angels, and the saints; his thought is fixed not so much on phenomenal things as on the invisible realm of spirits. This accounts for the paramount importance of theology for scholasticism, and the relative unimportance of the natural sciences. It also explains the failure of schoolmen to undertake an empirical study of subjects in which they have an interest, namely, psychology and ethics. They were less concerned with the description of how the soul acts than with the determination of its ultimate nature and destiny, and, in their opinion, the empirical analysis of the soul's contents contributed little to the understanding of its destiny. Nor did it seem possible to elicit from the world of experience an answer to the questions of ethics. The highest good is the blessed life in God— that is incontestable—but there are no empirical means of finding the best way to such a life, since it is bestowed by divine grace on those who do the will of God. Obedience to the will of God is the standard of right and wrong; what his will is cannot be determined by an analysis of experience but only by appeal to a divine revelation. Theology thus remains the basis of scholastic ethics; it cannot be replaced by psychology or any other empirical science.

The world about which the schoolman is chiefly concerned is not perceivable by the senses; it can be known only by rational thought. Logic, therefore, is a most important study, particularly deductive, syllogistic logic: the logic of the method which he employs in his pursuit of truth. In this field the schoolmen evinced great subtlety, not only in the analysis of logical processes, but, especially, in developing conceptions and distinctions which have, for better or for worse, become a part of our intellectual heritage. The scholastic philosophers contributed little to the theory of knowledge as distinguished from logic. They did not address themselves to the problems concerning the possibility and the limits of knowledge since, as a rule, they cherished an abiding, dogmatic confidence in the ability of reason to attain truth. The nominalists, to be sure, discussed the question of the validity of knowledge, but the nominalists are not typical schoolmen. A critical approach to the problems of the theory of knowledge, which was a major preoccupation of the Greek thinkers, and which we shall encounter again in modern philosophy, is largely in abeyance during the scholastic period.

Stages of Scholasticism. We shall distinguish in scholasticism three principal phases. (1) The *formative* period, beginning with the ninth and ending with the twelfth century, is largely influenced by Platonic conceptions; Platonism, Neoplatonism, and Augustinianism are the dominant philosophical tendencies of this phase. Ideas or universals are conceived, in Platonic terms, as the real essences of things and as prior to things (*universalia sunt realia ante res*). This is the theory of Platonic realism of which Anselm is the leading exponent. (2) The period of the *culmination* of scholasticism, the thirteenth century, witnesses the dominance of Aristotle's philosophy. Christianity allies itself with the great Greek thinker; universals are now conceived as real, not, however, as prior to things, but *in* them (*universalia sunt realia in rebus*). This teaching is called Aristotelian realism. The thirteenth century is the period of comprehensive systems; the leading thinkers of the period are Albert the Great and St. Thomas Aquinas. (3) The period of *decline* of scholasticism followed in the fourteenth century. Universals are now regarded not as the essences of things, but as mere concepts in the mind or as mere words or names: particular things alone are real, universals are real only in the mind and are hence *after* the things (*universalia sunt realia post res*). This is nominalism. John Duns Scotus and William of Occam are the leading exponents of nominalism, the implications of which are destructive of scholastic presuppositions. For scholastic realism the universe is, as it was for Plato and Aristotle, an ideal universe, a system of ideas or forms, which are somehow mirrored in the phenomenal world as the essential qualities of things. The real world is a rational, logical world, and its nature can, therefore, be thought out by the reason alone; the relational structure of the world is transparent to the reason of the human mind. The forms, which constitute the essential nature of classes of objects, are reflected in our thoughts or universal concepts. Now, if such ideas were merely thoughts in our minds, or, worse yet, were mere names, if there were nothing real corresponding to them, either in things or apart from things, then we could have no knowledge through them of things, no rational knowledge of the universe and of universals. Confidence in the power of reason to reach truth is seriously undermined by the nominalistic doctrine. With the advent of nominalism in the fourteenth century, the philosophy of the Middle Ages departs from its scholastic principles, and repudiates the underlying assumptions on which scholasticism rests. Realism and rationalism were intimately conjoined in the great systems of scholastic philosophy, and nominalism's devastating attack on the former seriously weakened the latter. Likewise, with the decline of scholasticism, the union between reason and faith, philosophy and religion, which was one of the great accomplishments of the scholastic synthesis, became less firm. The scholastic claim that the doctrines of faith and the deliverances of reason agree is gradually modified in two principal ways: the first view is that while some of the dogmas can be explained or rendered intelligible, others transcend reason; the second is that none can be explained for they are not objects of philosophical knowledge at all; the truths of religion lie beyond the reach of reason, and reason cannot fathom them. The latter view, which is the more extreme, amounts to an abandonment of scholasticism as such, and results in a deliverance of philosophy from servitude to dogmatic theology.

Sources of Scholasticism. The principal sources from which the early schoolmen drew their inspiration were Patristic literature, Greek philosophy, and, later, Arabian and Jewish speculations. The Greek philosophical material at their disposal, down to the middle of the twelfth century, consisted of Latin translations of: parts of Plato's *Timaeus* (by Cicero and Chalcidius), Aristotle's *Categories* and *On Interpretation* (by Boethius), and Porphyry's *Introduction to the Categories* (by Boethius and Victorinus). Plato's *Meno* and *Phaedo* were translated in the twelfth century. Of Roman philosophers they knew the writings of Boethius, Martianus Capella, Cassiodorus. Aristotle's *Analytics* and *Topics* became known in translation after 1128, and the metaphysical and physical works about 1200.

22. SCHOLASTICISM: ITS NATURE AND PROBLEMS

The Meaning of "Scholasticism." The diverse connotations of the word "scholasticism" make it desirable that we say something of its history and of the sense in which we shall use it. Scholasticism was applied in the time of Charlemagne to the teachings at the schools he established. A man designated as *scholasticus* might be supposed to be learned in the trivium (grammar, dialectic, rhetoric) and the quadrivium (arithmetic, geometry, music, astronomy), or in theology. The application was gradually broadened in the course of time, until, finally, the title was given to any learned person, whether in the sciences or in philosophy, and whether a teacher or not. Throughout most of the medieval period it was a title of respect; but in the Renaissance period it became a term of contempt. The writers of the Renaissance considered scholasticism barbaric on account of the presumed sophistry and pedantry of its representatives, and the alleged desiccation of its method.

Many modern historians of philosophy have tended to regard the Middle Ages as philosophically homogeneous, and have accordingly identified medieval philosophy and scholasticism. Some historians have based this identification solely on a chronological criterion; other historians have stressed the predominance of the didactic method, which they frequently assumed to be wholly deductive. Or again, the criterion has been the submission of reason to authority supposedly implicit in the theological orientation of most of the philosophy of the Middle Ages. But whatever standards were employed, the pejorative sense given the word scholasticism by the Renaissance has frequently been retained. In our own times, because of renewed interest in the philosophy of the Middle Ages, and, more particularly, because of the revival of the Thomastic philosophy, the original meaning of scholasticism has been reinstated, and many contemporary writers are proud to describe their philosophies as examples of a "new scholasticism."

The historian De Wulf represents this new attitude and has given good historical reasons for rejecting a definition of scholasticism in terms of chronology, method, connection with the great medieval schools and universities, or deference to the authority of revelation. He admits that the dominant philosophy of the Middle Ages contains all these elements, but insists that it is also a doctrinal tradition. Such diverse figures as Anselm of Canterbury, Abelard, Alexander of Hales, St. Thomas Aquinas, and Duns Scotus, despite many disagreements, accept pluralism, spiritualism, and a belief in liberty, personal immortality, and the objectivity of human knowledge. To this core of scholasticism he opposes various anti-scholastic philosophies which advocate pantheistic monism, materialism, moral determinism, impersonal immortality, and subjectivism. To the anti-scholastic tendencies listed by De Wulf may be added two other important medieval interests outside the tradition culminating in St. Thomas Aquinas' philosophy: mysticism and natural science. We shall, then, define scholasticism as the dominant philosophy of the Middle Ages, associated with cloister or cathedral schools, and later with the universities, and possessing considerable continuity of method, doctrine, and problems. Scholasticism is best thought of as the line of development culminating in St. Thomas Aquinas, since his philosophy marks a peculiar poise in the history of thought—as his time symbolizes a similar poise in the political sphere.

The Problems of Scholasticism. The essential continuity as well as the inner diversity of the scholastic tradition are best demonstrated by a survey of the development of certain central problems of scholasticism. For this purpose we have selected the following: (1) the relation between faith and reason, together with the not always identical question of the relation of revelation to reason; (2) the relation between the will and intellect; (3) the distinction between nature and grace—a problem which we may treat as ancillary to the first two; (4) the status of universals. To begin with any one of these problems is of course to find oneself very soon touching upon every one of the others.

Faith and Reason. In the period prior to St. Thomas, if we may oversimplify a highly diversified development, reason was ancillary to faith and had as its main purpose the rationalization of revealed truth. Most thinkers of this period felt that reason is quite competent to perform this function; indeed some of them, for example Berenger of Tours (999-1089), Roscelin of Compiègne (*ca.* 1050-1120), and Abelard (1079-1142), carry this confidence in reason to a point where reason often seems to run counter to, and to correct, faith; in these thinkers, somewhat overconfident use of reason tended to defeat its own initial purpose. Philosophy is identified by them with dialectic. Berenger of Tours had an abounding trust in the dialectical method: to appeal to dialectic is to appeal to reason. Reason is that in us which makes us images of God; hence, man's supreme good lies in following reason wherever it may lead him.

In a time that saw a restoration of the fervor of monastic life, there were, however, many who attacked the overweening dialectical pretensions of reason in the name of the truths of faith, and who urged that true knowledge is gained by adhering firmly to the truths of scripture. Chief among these is Peter Damian (1007-1072), who would not hear of imposing the puny necessities of human logic on the divine being. The opposition between reason and faith becomes intensified in the twelfth century, when we find on the side of reason Roscelin of Compiègne and Abelard and, on the side of faith, St. Bernard (1091-1153).

An intermediate position, which avoids the exaggeration of reason on the one hand and faith on the other, is represented by Lanfranc of Bec and Canterbury (1005-1089), a contemporary of Berenger, and St. Anselm (1033-1109). Berenger maintained that it is quite proper to confirm faith by reason, indeed, that dialectic can be used to sustain and confirm revelation, since there is no real contradiction between faith and reason when reason is properly employed. In the same spirit of moderation, St. Anselm accepts the wisdom of his master, St. Augustine, as embodied in the formula *credo ut intelligam* ("I believe in order that I may understand"), by which he means that of the two powers by which we attain knowledge, or apprehension, faith is the controlling one. Truth is so vast that the scriptures cannot claim to exhaust all the knowledge that is attainable by us; therefore, to comprehend by reason the faith contained in scripture is to approach closer to the vision of God. We are obligated not only to believe the mysteries of faith, but to force reason to comprehend them. There is scarcely an important truth of faith of which Anselm does not attempt to give a logical demonstration. In so doing he is much more confident of the power of reason than is St. Thomas, for the latter holds that there is a group of truths, such as the mysteries of the Trinity, the Incarnation, and the Redemption, quite incapable of justification by reason. The dominant tone before St. Thomas, then, is one of confidence in reason as an adjunct to faith.

For St. Thomas Aquinas, faith is a gift from the Creator, perfecting a finite nature which, without it, would be truncated. Man's finite nature has a supernatural end: a beatitude consisting of the love and direct knowledge of God. To such a supernatural end the finite nature of man ought to conform, but, because the end is supernatural, man's nature can never attain it without assistance. Although the grace that confers faith comes from outside, yet, because it comes from a Creator who is responsible for the existence of the creature in question, it works internally, and thus faith appears as intrinsic to the nature it perfects. A nature so perfected by faith has its intelligence perfected as well, and thus faith confers on the intellect, or reason, the ability to penetrate more deeply even in its own rational sphere. In this respect St. Thomas is at one with his master, St. Augustine, even though he differs from him in defining the precise extent to which reason may proceed unaided by faith.

The continuity of faith and reason, of grace and nature, is central to the thought of St. Thomas. In this context the important questions are: What can reason do when it is the reason of someone who possesses faith? What ought reason attempt to do? What are its concerns, and how should it limit itself? In his answers, St. Thomas insists throughout on the importance and the penetration of the intellect in its own sphere, when that penetration is helped by faith. There are only a few things to which reason cannot attain —for example, an adequate understanding of the Trinity. The main ingredients of St. Thomas' position are: the continuity of faith and reason; the amplitude of reason and the independence of its concerns—an independence which makes possible a natural theology founded on reason alone.

In the period after St. Thomas, there was less disposition to trust reason as a worthy auxiliary to faith, and thus revealed theology and faith became quite distinct from reason. This view so limits the scope of reason that, in natural theology at least, its province is meager or nonexistent. So discontinuous are the spheres of natural and revealed theology that reason, as exercised in the latter, is nothing but faith in disguise. The radical separation of faith and reason seems to be progressive. According to Duns Scotus (ca. 1270-1308), reason, though diffident and restricted in scope, is still considered to be in eventual harmony with the insights of revealed theology, but in the case of Occam and Nicolas of Autrecourt (about 1350), reason is forced to abdicate totally from theology. If we turn now to the distrust of reason which sets in after the thirteenth century, we encounter the doctrine of twofold truth, which may be interpreted as undermining either reason or faith, depending on whether emphasis is placed on the religious truths of faith or the secular truths of reason. The source of the theory of the twofold truth of the later Middle Ages may be traced principally to Siger of Brabant (ca. 1235-ca. 1281), the famous opponent of St. Thomas, who held that on certain questions two answers could be given, one by revelation, and one by reason, and that these answers may be contradictory. Siger, whether out of prudence, or out of a deference to religion understandable in even the most radical thinkers of those times, somewhat mitigates the opposition by reserving the name "truth" for the content of revelation. In its extreme form, the theory of the twofold truth holds that a doctrine may be true from the point of view of faith, even when our reason tells us that it is false.

Duns Scotus, unlike Siger, believes in the harmony of faith and reason: he considers theology founded on faith a practical science, more concerned with our salvation than our enlightenment, within which rational and necessary demonstrations are indeed possible, but only, in Anselmian fashion, when the articles to be demonstrated are first believed. To this practical science of theology is opposed the natural reason of philosophy, which is incapable of proving many of the truths of religion. Although Scotus does not yet go so far as to deny that the existence of God is susceptible to proof, this drastic step is taken by William of Occam in the fourteenth century. Occam's adoption of this extreme position results from his critical analysis of the human reason, and is prompted by a genuine desire to protect the truths of the faith against the destructive criticism to which rational proof is susceptible. According to Occam's nominalistic theory, our knowledge of the world of particulars yields only probability, even in such matters as the proof of the existence of God as a prime mover. But such probable knowledge is clearly inadequate for the purposes of natural theology. Occam is led by these considerations to exclude theology entirely from the domain of natural or rational knowledge, and thus to adopt the theory of the twofold truth. The closing period of the Middle Ages is characterized by a combination of empiricism, nominalism, skepticism, and religious faith in which the spirit of modern science can already be discerned, as also can the Reformation's attitude toward faith.

Relation of Will to Intellect. We find echoes of the faith *vs.* reason controversy when we turn to the related question of whether the higher of the two principal faculties of the soul is the will or the intellect; the Middle Ages thought of faith as primarily engaging the will, whereas reasoning, by definition, engaged the intellect. The question is whether action of the will is able to generate intellectual ideas, or whether the intellect on its own initiative presents the will with alternatives in the form of ideas. The question of the nature of that free will, which it is a major concern of all Christian philosophers to defend, is of course here involved. Any discussion of the will in scholastic philosophy is complicated by the connection between the will and a divinely ordained grace which supposedly moves the will.

The basic question at issue is whether the will is absolutely self-determining, or whether the will is itself determined by knowledge of the good. The lines of controversy are cleanly drawn between Augustinians, including Scotus and Occam, as advocates of the will, and Aristotelians, notably St. Thomas, as advocates of the intellect. This division, in the late Middle Ages, often coincides with the division between Franciscans and Dominicans.

St. Thomas Aquinas does not advocate the intellectualist position in its most extreme form; indeed, in his insistence on the importance of faith and love he has more in common with Augustine than is perhaps generally recognized. St. Thomas felt that it is better to love an object of the greatest magnitude than to know it imperfectly. He sees love of God as our highest function, and considers faith, which is a gift of grace, to be the mode of apprehension corresponding to this love. In faith and in the love of God, the will is the faculty which is most involved. In man's love of God, the operative power in the transaction, according to the doctrine of grace, is the *object,* God, rather than the *subject,* man. Despite this strong voluntaristic note in his doctrine of love and faith, on the specific issues concerning the relation between the will and the intellect in the individual man he aligns himself with the intellectualist position: in the moral and cognitive acts of man he assigns priority to the intellect over the will. In this life, and in respect to finite objects, possession by the intellect is a higher activity than possession by the will; hence, it is better to know than to believe. We should therefore seek to know and to demonstrate all that we can know, and such knowledge is theology when its object is the Deity. The will, however, must be ever alert, and we should be prepared to believe and love even when demonstration is impotent or would be an impertinence.

On the question of the relation between the faculties of will and intellect in a specific cognitive or moral act, there is a sharp opposition between the beliefs of Duns Scotus and St. Thomas. For the former, the intellect, whether of God or man, is associated with the determinate and the natural. Everything, then, if it is free, whether in God or man, belongs to will, which is a principle of indetermination; everything that is necessary or determinate is natural, and this includes the intellect. The voluntaristic theory of Scotus ascribes liberty to a spontaneous act of will, which, after deliberation, decides between alternatives. On this issue as on others, tendencies noticeable in Scotus are intensified in Occam; the latter holds that the very goodness of a good thing is derived from the decree of God.

The position of St. Thomas, while in general emphasizing the intellect, has certain features in common with the doctrine of Duns Scotus. Taking the will as the source of all movement in an entity, St. Thomas insists upon its absolute spontaneity or indetermination—freedom in its radical sense. The being may give or withhold its action—a man freely wills to think or not to think a certain good. We may argue that the will moves even the intellect to apprehend its object. St. Thomas offers a complex definition of free will in which indetermination, or indifference, is one of the characteristics of the will.[1] While the will is that in us which moves us to action, including the action which is knowledge, it can nevertheless only will a good which has been presented to it by the intellect. "The reason reasons about willing, and the will wills to reason." [2]

The complete description of this will that is said to be free must, then, include some account of its power to attain its object; and once more Aquinas attempts to preserve the freedom of the will even when the power seems to come from elsewhere:

. . . God moves everything in its own manner. . . . But it is proper to man's nature to have free choice. Hence in him who has the use of free choice God's motion to justice does not take place without a movement of the free choice; but He so infuses the gift of justifying grace that at the same time He moves free choice to accept the gift of grace in such as are capable of being moved thus.[3]

God helps us, as St. Augustine said, even to help ourselves. St. Thomas, like St. Augustine, is advocating a position which is neither extreme voluntarism nor strict intellectual determinism. The act of creation may be regarded as the sustaining of a creation from within or, as the phrase goes, it is creation *with* time, rather than *in* time. Thus the freedom of the creature is the act of a coadjutor in creation, and grace is a bridge between an infinite creator and a finite creation—a bridge clearly necessary to save the meaning of the "ought" with which the creature is confronted. In any case, the tendency of the late Middle Ages was toward a separation of will and intellect, faith and reason, grace and nature, incompatible with the earlier doctrine of freedom which sought a theory in which indetermination, value, and power mingled with and qualified the relations existing between will and intellect, and between free will and grace.

The Problem of Universals. The controversy over universals has its foundation in the following passage from Boethius' Latin version of Porphyry's Introduction to the *Categories* of Aristotle: "Next as to *genera* and *species,*

---

[1] *Summa Theologicae,* I-II, Q. 10, Art. 4.
[2] *Ibid.,* I-II, Q. 17, Art. 1.
[3] *Summa Theologicae,* I-II, Q. 113, Art. 3.

do they actually subsist, or are they merely thoughts existing in the understanding alone; if they subsist are they corporeal or incorporeal; are they
separate from sensible things or only in and of them? I refuse to answer;
these are very lofty questions unsuited to an elementary work." Porphyry's
warning on the difficulty of the problem went unheeded, and on his own
suggestive formulation of the problem, the early Middle Ages founded its
principal purely philosophical disputations. As we have seen, these disputes
were at first confined to certain restricted aspects of the Aristotelian logic,
and to Neoplatonic and Augustinian material; but this did not prevent the
formulation of extremely complex answers even before medieval philosophers
became acquainted with Aristotelian metaphysics, and thereby widened the
range of their speculations.

The answers given throughout the Middle Ages are of three types: (1)
Realism is the view that genera and species have a real subsistence, independent both of the mind that entertains them and the world of individuals
that may be presumed to exemplify them. In its extreme form, this doctrine
is combined with a derogation of the world of sense, and the ascription to
genera and species of a transcendent status that we may loosely designate
as Platonic. (2) At the other pole is *nominalism,* with its formula that only
the individual is real, construed in so strict a way as to imply that so-called
genera and species are simply names by means of which we designate
resembling individuals. In its extreme and more naïve form nominalism
insists that the general term is a mere name, a mere word, or even as a
mere sound. In its more subtle form, nominalism, while retaining the view
that these general terms are in any case mental, gives attention to the
meanings involved; the doctrine is then known as *sermonism* (Abelard)
or *terminism* (Occam). The version of the nominalistic doctrine which
recognizes meanings over and above mere words is sometimes referred to
by modern writers as *conceptualism.* (3) Mediating between nominalism and
realism is a third position, which depends for its formulation on the
Aristotelian analysis of the individual substance into components of form
and matter. This position, which is designated by its advocates as *moderate*
or *Aristotelian realism,* shares with nominalism only the disposition to
regard the individual as ultimate; but it agrees with realism in ascribing
to genera and species an independence of the knowing mind. This is not
the place to discuss the question whether Aristotle is not quite close to Plato
in so far as he insists that the immanent *form* confers actuality upon the
ultimate individual substance. We may note that this form is identifiable
with the essence of the individual; that the essence is that in the individual
which renders it definable; and that, therefore, the form is identifiable with

that which the individual has in common with other members of the same species. But we must then add that this form can nevertheless have a non-mental existence only as belonging to an individual concrete substance, composed of form and matter—a concrete substance in which the matter is the individuating factor. For the moderate realism of St. Thomas, which presupposes Aristotle's theory of knowledge, the individual is a composite of form and matter, of essence and existence; but in order for the mind to entertain the essence, and thereby give it the universality it lacks as an element in the concrete individual, there must be present to the knower an existing concrete individual, from which abstraction can be made. The universal, then, has a threefold existence; it exists *in* the individual, but not as a genuine universal; *after* its abstraction from the individual it has an added note of universality; and finally, under the influence of St. Augustine's exemplarism, genera and species are considered by St. Thomas *before* individuals, in the mind of God. But even this final doctrine preserves the intent of the Aristotelian emphasis on the individual, since the exemplars in God's mind are merely the ways in which aspects of God's essence may be imitated in an imperfect way by individual things. Realism in its extreme or Platonic form is the dominant solution of the problem of universals during the very earliest period of scholasticism. In the Neoplatonic version of John Scotus Erigena, the highest generality is associated with highest reality. In the course of the subsequent development of scholastic philosophy, however, nominalism very quickly comes to the fore. Nominalism is associated at first with Aristotle's logic which, being more formal and linguistic than his metaphysics, might easily give the impression that it relates primarily to words rather than to things. When nominalism made its first appearance, there was no suspicion that a nominalistic position tends to undermine the adequacy of our knowledge and thus, ultimately, threatens the entire scholastic program of providing a rational justification of the faith and creed. It was chiefly as a result of Roscelin's debate with Anselm who, being an Augustinian, is also a realist, that nominalism loses countenance in the early Middle Ages. Roscelin did not hesitate to insist that his nominalism renders suspect the formulation of the doctrine of the Trinity, if not the intent of our devotions, and the theologian St. Anselm is equally insistent that the articles of faith—felt to be demonstrable—require realism as a basis for this demonstrability. Many of Anselm's arguments—in particular the famous ontological argument—depend upon the assumption that degree of understood perfection is equivalent to degree of being; or, expressed differently, that it is possible to go from essence to existence.

Works on Scholastic Philosophy

C. Prantl, *Geschichte der Logik im Abenlande*, Vols. II-IV, 1855-70: *Die Logik im Mittelalter;* B. Haureau, *Histoire de la philosophie scholastique*, 3 vols., 1872-80; H. Siebeck, *Geschichte der Psychologie*, 1880-84; H. Rashdell, *Universities of Europe in the Middle Ages*, 3 vols., 1895; A. D. White, *A History of the Warfare of Science with Theology*, 1898; F. Paulsen, *German Universities*, trans. by F. Thilly and W. W. Elway, 1906; F. J. Picavet, *Esquisse d'une histoire générale et comparée des philosophies médiévales*, 1907; J. Rickaby, *Scholasticism*, 1908; H. O. Taylor, *The Classical Heritage of the Middle Ages*, 3rd ed., 1911, and *The Mediaeval Mind*, 2 vols., new ed., 1949; P. M. M. Duhem, *Le système du monde*, 1913-17; R. L. Poole, *Illustrations of the History of Medieval Thought and Learning*, 2nd ed., 1920; M. De Wulf, *Philosophy and Civilization in the Middle Ages*, 1922, and *History of Mediaeval Philosophy*, 3rd Eng. ed., trans. by E. C. Messenger, 2 vols., 1935-38; W. J. Townsend, *The Great Schoolmen of the Middle Ages*, 1922; G. B. Adams, *Civilization during the Middle Ages* in *Cambridge Mediaeval History*, 1922; M. Grabmann, *Mittelalterliches Geistesleben*, 1926-56; C. H. Haskins, *Studies in the History of Medieval Science*, 2nd ed., 1927; R. P. McKeon, *Selections from Medieval Philosophers*, 2 vols., 1929-31; G. Sarton, *An Introduction to the History of Science*, Vol. II, 1931; W. Betzendörfer, *Glauben und Wissen bei den grossen Denkern des Mittelalters*, 1931; H. Schaller, *Die Weltanschauung des Mittelalters*, 1934; L. Thorndike, *A History of Magic and Experimental Science*, 6 vols., 1934-43; S. H. Mellone, *Western Christian Thought in the Middle Ages*, 1935; E. Gilson, *The Spirit of Mediaeval Philosophy*, trans. by A. H. C. Downes, 1936; *La philosophie au moyen âge*, 2nd ed., 1944, and *Reason and Revelation in the Middle Ages*, 1938; E. Bréhier, *La philosophie du moyen âge*, 1937; E. C. Thomas, *History of the Schoolmen*, 1941; D. J. B. Hawkins, *A Sketch of Medieval Philosophy*, 1947; P. Vignaux, *La pensée au moyen âge*, 1948; C. S. J. Curtis, *A Short History of Philosophy in the Middle Ages*, 1950; G. Burch, *Early Medieval Philosophy*, 1950; F. C. Copleston, *Medieval Philosophy*, 1952.

23. JOHN SCOTUS ERIGENA: A NEOPLATONIC REVERSION

At the end of the fifth century a collection of writings appeared which were falsely attributed to Dionysius the Areopagite, the supposed first Bishop of Athens, but which breathe the spirit of Neoplatonism. They aroused great interest and exerted a profound influence on medieval thought. Among those who came under the spell of their mystical pantheism was John Scotus Erigena, who translated them into Latin and reared a system of philosophy upon their foundation. He was born in Ireland in 810, educated in the Irish schools, and called by Charles the Bald to head the Schola Palatina at Paris. The date of his death is unknown, though he is supposed to have lived until 877. His philosophy is presented in his work *De divisione naturae.*

A. Gardner, *John the Scot*, 1900; H. Bett, *Johannes Scotus Erigena*, 1925; E. von Erhardt-Siebold and R. von Erhardt, *Astronomy of Johannes Scotus Erigena*, 1940.

Pantheism. The theology of Scotus moves in the familiar atmosphere of Neoplatonic and Augustinian ideas. God is the beginning, middle, and end of all things; from him they come, in him and through him they exist, and to him they will return. He created the world out of nothing; he is the causeless first cause who produces all things out of himself. Or, as Scotus expresses it: Nature (as God) is an uncreated creator, the uncreated creating principle (*natura creans*). He created the world according to the plan or eternal patterns in his mind (the Logos), which is an expression of his being: his intelligence is responsible for the form and order in things, and continues to act on them. Or, as Scotus puts it: Nature (as Logos) is a created creator, while nature (as the things produced by the Logos) is created and noncreative. Everything, physical as well as mental, will return to God and be eternally at rest in him, for he is the ultimate goal of all creation; nature, in this aspect, is, according to Scotus, the uncreated and non-creating. God, as being, is Father; as Logos, or wisdom, Son; as life, Holy Ghost.

The universe is an expression or product of God's essence: everything—God's thought, the Logos, and the phenomenal world—proceeds from him. But the manifestation is not separate from God: it is his living garment, not something cast off by him. God and his creation are one; he is in his creation and his creation is in him. They are one and the same in the sense that he reveals himself in his creatures; the invisible and incomprehensible One makes himself visible. He that is without form and quality assumes both. The universe appears to man as a divided, manifold, and plural universe, as a *theophany;* but in its own nature it is one single undivided whole, a whole in which all opposites are reconciled.

God, then, is immanent in the world; but he is also transcendent. That is, Scotus is unwilling to conceive the universe as exhausting or even diminishing the divine nature. It is only a partial unfolding of the divine nature, and there is infinitely more in God than is expressed in nature. Just as one light can be seen and one voice heard by many without diminution of the light or sound, so all things share in God's existence without detracting from the fullness of his being. God's nature so transcends human comprehension that whatever terms we may employ fail to describe him: he is beyond anything language can express, far beyond all the categories of thought. Indeed, to predicate anything of him is to limit him; to affirm one quality is to negate another. He is superessential: he transcends goodness, deity, truth, eternity, and wisdom. He is the ineffable, incomprehensible, unknowable, and indefinable principle, of whom, to speak paradoxically, nothing and yet everything—since everything is an expression or manifestation of his nature—can be predicated.

From this pantheistic doctrine it would follow that man, too, is a manifestation of the divine principle; but Scotus is not ready to draw this conclusion, since it would imply human determinism and impute evil to God. Man is more than his phenomenal body, he is the microcosm, a living spirit, and is himself responsible for his fall from God. God cannot be the cause of evil; there is no idea of evil in God. Evil is, as St. Augustine had taught, nothing but the privation of good. Through a union with human nature, the Logos helped to redeem men by uniting them with God, by bringing them back to their original love of God.

Mysticism. As all things come from God, so all strive to return to him: he is both the source and goal of their existence. The return to God is made possible by mystical exaltation, by contemplating his divine nature, by rising above sense and reason and contemplating nothing but the incomprehensible transcendency of his being. In this state of mystical ignorance, we plunge into the divine darkness and lose ourselves in its life.

Scotus Erigena may be called a forerunner of scholasticism in so far as he aims to render the Christian conceptions intelligible by assimilating them to a universal system; and also in so far as his philosophy contains the germs of medieval realism. His thinking, however, was far too independent, and his teachings too little in harmony with orthodox views, to be welcome among the Christian scholars of his time; it was not to be expected that they would prefer the Pseudo-Dionysius to Augustine. More in accordance with the demands of the age was the work of Paschasius Radbertus, who presented Augustinian thoughts in simplified form.

24. The Beginnings of the Controversy over Universals

Early Schoolmen. The appearance of John Scotus Erigena was but a momentary spark of light in the medieval darkness; after his death came another long interval of intellectual quiet. The teachers of the "seven liberal arts" continued to present the traditional dialectic in the time-honored textbooks, and did not expend their efforts in the construction of theologies. They had their St. Augustine to fall back on, and, if pantheistically inclined, could revel in the pantheistic mysticism of the Pseudo-Dionysius, whose writings were now available in a Latin translation by Scotus Erigena, or study the books of Scotus himself. In their logical studies, however, the early schoolmen were giving some attention to a question which had an important bearing on both the theory of knowledge and metaphysics; and which was destined to become the paramount issue in the history of scholasticism. The question was, as Porphyry phrased it in his *Introduction,* whether universals (genera and species) are real substances or exist merely in the mind; whether, in case they are realities, they are corporeal or incorporeal; and whether they exist apart from concrete sensible things or in them. Porphyry formulates the problem of the substantiality of the Platonic ideas and Aristotelian forms, a problem that had played so significant a part in the theories of the great Greek philosophers. The various logical treatises which had been transmitted to the period we are now considering, gave different answers to the question. Some declared for Platonic realism (universals are realities *prior* to things), some for Aristotelian realism (universals are realities *in* things); others for nominalism (universals are mere names for particular things, not prior to them, nor in them, but *after* them). Porphyry was a decided realist; Boethius, Macrobius, and Chalcidius occupied a middle ground, while Martianus Capella was a clear and outspoken nominalist. John Scotus himself was a realist: he conceived universals to be existent, prior to particular objects as well as in them; the phenomenal world, since it is an expression of the thought of God, cannot exist apart from universals. Similar views were held by others during the ninth and tenth centuries in more or less undeveloped form, but not definitely worked out until later. Many of the logicians, unacquainted with Aristotle's works, accepted the Aristotelian position that individuals are the true realities, but interpreted it vaguely in a nominalistic sense without making clear to themselves what nominalism implied.

To be mentioned in this connection are: Eric of Auxerre; his pupil Remigius; the work *Super Porphyrium* by a pupil of Rabanus Maurus—all of the ninth century; Poppo, Reinhard, Notker Labeo, Gerbert (d. 1003 as Pope Sylvester II), Fulbert, Berenger of Tours (d. 1088). The interest in these subjects became so keen that some of the more conservative churchmen protested against the attempts of the dialecticians to subordinate the teachings of Scripture to the authority of dialectic; and Peter Damian (1007-1072) declared that logic should be *ancilla Domini,* the handmaiden of the Lord.

Roscelin's Nominalism. The full significance of the teachings of realism and nominalism and their bearing on metaphysics and theology were not understood until the second half of the eleventh century. Roscelin taught a pronounced nominalism and made it the basis of his interpretation of the Trinity. His argument was as follows: Particular substances alone exist, general concepts are mere names and words by means of which we designate particular objects. Hence, there is no single reality corresponding to the general name God; the notion of the Godhead, which we apply to the Trinity, is a mere name or word. There is not one substance God, but three particular substances or persons, who are equal in power.

The Meaning of Realism. This view was in direct opposition to the official trinitarian doctrine and aroused great indignation and opposition. The Council of Soissons (1092) condemned Roscelin's interpretation of the Trinity and compelled him to recant. Although nominalism as such was not included in the condemnation, it lost prestige and did not reappear until the fourteenth century. The schoolmen adopted, instead, Platonic realism, which, though modified and developed in various ways, remained the dominant conception throughout the twelfth century. It was well suited to ward off just such attacks as Roscelin had made on the Trinity, and to give rational support to the entire Church doctrine. If universals are real, if they are not mere tags or labels for groups of particular things, then the notion of the Trinity means more than three separate persons. The dispute over the question of universals was more than a logical quibble; far-reaching metaphysical and theological implications were involved in the answers. The realistic view that our general concepts, our logical thoughts, are not mere subjective ideas in the mind, but have a reality of their own apart from the mind, implies that the universe is rational and knowable. Thus truth is not mere subjective opinion; there is an objective, universally valid truth, which it is the business of philosophy to attain by means of conceptual thought. Realism also implies that there exist, besides particular individual phenomena which arise and pass away, permanent realities, which never die. The scholars of the Church found in this conception a splendid foundation upon which to rest their entire intellectual and ecclesiastical structure. God is such a universal idea, superior to and outlasting mere phenomenal existence; mankind is such a universal reality, which was corrupted in Adam and redeemed again in Christ; the Church is such an abiding entity, over and above the temporal members who compose it: an ideal whole and not affected in its essence by the coming and going of its parts. It was clearly not by a mere whim that the orthodox schoolmen shelved nominalism and rallied around the standard of Platonic realism: they chose the doctrine which in their eyes gave meaning to the Christian world-view and scheme of life.

25. ANSELM OF CANTERBURY: THE FIRST SCHOLASTIC SYNTHESIS

Anselm (1033-1109), Archbishop of Canterbury, opposes the nominalistic heresies of Roscelin in a system of thought based on Platonic and Aristotelian principles. He is the true type of the schoolman; firmly convinced of the truth of the dogmas and yet possessed of a strong philosophical impulse, he seeks to prove by reason what has to be accepted on authority. In his attempt to rationalize the faith, he includes in his theology not only such general propositions as the assertion of the existence of God, but the entire Church doctrine of salvation, the Trinity, the Incarnation, and the Redemption of man. We must believe the Catholic doctrine—that is beyond cavil—but we should also try to *understand* what we believe and *why* it is true; remembering always, however, that where intelligence fails us, it behooves us reverently to bow to faith.

Among Anselm's works we mention: *Monologium; Proslogium; Cur Deus homo?* These works and the monk Gaunilo's criticism of Anselm's ontological argument are translated by S. N. Deane, 1903.

R. W. Church, *St. Anselm*, 1888; A. C. Welch, *Anselm and His Work*, 1901; J. M. Rigg, *St. Anselm of Canterbury*, 1896; M. Rule, *Life and Times of St. Anselm*, 1883.

Proofs for the Existence of God. Anselm bases his celebrated proofs for the existence of God on the Platonic conception that universals have an existence independent of particular objects. In his *Monologium* (written *ca.* 1070) he employs the cosmological argument, which had already been advanced by St. Augustine, and which need not be repeated here. In his *Proslogium*, however, he offers another proof, also based on Platonic realism; it is the so-called ontological proof, with which his name has become linked in the history of thought. This proof consists in deducing the existence of God from the concept of God, in showing that the very idea of God implies his existence. The idea of God is the notion of something greater than which nothing can be thought—that is, the idea of a perfect being. Now, if God did not exist, this idea would not be the idea of the greatest thing thinkable; there would be something greater still. The idea of a being having existence is the idea of a more perfect being than the idea of one having no existence. Hence God, as the most perfect being, must exist. In this way, Anselm seeks to prove that the perfection of God implies his existence.

The conclusion, however, does not necessarily follow from Anselm's premises. His reasoning proves no more than that when we think of a being as existing, we are thinking of a being that is more perfect than a non-existent being. The notion of an existing being is the notion of a being that has more qualities than a being conceived as not existing. He does not prove that God exists, but merely that the idea of an existing God connotes more than the mere subjective idea of God. No doubt, the idea of God includes the idea of existence; but it does not necessarily follow from the *notion* of a perfect being, a notion which carries with it the idea of existence, that such a being actually exists. It should be noted, however, that the onto- logical argument will seem cogent to anyone accepting the realistic presup- position that universals have an extra-mental reality; the realistic theory of universals is thus an implicit premise of the ontological argument for God's existence.

The fallacy in Anselm's argument was exposed by the monk Gaunilo in his anonymously published book *Against the Reasoning in Anselm's Pros- logium*. The being of God in the mind, he declares, is the same as the being of any other thing in the mind, that is, so far as it is thought. In the same way in which Anselm proves the existence of God, one might prove the existence of a perfect island: defining it as the most perfect island which can be conceived, it follows by the Anselmian logic that a perfect island exists. Thomas Aquinas, more than a hundred years later, also subjected this argument to careful analysis and found it inconclusive. It was, however, frequently used in scholastic philosophy—e.g., by William of Auxerre and Alexander of Hales.

In the book *Cur Deus homo?* (written between 1094 and 1098), Anselm offers his theory of the scheme of redemption, which he conceives as a con- flict between the justice and mercy of God. The fall of Adam brought with it the sin of the entire human race. God's justice demands satisfaction, but his love prevents him from inflicting the punishment or suffering commen- surate with the sin. Christ, the God-Man, who is innocent of sin, sacrifices himself for man, thereby satisfying the demands of justice.

Contemporaries of Anselm. The theological applications of nominalism which Roscelin had made impressed on his contemporaries and successors the supreme importance of the question of universals. Anselm criticizes the nominalistic position from the point of view of realism, which, as we have pointed out, is admirably suited to his orthodox purpose. Universals are real; the particular objects constituting a class form a real unity. "The many men in the species are one man," just as "the many persons [in the Trinity], each single one of whom is perfect God, are one God." The question arises: What is the relation of this universal to the particular objects; what part do individuals play in the scheme? William of Champeaux (1070-1121), defending an extreme form of realism, holds that the genus and species to which an individual belongs are completely present in every individual, and that individuals differ from one another merely in their accidental properties, i.e., they do not differ *essentially* at all. Abelard retorted that if this were so, the same substance would have different, and even contradictory, properties; it would, for example, be in different places at the same time. If the universal "man" is completely in Socrates, he cannot be in Plato; if, however, we say he is also in Plato, then Plato must be Socrates, and Socrates must be in the place occupied by Plato as well as in his own. William of Champeaux, confronted with this objection, was forced to modify his theory, and insisted that it had not been his original intention to deny the essential differences of individuals; but it is more likely that he did not see the difficulties in which his realistic interpretation of universals involved him.

According to the work *De generibus et speciebus,* the author of which is unknown, but which is assigned to the early part of the twelfth century, the universal is inherent, not in the individual as such, but in all the individuals of the same species. Thus, the element common in all the particulars of a class is matter; that which differentiates it from other particulars of the same class—its individuality—is the form.

26. Peter Abelard and Twelfth-century Scholasticism

The most interesting figure among all these schoolmen is Peter Abelard (Abaelardus or Abeillard), who was born in 1079 in Pallet, and died in Paris in 1142, after many conflicts with the Church. He was a man of remarkable talents, and the most brilliant teacher of his time. He employed a method which consisted in giving after every important thesis discussed the views of opposing authorities (*dicta pro et contra*), leaving the solution of the problem to the reader himself, with suggestions of the principles for deciding the question. His pupil Peter the Lombard followed this method in a textbook on *Theology* which became the model for all succeeding medieval works of the kind.

Among Abelard's works are: *Epistolae; Introductio ad theologiam; Ethica; Sic et non; Dialogus inter philosophum, Judaeum et Christianum; Historia calamitatum* (autobiography). Abelard, *Letters,* trans. by C. K. Scott-Moncrieff, 1926. J. McCabe, *Life of Peter Abelard,* 1928; J. G. Sikes, *Peter Abailard,* 1932.

Abelard seems to occupy a middle ground between the nominalism of Roscelin and the original form of William of Champeaux's realism (both had been his teachers), but does not offer a definite solution of the problem. He opposes the realistic view that universals are real entities outside the mind of God: we cannot predicate a thing of a thing, yet we can predicate a universal of many things; hence a universal cannot be a thing. He equally rejects the nominalistic assertion that the universal is a mere word; it is a word only in so far as it is predicated of a class of objects, that is, in relation to the objects denoted; universals are not words (*voces*), but conceptual predicates (*sermones*). Perhaps he meant by this that universal ideas, which connote the properties common to a class of objects, are concepts in the mind, and that the terms or words used to express such concepts are *sermones.* This would be the view called *conceptualism,* and it is probably the position of Abelard. But he does not seem to have worked it out fully; he was chiefly interested in showing that universals are not entities apart from things, as well as that there are essential differences between things. It is not unlikely that Abelard was in doubt himself as to the correct view; his great admiration for both Plato and Aristotle made him perhaps feel that both were right. What he particularly desired to emphasize was that our thinking should be of things, that the purpose of speech is to express thought, but that thoughts must conform to things.

In his work *Introduction to Theology,* which was condemned at the Council of Sens in 1140, Abelard emphasizes the need of examining our faith in order that it may not be a blind faith; to this end he recommends training in logic and the use of logical methods in theology. Reason should precede faith, but not supersede it. He evidently believes that a strict logical proof of the dogmas cannot be given, and makes their acceptance an act of free will, for which we are to be rewarded in the future life by a knowledge of the grounds of faith. Abelard was thus firmly held in the grip of the scholastic method, and, in spite of the independence of his thought and his respect for reason, his attitude remains essentially scholastic. Reflect upon the dogma as profoundly as you can, he says, do not accept it until you have inquired into its reasons; but if, after you have doubted and inquired, it still does not seem reasonable to you, make up your mind to accept it nevertheless, for accept it you must.

The part of his *Theology* which aroused the greatest opposition and led to the condemnation of the book was his doctrine of the Trinity. In the Trinity, he said, the Father is the One, or Goodness; the Son is the Logos, or the Mind of God, containing the ideas; and the Holy Ghost is the World-Soul. He also characterizes the three persons as the power, wisdom, and good will of God.

In his Ethics Abelard emphasizes the importance of the good will. The rightness and wrongness of an act lie not in the deed, but in the intention of the agent; the act as such is indifferent, as are also natural inclinations to evil, which are due to original sin. "God considers not what is done, but in what spirit it is done; and the merit or praise of the agent lies not in the deed, but in the intention." Sin consists in our consent to evil recognized as such by us—in willing what we know to be wrong—and is, therefore, an act of free will. Morality, in other words, is a matter of conscience. So long as the agent acts in accordance with his conscience, in conformity with what he thinks is right, he may err, but he does not sin. His act is truly virtuous, however, only in case what he thinks is right *is* right, in case his subjective conviction agrees with objective principles of right. Abelard has in mind the distinction between subjectively moral and objectively moral acts. In a broader sense, everything is sin that is contrary to what is right; but in the narrow sense, only the conscious and voluntary pursuit of evil is sin.

But why is it sinful to consent to what is thought to be wrong? Because such consent implies a downright contempt of God, a disobedience of the divine will, a violation of his commands, which is the greatest of all sins. A good will is prompted by the love of God and acts in obedience to divine command. Such commands themselves Abelard regards as arbitrary deliverances of divine freedom; they differ for different times, but obedience to them is moral and is required. Here, again, we see how, in spite of occasional symptoms of independent thinking, the spirit of scholasticism triumphs in the end.

The School of Chartres. The school of Chartres, of which Bernard of Chartres and his brother Thierry were the heads, and which counted among its followers Bernard of Tours, William of Conches, Gilbert of Poitiers, Walter of Mortagne, and Adelard of Bath, studied and sought to develop the Platonic doctrines, so far as they were known at that time, sometimes in connection with Aristotle's views. Aristotle's *Analytics, Topics,* and *Fallacies* first became known to the schoolmen in Latin translations (1128). The school of Chartres exhibited a keen interest, not only in dialectical studies, but also in astronomy, mathematics, medicine, physics, physiological and psychological questions, books on which were being translated from the Arabic. A realism similar to Plato's was accepted by those who discussed the logical problems: universals, or concepts of genera and species (according to Bernard of Tours, also notions of particular things), exist in purity in the divine mind. To them matter in some way owes its form. Bodies are said to subsist in them as water exists in the bed of a river; "native forms" are introduced to explain bodies—forms which are related to the pure ideas in the divine mind as a thing is to its pattern; the nature of the relation is left undetermined. Material objects manifest the form or idea obscurely. The intellect can attend to the forms or common qualities in bodies by abstraction.[4]

The "Sentences." We have called attention to the method employed by Abelard in his teaching and writings, that of stating the opinions (*sententiae, sentences*) of different authorities on the subjects under discussion. The method was not a new one; it had been followed in a number of textbooks of theology, which were called *Sentences* or *Summaries of Sentences* (*Summae sententiarum*); among others are Robert Pulleyn's (d. 1150) *Sententiarum libri octo* and Hugo of St. Victor's *Summa sententiarum*. (The writers of such books were also called *Summists*.) Peter the Lombard (d. 1164), making good use of all these works, published a book *Libri quatro sententiarum*, which formed the basis of theological instruction for centuries to come, and won for its author the title *magister sententiarum*. The four books of this work discuss: God as the absolute Good; creatures; incarnation, redemption, and the virtues; the seven sacraments. Other Summists of this period are Robert of Melun, Hugo of Rouen (d. 1164), Peter of Poitiers (d. 1205), and Simon of Tournai. Alain of Lille (d. 1203, Alanus ab insulis) presents the subjects taken up in the *Sentences* in the form of a dogmatic system. In his *De arte fidei catholicae* and *Regulae theologicae* he employs the mathematical-deductive method, attempting to base theology on fundamental principles. In spite of his rationalistic ideal, however, Alain frequently betrays skeptical and mystical tendencies. The doctrines of the Church are more certain than all our worldly sciences, but not absolutely certain. If they were absolutely certain, there would be no merit in believing them.

John of Salisbury. The Englishman John of Salisbury (*ca.* 1115-1180), to whom we are indebted for information concerning many schoolmen of his age, criticizes the entire scholastic movement as dealing with fruitless con-

---

[4] Cf. Ueberweg-Heinze, *op. cit.*, §25.

troversies, and demands the reform of logic in his *Metalogicus*. In his book *Policraticus* he advocates realistic studies in education, and the absolute independence of the Church from the state. All knowledge, he thinks, ought to be practical; whatever does not help us either in acting on nature or in doing our duty, is useless. Our true good lies in a pious life; we should believe in the doctrines of the Church, even though we cannot prove them.

27. ANTI-SCHOLASTIC TENDENCIES IN THE TWELFTH CENTURY

Mysticism. The philosophical-theological movement which we have been describing has as its aim the rational interpretation of the Christian universe—of the universe as the orthodox churchman conceives it. The presupposition is that the purpose, nature, and operation of God can be made intelligible to reason, and that a system can be constructed on the basis of the Christian articles of faith. We have here a dogmatic rationalism or intellectualism, regulated by the official doctrine of the Church. Scholasticism as a completely rationalized theology, however, never gained undisputed possession of the Christian world; alongside of it, and often within it, we discover an anti-theological current, a reaction against the overrationalization of faith, a yearning for a more practical expression of the religious life. For this movement, religion is not merely a philosophy of religion, which finds its satisfaction in theorizing about the faith, but is religious faith as experienced; its chief desire is not to prove the existence of God and to define his nature, but to enter into other than intellectual relations with him. This mystical line of thought represents the conservative Augustinian element in Christianity and indeed the leaders of the first school of mystics were monks in the Augustinian cloister of St. Victor at Paris.

God, according to the mystics, is not reached by dialectic or logic, but by mystical contemplation; and it is the function of theology to tell us how such a state may be realized. Stressing, as they do, the inner faith of man, the inner experiences of the soul, they are naturally interested in an empirical study of the soul. Mysticism is practical theology teaching the art of mystical contemplation. But the mystics have their rational theology too, a theology in which the superrationality of faith is emphasized. As the school develops, mystical contemplation is accentuated and even exaggerated: for Richard of St. Victor it is far superior to knowledge; according to Walter, logic is the source of all heresies. Faith not only transcends knowledge, but contradicts it. Walter of St. Victor wrote a book *Against the Four Labyrinths of*

France (In quattuor labyrinthos Franciae), meaning Gilbert, Abelard, Peter the Lombard, and Peter of Poitiers, all of whom he regarded as heretics.

The highest goal of the mystic is "the mysterious ascension of the soul to heaven, the sweet home-coming from the land of bodies to the region of spirits, the surrender of the self in and to God." The road to this goal leads beyond sense perception and even conceptual thought to contemplation, in which the ideal object appears to the soul in its immediacy. There are three stages of knowledge: *cogitatio, meditatio,* and *contemplatio;* the very highest stage is superrational and praeterrational, bearing the mind to the profoundest mysteries of religion. In the most exalted form of knowledge (*alienatio mentis*), the individual consciousness comes to rest in contemplation. This supreme insight is an extraordinary favor of God; all that man can do is to *prepare* himself for the mystical "plunge into the ocean of infinite truth."

The chief representatives of orthodox mysticism are St. Bernard of Clairvaux (1091-1153), Hugo of St. Victor (1096-1141), Richard of St. Victor (d. 1173), and Walter of St. Victor. The mysticism of the twelfth century was continued by St. Bonaventura (1221-1274). Meister Eckhart (1260-1327), Johannes Tauler (1300-1361), and Johannes Ruysbroek (1283-1381) are pantheistic mystics, whose teachings are condemned by the Catholic Church as heretical.

R. A. Vaughan, *Hours with the Mystics,* 2 vols., 1888; F. von Hügel, *The Mystical Elements of Religion,* 2 vols., 1909, 2nd ed., 1923; R. S. Storrs, *Bernard of Clairvaux,* 1892; E. C. Butler, *Western Mysticism,* 1922.

Pantheism. The aim of the orthodox thinkers of the twelfth century was to rationalize faith, and to this end they had recourse to logic and metaphysics. Their rational endeavors rested on the desire to understand the things which the Church taught and they already believed. The traditional theology was based upon realistic preconceptions, which seemed to bring the results of philosophical thought into harmony with the doctrines of the Church. But even when men reason from the same premises, they often reach different conclusions. This happened constantly in the dogma-making period of Christianity; and it happened every now and then during the ages which followed. John Scotus, Roscelin, and Abelard did not succeed in making their thoughts square exactly with the official requirements. Among the heresies which attracted thinkers, pantheism had never quite lost its power: it found expression in Sabellianism, in the Pseudo-Dionysius, and in Scotus Erigena; and the mystics were not far from pantheism. Toward the close of the twelfth century, it appeared again and made some progress. Its chief representatives were the Abbot Joachim of Floris, Amalric or Amaury of Bennes who taught theology at Paris, and David of Dinant, of whose life we know very little. These pantheists reached their conclusions quite simply by deducing what they regarded as the logical implications of Platonic realism. If universals are real, then the highest universal, God, must be the most real being and everything else a manifestation of the divine essence. A realism of universals seems to imply a pantheistic conception of God and his relation to the world of particulars. Amalric taught with John Scotus Erigena that the world of changing and divisible phenomena, which has come from God, will ultimately return to God and abide in him as one unchangeable individual. Such pantheistic teachings found favor with many, and a sect of Amalricians was formed that spread over Switzerland and Alsace. The Church condemned the doctrines, exhumed the body of Amalric, who had been forced to recant before his death, and eradicated the sect. In 1225 it condemned Scotus Erigena as a heretic. In 1210 a provincial council at Paris prohibited the *Physics* of Aristotle, which had found its way at last into the Western world in a Latin translation from the Arabic.

The appearance of all these heretical tendencies is evidence of the growth of a spirit of independence, and an indication that the human mind was again getting ready to try its wings.

28. Symptoms of Unrest

Opposition to Scholasticism. We find, then, at the end of the twelfth century, besides the predominant scholastic philosophy, a number of opposing tendencies. On the one hand, some of the more conservative and orthodox schoolmen are opposed to the traditional system because it puts too much stress on dialectic; for them, it is not strict enough. On the other hand some thinkers, more independent than the schoolmen, reach conclusions antagonistic to the official Christian scheme of thought; for them it is too strict. Still others assume a skeptical attitude with respect to all attempts to construct a rational theology, either because they distrust reason as an ally of an inner living faith, or because the prevailing philosophical discussions do not seem to them to have any bearing on the real practical problems of the Church. In certain quarters the desire is felt for further knowledge concerning the relation of general ideas or universals to the world of particular objects; this desire develops into an interest in natural science, which is fed by Latin translations of Arabian scientific books.

Organization of Learning. There were many symptoms of unrest; the problems and difficulties were multiplying, and many thinkers were beginning to see how hard it was to demonstrate not only the positive dogmas of the Church, but the general propositions of theology as well. In spite of their bold syllogistic constructions, schoolmen often had to confess that the conclusions, though more certain than any worldly knowledge we might possess, still fell short of absolute rational certainty. And yet the fundamental conviction remained that the universe was a rational universe, that God acted intelligently and for the best, that there was truth if only one could make it out. But the goal of the search was fixed; it was sacrilegious and dangerous to tamper with the dogmas; there stood the powerful organization of the Church with its awful spiritual and temporal weapons, ready to discipline those who wandered too far afield. The intellectual activities of Christendom, too, were gradually made corporate and organic; out of the cathedral and monastery schools grew the universities, or corporations of scholars engaged in the study of theology and philosophy, medicine and law; and certain monastic orders formed compact philosophical schools, which, like the old Greek schools, continued for centuries to teach their favorite doctrines. Paris, the great international university, which owed its existence to the union of the theological school of Notre Dame and the school of logic at St. Geneviève, received its charter in 1208. The Dominican and Franciscan orders became the great teaching orders of the thirteenth century, nearly all the distinguished teachers and writers of that age belonging to the one or the other. These agencies—the Church, the universities, and the monastic orders—cooperated in the work of making secure the traditional doctrines of Christianity. The business of the individual thinker was to make reason and faith agree: this was not philosophy, but it was the task made necessary by the preconceptions of the times, and it was the path of least resistance.

The age was not ready to give up the dogmas, nor was it competent to construct a system of thought independently of religious and philosophical tradition; an adequate knowledge of the facts of experience was lacking. Empirical science was at a low ebb, modern scientific methods were unknown; it was an age of books, and there were no books from which such a knowledge might be obtained. The rise of empirical science had to await the more drastic revolutions of a later age—the age of the Renaissance.

Discovery of Aristotle. It was during the period we have been describing that a new world began to open up to Western Christendom, and that a new impetus was given to the study of scholastic philosophy. Greek works on mathematics, astronomy, and medicine, the writings of Aristotle and some of his Greek commentators (Alexander of Aphrodisias, Themistius), and the most celebrated Arabian and Jewish philosophers and commentators of Aristotle were becoming known in Latin translations from the Arabian texts. Around the year 1150 John Avendeath and Dominic Gundisalvi translated the chief works of Aristotle and of Jewish and Arabic philosophy from the Arabian into Latin; and between 1210 and 1225 nearly all the works of Aristotle, in translation from the Arabic, became known. These books were eagerly studied and at first interpreted, after the Arabic fashion, in the spirit of Neoplatonism.

The new Aristotelian literature was viewed with suspicion by the Church, partly, no doubt, on account of the odor of pantheism with which its Arabian expounders had surrounded it. At any rate, we find that the study of Aristotle's *Physics* and *Metaphysics* is expressly prohibited by the statutes of the University of Paris in 1215, and that Pope Gregory IX in 1231 forbids the use of the *Physics* until the work can be examined and expurgated. These proscriptions, however, do not seem to have had more than a passing effect; the books were read, and the foremost scholars of the period began to write commentaries on them. Translations from the original Greek versions of the chief works of the great Peripatetic were made later in the century, and the genuine Aristotle came in time to be distinguished from the Neoplatonic counterfeit of the Arabians.

Robert Greathead, Bishop of Lincoln, had translations made, especially of the *Nicomachean Ethics* (1250). William of Moerbecke translated Aristotle's works (including the *Politics*). Henry of Brabant translated certain works (*ca.* 1271). In 1254 the *Physics* and *Metaphysics* became parts of the curriculum of the University of Paris, the same university that had condemned them forty years before. Aristotle came to be regarded as "the rule of truth, as it were, in which nature demonstrated the highest perfection of the human mind," and as "the precursor of Christ in natural things as John the Baptist had been in matters of grace." Great encyclopedias appeared, based on the new philosophy, composed by Gundisalvi of Segovia (twelfth century), William of Auvergne, Robert Kilwardby, and, greatest of all, Vincent of Beauvais (d. 1264).

VIII

The Culmination of Scholasticism

29. ARABIAN PHILOSOPHY

Greek Sources. Western Europe first became acquainted with the Aristotelian writings through translations from the Arabian texts, and through the systems and commentaries of Arabian philosophers who interpreted Aristotle in the spirit of Neoplatonism. In 632 the followers of Mohammed, in their zeal to convert all unbelievers to the teachings of Islam, had set out to conquer the world; by the year 711 Syria, Egypt, Persia, Africa, and Spain were in their hands. In Syria the scholars of the new militant religion became acquainted with the Aristotelian philosophy, which, tinctured with Neoplatonism, had for centuries formed the chief object of study in the Eastern Empire among Christian theologians and heretical philosophers alike, and had been carried to Syria by the exiled Nestorian sect. Arabic translations were made, first from the Syrian, later from the Greek texts, not only of Aristotle's works, but of the works of commentators like Alexander of Aphrodisias, Themistius, Porphyry, and Ammonius, as well as of Plato's *Republic, Timaeus,* and *Laws* (876). The Arabians also studied translations of Greek works on mathematics, astronomy, medicine, and other natural sciences, and made valuable contributions to some of these fields. Aristotle came to the Arabian scholars in the Neoplatonic dress in which his later commentators had clothed him; there were also Pseudo-Aristotelian books of Neoplatonic origin which masqueraded under the name of Aristotle. Consequently, the Arabian scholars found little difficulty in interpreting the Peripatetic philosophy in terms of the emanation-theory of Neoplatonism.

T. J. De Boer, *History of Philosophy in Islam*, trans. by E. Jones, 1903; H. A. Wolfson, *Crescas' Critique of Aristotle*, 1929; P. K. Hitti, *History of the Arabs*, 4th ed., 1949.

Conflicting Schools. With the help of this literature the scholars of Islam succeeded in placing their religion on a philosophical basis and in creating a scholastic system not unlike, in its aim, that of the West. With them as with the Christians, the pivotal problem was the relation of divine revelation to human knowledge and conduct; the purpose of their science was to bring the teachings of the Koran into harmony with reason, and thus to rationalize the faith.

The questions which, at an early date, led to controversy among them, concerned the relations between divine predestination and human freedom, and of the unity of God to his attributes. The orthodox party accepted the teachings of the Koran without any attempt to justify them: there is one omnipotent, omniscient God, who has predetermined everything. Objections were urged against the traditional orthodox views by dissenters, or freethinkers, called Mutazilites, who made reason the test of truth. These thinkers came to feel the need of a philosophy, and so drew upon various Greek theories in support of their views, without, however, at once constructing a system of their own. In the tenth century there arose within the rationalistic school a reaction against philosophy in favor of orthodoxy; both the Aristotelian conception, with its impersonal reflective God and its eternal universe, and the Neoplatonic emanation-theory were rejected as out of harmony with the Islamic notion of a personal creator of the world. The Asharites, as these reactionaries were called after their leader Ashari (873-935), showed a great preference for a form of traditional atomism which modified certain of the essential principles of the atomic theory. Atoms were conceived as continuous creations of God, and the notions of causation and the uniformity of nature were discarded in order to save the absolute, arbitrary power of God, and to provide for the possibility of miraculous interference.

Those of the rationalistic school who remained faithful to philosophy developed a number of systems in which Aristotelian, Neoplatonic, and even Neopythagorean elements are combined in varying proportions. Some members of the school emphasized the Neoplatonic doctrines, bringing the practical, ethical, and religious teachings to the front; others accentuated the Aristotelian insights, insisting on the study of logic as a preparation for metaphysics, and constructing their metaphysics on what seemed to them a natural-scientific basis.

A typical example of Arabian Neoplatonism is the *Encyclopedia of Sciences,* a series of fifty-one treatises. It was produced in the tenth century by members of a religious-philosophical order called the Brothers of Sincerity, and exercised great influence throughout the Mohammedan world. This popular society, which reminds us of the old Pythagorean order in Italy, had as its ideal the perfection of the human soul in the likeness of God by means of philosophical study. Its ethico-religious teaching was based on the Neoplatonic emanation-theory, according to which all things flow from, and return to, the absolute unity of God. Man, the microcosm, the copy of the universe, must free himself from the bondage of matter and return, purified, to the source from which he sprang. The *Encyclopedia* culminates in occultism; the final part is given over to serious discussions of astrology, magic, alchemy, and eschatology.

In the book on the *Refinement of Morals,* Ibn Miskaweihi presents an ethical system which is a curious mixture of Platonic, Aristotelian, and Neoplatonic ideas, called Sufism, and which emphasizes the mystical side of Neoplatonism: the phenomenal world is viewed as an illusion and matter as the lowest emanation of Deity; by asceticism and ecstasy the soul penetrates the veil of illusion and is merged in God. Buddhistic influences are observable in that form of Sufism which teaches the absolute absorption of the individual soul into nothingness.

Rationalists. The other branch of the Arabian school, the chief representatives of which in the Orient are al-Kindi, al-Farabi, and Avicenna (d. 1037), insist on the importance of logic as an introduction to the study of philosophy, and emphasize the necessity of grounding metaphysics on a study of nature. But their conception of natural science is extremely crude, and permeated with fantastic notions, religious superstitions, and occult theories of all kinds. The interpretation of dreams, theurgy, alchemy, astrology, and natural magic are regarded by these men as legitimate parts of natural science; they believe in astral spirits, which they identify with the angels of the Koran and the Bible; nearly all of them are mystics. The only subjects not infected with superstition are logic and mathematics. It is not remarkable that these thinkers, for the most part, failed to grasp the real teachings of Aristotle and interpreted them as Neoplatonic; it was no easy task to discover the genuine Aristotle who had lain buried for centuries beneath the mass of Neoplatonic commentaries and interpretations.

In their logical studies, the Arabian philosophers generally exhibit good judgment and dialectical skill. They too are interested in the question which formed so important a part of Christian scholasticism, the question of universals. According to al-Farabi, universals have no existence apart from particulars, they are in things. Avicenna, likewise, holds that they do not exist as separate entities *prior* to things, except in the mind of God; in our own minds they exist *after* things, as abstractions from particulars; and they exist also *in* things, but not unmixed with their accidents.

In their metaphysics, al-Farabi and Avicenna make concessions to the demands of their religion. They try to weaken the Aristotelian notion of an eternal universe by making a distinction between necessary and potential existence. The eternal original being, which with Aristotle they conceive as intelligence (the primary and only direct product of God), is necessary and independent of any cause; everything else depends for its existence on this cause and is conditioned—that is, potential in God. The evolution of a world from its ground is a process of emanation. For al-Farabi, matter is a phase of this process; for Avicenna, it is eternal and uncreated. But according to both, creation means the actualization or realization of the potential in matter; form is somehow given to matter by God; God seems to place forms, as potencies, in matter and then to realize them, or bring them out, by means of his active intellect. This is, according to al-Farabi, a process in time. Avicenna held that the emanation of the lower from the higher is an eternal process, on the ground that the effect must be simultaneous with the cause, which is eternal; hence, the universe is eternal.

One of the numerous emanations from God is active or creative thought, the spirit of the lunar sphere, which gives everything the form it has been prepared to receive. And it is through this universal active intellect that the potential intellect is realized, or knowledge brought out in man. According to al-Farabi, the human intellect, thus actualized, becomes a simple immortal substance.

The goal of philosophy is to know God and to be like God, so far as this is possible. It can be reached, according to Avicenna, by instruction as well as by divine illumination; al-Farabi, however, regards a mystical union of the soul with God as "an old wives' tale."

Downfall of Philosophy in the East. Arabian philosophy comes to an end in the Orient at the turning point of the eleventh century. Al-Ghazzali attacks the teachings of the philosophers in the interest of the popular religion in his book, *Destruction of the Philosophers,* and denies the competence of philosophy to attain truth. He misses in the systems the doctrines especially emphasized by Islam orthodoxy: the theory of creation, the doctrine of personal immortality, and the belief in the absolute prescience and providence of God—the view that God knows and foresees all the minute occurrences of life and can interfere in them at any time. The appearance of al-Ghazzali's work not only silenced the philosophers, but led to the burning of their books by the public authorities.

The Spanish School. Arabian philosophy, however, continued its existence and flourished in the Moorish caliphate of Spain, particularly at Cordova, the seat of a celebrated school at which Mohammedans, Jews, and Christians studied without interference. The most important among the Arabian thinkers in the West are: Avempace, Abubacer, and Averroës (Ibn Roshd, 1126-1198). These men were physicians as well as philosophers. In the greatest of them, Averroës, whose ideas influenced Christian scholars, Arabian thought reaches its culmination.

Avempace denied individual immortality, regarding as immortal only the universal intellect which manifests itself in particular human minds. He also opposed mysticism; the ideal is, indeed, to rise beyond the lower stages of soul-life to complete self-consciousness, in which thought becomes identical with its object; but this goal is reached not by ecstasy, but through a gradual and natural development of our mental functions. With this Abubacer largely agrees in his philosophical romance, in which he describes the gradual evolution of the natural capacities of a human being, living alone on a desert island, and his final union with God by means of asceticism and ecstasy.

Averroës had a high opinion of Aristotle, regarding his intellect as the perfection of the human mind. His chief ambition was to reproduce the true Aristotle—an ambition, however, which he can hardly be said to have realized. The task was impossible for him—owing partly to the Neoplatonic preconceptions with which he approached the interpretation of the great Greek's teachings, partly because of the desire, characteristic of nearly every medieval philosopher, to accommodate his theories to the demands of his religion. At any rate, Averroës accepts the fundamental dogmas of the corrupted Aristotelianism of Islam: the emanation-theory and the doctrine of the universal intellect.

Forms, he teaches, are implicit in matter; not superadded, as al-Farabi and Avicenna had held, but unfolded, or evolved, or realized, by the action of higher forms, of which the highest is the divine intellect. Creation in the ordinary sense is, therefore, rejected. There is one universal active mind, which influences particular individuals and brings them to knowledge. This is explained by Averroës in the following manner: individual souls are naturally predisposed to such influence; by the action of the universal active mind the predisposed soul becomes a potential mind and so has implicit intelligence. The union of the universal mind with a soul capable of receiving it, yields an individualized soul: just as the sunlight is individualized or particularized by striking a body capable of receiving light, so a soul, capable of receiving intelligence, is individualized by the entrance into it of the universal spirit. By further action of the universal mind on this individualized soul, the knowledge implicit in the latter is made explicit or realized; it rises to the highest self-consciousness, and in this form becomes one with the universal spirit or absorbed in it (mysticism); it becomes a phase or element in the mind which is common to all human beings. In this sense, and in this sense only, is the individual soul immortal, not in the sense of personal immortality; the universal spirit alone is immortal. The universal mind itself Averroës conceives as one of the many emanations of God; it is an emanation of the spirit or mover of the sublunar sphere.

With all of the Arabian philosophers of his school, Averroës holds that the common man cannot grasp the whole truth, that in religion it is given to him in symbols which the philosopher interprets allegorically, but which the common man takes literally. Hence, a thing may be true in philosophy that is not true in theology, and vice versa. Thus, Averroës affirms that he necessarily infers the unity of intelligence by reason, but firmly holds to the opposite view by faith. Averroës was accused in his old age of teaching doctrines harmful to Mohammedanism and was banished from the court of the Calif of Cordova, whose physician he was.

It is not hard to understand why the Christian Church received with distrust the philosophical gifts of the Arabians. She had pantheistic heresies of her own to contend with, and had no desire to open the doors to the heresies of the infidels.

Jewish Philosophy. The different tendencies of Arabian thought which have been described above, greatly influenced, and are reflected in, the Jewish philosophy of the Middle Ages. Avicebron (Solomon ibn Gebirol), who lived in Spain during the eleventh century, offered a compendium of Neoplatonism in his book called *Fons vitae,* which became widely known among the schoolmen of Europe. The greatest Jewish philosopher of the period was Moses Maimonides of Cordova (Mose ben Maimun, 1135-1204), a follower of Aristotelianism and author of *Guide for the Perplexed* (*Moreh Nebûchim*). He accepts the authority of Aristotle for the sublunar sphere, but turns to Jewish revelation for knowledge of the divine, upholding the doctrine of creation out of nothing and the notion of an all-wise Providence in human affairs. He also teaches the freedom of the will and the immortality of the soul (that is, of the acquired active intellect).

30. The Influence of Aristotle

Scholasticism and Aristotle. Although the study of the Aristotelian philosophy gave scholasticism a new lease on life, it did not at once produce any great change in the philosophical conceptions of the times. Indeed, it was because Aristotle could be used to strengthen the prevailing scholastic system that he was so readily accepted. The chief aim of the schoolmen had always been to harmonize religion and philosophy; they now had a complete system of thought, the most developed product of Greek wisdom, ready at hand to form one of the partners of the union. It embraced all the branches of human knowledge, it reached definite conclusions, it presented them in clear and precise language, it had a fixed terminology; it impressed the schoolmen, as it impresses everyone, as the work of calm impersonal reason. It satisfied the scholastic bent for dialectic, giving reasons for and against every important thesis; it was the work of the master of logic.

There was much in the content of the Aristotelian teachings that fulfilled the demands of scholasticism; and where doctrinal agreement seemed to end, the scholastic mind had no difficulty in compelling harmony by convenient interpretations or by modifying doctrines to meet the official view. Aristotle taught the existence of a purely spiritual God, distinct from the universe and transcending it, yet the first and final cause of it—a theistic and dualistic conception which corroborated the Christian view. He offered a thoroughgoing teleological theory of nature, one that always appeals to common sense, and which was particularly attractive to an age beginning to take an interest in the study of nature. Here, then, seemed to be a system that organized the field of human knowledge as completely as the dogmatic system organized the field of revealed knowledge. It is not surprising that the "prince of those who know" soon became the greatest authority in "natural things," and that scholasticism now undertook to use him in support of the Christian world-view.

There were, it is true, serious points of difference between the Aristotelian system and the Christian philosophy, differences which made themselves felt in the course of the history of scholasticism. Aristotle taught the eternity of the universe, the Church creation out of nothing; Aristotle denied while the Church affirmed personal immortality; Aristotle's ethics was naturalistic, the Church's supernaturalistic. But where differences and difficulties between the two authorities appeared, the schoolmen harmonized, reconciled, modified, and supplemented them to suit their needs—and with brilliant results.

Augustinian Theology. The traditional theological movement of the twelfth century, however, did not come to an end with the advent of Aristotle. The dogma of the Church had developed under the influence of Platonic conceptions, and the Augustinian theology, which represented the first great synthesis of orthodox thought and Greek philosophy, continued to exercise an important influence. The function of scholasticism, at the beginning of the thirteenth century, was to assimilate the new material as best it could, to transform it in accordance with its own constitution—only to be itself gradually transformed in the process. Some of the Christian teachers, however, were very little affected by the new philosophy and remained true, in the main, to twelfth-century traditions. Among these were Alexander of Hales and Henry of Ghent. Others, like Albert the Great and St. Thomas Aquinas, sought a synthesis of the traditional theology with Peripatetic thought; still others, like Siger of Brabant, aimed at a pure Aristotelianism, as they understood it. The line of progress for the immediate future lay in the direction of the union of Peripatetic philosophy with the past achievements of scholasticism.

Alexander of Hales (d. 1245), an English Franciscan monk, was the first to make use of the new teachings to prove the old dogmas in a book of Sentences (*Summa universae theologiae*). Questions are asked and answered, and the answers demonstrated, syllogistically, by references to authorities. As authorities in matters of faith he appealed to the Latin Fathers, Ambrose, Augustine, Jerome; also the Venerable Bede, Alcuin, Anselm, the Victorines, Peter the Lombard, Bernard of Clairvaux; as authorities of reason, he invoked Plato, Aristotle, al-Farabi, Avicenna, al-Ghazzali, Cicero, Macrobius, Boethius, and Cassiodorus. In his theology, metaphysics, and psychology, Alexander betrays his Augustinian leanings, as well as his failure to penetrate very deeply into the thought of the new movement.

Albertus Magnus. Albert of Bollstädt was born in Lauingen, Württemberg, 1193, studied philosophy, mathematics, medicine, and theology at the universities of Padua and Bologna, and entered the order of the Dominicans (1222). He won great fame as a teacher of philosophy at Paris and Cologne, and became known as Albert the Great. He died in 1280. Albert wrote commentaries on Aristotelian writings, on the Scriptures, and Sentences; philosophical works and theological works: *De causis et processu univer-sitatis; De unitate intellectus contra Averroem; Summa theologiae; Paradisus animae.*

Works in 36 vols. J. Sighart, *Albertus Magnus,* 1857.

Albertus was the first doctor of the Church to offer a scholastic system based on Aristotle's philosophy. Arabian influences, however, are clearly discernible in his work. In discussing problems with a theological bearing, he also follows the *Guide for the Perplexed* of Maimonides, which seems to be more in harmony with the orthodox position than his other authorities. He showed a keen interest in natural-scientific studies, and has often been called the precursor of Roger Bacon in this field. In spite, however, of his insistence on experience in the study of nature, he lapses into the common scholastic habit of looking at nature through the eyes of Aristotle. Albert is noted for the breadth rather than for the depth of his learning, and was inferior to his great pupil, St. Thomas Aquinas, in critical acumen and speculative power.

Philosophical subjects, Albert says, should be treated philosophically, and theological subjects theologically. This tendency to separate the two fields, which foreshadows the later doctrine of twofold truth, is the result of a growing conviction on the part of many schoolmen that certain dogmas, like the doctrines of the Trinity and the Incarnation, cannot be demonstrated logically. The principle that nothing can come from nothing, for example, is true in physics, but not in theology; it is true of particular or secondary causes, but not true of ultimates. Augustine is his chief authority in matters of faith, Aristotle in natural science and rational theology, and he admits that the Greek thinker is not always in agreement with dogmatic theology.

His thought was developed and perfected, in a masterly manner, by his pupil St. Thomas, whose comprehensive system will serve as the best example of thirteenth-century scholasticism.

31. St. Thomas Aquinas: The Culmination of Scholasticism

Thomas, the son of Count Landolfo, of Aquino, was born in 1225 or 1227 at the ancestral castle near Naples, and was taught by Benedictine monks in the monastery of Monte Cassino. At an early age he joined the order of the Dominicans, against the protests of his father, and continued his studies at Paris and Cologne, where he became a pupil of Albert the Great. After the completion of his academic apprenticeship, he taught theology and philosophy at Cologne, Paris, Bologna, Rome, and Naples. During this period of travel and teaching, he devoted himself to the construction of the greatest system of Catholic thought that has ever existed. He died in 1274. He was called by his contemporaries the angelic doctor (*doctor angelicus*) and was canonized by Pope John XXII in 1323.

St. Thomas wrote commentaries on many works, among them those of Aristotle, and many philosophical and theological monographs. His chief works are: *Summa theologiae; Summa contra Gentiles; De regimine principum* (which is his only in part).

Trans. of *Summa Theologiae*, 1912-22; *Summa contra Gentiles*, 1923-24. A Pegis, *The Basic Writings of St. Thomas*, 1945, and R. McKeon, *Selections from Medieval Philosophy*, 2 vols., 1930, contain selections in English translation; P. Rouselot, *L'intellectualisme de Saint Thomas*, 3rd ed., 1924; M. Grabmann, *Thomas von Aquino*, 1920, trans. by V. Michel under title, *Thomas Aquinas*, 1928; E. Gilson, *The Philosophy of St. Thomas Aquinas*, 1924; D. J. Kennedy, *St. Thomas Aquinas and Medieval Philosophy*, 1919; M. De Wulf, *Medieval Philosophy Illustrated from the System of Thomas Aquinas*, 1922; A. E. Taylor, *Philosophical Studies*, 1934; A. C. Pegis, *St. Thomas and the Greeks*, 1939; M. C. D'Arcy, *Thomas Aquinas*, 1930.

Philosophy and Theology. The system of St. Thomas is typical of the movement we have been describing. Its fundamental aim is to demonstrate the rationality of the universe as a revelation of God. In its general outlines it agrees with the Augustinian metaphysics, accepting as guiding principles the teachings which had become the heritage of the Church. But it adopts Aristotle's method and operates throughout with Aristotelian conceptions: we hear again of *actus purus*, form and matter, actuality and potentiality, the four kinds of causes, and other Peripatetic principles of explanation. And yet, there is no tendency to weaken the validity of the Church's dogmas; the naturalism of Aristotle in no wise interferes with the supernaturalism of the Christian scheme of thought, so that no complaint can be made against the strict orthodoxy of St. Thomas.

Philosophy, according to St. Thomas, passes from facts to God; theology, from God to facts. He follows Albert in his distinction between reason and faith: dogmas like the Trinity, the Incarnation, original sin, the creation of the world in time, the sacraments, cannot be demonstrated by natural reason; they are not objects of philosophy, but matters of faith, revealed truths—beyond reason, but not contrary to reason. We cannot prove them, nor can we disprove them, but we can disprove objections to them. No necessary proof can be offered, for example, of the doctrine that the world was created in time; it is a matter of revelation, otherwise we should not know it; but there is nothing unreasonable in the doctrine. Only in case we already believe in the articles of faith can their reasonableness, their intelligibility, their plausibility, be made clear. Any attempt to give a rational proof of the mysteries of religion really detracts from faith, since there would be no merit in believing only what can be demonstrated to reason. Faith is a matter of will; the will commands acceptance; this compulsion St. Thomas explains as an inner instinct (God invites us to believe), or as coming to us from without, as the result of miracles.

The separation of revealed theology from natural or rational theology and philosophy was officially recognized by the University of Paris in a decree that "no teacher of philosophy shall consider any one of the specifically theological questions." It has since been accepted by orthodox Christianity, Catholic as well as Protestant. St. Thomas rendered a genuine service to philosophy by insisting on a distinction which eventually led to the elimination of such questions from philosophical discussions; Duns Scotus and his followers went a step farther in also withdrawing rational or natural theology from the jurisdiction of reason, thereby turning all problems concerning God over to faith.

Theory of Knowledge. St. Thomas' attitude on this question finds its partial explanation in his method and theory of knowledge, in which he largely follows Aristotle. Genuine knowledge is conceptual knowledge. Concepts, however, have their basis in sense perception: there is nothing in the intellect that was not first in sensation. The soul has different functions or faculties, the faculty of sensation, the faculty of active intellect (*intellectus agens*), and the faculty of potential intellect (*intellectus possibilis*), by virtue of which it can function in different ways. Each faculty of the soul is appropriate to that which it assimilates. Through sensation the soul receives copies or forms of particular objects, the so-called "sensible species." In order to be known or received by the potential intellect, which is entirely independent of the body, or hyperorganic, the sensible copy must be freed from everything material or corporeal. This is done by the active intellect, which fashions the sensible copy into an intelligible copy by abstracting from it such elements as conform to the nature of this intellect, for the soul can assimilate only what is conformable to its nature. The intelligible copy or "intelligible species," as St. Thomas calls it, is, therefore, not the copy of a particular object in space and time with all its accidental properties, but contains only the essential qualities; through it the potential intellect knows or conceives the universal notion of the thing. The mind could not know if it were not for sensation; nor could it know if it did not have the natural predisposition for forming universal notions on the occasion of sensation. St. Thomas' teachings take cognizance of both the sensational and conceptual aspects of our knowledge, of its particularity and its universality. He also emphasizes the active or spontaneous nature of our thinking, which is the source of its a priori character. The mind is predisposed to act in certain ways; knowledge is implicit in the mind and is made explicit when the mind is aroused to action by sensation.

Through the action of external objects on the soul, the raw material of knowledge is received and elaborated by the higher faculties of the mind into conceptual knowledge. Hence genuine knowledge, or science (*scientia*), has its basis in sense perception, in experience, and we can know only what we experience. Consequently, it is necessary for the philosopher to make the world of experience the starting-point of his explanation, to rise from an analysis of experience to the principles, or essence, of things. Such a science of being is metaphysics. Metaphysics abstracts from the particular objects their common qualities, and thinks in terms of universals. Hence, there can be science only where there are universals, only where there are particulars with common qualities. Since every spiritual being is a species of its own, there can be no universal notions of spiritual beings, and no genuine knowledge of them.

Metaphysics. Since science has the universal for its object, universals must be real, otherwise there could be no truth. But universals are not real in the sense of existing apart from particular objects: they are not "subsisting" things, i.e., they do not exist as entities. The universal exists in particular objects as the one in the many, as the essence of things, or their *quidditas,* their whatness, as St. Thomas calls it. At the same time he, like Albert, agrees with Aristotle in conceiving ideas, or forms, or universals as immanent in the mind of God, as well as abstractions from things in the mind of man.

Forms or universals are, therefore, necessary principles of explanation in metaphysics. They do not, however, taken by themselves, account for the world of natural objects; with Aristotle, St. Thomas introduces a second principle, matter: nature is a union of form and matter. The nature or substance of a corporeal being consists of form and matter: by substance he means that through which a thing is what it is; natural objects are what they are through matter and form. With the help of these two principles, St. Thomas attempts not only to account for the order and purposiveness in nature, but also to explain the existence of particular objects, or the plurality and diversity of things. Some realists regarded the form as responsible for the existence of particular individual objects, as *the principle of individuation;* according to St. Thomas, matter is the principle of individuation. The diversity of individuals of the same species depends on differences of bodily constitution; the *materia signata* or *materia individualis,* or definite quantity of matter which a particular natural object has, together with all the particular accidents peculiar to this particular quantum of matter, makes the particular individual object just what it is. In the case of man, it is because the soul is connected with a particular organic body that he is this particular person. Socrates is Socrates and no one else because of the particular matter peculiar to him.

Besides the forms which inhere in matter (inherent or material forms), there are those which can exist by themselves, and which do not need matter in order to be real (subsistent forms). Among these are pure spiritual beings, or angels, and human souls. Their substance or nature, that through which they are what they are, is not matter and form, but form alone: they owe their individuality to themselves.

Theology. God is pure form, pure actuality. We have a knowledge of God by faith, but we can also attain to knowledge of him by reasoning, in the manner already indicated; such knowledge, however, is indirect or mediate knowledge. In all our reasoning we pass from the known to the unknown, from the effect to the cause, from the conditioned to the unconditioned. We infer the existence of God from his creation, we can prove it only by the a posteriori method. St. Thomas rejects the ontological argument of Anselm and makes use of a number of proofs already employed by Aristotle, St. Augustine, and the Arabian philosophers. (a) Everything that is moved requires something to move it, every effect implies a cause: there must, therefore, be a first unmoved principle of motion, otherwise we should be compelled to go on *ad infinitum* in the causal series, and never reach the end. There must be something that exists *per se,* by itself, that does not need anything else through which it exists (Aristotle). (b) Natural objects are merely contingent, or possible; it is not necessary that this or that particular object exist; there must, however, be something that is not merely possible, but real, or necessary, something that forms the ground or basis of the contingent or possible, something that is absolutely necessary (al-Farabi). These two arguments constitute what Kant later called the cosmological argument. (c) Things form a graduated scale of excellence; there must be a highest form or degree of perfection to complete this series of more and less perfect objects. And since everything is caused by the first cause, the first cause must be the most perfect cause, the most perfect being, the cause of all perfect things in the universe (St. Augustine). (d) Everything in nature realizes an end or purpose. Such action implies an intelligence to guide it; a purposeful universe implies a great purposer, an intelligent God. The last two proofs are teleological proofs; they were in common use among the Greeks and the schoolmen.

God, therefore, is the first and final, or purposive, cause of the universe. He is pure actuality or energy; if he were mere potential being, something else would be required to make him actual or real, and he would not be the first cause. As pure actuality, God is absolutely simple and absolutely perfect; he is also absolute intelligence, embracing absolute consciousness and absolute will.

God created the world, including matter, out of nothing. For, if God is the first cause of all things, he must be the cause of both matter and form. And since he is pure spirit unmixed with matter, matter could not have emanated from him; he must have created it out of nothing. It cannot, however, be demonstrated philosophically that the world had a beginning in time, any more than it can be demonstrated that it had no beginning; both views are possible. Creation from nothing simply means that the world owes its existence to God, that God is its necessary cause; it does not imply either temporal or eternal creation. We are, therefore, dependent on revelation for the belief that the universe had a beginning in time. Time began with the creation of the world. God not only created the world, but is responsible for its existence at every moment of time: his creation is a continuous creation. He has chosen this world as the best of all possible worlds, for he can will only the best, since his will is determined by the good. His purpose in creation is to reveal himself in all possible ways, hence he creates all possible grades of being.

Psychology. God created nature, human souls, and angels. Angels are pure immaterial spirits, there being as many species of angels as there are individual angels. Natural objects are corporeal, in them form inheres in matter; there are plant souls and animal souls, but they have no existence apart from matter. Man is both pure spirit and matter; he is one person embracing two principles of being in the unity of a complete substance. The soul of man is an immaterial "subsistent" form, the entelechy of the body; it is organic, sensitive, and intelligent. The one soul, the formative or vital principle of the body, possesses three different capacities or functions: the moving function, the sensitive function and the intellectual function. The embryo has only the organic and sensitive soul; the intellectual soul is added at birth— God creates the soul as soon as the body is predisposed or ready to receive it. Intelligence and will constitute the essence of the human soul and differentiate it from other souls. Although it is intimately united with an organic body, its intellectual aspect is hyperorganic, wholly free from the body. In other words, the human being is a union of mind and body; the two are intimately connected, but evidently not so inextricably bound together as form and matter in nature in general. The soul is an intelligent, sensitive, and vital principle, a trinity which forms and moves the body predisposed to such action, as well as feels, thinks, and wills.

The intelligent soul can, therefore, exercise its functions without a body; it is immortal: "After the dissolution of the body it can remain active." There is not one universal intelligence, as the Arabians held; if there were, man would be neither a rational nor a moral being, his thinking and willing would be the work of something distinct from him. The individual soul continues after death to exist in all its parts, as intellect, sense soul, and organic soul—for these constitute one single soul—and forms a new body for itself like its old one.

The arguments for immortality used by St. Thomas are the old Platonic arguments which had become the common property of the Christian and Arabian world. The human soul knows universals and is, therefore, immaterial, hence separation from the body cannot destroy it; and since it is an actual form (a living principle), it cannot perish, for actuality (life) implies continued existence. Moreover, the soul's desire for immortality is another reason for its imperishableness; every natural desire must be satisfied.

Corresponding to sensible knowledge and supersensible or rational knowledge, man has sensuous desire, and rational desire or will. He is not absolutely determined in his desires and actions by sense impressions as is the brute, but possesses a faculty of self-determination, whereby he is able to act or not to act. But in order that the will may decide, it must have before it the notion of the good. Hence, intelligence moves the will, but does not compel or coerce it; it moves the will by placing before it an object, a purpose or an end. The will, on the other hand, is "the prime mover in the kingdom of the soul" in the sense that it prompts intelligence and sensibility to action; over organic life it has no control. Intelligence and will, therefore, mutually determine one another, according to St. Thomas, but the intellect takes precedence over the will. The will is determined by what intelligence conceives to be the good, by a rational purpose. This, however, is not compulsion; compulsion exists where a being is inevitably determined by an external cause. Man is free because he is rational, because he is not driven into action by an external cause without his consent, and because he can choose between the means of realizing the good or the purpose which his reason conceives.

Ethics. The ethics of St. Thomas are a fusion of Aristotelian and Christian elements. Their underlying assumption is that God made everything for a purpose—for the purpose of revealing his goodness in creation—that the nature of everything points in the direction of this purpose, and that every creature will realize the divine idea and reveal the goodness of God by realizing its true being. Objectively considered, the highest good, therefore, is God; subjectively considered, the good for creatures is their greatest possible perfection, or likeness to God. St. Thomas agrees with Aristotle that the supreme good for man, which he calls blessedness (*beatitudo*), consists in the realization of his true self. Irrational beings are determined by natural or sensuous impulses, implanted by God, to realize their goal; while rational beings seek to realize it consciously and voluntarily. The highest form of action is speculation or contemplation, and the highest object of speculation is God. Hence, man realizes his true self—his perfection and the highest blessedness—in the knowledge of God. But there are many ways of knowing God. We have a kind of natural, immediate, unreflecting knowledge of God; this, however, cannot give us complete happiness because it is not perfect activity. We may attain a knowledge of him by reasoning, but not all human beings can reach it in this way, and, besides, it is not sufficiently certain. We may know him by faith, but faith depends on will, and lacks self-evidence. The highest knowledge of God is intuitive: this is attained only in the hereafter and endures forever; it yields supreme happiness and is the supreme goal of human striving. They are most like God who know God as God knows himself.

We have here the Christian completion of the Aristotelian ethics. For Aristotle the supreme good was speculative knowledge, philosophy, the pure contemplation of God. The philosopher, or wise man was, after all, his ideal. For St. Thomas, too, knowledge of God is the highest good, but it is gained by intuition: it is a beatific vision, possible only in the life to come. In this sense it is a supernatural good; supernatural, also, in the sense of being a supernatural gift of grace. Since blessedness is nothing but the attainment of the highest good, there can be no blessedness without happiness (*delectatio*). Love is another concomitant of blessedness: we cannot contemplate God without loving him.

St. Thomas, in his ethics, does not confine himself to the discussion of the *summum bonum,* but enters upon a careful analysis of moral conduct and a full treatment of the virtues. Acts are called moral which are the result of deliberation and choice; the acts, in other words, of free, rational beings. The goodness or badness of an act depends on the object at which it aims, the purpose or intention of the agent, and the circumstances. These must conform to the rule of reason, which is the principle of human conduct. The supreme criterion of moral conduct is the reason of God, the eternal or divine law (*lex aeterna*), the laws of the Old and the New Testament. The law of the Old Testament has an earthly goal, demands just works, and has fear for its motive; the law of the New Testament has a heavenly goal, demands holiness of will, and its motive is love. The law of God, however, is not an arbitrary law; God cannot will anything but the good. Besides the eternal law, there is natural or human law (*lex naturae*), the law which is written in our hearts. Hence, in order to be good, an act should conform to reason quickened by divine law or natural law, as the result of instruction or infusion.

Conscience is explained by St. Thomas in the medieval fashion. The intellect is speculative and also practical; reason is endowed with both theoretical and moral principles. As the faculty of moral principles, reason is called *synteresis*. The synteresis furnishes the major premise of a syllogism: all evil ought to be avoided; an inferior kind of reason supplies the minor premise: adultery is evil; conscience (*syneidesis*) draws the conclusion: adultery ought to be avoided.

It must be remembered that the immoral character of an external act depends exclusively on the will; an act may be good as such, but it may be turned to an immoral purpose and so be bad. An external act, however, which as such is evil, can never be made good by the will directing it to a good end. Thus, St. Thomas emphatically rejects the doctrine that the end justifies the means. As to the so-called "passions of the soul," the appetites of sense, these are not always morally bad; they are so only when they fail to conform to the rule of reason.

St. Thomas follows Aristotle's treatment and classification of the virtues, supplementing them, however, with Christian conceptions. No virtue is inborn; all virtues may be acquired by the performance of virtuous acts. Such acquired virtues lead to imperfect or incomplete happiness, which is possible in this life. In order to realize eternal blessedness, a supernatural principle of grace must be added to the soul by God, a higher form which makes possible a higher perfection and a higher being. Certain supernatural virtues are poured into man, or infused, by God: the three theological virtues, faith, hope, and charity. Without these, the supernatural goal cannot be reached. The ethical virtues, too, in order to help us realize the life of blessedness, must needs be implanted by God; as mere acquired virtues they are of no avail in this regard. Love is the highest of the infused virtues, the perfect form of all the virtues.

The contemplative life is, as we have seen, the highest, the most blessed, and the most enjoyable life. The state of contemplation can be reached even in this world. Through the illuminating influence of God a state of rapture may be produced, in which the soul is freed from its senses and organs, and lost in pure contemplation (mysticism). The contemplative life is not only superior to the practical life, but also more meritorious. It is grounded on the love of God, while the practical life is grounded on the love of man. In so far as the active life aims at externals, it is a hindrance to the speculative life; in so far as it is engaged in the control of the senses, it promotes it.

The safest and quickest way to blessedness is the total abandonment of earthly goods and the pursuit of eternal life. This course cannot be commanded, it can only be advised: there are certain evangelical counsels (*consilia evangelica*), such as poverty, celibacy, and obedience, by following which a higher perfection is attained. For St. Thomas as for Augustine and, indeed, for all the priests of the Church, the monastic or ascetic life is the ideal life; this, however, is only for the few; for the great mass of men, who live in the world, a less exacting goal is set.

Thus the moral philosophy of St. Thomas Aquinas incorporates the contrasting features of both Greek and medieval ethics, but the medieval ideal gains the ascendency. For the Greek moral philosopher the highest good is always some phase or achievement of our earthly human life, be it virtue or happiness; something, moreover, that may be attained in a perfectly natural manner, through the exercise of virtue and with the aid of human reason. According to the medieval theologian, the *highest* good is not a life in this world—our earthly existence is but a pilgrimage to God—but eternal blessedness in the life to come. The attainment of the goal does not follow naturally and necessarily from the performance of virtuous conduct, but depends on the supernatural grace of God himself. The ideally good man is not the wise man, but the holy man, the man who, inspired by love and respect of God, conforms completely to the will of God. The state of holiness can be best attained in the monastery, away from the temptations and complications of the world.

Like St. Augustine, St. Thomas regards evil as privation. In so far as a thing acts according to its nature, which is good, it cannot cause evil. Evil is due to defective action on the part of the form, or cause, or to the defective state of matter, the effect. In the case of moral evil, the defect lies in the will, which lacks the direction of the rule of reason and of the divine law. All things aim at good, hence whatever evil they realize is outside their intention. This is particularly true of free rational beings. Whatever they strive for, they regard as good; and though it may be evil, they do not desire it because it is evil but because they view it—though erroneously—*sub ratione boni*.

St. Thomas caps his ethical system with a doctrine of salvation that follows Augustine and the orthodox theology. In the Aristotelian metaphysics, the lower stages of existence are conceived as the *matter* of the next higher stages, which are *forms* in relation to them; and so on to the end of the series. St. Thomas embraces this doctrine in calling the natural man the matter and preparation for the spiritual man, the man in whom the grace of God operates and who, therefore, can rise to a still higher state of perfection than is possible to the Aristotelian man. Through Adam's sin man's nature was corrupted and his guilt transmitted to his descendants (the doctrine of original sin), and only divine grace can redeem him. The sacraments of the Church are the organs or instruments through which God bestows his grace. God endows with grace those who are to be saved. This does not, in his opinion, abolish the freedom of the will, because grace can act in man only with the cooperation of his will. God is not responsible for man's failure to return to him; he foresees that certain persons will abuse their freedom and do evil; he permits it and predestines such persons for punishment. The goal of all ethical and religious progress, however, is universal resurrection, in which is included the resurrection of the body.

Politics. In his theory of the State, St. Thomas fuses Aristotelian conceptions with the ideals of the Christian polity already set forth in St. Augustine's *City of God*. Man is a political being and seeks life in society. The purpose of all government is the common weal; this is possible only in a society in which there is internal unity or peace and security against external foes, and can best be attained by a centralized government, or monarchy. The monarchy must be so constituted as to prevent tyranny; but even in case of extreme oppression, regicide and revolution are never justifiable. The remedy should be sought by legal means, in accordance with the constitution—for the political order is a divine order; when that is not possible, the outcome must be left to God.

The ruler should keep in view the divine purpose and enable his subjects to realize the highest good. But since the highest good of mankind is eternal blessedness, the Church and its head, the pope, who is God's vicegerent on earth, are superior to the secular power. In spiritual affairs, therefore, the temporal rulers are subordinate to the priests; they are vassals of the Church, and their subjects do not owe them loyalty after they have been excommunicated. The State is no longer regarded as the result of the sinful nature of man, as in Augustine's *City of God,* but is a divinely established institution.

Followers of St. Thomas. Among the followers of St. Thomas are the following: Gottfried of Fontaines, Aegidius Colonna, Thomas of Strasburg, Hervé de Nedellec, Thomas Bradwardine, Capreolus, Dominicus of Flanders, Thomas de Vio (Cajetanus). Dante (1265-1321), in his *Divina Commedia,* is an enthusiastic follower of Thomist philosophy.

A modified Thomism was taught by the Jesuit Molina, Gabriel Vasquez, and Francis Suarez. Francis Vittoria and Bañez advocated the original Thomistic views.

The Dominicans made St. Thomas "the doctor of the order" in 1286. The Jesuits adopted his teachings at the foundation of their order by Loyola (1534), but later departed from them. Pope Leo XIII made the philosophy of St. Thomas the official philosophy of the Catholic Church and ordered the publication of a new edition of his works. Thomism is today the leading philosophical system of Catholicism.

32. Some Anti-Scholastic Tendencies: Mysticism, Pantheism, and Natural Science

Mysticism. In addition to the great scholastic systems of Albertus Magnus and St. Thomas, we find in the thirteenth century the same supplementary and antagonistic movements which we noted in our survey of twelfth-century thought: mysticism, logical and scientific studies, and pantheism continued to attract many scholars of the Church.

John Fidanza (1221-1274), called St. Bonaventura, a pupil of Alexander of Hales, belonged to the Franciscan order, in which Augustinianism was popular. Although he wrote Sentences and exegetical works, he is particularly noted as a mystic. His leanings are toward the Augustinian-Platonic mode of thought, and his mysticism does not essentially differ from that of the school of St. Victor. His chief mystical work is the *Itinerarium mentis ad Deum.*

The way to God leads from *cogitatio* through *meditatio* to *contemplatio-*

In contemplation we pass through several stages: we contemplate God in the corporeal world, then in our own inner life, and rise from this to the immediate vision of God himself. On the highest stage the soul transcends itself, enters upon a state of holy ignorance, and becomes one with the divine will through love. The preparation for such a state of ecstasy, which is a gift of divine grace, is a life of holiness and prayer. St. Bonaventura, himself a member of the mendicant order of St. Francis of Assisi, regards the ascetic life in the monastery, with its vows of poverty, chastity, and obedience, as the supreme form of Christian perfection.

E. Gilson, *La philosophie de Saint Bonaventure,* 1924, trans. by D. I. Trethowan and F. J. Sheed under the title, *The Philosophy of St. Bonaventure.*

Logic. Among the writers who occupied themselves with the study of logic and grammar are William of Shyreswood (d. 1249), Lambert of Auxerre (d. 1250), and Peter of Spain (most likely identical with Pope John XXI, who died in 1277). Peter wrote a textbook on logic, *Summulae logicales,* which largely follows Aristotle and Boethius, and which for centuries remained an authoritative work on the subject. Nicolas of Paris, who taught at Clos-Bruneau from 1250-1263, combined grammar and logic in his *Syncategoremata.*

Natural Science. As has been pointed out before, the interest in natural science was combined with scholastic philosophy, the dominant intellectual interest of the Middle Ages.

During the thirteenth century the pre-occupation with scientific studies continued, although Roger Bacon, one of the leaders of the movement, complains of the scant attention paid to such things outside of Oxford. Among those whom we have already mentioned as encouraging an interest in nature were Adelard of Bath and Albert the Great. In England, the mathematical and physical sciences were cultivated. Albert, Vincent of Beauvais, and Roger Bacon devoted themselves to geographical studies. The scientific men of the times believed that the earth was a sphere—a view which was condemned by the Church—and that the Mediterranean basin occupied the center of the earth. They supposed that India was reached by a westward sea route; indeed, Columbus died in the belief that he had discovered the western part of India.

The names which have been recorded in the list of students of science are: Alexander Neckam (d. 1217), Alfred Sarchel (who wrote a treatise on the motion of the heart, about 1225), John Peckham (d. 1292), Roger Bacon (*ca.* 1214-1294), Witelo (b. *ca.* 1230), and Dietrich of Freiberg (a teacher at

Paris from 1265 to 1269). In Witelo and Dietrich the natural-scientific interest is combined with Neoplatonic leanings.

Roger Bacon. The most brilliant and independent figure of this group is Roger Bacon, who is a curious mixture of the medieval and the modern scholar. Bacon, who was a Franciscan monk and received his training at Oxford and Paris, devoted himself especially to the study of mathematics (which he regarded as the foundation of all scientific study and in which he included arithmetic, geometry, astronomy, and music) and the physical sciences, among which he enumerates perspective, alchemy, agriculture (the science of plants and animals), medicine, astrology, and magic. He also regarded the study of languages, Greek, Hebrew, Arabic, and Chaldean, as indispensable to theology and philosophy. Metaphysics he defined as the science of first principles. Bacon recorded his thoughts in an encyclopedic work, the *Opus majus.*

Of the two methods of knowledge, demonstration and experience, Bacon lays stress on the latter, "for without experience, nothing can be sufficiently known." Experience, however, is twofold: human or philosophical, which depends on the external senses, and inner illumination or divine inspiration, through which we reach "knowledge not only of spiritual things, but of corporeal matters and the sciences of philosophy." By means of such inner experience we may also rise, through seven stages, to a condition of ecstasy or mystical knowledge "of spiritual things and of all human sciences," in which he who has the experience discerns much which man cannot express in language.

Bacon's scientific attitude is far removed from the spirit of modern science. Together with much that anticipates it, he offers a mass of fantastic ideas and superstitions: astrology is mixed with astronomy, magic with mechanics, alchemy with chemistry; and the doctrine of twofold experience opens the door to all kinds of possibilities harmful to the development of experimental science; he did, however, study and observe nature.

Roger Bacon, *The Opus Majus,* trans. by R. B. Burke, 2 vols., 1928; W. R. Newbold, *The Cipher of Roger Bacon,* 1928; F. W. Woodruff, *Roger Bacon,* 1938.

The Doctrine of the Twofold Truth. In addition to its mystical and natural-scientific tendencies, which did not always accommodate themselves to scholasticism, the thirteenth century exhibits signs of opposition to the entire Church philosophy. Under the influence of Averroës, a number of thinkers distinguish between philosophical truth and theological truth, holding that though these may contradict one another, each is true in its own sphere. This device did not deceive the authorities of the Church, and some of the heretical propositions advanced in this way were condemned in 1240 by the Bishop of Paris. John of Brescia proclaimed a number of heresies in 1247 with the plea that they were offered not as theological but as philosophical truths. The Bishop of Paris, Etienne Tempier, again, in 1270 and in 1277, rejected the doctrine of twofold truth and condemned a long list of theses taught in the Faculty of Arts at the University of Paris, among them propositions denying the Trinity, the resurrection of the body, the suffering of the soul by fire, the supernatural nature of ecstasies and visions, creation in time, and the need of grace as means to happiness. An exaggerated version of the doctrine of twofold truth was proposed at about the same time by Siger of Brabant, who tried to show the impossibility of demonstrating a number of "theologically" self-evident propositions, by proving their opposite: for example, that there is no God, no certain knowledge, no moral responsibility, no principle of contradiction, and that an unsupported object will not fall.

Raymond Lully. Raymond Lully (1235-1315; *Ars brevis, Ars magna*), who opposed such heresies, may be cited to show that faith in the capacity of reason to solve all problems had not entirely disappeared. In his opinion, reason not only reaches no conclusions contradicting the Christian faith, but is able to demonstrate with absolute certainty all the mysteries of religion. He invented what he called "the great art," a method by means of which one might "without the effort of learning and reflection give information concerning all questions of knowledge." The method consisted in placing a series of nine concepts and questions on seven movable concentric disks and manipulating the disks in such a way as to produce answers. With this barren mechanical device he succeeded in winning a large and enthusiastic following, which continued to believe in the "great art" down to the seventeenth century.[1] Lully's attempts to rationalize the Christian dogma proved ineffectual, and the widespread prevalence of the doctrine of twofold truth was a symptom of the failure of the synthesis of theology and philosophy which presaged the ultimate decline of scholasticism.

---

[1] Cf. Kercher, *Raimund Lullus.*

IX

The Decline of Scholasticism
After the Thirteenth Century

33. JOHN DUNS SCOTUS

Opposition to St. Thomas. Although the Thomistic philosophy became the official doctrine of the Dominican order and gained many adherents, its supremacy did not remain undisputed. The Franciscan schools, whose first great teachers were Alexander of Hales and St. Bonaventura, adhered to the Augustinian-Platonic tradition and, although they did not explicitly repudiate Aristotelianism, they opposed many of the arguments and conclusions of the new system. Soon Christian scholars were divided into two rival camps. The Franciscans emphasized the practical, emotional, mystical, personal, and devotional side of religion; for them the intellect was of less importance than the will, the ethical-religious content of Christianity more significant than theoretical constructions of the faith. It is not surprising, therefore, that many critics and opponents of the new scholasticism should have sprung from this order.

A number of possibilities were open to the dissenters: (1) to attack certain principles of the dominant philosophy; (2) to reject as unsuccessful the union of Christianity with Aristotelianism; (3) to deny the demonstrableness of the faith; (4) to deny the possibility of scholasticism altogether. By adopting the first three of these positions, John Duns Scotus paved the way for the acceptance of the fourth and thus assisted in the overthrow of the scholastic system.

Among those who joined the opposition to Thomism were the following, some of whom have already been mentioned in other connections: Peckham, Warro, Kilwardby, William Lamarre (who wrote *Correctorium fratris Thomae*, in 1284), Richard of Middletown, Henry of Ghent, Siger of Brabant, Matthew of Aquasparta, Peter John Olivi, Roger Bacon, and William Durand of St. Pourcain.

The spirit of opposition to the Thomistic system found expression in the thought of John Duns Scotus.

John Duns Scotus, born *ca.* 1274, was a native of England or Ireland and a member of the Franciscan order. The exact place and date of his birth are not known. He studied at Oxford, where he showed an aptitude for mathematics, and became a teacher at Oxford, Paris, and finally at Cologne, where he died in 1308. His fame rests not so much on his constructive ability as on his dialectical skill and critical acumen; his title, "the subtle doctor," was well earned. He was influenced by Roger Bacon and Alexander of Hales, and regarded St. Augustine and St. Anselm as the highest authorities. The Franciscans made him the doctor of their order.

Among his works are: *Opus Oxoniense* and *Opus Parisiense* (lecture notes published by his pupils at Paris); *Quaestiones quodlibetales. Works,* 26 vols., 1895.

C. R. S. Harris, *Duns Scotus,* 2 vols., 1927.

Faith and Knowledge. The philosophy of Duns Scotus is based on the following presuppositions: The dogmas are beyond dispute; faith is the basis of the highest truth; love is the fundamental virtue; faith and love are based on the will, and are the conditions of the vision of God; the will is superior to the intellect. He agrees with St. Thomas that there can be no conflict between the truths of faith and the truths of reason; and he avails himself of philosophical knowledge to support his own theories and to criticize those of his adversaries. In his opinion, also, reason is incapable of explaining the mysteries of religion and must be supplemented by faith. But Duns Scotus goes far beyond St. Thomas in restricting the sphere of reason; his mathematical studies had taught him what constituted real demonstration, and he did not consider propositions pertaining to the divine nature, the divine purpose, the divine prescience and predestination, the immortality of the soul, and the like, susceptible of rational demonstration. On such matters, he held that faith alone can give us certainty. Faith may not entirely exclude doubt, but it does exclude convincing doubt. The aim of theology is practical, not theoretical. Without a revealed doctrine, which is the concern of theology, we could not know the purpose of God toward man, for science cannot tell us this. Theology has its own principles and, since it is concerned with the highest possible object, namely God, it takes precedence over all the sciences. Philosophy, too, has its own principles; it is an independent science, in no way subordinate to theology.

In this teaching a clean separation is made between revealed theology and philosophy, which if consistently adhered to leads to the emancipation of

philosophy from its servitude to theology. Duns Scotus made the separation
in the interest of faith, but, in so doing, he opened the way for the liberation
of philosophy. He was so thoroughly convinced of the truth of revealed theology that he feared no danger from rational thought; he was confident that
reason, if properly employed, could not fail to be in harmony with religion.
Reason, it is true, could not demonstrate the dogmas, but neither could it
disprove them. For thinkers of a less firm faith than Scotus, there were
other possibilities: reason might reach conclusions conflicting with dogma;
and then it would be necessary either to accept or pretend to accept both
reason and faith, or to abandon the dogma itself. Each of these alternatives
was chosen by some thinkers of the period.

The Doctrine of Universals. In his doctrine of universals, Duns Scotus largely
followed the theory of his time, which St. Thomas, too, had accepted. Universals exist *before* things, as forms in the mind of God; *in* things, as their
essence or general nature; and *after* things, as abstract concepts in our
minds. Universals are not mere ideas in finite minds and, thus, conceptual
knowledge has a real object. If universals had no extra-mental reality, all
science would be reduced to mere logic. The principle that governs Duns
Scotus is that thought and reality agree, that logical notions and distinctions
are not mere acts of thought, but have a reality corresponding to them. It
is not necessary, however, that the correspondence between knowledge and
objects be one of identity, or even that the one should be an exact copy of
the other. We could not think at all if we did not begin with particular
objects; yet, starting from particulars, we think in universal terms. Accepting the logical distinction between the genus and the species, we find that
the genus necessarily implies the species, and that a species in turn necessarily implies individuals. There is an individual difference distinguishing
individuals from one another, as there is a specific difference differentiating
species. The process of differentiation can go no further than the individual,
for we cannot logically divide the individual: every individual or particular
thing is an indivisible unity, an ultimate reality, the terminus of logical and
metaphysical differentiation. It is the individual difference which constitutes
a particular individual; just as the species is the genus plus the *specific* difference, so the individual is the species plus the *individual* difference. The
universal nature, or essence, or *whatness* (*quidditas*) is here supplemented
by the individual nature, by *thisness* (*haecceitas,* as later writers expressed
it). Just as *man* is derived, logically, from animal by the addition of the specific difference—*humanity*—to life, so Socrates comes from man by the addi-

tion to the universal and specific essence, of the individual character, *Socratitas*. The *principle of individuation,* declares Duns Scotus, is to be found in this individual difference and not, as St. Thomas had thought, in matter. The particular thing is what it is, not because of its matter—if that were so, the members of the same species would all be the same—but because of its individual nature, its individuality. This individuating difference is not a thing (*res*) or entity added to the general characteristics of an object, nor merely a logical differentia, but a quality or character conjoined with the general characteristics, and inherent or imminent in them.

By descending from universals or general concepts we finally reach individuals; but, proceeding in the opposite direction, we reach the universal or transcendent concepts, the highest of which is being (*ens*), since it can be predicated of everything else. Besides being, there are other transcendent concepts—the most general predicates which we can apply to things—such as unity, goodness, truth; identity and diversity; contingency and necessity; actuality and potentiality.

Theology. With St. Thomas, Duns Scotus holds that we can infer the existence of God only a posteriori or from his works—the proof is latent in every rational, created spirit, and requires only to be made actual. The doctrine of divine omnipotence and of God's creation of the world out of nothing cannot, however, be proved. God is pure form or actuality, in whom everything is explicit and nothing merely potential, otherwise he would not be an absolutely perfect spiritual principle. God's knowledge is a living intuition of everything real and possible. From the fact of the world we infer the existence of a first cause to which, of necessity, we must ascribe conscious knowledge and purpose. We cannot, however, from the divine nature or being deduce a priori all truths embraced in God's intelligence. Only such arguments as are based on a posteriori evidence have rational certainty for Scotus; all other forms of speculation indulged in by the schoolmen of his day are rejected by him. There are a posteriori grounds for ascribing will to God in addition to intelligence. God's will is infinite and absolute: in a single act he can will everything possible to him, and he is absolutely free to will or not to will. This doctrine, though it is difficult to conceive, must be accepted as a Christian dogma. God willed the world and must have willed it eternally, otherwise there would have been a time when he did not will it and this would imply change and imperfection in God. God alone is pure form; everything else is a union of form and matter, actuality and potentiality. All created spirits, including the angels and the human soul, have matter as well as form. This doctrine was one of the points of dispute between Scotists and Thomists. Scotus is here asserting that potentiality is associated with materiality, that only God, as an actual or realized spirit, is pure form.

Psychology. The psychology of Duns Scotus, like the rest of his philosophy, shows many points of agreement with St. Thomas. Yet their respective interpretations of the soul and its faculties display many subtle differences. Scotus holds that soul and body exemplifying form and matter respectively constitute a substantial unity in man, but that the soul itself is also a union of form and matter; and the body, too, as the particular body of a particular soul, has its form. He also holds that the different faculties of the soul are distinguished from the essence of the soul and from one another, and yet, that there is one soul with its diverse faculties or functions. The radical difference between the views of the two thinkers on the relative importance of the will and the intellect was the source of a major controversy between Thomists and Scotists. Although St. Thomas recognizes the importance of the will in the economy of the soul, the intellect takes precedence over the will in his system. The intellect, the more abstract and simple function, is the higher faculty, the distinguishing mark of the rational being, which, as we have seen, determines the will with respect to the highest good. With Duns Scotus the will is superior to the intellect. The will would cease to be will if it were necessarily determined by knowledge. It has power of assent (*velle*) and denial (*nolle*). Imagination and intelligence are the indispensable preconditions (*causae sine quibus non*) of acts of will, but not their determining causes: the will can decide in favor of temptations of sense or in favor of the moral conscience; it is a free will (*liberum arbitrium*).

This account of the psychology of the will implies that it can, without the aid of divine grace, act in accordance with the demands of natural morality. Scotus accepts this conclusion, but points out that eternal life cannot be won without faith, hope, and love, which are gifts of grace, and which enable the will to perform the acts demanded by God. For St. Thomas eternal blessedness consists in the contemplation of God; for Scotus it is centered in love, which is an act of will in which we are directly united with God. The vision of God is the material cause, or condition of blessedness. Knowledge is an instrument of the will, but will and love, which is a function of the will, are ends in themselves. St. Thomas says that if we had our choice between intellect without will and will without intellect, we should choose the former; Scotus says we should choose the latter. The will is the higher, nobler, more worthy faculty of the soul, it is absolutely free in its action and not determined by the idea of the good; it chooses the good freely.

God and the Moral Law. Duns Scotus extends his voluntarism from man to God. In God, too, the will is superior to the intellect, he is not determined by his reason. Hence, we cannot know his purposes and understand his acts by rational deductions from principles. It was not necessary for him to create a world, and he could have created a different one from this if he had so willed. Nor is he bound by the order he has established; he can change it, *at will,* without incurring guilt. Whatever he wills and establishes is right (*lex recta*). The universe, therefore, is not rational in the sense of being the necessary outcome of rational thought; if it were, we could reason the whole thing out ourselves, think the thoughts of God after him, and confidently predict the course of events. Because all things are contingent on the will of God, nothing in the universe is rationally necessary.

Similarly, the divine commandments which concern our life in the world and our relations with one another are not necessary commandments: God does not command us to act in certain ways because the rules are self-evident to reason or necessary; on the contrary, they are necessary because God prescribes them. He could have made a society in which murder and polygamy and the violation of property rights would not be wrong. We cannot deduce these laws from an absolute moral law, we cannot derive them from the command of brotherly love, because they do not follow necessarily from it, and, besides, the law of love is not a law of nature; nor can we prove that the love of God is a law of nature. Scotus does, however, regard certain laws of the Decalogue, the first four commandments, as necessary. In principle, this, of course, amounts to an abandonment of the entire theory of the arbitrary will, for if God is bound by necessary laws in any one case, he is not absolutely free. Scotus justifies the exception in this way: that man should have no other gods but God, that he should not take his name in vain, that he should worship him, are self-evident laws; they follow from God's love of himself, and God must love himself; they are not merely the commands of an arbitrary will.

Since God is omnipotent, his decrees must be fulfilled. Among his irrevocable decrees are the reward of the good and the punishment of the wicked. But who in particular is to be rewarded, and who punished, is not settled. Here we are dealing with particular decisions, not general laws, and, in these cases, God may change his mind and will otherwise, since he is absolutely free. The divine will is absolutely just because what it wills is absolutely just. Scotus is the great medieval exponent of theological ethics of the voluntaristic type: the source of the moral law is traced to the free decrees of the will of God.

Among the pupils of Duns Scotus are John de Bassolis, Antonius Andreae, Francis de Mayronis, and Walter Burleigh.

34. THE REVIVAL OF NOMINALISM

St. Thomas and Duns Scotus both limited the sphere of provable truth. Doctrines which had been regarded as demonstrable by schoolmen before them, were relegated to the domain of authority and faith. Scotus went even farther than St. Thomas in this direction, as we have seen; he not only circumscribed the boundaries of philosophy, but subjected the arguments which had been offered in support of Christian dogma and natural theology to a searching and destructive criticism. We find him exercising a strict censorship over the intellectual activities of the schoolmen, distinguishing carefully between what is valid and what is invalid in their reasonings, and keeping thought within what appeared to him its legitimate bounds. He does not lack confidence in human reason; indeed, he has an abiding faith in it and employs the methods of logic in theology as well as in philosophy. But he is emphatic in his insistence that the articles of faith, though capable of rational treatment once we are in possession of them through revelation, cannot be acquired and demonstrated by the unaided natural reason.

This view suggested to some thinkers a further and more radical advance: they simply wiped the field of provable theological truth from the scholastic map. Nothing in theology can be demonstrated, they held; theology is not a science at all, the dogmas are not only incapable of proof, they cannot even be rendered intelligible. Instead of endeavoring to rationalize them, we should obediently believe them; though there may seem to be neither rhyme nor reason in them, they are true nevertheless; it is meritorious to believe what cannot be demonstrated.

The moderate realism of St. Thomas and Duns Scotus suggested a modification of the theory of universals in the direction of nominalism. If the particular object is, as Scotus says, the "ultimate reality," if individuality consists not merely of accidental characteristics, but is the final realization of the universal, then the particular object is the only true and genuine reality and, for us, the only object of scientific study. Such scientific study confirms the view, so it was argued, that general concepts or universals are not real in the scholastic sense at all, but mere abstractions of the thinking

mind, mere ways of designating qualities which are common to many particular things. This is a revival of the doctrine which appeared in Roscelin
at the threshold of scholasticism, and which also marks its end: namely, the
doctrine of nominalism.

William of Occam. Among those who drew these conclusions and laid the
foundations for a new nominalistic philosophy are the Franciscan Peter
Aureoli, and the Dominican William Durand, once a follower of St. Thomas.
The great leader of the movement, however, called by his followers the
"venerable inceptor" and "invincible doctor," was William of Occam, or
Ockham.

The English Franciscan William of Occam was born *ca.* 1280. He was probably
a pupil of Duns Scotus at Oxford, and it is certain that he taught at Paris for a few
years. In the conflict which was raging in his day between Church and state, he sided
with the nationalists and enjoyed the protection of Louis of Bavaria, at whose court he
died in 1347.

Among his books are four books of *Sentences; Summa totius logices; Quodlibeta
septem; Centiloquium theologicum;* and works on the power of the State and the
Church.

E. Moody, *The Logic of William Ockham,* 1935; S. Tornay, *Ockham: Studies and
Selections,* 1938; E. F. Jacob, *Ockham as a Political Thinker,* 1936.

According to William of Occam, only particulars exist and all our knowledge begins with them. Hence follows the importance of what he calls
intuition, or perception, through which we become aware of the existence
of a thing and which we express in judgment (*actus intellectus*). We abstract from the particular objects the qualities common to them, and so
form universal concepts. We have no special faculty of the mind, or intellect,
for this; we naturally abstract when two similar objects are presented to us.
Such universals, however, exist merely as ideas or thoughts in the mind,
and are expressed in words or conventional signs which designate many
particular similar things. Science, therefore, is wholly concerned with signs,
or rather terms (*termini*), a term being a word plus its meaning. This does
not mean, however, that our judgments are concerned with ideas only; they
are also concerned with things.

Universals, consequently, have no existence outside the mind, and are
not inherent *in* things; to assume extra-mental universals, as the realists do,
is to make entities of abstractions, or to hypostatize ideas, and thereby to
involve ourselves in all kinds of absurdities. *Entia non multiplicanda praeter
necessitatem:* entities or principles should not be unnecessarily multiplied.

This principle, which is known as "Occam's Razor," because it shaves off the superfluous universals, had already been enunciated by Peter Aureoli. Nor do universals exist, in the mind of God, as substances or entities; like ourselves, he has knowledge of particular things, which alone have real existence.

Intuitive knowledge includes, besides sense perception, a knowledge of one's own inner states—"intellections, acts of will, joy, sorrow"—which is more certain than sense perception. We do not, however, gain a knowledge of the nature of the soul in this way, but merely observe its activities. In addition to such direct knowledge we have, also, what Occam calls "abstractive" knowledge, by which he means the knowledge we acquire by deductive reasoning or the syllogism, and which is necessarily true. The principles forming the basis of our arguments, however, are derived from experience by induction. Experience, then, is the source of our knowledge, and all knowledge that transcends experience is a mere matter of faith. It is impossible to demonstrate the existence of God either ontologically in the manner of Anselm, or from experience. Even the latter method does not yield more than probability, as all the principles which it employs, such as the notion of the impossibility of an infinite regress, are unproved assumptions. Still, the existence of God is probable on rational grounds, whereas the articles of faith cannot even be rendered intelligible to reason. It is impossible to rationalize the Christian dogmas; all we can do is to believe them. Hence, there is no such thing as a science of theology; we are wholly dependent on revelation for the certainty of the truths of religion. Philosophy and theology no longer play into each other's hands.

God is an omnipotent being, bound by no law, free in thought, will, and action. He could have established other rules of morality than those which have been prescribed: there is nothing self-evident about them, they are binding on us only because he has willed them. In us, as in him, the will is superior to the intellect.

Nominalism vs. Realism. We find in these views the abandonment of the fundamental principles of the entire scholastic enterprise, the original goal of which had been the rationalization of the Christian faith, the union of philosophy and theology. The whole undertaking is now declared to be not only presumptuous, but futile; scholastic theology is a pseudo-science, the entire contents of faith are inaccessible to reason. The pious Franciscan who promulgated these thoughts, and those who accepted his teachings as a whole, held all the more obstinately to their faith in the wreck of theology; but men of different temperament refused to give up the attempt to rationalize their universe. The battle between the Thomists and Scotists was now transformed into one between realists and nominalists, and was waged with extreme bitterness. In 1339 the University of Paris prohibited the use of Occam's books, and in 1340 rejected nominalism; more than a century later (1473), all the teachers at the university were bound by oath to teach realism. Other universities, however, were established, in which the nominalists found ample opportunity to express their opinions: Prague in 1348, Vienna in 1365, Heidelberg in 1386, Cologne in 1388; and the controversy lasted over a hundred years.

Followers of Occam. Among the followers of Occam are: John Buridan, who discussed the freedom of the will; Albert of Saxony, who wrote on logic and physics; Gregory of Rimini, Nicolas d'Oresme, Marsilius of Inghen, Heinrich Hembucht, and Gabriel Biel, who gave a systematic exposition of Occam's teachings and is called the "last of the schoolmen."

Pierre d'Ailly regarded inner perception as more certain than sense perception and recognized the scientific certainty of deductive reasoning, such as is employed in mathematics, which is based on the principle of contradiction. Robert Holcot (d. 1349) insisted on the consistent development of philosophical thought, regardless of its consequences for the dogma. Nicolas of Autrecourt criticized the notion of causality and, opposing Aristotle, accepted the atomistic theory and the doctrine of the eternal recurrence of worlds. John Gerson (1363-1429) based his mysticism on nominalistic premises, and emphasized the importance of revelation and faith as means of knowledge.

M. H. Carré, *Realists and Nominalists*, 1945; J. R. Weinberg, *Nicolas of Autrecourt, A Study in 14th Century Thought*, 1948.

35. FOURTEENTH-CENTURY MYSTICISM

Orthodox and Heretical Mystics. We have frequently shown, in considering the different tendencies characteristic of the Middle Ages, how mysticism accompanied scholasticism as a shadow. Many minds refused to be satisfied with a science of God that brought them no nearer to him; a theology meant nothing to them unless it could give them personal experience of the divine being. The current theological thought in the fourteenth century was altogether favorable to this religious movement; the more impotent reason became in grasping and explaining the mysteries of religion, the greater became the emphasis on feeling and will.

During the fourteenth century we find two branches of mysticism: a Latin mysticism, which is submissive to the Church and follows the path marked out by the Victorines and St. Bonaventura; and a Germanic mysticism, which assumes a more independent attitude toward the doctrines and government of the Church. To the former branch belong Pierre d'Ailly (1350-1425), his pupil John Gerson, and Raymond of Sabunde, whom we have already mentioned at the end of the preceding section. The Germanic school includes Eckhart or Eckehart (1260-1327); Heinrich Seuse or Suso; Johannes Tauler (1300-1361); the anonymous author of the *German Theology;* and the Dutch mystics: Jan van Ruysbroek (1293-1381), Gerhard de Groot, the Brothers of the Common Life, and Thomas à Kempis (Thomas Hamerken of Kempen, 1380-1471), the celebrated author of the *Imitation of Christ.*

Meister Eckhart. The greatest figure in the whole movement is Meister Eckhart, a Dominican teacher who died in the prison of his order. Although the Thomist system forms the metaphysical groundwork of his mysticism, Neoplatonic elements, which had their source in the writings of the Pseudo-Dionysius, are present to a marked degree. In his Latin writings, Eckhart presents his views in technical form and in the scholastic tradition, while in his German sermons and tracts he gives them more personal, emotional, and popular expression. In the latter, the ethical and psychological features are strongly emphasized, and it was through them that he exercised his powerful influence; he was at his best when he was appealing to the congregation rather than to the scholars. His interest, however, is always speculative; he does not, like most mystics of the fourteenth century, emphasize primarily the mystical absorption in God, but offers a rational interpretation of the whole Christian scheme of life. His mysticism is intellectual.

With Neoplatonism, Eckhart regards God as an inconceivable, indefinable spiritual substance, a limitless potency in which all things are united. The beginning and the end is the hidden darkness of the eternal Godhead, unknown even to itself. God, as the inexpressible, transcendent being, cannot reveal himself; he becomes manifest only in the Trinity. In an eternal process the three persons flow from the divine nature and return to it. The Deity can become God only by thinking of himself, and in order to think himself he needs the Trinity and the world. God must know himself, act and communicate himself, and will the good. All this Eckhart conceives as a timeless and unchanging process; he first applies human categories to the Absolute, and then withdraws them as unsuitable to a transcendent being.

The world rests in the Absolute; in him dwells the system of eternal ideas, much as a work of art exists in the mind of a creative artist. The world is an eternal creation; all things are in God, and God is in all things. The finite mind perceives plurality; the timeless and spaceless mind seizes all things in their unity; in God's mind everything is eternally *now*. Eckhart seeks to avoid pantheism by distinguishing between the unified ideal world and the world of creatures. The temporal world, a copy of the ideal world, was created out of nothing; it is the overflow of the divine essence, yet it is contained in the divine essence; it is in God and yet not identical with God, and thus its imperfections do not touch him. God cannot be conceived without creatures; he can no more do without them than they without him. God requires most of all the soul of man, in which he finds his true rest.

Knowledge is the highest function of the soul; and the highest stage of this knowledge is superrational. By a supernatural contemplation, transcending space and time, the soul seeks to become one with its object, God. The soul is able to rise beyond the plural, the temporal, and the external because it contains a divine "uncreated spark"; and thus its union with the divine mind is not man's own act but an act of God within man's soul. The whole process of knowledge is an ascent from particulars to unity; it does not stop until it has passed beyond all differences and has entered "the silent desert into which no difference has ever penetrated, which is immovable and supreme over all oppositions and divisions."

Morality consists in bringing the soul back to God. To accomplish this, man must negate his individuality, which, after all, is a mere accident, a nothing: "Put off the nothing, and all creatures are one." "Whoever would see God must be dead to himself and buried in God, in the unrevealed desert Godhead, to become again what he was before he was." "The highest degree of self-estrangement is poverty. He is poor who knows nothing, desires nothing, and has nothing. So long as a man still has the will to do God's will or craves God or eternity or any particular things whatsoever, he is not yet quite poor, and not yet quite perfect." "Act for the sake of acting, love for the sake of loving; and even if there were no heaven or hell, love God for his goodness." "Morality consists not in doing, but in being." Love, which is the striving for the good, is the principle of all the virtues; when the spirit of love is present, right action is the inevitable result. Salvation does not depend on outward forms of conduct like fasting and mortifying the flesh; goodness depends only on the spirit in which the deed is done. All virtues are one and there are no degrees of virtue; so long as one is capable of doing anything contrary to God's will, he does not yet possess the love of God. A person should not spend all his time in contemplation; mere contemplation without moral action would be selfish. Anyone, in a state of ecstasy, knowing of a poor man needing relief, should put an end to his ecstasy and serve his needy brother.

Through grace, man becomes reunited with God. As an individual, he contributes to God's goodness by returning to him and thus enabling him to communicate with himself. God cannot know himself without the help of the individual soul. Insofar as man is immanent in the essence of God, he can perform his works through him; and everything that is an object of his understanding becomes so through man. In returning to God, man becomes one with God again; God has entered into man's being in order that he, in turn, may become God.

The followers of Eckhart neglected the speculative side of mysticism, in which he was particularly interested, and exaggerated the practical religious side. The substance of Eckhart's mysticism is reproduced in a book composed in Frankfort-on-the-Main, and later discovered by Luther, who published it under the title *Eine deutsche Theologie* (*A German Theology*). The work made a deep impression on the great reformer.

36. The Progress of Secularism and Free Thought

Medieval Rationalism. The main historical mission of the Middle Ages was to transmit and to develop the classical Christian culture. The task was performed by the Church, of which the people were the spiritual wards. It was inevitable, however, that the children should grow into manhood and the days of tutelage end. This time had now arrived, and a new phase in the history of philosophy began. It must not be supposed, however, that there was a sudden break—such breaks rarely occur in history. The new period was simply the outcome of a long process of evolution, and carried over from the past many of its characteristics. Scholasticism itself had been the result of a yearning for rational insight, of a desire to understand and find reasons for the new faith. It represented the same spirit of reflection and inquiry which had led to the construction of great metaphysical systems in the golden age of Greek thought. It is true that the goal of its search was fixed by faith and that philosophy served as its handmaiden; but within its circumscribed bounds human reason had a fairly free swing.

The attitude of the Middle Ages toward rational knowledge was by no means the same as that of the early Christians. Primitive Christianity did not glorify the intellectual achievements of man, or expect to enter the kingdom of heaven through the portals of speculative reason. "Where is the wise? Where is the scribe? Where is the disputer of this world?" St. Paul asks, "Hath not God made foolish the wisdom of this world?" This is not the spirit of the scholastic Middle Ages. The Fathers and the Doctors of the Church are eager to understand, they are bent on rationalizing their faith; they desire to know God by wisdom. If they did not study the world as we study it, and did not pursue truth in the independent manner of the Greeks, it was because they were so thoroughly convinced of the absolute truth of their premises, the doctrines of the faith. These were their data, with these they whetted their intellects, these they sought to weld into a system. Their interest lay in a transcendent world and in the relation of our earthly life to the spiritual kingdom; the occurrences of nature left them cold except in so far as they saw in them the workings of the divine plan. What cared they for petty details so long as they understood the really valuable transcendent truths? The Church did not oppose scientific studies as such; it was convinced that no facts could be discovered which would not confirm the great and fundamental truths, and so it brushed them aside.

The Rise of Nationalism. Despite the power of the Church, the spirit of independence and opposition to authority was never entirely extinguished, though it lay smoldering for a long time. It manifested itself in the political sphere in the struggles of Church and state, which began early and were carried on with fierceness on both sides. The victory passed from popes to emperors and kings and back again. The reign of Gregory VII (1077) marks a triumph for the Church: Henry IV of Germany goes to Canossa to do penance and to pay homage to the pope. The power of the Church reached its climax during the papacy of Innocent III (1198-1216); but from that time on it declined. Philip IV of France (1285-1314) met with success in his war with Pope Boniface VIII and caused the removal of the Papal See to Avignon, where it remained from 1309 to 1376. It was during this period that the independent movements of nominalism and German mysticism made great headway. The great schism in the Papacy lasted from 1378 to 1415; during these years two popes ruled, at one time three. The Babylonian captivity at Avignon and the schism were terrible catastrophes for the Church; how could she claim either temporal or spiritual supremacy when she was divided against herself? The unfortunate situation suggested to the University of Paris the idea of a national Church; if the world could go on with two popes, why might not each nation have its own primate? Objection was also raised to the absolutism of the pope within the Church itself, and the demand made that since the Church is superior to the pope, he ought to be subordinate to a council.

Here we have the struggle between nationalism and ecclesiasticism, and between democracy and absolutism. Back in the twelfth century Arnold of Brescia had opposed the temporal power of the Church and established a republic in Rome, but it was short-lived and Arnold died on the scaffold (1155). At first the Church writers sided with the Church, but gradually opposition to the temporal power of the Roman See arose even within the ranks of the Church itself.

Among those favoring Church supremacy were nearly all the old orthodox schoolmen, and, during the fourteenth century, Augustinus Triumphus and Alvarus Pelagius. Dante (1265-1321), in his *De monarchia,* favors the supremacy of the Emperor in worldly affairs, and of the pope in spiritual affairs. Joachim of Floris, William of Occam, Wyclif, and Marsilius of Padua, all oppose the temporal power of the Church. Marsilius teaches an imperialistic theory of the State, the doctrine of popular sovereignty, and the contract theory.

Heretical Tendencies. On the doctrinal side, the heretical tendencies which accompanied early attempts to make a platform for Christianity never disappeared. In tracing the evolution of the dogma, we have already called attention to numerous sects whose teachings were antagonistic to orthodox doctrines. Marcion, a fervent adherent of the Pauline faction of the new religion, who condemned everything Jewish and Petrine, became the father of a movement that continued in one form or another for centuries. We find the descendants of the Marcionites, the Paulicians, in Armenia and Asia Minor from the fifth century onwards; the Bogomils in Bulgaria from the tenth on. In the eleventh century, a sect called Cathars or Cathari, with similar teachings, appeared in southern France. For centuries the Church waged a relentless war against the Albigenses, as the sect came to be named, and with the aid of the terrible Inquisition succeeded in destroying it, root and branch. In the twelfth century a similar sect arose in northern Italy, the Waldenses, founded by Peter Waldo in 1170, which, under the name of the Vaudois, still exists today. Waldo emphasized the doctrine of justification by faith, preached repentance, favored sermons rather than ritual, opposed the confessional, dispensations, relics, worship of saints, and transubstantiation. He made the Bible the criterion of faith, and had the New Testament translated for general study.

In the fourteenth and fifteenth centuries we have the great reform movements inaugurated by Wyclif (1327-1384) in England and continued by John Huss (1369-1415) in Bohemia. Wyclif opposed the Church system, worship of the saints, celibacy of the clergy, monasticism, the mass, transubstantiation, hierarchical government, the primacy of the pope; he demanded a return to the original congregational organization and the independence of Church and state. With the desire for religious reform came a desire for political and social reforms: Wat Tyler in England and Thomas Münzer in Germany became the leaders of social revolution.

The Spirit of Free Inquiry. Signs of a similar independence of thought are found in those who refuse to accept the orthodox philosophy. We have already spoken of the pantheism of Scotus Erigena, which was anathema to the Church, and of the pantheists Joachim of Floris, Simon of Tournay, Amalric of Bennes, and David of Dinant, who exhibited a remarkable freedom in their thinking. The pious mystics of St. Victor shake the very foundations of scholasticism in denying the possibility of a union of reason and faith, of science and religion. Even among the regular schoolmen we find liberal tendencies in the twelfth century. The fact is that when men begin to think, they are apt, in spite of their orthodoxy, to run counter to the prescribed doctrine now and then. Anselm, whose sole aim was to rationalize faith, comes dangerously near, at times, to contradicting the dogmas of the Church, as St. Augustine and Scotus Erigena had done before him. Roscelin's reflections on universals led him into an out-and-out heresy. The entire life of Abelard impresses one as a conflict between intellectual integrity and loyalty to the Church. Sparks of the spirit of independence are visible in the writings of Bernard of Chartres, William of Conches, Gilbert of Poirée, and John of Salisbury, all bishops of the Church; and the discussions in Peter the Lombard's *Sentences* betray an intellectual curiosity which augured well for the future of independent thought. Many of the questions which the thinkers of the age considered with all seriousness, seem barren and foolish to us today; but that is due to our radically altered outlook on life; considered in their medieval religious context, they represent the activity of the inquiring mind.

The thirteenth century turns from Platonic to Aristotelian realism. The interest which it showed in Aristotle was itself a sign of freedom of thought. Aristotle was a pagan, and, besides, the knowledge of his writings had come to the Western world from the "infidel" Arabians. The Church, quite naturally, at first condemned his philosophy, but soon adapted it to its needs, and made it the official ecclesiastical system. The new world-view helped to strengthen the bonds of union between reason and faith, which were being loosened at the beginning of the thirteenth century. In this respect, it is true, Aristotelianism served as an antidote to the liberal tendencies of the age and temporarily stemmed the tide of free thought. At the same time, it contained within itself elements that proved dangerous to scholasticism and ultimately encouraged the spirit of independent inquiry. By placing a heathen philosopher on so high a pedestal, the Church widened the intellectual horizon of men and increased their respect for the achievements of antiquity. The Aristotelian system also helped to arouse an interest in the study of nature, and this in time proved to be a great stimulus to free inquiry. It formed the bridge from Platonic realism to nominalism, and thus to modern science. Aristotle's philosophy was natu-ralistic, Christian thought supernaturalistic; and although St. Thomas Aquinas attempted to supplement Aristotle's world-view by Christian super-naturalism, the contradiction between the two lines of thought remained; and, when it was brought out, as it had to be sooner or later, the great respect in which Aristotle had come to be held made his heterodox theories palatable.

Aristotle's philosophy, therefore, was a "Greek gift" after all, and led to the ultimate dissolution of scholasticism. St. Thomas constructed, on an Aristotelian basis, a system which was acceptable to the Church; Duns Scotus, who, incidentally, was not canonized, believed that he was true to Aristotelianism in opposing the rationalistic, realistic, and deterministic conceptions of St. Thomas. Scotus, in emphasizing the reality of particulars, enhanced the importance of the individual human being and the worth of the individual conscience. His doctrines also paved the way for empiricism and nominalism.

William of Occam boldly developed certain implications of the Scotist teaching and attacked the very foundations of scholastic thought. If uni-versals are not real, they are mere words; if theology is a barren science, let the Church cast it off. Faith should take the place of reason. Let us dissolve the Church's alliance with reason and the world, and return to the simple belief and the democratic organization of the spiritual Church of Apostolic times.

Mysticism had always shown a distaste for rational theology. But in spite of their anti-rationalistic leanings, the mystics of the twelfth and thirteenth centuries remained true to the established doctrines of the Church. In the fourteenth and fifteenth centuries, however, they became pantheistic and nominalistic, as we have seen, and their teachings, though offered in the interests of a spiritual religion, greatly weakened the scholastic system and the influence of the visible Church.

PART THREE

Modern Philosophy

X

Philosophy of the Renaissance

37. The Spirit of the Renaissance

The Revolt Against Authority. The tendencies we have outlined—the development of nationalism, the heretical currents of thought, mysticism, the antagonism to the scholastic alliance of theology and philosophy—are the forerunners of two great reform movements called the Renaissance and the Reformation. The times were beginning to find fault with the old traditions, with the old language and literature, the art, the theological systems, the political relations of Church and State, the authoritarian religion. The spirit of reflection and criticism, which had been silently quickening, finally broke out in open revolt against authority and tradition: in the revolt of nation against Church, of reason against prescribed truth, of the individual against the compulsion of ecclesiastical organization. The conflict between Church and State had been settled in favor of the State; but within both Church and State themselves the desire for political, economic, religious, and intellectual liberty found partial realization in the Renaissance and Reformation, expressing itself in modern philosophy and in other manifestations of the struggle for human liberty and enlightenment.

The authority of the Church over the mind of man gradually weakened and the individual began to assert his intellectual independence. Reason supplanted authority in philosophy, and the belief began to prevail that truth is something to be won by free and impartial inquiry instead of being decreed by authority. The interest of medieval philosophers had largely centered on supernatural things; the new age turned its gaze from heaven to earth, and natural science gradually pushed its way to the front. The same independent spirit became manifest in religion: the individual threw off the fetters of the Church and appealed to the Bible and conscience. He refused to accept an institutional intermediary between himself and his God, and attempted to attain an immediate, personal communion with the object of his faith.

Humanism. When man turned his back upon the past and yearned for new things, two ways lay open to him: he could either create new forms of life, art and thought, or revert to the models of antiquity. The latter course was chosen first. Accustomed as the medieval mind had been to authority and tradition, it was unable at once to strike out along new paths. The intellectual reformers turned to classical antiquity for inspiration; the culture of Greece and Rome is revived or reborn (Renaissance) and humanity is rediscovered (humanism).

With the fifteenth century comes the awakening of the Western world to an appreciation of the long neglected heritage of classical civilization. A hundred years earlier, the Italian poets Dante (1265-1321), Boccaccio (d. 1375), and Petrarch (d. 1374) had cultivated a taste for the classics, and had used the mother-tongue as a literary medium. Laurentius Valla now purifies the barbarous Church Latin and makes Cicero and Quintilian the models for Latin style. Manuel Chrysoloras is the first Greek to become a public teacher of the Greek language and literature in Italy; and his pupil Leonardus Aretinus, the translator of Platonic and Aristotelian works, arouses a widespread interest in Greek studies among the Italians. In 1438 and, later, after the fall of Constantinople (1453), Greek scholars flock to Italy, and the treasures of art and literature which had been preserved, enjoyed, and studied in the Eastern Empire while the Occident was steeped in "Gothic barbarism" are revealed to the willing pupils in the West. Humanism finds its way into the ecclesiastical and secular courts, and spreads until even the universities are touched by its influence. The popes themselves are affected by the new culture; Nicolas V (1447-1455) founds the Vatican Library, Julius II (1503-1513) rebuilds the church of St. Peter, and it is said of Leo X (1513-1521) that he found more pleasure in the study of the classics than in Christian theology. Interest is aroused in human achievements; human talents are no longer counted as insignificant or despicable and man is glorified, human genius exalted, and honors are showered upon the poets, orators, and historians of the times. Art and architecture are humanized, medieval art, expressive of the spirit of world-denial, suffering, and death, gives way to the art of Renaissance, which is an expression of the natural joy of life.

The systems of the ancient Greeks are studied and imitated. The entire scholastic method is attacked as barren logomachy or word-wisdom and dialectical hairsplitting, and efforts are made to devise a new logic. Occasionally original theories are formulated, but they are generally crude and inevitably relapse into the old traditional way of looking at things. The scholastic elements are, however, gradually sloughed off; the ancient patterns are no longer slavishly followed, thought becomes more independent and original, until, at last, the Renaissance ushers in the phase of development which is called modern philosophy.

General Works on Renaissance Philosophy

K. Fischer, *History of Modern Philosophy*, Vol. I, Introduction, chaps. v, vi, 1887; H. Höffding, *History of Modern Philosophy*, Vol. I, 2nd ed., 1915; W. H. Hudson, *The Story of the Renaissance*, 1912; *Cambridge Modern History*, Vol. I; J. A. Symonds, *The Renaissance in Italy*, 7 vols., 1900; J. Burckhardt, *The Civilization of the Renaissance*, 2 vols., trans. by S. G. C. Middlemore, 1878-80; W. H. Woodward, *Studies in Education During the Age of the Renaissance*, 1906; H. O. Taylor, *Thought and Expression in the Sixteenth Century*, 1920; F. Ueberweg, *Grundriss der Geschichte der Philosophie*, 12th ed., Vol. III, 1924; A. Riekel, *Die Philosophie der Renaissance*, 1923; E. Cassirer, *Individuum und Kosmos in der Philosophie der Renaissance*, 1927; E. McCurdy, *The Mind of Leonardo da Vinci*, 1928; J. O. Riedl, *A Catalogue of Renaissance Philosophers, 1350-1650*, 1940; E. Cassirer, P. O. Kristeller, and J. H. Randall, Jr., *The Renaissance Philosophy of Man*, 1948; W. K. Ferguson, *The Renaissance in Historical Thought*, 1948.

38. PLATONIC AND ARISTOTELIAN INFLUENCES

Platonism. The first important task undertaken was the study of the ancient philosophers. A Greek named Pletho came to Italy in 1438 to participate in a council called together at Florence to discuss the union of the Eastern and Western Churches. Persuaded by Cosimo de' Medici to remain in Italy, he established the Florentine Academy (1440) for the purpose of teaching and defending the Platonic philosophy. The entire body of Plato's works was for the first time accessible to Western scholars, and Plato was accounted by the reformers of the period a rival of Aristotle as the official philosopher of the Church. But they interpreted the great idealistic system after the fashion of the entire East as Neoplatonism. Pletho, who wrote a book comparing the doctrines of Plato and Aristotle, was so intensely Hellenistic that he sought to revive the old Greek cults in an allegorized Neoplatonic form.

Pletho was followed by Bessarion (author of a work entitled *Against the Calumniators of Plato*, 1469), who defends Plato against his Aristotelian compatriots, Gennadius, Theodorus Gaza, Georgius of Trebizond. His pupil Marsilio Ficino (1433-1499), a Florentine who regarded Plato's philosophy as the quintessence of wisdom and the key to Christianity, succeeded him. Ficino edited and translated Plato and the Neoplatonists, and wrote commentaries on them. All these thinkers were opposed to the scholastic system of philosophy.

N. A. Robb, *Neoplatonism in the Italian Renaissance*, 1935; P. O. Kristeller, *The Philosophy of Marsilio Ficino*, 1943.

Nicolas of Cusa. The only original system of thought to come out of the fifteenth century, one which does not follow the beaten track of scholasticism, is that of Nicolas of Cusa (Krebs of Kues or Cusa, 1401-1464). Nicolas was educated by the Brothers of the Common Life at Deventer, studied mathematics, jurisprudence, and theology at Heidelberg and Padua, and became a bishop and cardinal of the Church. Like many philosophies of the Renaissance and even of the earlier period, Nicolas of Cusa's world-view is a mixture of medievalism and modern thought. It shows the influence of German mysticism, Neoplatonism, and the Pythagorean number-theory, and oscillates between pantheism and the Christian dualistic conception of God and the world.

De docta ignorantia, 1440; *De conjecturis*, 1440; *De pace seu concordantia fidei*, 1453 (a remarkable example of the spirit of religious tolerance). See E. Van Steenberghe, *Le Cardinal Nicholas de Cusa*, 1920; De Gandillac, *La Philosophie de Nicholas de Cusa*, 1941.

Nicolas shares the nominalistic theory of the incompetence of reason as a source of knowledge of God. He holds, however, that we can have an immediate intuition of him, a "vision without comprehension," as the mystics taught, and that this may be reached by ecstasy. He calls this a state of learned ignorance (*docta ignorantia*), in which discursive thought is transcended. God is the infinite substance of all that is real in things; in him essence and existence, potentiality and actuality are one; he is pure and infinite actuality, absolute potentiality, absolute knowledge, absolute will, absolute goodness. In him all contradictions are comprehended; he is the *coincidence of opposites*, and cannot, therefore, be grasped by conceptual thinking. Indeed, negations alone are true and affirmations inadequate in theology. Nicolas is unwilling to qualify God in any way: the infinite God can be attained only by one who knows that he is ignorant of him.

The world is the explication of God, unity differentiated into plurality; it is the copy of God, an animated whole, in every part of which he is present in the fullness of his power. He is the maximum in that he is unlimited and embraces all things; he is the minimum in so far as he is present in every particular thing. In the sense that God is potential in everything, "each actual thing is a contraction of all things." All this is thoroughgoing pantheism, and, as it stands, would be pure heresy. Nicolas, however, tries to square his theory with orthodox dualism by conceiving the world as different from God: the essence of things is not identical with the divine essence; things are finite and do not completely realize the divine ideas; they are contingent, and do not follow necessarily from God's being.

The True Aristotle. While some thinkers of the Renaissance were reviving Plato, others were becoming acquainted with the real Aristotle, and were beginning to note the differences between him and the scholastic conception of him, which had been influenced by the Neoplatonic interpretations of the Arabians. The Aristotelians split into two parties—some following Averroës, others Alexander of Aphrodisias—in the interpretation of the Peripatetic system, and tactfully criticized the Aristotle of the Church. Thus Pietro Pomponazzi, a professor at Padua, in his book, written in 1516, *De immortalitate animae*, declares that Aristotle did not teach personal immortality, that such a thing is physically impossible and morally unnecessary. Other works of Pomponazzi are: *On Magic; On Fate, Free Will*, etc.

A school of Averroists existed at Padua in northern Italy which was largely composed of physicians and natural scientists who interpreted Aristotle in the Averroistic sense, accepting the doctrine of one universal intellect and denying the immortality of the soul. When the new Aristotle became known, however, the school changed its position, and followed the interpretation of Alexander of Aphrodisias.

An attempt was also made to reconcile Platonism and Aristotelianism— from the Platonic side by John Pico of Mirandola, and from the Aristotelian side by Andreas Caesalpinus. Other thinkers of the times sought to revive Epicureanism and Stoicism; the latter in its Roman form became quite popular with the educated classes.

See A. H. Douglas, *The Psychology and Philosophy of Pietro Pomponazzi*, 1910.

Reform of Science, Philosophy, and Logic. The Spaniard Ludovico Vives (1492-1540) opposes not only the scholastic system, but its entire method of substituting authority for experience. The nominalistic philosophy of the late Middle Ages had prepared the way for such a view. He severely criticizes scholastic sophistry in his dialogue *Sapiens*, and in his main work, *De disciplinis*. Instead of confining ourselves to Aristotle in the study of natural science, he thinks we should make independent investigations of nature; instead of indulging in metaphysical speculations, we should observe the phenomena themselves and reflect on our observations. He also recommends an empirical study of the soul; we ought to inquire not into the essence of the soul, but should attempt to discover how it acts. In Vives' metaphysics, as in the scholastic, God is the central concept. The nominalistic influence is evident, however, in his adoption of a critical attitude toward ultimate problems, in his placing greater value on the ethical significance of belief in God and the immortality of the soul than on the arguments advanced for them.

Peter Ramus (Pierre de la Ramée, 1515-1572), who was influenced by Vives, also attacks the Aristotelian logic in his *Animadversions on Aristotle's Dialectic,* 1543, accusing Aristotle of corrupting the natural logic of the human mind, and holding him responsible for the barren dialectical method current in the universities. In the *Foundations of Dialectic,* published at the same time, he offers a new logic, which is to be an art of disputation (*ars disserendi*), and shall consist in first finding a principle and then establishing its proof. In a later work he rejects as spurious the *Organon* ascribed to Aristotle, and calls himself the only genuine Aristotelian. In criticizing the scholastic methods of instruction and demanding educational reform, he is the forerunner of Bacon, Descartes, Locke, and, indeed, of nearly all the early modern philosophers who chafed under the curriculum of the Schools. He, more than anyone else, personifies the spirit of humanism in the field of education.

39. Philosophy of Nature and Natural Science

Occultism. We have spoken in the preceding pages of the interest in the study of nature which was beginning to manifest itself in this age of enlightenment. The desire to unravel the mysteries of the external world assumed a fantastic and charlatanical form in many of the bolder spirits of the times. Instead of employing the method of observation and experiment, they hoped, in their impatience, to penetrate the secrets of nature by occult means, by a special inner revelation superior to sense perception. To this group belong the Platonist John Pico of Mirandola (d. 1494), his nephew Francis (d. 1533), and Reuchlin (*De verbo mirifico,* 1494). They were enthusiastic students of the Jewish Cabala, or secret emanation-theories, which had been studied by the Jews ever since the ninth century, and which were popularly supposed to go back to Abraham.

Others, not content with penetrating the secrets of nature in this way, were eager to gain power over it, to compel it to do their bidding. Regarding nature as the manifestation of occult forces, they believed it possible to control natural phenomena by coming into communion with these spirits. They expected to accomplish their purpose by means of secret arts and symbols, mystic formulae of all kinds, or by discovering the hidden numbers in which, according to the Pythagorean teaching, the book of nature is written. This is magic or theurgy. Since the planets, too, are under the domination of spirits, astrology forms an important part of the doctrines of the occultists. They were also deeply interested in alchemy—the magical transformation of metals, the art of making gold. Alchemy was placed in the service of medicine, and all kinds of secret compounds and tinctures, mixed in the most fantastic ways, were used to cure disease. The aim of the entire movement was a search for the philosopher's stone, with the aid of which the profoundest secrets of nature were to be fathomed and complete control gained over it.

Agrippa of Nettesheim and Theophrastus of Hohenheim (1493-1541), called Paracelsus, were leading figures in this group of magicians. Among later followers of Paracelsus are: R. Fludd, John Baptista van Helmont, and Francis Mercurius van Helmont.

Paracelsus. The philosophical foundation of Paracelsus' conception of nature is Neoplatonism. Man is the microcosm, and nature the macrocosm; we can understand the universe only by studying man, and man only by studying the universe. Man possesses an elementary, or terrestrial or visible body, and a sidereal, or astral or invisible body (the spirit), which comes from the region of the stars, and a soul, which originates in God. Hence, there are three great sciences: philosophy, astrology, and theology. These, together with alchemy, form the basis of the science of medicine, and the physician should have knowledge of all of them. The so-called four elements, earth, water, fire, air, are composed of three basal substances, sal (the solid principle), mercury (the liquid), and sulphur (the combustible). Each of the four elements is ruled by elemental spirits: earth by gnomes, water by undines, air by sylphs, and fire by salamanders. Each particular thing has an archeus ruling it, and disease is the checking of this vital force by terrestrial and astral forces in opposition to it. The secret of medicine is to aid, by means of alchemy and magic, the struggle of this vital force against its enemies.

This fantastic conception of nature, which presents a curious mixture of supernaturalism and naturalism, of mysticism and science, is finely portrayed by Goethe in his *Faust*. Faust personifies the spirit of the Renaissance: the insatiable thirst for knowledge, the primitive methods of gaining it, the medieval prejudices and superstitions, the ensuing skepticism, the keen longing for the exuberance of life—all these are the characteristics of a man standing on the threshold of a new era.

There was nothing to cause astonishment in doctrines of the kind put forth by Paracelsus and his followers. The view of nature as the abode of occult magic forces harmonized with the popular beliefs. Miracles were not unusual: saint after saint performed them during his life, and his relics exerted magic influence after his death. Why should not men who occupied themselves with the hidden forces or the black arts be able to perform wonderful things? At the end of the fifteenth century a theologian named Jacobus Sprengel wrote a book on witchcraft, *Malea malefica,* in which he discussed, with all seriousness and in a scientific manner, the causes of witchcraft, its effects, and the remedies to be used against it.

In spite of its extravagances and superstitions, this movement contributed to progress. In so far as it attempted to study and control nature, it was a precursor of modern science. The followers of the magic arts were still enamored of the occult theories and practices of medievalism, but their faces were turned toward the future. In the course of time the extravagant elements are shed one by one: alchemy evolves into chemistry, astrology into astronomy, magic into experiment; and the mystical Pythagorean number-system fosters a taste for mathematics. It was an astrological motive that induced Copernicus to inquire into the mathematical order of the heavens. What appears the longest way round is sometimes the shortest way home.

Philosophy of Nature. In Italy we find a number of nature philosophers who, though not entirely free from the old superstitions, such as alchemy and astrology, were imbued with the true scientific spirit. Jerome Cardan or Girolamo Cardano (1501-1576), a celebrated physician, mathematician, and scientist, tries to explain all things naturally. There are three elements, not four: earth, air, water; fire is not a substance at all, but an accident or property of heat, produced by motion. The world has a soul, which is identical with light and heat.

Bernardino Telesio (1508-1588, *De rerum natura*) attempts to reform natural science by liberating it from Aristotle and the ancients, and basing it on observation. Although his philosophy far surpasses the other nature-systems of the Renaissance, it is not free from Greek influence; traces of the

Pre-Socratic "physiologers" and of the Stoic metaphysics are noticeable in it. He adopts as his principles of explanation matter—which was created by God and remains constant in quantity—and force, with its opposing elements, heat and cold. Heat causes expansion and rarefaction in matter, and is the source of all life and motion; cold contracts and condenses, and is the cause of all fixity and rest. The universe owes its existence and changes to the constant opposition between these two principles. Even the soul (*spiritus*) is explained mechanically and materially by Telesio; it is a fine stuff consisting of heat, concentrated in the brain but diffused over the entire body. The soul is the principle which holds the parts of the organism together and initiates their motion. In addition to the material soul there is an immortal soul, which is superadded by God. In his ethics Telesio teaches that self-preservation is the sole object of man's striving.

Telesio was the founder of a natural scientific society at Naples, the Telesian Academy. Francis Patrizzi (1529-1597) combines Neoplatonism with the Telesian principles.

The Scientific Movement. The interest in external nature, which so frequently revealed itself during the Middle Ages and assumed such curious shapes, culminated in the scientific movement of which Leonardo da Vinci (1452-1519), Copernicus (1473-1543), Galileo (1564-1641), Kepler (1571-1630), and Newton (1642-1727) are the chief representatives. The occult and magic elements are completely eliminated by these thinkers, and the attempt is made to explain the phenomena of nature in a perfectly natural way. The old Aristotelian principles of explanation—the forms or essences working on matter and causing it to realize the ends or purposes of the forms—are discarded for the mechanical explanation: all natural occurrences are caused by the motion of bodies, according to fixed laws. The secret of the planetary motions is revealed by mathematics: Kepler discovers the orbits of the planets, and as a result astrology becomes astronomy. Robert Boyle introduces the atomic theory into chemistry and, though himself an alchemist, puts an end to alchemy. This entire anti-teleological line of thought reaches its climax in the Darwinian theory of the nineteenth century, which seeks to explain organic forms causally and mechanically, without any appeal to vital force or purpose of any kind in the things or outside of them.

Galileo. Galileo was thoroughly acquainted with the theories of Democritus, whom he considered superior to Aristotle in philosophical acumen. All change he regarded as merely relative to the parts of objects; there is neither origin nor decay in the strict sense, everything being the result of the movement of atoms. Sensible qualities are subjective and are based on quantitative relations; all qualities are explained by quantities. Hence mathematics, which deals with quantitative relations, is the highest science: "the book of the universe is written in mathematical characters." Whatever we can measure we can know; what we cannot measure we cannot know; we can reduce the relations of motion to mathematical formulae, hence we can explain occurrences in terms of motion and its laws. These laws, which form the basis of the study of mechanics, are discovered and formulated by Leonardo, Kepler, and Galileo. Their work confirms the Copernican or heliocentric theory of astronomy, according to which the earth is no longer conceived as the immovable center of the universe, but, with all the planets, as revolving around the central sun. The Copernican theory, though at first favorably received by the Church, was later condemned as "pernicious to Catholic truth" and placed on the Index in 1616. Galileo was forced to recant the Copernican theory in 1633, and remained under the surveillance of the Inquisition until his death in 1641. With the discovery by Sir Isaac Newton (1642-1727) of the law of gravitation in 1682, the Copernican theory receives further confirmation: the laws of planetary motion which Kepler formulated were found to be implications of the law of gravitation and the other laws of physical mechanics.

Galileo rejects authority and mystical speculation in matters of science and declares that all general propositions should rest on observation and experiment; but, he says, experience needs to be supplemented by the understanding. We subsume facts under laws; we reduce facts to their simple and necessary causes by abstracting from accidental circumstances; all these are operations of *thought*. The ideal method of investigation employs observation, experiment, and thought.

Pierre Gassendi (1592-1655) revived the doctrines of Epicurus and Lucretius, and opposed the corpuscular theory of Descartes. At the same time, he supplemented his mechanical theory with theological notions, making God the initiator of motion. Père Mersenne (1588-1648) and Robert Boyle (1627-1691) sought to reconcile Gassendi's atomism and Descartes's corpuscular view. Boyle introduced atomism into chemistry, but regarded it merely as an instrument of method, not as a philosophical theory of the universe. The world points to an intelligent creator and designer, who initiated the motion. Newton held a similar theistic view.

Works on Renaissance Science

Galileo, *Dialogues Concerning Two New Sciences,* trans. by H. Crew and A. de Salvio, 1939; Copernicus, *Commentariolus,* trans. by E. Rosen, 1939; H. Höffding, *A History of*

Modern Philosophy, 2nd ed., 1915, trans. by B. E. Meyer, Vol. I, pp. 161ff.; E. A. Burtt, *The Metaphysical Foundations of Modern Physical Science,* 1925; E. Mach, *The Science of Mechanics,* trans. by T. J. McCormack, 1919, 1942; L. Thorndike, *A History of Magic and Experimental Science,* Vols. III, VI, 1934-41; R. Lenoble, *Mersenne ou la naissance du mécanisme,* 1943; G. S. Brett, *The Philosophy of Gassendi,* 1908.

40. GIORDANO BRUNO AND TOMMASO CAMPANELLA

In the writings of the Italians Giordano Bruno (1548-1600) and Tommaso Campanella (1568-1639) we have comprehensive systems of metaphysics, conceived in the spirit of the new age.

Bruno. Bruno marveled at the immensity of the new astronomical universe, and regarded the fixed stars as planetary systems like our own. God is immanent in the infinite universe, the active principle (*natura naturans*); he expresses himself in the living world (*natura naturata*), which follows from him with inner necessity. With Cusa, he conceived him as the unity of all opposites, as the unity without opposites, as the one and the many, whom the finite mind cannot grasp.

Bruno was originally a monk of the Dominican order, but he later left it and journeyed from city to city, a restless wanderer until he again set foot on Italian soil, in 1592, when he was imprisoned by the Inquisition. Refusing to renounce his convictions, he was burned at the stake (1600) in Rome, after an imprisonment of seven years.

Della causa, infinito, ed uno; De triplici, minimo et mensura; De monade, etc.; Plumptre, *Life and Works of Bruno,* 2 vols., 1884; J. L. McIntyre, *Giordano Bruno,* 1903; W. Boulting, *Giordano Bruno,* 1916; R. Hönigswald, *Giordano Bruno,* 1912; C. Martin, *Giordano Bruno,* 1921.

The old Aristotelian forms, however, were not discarded in Bruno's system. Each star is moved by a form or soul, and there is soul and life in all things. Form without matter does not exist, the two together constituting a unity; but forms arise and pass away in matter. All particular things change, but the universe remains constant in its absolute perfection.

To these teachings Bruno added a doctrine of monads, or monadology, that reminds us of the Stoic germ-theory. Things are composed of uncaused and imperishable elementary parts called monads, which are both mental and physical. The soul itself is an immortal monad, and God is the monad of monads.

Campanella. Tommaso Campanella (1568-1639) was also a Dominican monk; he, too, was persecuted by the Inquisition, spending twenty-seven years of his life in prison on account of political ideals which he never attempted to put into practice. He is a child of his age in that his thoughts both hark back to the past and point forward to the future. He tells us to study nature directly and not from books, that all our philosophical knowledge is based on sensation, that all higher forms of cognition are merely different forms of sensation. At the same time, nature is a revelation of God and faith is a form of knowledge—the source from which theology springs.

Philosophia sensibus demonstrata; Universalis philosophia, etc.; *Civitas solis.*

In sensation we become aware of our own existence, of our own states of consciousness—of how things affect us, not of what they are in themselves. With St. Augustine before him and Descartes after him, Campanella finds in consciousness the pivot of certainty: whatever else we may doubt, we cannot doubt that we have sensations and that we exist. Introspection also reveals to us the three primal attributes of the soul: power, cognition, and will (*posse, nosse, velle*), which, in their perfection, are likewise the attributes of God: omnipotence, omniscience, and absolute goodness. Campanella's argument here is that since God is the ground of all things and man the little world (*parvus mundus*), the divine qualities must attach to the human soul in a finite degree. The same three principles are present in all being: in the lower forms of existence—that is, when mixed with non-being—they appear as impotence, ignorance, and malice. The world, in other words, is conceived, with Neoplatonism, as a series of emanations from God; he has produced the angels, ideas, spirits, immortal human souls, space and bodies. We have an immediate knowledge of God, and he reveals himself also in the Bible; but we can prove his existence from our notion of an infinite being, an idea which we could not have produced ourselves and which therefore implies an infinite cause. This argument plays an important rôle in the later Cartesian system.

In his *City of the Sun* (*Civitas Solis*) Campanella offers a socialistic theory of the State that recalls Plato's *Republic*. It is a State of enlightenment—a city of the sun—in which power is governed by knowledge; the principle of equality prevails in it, there being no class distinctions except those based on superiority of knowledge. Philosophers or priests are the rulers, and the City of the Sun is a universal papal monarchy with religious unity, dominating the secular State. Education, which is to be universal and compulsory, will be based on mathematics and natural science, and the pupils are to receive special training for their different occupations. Campanella also recommends learning by play, open-air schools, and instruction by means of object lessons.

41. New Theories of the State; Philosophy of Religion; Skepticism

Scholastic Theory of the State. The Renaissance attempted to work out a new theory of the State, one that would be independent of theology and of Aristotle, exhibiting, in this respect, the same opposition to authority and tradition that characterizes the other fields of thought. The orthodox school-men had, as we have seen, defended the temporal power of the ecclesiastical hierarchy and the subordination of State to Church. Writers like St. Thomas Aquinas justified papal supremacy by arguments resting on Christian and Aristotelian premises. The purpose of all human government, they held, is welfare; a ruler who serves that end is good, one who does not is bad and may be deposed. Since the supreme welfare of a people is its spiritual welfare, a sovereign who refuses to accept the Christian dogma, or even places himself in opposition to the Church, endangers the true good of his subjects, and such a course justifies rebellion. The Church is of divine origin; it is the vicegerent of God on earth and the court of last resort in matters of faith, and its function is to propagate the Christian religion. The State is, therefore, in the last analysis, subservient to the Church, and politics, like philosophy, is the handmaiden of theology.

Machiavelli. As has already been pointed out, this political theory and the efforts to put it into practice were opposed by the secular powers, and, in the centuries witnessing the decline of the papacy, even by Catholic writers themselves. During the period of the Renaissance and the Reformation, the opposition to the Catholic idea grew stronger, and the foundations were laid for the political theories which have played such an important rôle in modern history. The most radical attack came from the Italian diplomat Niccolò Machiavelli (1469-1527), secretary of the Chancellery of the Council of Ten at Florence, who had gained a discouraging insight into the political corruption of the Roman Curia and the Italian governments, and who presented his views in his *History of Florence* (1532), *Essays on the First Decade of Livy* (1532), and *The Prince* (1515).

The Prince, trans. by N. H. Thomson, 3rd ed., 1913. Essay on Machiavelli in *Cambridge Modern History*, Vol. I; P. Villari, *The Life and Times of Niccolò Machiavelli*, trans. by L. Villari, 1891; V. Marcu, *Accent on Power: The Life and Times of Machiavelli*, 1939; D. E. Muir, *Machiavelli and His Times*, 1936.

Machiavelli's ideal was a united, independent, and sovereign Italian nation, absolutely free from the domination of the Church in politics, science, and religion. Christianity, he held, discourages political activity on the part of the citizen and makes him passive; hence, the old Roman religion, which produced patriots, is preferable. The best form of government would be a republic of the type so brilliantly exemplified in Sparta, Rome, and Venice. Such a constitution is possible only where public spirit exists; political freedom is possible only where men are pure.

In times of corruption, however—like those in which Machiavelli lived—an absolute despotism is needed to realize the ideal of a strong and independent State, and civic freedom must be sacrificed. How terrible the political conditions of his country were, may be seen from a study of the history of the countless petty despots of Renaissance Italy.[1] Under these circumstances, it is right for the Prince to employ whatever means will lead to the nationalistic goal; force, deceit, severity, breach of the so-called moral laws are all justified by the great end; anything is preferable to the existing anarchy and corruption.

Machiavelli's political thought expressed a longing for a rational Commonwealth and an abhorrence of the corrupt secular and ecclesiastical politics of his day. His advocacy of political despotism was rooted in his pessimistic conception of human nature which, in his opinion, hunger alone makes industrious and law virtuous. He saw no way out of the corruption and disorder of his age except by meeting force with force, trickery with trickery, and by fighting the devil with his own weapons; and he condemned halfway measures in the pursuit of the goal. He justified in theory what many politicians of Church and State have practiced and continue to practice to this day, but he justified it only because he saw no other way of saving the State.

The New Politics. The aim of the new politics was to construct a political theory independent of theology and the Church and in harmony with the new ideal of a sovereign State. The problem was not merely theoretical; the existence of different Christian sects naturally suggested the question of the relation of these bodies to the State and the Prince, and made a consideration of the meaning and source of sovereignty a practical necessity. In working out a new political philosophy, many of the theories of the medieval thinkers to whom we have referred were utilized and developed: the contract theory, the theories of popular sovereignty and the sovereignty of the ruler, and the ideas of natural law and natural rights. Lines of thought were marked out which led to the theories of Hobbes on the one hand, and those

[1] Cf. Burckhardt, *The Civilization of the Renaissance.*

of Locke and Rousseau on the other; thus the new politics led in its practical application to both absolutism and democracy.

Jean Bodin (1530-1596) teaches that the State rests on a social contract by which the popular sovereignty has been irrevocably transferred to the ruler. Johannes Althusius (1557-1638) regards the contract as conditional on the ruler's observance of his part of it; the sovereignty of the people cannot be alienated, the authority of the ruling functionary or functionaries is revocable; and the prince who violates the contract may be deposed or executed. The idea gains ground, partly owing to religious oppression, that the State ought not to interfere with the religious convictions of its citizens, and the right of revolution is upheld. Alberico Gentile (1551-1611) discusses the law of war in his book, *De jure belli* (1588), and Sir Thomas More offers a socialistic ideal of the State in his *Utopia* (1516).

The theory of absolutism is accepted in moderate form by Hugo Grotius (Huig van Groot, 1583-1645), a leader of the aristocratic party in Holland, and Samuel Pufendorf (1632-1694). Grotius is the author of the celebrated work *De jure belli et pacis* (1625), in which he presents a theory of natural rights that is an inheritance from Stoicism and Roman law. The natural or unwritten law (*jus naturale*) is rooted in the rational nature of man, it is unalterable and God himself cannot change it; positive law (*jus voluntarium* or *civile*) arises in history as the result of voluntary enactment, and is based on the principle of utility. Society owes its origin to the social nature of man, which is the source of neighborly love and of all other duties. In society natural rights are limited by regard for social welfare; whatever is conducive to the existence of social life is also a natural right. The State, therefore, is not an artificial creation of God but a natural institution; it rests on reason and human nature. Since the State depends on the free consent of its members, that is, on contract, the rights of the individual can never be abrogated. The people have sovereignty but may surrender it, for all times, to a monarch or a ruling class. War between nations is justifiable only in case of violation of natural rights, but should be carried on humanely.

Other writers on politics are: Ayala, Oldendorp, Nicolas Hemming, Benedict Winkler. Pufendorrf is a follower of Grotius and Hobbes, and introduces the notion of natural law into Germany; sovereignty implies unity of will and, therefore, the absolute right of the monarch.

Among the orthodox writers, the Protestants Luther and Melanchthon conceived the State as of divine origin, while the Jesuits Bellarmin and Juan Mariana advocated the contract theory and the doctrine of popular sovereignty.

Translation of Grotius, *De jure belli et pacis,* by W. Whewell, 3 vols., 1853; J. Bodin, *Method for the Easy Comprehension of History,* trans. by B. Reynolds, 1945.

Evolution of the Modern State. These theories reflect the evolution of political ideas and political institutions from the medieval period. In the Middle Ages the State did not possess sovereignty in the sense in which modern states possess it. The medieval ruler had certain limited rights, as did the feudal lords, but there was frequent conflict between emperors and kings and their vassals, and the power of the ruler depended on the good will of his vassals and on his military strength. In Germany and Italy the centralized State gradually divided into a loose federation of states after the breakdown of the feudal system and of the territorial lords. In France the tendency was the other way—from a loose federation of states to a unified State or nation with an absolute king. England remained centralized, but the king's power declined as the power of the people grew. In any case, the idea of the sovereignty of the State was only gradually developed, and it was only as the result of historical evolution that the State extended its functions and became modern. The tendency at the beginning of the modern era was towards absolutism, which reached its climax in the last half of the seventeenth and the first half of the eighteenth century; the power of the ruler was, theoretically, unlimited, the subject receiving whatever rights he might have from the State, which was incarnate in the ruler: *L'état, c'est moi*—so Louis XIV declared. The notion of the sovereignty of the State has remained intact; but the opposition to absolutism which was reflected in the theories of Althusius, Locke, and Rousseau continued to gain ground and ended in the establishment of the constitutional monarchies and democracies of our era.

Natural Religion of Herbert of Cherbury. The new philosophy of the Renaissance offers, as we have seen, natural or rational instead of supernatural explanations of things; it applies its rationalistic method not only to metaphysical systems, but also to fields of thought such as politics and religion. Herbert of Cherbury (1583-1648; *De veritate,* etc., 1624; *De religione gentilium,* 1645) evolved a philosophy of religion based on a theory of natural knowledge and independent of any positive or historical religion. He regarded as rational or natural truths common to all religions, that there is one God, that he ought to be worshiped, that worship consists of piety and virtue, that we must repent of our sins, and that there are present and future rewards and punishments. These, in other words, are the beliefs to which a natural man, unhampered by prejudices and following his own reason, would come; they are truths implanted by nature. They belong to the group of *notitiae communes* or universal notions, which are of divine origin and have as their distinguishing marks priority, independence, universality, certainty, necessity—in the sense of utility—and immediacy. This original natural religion of man has, according to Herbert, been corrupted by priests, but Christianity has done much to restore it. Though it may be supplemented by revelation, the revelation must itself be rational. Herbert of Cherbury is the predecessor of the deists and the advocates of the theory of natural or rational religion in the eighteenth century.

Skepticism. A note of skepticism similar to that heard in nominalism and mysticism is found in a number of French thinkers of the Renaissance, who were influenced by Greek skeptical writings. Thus Michel de Montaigne (1533-1592), the author of the celebrated *Essays*, doubts the possibility of certain knowledge, for reasons with which we have become familiar in our account of Greek skepticism. He despairs of reason and recommends a return to uncorrupted nature and revelation. Although we cannot have knowledge he urges that we do our duty and submit to the divine commands. According to Pierre Charron (1541-1603), the skeptical attitude keeps alive the spirit of inquiry and leads us to faith in Christianity, the true religion. He emphasizes the practical ethical side of Christianity. Francis Sanchez, too, denies the possibility of absolute knowledge; finite beings cannot grasp the inner essence of things or understand the meaning of the universe as a whole; but he holds that we can know secondary causes through observation and experiment. Later French skeptics are La Mothe le Vayer and the Bishop Pierre Huet. Joseph Glanvil, Hieronymus Hirnheim, of Prague, and Pierre Bayle (1647-1706), author of the *Dictionnaire historique et critique* (1695) is, in some respects, affiliated with the same movement.

Montaigne's *Works*, ed. by Hazlitt, 1902; *Essays*, trans. by Trechmann, 1946. Cf. L. Lévy-Bruhl, *Modern Philosophy in France*, trans. by G. Coblence, 1899; J. Owen, *The Sceptics of the French Renaissance*, 1893; A. Gide, *Living Thoughts of Montaigne*, 1939.

42. RELIGIOUS REFORM

Spirit of the Reformation. The Italian Renaissance rebelled against authority and the scholastic system, and found inspiration in the literary and artistic products of classical antiquity. It was the protest of the mind against intellectual coercion. The German Reformation was a religious awakening, or renaissance—the protest of the heart against the mechanization of faith.

As humanism had turned to ancient philosophy, literature, and art for help, so religion now turned to the Bible and the simple faith of the early Fathers, especially St. Augustine, for support. In place of scholastic theology, the elaborate system of indulgences, and the ritual of the Church, the Reformation emphasized inner religion and personal worship: justification by faith instead of justification by works. It resembles the Renaissance in its contempt of "barren scholasticism," its opposition to ecclesiastical authority and temporal power, and in its exaltation of the human conscience; but it does not go with it in its glorification of the intellect, nor share its optimistic joy of life. Luther had come under the spell of the nominalistic mystics and shared the suspicions of primitive Christianity that reason is blind in matters concerning the salvation of our souls. He believed that a thing may be false in philosophy and yet true in a theology rooted in faith, and he despised the scholastic no less than the true Aristotle.

But in spite of the anti-rationalistic attitude of the leader of the Reformation, the new religious movement fostered the spirit of critical reflection and independent thought no less than the Renaissance had done. In refusing to accept the Church as the arbiter of Christian faith, and in appealing to the Bible and the individual conscience, it gave reason the right to sit in judgment on religious dogma and encouraged rationalism and individualism. This is not what Luther had aimed at, but it was an inevitable practical consequence of his protest against the authoritative Church and its theology, a consequence which Protestantism at large did not hesitate to draw. Indeed, the reformers themselves differed in their interpretation of important Christian dogmas, and the new church soon divided into separate sects: Luther accepted the mystical presence of Christ in the Eucharist; Zwingli, the most liberal of the reformers, regarded the sacraments as symbols; and Calvin taught the doctrine of predestination, which the Catholic Church had refused to accept in spite of her respect for the great St. Augustine.

P. Smith, *The Age of Reformation*, 1920; E. M. Hulme, *The Renaissance, the Protestant Revolution and the Catholic Reformation*, rev. ed., 1924; C. Beard, *Reformation in the Sixteenth Century in Relation to Modern Thought and Knowledge*, 1927; H. S. Lucas, *The Renaissance and the Reformation*, 1935; J. Mackinnon, *Origins of the Reformation*, 1939.

Protestant Scholasticism. Although Luther had rejected scholastic philosophy as barren word-wisdom, the new church soon felt the need of rationalizing her faith; in other words, of constructing a scholastic system of its own. The appeal to the Bible and the faith of primitive Christian times opened the door to all kinds of fantastic sects which interpreted the Christian teachings according to their own lights, as happened in the case of the Anabaptists and Iconoclasts. With the organization of a new church, a religious platform became a practical necessity; the movement which had sprung from mysticism, and had arisen as a protest against the mechanization of religion, now forgot its origin and began to evolve its own dogma. Soon even Luther began to see the need for a philosophical support of the Reformation. The theologian who undertook the work of constructing a "Protestant system" in Germany was Melanchthon (1497-1560). He selected as most suitable for his task the Aristotelian world-view, "as that species of philosophy which has the least sophistry and the right method." The Epicureans were too godless for him, the Stoics too fatalistic, Plato and Neoplatonism too vague and heretical, the Middle Academy too skeptical. Melanchthon wrote the textbooks of Protestantism, using Aristotle as his guide, and became the *praeceptor Germaniae*. His books were used in Germany throughout the seventeenth century.

The philosophy of Nicolaus Taurellus (1547-1606) is a Protestant attempt to construct a scholastic system on an Augustinian basis. Its opposition to Aristotelianism represents the protest of the Augustinian mystical wing of Protestantism against the official doctrine of the Church. The conception of the universe as an order governed by law without divine interference shows the influence of the new natural science. Calvin likewise goes back to St. Augustine, as do also the Catholic Jansenists of Port Royal, while Zwingli follows Neoplatonism.

Mysticism of Jacob Boehme. Mysticism, however, continued to find a refuge among the common people; and its chief representatives, men like Osiander, Caspar Schwenkfeld, Sebastian Frank (d. 1545), and Valentin Weigel, protested against the scholasticism and formalism of the Reformation, as Luther himself had once thundered against Rome. At the beginning of the seventeenth century, mysticism again finds its voice in the comprehensive system of an uneducated German cobbler, Jacob Boehme (1575-1624), in his work *Aurora*.

Troubled by the fact of sin in the world, Boehme attempts to account for it as a necessary phase in the process of divine self-expression. Everywhere in reality he finds oppositions and contradictions: there is no good without evil, no light without darkness, no quality without its opposite. Since all things come from God, he must be the primal ground of all opposition; in him all the contrarieties of nature must lie concealed. Conceived as the original source of things, he is an undifferentiated, unqualified, motionless being: absolute quiescence, all and nothing, the fathomless ground, the primal objectless *will*. In order that this principle may manifest and know itself, it must become differentiated, it must have something to contemplate; as light needs darkness in order to be revealed, so God cannot become conscious of himself and express himself without an object. The blind craving of the divine will gives rise to the oppositions which confront us in existence.

The significant teachings of Boehme's world-view are that the universe is a union of contradictions, that life and progress imply opposition, that the ground of all reality lies in a spiritual principle, that this principle is not fundamentally intelligence, but a groundless will, and that existence is a procession from darkness to light. Boehme attempts to trace the evolution of this process, combining Christian theological ideas—Trinity, angels, fall of Lucifer, fall of man, plan of salvation—with all kinds of fantastic notions derived from the magical nature-philosophy of Paracelsus, which had found their way into German Protestant mysticism. As in Neoplatonism, the process must retrace its steps and return to its source: the concrete material world, which is the result of Lucifer's sin and a caricature of God, finds its way home to God; the material garment is cast off, and God contemplates the essence of things in their naked purity.

43. The Spirit of Modern Philosophy

Characteristics of the Modern Era. The history of the new era may be viewed as an awakening of the reflective spirit, as a quickening of criticism, as a revolt against authority and tradition, as a protest against absolutism and collectivism, as a demand for freedom in thought, feeling, and action. The leaven which had begun to work in the transition period of the Renaissance and the Reformation continued active throughout the following centuries and has not yet come to rest. The political conflict was settled in favor of the State, and the State gradually took the place of the Church as an organ of civilization: ecclesiasticism gave way to nationalism. Within the State itself there appeared a growing tendency towards constitutionalism and democratic institutions, which is still manifested in present-day demands for equal rights and social justice. The spirit of independence which had raised its voice against the authority of the Church in time attacked the paternalism of the State, and the doctrine of political non-interference became the ideal of the individualist. The same spirit found expression in the economic sphere: slavery, serfdom, and the old guild system gradually disappeared, the individual threw off his fetters, and demanded to be let alone in working out his economic salvation. This modern theory of economic individualism is commonly referred to as the *laissez faire* (let alone) doctrine.

We are confronted with the same phenomenon in the empire of the intellect, with the same antagonism to tutelage, the same demand for a free field. Reason becomes the authority in science and philosophy. As we pointed out before, the notion begins to prevail that truth is not something to be handed down by authority or decreed by papal bulls, but something to be acquired, something to be achieved by free and impartial inquiry. The gaze is turned from the contemplation of supernatural things to the examination of natural things, from heaven to earth—theology yields her crown to science and philosophy. The physical and the mental world, society, human institutions, and religion itself are explained by natural causes. What characterizes the higher intellectual life of the period following the Middle Ages is an abiding faith in the power of human reason, an intense interest in natural things, a lively yearning for civilization and progress. Knowledge, however, let it be noted, is esteemed and desired not only for its own sake, but also for its utility, for its practical value: knowledge is power. Nearly all the great leaders of modern thought, from Francis Bacon onward, are interested in the practical applications of the results of scientific investigation, and look forward with an enthusiastic optimism to a coming era of wonderful achievement in the mechanical arts, technology, medicine, as well as in the field of political and social reform.

The individual likewise throws off the yoke of the Church in religion and morals; the appeal to reason in matters of the intellect is matched by an appeal to faith and the conscience in matters of belief and conduct; he refuses to accept an intermediary between himself and his God. However Luther may have differed from the leaders of the Renaissance, the influence of the Reformation eventually helped to quicken the spirit of religious, moral, and intellectual independence and contributed its share to the emancipation of the human soul from external authority.

Modern philosophy, in its beginnings, breathes the spirit of the modern times, the characteristics of which we have endeavored to describe. It is independent in its search for truth, resembling ancient Greek thought in this respect. It is rationalistic in the sense that it makes human reason the highest authority in the pursuit of knowledge. It is naturalistic in that it seeks to explain inner and outer nature without supernatural presuppositions.

It is, therefore, scientific, keeping in touch with the new sciences, particularly with the sciences of external nature.

Although modern philosophy arose as a protest against the old scholastic system, it did not, and could not, completely break with the past. Traces of the scholastic philosophy remain in its blood for a long time to come. The early modern thinkers constantly criticize the scholastic method, but many of the old conceptions are bodily taken over by them, and influence both their problems and their results. The theological bias is not entirely absent: Bacon, Descartes, Locke, Berkeley, and Leibniz all accept the basal doctrines of Christianity. It is true, we are not always able to judge the candor of their protestations, but even insincerity in this regard would be a proof of the theological influence.

Empiricism and Rationalism. Modern philosophies have been classified as rationalistic or empiristic according as they accept reason (*ratio*) or experience as the source and norm of knowledge. To avoid misapprehension, however, several points should be emphasized. (1) If by rationalism we mean the attitude which makes reason instead of revelation or authority the standard of knowledge, all modern systems of philosophy are rationalistic; indeed, it is this characteristic which enables us to classify them as modern. To be sure, there are modern world-views which seek the source of truth in feeling, faith, or intuition rather than in the intellect; but even these faith- or feeling-philosophies endeavor to construct theories which shall justify to reason their methods of reaching the truth and the objects of their faith. (2) On the other hand, we may mean by rationalism the view that genuine knowledge consists of universal and necessary judgments, that the goal of thought is a *system* of truths in which the different propositions are logically related to one another. This is the mathematical conception of knowledge, which is accepted by nearly all modern thinkers as the ideal; whether they believe in the possibility of realizing it or not, they consider genuine only such knowledge as conforms to the mathematical model. (3) There is, further, the question concerning the *origin* of knowledge, which receives different answers in modern philosophy: (a) Genuine knowledge cannot come from sense perception or experience, but must have its foundation in thought or reason: certain truths are natural or native to reason: innate or inborn or a priori truths. Truths which have their origin in the mind itself are valid truths. This view, too, has been called rationalism, although some writers prefer to name it intuitionalism or apriorism. (b) There are no inborn truths: all knowledge springs from sense perception or experience, and hence so-called necessary propositions are not necessary or absolutely certain at all, but yield only *probable* knowledge. This view has been called empiricism or sensationalism.

The empiricists may accept rationalism in the first and second senses; they may consider only such knowledge genuine as gives us absolute certainty, and, at the same time, deny the possibility of attaining real knowledge except perhaps in mathematics. If by empiricism we mean that our world of experience is the object of philosophy, that philosophy has to interpret it, then all modern philosophy is empirical. If we mean by it that we cannot know without experience, that *pure* thought, or thought absolutely independent of sense perception, is impossible, then, again, modern philosophy is largely empirical.

Keeping all this in mind, we may characterize philosophers as rationalists (apriorists) or empiricists (sensationalists), according to the answers they give to the question of the origin of knowledge. Closely connected with the question of the origin is the question of the certainty or validity of knowledge. Both schools of early modern times agree that sense knowledge is not absolutely certain; rationalists declare that only rational or a priori truths, clearly and distinctly perceived truths, are certain; empiricists generally deny that there are such a priori truths, and hold that clearly and distinctly perceived truths are not necessarily certain. We may, therefore, classify Descartes, Spinoza, Malebranche, Leibniz, and Wolff as rationalists; Bacon, Hobbes, Locke, Berkeley, and Hume as empiricists. The rationalists are the intellectual descendants of Plato, Aristotle, and the realists among the schoolmen in their general theory of knowledge and the empiricists are the continuers of the nominalistic traditions. We must bear in mind, however, that these thinkers are not always consistent in their doctrines; we shall be guided in our rough classification by their general attitude toward the problem of the origin of knowledge.

Besides these movements, we find also the customary accompaniments with which we have become acquainted in medieval philosophy: skepticism and mysticism (faith-philosophy), both of which may develop from the soil of either empiricism or rationalism. David Hume's skeptical conclusions may be regarded as the result of certain empirical presuppositions of Locke, and Pierre Bayle's as the application of the rationalistic ideal of Descartes. Mysticism may flourish in both fields, as we have seen; many of the medieval nominalists were mystics, and many modern mystics build upon rationalistic foundations. In addition to all these currents, the old scholastic philosophy has persisted among Catholic scholars.

Works on Modern Philosophy

General Histories: J. Royce, *Spirit of Modern Philosophy*, 1892; R. Falckenberg, *History of Modern Philosophy*, trans. by A. C. Armstrong, 1893; R. Adamson, *Development of Modern Philosophy*, 1903; H. Höffding, *A Brief History of Modern Philosophy*, trans. by C. F. Sanders, 1912; and *History of Modern Philosophy*, 2 vols., trans. by B. E. Meyer, 1924; M. W. Calkins, *Persistent Problems of Philosophy*, 1925; W. Windelband, *Geschichte der neueren Philosophie*, 2 vols., 1899; F. Ueberweg, *History of Philosophy*, trans. by G. S. Morris, 2 vols., 1903; A. S. Dewing, *Introduction to the History of Modern Philosophy*, 1903; E. A. Singer, *Modern Thinkers and Present Problems*, 1923; H. W. Dresser, *A History of Modern Philosophy*, 1928; B. A. G. Fuller, *A History of Modern Philosophy*, 1938; D. W. Gotschalk, *Metaphysics in Modern Times*, 1940; W. K. Wright, *A History of Modern Philosophy*, 1941; J. H. Randall, *The Making of the Modern Mind: A Survey of the Intellectual Background of the Present Age*, rev. ed., 1941; A. Castell, *An Introduction to Modern Philosophy in Six Philosophical Problems*, 1943.

Special Works: E. Cassirer, *Das Erkenntnisproblem in der Philosophie und Wissenschaft in der Neueren Zeit*, 5 vols., 3rd ed., 1923; Jodl, *Geschichte der Ethik*, 2 vols., 4th ed., 1923-30; W. A. Dunning, *Political Theories from Luther to Montesquieu*, 1905; W. E. H. Lecky, *History of the Rise and Influence of the Spirit of Rationalism in Europe*, 7th ed., 1875; H. Laski, *Political Thought in England from Locke to Bentham*, 1920; A. O. Lovejoy, *The Great Chain of Being*, 1942; A. C. McGiffert, *Protestant Thought before Kant*, 1911; E. Cassirer, *An Essay on Man*, 1944, and *Substance and Function*, 1923; A. N. Whitehead, *Science and the Modern World*, 1925; E. Zeller, *Geschichte der deutschen Philosophie seit Leibniz*, 1875; Carl Siegel, *Geschichte der deutschen Naturphilosophie*, 1913; M. Ettlinger, *Geschichte der Philosophie von der Romantik bis zur Gegenwart*, 1924; S. H. Mellone, *The Dawn of Modern Thought*, 1930; P. Smith, *A History of Modern Culture*, 2 vols., 1930; A. Wolf, *A History of Science, Technology and Philosophy in the 16th & 17th Centuries*, 1935; G. H. Mead, *Movements of Thought in the 19th Century*, 1936; G. Sarton, *The Study of the History of Science*, 1936; G. Sarton, *The History of Science and the New Humanism*, 1937; A. Wolf, *A History of Science, Technology and Philosophy in the 18th Century*, 1939; J. Needham, and W. Pagel (eds.) *Background to Modern Science*, 1940; R. D. Rosenfield, *From Beast-Machine to Man-Machine*, 1941; H. Miller, *An Historical Introduction to Modern Philosophy*, 1947.

Selections from Writings of Philosophers: B. Rand, *Modern Classical Philosophers*, 1926; D. S. Robinson, *An Anthology of Modern Philosophy*, 1931; T. V. Smith and Marjorie Grene, *From Descartes to Kant*, 1940.

XI

The Beginnings
of Modern Philosophy

44. Francis Bacon

Francis Bacon (1561-1626) devoted himself to law and politics, although, so he himself tells us, his chief interests lay along the lines of the studies to which he gave his leisure hours. Important offices and high honors were conferred upon him by Queen Elizabeth and King James I—he was made Baron Verulam and Viscount St. Albans, and became Lord Chancellor. In 1621 he was accused of having accepted gifts from litigants in his official capacity as a judge, an offense to which he confessed guilty but which, he declared, had never influenced his decisions. He was found guilty, sentenced to imprisonment, heavily fined, and deprived of office, but received the king's pardon, and retired to private life.

Among the English predecessors of Bacon were: Everard Digby (d. 1592), professor of logic at Cambridge, who aroused an interest in the study of philosophy in his country. His Neoplatonic doctrine, which he combined with Cabalism, was opposed by Sir William Temple (1553-1626), who followed the logic of Peter Ramus in opposition to Aristotle.

Bacon's celebrated *Essays* appeared in 1597, an enlarged edition in 1625; the Latin translation of them bears the title *Sermones fideles*. Among his other works are: *The Advancement of Learning,* 1605 (the Latin enlarged and revised edition is entitled, *De dignitate et augmentis scientiarum,* 1623) and the *Novum Organum,* 1620 (the new "organon" or instrument of knowledge in contrast to the organon of the traditional Aristotelian logic). Complete works, in Latin and English, by J. Spedding, R. L. Ellis, and D. D. Heath, 14 vols., 1857-74.

J. Spedding, *Life and Times of Francis Bacon,* 2 vols., 1879; R. W. Church, *Bacon,* 1909; E. A. Abbot, *Bacon,* 1885; T. Fowler, *Bacon,* 1881; J. Nichol, *Francis Bacon, His Life and Philosophy,* 1888-89; I. Levine, *Francis Bacon,* 1925; C. D. Broad, *The Philosophy of Francis Bacon,* 1926; A. E. Taylor, *Francis Bacon,* 1926; E. Lewalter, *Francis Bacon,* 1939; K. R. Wallace, *Francis Bacon on Communication and Rhetoric,* 1943; F. H. Anderson, *The Philosophy of Francis Bacon,* 1948.

The Reform of Science. Francis Bacon is, in many respects, a typical representative of the modern spirit. He is opposed to the ancient authorities, to Aristotle and Greek philosophy no less than to the barren philosophy of scholasticism. The eye of the mind, he tells us, must never turn away from the things themselves, but must receive the images as they truly are—undistorted by past theories.

The past has accomplished nothing; its methods, foundations, and results were wrong. We must begin all over again, free our minds of transmitted and inherited prejudices and opinions, go to the things themselves rather than follow opinions—in short, do our own thinking. The model of knowledge is natural science, the method is induction, and the goal the art of invention. So little progress has been made in twenty-five hundred years because the right methods of acquiring knowledge have not been adopted. Some have used the method of demonstration, but they started from principles that had been hastily formed or taken on trust. Others follow the way of sense, but the senses, left to themselves, are faulty; still others despair of all knowledge, but this attitude, too, is dogmatic and unsatisfactory. We must begin the work anew and raise or rebuild the sciences, arts, and all human knowledge on a firm and solid foundation. This ambitious enterprise is the Great Instauration.

All these ideas are characteristically modern, as are also Bacon's supreme self-confidence and optimism. The very failures of the past inspire him with the hope and belief that an era of glorious achievement is at hand, that great things are going to happen, that with the abandonment of the fruitless science of the past the face of the earth and of society will be changed. Bacon's vision of a new social order grounded on science and technology is portrayed in his *New Atlantis*. The practical goal is constantly emphasized, "the end always to be kept in view is the application of the truth acquired to the good of mankind."

Bacon did not advance the cause of natural science by his own experiments nor, indeed, was he sufficiently acquainted with mathematics to appreciate the work of the great astronomers of the new era. And it is questionable whether his theory of method exercised any appreciable influence on experimental science; science had advanced too far for that. In his own country William Gilbert (1540-1603), the well-known author of the book *De magnete* (1600), had employed the inductive method in his researches before the appearance of Bacon's writings on the subject. Bacon does, however, deserve the title of the "trumpeter of his time," which he applied to himself, for he gave conscious expression to the new scientific spirit. He understood and emphasized the importance of systematic and methodical observation and experimentation in natural science; the other and most important phase, mathematics, he mentions and considers essential, but fails to make use of in his theory because he lacked sufficient knowledge of it.

Inductive Method. Bacon thinks that the fruitlessness of science and philosophy in the past was due to the absence of a proper method. The understanding, when left to itself, possesses but little power—like the hand unassisted by tools and instruments. We must devise a new way of reaching knowledge, a new instrument or organ for the mind, a new logic, a *novum organum*. The old syllogistic logic is useless for scientific discovery. It only assists in confirming and rendering inveterate the errors founded on vulgar notions rather than in seeking after truth.

But before describing his method in detail, Bacon insists that the mind clear itself of all false opinions, prejudices, or *idols,* of which there are four kinds. The idols of the tribe (*idola tribus*) are such as inhere in the very nature of the human mind, among them being the appeal to final causes (teleology) and the habit of reading human desires into nature. The idols of the den (*specus*) are peculiar to the particular individual, to his disposition, education and intercourse, his reading, the authority of those whom he admires, and the like. The idols of the market (*fori*) are the most troublesome of all; they come from the associations of words and names. Words are often used as names of things which have no existence; or they may be the names of actual objects, but confused, badly defined, and hastily abstracted from things. The idols of the theater (*theatri*) are the result of false theories or philosophies.

Of such idols the mind must be freed and cleared; it must approach the task of knowledge pure and unadulterated. The end in view, let it be remembered, is to discover principles, not to conquer adversaries by words, but nature by works. We cannot realize this end without knowing nature; in order to produce effects, we must know causes. Our present syllogistic methods will be of no avail in furthering this task; the syllogism accomplishes only the arrangement of matters already discovered—the systematization of truths gained by some other method. It consists of propositions, propositions consist of words, and words are signs of ideas. If our basic ideas are confused and carelessly abstracted from things, as is often the case, the whole superstructure of knowledge lacks solidity. The concepts, principles, and axioms used in the syllogism are, to be sure, based on experience—as indeed all concepts, principles, or axioms are; but, all too frequently, the experience is vague and faulty, and our concepts are hasty generalizations. Our only hope, then, is genuine induction. We must ascend gradually and in an orderly and methodical way from experience to propositions of higher and higher generality until we finally come to the most general and best-defined axioms. In the pursuit of knowledge, we must combine the experimental and the rational faculties.

Induction does not consist in simple enumeration, which is a childish procedure. The aim of human knowledge is to discover the *form* or true basis of a given nature or quality. By "form" Bacon means not the same as the realists, not abstract forms or ideas. Matter rather than forms, he tells us, should be the object of our attention; nothing exists in nature besides individual bodies which act according to fixed law. In philosophy the investigation, discovery, and explanation of a quality or a fact by a law is the foundation of knowledge as well as of operation. This law he calls *the form,* a term which had come into general use; Telesio, whom Bacon mentions, speaks of heat and cold as active forms of nature. The form of heat is the law of heat; it is that which determines or regulates heat wherever heat is found, that on which heat depends. Whoever knows the forms understands the unity of nature even in the most unlike substances; he knows what in nature is constant and eternal and universal, and opens broad roads to human power, such as human thought can scarcely comprehend or anticipate. Bacon declares that the form or cause of heat is the motion of the small particles of the body. The investigation of forms or causes which are eternal and immutable constitutes metaphysics; the investigation of efficient cause and matter, and of the latent process and latent configurations, constitutes physics. The application of the knowledge of forms or fundamental laws of nature leads to the highest kind of invention. Bacon calls the application of metaphysical knowledge "magic" (the term is evidently suggested by the language of alchemy—the art of making gold). The application of knowledge of material and efficient causes is mechanics or practical physics. In his emphasis on the application of metaphysical and physical knowledge to invention and the control of nature, Bacon is clearly foreshadowing the modern concept of a technology based on science.

The causes or laws, then, which science seeks to discover are "forms," and these are found by three inductive procedures. (1) The form of a nature or quality (heat, for example) is such that, given the form, the quality invariably follows. It is, therefore, always present when the quality is present, and universally implies it, and is constantly inherent in it. A quality being given, we must first determine all the known instances which agree in this quality, though in other aspects they be most unlike; these are the so-called "positive instances." This enumeration is Bacon's Table of Essence or Presence, which clearly anticipates Mill's Method of Agreement. (2) The form is such that, if it be taken away, the quality invariably vanishes; it is always absent when the quality is absent, implying its absence and inherent in nothing else. Accordingly, we must review the instances in which the given quality is wanting—the so-called "negative instances." The negative instances should be joined to the positive, and the absence of the given quality noted in those subjects which are most akin to the instances in which both the quality and the form are present. Bacon calls this enumeration the Table of Deviation or of Absence in Proximity, and it, in turn, foreshadows Mill's Method of Difference. (3) Lastly, we take the cases in which the object of our inquiry is present in a greater or less degree, either by comparing its increase and decrease in the same object, or its degree in different objects. This is the Bacon's Table of Degrees or Comparative Instances—the prototype of Mill's Method of Concomitant Variations. Bacon mentions a number of auxiliary methods and techniques of inductive inquiry employed by the mind in discovering forms, e.g., rejection, use of "first vintages" or hypotheses, citation of crucial or "prerogative instances," etc., but these aspects of the inductive theory are not systematically worked out by him.

Program of Philosophy. Bacon held that mankind must begin the work of science anew. He did not himself offer a complete theory of the universe; his office was merely to stake out the ground and point the way to new achievements. To this end he planned his great work, or *Instauratio magna,* consisting of six parts, only two of which were completed: the *Encyclopedia* or *Advancement of Learning,* and the *Novum Organum.* He divides the field of knowledge, or "the intellectual globe," into history, poesy, and philosophy, according to the faculties of the mind employed—namely, memory, imagination, and reason—and subdivides each into numerous specialized branches.

Philosophy is the work of reason; it deals with abstract conceptions derived from impressions of sense, and its task is the composition and division of these conceptions according to the laws of nature and fact. It embraces primary philosophy, revealed theology, natural theology, metaphysics, physics, mechanics, magic, mathematics, psychology, and ethics. Primary philosophy busies itself with the concepts and axioms common to several sciences, with what we should now call basic scientific categories and presuppositions of science. Metaphysics has two functions: to discover the eternal and immutable forms of bodies, and to discuss purposes, ends, or final causes. In physics, final causes have no place; Democritus wasted no time on them and consequently, Bacon declares, penetrated more deeply into nature than Plato and Aristotle, who were preoccupied with them. The doctrine of final causes has no practical value, but is a barren thing, like a virgin consecrated to God. Mathematics is a branch of metaphysics— being a science of quantity, which is one of the essential, most abstract, and separable forms of matter. Mathematics and logic both ought to be handmaids of physics, but instead they have come to domineer over physics. Bacon does not deny, however, that mathematics is of great importance to metaphysics, mechanics, and "magic."

Philosophy of Man. Philosophy comprises human, and civil or political philosophy. In the former we consider man as a separate individual; in the latter he is a member of society. Human philosophy studies body and soul, and their relation. Among its topics are the miseries and the prerogatives or excellencies of the human race, physiognomy and the interpretation of natural dreams, the effect of bodily states on mind, e.g., in madness or insanity, the influence of mind on body, the proper seat and habitation of each faculty of the mind in the body and its organs, and also "medicine, cosmetic, athletic, and voluptuary." Bacon embraces in human science all knowledge of man as a psycho-physical individual; his is a comprehensive philosophical anthropology which draws upon the more specialized psychological and physiological inquiries. In envisaging a comprehensive science of man, Bacon founded scientific humanism, which was far removed from the classical humanism of Renaissance philosophers, and destined for a twentieth-century revival by philosophers like John Dewey.

The human soul has a divine or rational, and an irrational part. All problems relating to the former must be handed over to religion. The sensitive soul is corporeal, attenuated by heat and rendered invisible, and, in the case of the more highly developed animals, resides chiefly in the head. The faculties of the soul are understanding, reason, imagination, memory, appetite, will, and all those with which logic and ethics are concerned. The origins of these faculties must be physically accounted for. Bacon's treatment of the questions relating to voluntary motion and sensibility is suggestive. How can so minute and subtle a breath as the material soul initiate motion in bodies so gross and hard as the physical objects which man handles and manipulates? What is the difference between perception and sense? Bacon finds a manifest power of perception even in inorganic bodies, and a kind of appetite to choose what is agreeable, and to avoid what is disagreeable to them: the loadstone attracts iron, one drop of water unites with another, one body "feels" the impact of another, perceives the absence of a body that is removed from its environs; perception is diffused through all nature. Bacon's willingness to indulge in such speculations shows how hard it was for the man of his time to divest himself of the old medieval conception of an animated nature.

Logic treats of the understanding and reason; and ethics, of the will, appetite, and affections; the one produces resolutions, the other actions. The logical arts are inquiry or invention, examination or judgment, custody or memory, elocution or delivery. The study of induction belongs to the art of judgment. Ethics describes the nature of the good and prescribes rules for conforming to it. Man is prompted by selfish and social impulses. Individual good—self-preservation and defense—differs radically from social good and frequently conflicts with it, although, at times, they may coincide. The social good is called duty, and it is the business of the science of government to discover the fountains of justice and public good and to reinforce their claims even when they conflict with the interests of the individual.

Philosophy, in the broad sense, is the apex of the pyramid of knowledge. It is founded on the just, pure, and strict inquiry into all the subjects of study already proposed by Bacon. His purpose was not to offer a universal system, but "to lay more firmly the foundations and extend more widely the limits of the power and greatness of man." He did not believe that the time had come to propound a speculative theory of the universe; indeed, he seemed to have been doubtful of the possibility of reaching such knowledge at all.

Metaphysics and Theology. Bacon divides theology into natural, and inspired or revealed theology. Natural theology is that knowledge, or rather rudiment of knowledge, concerning God, which may be obtained by the light of nature and the contemplation of God's creatures. The limitations of natural theological knowledge, when rightly drawn, are such that, although theology suffices to refute atheism, and to give information regarding the laws of nature, it does not suffice to establish religion. "It is an assumed truth and conclusion of experience that a little or superficial knowledge of philosophy may incline the mind of man to atheism; but a farther proceeding therein doth bring the mind back again to religion." Yet, such a study does not yield a perfect knowledge of God; nor can we adapt the heavenly mysteries to our reason. Knowledge derived from the senses—and all science is so derived—cannot help us here: "The senses are like the sun, which displays the face of the earth, but shuts up that of the heavens." Here we must appeal to sacred or inspired theology. "Sacred theology is grounded only upon the word and oracle of God and not upon the light of nature. . . . So then the doctrine of religion, as well natural as mystical, is not to be attained but by inspiration and revelation from God." [1] This applies not only to the great mysteries of the Godhead, but also to the true interpretation of the moral law, a large part of which is too sublime to be attained by the light of nature. Bacon, therefore, repudiates the attempt of the schoolmen to deduce the truth of the Christian religion from the principles of the philosophers; the scholastic union between science and faith is a failure. Once the articles and principles of religion have been postulated, however, we can by reason deduce inferences from them. If we accept the premises, we must accept the conclusions. "Thus in chess or other games of like nature, the first rules and laws of the play are merely positive postulates, which ought to be entirely received, not disputed: but the skillful playing of the game is a matter of art and reason."

The cleavage which Bacon makes between theology and philosophy is the inheritance of the closing Middle Ages; by relegating the dogmas to a separate territory, the field was left free for philosophy. His attitude toward theology is really one of indifference. It may surprise us that he devotes so much attention to such subjects as astrology, dreams, divination, etc., but these things were widely believed in his day, and a scientific treatment of them did not seem out of place at the time.

Bacon as an Empiricist. Although Bacon's empiricism is not thoroughly and consistently worked out, we may class him among the members of that school. He holds that all our knowledge, except revelation, is derived from sensation; only particulars exist. Mind or reason acts on the materials fur nished by the senses; knowledge is rational as well as experimental, but reason has no truths of its own. At the same time, he speaks of mental faculties as though they were a priori endowments. The soul is material, and yet there is a rational soul, about which, however, we know nothing,

[1] *Advancement of Learning*, Bk. II. See Spedding, Ellis, and Heath edition of *Philosophical Works*, Part III, pp. 394-95.

and which belongs to the domain of religion. Teleology is banished from physics and becomes a part of metaphysics.

45. THOMAS HOBBES

Thomas Hobbes (1588-1679) studied scholasticism and the Aristotelian philosophy at Oxford, traveled extensively on the Continent as the tutor and companion of young English noblemen, and became acquainted, in Paris, with Descartes, Gassendi, and Mersenne. He fled to France in November 1640, after the assembling of the Long Parliament, returning in 1651 to make his peace with Cromwell.

Among his works are: *Elementa philosophica de cive*, 1642; *De corpore*, 1655; *De homine*, 1658; *Leviathan*, 1651; *Elements of Law, Natural and Politic* (consisting of *Human Nature* and the *Body Politic*, written in 1640), ed. by Tönnies, 1888; and the two treatises on *Liberty* and *Necessity*, 1646 and 1654; works ed. by J. Molesworth, 1839-45, five Latin and eleven English volumes; *Elements of Law, Behemoth, Letters*, ed. by F. Tönnies, 1888-89; *The Philosophy of Hobbes* (selections ed. by F. J. E. Woodbridge), 1903; *The Metaphysical System of Hobbes* (selections ed. by M. Calkins), 1905; G. C. Robertson, *Hobbes*, 1886; L. Stephen, *Hobbes*, 1904; A. E. Taylor, *Thomas Hobbes*, 1909; F. Tönnies, *Thomas Hobbes: Leben und Lehre*, 1926; B. Landry, *Hobbes*, 1930; J. Laird, *Hobbes*, 1934.

Aim and Method. One of the boldest and most typical representatives of the modern spirit is Thomas Hobbes. Like all the modern reformers of philosophy he attempts to break completely with the past; the weeding out of inveterate opinions is the first task of philosophy. Greek philosophy is to him an aberration. Like Bacon, he accentuates the practical utility of science and philosophy: the end of knowledge is power. He denies completely the scientific character of theology: there can be no science of God, no doctrine of angels. He also repudiates the spiritualistic notion of the soul, which is basic in the thought of his contemporary Descartes and which had been introduced by Bacon into his physiological psychology as a kind of appendage. He accepts, instead, the new natural science of Copernicus, Galileo, and Harvey, whom he regards as the founders of science, and, in his materialistic philosophy, fearlessly deduces the consequences of the mechanical theory. An ardent admirer of mathematics, though not a great mathematician, Hobbes looks upon the method of geometry as the only one capable of giving us certain and universal knowledge. Natural and political history, since they fail to exemplify the mathematical ideal, are not sciences, and historical knowledge is the product of experience, not of ratiocination. While his rationalistic ideal of knowledge is like that of Galileo and Descartes, he is, like Bacon, an empiricist in his theory of the origin of knowledge. He finds it difficult, however, to reconcile his rational-ism with his empiricism, and the presence of both tendencies in his system is responsible for many confusions and inconsistencies. In his own estima-tion, his chief contribution to thought is his theory of the State; civil phi-losophy, he proudly tells us, is no older than his book *De cive*.

Theory of Knowledge. Philosophy, according to Hobbes, is a knowledge of effects from their causes and of causes from their effects; his method is, therefore, partly synthetic, partly analytic. That is to say, we may proceed from sense perception or experience to principles (analysis), or from primary or most universal propositions—or principles which are manifest in them-selves—to conclusions (synthesis). In order to be genuine science or true demonstration, reasoning must take its beginning from true principles, mere experience not being science. Nominalist that he is, Hobbes also defines reasoning as a kind of calculation: reasoning is a conceptual arithmetic—the logical addition and substraction of concepts agreed upon for mark-ing and signifying our thoughts.

The problem, therefore, is to find a first principle, a starting-point for our reasoning, a cause on which to ground all effects. This Hobbes finds in motion. Every body of which we can know the causes and effects is subject-matter for philosophy. There are natural bodies, and artificial bodies or the commonwealth, a body made by man. Hence, we have natural phi-losophy (physics and psychology), and political philosophy, which is made up of ethics and politics proper. Primary or first philosophy is a science of the fundamental principles or definitions of all science; it is a kind of prelude to the other branches, treating of space, time, body, cause, effect, identity and difference, relation, quantity, and the like. By analyzing particular things, we ultimately reach their most universal properties and at once know their causes, since these are manifest of themselves, having but one universal cause—motion. The last things cannot be demonstrated until the first are fully understood. Hence, philosophy is the science of the motions and actions of natural and political bodies, and everything can be explained by motion: the nature of man, the mental world, and the State, as well as the occurrences of physical nature, can be explained mechanically.

Whence do these principles arise, how does our knowledge originate? The origin of all our thoughts are the senses. Sensations persist or are retained in memory which Hobbes describes as "decaying sense." The mem-ory of many things is experience. Images or thoughts succeed one another in the mind, whence we have a train of thoughts, which can be regulated by desire and design. The function of speech is to transfer our mental discourse into trains of words, which helps us to register our thoughts as well as to communicate them to others. In the right definition of names lies the first use of speech, which is the acquisition of science. In science we use universal terms, but the things themselves are not universal, there is nothing called "man" in general (nominalism). Hence, neither knowledge of fact nor knowledge of consequence is absolute, but conditional.

Whereas Bacon emphasizes the rôle in knowledge of experience and induction from experience, Hobbes shows the need of demonstration or the deductive method. But holding, as he does, that the principles from which we reason have their source in sense, he loses his firm faith in the possibility of any method to reach absolute knowledge. Locke later on strengthens these doubts by declaring that we can have no science of bodies at all.

Knowledge, then, has its origin in sense impressions. Now, what is sensation and how is it caused? Through our sense-organs we receive different sensations: colors, sounds, tastes, smells, etc. These processes are caused by the action of some external object on the organs of sense. Motion is produced in the organ and carried through nerves into the brain and thence into the heart. There a reaction ensues (an endeavor outward) which makes it appear that there is some outward object. The sensations, then, are nothing but motions in the brain, or spirits, or some internal substance of the head. The sensation, or image or color is but an appearance, an apparition of the motion, agitation, or alteration which the object works in the brain. Sensations are not qualities of things themselves; they are but motions in us. Now, since only motion can produce motion, there can be nothing outside except motion. All sense is fancy, but the cause is a real body. There is no similarity between the cause of the sensation and the sensation or appearance. The reality outside is a moving reality; we perceive it as color or sound. Our picture of the world obtained through sensation is not the real world.

If this is true, how do we know what is the nature of the world? Hobbes does not answer this problem, for it did not disturb him; he dogmatically assumes with the scientists of his day that the world is a corporeal world in motion. As we shall see later, Descartes attempted to prove the existence of an extended moving reality deductively, from the self-certainty of consciousness; but the English empiricist was not troubled by skeptical doubts with respect to external things.

Metaphysics. A real world of bodies in space exists; there is real space besides imaginary space, or the idea of space produced by the object; the real magnitude of a body causes the idea or phantasm of space in the mind; in this sense imagined space is an accident of the mind. No body can be conceived without the accident of extension and figure; all other accidents —rest, motion, color, hardness, and the like—continually perish and are succeeded by others, yet in such a way that the body never perishes. Motion is defined as a continuous relinquishing of one place and acquiring of another. It can have no other cause than motion. When one motion produces another, it does not mean that one accident goes out of one object into another, but that one accident perishes and another is generated. A body is said to act or work on—*do* something to—another body, when it either generates or destroys some accident in it. This is the relation of cause and effect. The efficient cause of all change and motion is motion. Power is not a certain accident that differs from all acts, but is called power because another act shall be caused by it afterwards. The question of the beginning of motion cannot be answered by philosophers, but only by "those that are lawfully authorized to order the worship of God." When he created the world, God gave to all things whatever natural and special motion he thought good.

There are not, as the schoolmen had held, any incorporeal substances or spirits in addition to bodies. Substance and body are identical, hence to speak of incorporeal substances is to speak of incorporeal bodies, which is a contradiction in terms or an absurdity of speech. Besides, if there were spirits or souls, we could not know them, for all our knowledge is based on sensation, and spirits presumably do not affect the senses. The Bible does not teach that there is an incorporeal or immaterial soul, but rather supports those who hold angels and spirits to be corporeal. God himself, Hobbes is inclined to think, is body or a corporeal being. That there is a God we know and can prove in the causal way, but *what* he is we do not know.

Psychology. Hobbes offers various conceptions of the mind. Mind is motion in the brain; or it is an internal substance in the head, a subtle body. Images or ideas are motions in the brain and heart, motions of a material substance. This is complete materialism. But when he speaks of mental processes as "appearances" or apparitions of motions, as accidents of the mind, but "not like motions," he modifies his materialism: states of consciousness here are no longer motions, but the effects of motions. Such a view is called by modern writers epiphenomenalism: consciousness is an after-appearance.

Besides the faculty or power of knowing, there is a motive power, the power by which the mind gives animal motion to its body. Motion proceeds from the head to the heart; when it helps the vital motion there, it is delight or pleasure, when it hinders it, it is pain. Pleasure and pain arouse *appetite* or *desire,* and *aversion:* appetite is an endeavor toward, aversion an endeavor away from, something. Some appetites and aversions, such as appetite for food, are inborn with us; the rest are acquired by learning and experience. All delight or pleasure has its source in appetite, hence there can be no contentment except in the progressive satisfaction of appetites. Felicity or continued happiness consists not in having prospered, but in the process of prospering.

That which pleases a man he calls good, what displeases him, evil. Men differ in constitution, and, therefore, in their judgments concerning good and evil. There is no such thing as absolute goodness, for goodness is always relative to individual men; even God's goodness is goodness in relation to us.

The imagination is the first beginning of all voluntary motion. The alternate succession of appetite and aversion is called deliberation; in deliberation the last appetite or aversion is called will: will to do or will not to do. All other appetites to do and to refrain from doing are called intentions and inclinations, but not acts of will. Will in man is not different from will in other animals. The causes of our appetites and aversions are, therefore, also the causes of our will. Our will is the effect of sense, memory, understanding, reason, and opinion. The will, including each inclination arising during deliberation, is as much necessitated and dependent on a sufficient cause as anything else. It is not free but caused; to call an agent free means he has made an end of deliberating, and can do if he will, and forbear if he will; liberty is the absence of external impediments. A man is free to act, but not free to will as he wills, he cannot will to will. To say I can will if I will, is absurd.

Politics. Now that we know the nature of man, we are ready to understand the meaning of the State and of law. We may study civil and moral philosophy synthetically, by beginning with principles—say, the knowledge of human motives (motions of the mind)—and deduce from them the necessity of establishing a commonwealth and rights and duties. We can, however, also reach the principles analytically, by induction, or by observing the motives in ourselves. It is right and reasonable for a man to use all means and do whatever is necessary for the preservation of his body. He, therefore, has *by nature* the right to do whatever he pleases to whom he pleases, to possess, use, and enjoy all things within his reach. Nature has given all things to all men, hence right and profit (*jus* and *utile*) are the same thing. But in a state of nature, where every man is striving for such power, where it is just for every man to invade another man's right and to resist invasion of his own, there will be a state of perpetual war of all against all (*bellum omnium contra omnes*). In such a state of war nothing can be unjust; the notions of right and wrong, justice and injustice have no place there. Where there is no common power, there is no law; where no law, no injustice. Force and fraud are the cardinal virtues in war; justice and injustice are qualities that apply to men in society, not in solitude. Aristotle had taught that man is a social animal, that the social instinct leads him to form societies. This Hobbes denies. Man, he says, is a ferocious animal: *Homo homini lupus.* Competition for riches, honor, and power inclines a man to contention, enmity, and war, because only in this way can one competitor fulfill his desire to kill, subdue, supplant, or repel his rivals. In such a state of hostility and war, no man can hope for sufficient might to preserve himself for any length of time. His desire for power defeats itself, for to practice injustice creates a state in which the very end he aimed at is thwarted. There is, consequently, a certain absurdity in acts of injustice and injury, for to commit an act of injustice is to undo voluntarily that which from the beginning has been voluntarily accepted. Although injustice is illogical or irrational, Hobbes is not so optimistic as to believe that man will be ruled by reason alone; only the fear of consequences can make him keep his word and abide by the dictates of reason.

Reason dictates that there should be a state of peace and that every man should seek after peace. The first precept of reason, or *law* of nature, commands self-preservation; the second, that man lay down his *natural* right and be content with as much liberty for himself as he is prepared to allow others in the interests of peace and security. When he has relinquished his natural right, it is his *duty* not to nullify that voluntary act. Man, however, transfers his right in consideration of some right reciprocally transferred to him, or for some other good. Consequently, no man can be expected to transfer certain rights, such as the right of self-defense, since he transfers his right for the very purpose of securing his life and this mutual transferring of right is called *contract*. The third law of nature is that men keep the covenants they have made and this constitutes the fountain and original of justice, for where no covenant has been made, no right has been transferred, and no action is unjust. But where there is fear by either party that the covenants will not be maintained, the covenants are invalid, and there can be no injustice. It follows that before just and unjust can have any meaning, there must be some coercive power to compel men equally to the performance of their covenants, by the threat of some punishment. There is no such power before the erection of a commonwealth; hence, where there is no commonwealth there is nothing unjust.

The laws of nature are immutable and eternal; injustice, ingratitude, arrogance, pride, iniquity, and the rest can never be made lawful. For it can never be that war shall preserve life and peace destroy it. The science of these laws is the only true moral philosophy. For moral philosophy is nothing else but the science of what is good and evil, in the conservation and society of mankind. These laws are called *natural* laws because they are dictates of reason; they are called *moral* laws because they concern men's manners toward one another; they are also *divine* laws in view of their author.

The only way to erect a commonwealth and insure peace is to confer the total power and strength of men upon one man or assembly of men, whereby all their wills, by a majority vote, coalesce into one will. This is more than consent or concord; it is a real unity of all in one and the same person, made by covenant, of every man with every man. The multitude so united in one person is called a commonwealth; it is the great Leviathan, the mortal god, from which the sovereign derives his supreme power.

The subjects cannot change the form of government, the sovereign power cannot be forfeited; no one can protest against the institution of the common sovereign, declared by the majority. He has the sole right of making rules by legislation, the right of jurisdiction, of making war and peace, choosing counselors and ministers, rewarding and punishing, as well as the right of deciding the doctrines fit to be taught his subjects. These rights are incommunicable and inseparable. Other rights the sovereign may confer, e.g., the power to coin money. The evils that may follow from such absolute sovereignty cannot be compared with the miseries and horrible calamities of civil war, the dissolute condition of masterless men.

The sovereign power may reside in one man, or in an assembly of men (monarchy, aristocracy, democracy). The monarchy is the best form: in the king the public and private interest are most closely united, and he can act more consistently than a body of men. But the sovereign power, wherever placed, ought always to be absolute. Some things, however, the subject may refuse to do: every subject has liberty in all things, the right to which cannot be transferred by contract; he is not bound to injure or kill himself, confess his crime, kill any other man, etc. Among such rights Hobbes does not include the right of religious liberty: the religion is determined by the State and is obligatory upon the subjects. God speaks by his vicegerents or lieutenants here on earth, by sovereign kings or others having sovereign authority. The appeal to the private conscience causes trouble; we need a common tribunal to decide how to act if we are to have peace. Hobbes' theory of the State may be regarded as a philosophical defense of the English monarchy of the Stuarts against the demands of the people. The sovereign can do no injury, for he represents the subject who has given him authority. He may commit iniquity, but not injustice or injury in the proper meaning of the term. The obligation of subjects lasts as long and no longer than the power by which the sovereign is able to protect them. The duty of the sovereign consists in the good government of the people; when his acts tend to hurt the people in general, they are breaches of the law of nature or of the divine law.

Works on English philosophy

W. R. Sorley, *Beginnings of English Philosophy*, in *Cambridge History of English Literature*, vols. IV, ff.; T. M. Forsyth, *English Philosophy*, 1910; K. Fischer, *Bacon of Verulam and His Successors*, trans. by J. Oxenford, 1857; A. Seth Pringle-Pattison, *On Scottish Philosophy*, 1885; L. Stephen, *History of English Thought in the Eighteenth Century*, 2 vols., 1876-1925, and *The English Utilitarians*, 3 vols., 1900; E. Albee, *History of English Utilitarianism*, 1902; Selby-Bigge, *British Moralists* (selections from writings), 1897; W. Graham, *English Political Philosophy from Hobbes to Maine*, 1899; J. J. Rickaby, *Free Will and Four English Philosophers*, 1906; C. W. Eliot, *English Philosophers of the Seventeenth and Eighteenth Century*, 1910; J. W. Hudson, *The Treatment of Personality by Locke, Berkeley and Hume*, 1911; J. Seth, *English Philosophers and Schools of Philosophy*, 1912; W. R. Sorley, *A History of English Philosophy*, 1920; E. A. Burtt, *The English Philosophers from Bacon to Mill* (writings of the British Philosophers), *Modern Library*, 1939; G. Kennedy, *Bacon-Hobbes-Locke* (Selections), 1937.

XII

Continental Rationalism

46. René Descartes

René Descartes (1596-1650) was born at La Haye, Touraine, the son of a noble family. He was educated by the Jesuits of La Flèche, learning ancient languages, scholastic philosophy, and mathematics. In this latter study alone he found the certainty and clearness he craved; the others did not satisfy him, and he abandoned them upon leaving school (1612), to seek only after such science "as he might discover in himself or in the great book of the world." He traveled, pursued the diversions of a man of the world, entered the armies of Maurice of Nassau (1617) and General Tilly (1619), and mingled with all sorts and conditions of men. During this entire period his intellectual interests never flagged; we frequently find him in meditative retirement, even at the headquarters of the army. The problem that stirred him was how to reach such certainty in philosophy as characterizes mathematics; he prayed for divine illumination, vowing a pilgrimage to the shrine of Loretto in case his prayer should be answered. Leaving the army in 1621, Descartes devoted himself to travel and study (1621-1625), and spent three years in Paris with scientific friends (1625-1628); but feeling the need of solitude, he withdrew to Holland, where he busied himself with the preparation of his works (1629-1649). In 1649 he accepted the invitation of Queen Christina of Sweden, who was deeply interested in philosophy, to come to Stockholm; the climate, however, undermined his health, and he died after a year's stay there.

Among Descartes' works are the *Discours de la méthode* (which appeared with *Dioptrics, Meteors,* and *Geometry* in a series of *Philosophical Essays*), 1637; *Meditationes de prima philosophia,* to which were added objections by several learned men, Arnauld, Hobbes, Gassendi, and others, together with rejoinders by the author himself, 1641; *Principia philosophiae,* 1644; *Les passions de l'ame,* 1650. The *Discours* and *Passions* were written in French, the *Meditations* and *Principles* in Latin. The book *Le monde ou traité de la lumière,* begun in 1630, was not published by Descartes; the condemnation of Galileo by the Inquisition in 1632 deterred the timid and peace-loving philosopher from completing it. It and the *Traité de l'homme* appeared in 1644; *Letters,* 1657-1667; posthumous works, 1701.

Works ed. by V. Cousin, in French, 11 vols., 1824-26; some unpublished writings by Foucher de Careil, 2 vols., 1859-60; C. Adam and P. Tannery, *Œuvres complètes,* 13 vols., 1896-1911; trans. of *Meditations,* and selections from *Principles* by J. Veitch (used in this book), 1905; *The Philosophical Works of Descartes,* 2 vols., trans. by E. S. Haldane and G. R. T. Ross, 1911-12; Descartes: *Selections,* ed. by R. M. Eaton, 1927.

K. Fischer, *Descartes and His School,* trans. by J. P. Gordy, 1887; N. Smith, *Studies in Cartesian Philosophy,* 1902; E. Boutroux, "Descartes and Cartesianism," in *Cambridge Modern History,* Vol. IV, chap. xxvii; E. Boutroux, *Historical Studies in Philosophy,* trans. by F. Rothwell, 1912; P. G. Natorp, *Descartes' Erkenntnistheorie,* 1882; E. S. Haldane, *Descartes, His Life and Times,* 1905; L. Lévy-Bruhl, *History of Modern Philosophy in France,* trans. by G. Coblence, 1899; L. Brunschvicg, *Descartes et Pascal,* 1944; S. V. Keeling, *Descartes,* 1934; M. J. Mahony, *Cartesianism,* 1925; E. Gilson, *Le rôle de la pensée médiévale dans la formation du système cartésien,* 1930; J. Maritain, *Le songe de Descartes,* 1932; A. B. Gibson, *The Philosophy of Descartes,* 1932; S. V. Keeling, *Descartes,* 1934.

Descartes' Problem. Descartes, like Bacon, resolutely sets his face against the old authorities and, like him, emphasized the practical character of philosophy. "Philosophy is a perfect knowledge of all that man can know, as well for the conduct of his life as for the preservation of his health and the discovery of all the arts." Unlike the English empiricist, however, he took mathematics as the model of his philosophical method. He offers not merely a program of human knowledge, but sought to construct a system of thought which would possess the certainty of mathematics. In his conception of external nature, he was in agreement with the great natural scientists of the new era: everything in nature—even physiological processes and emotions—must be explained mechanically, without the aid of forms or essences. At the same time, he accepted the fundamental principles of the time-honored idealistic or spiritualistic philosophy and attempted to adapt them to the demands of the new science: his problem was to reconcile the mechanism of nature with the freedom of God and the human soul.

Classification of the Sciences. The first part of true philosophy, according to Descartes, is metaphysics, which contains the principles of knowledge, such as the definition of the principal attributes of God, the immateriality of the soul, and of all the clear and simple ideas that we possess. The second is physics, in which, after finding the true principles of material things, we examine, in general, how the whole universe has been framed; then, in particular, the nature of the earth and of all the bodies most commonly found upon it, as air, water, fire, the loadstone and other minerals; next the nature of plants, animals, and, above all, man, in order hereafter to be able to discover the other sciences that are useful to us.

Thus philosophy as a whole is like a tree whose roots are metaphysics, whose trunk is physics, and whose branches, which issue from this trunk, are all the other sciences. These reduce themselves to three principal ones, viz. medicine, mechanics and morals—I mean the higher and most perfect moral science which presupposing a complete knowledge of the other sciences, is the last degree of wisdom.[1]

The first part of Descartes' book, *Principles of Philosophy,* contains the metaphysics, the other three parts take up "all that is most general in physics." [2]

Method and Criterion of Knowledge. Descartes' aim is to find a body of certain and self-evident truths, such as everyone endowed with common sense and the faculty of reasoning will accept. Such knowledge scholastic philosophy was unable to give us; there are many different opinions on one and the same subject, and we look in vain for certainty from this source. The other sciences, taking, as they do, their principles from scholastic philosophy, can build nothing solid upon such unstable foundations. Instead of clear and certain knowledge, we receive a lot of false opinions and are involved in error and doubt. There is not a single subject in philosophy that is not still being disputed. Hence, if we would have anything firm and constant in the sciences, we must get rid of these opinions and build the edifice of knowledge anew from its foundations.

Instead of accepting the traditional views, we must study the great book of the world. "We shall never become philosophers even though we should read all the reasonings of Plato and Aristotle if we cannot form a sound judgment upon any proposition." [3] To know the opinions of others is not science, but history; a man should do his own thinking. But how shall we proceed in our attempts to reach clear and certain knowledge, what *method* ought we to follow? The example of mathematics gives us a hint of the order to be pursued in our reasonings; the mathematicians alone have been able to find certain and self-evident propositions. We accept without debate the statement that twice two is four, or that the sum of the angles of a triangle is equal to two right angles. If we could discover similar truths in philosophy, there would be an end to countless disputes and controversies: we should be able to prove the existence of God, the immortality of the soul, the reality of an external world, and we should succeed in laying secure foundations for the sciences.

[1] Author's letter to the translator of his *Principles of Philosophy,* which serves as a Preface to the book. Haldane and Ross translation of *The Philosophical Works of Descartes,* Vol. I, p. 211.

[2] *Op. cit.,* Vol. I, p. 212.

[3] *Rules for the Direction of the Mind,* Rule II.

How do we proceed in mathematics, what is the method pursued? We begin with axioms, or principles which are self-evident, which everyone accepts who hears and understands them. From these principles as our starting-point we deduce other propositions which logically follow from them, and which are just as certain as the former, provided no mistake has been made in the reasoning. That is, we begin with simple propositions that are self-evident, and pass from these to more complex ones; our method is synthetic or deductive.

This method must be extended to philosophy. We should proceed from absolutely certain first principles, from propositions which are clear and self-evident, and pass on to new and unknown truths which are equally certain. We look in vain for such truths in the traditional scholastic systems, for in them we find nothing but a mass of divergent opinions. Besides, we cannot accept any truth on the authority of others alone; we must search after it ourselves, never receiving anything as true which we do not clearly and distinctly perceive to be so. We should be on our guard against being influenced by our prejudices, and by transmitted beliefs which have been impressed upon us in our childhood by our parents and teachers. Many of these opinions have been found by experience to be false; perhaps all of them are. Neither can we have faith in our sensations, for these often deceive us, and how do we know that they correspond to anything real? But can we not be sure that our own bodies and actions are realities? No, we cannot be certain even of these; for we are often deceived, we dream, and in our dreams we believe we have realities before us, whereas they are nothing but illusions. Perhaps we are dreaming now, at this present moment; we have no means by which we can with certainty distinguish between waking and dreaming. For all I know, an evil spirit may have made me in order to deceive me. His world which I picture to myself may exist only in my imagination; perhaps it has no existence outside my mind. Even the demonstrations of mathematics may be doubted, for we have sometimes seen men fall into error in such matters and admit as absolutely certain what to us appeared false.

There is no idea of which I can be entirely certain. "I suppose, accordingly, that all the things which I see are false; I believe that none of those things which my deceptive memory presents to me are true; I suppose that I have no senses; I believe that body, figure, extension, motion, and place are nothing but fictions of my mind. What is there then that can be thought true? Perhaps only that nothing in the world is certain." [4]

[4] *Meditation II.*

But one thing *is* certain, and that is that I doubt, or think; of that there can be no doubt. It is, indeed, a contradiction to suppose that that which thinks does not exist at the very time when it thinks. Descartes does not appeal to an empirical psychical fact, the mind's awareness of itself; but reasons logically that doubt implies a doubter, thinking a thinker, a thinking thing (*res cogitans*) or spiritual substance; thus he reaches what seems to him a rational, self-evident proposition. To doubt means to think, to think means to be; *cogito, ergo sum*—I think, therefore I am. "It is the first and most certain knowledge that occurs to one who philosophizes in an orderly manner." [5] Here is the principle we have been seeking—a certain, self-evident starting-point for our metaphysics. This proposition also furnishes us with a criterion or test of truth. This one proposition is absolutely certain, true, clearly and distinctly perceived; hence, I can establish as a general rule that all things which are like it, clearly and distinctly perceived, are true.

Proofs of the Existence of God. We now have a fundamental principle and a criterion of true knowledge. What else can we know? It is doubtful whether anything can be certain, so long as we are confronted with the possibility of a deceiving God; we do not know as yet whether there is a God, and, if there is, that he is not a deceiver. This difficulty must be removed. Some of our ideas appear to be innate, some are our own inventions, most of them seem to have been received from without. Certain ideas we regard as effects or copies of an external world. But all this may be illusion. One of the ideas I find in myself is the idea of God. Now, nothing can come from nothing, whatever exists must have a cause for existing; this, too, is a self-evident proposition. Moreover, the cause must be at least as great as the effect, there must be at least as much reality in it. That which contains greater reality in itself and which is the more perfect, cannot be a consequence of, and dependent on, the less perfect. Hence, I myself cannot be the cause of the idea of God, for I am a finite, imperfect being, while the idea of God is the idea of a perfect, infinite being. It must have been placed in me by an infinite being, or God, and hence God must exist. This proof for the existence of God is not the ontological proof of Anselm, but a causal proof, which begins with the idea of a perfect being existing in my mind. It is not argued that such a being exists merely because we have a concept of him, but, rather, that from the idea of such a being we can necessarily infer the existence of that being as the *cause* of the idea. The argument differs from the ontological proof in two respects: (1) its starting point is not the concept of God as a formal

[5] *Principles of Philosophy,* Part I, Princip. VII.

essence, but the actual existing idea of God in the mind of a man; (2) it proceeds by causal inference from the idea of God to God himself and not, as in the case of the ontological argument, by strict formal implication from the essence of God to his existence.

But, it may be urged, the concept of infinity is a mere negative concept—the denial of perfection. This cannot be so, according to Descartes, for the idea of finitude implies the idea of infinity, or of God; how could I doubt or have desires if I did not have in myself the idea of a being more perfect than myself, by comparison with whom I recognize the defects of my nature? Doubt implies a standard of truth, imperfection a standard of perfection.

Again, I could not have been the cause of my own existence; for I have an idea of perfection, and if I had created myself, I should have made myself perfect, and, moreover, I should be able to preserve myself, which is not the case. If my parents had created me, they could also preserve me, which is impossible. Finally, it also follows from the very notion of God as a perfect being that he exists. It is not in my power to conceive a God without existence, that is, a being supremely perfect and yet devoid of an absolute perfection. This is the ontological argument used by both Anselm and Augustine.

It is also unthinkable that the divine perfections, which I conceive, should have more than one cause, for if these causes were many, they would not be perfect; to be perfect there must be one cause only, one God. God must be self-caused, for if he is the effect of another being, then that being is the effect of another, and so on *ad infinitum*: we have an infinite regress and never can reach a causal explanation of the effect with which we began.

The idea of God I have received from God; it is innate. God is not only the cause, but the archetype of our existence; he has created man in his own image. We need not wonder that God in creating us should have placed this idea in us, to serve as the mark of the workman imprinted on his work. If God did not exist, we could not possibly be what we are, nor could we have an idea of God. We know more of God himself and of the human mind than we know of corporeal objects. Reflecting upon the idea of God, we perceive that he is eternal, omniscient, omnipotent, the source of all goodness and truth; the creator of all things. He is not corporeal and does not perceive by means of the senses, as we do. He has intellect and will, but not like ours; and he does not will evil or sin, for sin is the negation of being. This is the usual theistic position with which we have become acquainted in scholasticism. Descartes agrees with Duns Scotus that we can accept reason only in so far as it does not conflict with revelation. He also holds with him that God could have arranged the world otherwise than it is; and that a thing is good because God makes it so; he does not make it so because it is good.

Truth and Error. We have thus far discovered several self-evident truths: I exist; whatever is clearly and distinctly perceived is true; nothing can be without a cause; the cause must contain at least as much reality and perfection as the effect; God exists; God is perfect and cannot deceive us. How, then, does it come about that we are ever deceived, that we ever err at all? In the first place, the power of distinguishing the true from the false, which God has given us, is not infinite. Moreover, error depends on the concurrence of two causes, namely, the faculty of cognition and the faculty of election, or the power of free choice—understanding and will. By understanding alone, I neither affirm nor deny anything, but merely apprehend the ideas regarding which I may form a judgment; no error, properly so-called, is found in it. Neither is the will itself the source of error, for it is exceedingly ample and perfect of its kind. The source of error is the disparity between the finitude of the human intellect and the infinitude of the human will. Errors are due to our failure to restrain the will from judging a thing when we do not conceive it with sufficient clearness and distinctness; by choosing the false instead of the true and evil instead of good, the will falls into error and sin.

Existence of the External World. Another problem demanding consideration is that of the external world. We imagine that there are bodies outside of us. How can we know that they actually exist? We have feelings of pleasure and pain, appetites, and sensations, which we refer instinctively to bodily causes. But since our sensations often deceive us, and, since our desires and appetites are often misleading, we cannot prove the existence of bodies from the existence of such experiences. Yet, if God induced in us a deeply rooted conviction of the existence of an external world, when no such world existed, he could not be defended against the charge of being a deceiver. The existence in my mind of illusions of sense and even hallucinations and dreams is, however, compatible with the divine goodness, since God has endowed me with the power of intellect to dispel and correct such delusions. Thus, God is not a deceiver, but a truthful being, and our sensations must, therefore, be caused by real bodies.

What are bodies? Bodies exist independently of our thinking; they do not need our existence in order to exist. Such an independent thing is called a substance. By substance we can mean nothing else than a thing which so exists that it needs no other thing in order to exist. In reality, only one such being—God—is substance in the absolute sense. Descartes, strictly speaking, affirms one absolute substance—God—and two relative substances—mind and body. The two relative substances exist independently of one another, but both depend on God. They are fundamentally different from one another, and we know them only through their attributes. The essential characteristic or property of substance, that which necessarily inheres in it, is called the attribute. The attribute is the quality without which the substance cannot conceivably exist. But the attribute can manifest itself in different ways or modes or modifications. Substance and attribute can be conceived without modes, but modes cannot be conceived without substance and attribute. We cannot conceive figure without extension, nor motion except in extended space; nor imagination or will, except in a thinking thing. We can, on the other hand, conceive extension without figure or motion, and thought without imagination or sensation. The substance cannot change its attributes, but it can change its modes: a body will always be extended, but its figure need not remain the same.

What, then, is the nature of external things? What we clearly and distinctly perceive in body is the essential attribute of body. Sounds, colors, taste, smell, heat and cold are not attributes of body: we are unable to conceive these clearly and distinctly, they are confused; what we sense is not the body's true reality. The attribute of body is extension, and nothing else; body and extension are identical. Extension is a spatial continuum of three dimensions, length, breadth, and thickness; every body is a limited spatial magnitude. There is no empty space or vacuum, for, wherever there is space, there is body. Space is infinitely divisible; there are no ultimate parts of space, hence matter is infinitely divisible, i.e., there are no atoms. The smallest parts of bodies are still further divisible; they are not atoms, but corpuscles. Nor can extension stop anywhere, for the corporeal world is infinite.

All the processes of the external world are modifications or modes of extension; extension may be divided without end, the parts may be united and separated, whence arise different forms of matter. All variation of matter, or diversity of form, depends on motion. Motion is the action by which a body passes from one place to another. It is a mode of the movable thing, not a substance. All occurrence is transference of motion from one part of space to another. "Motion is the transporting of one part of matter or of one body from the vicinity of those bodies that are in immediate contact with it, or which we regard at rest, to the vicinity of other bodies." The physical world can be explained in terms of mechanics. There is no action at a distance—

all occurrences are due to pressure and impact. Hence, there must be a universal ether to account for the facts of astronomy.

Body conceived as mere extension is passive and cannot move itself; we must, therefore, have recourse to God as the first cause of motion in the world. "God originally created matter along with motion and rest, and now by his concourse alone preserves in the whole the same amount of motion that he then placed in it." This view of the prime mover was widely held in the time of Descartes and later. It is the old Aristotelian conception which Galileo and Newton both accepted. To insure against divine interference with the world, however, which would mean the abandonment of the mechanical theory and a relapse into scholasticism, Descartes holds that God has given the world a certain amount of motion: motion is constant. We have here the germ of the theory of the conservation of energy. The physical magnitude called "motion" by Descartes, the constancy of which he asserts, is presumably what physicists call momentum or quantity of motion—the product of mass and velocity. In asserting the constancy of motion, Descartes is not making the palpably false claim that velocity of motion is a constant. Bodies cannot of themselves initiate or stop their motion; they can neither increase nor decrease the amount of motion in the physical universe, and hence the quantity of motion and rest must remain the same.

Since God is immutable, all changes in the world of bodies must follow constant rules, or laws of nature. All laws of nature are laws of motion. All differences in bodies are explained by different relations of the parts: solid bodies are bodies in which the parts are united and at rest; fluids are bodies in which the parts move.

Relation of Mind and Body. Mind is diametrically opposed to body. The attribute of body is extension: bodies are passive; the attribute of mind is thinking: mind is active, free. The two substances are absolutely distinct: mind is absolutely without extension, and no body can think. We cannot conceive of mind or soul without thought: the soul is *res cogitans;* I have a clear and distinct idea of myself in so far as I am only a thinking and unextended thing. Hence, it is certain that I, that is, my mind, through which I am what I am, is entirely and truly distinct from my body, and may exist without it. I can clearly and distinctly conceive of myself as entire, without the faculties of imagining and perceiving; but I cannot conceive these without conceiving myself, that is to say, without an intelligent substance in which they reside. Imagination and perception are, therefore, distinct from myself, as modes are from things. In thought, however, Descartes includes will, and evidently also such higher emotions as are not the result of the union of body and mind. He tells us in his *Discourse on Method* that a thinking thing is one that doubts, understands, conceives, affirms, denies, wills, refuses, imagines as well as feels. Thought is by no means restricted to the intellectual or even cognitive activities of mind—it embraces everything which we now label "consciousness." I clearly perceive that neither extension nor figure, nor local motion nor anything similar that can be attributed to body, pertains to my nature as a thinking thing. The knowledge I have of my own mind precedes that of any corporeal thing and is more certain, since I may doubt whether there is any body in existence, while I already perceive that I think.

What particularly attracted Descartes to this extreme dualism was that it left nature free for the mechanical explanations of natural science. Mind is eliminated from nature and given an independent territory of its own. Physics is allowed to go its own way, all purposes or final causes are banished from its domain. A division is made between mind and body similar to the division made between theology and philosophy in days of scholasticism. This teaching Descartes applies to the entire organic world, even to the human body. The human body is, like the animal body, a machine. The moving principle of the body is the heat in the heart; the organs of motion are the muscles; the organs of sensation, the nerves. Animal spirits are distilled in the blood in the heart and rise through the arteries into the brain, and thence into the muscles and nerves. All the functions of the body follow naturally, in this machine, from the arrangement of the organs—as necessarily as the movements of a watch follow from its pendulum and wheels. It is not necessary to assume the presence in man of a sensitive soul or any principle of vital motion other than the blood and the animal spirits. Descartes repudiates the vitalism of Aristotle and the schoolmen, and offers instead a mechanical theory of organic nature.

If these two substances exclude one another, it follows that there can be no interaction between them: mind cannot cause changes in the body, and body cannot cause changes in the mind. Descartes, however, does not consistently draw the consequences of his premises. There are certain facts which point to an intimate union between body and mind in man: appetites of hunger and thirst; emotions and passions of the mind which are not exclusively mental affections; sensations of pain, color, light, sound, etc. These we cannot refer to the body alone or to the soul alone, but must explain by the close and intimate union of the two. The union is not to be conceived as analogous to that of the pilot to his vessel. Mind and body compose a *sub-*

stantial unity. All the sensations just mentioned are merely confused modes of consciousness, the result of this union; man is not a pure spirit. Motion in animals, and often in ourselves, occurs without the intervention of reason; the senses excited by external objects simply react to the animal spirits and the reactions are mechanical—the animal is nothing but a machine. But in man bodily motion may produce sensations. If I were merely a thinking being, if my soul were not somehow intimately conjoined with my body, I should, for example, *know* that I am hungry, but not *feel* hungry. I should not have sensations and feelings which are confused modes of consciousness resulting from the intimate union of body and mind.

Just how this intimate union is to be conceived, is not made clear by Descartes—and, indeed, it is not possible within the framework of his dualism. Descartes warns us against confounding mind and body with one another. Thought and extension, he says, are combined, in man, in unity of composition, but not in unity of nature: the union should not be compared with a *mixture* of two bodies. He teaches that "thought can be troubled by the organs without being the product of them"; sensations, feelings, and appetites are disturbances in the soul resulting from its union with the body. In spite of the union, however, body and soul remain distinct; God has put them together, but they are so separate in their nature that either could be conserved by God apart from the other. Descartes seems to adopt the position that the relation between mind and body is not such that a physical state *becomes,* produces or *causes* a mental state, or vice versa, but rather that the mind is simply troubled by organic processes. His obscurity and vacillation on this point are due to his desire to explain the corporeal world on purely mechanical principles, and at the same time to leave a place for the action of a spiritual principle. The facts of experience point to an intimate connection between the two worlds which his clear-cut distinction between them seems to render impossible.

Descartes at times accepts the theory of causal interaction without hesitation. The soul, though united with the whole body, has its principal seat in the pineal gland of the brain. Movements in the animal spirits are caused by sensible objects and transferred to the pineal gland; in this way sensations are produced. The soul can also move the gland in different ways; this motion is transferred to the animal spirits and conducted by them over the nerves into the muscles. Here the relation of mind and body is clearly conceived as causal: through the mediation of the pineal gland a certain interaction between mind and body takes place. But Descartes does not succeed in showing how this interaction is compatible with his metaphysical dualism of thinking and extended substance.

Psychology of the Emotions. The soul, according to Descartes, does not consist of separate souls or faculties, but is a single principle expressing itself in various ways: the same soul that feels also reasons and wills. He distinguishes between its active and passive phases, the actions and passions of the soul, as he calls them. The former are our volitions or acts of will, which depend on the soul itself: I am free to will to love God, to affirm or deny propositions, to revive memories, to create pictures in the imagination, or to move my body. The latter include sensations and their copies, appetites, pain, heat, and other bodily feelings, which are referred either to external objects or to the body. The voluntary or active states are absolutely in the power of the soul and can only be indirectly changed by the body, whereas the passive states depend absolutely on their physiological causes and can be changed by the soul only indirectly, except in those cases in which the soul is itself their cause. There are, however, other states, or "perceptions, . . . of which we feel the effects as in the soul itself." These are the sentiments of joy, anger, and the like, which are passions in the restricted sense of the term; they are perceptions, or sentiments or emotions of the soul, which we refer particularly to it and which are caused, supported, and strengthened by certain movements of the animal spirits. The principal effect and use of such passions, however, is to incite and dispose the soul to will the things for which they prepare the body: fear incites the will to flee, courage to fight, and so on. The passions have as their immediate cause the movements of the animal spirits which agitate the pineal gland, but they can sometimes be caused by the action of the soul, which wills to conceive such and such an object; thus I may arouse feelings of courage in myself by analyzing the situation.

The so-called conflicts between natural appetites and will are explained as oppositions between movements, which the body by its spirits, and the soul by its will, tend to excite in the pineal gland at the same time. Everyone can recognize the strength or weakness of his soul by the outcome of such conflicts. But there is no soul so feeble that it cannot, if well conducted, acquire an absolute power over its passions. The power of the soul, however, is inadequate without the knowledge of truth.

Descartes enumerates six primary passions: wonder, love, hate, desire, joy, and sorrow, of which all the rest are species. They are all related to the body, their natural use being to incite the soul to consent and contribute to the actions which tend to preserve the body or to render it in some way more perfect; and in this sense joy and sorrow are the first to be employed. For the soul is directly turned from harmful things only by the feeling of pain, which produces the passion of sorrow; then follow hatred of the cause of the pain and the desire to be freed from the pain.

Our good and evil depend chiefly on the inner emotions excited in the soul by itself. So long as the soul has something within it to satisfy it, all the troubles which come from without have no power to hurt it. And, in order that it may have this inner satisfaction, all that is needed is to follow virtue exactly. We note here the Stoic influence on Descartes' ethics. Stoicism was the current ethical theory in the Renaissance and remained popular far into modern times.

Bacon had suggested a mechanical theory of mental states, and Hobbes had made mechanism the basis of his entire philosophy. Descartes attempts to apply it in detail to a large portion of our psychic life, but he does not use it to explain all our mental processes. Mind itself is a distinct entity, having the power of understanding and will. Moreover, all the "perceptions," of which Descartes speaks—sensations, appetites, emotions—are states of mind, not motions; and some passions are purely mental, not caused by organic activities at all. The will is independent of bodily states and can of its own accord produce such states. The will is free, and the ethical ideal of the soul is to make itself free from external influences.

The Theory of Innate Ideas. The aim of Descartes is to reach clear and certain knowledge, such as arises when we judge that it is impossible for a thing to be otherwise than as we conceive it. We have such necessary knowledge in the demonstrations of mathematics, and also in philosophy, if we follow the proper method. Certainty is a property of truths which are clearly and distinctly perceived. Now, certain knowledge cannot spring from the senses, for the senses do not reveal what things are in themselves, but only how they affect us. Colors, sounds, taste, odors, do not belong to the object. What the real object is, what it is when stripped of the qualities the senses ascribe to it, we can know only by clear and distinct thinking. If we cannot derive true knowledge from sense experience, if genuine knowledge is the result of reasoning from certain basal concepts and principles, these must be inherent in the mind itself—i.e., innate or a priori. The mind has its own standards or norms, which guide it in the pursuit of truth. Principles of knowledge can become explicit only in the course of experience, as the mind exercises itself in thought, but they are somehow present from the beginning. Descartes' basal idea is that reason has its natural norms; how they are present, he is not sure; here, again, he vacillates. By innate knowledge he means at times ideas or truths impressed upon the mind, principles which the soul finds in itself, and at other times, the native capacity of the soul to produce such knowledge in the course of human experience. The polemic of Locke against the doctrine of innate ideas contributed to greater clarity and definiteness with regard to the whole problem, and compelled Leibniz and Kant to present rationalism in a different form.

Descartes' rationalism and apriorism did not hinder him from paying ample attention to experience. He did not work out a systematic theory of knowledge; he was interested in discovering a method of truth rather than in a detailed discussion of epistemological problems. In spite of his studied skepticism, he was a dogmatist in the sense of believing in the competence of reason to attain certain knowledge. He was a realist in accepting the existence of an external world, the true nature of which, however, can be discovered only by rational thinking.

47. SUCCESSORS OF DESCARTES

Difficulties in Descartes' Philosophy. The Cartesian philosophy presented many difficulties and provoked a host of problems which kept thinkers busy for centuries to come. If God and nature are two distinct and independent realities, as the theory demands, there can be no real converse between them, and God cannot impress the idea of himself upon the mind of man, nor can man know anything of God. It is also inexplicable how God, a pure spirit, should be able to impart motion to matter. These perplexities Descartes sometimes seeks to escape by distinguishing between the substantiality of God and that of souls and bodies: God is the only real substance, all other things are dependent on God, effects of his causality, his creatures. In nominally abandoning the dualism inherent in the system, Descartes opens the way for the pantheism of Spinoza.

Another difficulty in the Cartesian philosophy—one which Spinoza sought to remedy—is that Descartes endowed man with free will without being able to explain the "great mystery" by his philosophy. Another chasm yawns between man and nature, or mind and body. If mind and body are totally distinct, how can any communication take place between them? By hypothesis, interaction is impossible, and yet such interaction is assumed as a fact. We have, therefore, a double contradiction here: God is the only true substance; souls and bodies are his creations, they are independent substances, and yet they act on one another. Moreover, if the bodies of animals are machines, why are not human bodies machines also?

Descartes' philosophy is an attempt to harmonize the mechanical theory of modern science, which it was impossible to ignore, with the spiritualistic theology and metaphysics which had appeared with Christianity. Nearly all of Descartes' difficulties are caused by this task of reconciliation; the function of his successors consisted either in pointing them out or in discovering ways of escaping them. It was possible to avoid the dualism of the system: (1) by eliminating nature as an independent reality and teaching absolute idealism (Malebranche); (2) by eliminating mind as an independent reality and accepting materialism (Hobbes, La Mettrie, and the French materialists); (3) by making both mind and matter manifestations of an absolute substance, God or nature (Spinoza). Or it was possible to retain the dualism and frankly deny the possibility of interaction (parallelism). In addition to the metaphysical problems, questions concerning the origin, nature, and method of knowledge demanded further attention; and in this work English empiricism and French sensationalism were leading participants.

The philosophy of Descartes met with bitter opposition from the Jesuits—his writings were placed on the Index in 1663—and from the Calvinists in Holland, and was prohibited in the universities of Germany. It gained followers, however, in the new Dutch universities, particularly among the theologians, and in France, where it was taken up by the Oratory of Jesus. Among those who were interested in the metaphysical problems suggested by Cartesianism, especially in the problem of the relation of mind and body, were the following: Regis (1632-1707), De la Forge, Cordemoy, Bekker (1634-1698), who tries to prove on Cartesian principles the impossibility of demonology, witchcraft, magic, and other superstitions; and Arnold Geulincx (1625-1669). Clauberg (1622-1665) holds that the soul cannot produce movements in the body, but can direct such movements as the driver guides his horses. Antoine Arnauld (1612-1694), author with Nicole of the *Art de penser,* or the Port Royal Logic as it came to be called, and a follower of Jansenism, accepted the philosophy of Descartes.

Occasionalism. Most of these Cartesians reject the theory of interaction, or *influxus physicus,* as it was called, and have recourse to the will of God in explanation of the body-mind relation. Body and mind are distinct; the will does not move bodies—how could it? The will is the occasion for a change in the external world—a change which God himself brings about. Nor can physical occurrences produce ideas in us: they are only the occasional causes (*causae occasionales*) for God's producing them in us. This view, which has been called occasionalism, is a form of parallelism; it holds that mental and physical processes are not causally related but run parallel to one another. The occasionalistic philosophy explains parallelism by the continuous interference of God. We have here the beginnings of the criticism of the notion of causation which culminated in Hume's skepticism: how can a mental cause produce a physical effect, or vice versa?

Arnold Geulincx. Geulincx explains the matter somewhat differently. It is true, he holds, that we cannot act on the physical world, nor can the physical world act on us. Yet our volitions are not the occasion for creating movements, nor movements the occasion for creating ideas, by a special act of God. Nor did God pre-establish the harmony between body and soul. God knows what I am going to will, although my will is free; and the entire universe has been arranged in accordance with that knowledge.

He bound together these most diverse things (the motion of matter and the choice of my will), . . . so that when my will wills, such a motion as it wills occurs, and on the other hand when the motion occurs, the will wills it, without any causality or influence of the one upon the other; as in the case of two clocks which are carefully adjusted together to the daily course of the sun, as often as the one strikes and tells us the hours, the other strikes in the same way and indicates the same hours, and *that* apart from any causality . . . but solely on account of the connection which comes from the fact that both are made by the same art and with the same workmanship.[6]

In the above passage, Geulincx employs the famous simile of the two clocks to illustrate his occasionalism—a simile which Leibniz later borrowed from Geulincx to elucidate his own closely allied theory of pre-established harmony. Occasionalism and pre-established harmony are both attempts to avoid the difficulties of Descartes' theory of causal interaction between soul and body. Geulincx also deviates from Cartesianism in his conception of knowledge: I cannot know things as they are in themselves; God alone has knowledge of them, whereas I know only my own ego.

Works by Geulincx: *Saturnalia*, 1653; *Logica*, 1662; *Ethica*, 1664; *Entretiens sur la métaphysique et sur la religion*, 1688; *Metaphysica*, 1691; Philosophical works, ed. by J. P. N. Land, 3 vols., 1891-93.

The Idealism of Malebranche. Nicolas Malebranche (1638-1715) looks at the problem presented by Descartes from another angle. He was a member of

---

[6] *Ethics*, Tract I, Land ed., Vol. III, p. 211, trans. by R. Latta in Leibniz, *The Monadology, etc.*, p. 30, note.

the Oratory of Jesus, among whom the doctrines of St. Augustine were popular. The reading of Descartes' *Traité de l'homme* led him to devote himself to the study of the entire system. Although his aim was to reconcile religion and philosophy, Augustinianism and Cartesianism, his books were placed on the Index. His chief works are: *De la recherche de la vérité*, 1675; *Traité de la nature et de la grâce*, 1680; *Traité de la morale*, 1684; *Entretiens sur la religion et métaphysique*, 1688; *Traité de l'amour de Dieu*, 1697.

Works ed. by J. Simon, 4 vols., 1871; N. Malebranche, *Dialogues on Metaphysics and on Religion*, trans. by M. Ginsburg, 1923; R. W. Church, *A Study in the Philosophy of Malebranche*, 1931; A. A. Luce, *Berkeley and Malebranche*, 1934.

If thought is something utterly distinct from motion, Malebranche asks, how can motion produce sensation, and how can mind perceive real extension if such there be? The thing seems impossible. Spiritual things are spiritually discerned, only like knows like. What we see is not the real world or extension, but a world of ideas, an intelligible world in ideal space. The ideas are in God, and God is spirit with spiritual attributes only. A real body, or created space, cannot affect mind; nothing but an ideal body, the idea of a body, can do so. We see all things in God, not in an extended God, but in a thinking God; and the things we see are ideas, not the extended material objects themselves. Thus far, Malebranche's theory is an idealistic pantheism, and if he had stopped here, the verdict of the historians of philosophy who call him a "Christian Spinoza" might seem partly justified. He does not hold, however, that there is one universal substance, but that there is only one supreme Reason embracing the ideas of all possible things. The material world is *terra incognita;* whether it exists or not, we do not know. The *idea* of matter, and not matter itself, is the real immediate object of my mind; I cannot know that matter exists except through natural or supernatural revelation. "If God had destroyed the created world, and would continue to affect me as he now affects me, I should continue to see what I now see; and I should believe that this (created) world exists, since it is not this world that acts on my mind." We believe in such a world because revelation tells us of its existence. Malebranche's system would be pantheism if he had rejected this unknown counter-world whose face is turned away from us; but it would be idealistic pantheism, and not the naturalistic pantheism of Spinoza.

Malebranche's discussions of the problem of causation anticipate the criticisms later made by Hume, who was acquainted with the French Platonist's doctrine. We cannot derive the notion of necessary connection of cause and effect from outer or inner experience: our right to assume necessary connection lies in the reason; necessary causation is implied by a universal being.

The Mysticism of Pascal. In Blaise Pascal (1623-1662; *Lettres provinciales,* 1657, *Pensées sur la religion,* 1669), a gifted mathematician and physicist, mysticism is combined with a partial skepticism. Pascal, who sympathized with the Jansenists of Port Royal—reformers within the Catholic Church inspired by St. Augustine—accepted the Cartesian dualism with its mechanical conception of nature. He also recognized the validity of certain first principles, e.g., the existence of space, time, motion, number, matter. But knowledge of ultimates he declared to be beyond our ken; we know neither the reason for, nor the goal of, things; we cannot demonstrate the existence of God nor the immortality of the soul. In the absence of proof of God's existence, Pascal proposes his famous wager: either God exists or He does not exist; if you wager that He exists, and He in fact does exist, you gain all; if you lose the wager because He in fact does not exist you lose nothing. In wagering on God's existence, your stake is zero, your reward, if God exists, is infinite. Reason ends in doubt and leaves unsatisfied our deepest interests. However, in religious feeling we directly experience God and find peace: "The heart has its reasons which reason does not know." Everything natural—human nature and human society—is sinful and corrupt; divine grace, revelation, and the authority of the Church alone can save us.

Pensées, trans. by W. F. Trotter (Everyman's Library), 1908; H. F. Stewart, *Pascal's Pensées, with an English Translation,* 1950.

M. Duclaux, *Portrait of Pascal,* 1927; C. C. Webb, *Pascal's Philosophy of Religion,* 1929; M. G. Bishop, *Pascal,* 1936; D. M. Eastwood, *Revival of Pascal,* 1936; H. F. Stewart, *Secret of Pascal,* 1941 and *Pascal's Apology for Religion,* 1942.

The Skepticism of Bayle. Pierre Bayle (1647-1706; *Dictionnaire historique et critique,* 1695, *Système de la philosophie,* 1737) employs the Cartesian criterion of clear and distinct ideas as the test of truth in a searching criticism of philosophical and theological dogmatism. With remarkable dialectical skill he lays bare inconsistencies of fact and reason in the doctrines of religion, and calls attention to the opposition between reason and revelation, science and religion. Religion is limited to revelation, but revelation itself must submit to reason, and the historical facts on which it is based must be subjected to critical examination.

Bayle greatly influenced Leibniz and other representatives of the German Enlightenment. His destructive criticism proved a potent influence on Hume and philosophers of the French Enlightenment of the eighteenth century who drew copiously from his great work. In 1767 Frederick the Great wrote to Voltaire: "Bayle began the battle. A number of Englishmen followed in his wake. You are destined to finish the fight."

48. BENEDICT SPINOZA

Baruch (Benedict) de Spinoza (1632-1677) was born in Holland, the son of a wealthy Portuguese Jewish merchant. He studied Hebrew literature with the intention of becoming a rabbi, but found as little to satisfy him in Jewish philosophy as Bacon and Descartes had found in the Christian system. In his state of doubt he became acquainted with the works of Descartes and renounced Judaism. Expelled from the synagogue (1656) and forced to leave Amsterdam, he took up his abode in various Dutch towns and finally settled at The Hague (1669), where he gained his livelihood by grinding lenses. In his profound love of truth, his unselfishness, and his simple mode of life, he exemplified the virtues of the philosopher. But his pantheistic system aroused intense and almost universal indignation, and Spinoza was for centuries despised as an atheist. The only work of his that appeared under his own name during his lifetime was the exposition of Descartes' system, *Cogitata metaphysica* (1663). The *Tractatus theologico-politicus*, in which he critically examined the Mosaic authorship of the Pentateuch, and advocated freedom of thought and the separation of Church and State, was published anonymously. His posthumous works, including the *Ethics, Tractatus politicus, Tractatus de intellectus emendatione,* and *Letters,* appeared in 1677. A Dutch translation of the *Short Treatise* (*Tractatus brevis de Deo et homine eiusque felicitate*), his earliest work, was found in 1850; the original Latin and Dutch texts have been lost.

Edition of works by J. Van Vloten and J. P. N. Land, 2 vols., 1882-83; trans. of chief works by R. H. M. Elwes, 2 vols., 1883, rev. ed., 1906; of *Ethics,* by W. H. White, 1910; of *Cogitata metaphysica* by H. H. Britain, 1905; of *Short Treatise on God, Man and His Well-Being* by A. Wolf (with Life), 1910; of *Selections,* by G. Fullerton, 1892, 2nd ed.; *The Correspondence of Spinoza,* by A. Wolf, 1927; *Spinoza: Writings on Political Philosophy,* ed. by B. A. G. Balz, 1937; *Spinoza: Selections,* ed. by J. Wild, 1930. (Elwes and White translations are quoted in this book.)

J. Caird, *Spinoza,* 1914; J. Martineau, *A Study of Spinoza,* 1895; F. Pollock, *Spinoza, His Life and Philosophy,* 2nd ed., 1899; H. Joachim, *A Study of the Ethics of Spinoza,* 1901; R. A. Duff, *Spinoza's Political and Ethical Philosophy,* 1903; R. McKeon, *The Philosophy of Spinoza,* 1928; L. Roth, *Spinoza,* 1929; J. Ratner, *Spinoza on God,* 1930; H. A. Wolfson, *The Philosophy of Spinoza,* 2 vols., 1932; D. Bidney, *The Psychology and Ethics of Spinoza,* 1940; H. H. Joachim, *Spinoza's Tractatus de Intellectus Emendatione; A Commentary,* 1940; S. Alexander, *Spinoza and Time,* 1927; C. D. Broad, *Five Types of Ethical Theory,* 1934.

The origin of Spinozism has been sought by different students of his doctrines in different sources: in Averroism, in the cabalistic and pantheistic literature of the Middle Ages, in the writings of the Jewish scholars Moses

Maimonides and Creskas,[7] in the speculations of Giordano Bruno. Whatever influence any or all of these teachings may have had on him, it would seem that the philosophy of Descartes furnished the building stones of his system. The problems which occupy his attention, and which he tries to solve, grew out of the theories of the great French rationalist, and the pantheistic conception which characterizes his own solution was a logical consequence of the Cartesian notion of God as the absolute substance. It is possible, however, that the Neoplatonism of the medieval Jewish thinkers led him to appreciate the pantheistic possibilities of the Cartesian system.

Rationalism. Descartes is a dogmatist and a rationalist: he believes in the power of human reason to reach sure and universal knowledge. With the help of self-evident concepts and principles, which have their seat in the mind, he undertakes to construct a universal theory as binding on reason as the propositions of geometry. Spinoza shares this faith; for him, too, the goal of philosophy is the complete knowledge of things, and this can be reached by clear and distinct thinking. If we proceed from self-evident principles and prove every step in the argument, we can fashion a body of truths as certain and universal as mathematics. Descartes had given an illustration of the application of the geometric method in the appendix to his *Meditations.* Spinoza follows the same method in *Cogitata metaphysica,* an exposition of Descartes' philosophy, and in his *Ethics,* his chief work. He begins with definitions and axioms and proceeds to propositions which he demonstrates in the geometrical order (*ordine geometrico*), each proposition occupying the exact place in the argument appropriate to it. To the propositions are added corollaries, which are necessary consequences of propositions, and scholia, in which propositions are discussed at greater length and in a less formal manner. His strict adherence to the mathematical method greatly influenced Spinoza's thought, as we shall see later on.

In aim and in method, then, Spinoza follows the example set by Descartes. He is also interested in the same problems as his predecessor, but seeks to solve them in a more consistent and systematic way. Descartes distinguishes sharply between God and nature, between mind and body: thought is the attribute of mind, extension the attribute of body. Body and mind are mutually independent substances, but he declares that God is the sole absolutely independent substance. Spinoza takes the idea of substance and works out its implications with logical consistency. If substance is that which needs

---

[7] Maimonides holds that to conceive God as the bearer of many attributes would destroy his unity, while Creskas defends this view.

nothing other than itself in order to exist or to be conceived, if God is *the* substance and everything else dependent on him, then, obviously, there can be no substance outside of God. Consequently, thought and extension cannot be separate substances, but must be attributes of the one single independent substance which is God. Everything in the universe is dependent on him; God is the cause and bearer of all qualities and events, the one principle in which all things find their being. He is the one thinking and extended substance; the dualism of substances has disappeared, but the dualism of attributes remains. There can be no interaction between the two attributes, between mental and physical processes; the two series are parallel to each other and never intersect. Wherever there are mental processes, there must be physical processes, and vice versa; and the order and connection of the physical realm is the same as that of the psychic realm. Dualism gives way to monism, theism to pantheism, interactionism to parallelism.

Method. The problem of the nature of the world is handled by Spinoza like a problem in geometry. Everything is said to follow from the first principle or ground of the universe as necessarily as the propositions of geometry follow from their logical presuppositions. Just as in a mathematical reasoning the conclusions are not mere temporal effects but eternal consequences of a principle, so things follow from the first cause, not as an evolution in time, but eternally, *sub specie aeternitatis.* Time is a mere mode of thought, *modus cogitandi;* there is no before and after, but only eternity. Cause is reason, *causa = ratio;* no distinction is made between rational or logical ground and real ground. Thought and being are identical. In reality, one thing follows another or is caused: the universe is a causal chain in which each link is necessarily connected with the preceding link, just as in a process of reasoning every conclusion is grounded on premises. Moreover, just as a proposition is the necessary consequence of some other proposition in a mathematical demonstration, so, in nature, everything is the necessary effect of something else, and the whole is an interrelated system in which every member has its necessary place. Thus, Spinoza's system is strictly deterministic. Again, as there is no purpose or design in mathematics, there is no purpose or design in nature; in this sense, the system is anti-teleological. How could there be design in God? Thought and extension are co-eternal attributes of the underlying substance, and hence thought cannot precede extended nature as its final cause. To ascribe purpose to God is to give precedence to thinking, and thinking, as an attribute or manifestation of God, is on the same level as extension.

The Universal Substance. Spinoza's philosophy is presented in its most developed form in his *Ethics*. This work is divided into five parts, each dealing with the following topics: (1) God; (2) the nature and origin of mind; (3) the nature and origin of the emotions; (4) human bondage and the power of the emotions; (5) the power of the intellect or human liberty. The starting-point of thought is the definition of substance. Substance is that which exists in itself or independently of anything else, that which does not need the conception of any other thing in order to be conceived: nothing can be conceived without presupposing substance, while substance can be thought without presupposing anything else; it is the absolutely independent underlying principle.

From the definition of substance certain consequences necessarily follow. If substance is absolutely independent being, it must be infinite, for otherwise it would not be independent. There can be only one such being, otherwise, again, it would be limited by others and not independent. It is self-caused, *causa sui*, for if it were produced by anything else, it would be dependent on that. It is, therefore, free in the sense that nothing outside of it can determine it; it is self-determined, in that all its qualities and actions follow from its own nature as necessarily as the properties of a triangle follow from the nature of a triangle. Individuality or personality cannot be ascribed to substance, for these imply determination or limitation: all determination is negation. Hence, neither intelligence nor will, in the human sense, belong to it; it does not think and plan and decide, it does not act according to conscious purpose or design—such teleology is entirely foreign to its nature. "I confess," says Spinoza, "that the view which subjects all things to the indifferent will of God and makes them depend on divine caprice, comes nearer the truth than the view of those who maintain that God does everything for the sake of the good. For these persons seem to place something outside of God which is independent of him, to which he looks as to a model while he is at work, or at which he aims as if at a mark. This is, indeed, nothing else than subjecting God to fate, and is a most absurd view of him whom we have shown to be the first and only free cause of the essence and existence of things." [8]

This single, eternal, infinite, self-caused and necessary principle of things is called God or nature, God is not, as Descartes held, apart from the world an external transcendent cause acting on it from without (theism), but *in* the world, the immanent principle of the universe. God is in the world and

[8] *Ethics,* Part I, Prop. XXXIII, Scol. II.

the world in him, he is the source of everything that is (pantheism). God and the world are one. Cause and effect are not distinct here; God does not create in the sense of producing something separate from, and external to himself, something that can exist apart from him; he is the permanent substance, or substratum or essence *in* all things. As the active principle or source of all reality, Spinoza, using an old scholastic term, calls him *natura naturans;* as the plurality of objects, the effects or products of the principle, he calls him *natura naturata.*

Attributes of God. How else shall we define nature, or God; what are the attributes of universal reality? By attribute Spinoza means that which the intellect perceives as constituting the essence of substance. Some interpreters, including Hegel and Erdmann, consider attributes forms of our knowledge, not really belonging to God, but attributed to him by human thought. This is the idealistic interpretation of the doctrine of attributes. Others, among them K. Fisher, regard the attributes as real expressions, actual components of God's nature, not merely as human modes of thought. The second, or realistic interpretation, is probably the correct one. Spinoza, the rationalist, accepted necessary forms of thought as having objective validity: What reason compels us to think has more than mental reality. And yet he felt a certain hesitancy in ascribing definite attributes to the infinite ground of things, since all determination is negation. But he tried to avoid this difficulty by ascribing to the infinite substance an infinite number of attributes, every one of which is infinite and eternal in its essence. God is so great that he is conceived as possessing infinite attributes in an infinite degree. The infinitude of God is of the second order: he possesses an infinite number of attributes—each of which is infinite in extent.

Of these infinite attributes, the mind of man can grasp but two. Nature expresses itself in an infinite number of ways, of which only extension and thought are knowable by man, who is himself a physical and mental being. God or nature, therefore, is *at least* both bodily and mental. Wherever, then, there is space or matter, there is soul or mind, and vice versa; the two attributes, being essential to the nature of substance, must be present wherever the substance is found, that is, everywhere. Each of the two attributes is infinite in its own kind, but not absolutely infinite—neither thought nor extension is the sole attribute; since there are infinitely many attributes of God, none of them can be called absolutely infinite. These attributes are absolutely independent of one another and cannot influence each other: mind cannot produce changes in body nor the body changes in mind. "When two things have nothing in common with one another, the one cannot be the cause of the other." [9] Spinoza thus accepts the doctrine of the occasionalists and of Malebranche, that only like can produce like, that mind cannot produce motion nor motion mind.

We cannot explain the mental by the physical, as materialism does, nor the physical by the mental, as idealism does. Both the mental and the physical realms, the world of thought and the world of motion, are manifestations of one and the same universal reality, and are of equal rank; neither is the cause nor the effect of the other, both are the effects of the same cause, both flow from the same substance. The one indivisible nature, or God, regarded in one of his aspects, is a space-occupying, moving thing; in another aspect, it is an ideal world. This is what may be called a double-aspect theory; it is likewise a form of psycho-physical parallelism: the order and connection in the one realm are the same as in the other. To our notion of a circle there corresponds a real circle existing in nature.

The Doctrine of Modes. Attributes appear in specific ways or modes. Modes are defined as "the affections or modifications of substance, or that which is in another thing through which also it is conceived." [10] That is, a mode or modification cannot be conceived except as the mode of a thing. The attribute of extension manifests itself in particular figured bodies, thought expresses itself in particular ideas and acts of will. We never have abstract thought as such, a barren stretch of thought, nor abstract extension as such, but always particular ideas and particular bodies. We cannot, however, think the latter apart from attributes—motion or rest, for example, without extension; intellect or will, without mind.

Individual minds and individual bodies are finite temporal modes of substance—the former under the attribute of thought, the latter under the attribute of extension. The eternal infinite substance expresses itself forever in definite ways, in an eternal and necessary system of physical and mental forms, in a system of ideas and in a system of bodies. Spinoza calls this infinite and necessary system of ideas, the totality of all ideas, the absolutely infinite intellect; the system of modes of extension he calls motion and rest. Motion and rest are the modes of extension, since there can be no motion without extension. The infinite intellect of God and the system of motion and rest together constitute the *face of the whole universe*, which always remains the same, although its parts undergo constant change.

[9] *Op. cit.,* Part I, Prop. III.
[10] *Op. cit.,* Part I, Def. V.

Nature, as a whole, may here be compared to an individual organism, the elements of which come and go, but whose form or "face" remains the same.

The particular finite objects and minds are not direct effects of the substance of God; each finite thing has its efficient cause in some other finite thing, and so on *ad infinitum*. The particular bodies form a chain of interconnected members, a strict causal nexus, and the particular ideas form a similar chain. The particular idea in my mind owes its existence to some other idea, and so on; the particular physical object before me owes its existence to some other physical object. Yet not a single thought or body could exist were it not for the permanent underlying reality to which all things belong, of which all are manifestations. Spinoza is well aware that we cannot logically derive this or that particular thing, the finite mode, from the notion of substance; that we can never deduce particulars from concepts. Given the concept of an infinite extended and thinking substance, we cannot prove that such and such an individual necessarily follows. But we can say, Spinoza believes, that given such a substance, thoughts and bodies necessarily follow. As all the properties of the triangle follow from the definition of the triangle, so all the properties of the universe follow necessarily from the concept of substance. We cannot, however, deduce from the concept of the triangle the existence, number, size, and shape of different triangles. Similarly, we cannot deduce from the notion of substance or God the existence, number, and properties of the different finite objects in the world, the so-called modes or forms in which substance appears, the particular concrete men, plants, and bodies now existing. These do not follow necessarily from the idea of substance, they are contingent and accidental as regards the abstract concept of God. Spinoza explains individual things as effects of other individual things. In the explanation of one particular by another, we are confined to the ordinary scientific explanation, which does not go very deep; rational explanation, *sub specie aeternitatis,* is out of the question at this level. Spinoza's rationalism does not pretend to deduce the details of physical or psychological nature from the abstract concept of God, nor from the concepts of pure extension and pure thought. He is asserting only that each is a system of interrelated parts.

Conceived under the form of eternity, God literally *is* his infinite attributes; conceived under the form of time, or through the imagination, God is the world. To the senses and the imagination, nature appears in the form of isolated separate phenomena, but that is an inadequate and superficial way of viewing it; to the understanding, nature is one universal substance and the particular phenomenon only a limited form of it, a negation of all the other forms in which substance expresses itself. No mode, then, can exist except as the mode or modification of a substance; the substance is the abiding principle, the mode is transitory. The particular mode, therefore, is not permanent; it is but a temporal expression of the substance.

Spinoza's doctrine of modes is determined by his rationalistic presuppositions. Logically, we cannot deduce the particular finite modes from the concept of God, hence they have no true reality, and are not essential. Yet it is hard to see why Spinoza is not committed to the position that particular modes should be necessary consequences of substance since they have their source in it, and since everything flows necessarily from it. Spinoza's difficulty arises from his attempt to explain the universe logically. Influenced by the method of geometry, he holds that things follow eternally from the first principle, which would make change and evolution impossible; experience, however, convinces him that there is change. In order to do justice to both logic and the facts, Spinoza invents the distinction between the infinite or eternal modes and the finite or temporal modes of God.

The Human Mind. According to Descartes, there are corporeal substances and soul-substances, which act on one another. According to Spinoza, there is but one substance or principle, on which all processes, both physical and mental, depend and from which they proceed. In his opinion, there can be no such thing as a soul or ego, a spiritual substance that has thoughts, feelings, and volitions; the mind exists as a complex mode consisting of its thoughts, feelings, and volitions—and these states of mind are themselves not effects of bodies or of bodily processes; mind and body do not influence one another, there is no interaction between them. Ideas or states of mind correspond to bodily processes, the two series are parallel—indeed, they are modally identical. The mind and its body are processes of one and the same thing expressed in two different ways.

All things, therefore, are modes or forms of matter and modes or forms of mind. Where there is body, there are ideas or mental phenomena; wherever there are mental processes, there are bodies. Spinoza, therefore, calls the human mind the idea of the human body; a body is an object or process in space corresponding to an idea. The human body is very complex, it is made up of many parts. So, too, the human mind is composed of many ideas. The human mind is not only the idea of the body, but is at the same time conscious of its own actions, or self-conscious; hence Spinoza calls it "the idea of the idea of the body," or an "idea of the mind." The mind, however, knows itself only in so far as it perceives the ideas of the modifications of the body.

The order and connection of ideas is the same as the order and connection of things; the order and connection of the actions and passions of the body is coincident with the order and connection of the actions and passions of the mind. Idea is correlated with its object: *idea* with *ideatum*. All ideas or thoughts in the universe form a unified mental system corresponding to the natural system. Every mind is a part of the infinite intellect, which is composed of an infinite number of minds and their ideas and is an eternal mode of the thought of God. If all this is true, and if the physical order or nexus is causal, the mental series must also be causally determined.

Nothing can happen in the body unless there is a corresponding mental state; in this sense, the human mind must perceive everything that happens in the human body. The mind has no way of knowing the body itself, nor that the body exists, except through ideas corresponding to such modifications of the body. In the same way, the mind knows the existence and nature of other bodies because its body is affected by them. Such knowledge by sense perception, however, is not clear and distinct, but confused; we gain no *adequate* knowledge of our own body or of external bodies through these ideas. To the extent that the mind is determined from without, by a chance coincidence, its knowledge is confused; only in so far as it is determined from within does it contemplate things clearly and distinctly.

Theory of Knowledge. Spinoza's theory of the mind and its relation to the body provides the metaphysical basis of his theory of knowledge, which he discusses in Part II of the *Ethics* and in his work: *On the Improvement of the Understanding*. Spinoza distinguishes three principal levels of cognition. (1) Obscure and inadequate ideas have their source in sensation and the imagination; they depend on sense perception, which has, as its objects, the modifications of the body. Uncritical experience and mere opinion do not yield genuine knowledge. (2) We also have adequate knowledge, clear and distinct ideas, rational knowledge. Reason contemplates things as they really are, knows their necessary connection, conceives them under the form of eternity. It comprehends the universal essences of things and understands these in their relation to God's being: such knowledge is self-evident. The criterion of truth is its intrinsic clarity; just as the light reveals both itself and the darkness, so truth illuminates itself and error. (3) Intuitive knowledge Spinoza calls the highest kind of knowledge; it is hard to say, however, just how it differs from the preceding stage. By it everything is conceived as necessarily grounded in God's being and following from it: "It advances from an adequate idea of the objective essence of certain attributes of God to the adequate essence of things." The imagination does not see things whole; it loses itself in details, does not grasp the unity of phenomena, does not understand their meaning. It is the source of prejudice, illusion, and error; it gives rise to the belief in so-called general ideas existing independently of individuals, in final causes or purposes in nature, in spirits, in a God having a human form and human passions, in free will, and other errors. Reason and intuitive knowledge repudiate all such products of the imagination as inadequate; they alone enable us to distinguish between truth and error. Whoever has a true idea knows that he has it.

Spinoza conceives error as defect of knowledge. No idea is either true or false as such; what makes an idea true is the presence of an appropriate object; an idea is false when the object is not present. We fall into error when, having an illusory idea, we lack the knowledge that the idea is a mere illusion.

Intellect and Will. In so far as the soul knows ideas, it is intelligence or intellect; in so far as it affirms and denies what is true and false, we call it will. Neither the intellect nor the will is a faculty of the mind; there are no soul-faculties, only ideas exist in the mind. The soul is reduced to ideas, it is an idea of the body: it mirrors physiological processes. No ultimate distinction is made by Spinoza between knowing, feeling or emotion, and willing. Volitions, too, are nothing but ideas of things; the particular act of will and the particular idea are identical. Hence, intelligence and will are essentially the same: the will is an idea affirming or negating itself. This act of affirmation or negation, which is an act of judgment, is not, as with Descartes, an act of free or capricious choice, but is determined by the idea itself. There is no such thing as free will; everything in nature is determined, everything follows necessarily from something else and all things are ultimately conditioned by the universal substance. The human soul is merely a mode of the divine thought; besides, every particular act of will is a mode of thought determined by another mode. Moreover, there is no causal relation between mind and body: the will cannot move the body. Everything physical may be explained in a physical context in conformity with mechanical laws. The decision of the will and the corresponding movement of the body are one and the same thing considered in two diverse contexts: considered under the attribute of thought we call it decision, under the attribute of extension we call it action. Man thinks he is free because he is ignorant of the causes of his decision. Thus the falling stone, if it suddenly became conscious, would regard itself as free. Spinoza defines free will, in the case of human beings, in terms of caprice or indeterminacy and denies its possibility; in the case of God, however, Spinoza defines freedom as action in accordance with his nature, and he ascribes freedom of this sort to God.

Will and intelligence, then, are identical. Corresponding to the stages of the intellect—sensation or imagination and reason, we have different stages of the will: passions and will proper. The passions, which literally represent the passive side of the human mind, are confused and inadequate ideas corresponding to physiological states. To our ignorance and confusion are due the passions of love, hate, hope, and fear. In so far as the mind has clear and distinct (adequate) ideas, in so far as it has knowledge and understanding, it is not passive but active: it is rational. Spinoza's main polemic is against absolute freedom of choice or a groundless will; he is not prepared to deny all significance to freedom as applied to man. When the soul comprehends the meaning of things, or has adequate ideas, it has no passions and ceases to be in bondage. The more confused a man's knowledge, the more he is passion's slave, the more limited, the more impotent and dependent he is. The clearer his knowledge, the more rational he is; the better he understands the universe in all its relations, the freer he will be from passions and the less dependent on them. To know means to be free from hate and fear, anger and envy, even from love and hope, pity and repentance. He who knows the true causes of things or sees them in their necessary relations to God, will love God: this intellectual love of God (amor intellectualis Dei) is the love of God for himself, for man is a mode of God. Man must not expect God to reciprocate this love.

The passions are not errors of human nature, but properties necessarily belonging to it; hence they must be studied as if they were "lines, surfaces, and bodies." There are three fundamental passions: desire, joy, sorrow. The basis of all passion is the desire for self-preservation. Every thing strives to maintain itself in its being; in man, too, there is such striving (appetitus) to preserve the bodily and mental life. What human nature strives for, the human mind is conscious of; this conscious striving is voluntas, will, when related to soul alone; or cupiditas, conscious appetite, when related to soul and body. What promotes our desires is good, the opposite bad. Every man, therefore, aims to increase his being; when it is intensified, he feels joy, otherwise sorrow. Joy is the transition from lesser to greater perfection; sorrow, the transition from greater to lesser. Joy is not perfection itself; if a man were born perfect, he would not have the feeling of joy. Man seeks to preserve the joyful feelings and to rid himself of sorrow. We love whatever causes pleasure in us, we hate what injures us. Hope or fear is aroused by the anticipation of future pleasure or pain. The individual believes he is the cause of his own acts, hence he feels self-satis-faction when they are pleasant and remorse when they are painful. The more active we are the more pleasurable our feelings, and the greater our sense of power. Hence, such emotions as envy and pity are bad for us, they lower our sense of power and our vitality. Like Descartes, Spinoza is one of the forerunners of modern physiological psychology.

Ethics and Politics. The impelling motive of Spinoza's thought was ethical and religious: "The mind's highest good is the knowledge of God, and the mind's highest virtue is to know God." The end can be attained only through philosophy; ethics must be based on metaphysics. The system culminates in ethics: the title of Spinoza's chief work is *Ethics*. With Hobbes, he starts out from egoistic premises, but modifies them in such a way as to weaken their effect. Every being strives to preserve its own being, and this striving is virtue. Virtue is, therefore, power; everything that tends to diminish the power of the body or mind is bad: pity and sorrow are bad, joy is good. Nature demands nothing contrary to nature, hence it demands that a man love himself and strive for whatever is useful to him or leads to his greater perfection. The power of nature is the power of God himself; each individual, therefore, has the highest right to whatever he regards as useful to himself and to appropriate it in every way, whether by force, strategy, or entreaties. With perfect right the larger fishes take possession of the water and devour the little ones. So far, the doctrine is bald egoism: might makes right. Spinoza, however, does not stop here. Virtuous action is rational action: it is only when the soul has adequate ideas, or knows, that it may be said to be really acting. Passion is not power, but weakness, slavery. Every man should seek what is *truly* useful to him, and reason tells him that nothing is useful to the soul except what is a means to knowl-edge. In life it is before all things useful to perfect the understanding or reason; in this alone man's highest happiness or blessedness consists; indeed, blessedness is nothing else than contentment of spirit, which arises from the intuitive knowledge of God. To perfect the understanding is nothing other than to understand God, his attributes, and the actions which follow from the necessity of his nature.

Moreover, there is nothing more useful to man, in his desire to perfect his being, than unity of purpose among men, nothing more excellent than that all men shall agree in all matters and that, consequently, their minds shall form one single mind and their bodies one single body. Nothing assists a man to preserve his real being more than another rational man who seeks his own true utility; hence, men will be most useful to one another if each will seek his own true good or act under the guidance of reason. Consequently, men who are governed by reason desire nothing for themselves which they do not also desire for the rest of mankind, and hence are just, faithful, and honorable in their conduct. Whatever is good for other men is also good for me. Hence, love of enemy is good; hatred, anger, revenge, envy, and contempt are evil. Humility, self-denial, remorse, and hope are not good, though they may prepare weak-minded persons for a more rational life.

In the state of nature every man has the right to do what he can; might makes right. But conflict would arise in such a situation, for men would overshoot their powers; hence it is necessary that men relinquish their natural rights in order that all may live in peace (social contract). This is achieved in the State, which limits natural rights and the caprice of the individual in the interest of general welfare. It is only in organized society that justice and injustice, merit and guilt have meaning; that is to say, morality is justified on the ground that it makes social life possible.

Spinoza's ethics is individualistic in the sense that its fundamental motive is the desire for individual perfection or happiness. A man should seek his own interest, and his highest interest is knowledge of the universe or God, which brings peace of mind; it is to each man's interest to have regard for the welfare of others. Spinoza's ethics is universalistic, since he teaches that the highest good of the mind is the knowledge of God and the highest virtue of the mind is to know God. The supreme good is the love of God which comes from an adequate knowledge of him.

Intellectual Love of God. Our highest good consists in the intellectual love of God, which is eternal, like reason itself. We feel and know by experience that we are eternal, and this existence of the mind cannot be limited by time nor manifested through duration.

The term God is variously employed in Spinoza's system: He is identified with the universe, or he is identified with his attributes, or he is the absolute unified substance with its infinite attributes, or he is the unified substance itself, higher than these attributes. His real meaning probably is that God is the universe conceived as an eternal and necessary unity. Spinoza expressly denies personality and consciousness to God. He has neither intelligence, feeling, nor will; he does not act according to purpose, but everything follows necessarily from his nature, according to law; his action is causal, not purposive. God's thinking is constituted by the sum-total of the ideas in the world. He has the power or attribute of thought which expresses itself in the absolutely infinite intellect or in the eternal and necessary modes of thinking, and these, in turn, express themselves in human minds.

XIII

The Development
of British Empiricism

49. John Locke

John Locke (1632-1704) studied philosophy, natural science, and medicine at Oxford. He was repelled by the scholastic methods of instruction which still prevailed at the university, but found great satisfaction in the writings of Descartes. For many years (1666-1683) he was in the service of the Earl of Shaftesbury, as secretary and as tutor to his son and grandson, and followed his patron to Holland into exile. Returning to England (1689) after the deposal of James II and the ascension of William of Orange to the throne, he held several important public offices, and spent the remaining years of his life (1700-1704) in the household of Sir Francis Masham, whose wife was the daughter of the philosopher Cudworth.

Collected Works, 1853; philosophical works, edited by St. John in Bohn's Library. *An Essay Concerning Human Understanding,* ed. by A. C. Fraser, 2 vols., 1894; *Treatise of Civil Government and a Letter Concerning Toleration,* Charles L. Sherman, ed., 1937; M. W. Calkins, ed., *John Locke—Selections,* 1917; S. P. Lamprecht, ed., *John Locke—Selections,* 1928.

H. R. Fox Bourne, *Life of Locke,* 2 vols., 1876; T. Fowler, *Locke,* 1880; A. C. Fraser, *Locke,* 1890; S. Alexander, *Locke,* 1908; M. M. Curtis, *Outline of Locke's Ethical Philosophy,* 1890; F. Thilly, "Locke's Relation to Descartes," in *Phil. Rev.,* IX, 6; V. Cousin, *La philosophie de Locke,* 1861; J. Gibson, *Locke's Theory of Knowledge and Its Historical Relations,* 1917; R. I. Aaron, *John Locke,* 1937; W. Kendall, *John Locke and the Doctrine of Majority Rule,* 1941; C. R. Morris, *Locke, Berkeley, Hume,* 1946.

Locke's Problem. Hobbes, as we have seen, was a rationalist in his ideal of knowledge, holding with Descartes that mere experience will not give us certainty. At the same time, he agreed with his compatriot Bacon that sensation is the source of knowledge. These two lines of thought in Hobbes' philosophy did not seem to fit together; the sensationalistic origin of knowledge appeared to undermine the rational validity of knowledge and to

333

destroy its certainty. Hobbes himself felt the difficulty and was led by it to occasional skeptical conclusions concerning physics. To John Locke this problem becomes the all-important one; in him philosophy turns to the theory of knowledge and undertakes an examination of the nature, origin, and validity of knowledge; his philosophy was indeed "an essay concerning human understanding," as is indicated by the title of his chief work.

Origin of Knowledge. Philosophy, according to Locke, is the true knowledge of things, including the nature of things (*physics*), that which man ought to do as a rational voluntary agent (*practica,* or ethics), and the ways and means of attaining and communicating such knowledge (*semiotics,* or logic). As the most important of the three, Locke regards the problem of knowledge, holding that before we set ourselves upon inquiries, it is necessary to examine our own abilities and see what our understanding is, or is not, fitted to deal with. This he undertakes to do in his main work, *An Essay concerning Human Understanding.* But, he declares, we must first study the origin of our ideas to tell what knowledge is certain, and what the limits of our knowledge are. Much depends on discovering the source from which our knowledge springs, for if it is true, as Descartes and many others held, that we have an innate knowledge of principles, there would seem to be no reason for questioning its validity. The problem of innate ideas is, therefore, taken up by the English thinker in the first book of his *Essay,* which was written last.

Assuming that the mind must be conscious of its innate principles, if there be any—since nothing can be said to be in the mind of which it is unconscious—Locke proceeds to refute the doctrine of inborn truth. There are no speculative or practical principles present to the minds of men, and even if there were, they might have been acquired in the same way as other truths. If a principle can be imprinted on the soul without being known, it is impossible to distinguish between what is native and what not. It cannot be said that we first become aware of such truths when we begin to exercise our reason, for children, the uneducated, and savages are a long while in possession of their reason without knowing them. Nor is immediate assent to a proposition proof of its primitiveness. The moral laws cannot be called innate, for they are not self-evident or universally recognized, and do not impel men to action. What to many people is sin, is duty to others. To say that such ideas have been gradually obscured through prejudice, education, and custom, is to deny their universal acceptance. If we hold that they cannot be obliterated, they ought to appear in all men, and most clearly in children and the uncultured. That the idea of God, on which Descartes lays such emphasis, cannot be innate is proved by the fact that entire tribes either lack the idea and knowledge of God or have no clear impression of him. But even if all mankind had a notion of God, it would not follow that the idea of him is innate. The ideas of fire, the sun, heat, or number are not proved to be innate on the grounds that they are so universally received and known amongst mankind. A rational creature reflecting on the visible marks of divine wisdom and power in the works of creation, cannot miss the discovery of a deity, but this does not establish the innateness of the idea of God.

In short, ideas and principles are just as little innate as the arts and sciences. The mind, in its first state, is a *tabula rasa,* a "dark chamber," an "empty cabinet," "white paper," void of all characters, without any ideas. The question now is, how does it come to be furnished? Whence does it derive all the materials of reason and knowledge? To this Locke answers in one word—"experience"; all our knowledge is founded on, and ultimately derived from, experience. The two sources of all our ideas are *sensation,* through which the mind is furnished with sensible qualities, and *reflection,* or internal sense, which supplies the mind with ideas of its own operations, such as perception, thinking, doubting, believing, reasoning, knowing, willing. The primary capacity of the human mind is intellect's ability to receive the impressions made on it, either through the senses by outward objects or by its own operations when it reflects on them. By idea Locke means whatsoever the mind directly apprehends, or which is the immediate object of perception, thought, or understanding.

The ideas thus received are *simple ideas,* which the mind has the power to repeat, compare, and combine in endless variety, and thus to make at pleasure new *complex ideas.* Yet no understanding has the power to invent or frame one new simple idea. Some simple ideas enter our minds by one sense only, e.g., ideas of color, sound, taste, heat, cold, solidity; some are conveyed into the mind by more senses than one, e.g., space or extension, figure, rest, and motion which enter through both sight and touch. Some are received by reflection only, that is, the mind observes its own operations on those ideas it already has, and gets others in this way, e.g., it notices its operations of perception, retention and recall in memory, discerning, comparing, compounding, naming, and abstracting. Some ideas, finally, we receive through both sensation and reflection—among these are pleasure and pain or uneasiness, power, existence, unity, succession, and duration.

Although many of our ideas of sensation resemble external qualities, the majority are not the likenesses of something existing outside ourselves, the exact images and resemblances of something inherent in the object. The power which objects have to produce definite ideas in us, we call qualities. Now, some of these qualities belong to the objects themselves, are utterly inseparable from them; they are called by Locke *original* or *primary qualities;* among them are: solidity, extension, figure, motion or rest, and number. Qualities such as colors, sounds, tastes, which are nothing in the objects themselves except powers to produce various sensations in us by their primary qualities, are called *secondary qualities.*

All our simple ideas are received through the two avenues of sensation and reflection; from these simple ideas all our knowledge is derived, just as the words are made out of the twenty-six letters of the alphabet. External and internal sensation alone are the windows by which light is let into the dark room of the understanding. The mind can, by its own power, put together these simple ideas and make new *complex ideas;* it can bring two ideas together, view them together, and thereby frame ideas of relations; and finally, it can separate ideas from all other ideas which accompany them in their real existence; this operation is called abstraction. The mind is passive in the reception of all its simple ideas, but exerts power over them in the acts just described.

The endless number of complex ideas may all be embraced under three heads: modes, substances, and relations. Our *ideas of modes* are complex ideas which do not contain in themselves the supposition of subsisting by themselves, but are considered as dependencies on, or affections of, substances, e.g., triangle, gratitude, murder. A *simple mode* consists of variations of the *same* simple idea, repeated in different combinations without the mixture of any other; thus a dozen or a score is a mode obtained by the successive addition of units. *Mixed modes* are compounded of simple ideas of *several* kinds, put together to make one complex one, such as beauty, which consists of a certain composition of color and figure, causing delight or pleasure in the beholder. By taking the simple idea of space and compounding it, we get the simple modes of immensity, figure, place, infinite expansion; hours, days, years, time and eternity, are simple modes of duration. There are also simple modes of thinking or of the operations of the mind.

Our *ideas of substances,* too, are complex ideas made up of simple ideas, put together by the mind. The complex idea of a substance consists of a combination of ideas of qualities, supposed to represent a distinct particular thing, and the confused idea of a support or bearer of these qualities. Thus, the idea of the substance *lead* consists of this supposed or confused idea of a bearer, to which are joined ideas of a certain dull whitish color, certain degrees of weight, hardness, ductility, and fusibility. We notice that certain simple ideas derived from sensation and reflection constantly go together; we suppose they belong to one thing and call them, so united, by one name. We cannot imagine how these qualities or ideas could exist by themselves, so we suppose that there is a substratum wherein they do subsist and from which they result; this substratum, we call substance. We have ideas of material and spiritual substances, and of God.

The mind also gets certain *ideas of relation* by comparing one thing with another: the mind first brings or sets one thing by another, and then, directing its attention from one to the other, discerns a relation between them.

All things are capable of relation, and all ideas of relation are made up of simple ideas. The *idea of cause and effect* is the most comprehensive relation subsisting among ideas; it is a relation derived both from sensation and reflection. Through our senses we learn that things change, that qualities and substances begin to exist, that they owe their existence to the operation of other qualities and substances. We call that which produces any simple or complex idea *cause;* that which is produced, *effect:* thus, heat is the cause of the fluidity of wax. Cause is that which makes another thing—either simple idea, substance, or mode—begin to be; effect is that which had its beginning from some other thing. Different kinds of causation are creation, generation, making, alteration. To form the idea of cause and effect, it suffices to consider any simple idea or substance as beginning to exist by the operation of some other, even without knowing the manner of that operation. The idea of cause and effect is the most comprehensive and hence scientifically important relation, but there are countless other relations, relations of time, place, and extension, relations of identity and diversity, moral relations, and so on.

Nature and Validity of Knowledge. The materials of our knowledge, then, are furnished to the mind by sensation and reflection; the mind acts on them and makes complex ideas. The question arises, What cognitive value do such ideas have, what conditions must they fulfill in order to be knowledge? Ideas should be *clear* and *distinct,* because confused and obscure ideas make the use of words uncertain. *Real* ideas are such as have a foundation in nature, and which are in conformity with the real existent things with which they correspond and which are their archetypes. Our simple ideas are all real, not because they are all images or representations of what exists —only the primary qualities of bodies are that—but because they are all the effects of powers outside our minds. Mixed modes and relations have no reality other than in the minds of men, they do not claim to be copies of things really existing; they are real only in that they are so framed that there is a possibility of something existing conformable to them. They are themselves archetypes, and so cannot be chimerical unless inconsistent ideas are jumbled together in them. But our complex ideas of substances are intended by us to be representations of external substances, and they may really be such; they are, therefore, real only in so far as they are such combinations of simple ideas as are really united, and coexist, in things outside us. Ideas are *adequate* which perfectly represent the archetypes from which the mind supposes them to have been taken, while *inadequate* ideas are but a partial or incomplete representation of these archetypes. Simple ideas and modes are all adequate; but ideas of substances are all inadequate, because they seek to copy things as they really exist, but never quite succeed in doing so. Whenever the mind refers any of its ideas to things extraneous to them, the ideas are then capable of being called *true* or *false;* the mind, in referring ideas to things, makes a tacit supposition of their conformity to those things, and this supposition may be true or false.

All knowledge is gained by means of ideas, and our most certain knowledge is nothing but the perception of the connection or agreement, and repugnancy or disagreement, of any of our ideas. We perceive that white is not black, that the idea of white and the idea of black do not agree. There are different degrees of evidence in knowledge. Sometimes the mind perceives the agreement or disagreement of two ideas by direct inspection, without the intervention of any other ideas. This is *intuitive* knowledge. The mind perceives at once that white is not black, that a circle is not a triangle, that three is greater than two. This is the clearest and most certain knowledge of which human frailty is capable; it need not be proved and cannot be proved; it is irresistible, self-evident. On the certainty of direct intuition depends whatever certainty and evidence our knowledge possesses. Sometimes our mind, though it is unable to perceive the agreement or disagreement between two ideas immediately, can establish it indirectly by comparing them with one or more other ideas. This knowledge by intervening ideas is called mediate, rational, or *demonstrative* knowledge. Its proofs are certain, yet its evidence is not quite so clear and bright, nor the assent so ready as in intuitive knowledge. Every step in demonstrative knowledge must have intuitive certainty, in order that the conclusion may be certain. Such demonstration is employed in mathematics and wherever the mind can perceive the agreement or disagreement of ideas by the help of intermediate ideas. In both intuitive and demonstrative knowledge we have certainty; whatever falls short of one of these is faith or opinion, but is not knowledge in the strict sense.

What shall we say of our knowledge of the external world? We have in the mind *ideas* of external objects; that we have them is as certain as anything can be. But is there anything more than the ideas; can we with certainty infer the existence of any extra-mental reality which corresponds to them; is there a real world outside? Sometimes, as in dreams, we have ideas to which nothing corresponds at the time. Ordinary perception— when we are awake and presumably subject neither to hallucination nor illusion—affords a kind of evidence which is beyond any reasonable doubt; our knowledge of the particular existence of finite, external things, thus goes beyond bare possibility, and yet does not reach perfectly intuitive or demonstrative knowledge. Locke calls it *sensitive* knowledge. I have no self-evident knowledge of real existence except of myself and God; my own existence I know by intuition, the existence of God is made clearly known to me by reason. The apprehension I have by my senses of the existence of things outside me, though not so certain as intuitive knowledge or the deductions of the reason, yet has an assurance that entitles it to the name of knowledge. But besides this assurance provided by the senses themselves, we have the further confirmation that perceptions differ intrinsically from memory-images, that they are often accompanied by pain, and that the senses corroborate one another's testimony.

The Limits of Knowledge. What, then, is the extent of our knowledge? Since it is a perception of agreement or disagreement of our ideas, it follows that our knowledge cannot reach further than our ideas. Where ideas are wanting, there can be no knowledge; we are limited to the dull and restricted information received from a few and not very acute ways of perception. But our knowledge is even narrower than our ideas; not only can we not go beyond what we experience, but we neither have nor ever shall have as extensive a knowledge of our ideas as we desire. We do not experience everything we are capable of experiencing, nor do we understand everything we actually perceive. Our ignorance is due, in the first place, to a want of ideas. Beings more perfect than ourselves, possessing organs of sense more acute and differently constituted from ours, may have a greater variety of simple ideas than we have. Moreover, some things are too remote for our observation, others too minute. Then, again, we cannot discover any necessary connection between many of our ideas: we do not see what connection there is between the figure, size, or motion of the invisible parts of a body and its color, taste, or sound; we do not understand the relation between the yellow color, the weight, the malleableness, the fixedness and the fusibility of gold, so that knowing one or two or more of these qualities, we can know that the others must be there. Given the definition of a triangle, it will follow necessarily that the sum of its angles is equal to two right angles; that is a self-evident proposition, which is true of everything called a triangle. But from my idea of gold as a yellow metal having a certain weight, I cannot deduce with certainty the fact that it is malleable. Observation tells me that it is malleable, but that all gold is malleable is not a self-evident truth. The only knowledge that really satisfies me is knowledge of universal self-evident truths; but there are large areas of experience in which such knowledge seems unobtainable.

Another limitation of our knowledge is apparent when we consider "real" knowledge, consisting of our ideas which, in some way, agree with the realities of things. All simple ideas represent things outside, because they must necessarily be the product of things operating on the mind. We know that there are bodies outside which arouse in us the sensation white; though we may not know what it is that produces the sensation in question, and how it is done, yet we do know that something does it. But our complex ideas, though they too, for the most part, give us knowledge, are not intended to be copies of anything, nor referred to the existence of anything as originals; they are patterns or archetypes of the mind's own making. The mind of its own free choice combines ideas without considering any connection they may have in nature. Such systems of complex ideas framed by the mind give us certain knowledge, such as we have in mathematics. The mathematician forms an idea of a triangle or a circle; these are ideas in his mind, made by himself. The propositions which he deduces logically from these definitions are true and certain. If there is such a thing as a triangle, these propositions are bound to be true of it wherever it exists. But that a real or actual triangle exists in nature cannot be established by such ideas.

The case of our complex ideas of substances, however, is different. Our ideas of substances are supposed to be copies of archetypes to which the ideas refer. If the qualities we put together in our ideas of substance co-exist in nature, if, for example, there is something in nature having the qualities yellow, malleable, fusible, fixed, etc., then the idea of this substance is the object of real knowledge. And we may say, whatever simple ideas have been found to coexist in any substance may with confidence be joined together again. But it is to be noted that we can make no universal propositions concerning substances, because we do not see any necessary connection between the ideas put together. Experience tells us that certain qualities coexist in an unknown bearer or substratum; but we cannot discover the dependence of these qualities on one another, and we cannot infer from the qualities we observe going together what other qualities *must* go with them. There is not a single general affirmation about gold that we can know to be certainly true—true in the sense of being absolutely self-evident. If we could discover a necessary connection between malleableness and the density of gold, we might make a certain universal proposition in this respect, and say: All gold is malleable. The truth of the proposition would then be as certain as the truth: the sum of the angles of a triangle is equal to two right angles. There is another difficulty in the case of substances which complicates the problem. The substances in nature are not independent, isolated things; their qualities depend, for the most part, on many unobservable conditions in nature. Whence the forces come that keep all these curious machines in motion and repair, how they are conveyed and modified, is beyond our perception and appreciation. To understand them aright, therefore, we must understand the universe as a whole. But we cannot even discover the size, figure, and texture of their minute and active parts, much less the different motions and impulses produced in them by the action of other bodies. Hence, we do not know what changes the primary qualities of one body regularly produce in the primary qualities of another, nor how they are produced. We do not know what primary qualities of a body produce such and such sensations or ideas in us; we do not perceive the necessary connection between these primary qualities and their effects. Universal certainty is unattainable in this area of knowledge, and we must content ourselves with *probability*. "As to a perfect science of natural bodies (not to mention spiritual beings), we are so far from being capable of any such thing that it is lost labor to seek after it." [1]

Absolute certainty of a general sort is, therefore, never to be found except in the agreement and disagreement of our ideas. It is the contemplation of our own abstract ideas that alone is able to afford us general knowledge. We have no self-evident propositions as to real existence—except in the case of God and ourselves—and can build no science of existential truths.

---

[1] *An Essay Concerning Human Understanding*, Bk. IV, ch. III, sec. 29.

Most of the propositions we reason and discourse about and act upon are such that we cannot have certain knowledge of their truth. Yet some of them border so closely upon certainty that we have no doubt at all about them, but assent to them firmly. There are different degrees of probability of statements of fact, depending upon their conformity with our own experience and the testimony of others' experience. The bare testimony of revelation, however, Locke regards as the highest certainty; our assent to it is faith. Faith is a settled and certain principle of assent and assurance, and leaves no room for doubt or hesitation. But we must be sure that it *is* a divine revelation. Consequently, our assent can be rationally no higher than the evidence of its being a revelation. No proposition can be received for divine revelation if it be contradictory to our clear intuitive knowledge; faith can never convince us of anything that contradicts our knowledge. There can be no evidence that any traditional revelation—in the words in which we receive it and in the sense in which we understand it—is of divine origin. Truths of revelation are never as clear and certain as the principles of reason. But things which are beyond the discovery of our natural faculties, and *above* reason, are, when revealed, the proper matter of faith. Thus, the belief that the dead shall rise and live again, is purely a matter of faith with which reason has nothing to do directly.

Metaphysics. We have heard Locke's answers to the questions concerning the origin, validity, and limitations of knowledge; let us now consider the general world-view to which he stands committed. He did not work out a complete theory of reality in a separate book; his theory of knowledge, as developed in his *Essay,* rests on metaphysical presuppositions which may readily be discovered.

In spite of the restrictions which he places upon knowledge and of his frequent skeptical misgivings, he adopts, with variations, a metaphysical position in substantial agreement with that which Descartes had organized into a system. The world is composed of substances, of supports or bearers of powers, qualities, and actions in which the latter inhere and from which they flow. Substances, the grounds and causes of qualities and acts, are of two kinds, bodies and souls. A body is a substance whose attributes are extension, solidity or impenetrability, and mobility or the power of being moved. These are its primary qualities, which we receive through our senses. Hence, there can be a vacuum—pure space without body; the fact that we can conceive space without solidity and motion proves the existence of the vacuum. Besides material substances, there exist spiritual substances, or souls. The soul is a real being; its qualities are thinking or the power of perception, and will or the power of setting the body in motion. These qualities we know through reflection. Thinking, however, is not the essence, but the action of the soul. The soul is an immaterial or spiritual substance, analogous to corporeal substance. I frame the idea of a bodily substance by putting together certain corporeal qualities and supposing a support for them; I form an idea of soul-substance by reflecting upon the operations of my own mind—such as thinking, understanding, willing, knowing, and the power of beginning motion—and joining these to a support or bearer. It is as absurd to say that there is no spirit because we have no clear and distinct idea of the substance of a spirit, as it would be to deny the existence of body because we have no clear and distinct ideas of matter as a substance or bearer of qualities. "It is plain then that the idea of corporeal substance in matter is as remote from our conceptions and apprehensions as that of spiritual substance or spirit: and therefore, from our not having any notion of the substance of spirit, we can no more conclude its nonexistence than we can for the same reason deny the existence of body. . . ." [2] Indeed, if anything, I know more certainly that there is a spiritual being within me that sees and hears than that there is some corporeal being outside me. Moreover, incogitative matter and motion could never produce thought; it is impossible to conceive that matter, either with or without motion, could, in and of itself, have sensation, perception and knowledge.

Pure spirit or God is active only, matter is passive only; but man's soul is both active and passive. It has the power to move the body, as experience shows, and it is passive in relation to the bodies outside which produce changes in the soul; indeed, all our ideas are due to the action of the body on the mind. This is the theory of interaction. It is true, we do not know *how* this is done, but neither do we know how one body moves another. Indeed, we have a much clearer idea of the active power of moving in spirit, than in body; a thinking thing is more easily conceived than an extended thing.

Mind and body exist as real beings, and interact. Bodies act on mind and produce sensations of color, sound, touch, solidity, extension, etc. Of these, the secondary qualities do not faithfully represent the reality outside; objects are not colored, sounding, fragrant, savory; these are the effects produced on the mind by solid extended objects; the ideas of extension, solidity, and motion are copies of real qualities existing in things. Bodies are solid ex-

---

[2] *An Essay Concerning Human Understanding*, Bk. II, ch. XXIII, sec. 5.

tended things that move. But, so far as we can judge, body is able only to strike and affect body; and motion, according to the utmost reach of our ideas, is able to produce nothing but motion. To assert that a bodily state produces pleasure or pain, or the idea of color or sound, is to go beyond reason and our ideas, and ultimately to attribute the influence wholly to the good pleasure of our Maker. Locke here encounters a fundamental difficulty for his philosophy—the conflict of the theory of mechanism with the apparent facts of experience. If motion can produce nothing but motion, how can it produce states of consciousness in us? To meet this difficulty, Locke tells us that God has annexed those apparent effects of motion which we cannot conceive motion to have produced. In adopting this position, he has relapsed into occasionalism. He is likewise confronted with the equally difficult problem of explaining how mind can start a motion, how the will can cause an act to take place. But he brushes aside both these difficulties by declaring that to understand how motion produces sensation or volition motion, is no more baffling than to understand how one motion produces another motion. Experience tells us every moment that the thing is done.

Locke has occasional misgivings not only concerning the problem of interaction, but also on the question of the immaterial nature of the soul. His general position seems to be that mental processes cannot be the action of bare insensate matter, that there could be no sensation without an immaterial thinking being, and that there is within man a spiritual being that sees and hears. At the same time, he is sometimes in doubt about the nature of this being that thinks in each of us. Perhaps it is material—perhaps a material being is capable of thinking. Since we do not know the real nature of any substance, how can we be sure that solid material beings are incapable of thinking, and that thinking beings are not extended? Perhaps we shall never know whether or not any mere material thinks. We do not know wherein thinking consists, nor to what sort of substances God may have been pleased to give that power which may indeed reside in any created being, including body. God has annexed effects to motion which we cannot intellectually conceive; why could he not have given to certain systems of created matter, namely, those constituting bodies, some degree of sensation, perception, and thought?

We have called attention to some of the difficulties, obscurities and inconsistencies in Locke's system. Beneath these we discern the outlines of his metaphysics. His theory remains, in the main, dualistic: there are two substances, the material and the mental—"incogitative and cogitative." In this he agrees with Descartes, except that he makes solidity or impenetrability, rather than extension, the essential attribute of body. Like Descartes, he also accepts the "corpuscularian" hypothesis as the best explanation of the facts. There are extremely small bodies having bulk, figure, and power of motion. These insensible corpuscles are the active parts of matter and the great instruments of nature, on which depend not only all the secondary qualities of bodies, but also their natural operations. But we have no distinct precise ideas of their primary qualities. No one has ever pretended to perceive their distinct bulk, figure, or motion, and no one understands the tie that binds them together. If we could discover the figure, size, texture, and motion of the minute constituent parts of any two bodies, we should know how they would operate one upon another, as, in geometry, we know the properties of a square or triangle from its geometrical structure. We do not know these things; we do not know what bonds hold these corpuscles together, what cement makes them stick together so firmly; we do not know how one moves the other, how motion is transferred from one to another. Consequently, this corpuscular hypothesis advances our knowledge of corporeal substances very little. So long as we do not see the necessary connections between the qualities and powers of bodies, our knowledge remains scant. Hence, there is no science of bodies in the real sense of the term, and Locke sees little prospect of its early realization. What Locke no doubt envisaged—however vaguely—was a science similar to modern physical chemistry, in which the chemical properties, though not strictly deducible from the physical, are explained and interpreted by reference to the latter. It is interesting to note also that Locke's corpuscular theory of matter, unlike the atomic theory, does not envisage ultimate and indivisible particles of matter.

Besides the two substances, body and mind, there is another spiritual substance, God. We have no innate idea of God, but we may, by the right use of our natural abilities, attain a knowledge of him. It is as certain that there is a God as that the opposite angles formed by the intersection of two straight lines are equal. We form the idea of God by taking the ideas which we derive from experience of existence and duration, knowledge and power, pleasure and happiness, etc., and enlarging each of these to an infinite degree; and by finally combining together these infinite ideas. Thus Locke explains the genesis of the idea of God, but he does not claim to know God's real essence. Locke's account of the origin of the idea of God—like his theory of all other ideas of sense or reflection or both—remains obstinately empirical and nominalistic; in this aspect of his philosophy he makes no concessions to rationalism and the realism of universals.

Locke offers the usual causal and teleological proofs of God's existence. Man knows with certainty that he himself exists. He also knows that bare nothing cannot produce real being. Hence if there is real being—and man knows that *he* is real being—there must have been something to produce him. Moreover, that which owes its being and beginning to another being must derive everything it has from the being that made it. The eternal source of all being, then, must be the source and origin of all power, hence it must be all-powerful, and, for the same reason, it must be all-intelligent. Unthinking matter cannot produce a thinking being; howsoever we may conceive God, we cannot conceive him as material. If God has made the knowing beings, he has also made the less excellent pieces of this universe, which establishes his omniscience, power, and providence. If it be asked how we can conceive God as making something out of nothing, Locke replies that we can as little conceive how thought can produce motion, and yet we cannot deny that it does.

Ethics. In harmony with his general philosophical empiricism, Locke offers an empirical theory of ethics, which ends by being an egoistic hedonism. There are no innate practical or moral truths, any more than there are innate theoretical truths. We make moral judgments without having any rules "written on our hearts."

Men attain knowledge of moral rules and are convinced of their obligation to conform to them, in the same way in which they come to know other things—namely, by experience. Moreover, men learn such rules through their education, environment, and the customs of their country. We instill into the minds of children those moral doctrines which we would have them retain and profess; and our children, when they grow up, find these truths present in their consciences and, unable to recall how they were originally instilled, regard them as imprinted by God and nature. Conscience is nothing but our opinion of the rightness and wrongness of our own actions in the light of such acquired moral knowledge. "And if conscience be a proof of innate principles, contraries may be innate principles, since some men with the same bent of conscience prosecute what others avoid." [3]

The question now arises: How did such moral laws originally come to be established, how has the knowledge of right and wrong been acquired? Pleasure and pain are the great teachers of morality, according to Locke.

[3] *An Essay Concerning Human Understanding,* Bk. I, ch. III, sec. 8.

Nature has placed in man a desire for happiness and an aversion to misery, and these are natural tendencies, or practical principles, which influence all our actions; but they are inclinations and not truths of the understanding. We call that good which is apt to cause pleasure in us, and evil that which is apt to cause pain. Everyone constantly pursues happiness and desires whatever contributes to it; it is this desire or uneasiness which determines the will. Happiness in its fullest extent is the utmost pleasure we are capable of, and misery the utmost pain. Now, certain modes of conduct produce public happiness and preserve society, and also benefit the agent himself. God has joined virtue and public happiness together and made the practice of virtue necessary to society. Men discover these forms of virtuous behavior, and embody them in rules of practice. Everyone reaps advantage to himself from the observance of the moral rules and, therefore, recommends them.

It would be futile for one intelligent being to prescribe a rule for the actions of another if he did not have the power to reward obedience and punish disobedience by some good or evil that is not the natural consequence of the act itself. There would be no need of a law if the natural consequences of actions had sufficient motive force to induce them. The laws of society determine the wills of men by rewards and punishments, pleasure and pain, and are enforced by the will and power of a lawgiver. There are three sorts of law: divine law, civil law, and the law of opinion or reputation. The divine law is the law which God has set for the guidance of the actions of men, whether promulgated to them by the light of nature or the voice of revelation. God has the power to enforce this law by rewards and punishments of infinite weight and duration in another life. Divine law is the basis of duties and sins. The civil law is the rule set by the commonwealth, and is accompanied by legal rewards and punishments; civil law is the basis of the notions of crime and innocence. But the great majority of men govern themselves chiefly, if not solely, by the law of fashion or private censure. Commendation and disgrace are strong motives, causing men to accommodate themselves to the opinions and rules of those with whom they converse. No man who offends against the fashion and opinion of the company he keeps can escape the punishment of the dislike and censure of his fellows. Virtue is everywhere thought praiseworthy; and nothing which lacks public esteem is called virtuous. Men compare their actions with these laws or rules and, according to their agreement or disagreement with them, call them good or evil. The true sanction of virtue, however, is the will of

God; the will and law of God constitute the only ultimate touchstones of morality.

In the main, virtues and vices are everywhere the same, and correspond with the unchangeable rule of right and wrong established by the law of God. Obedience to the laws of God secures and advances the general good of mankind; and hence no rational human beings, caring for their own interest, could fail to commend the right and blame the wrong.

Locke's ethics is the old Greek hedonistic interpretation of morality, supplemented and reinforced by a narrow conception of Christian theology. Virtue is nothing else but doing of good either to oneself or to others. The most lasting pleasures in life consist in health, reputation, knowledge, doing good, and the expectation of eternal and incomprehensible happiness in another world.

Locke shows how we may derive our moral knowledge from experience. He believes that we may also reach it by reasoning from certain first principles, i.e., by demonstration. Moral truth—like mathematical truth—is capable of demonstration.

The idea of a supreme Being, infinite in power, goodness, and wisdom, whose workmanship we are, and on whom we depend; and the idea of ourselves, as understanding, rational beings, would, I suppose, if duly considered and pursued, afford such foundations of our duty and rules of action as might place morality among the sciences capable of demonstration. . . . Where there is no property there is no injustice, is a proposition as certain as any demonstration in Euclid. . . . No government allows absolute liberty; the idea of government being the establishment of certain rules or laws which require conformity to them, and the idea of absolute liberty being for any one to do whatever he pleases, I am as capable of being certain of the truth of this proposition as of any in mathematics.[4]

Locke recognizes three modes of moral knowledge: we have an empirical knowledge of right and wrong, a demonstrative knowledge, and a revealed knowledge, all of which agree. God has so arranged it that, given a desire for happiness in human nature, man will evolve a moral code to promote his happiness. God has also endowed him with reason which will enable him to acquire moral truth by demonstration. And, finally, he has revealed in the Scriptures the same laws which can be reached by experience and reason.

Free Will. Freedom, according to Locke, is an idea pertaining not to volition or preference, but to the person, having the power of doing or forbearing

[4] *An Essay Concerning Human Understanding,* Bk. IV, ch. III, sec. 18.

to do according as the mind shall choose or direct. The free will problem is, in Locke's opinion, meaningless; for the concept of freedom has significant application to man's power of action but not to his will. We cannot say that a man's will is free, "it is as insignificant to ask whether a man's will be free, as to ask whether his sleep be swift or his virtue square." The will is one power or ability, namely, the power of an agent to think his own actions and to prefer their doing or omission; freedom is another power or ability, the power to do or forbear doing any particular action according as he himself wills. So that when we ask: Is the will free? we are really asking: Has one power another power? which is an absurdity. A man is free so far as he has power to think or not to think, to move or not to move according to the preference or direction of his own mind. Wherever he has not the power to do or forbear any act according to the determination or thought of the mind, he is not free, though perhaps his act may be voluntary. It is some pressing uneasiness that successively determines the will and sets us upon those actions we perform. This uneasiness is desire, an uneasiness of the mind for want of some absent good. God has put into men the uneasiness of hunger and thirst and of other natural desires, to move and determine their wills for the preservation of themselves and the continuation of the species. The most pressing uneasiness naturally determines the will, and the desire, in its turn, is directed toward happiness. Locke's account of human motivation interprets happiness, desire and volition in their relation to one another, but finds no place in the scheme for free will.

Political Philosophy. Locke's theory of the State is presented in his *Two Treatises on Government,* the first of which is a refutation of Sir Robert Filmer's absolutistic work, *Patriarcha,* in which Filmer derives patriarchal authority in the State from a divine unalterable right of sovereignty, inherited from Adam. In the second treatise he discusses "the true original, extent and end of civil government." He opposes the view that the best government is absolute monarchy, that kings have a divine right to absolute power, and that mankind has no right to natural freedom and equality. Men are naturally in a state of perfect freedom to order their actions and dispose of their possessions as they think fit, within the bounds of the law of nature, without asking leave, or depending on the will of any other man. They are also in a state of equality of nature, no man having more power and jurisdiction than another. The law of nature or reason teaches all mankind that, all being equal and independent, no one ought to harm another in his life, liberty, and possessions.[5] The basis of Locke's philosophy is ego-istic: everyone is bound to preserve himself and to preserve the rest of man-kind when his own preservation is not endangered. In a state of nature everyone has the power to punish transgressions of that law of nature, to preserve the innocent, to restrain offenders, and to take reparation for in-juries done him. Each transgression may be punished to that degree of severity which will suffice to make it an ill bargain to the offender, give him cause to repent, and deter others from doing the like.

The state of nature is not, as Hobbes had supposed, a state of war, but a state of peace, good-will, and mutual assistance. God so made man that convenience and inclination drove him into society, and fitted him with understanding and language to enable him to continue to enjoy it. But there is lacking in a state of nature an established, settled, known law, en-forced by an impartial judge with acknowledged authority and power to en-force the sentence, when right, and give it due execution. We have political or civil society whenever a number of men unite in one society—each relin-quishing his executive power under the law of nature, and transferring it to the public—to form one people, one body politic under one supreme government. Locke subscribes to a form of the contract-theory of the origin of society.

According to Locke's view of the nature of the social contract, absolute monarchy is inconsistent with civil society. For if the prince holds both the legislative and executive powers, there is no judge who may fairly, impar-tially and authoritatively decide issues, and there are no rules to which ap-peal can be made. In an absolute monarchy, the subject is the slave of one man; but no one should be subjected to the political power of another with-out his own consent. When any number of men have, by the consent of every individual, formed a community, they have thereby made that com-munity one body, having power to act as such, i.e., in accord with the will and determination of the majority. But after such a society has been formed, every man puts himself under an obligation to everyone of that society to submit to the rule of the majority. There would be no real contract if, after the contract has been made, everyone were left free and under no ties except those which bound him in a state of nature. Though unanimous consent is

[5] Locke incorporated some of his equalitarian ideals in the first constitution for the Carolinas which was drafted in 1669, and in which King Charles II had bestowed the Carolinas upon a number of noblemen, among them Locke's patron, the Earl of Shaftesbury. The document is not, however, as democratic in every respect as Locke's political philosophy required.

next to impossible, approximation to unanimity is frequently attainable and, indeed, all the governments of the world that had their beginning in times of peace were established by the consent of the people.

A man consents to give up his unlimited freedom and power, because the enjoyment of it is very uncertain and constantly exposed to the invasion of others; all being kings as much as he—since every man is his equal—and the majority no strict observers of equity and justice, the enjoyment of the property he has in this state is very unsafe and insecure. If it were not for the viciousness and corruption of degenerate men, there would be no need of any society but the state of nature. The great and chief end of men's uniting into a commonwealth is the mutual preservation of their lives, liberties, and estates. Hence the power of society can never be supposed to extend farther than is required by the common good.

The first and fundamental *natural* law, which is to govern even the legislative authority itself, is the preservation of society and—so far as is consonant with the public good—of every person in it. The first and fundamental *positive* law of all commonwealths is the establishing of the legislative power. This power is not only supreme, but is sacred and unalterable in the hands in which it has once been placed by the community; nor can the edict of anyone else have the force and obligation of a law, unless it have the sanction of that legislative power which the public has chosen and appointed. But the legislative power cannot have absolute and arbitrary control over the lives and fortunes of the people; it is limited to what promotes the public good of society. The laws of nature do not cease in society, they stand as eternal rules for all men, legislators as well as others. Hence the legislative power has no right to enslave, to destroy, or purposely to impoverish the subjects. Again, it cannot assume power to rule by extemporary, arbitrary edicts and decrees; standing laws are needed. Furthermore, the supreme power cannot take a subject's property without his consent; taxes can be levied only by consent of the majority. Lastly, it cannot delegate the power of making laws to other hands.

It is not desirable that those who have powers of making the laws should also have power to execute them. The federative power is the power of war and peace, the power to enter leagues and alliances, and to engage in all transactions with all persons and communities outside the commonwealth. The federative and executive powers are almost always united, and it is best that they should be placed in one hand. To the executive is delegated the supreme execution of the laws. The legislative power may, when it finds cause, take both the executive and federative powers out of the hands in which it has placed them, and punish any maladministration. It is supreme, but it is a fiduciary power which is restricted to acts for certain specified ends. The people, in Locke's theory, have a supreme power to remove and alter the legislative when they find it acting contrary to the trust reposed in it. But whilst the government exists, the legislative is the supreme power. The power of choosing it rests with the people. Not the prince, as Hobbes had taught, but the legislative agency is the soul of the commonwealth, and the legislative power represents the people; the people are the sole judge as to whether the prince or the legislative power has acted contrary to the people's trust.

Theory of Education. Like all great philosophers of the modern era, Locke finds fault with the methods of instruction which had come down as a heritage from scholasticism, and presents a new program of education based on his empirical psychology and ethics. The soul being at birth devoid of all principles except the desire for pleasure and the power to receive impressions, the purpose of education is to learn by experience and to realize happiness. In order to attain it, a healthy body and sound sense organs are requisite; the body must be hardened by exercise and habit. He prescribes physical training for the child and considers a frugal mode of life imperative. The individuality of the child is to be developed in a natural manner; hence, private instruction is preferable. Locke also emphasizes the importance of object lessons, of learning by play, and of arousing the pupil's mental activities; study is to be made a delight. Above all, the social end of education should not be lost sight of: the youth is to be trained to become a useful member of society.

50. LOCKE'S INFLUENCE

Extent of Locke's Influence. Locke's teachings form the starting-point of many schools of thought, and his influence, like that of Descartes, extended far beyond his age and the boundaries of his country. The remark which Schiller once made of a great man applies to him: he had marrow in his bones to last for centuries. His *Essay* was the first attempt at a comprehensive theory of knowledge in the history of modern philosophy, and inaugurated the movement which produced Berkeley and Hume and culminated in Kant. His empirical psychology became the source from which the English associationism of Browne and Hartley and the French sensationalism of Condillac and Helvetius drew their nourishment. His ethical philosophy was continued and corrected by the work of Shaftesbury, Hutcheson, Ferguson, Hume, and Adam Smith. His theory of education influenced the great French author Rousseau and, through him, the entire world. His political ideas found brilliant elaboration in Voltaire's writings, in Montesquieu's *Esprit des lois,* and a radical reformulation in Rousseau's *Contrat social;* while the spirit of his entire thought gave an impetus to the religious movement of the deists in England and in France. In Locke the forces that were making for enlightenment were concentrated and reflected more faithfully than in any thinker before him. He represents the spirit of the modern era, the spirit of independence and criticism, of individualism, of democracy, the spirit which had sought utterance in the Reformation and in the political revolutions of the sixteenth and seventeenth centuries, and which reached its climax in the Enlightenment of the eighteenth century. No modern philosopher has been more successful than he in impressing his thought on the minds and institutions of men. We shall survey Locke's influence in each of the following spheres: (1) religion, (2) theory of knowledge, (3) ethics, (4) economics.

Theological Influence. Deism begins, as a vital movement, with Locke's book on the *Reasonableness of Christianity* (1695). Locke had set up reason as the ultimate test of revelation; revealed truths are absolutely certain, of that there is no doubt; but human reason is the criterion of revelation itself. Locke agreed with Herbert of Cherbury, in accepting as true certain propositions of natural or rational theology; but he did not regard them as innate. The deists apply Locke's ideas by subjecting revelation to rational standards, and seeking the true revelations of God in the laws of nature. On this basis, Christianity is fashioned into a rational religion; it is not mysterious, it is as old as creation itself. In 1696 John Toland writes *Christianity not Mysterious,* a book which was condemned by the Anglican Church. In his *Letters to Serena* (1704) and *Pantheisticon* (1720), he accepts a nature religion, which he calls *pantheism* (a term coined by him). A. Collins writes his *Discourse of Free Thinking* (1713), in which he opposes the interference of the Church with critical discussions of the Bible. Other deistic works are: Tindal, *Christianity as Old as the Creation* (1730); Woolston, *Six Discourses on the Miracles of Our Savior* (1727-1730); Chubb, *The True Gospel of Jesus Christ* (1738); Morgan, *The Moral Philosopher* (1737). Conybeare (1732) and Joseph Butter (1736) defend revealed religion against the rationalistic theology of deism.

Sensationalism and Associationism. In his account of the origin of knowledge, Locke distinguishes between sensation and reflection. He also endows
the mind with certain powers or faculties which act on the materials of sense.
Locke's empiricism is not sensationalism, since he admits reflection in addition to sensation as a basic mode of experience; his empiricism is, however,
the historical source and main inspiration of later English and French sensationalism. The attempt is made by many of his followers to explain all
mental processes, reflection as well as the higher faculties, as transformed
sensations; reflection and the powers of the understanding are reduced to
sensation. Peter Browne, Bishop of Cork (d. 1735), presents this view in
The Procedure, Extent, and Limits of the Understanding (1728), and it is
worked out in detail by the French priest, Etienne de Condillac (1715-1780)
in his *Traité des sensations* (1754). Condillac tries to show how a hypothetical being endowed with but a single sense—smell, for example—would
develop, in turn, attention, memory, comparison, pleasure and pain, passion,
desire, will. From comparison, which is nothing but the multiplication of
sensations, arise judgment, reflection, reasoning, and abstraction, that is, understanding. Reflection is reducible to sensation and the ego is simply the
sum of the sensations which we now have and those which we have had. In
order, however, to obtain the idea of an external world, with its extension,
form and solidity, the sense of touch is needed. This sense yields us knowledge of objective reality; it assures that there is something other than ourselves, but what its nature is, we do not know.

Sensationalism, in some form or other, became popular in England and
in France. Among its followers were Hartley, Priestley, Erasmus Darwin,
James Mill, J. Bentham, Helvetius, Condorcet, Volney, the Encyclopedists,
and the materialists. Charles de Bonnet (1720-1793) teaches a moderate sensationalism, but regards all mental operations, the higher as well as the
lower, as dependent on brain vibrations, which cause reactions in an immaterial soul. Helvetius applies sensationalism to ethics.

The law of the association of ideas, according to which ideas are associated
in the mind in a certain regular order, had been anticipated by Aristotle and
Hobbes and discussed by Locke and Gay; it was elaborated and formulated
into a philosophical system by David Hartley (1705-1757) in his *Observations on Man, His Frame, His Duties, His Expectations* (1749). This law,
combined with the doctrine that all our ideas are copies of sensations, has
been employed as the chief principle of explanation of mental life by the
followers of empiricism, and by many modern psychologists. In ethics, it has
been used to account for the moral sentiments: man learns to associate his

pleasures with that which pleases him; the moral sentiments procure for him many advantages, and he gradually transfers his affections from these to the things which procure them, and in this way comes to love virtue for virtue's sake. The law of association of ideas applied to ethics affords a plausible account of the origin of conscience and of the moral sentiments, and thereby promotes the cause of empiricism in ethics.

Condillac, *Treatise on Sensations,* trans. by G. Carr, 1930; Z. Schaupp, *The Naturalism of Condillac,* 1926.

Ethical Theory. English empiricism derived the knowledge of right and wrong from experience and based morality on the impulse of self-preservation or the desire for happiness. Bacon, it is true, had not overlooked the social instinct, but Hobbes and Locke conceived human nature as fundamentally egoistic and made morality a matter of enlightened self-interest. Rationalistic thinkers like Cudworth, Clarke, and Wollaston protested against such empirical and egoistic conceptions; to deny that I should do for another what he in the like case should do for me, Clarke said, "is as if a man should contend that though two and three are equal to five, they are not equal to two and three." Richard Cumberland (*De legibus naturae,* 1672), who may be regarded as the founder of English utilitarianism, refused to accept the rationalistic doctrine of innate moral knowledge; but he regarded as false the egoistic conception of man, as a mere bundle of selfish impulses: man has sympathetic feelings, or benevolence, as well as selfish feelings. Social life or the common welfare is the highest good, and we are fitted for it by social feeling and rationality.

The English moralists succeeding Locke base moral knowledge primarily on feeling or impulse rather than reason or innate ideas of right and wrong; but they regard capacity for these feelings as a native endowment of human nature. According to Lord Shaftesbury (*Characteristics,* 1711), man possesses self-affections and social affections; virtue consists in the proper balance between the two, and the moral sense tells us whether they are in harmony or not. Francis Hutcheson (1694-1747) works out these ideas in systematic form in his *Inquiry into the Ideas of Beauty and Virtue* (1725), and *System of Moral Philosophy* (1755), and is the first to make use of the utilitarian formula, "the greatest happiness for the greatest number." To the same school belong David Hume (*Inquiry Concerning the Principles of Morals,* 1751), Adam Ferguson (*Institutes of Moral Philosophy,* 1769), and Adam Smith (1723-1790), the author of *Theory of the Moral Sentiments* (1759), and *Wealth of Nations* (1776), who finds the source and criterion of the moral law in sympathy. All these writers emphasize the importance of the emotive and impulsive side of man's nature: our ethical judgments and actions are rooted, not in reason, but in feeling. Most of them may be classed as moral intuitionists, in that they subscribe to the immediacy and quasi-sensuous character of moral knowledge. Either the worth of motives and acts is disclosed to a native moral sense, or the moral judgment is based on the feeling of sympathy. They all agree in regarding the general welfare as the highest good, and in this doctrine they anticipate the later utilitarians.

Joseph Butler (*Fifteen Sermons upon Human Nature*, 1726, *Dissertation upon Virtue, Analogy of Religion*, 1736) follows this school in its general teaching, but lays greater emphasis on the conscience, which he conceives not as a feeling (moral sense), but as a principle of reflection.

There is a superior principle of reflection or conscience in every man, which distinguishes between the internal principles of his heart as well as his external actions; which passes judgment upon himself and them, and pronounces determinately some actions to be in themselves just, right, good, others to be in themselves evil, wrong, unjust: which, without being consulted, without being advised with, magisterially exerts itself, and approves or condemns him the doer of them accordingly.[6]

If conscience had strength as it has right, it would govern the world. He also finds in individual happiness the ultimate rational standard, though not necessarily the psychological motive of right and wrong. Conscience or duty and self-love or interest, if we understand our true happiness, always lead us the same way; they coincide perfectly for the most part in this world, and entirely and in every instance if we take in the future and the whole. Our ideas of happiness and misery are nearest and most important to us. In the light of calm consideration, we can neither justify to ourselves the pursuit of what is right and good, as such, nor any other pursuit, until we are convinced that it will be for our happiness, or at least not contrary to it.

William Paley, in his *Principles of Moral and Political Philosophy* (1785), rejects the moral sense, and declares that actions are to be estimated according to their consequences. Whatever is expedient is right. "Virtue is the doing good to mankind, in obedience to the will of God, and for the sake of everlasting happiness."[7]

In opposition to Shaftesbury, Bernard Mandeville (*The Grumbling Hive:*

[6] *Fifteen Sermons upon Human Nature, Sermon II.* Cf. B. Rand, *The Classical Moralists*, p. 383.

[7] *The Principles of Moral and Political Philosophy*, Bk. I, chap. VII. Cf. B. Rand, *The Classical Moralists*, p. 479.

or *Knaves Turned Honest*, 1705, *The Fable of the Bees: or Private Vices Public Benefits*, 1714), tries to show that selfishness (private vices) contributes more to the public good than benevolence. The Frenchman Helvetius (*De l'esprit*, 1758, *De l'homme*, 1772) follows Hobbes and Mandeville in making egoism the sole motive of human action, and enlightened self-interest the criterion of morals. The only way to make a man moral is to make him see his own welfare in the public welfare, and this can be done by legislation only, i.e., by proper rewards and punishments. The science of morals is nothing but the science of legislation. This theory is, after all, the Lockian theory stripped of its theological additions.

Economic Theory. This individualistic view, which is found in Locke and Paley, and which also appears in Butler's theory, is reflected in the economic theories of the French physiocrats (François Quesnay, 1694-1774; A. Turgot, 1727-1781) and in Adam Smith's *Wealth of Nations;* all of these oppose the old mercantile system which sprang up in Europe at the close of the Middle Ages. The new economic philosophy is based on the idea that the individual has a natural right to exercise his activity in the economic sphere with the least possible interference from society (*laissez faire*). The assumption is that with unrestricted competition and with the removal of unnatural restraints—such as monopolies or privileges—the freedom of exchange, the security of contract and property, enlightened self-interest will promote not only the good of the individual, but also the public welfare. The conception of *laissez faire* is an expression of the general theory of natural rights and demands an open road for the individual in the pursuit of life, liberty, and happiness, holding that this will lead to social justice: in the words of Adam Smith, "the simple and obvious system of natural liberty establishes itself of its own accord." The theory rendered service in helping to discredit and overthrow the old economic system and to deliver the individual from harmful restraints. The origin of economic liberalism of the *laissez-faire* type may be traced to the ethical and political individualism of Locke's philosophy.

Shaftesbury's Characteristics, ed. by J. M. Robertson, 2 vols., 1900; Fowler, *Shaftesbury and Hutcheson*, 1900; B. Rand, *Life, Unpublished Letters and Philosophical Regimen of Anthony, Earl of Shaftesbury*, 1900.

Butler, *Works*, ed. by Gladstone, 2 vols., 1896, 2nd ed., 1910; W. L. Collins, *Butler*, 1881; W. J. Norton, Jr., *Bishop Butler, Moralist and Divine*, 1940.

51. George Berkeley

George Berkeley(1685-1753)was born in Ireland; he studied at Trinity College, Dublin, traveled, and became Bishop of Cloyne in 1734. In 1732 he was sent to Rhode Island to establish missions. Among his works are: *An Essay towards a New Theory of Vision* (1709), *A Treatise Concerning the Principles of Human Knowledge* (1710), *Three Dialogues between Hylas and Philonous* (1713), *Alciphron, or the Minute Philosopher* (1732).

> *Complete Works,* ed. by A. C. Fraser, 4 vols., 1871, 2nd ed., 1901; *Selections from Berkeley,* ed. by Fraser, 5th ed., 1900; *Essay, Principles, Dialogues,* ed. by M. W. Calkins, 1929; Berkeley, *Principles* and Hume, *Treatise,* ed. by P. Wheelwright, 1935.
>
> A. C. Fraser, *Berkeley and Spiritual Realism,* 1908; T. H. Huxley, *Hume, with Helps to the Study of Berkeley,* 1894; G. D. Hicks, *Berkeley,* 1932; J. M. Hone and M. M. Rossi, *Bishop Berkeley, His Life, Writings, and Philosophy,* 1931; G. A. Johnston, *The Development of Berkeley's Philosophy,* 1923; J. Wild, *George Berkeley: A Study of His Life and Philosophy,* 1936; G. D. Hicks, *Berkeley,* 1932; B. Rand, *Berkeley's American Sojourn,* 1932; A. A. Luce, *Berkeley and Malebranche,* 1934; C. R. Morris, *Locke, Berkeley, Hume,* 1946.

Berkeley's Problem. We shall now consider the main tradition of philosophical empiricism which developed from Locke's theory of knowledge. Locke taught that bodies produce sensations in the mind which include extension, solidity, motion, color, sound, taste, smell, touch. Some of these, the primary qualities, are copies of the qualities of things; others are the effects on us of powers in things. Sensations furnish the materials of the mind, the alphabet of all our knowledge. The soul acts on them, arranging, uniting, separating, and relating them; it also reflects on its own operations. All our knowledge, therefore, is confined to the facts of experience; we have a direct knowledge only of our ideas. We also know that there is an external world, but this knowledge is not as self-evident as the knowledge of our own ideas.

Berkeley makes use of the basal empiricism of Locke to establish idealism and thereby refute materialism and atheism. If, as Locke claimed, the basis of our knowledge is sensation and reflection, and we know only ideas, how can we know a world of bodies, a material world outside us? We are limited, so far as our knowledge of matter is concerned, to our states of consciousness; we cannot compare our ideas with these corporeal substances; we do not know what they are or even that they are.

Even if there were matter, it is difficult to see how, in terms of Locke's theory, we could know it. If we accept his presuppositions we become entangled in skepticism. Besides, if there is an independent substance like matter and a world of pure space, then there is an infinite, eternal and immutable reality existing alongside of God and limiting him—even tending to negate the very existence of God. The belief in matter, therefore, leads to atheism and materialism. The seeds of skepticism, atheism, and irreligion are contained in the view that matter, or a world of bodies, exists. We can avoid these implications only by getting rid of the premise from which they spring —the assertion that matter exists. We can explain the universe without such a premise: given God, the supreme Spirit, and other spiritual beings, we can account for all the facts. The paramount question for Berkeley, therefore, is: Does an extra-mental world exist, is there an independent world of matter?

Berkeley is confident of the capacity of the human mind to cope with the problem of knowledge. It is a mistake, he says, to hold that our ignorance is due to the limitations of our human faculties; providence usually furnishes the means of satisfying the appetites which it implants in its creatures—provided these appetites are rightly used. Hence we may be confident that the desire for knowledge can be satisfied by a proper use of our faculties, and that we can deduce from true principles tenable conclusions. It is well worth our while, therefore, to make a strict inquiry concerning the principles of human knowledge, to sift and examine them on all sides.

Rejection of Abstract Ideas. The chief reason for the opinion that external objects (houses, mountains, rivers) have a natural or real existence, distinct from being perceived, is the doctrine that the mind can frame abstract ideas. But the mind is, in fact, incapable of framing abstract ideas. We can imagine, or represent to ourselves, the ideas of the particular things we have perceived, and we can variously divide and compound them. But we cannot, for example, find in our thoughts an idea corresponding to the description of the general idea of a triangle, of a triangle that is "neither oblique nor rectangular, equilateral, equicrural, nor scalenon, but all and none of these at once." It is true that a man may consider a figure merely as triangular without attending to the particular qualities of the angles or relations of the sides; so far he may abstract. But this will never prove that he can frame an abstract idea of a triangle. Similarly, we cannot frame the idea of motion, distinct from the body moving, and which is neither swift nor slow, curvilinear nor rectilinear. There are general ideas, to be sure, in this sense—a general idea is one which, considered in itself, is particular, but which becomes general by being made to represent or stand for all other particular ideas of the same sort. We use one name or sign for all particular ideas of the same sort, and because we use one name, we come to believe there is one abstract idea corresponding to it. Such supposedly abstract ideas are not necessary for the communication nor for the enlargement of our knowledge—general ideas suffice for the discovery and communication of all mathematical, scientific and philosophical truth.[8] The idea of a world without the mind, that is, of a real world of matter, is such an abstract idea. We separate the sensible objects from their being perceived and conceive of matter as existing unperceived. But such unperceived existence is impossible. We cannot see or feel anything without an actual sensation of that thing, nor can we conceive any sensible thing or object distinct from the sensation or perception of it. One of Berkeley's objections to unperceived matter is that it is an abstraction; the doctrine of abstract ideas thus underlies one of his arguments for the non-existence of matter.

Berkeley agrees with Locke that the objects of human knowledge are either actually imprinted on the senses, or are such as are perceived by attending to the passions and operations of the mind; or, lastly, ideas formed by the help of memory and imagination. These ideas we compound, divide, or merely represent. Besides ideas there is likewise something which knows or perceives them, and exercises diverse operations—as willing, imaging, remembering—upon them. This perceiving, acting being is mind, spirit, soul, myself. It is entirely distinct from my ideas, it is a thing wherein they exist or whereby they are perceived, for the existence of an idea consists in being perceived.

To Be Is to Be Perceived. Now, everybody will grant that our thoughts and passions and the pictures of the imagination do not exist outside the mind; they are all in the mind, their existence consists in their being perceived or known by the mind. The same thing, however, is true also of our sensations; here, too, existence is identical with perception: *esse = percipi*. When I say the table I write on exists, I mean that I can see and feel it. When I say it exists when I am out of the room, I mean that if I were in the room I might perceive it, or that some other mind actually does perceive it. To say things exist when no mind perceives them, is perfectly unintelligible. Hence, to exist means to be perceived, to be in the mind. Bodies, therefore, have no existence without a mind; their *being* consists in being perceived or known; so long as they are not perceived by me or do not exist in my mind or that of any other created spirit, they have no existence at all, or else exist only in the

---

[8] Berkeley's rejection of abstract ideas in favor of general ideas is a commitment to the nominalistic position. This nominalistic doctrine—though he modified it in later years in *Alciphron*—underlies the main idealistic argument of the *Principles*.

mind of some eternal spirit. It is a contradiction in terms to say that matter exists unperceived by any mind.

The impossibility of an unperceived body follows necessarily from the idea of body as held by Locke. A body is a solid, extended, figured substance having the power of motion, a certain color, weight, taste, smell, and sound. Certain of its qualities, however, do not inhere in it; color, sound, taste, smell are the effects of the body produced in a perceiving subject; they are qualities residing not in the body itself, but *in me;* we call them secondary qualities. Extension, figure, solidity, motion, rest are said to be qualities inherent in the substance, or body, itself; they are the primary qualities. But, says Berkeley, these so-called primary qualities are just as secondary as the others. The ideas of extension and solidity I get through the sense of touch; they are sensations in my mind also. I cannot separate my idea of extension from the idea of color and other secondary qualities; I never perceive an extended thing which is not at the same time colored, and so on. The primary qualities are inseparably united with the secondary; I cannot abstract the latter and leave behind an extended solid substance, which is that and nothing else. I have no abstract idea in my mind of such a substance. But surely, there must be something outside which supports, or underlies, these qualities—a substance? That, again, says Berkeley, is a mere abstraction; there is no meaning whatever in the words material substance. Even if it were possible for such a solid, figured, movable substance to exist outside the mind, how could we know it? Moreover, all our ideas or sensations, or the things perceived, are inactive, and have no power to do anything; hence extension, figure, motion, all of which are ideas, cannot be the cause of sensations.

The World of Spirits. But, you say, there must be some cause of the sensations or ideas in my mind. And so there is, and this cause must be an active substance. It cannot, however, be a material substance, for there is no such thing; hence it must be an incorporeal, active substance or Spirit. A spirit is one undivided, active being, which in so far as it perceives ideas, is called *understanding;* in so far as it produces or otherwise operates upon them, it is called *will.* There can be no *idea* formed of soul or spirit, because all ideas are passive and inert, whereas spirit is active and creative; hence we can have no idea or image or likeness of that which acts. We cannot *perceive* the spirit itself, but only the effects which it produces. Still, we have some *notion* of soul or spirit and the operations of the mind, such as willing, loving, hating, in as much as we understand the meaning of these words. Notion—in contradistinction to idea—is the technical term by which Berkeley designates the vehicle or medium of our apprehension of minds and their operations. I have notions of my own mind and its operations, of other finite minds, and of God's mind.

Some ideas I can make and unmake at pleasure; in this respect my mind is active and I have power over my own thoughts. But over my sensations I have no such power. I open my eyes: it is not in my power to choose whether I shall see or not, nor to determine what particular objects shall present themselves to my view. The ideas imprinted on my senses are not creatures of my will. Hence, there is some other will or spirit that produces them. The ideas of sense are stronger, more lively and distinct than those of the imagination; they have likewise a steadiness, order, and coherence and are not excited at random, as are those which are the effects of human will, but appear in a regular train or series, whose uniform connection sufficiently testifies to the wisdom and benevolence of their Author. Now, the uniform rules in conformity with which the supreme Mind excites in us the ideas of sense, are called the *laws of nature;* and these we learn by experience, which teaches us that such and such ideas are attended by such and such other ideas in the ordinary course of events. God, in other words, arouses in us ideas in a constant and determinate order; he has connected with the idea of food the idea of nourishment; with the idea of sleep, the idea of refreshment; with the visual sensation of fire, the bodily sensation of warmth. If there were no such regular order in our sensations, we would be eternally at a loss to know what to expect next and would not know how to act; that there is such regularity in the flow of our sensations enables us to regulate our actions for the benefit of life. We notice this connection between our ideas and erroneously come to believe that the ideas cause each other, that fire produces warmth, that sleep causes refreshment, that collision of bodies causes sound. The ideas imprinted on the senses by God are called *real* things; and those excited in the imagination, being less regular, vivid, and constant, are more properly termed *ideas* or *images* of things which they copy or represent. But our sensations are ideas, nevertheless; they exist in the mind; they are simply more vivid, strong, orderly, and coherent ideas than our images; they are also less dependent on the thinking substance which perceives them, for they are excited by the will of another, more powerful spirit.

Objections Answered. Berkeley is well aware of the difficulties of his idealistic hypothesis. What becomes of the sun, moon, stars, houses, mountains, rivers, trees, and stones, on this hypothesis? Are they but chimeras or illusions of the fancy? Not at all, he replies. They exist in the sense indicated above, they are real in that God arouses these sensations in us in a regular coherent order. Material substance, too, is real in this sense, if we mean by it a combination of sensible qualities, such as extension, solidity, weight, and the like. If we mean by matter a support of accidents or qualities outside the mind, it does not exist even in the imagination. But does this not mean that we eat and drink ideas, and are clothed with ideas? We eat and drink and are clad with the immediate objects of sense, which cannot exist unperceived or external to the mind. It is more proper, therefore, to call them things rather than ideas. But how do we externalize things and see them at a distance? This is the problem discussed in Berkeley's *Essay towards a New Theory of Vision,* in which he holds that distance, or "out-thereness" is not immediately perceived by sight, nor even apprehended or judged solely by lines and angles in the field of vision. Ideas of sight or visual sensations come to suggest to us certain ideas of touch and locomotion. When the object seems indistinct and small, experience has taught us that it is far off, at a distance, that we must walk far to get a distinct and larger picture. The idea of space accordingly results from the correlation of sensations of different senses— particularly vision and touch.

But does not everything disappear when I close my eyes? The things are no longer perceived by me, hence they ought no longer to exist. But, Berkeley points out, I may say when I close my eyes that things continue to exist in so far as they are perceived by other minds, including the divine Mind.

Again, does not this idealism do away with the whole corpuscular philosophy? Berkeley answers that there is no phenomenon explained by that hypothesis which cannot be explained without it. No one really knows how matter operates on a spirit or produces any idea in it. Besides, the natural philosophers do not account for things by corporeal substance, but by figure, motion, and other qualities, which are, in truth, no more than mere ideas and cannot, therefore, be the cause of anything.

Would it not be absurd to speak in the language of this new theory and to say a spirit heats instead of fire heats? Berkeley replies: "in such things we ought to think with the learned and speak with the vulgar." Those who accept the Copernican theory still speak of the sun rising. It is said, however, that the whole world believes in matter; is the whole world mistaken? But does the whole world really believe in it? Probably not. The truth is, men have no speculative opinion at all about matter in the philosophical sense. Besides, universal consent would not be proof of the correctness of a philosophical position. Men assumed that their sensations had an existence inde-

pendent of the mind because they themselves were not the authors of them.
They did not dream that this belief involved a contradiction in terms. They
supposed that qualities existed outside the mind and that, therefore, an unthinking substance was needed. Then they realized that secondary qualities
had no extra-mental existence. Since, however, the primary qualities do not
exist outside the mind either, substance becomes unnecessary. If you say, perhaps there is a substance having qualities as incomprehensible to us as color
is to a man born blind, we ask: What is the advantage of disputing about an
unknown support of unknown qualities, about something we know not
what and know not *why?* Besides, if we had a new sense to perceive these
qualities, we should encounter the same difficulties over again. If matter is
defined negatively as "an unknown somewhat—neither substance nor accident, spirit nor ideal—inert, thoughtless, indivisible, immovable, unextended,
existing in no place" then it is indeed nothing. If you distinguish it from
nothing by giving it existence, quiddity, entity, then, says Berkeley, this idea
is incomprehensible "trifling with words."

Knowledge of Ideas, Spirits, and Relations. Spirits, then, are active, indivisible substances; ideas are inert, fleeting, dependent things which subsist
not by themselves, but are supported by or exist in minds or spiritual substances. We comprehend our own existence by inward feeling or reflection,
and that of other spirits by reason. We may be said to have some knowledge
or *notion* of our own minds, of spirits, and active beings, whereof, in a strict
sense, we have no *ideas*. In the same way we know and have a notion of
relations between things or ideas—relations which are distinct from the
ideas or things related, inasmuch as the latter may be perceived by us without our perceiving the former. Berkeley holds that *ideas, spirits,* and *relations*
are all objects of human knowledge and subjects of discourse; and that "the
term idea would be improperly extended [if used] to signify everything we
know or have any notion of. Ideas imprinted by the senses are real things
. . . but they cannot subsist without the minds which perceive them"; they
are not replicas of an archetype existing outside the mind. They may, indeed,
be called external in the sense that they are not generated within the mind
itself, but imprinted by a spirit distinct from that which perceives them.
Sensible objects may also be said to be "without the mind" in the sense that
when I shut my eyes the things still exist; but they must be in another mind.

Refutation of Dualism, Atheism, and Skepticism. This idealistic theory,
Berkeley declares, banishes from philosophy several obscure and difficult
questions: Whether corporeal substances can think? Whether matter is in-

finitely divisible? How it operates on spirit? It reduces human knowledge to knowledge of *ideas* and knowledge of *spirits*. It gets rid of the dualism of *intelligible* objects, or objects in the mind, and *real* objects, or objects outside the mind. This dualism is the root of skepticism, for how can we know that the things which are perceived are conformable to the things which are not perceived? If color, figure, motion, extension, and the like are referred to things outside the mind, we perceive appearances only, not the real qualities of things; this distrust of the senses leads to skepticism. Berkeley believes that the idealistic theory dispels all such doubts.

The doctrine of matter is also the cause of atheism; give up materialism, and the whole fabric of atheism disintegrates. If a self-existent, inert, unthinking substance is the root and origin of all things, we exclude freedom, intelligence, and design from the formation of the world. Dispense with matter and your Epicureans, Hobbes, and others of their kind are deprived of their pretense of plausibility. Idolatry, too, stands and falls with matter, for if objects of sense are merely so many sensations in the mind, then it is scarcely likely that men will fall down and worship their own ideas. Also, take away material substance and mean by body what every plain ordinary person means by the word—that which is immediately seen and felt, which is only a combination of qualities or ideas—and every objection to bodily resurrection comes to nothing. In brief, eliminate the hypothesis of matter, and atheism, idolatry and irreligion lose their basis and support.

Another source of error is the doctrine of the *abstract ideas*. Everybody knows what time, place, and motion, taken in particular or concretely, are; but after they have passed through the mind of a metaphysician, they become too abstract and fine to be apprehended by men of ordinary sense. Time abstracted from the succession of ideas in our minds is nothing, hence the duration of any finite spirit must be estimated by the number of ideas or actions succeeding each other in the same spirit or mind. That the soul always thinks is a simple consequence of the identification of time with the succession of ideas in the mind. The rejection of abstract ideas also implies that where extension is, there color is also, i.e., in the mind. The archetypes of extension and color can exist only in some other mind, and the objects of sense are nothing but sensations combined, blended together in a concrete nexus. None of these entities—time, space, sense qualities, etc.—can be supposed to exist unperceived. We cannot frame an idea of pure time exclusive of the sequence of ideas, nor of pure space exclusive of all extended sensations. Pure space means the ability of the limbs of my body to move in all directions without the least resistance.

The skeptics triumph in natural philosophy. They say we do not know the real essence, the internal qualities and constitution of things. There is something in every drop of water, in every grain of sand, which it is beyond the power of human understanding to fathom or comprehend. This complaint is groundless. There is no inward essence of things whence their discernible qualities flow and whereon they depend. It is also a vain labor to endeavor to explain appearances or qualities, the production of color and sound, for example, by the figure, motion, weight, and like qualities of insensible particles. There is no other agent or efficient cause than *spirit;* motion, like all other ideas, is perfectly inert.

The great principle in vogue in Berkeley's time was that of attraction. The word, says Berkeley, does not mean anything but the effect itself; it does not tell us anything as to the manner of the actions whereby it is produced, or the cause which produces it. Many pronounce gravitation universal: to attract and to be attracted by every other body is said to be an essential quality inherent in all bodies. There is nothing necessary or essential in gravitational attraction—it depends entirely upon the will of the Governing Spirit, who causes certain bodies to cleave together or tend towards each other, according to various laws. Hence, it is vain to seek for a natural efficient cause distinct from mind or spirit. The whole creation is the workmanship of a wise and good Agent, and philosophers should concern themselves solely with the final causes of things: they should try to discover the various ends to which things are adapted, and for which they were originally contrived. There is no reason why observations and experiments should not be made. "That they are of use to mankind and enable us to draw general conclusions, is not the result of any immutable habitudes or relations between things themselves, but only of God's goodness and kindness to men in the administration of the world. By a diligent observation of phenomena within our view, we may discover the general laws of nature, and from them deduce the other phenomena; I do not say *demonstrate,* for all deductions of that kind depend on the supposition that the Author of Nature always operates uniformly and in a constant observance of those rules we take for principles: which we cannot evidently know." [9] The rules of morality, however, which have a necessary tendency to promote the well-being of mankind, Berkeley thinks can be demonstrated, and possess the same immutable, eternal truth as the propositions of geometry.

[9] *A Treatise Concerning the Principles of Human Knowledge,* sec. 107.

Arthur A. Collier (1680-1732), a contemporary of Berkeley, in his *Clavis Universalis* (1713), making Malebranche's system his starting point, attempts from the standpoint of rationalism to prove the non-existence of an external world. *Clavis Universalis,* ed. by E. Bowman, 1909; G. Boas, *The Major Traditions of European Philosophy,* contains a good account of Collier.

52. DAVID HUME

David Hume, born in Edinburgh in 1711, studied law, served as secretary to General St. Clair and later to Lord Hertford (1763-1766), became librarian to the Faculty of Law in Edinburgh (1752-1757), and Under-Secretary of State (1767-1769). He wrote his chief work, *Treatise on Human Nature,* in three books, during his first residence in France (1734-1737), but the work made no impression upon the public; it "fell dead-born from the press," as Hume says. He afterwards worked it over, in more popular form, and published three essays corresponding to the three parts of the original *Treatise;* but his fame during his lifetime rested upon his achievements as a historian rather than on his philosophical works. During his second sojourn at Paris, as a member of the English Embassy, he met Rousseau, Diderot, Holbach, Turgot, and d'Alembert, and induced Rousseau to visit England. He died in 1776.

Among his works are: *Treatise on Human Nature* (1739-1740); five volumes of *Essays:* 1. *Essays, Moral, Political and Literary,* 1741-1742; 2. *Inquiry Concerning Human Understanding,* 1748 (an essay dealing with the topic of Book I of the *Treatise*); 3. *Inquiry Concerning the Principles of Morals,* 1751 (corresponding to Book III of the *Treatise*); 4. *Political Discourses,* 1752; 5. *Four Dissertations,* 1757, including *A Dissertation on the Passions* (on the same topic as Book II of the *Treatise*) and *Natural History of Religion.* Posthumous works: *My Own Life* (published by Adam Smith), 1777; *Dialogues Concerning Natural Religion,* 1779; *Suicide* and *Immortality of the Soul,* 1783. His *History of England* appeared 1754-1762.

Works, ed. by Green and Grose, 4 vols., 1874, new ed. 1909; *Essays and Principles of Morals,* ed. by Selby-Bigge, 1894; *Dialogues Concerning Natural Religion,* ed. by N. Kemp Smith, 1935; *Treatise,* Book I, together with Berkeley's *Principles,* ed. by P. Wheelwright, 1935.

T. Huxley, *David Hume,* 1879; T. H. Green, *"Introduction" to Hume's Works* (contains criticisms of Hume), 1882; W. B. Elkin, *Hume: the Relation of the Treatise and the Inquiry,* 1904; C. W. Hendel, ed., *Hume: Selections,* 1927; M. S. Kuypers, *Studies in the Eighteenth Century Background of Hume's Empiricism,* 1930; N. K. Smith, *The Philosophy of David Hume,* 1941; C. W. Hendel, *Studies in the Philosophy of David Hume,* 1925; J. Laird, *Hume's Philosophy of Human Nature,* 1931; B. M. Laing, *David Hume,* 1932; H. H. Price, *Hume's Theory of the External World,* 1940; J. Greig, *David Hume,* 1932; R. W. Church, *Hume's Theory of Understanding,* 1935; C. Maund, *Hume's Theory of Knowledge,* 1937; R. M. Kydd, *Reason and Conduct in Hume's Treatise,* 1946; C. R. Morris, *Locke, Berkeley and Hume,* 1946.

Hume's Problem. Locke had taught that we have certain knowledge of our ideas, demonstrative knowledge of God and of morality, and practically certain knowledge of the external world of bodies. Berkeley denied the existence of a material world and limited our knowledge to ideas, relations, and spiritual beings. David Hume accepts the empirical theory of the origin of knowledge and the Berkeleyan view that *esse* = *percipi,* and draws what seem to him the logical conclusions. If all we can know are our own impressions, we have no right to assert the reality either of material or of spiritual substances. We find no impressions that justify the assumption of *any kind* of substance. And we discover nothing in our experience that justifies our notion of necessary connection or causation; cause and effect can mean nothing more than a regular succession of ideas. Metaphysics, theology, and natural science cannot yield universal and necessary knowledge; the sciences of God, the universe, and the soul are impossible, as rational sciences. We can know only what we experience, and we can reach only probability in this field. Hume agrees with Descartes, Hobbes, and Locke in requiring that genuine knowledge must be self-evident; but he finds no such knowledge anywhere except in mathematics, which merely analyzes its own concepts.

Hume's view is empirical: our knowledge has its source in experience; it is positivistic: our knowledge is limited to the world of phenomena; it is agnostic: we know nothing of ultimates, substances, causes, soul, ego, external world, universe; it is humanistic: the human mental world is the only legitimate sphere of science and enquiry.

Science of Human Nature. All sciences, says Hume, have a relation to human nature. The sole end of *logic* is to explain the principles and operations of our reasoning faculty and the nature of our ideas; *morals* and *criticism* relate to our tastes and sentiments; and *politics* studies men as united in society and dependent on each other. Even mathematics, natural philosophy, and natural religion are products of the powers and faculties of men. Hence, we ought to study human nature itself, in order to find the principles which regulate our understanding, excite our sentiments, and make us praise or blame any particular object, action, or behavior. What, we ask, is the source of our distinctions between truth and falsehood, vice and virtue, beauty and deformity? The science of man, or moral philosophy, as Hume calls it, is the only solid foundation we can give to the other sciences, and must be based on experience and observation; the "experimental method of reasoning" must be introduced into philosophy. Hume attempts this task in his *Treatise on Human Nature,* of which Book I treats of the understanding, Book II of the passions, and Book III of morals. The same subjects are discussed in the *Inquiry concerning Human Understanding, Dissertation on the Passions,* and *Inquiry concerning the Principles of Morals.*

The most important task is to inquire into the nature of the human understanding, to analyze its powers and capacities, to show that it is not fitted for the abstruse and remote subjects which traditional philosophy has set before it; in other words, we must cultivate true metaphysics—the science of the understanding—in order to destroy the false and adulterate kind which attempts to penetrate into realms inaccessible to the intellect. Even if we could do no more than offer a "mental geography," a delineation of the distinct parts and powers of the mind, there ought to be, to say the least, as much satisfaction in that as in studying the system of the planets. But why may we not hope to discover the secret springs and principles by which the mind is actuated in its operations? May not a Newton of the mental sciences arise who will discover a universal and general principle of the mind comparable to the law of gravitation in physics?

Origin of Knowledge. The chief problems that occupy Hume are those of the origin and nature of knowledge. What is the source of our knowledge; what degree of certainty does it possess; what are its extent and limitations? What are the meaning and value of the categories of knowledge, such as substance and causality? Of all these questions the basic one for Hume is the question of the origin of knowledge. All the materials of our thinking are derived from outward and inward impressions. By impressions we mean our more lively perceptions, when we hear or see or feel or love or hate or desire or will: that is, all our sensations, passions, and emotions as they make their first appearance in the soul. All our thoughts or *ideas* are copies of such impressions: they are the less lively perceptions, the faint or feeble perceptions of which we are conscious when we recall or reflect on any of the sensations or any other impressions just mentioned. Outward impressions, or sensations, arise in the soul from unknown causes, while the inward impressions are frequently occasioned by our ideas. For example, we have an impression of heat or cold, pleasure or pain, of which a copy, or idea, remains. This idea of pleasure or pain produces new impressions: desire and aversion, hope and fear, which are impressions of reflection. These, again, are copied by the memory and imagination. From such impressions, all our knowledge is derived. Knowledge results from compounding, transposing, augmenting, or diminishing the materials furnished us by the senses and experience. The mixture and composition of the impressions alone belongs to the mind and will. Analysis shows that every idea which we examine is copied from similar impressions. Moreover, where there are no impressions, there can be no ideas; a blind man can have no notion of color, nor a deaf man of sound. Hence, we should always ask ourselves in examining the meaning of philosophical terms: From what impression is the supposed idea derived?

Our thoughts or ideas, however, are not entirely loose and unconnected, or joined by chance; they introduce one another with a certain degree of method and regularity; there is a bond of union between them, one calls up another. A picture naturally leads our thoughts to the original (resemblance), the mention of one room in an apartment suggests an adjoining one (contiguity), the thought of a wound calls up the idea of pain (cause and effect). This is the phenomenon called *association of ideas*. The principles or laws of association are resemblance, contiguity in time and place, and cause and effect. Thoughts, in other words, tend to call up thoughts of like things, of things contiguous in time and place, and of things related as cause and effect.

Relation of Cause and Effect. All our reasonings concerning matters of fact are based on the relation of *cause and effect;* that is, we always seek a connection between a present fact and another. A man finds a watch in a desert island: he concludes from the product to the cause, and infers that men have once been there. On our search for causes and effects depend our speculations and practice. It is, therefore, of cardinal importance that we study this relation. How do we arrive at the knowledge of cause and effect, and what is the validity of this knowledge, what the nature of its evidence?

We do not reach a knowledge of this relation by a priori reasonings. Adam could not have inferred a priori, prior to experience, from the light and warmth of fire, that it would consume him. The mind cannot deduce the effect from the supposed cause; no amount of reasoning will enable us to discover a priori the explosiveness of gunpowder or the magnetic attraction of the loadstone. For the effect is totally different from the cause and can never be discovered in it. We cannot *demonstrate* that a certain cause must have a certain effect or that it must always have the same effect; we cannot prove by reason that bread nourishes and fire warms, as we can a mathematical proposition. There is no necessary connection between bread and nourishment, such that the conception of the one necessarily implies that of the other; if there were, we could, without experience, infer the effects from the first appearance of these qualities, just as we can conclude from the concept of a triangle that the sum of its angles is equal to two right angles. There is nothing logically contradictory in assuming that fire will not warm nor bread nourish nor gunpowder explode.

Our knowledge of the relation of cause and effect is based on observation and experience. We observe that objects succeed one another, that similar objects are constantly conjoined, that heat follows flame, cold snow, that the motion of one billiard ball is attended by the movement of the other. Having found, in many instances, that any two kinds of objects have always been conjoined, we infer that the objects are causally related, that one is the cause of the other. That is, we are led to expect upon the appearance of the one, the appearance of the other; the mind is led by habit or custom to believe that the two objects in question are connected, that they will always go together. After the constant conjunction of two objects, such as heat and flame, weight and solidity, we are determined by custom to expect the one from the appearance of the other. Our experience of the constant conjunction of objects, in other words, produces a belief in their connection. This belief is an operation of the mind, a species of natural instinct, as unavoidable as feeling the passion of love when we receive benefits. We cannot define belief except as a feeling of which everyone knows the meaning, because every man is conscious of it. In the *Treatise* Hume is still uncertain as to the psychology of belief: he connects it with the imagination, but the matter remains obscure and unsatisfactory to him. Nature, apparently, has not entrusted to the fallible deductions of reasoning the operation of the mind by which we infer like effects from like causes and vice versa, but has secured it by an instinctive or mechanical tendency.

A cause may, accordingly, be defined as an object followed by another, and whose appearance conveys the thought of that other. This definition, however, does not satisfy some metaphysicians. For them a cause is something productive of another thing; there is something in the cause by which it is enabled to produce the effect, a secret power, force, or energy. There is a tie that binds the cause to the effect, a necessary connection between cause and effect, such that if we knew the power, we could foresee the effect even without experience, and might, on the very first occasion, pronounce with certainty concerning it, merely by dint of thought and reasoning. If this were true, we could deduce the effect from the cause; a knowledge of the cause would necessarily carry with it a knowledge of the effect and we should know at once, without any experience, how an object would act.

But what do the terms power, force, energy, necessary connection mean, and what right have we to employ them? To answer this question, we must analyze our idea of power or necessary connection. We cannot *think* of anything which we have not antecedently *felt* either by our external or internal senses. Now what is the *impression* on which this idea of power depends, how do we get it? When we look at external objects and consider the operation of causes, we never discover any power or necessary connection, any quality which binds the effect to the cause and renders the one an infallible consequence of the other. We only find that the one does actually follow the other. The impulse of one billiard ball is attended with motion in the second: this is all that appears to the *outward* senses. From the first appearance of an object we can never conjecture what its effect will be. The force in the universe which actuates the whole machine is entirely concealed from us. We know that heat is a constant attendant upon flame, but what the connection is between them we cannot imagine. Nor do we get the idea of power from reflection on the operation of our own minds; it is not copied from any *internal* impression or experience. But, it may be asked, are we not every moment conscious of internal power, do we not feel that by a simple command of our will we can move the organs of the body or direct the faculties of the mind? An act of volition produces motion in our limbs or generates a new idea in our imagination. Are we not acquainted with the influence of the will in our inner consciousness? Thus we acquire the idea of power or energy; and we are certain that we ourselves and all other intelligent beings are possessed of power.

Let us examine this view, says Hume. It is true, we do influence the organs of the body by volition. But we are not conscious of the means by which this is effected; we never are, and never can be, directly conscious of the energy by which the will does this. The power is utterly concealed from us here, as in the case of natural events. The motion of the body follows upon the command of the will, that is all experience tells us; how it is done is a mystery. Experience does not tell us the secret connection which binds together the will and its act and renders them inseparable. Indeed, the entire relation between mind and body is mysterious; we do not discern any inner connection between the mind as cause and the body as effect which renders the one an infallible consequence of the other. It is equally impossible to know how our will controls our thinking, the power by which the mind produces ideas. We do not discover any such power; all we know is that the will commanded an idea and the event followed.

To sum up: We can never discover any power at all, all we see is one event following another. We cannot observe or conceive the tie that binds together volition and bodily movement; we do not experience the energy by which the mind produces its effect. The same is true of natural events. One event follows another; we can never observe a tie between separate events. They are *conjoined* but never *connected*. We receive no *impression* of such a tie, or power, or connection, hence we can have no *idea* of it. Employed in this way, these words are devoid of meaning. But they have a meaning when used in their proper sense: when we say one object is connected with another, we mean that they have acquired a connection in our thought. As has been said before, the mind is led by *habit,* on the appearance of one event, to expect its usual attendant and to believe that it will exist. This connection, therefore, which we feel in the mind, this customary transition of the imagination from one object to its usual attendant, is the sentiment or impression from which we form the idea of power or necessary connection.

According to Hume, then, objects are not necessarily connected, but the ideas are connected in our mind by association. The association is the result of repetition, of custom or habit. Two ideas have gone together so often that when one appears, it suggests the other. We have here not logical but psychological necessity, and this psychological necessity depends on experience. The process is the same in animals, in children, and among the majority of men and philosophers.

Another basic concept or category of human thought is that of *substance.* We cannot forbear looking at colors, sounds, tastes, figures, and other properties of bodies, as existences which cannot subsist by themselves, but which require a subject of inhesion to sustain and support them. The imagination feigns something unknown and invisible which it supposes to continue the same despite all variation of quality. This unknown something is the substance; its qualities are called accidents. Many philosophers also posit occult qualities and substantial forms. But all these are fictions, they are like specters in the dark. We have no idea of anything but a perception; a substance is entirely different from a perception; therefore we have no idea of a substance. Every quality, being a distinct thing from every other quality, may be conceived to exist apart, and may indeed exist apart, not only from every other quality, but from that unintelligible chimera—substance.

Validity of Knowledge. All our ideas or thoughts, then, are copies of impressions, all knowledge is derived from experience. Now let us ask: What is the validity of such knowledge, what is the nature of its evidence? All the objects of human knowledge may be divided into two kinds: relations of ideas and matters of fact. Of the first kind are the truths of geometry, algebra, and arithmetic, and, in short, every affirmation which is either intuitively or demonstratively certain. That the square on the hypotenuse is equal to the sum of the squares on the other two sides is a proposition which expresses a relation between these figures. That three times five is equal to half of thirty expresses a relation between these numbers. Propositions of this kind are discoverable by the mere operation of thought, without dependence on what is existent anywhere in the universe. Even if there had never been a circle or a triangle in nature, the truths demonstrated by Euclid would forever retain their certainty and self-evidence.

All evidence of matters of fact which lies beyond the testimony of sense or memory is derived entirely from the relation of cause and effect. Our knowledge of cause and effect is derived, as we saw, from experience: custom leads us to infer that objects which our experience tells us are frequently conjoined, will always be so; but custom is an instinct and instinct may mislead us. Our evidence of the truth of matters of fact is not comparable to the evidence we have in mathematics. The contrary of every matter of fact is still possible, for its occurrence would involve no contradiction. That the sun will not rise tomorrow is no less intelligible a proposition, and implies no more contradiction than that it will rise. Here we are dealing not with certain, self-evident knowledge, but with probability.

Of substances we have no idea whatever, and they have no place in knowledge. But, it may be asked, why trust imagination in the case of causes and not in the case of substance? Hume's answer is that we must distinguish between principles which are permanent, irresistible, and universal, such as is the customary transition from causes to effects, and the principles which are changeable, weak, and irregular, such as substance, substantial forms, accidents, occult qualities. The former are the foundation of all our thought and action, so that, in their absence, human nature would inevitably perish and go to ruin. The latter are neither unavoidable for mankind nor necessary and useful in the conduct of life.

Thus we have no absolute, self-evident or certain knowledge of matters of fact; our knowledge never reaches absolute certainty. We base our conclusions on experience, we believe the future will be like the past, but we have no absolute assurance that things will not change. Life, however, would be impossible unless we acted on the belief that nature is regular and uniform; no practical good can come of our skepticism; practice is the best cure for all skeptical reflections.

Knowledge of the External World. The testimony of the senses alone is not to be trusted implicitly; we must correct their evidence by reason. We trust our senses by a natural instinct and accept an external universe without reasoning, almost before the use of reason. We assume it to exist even if every sensible creature were annihilated. The slightest philosophical reflection, however, suffices to destroy the instinctive opinion of all men. Nothing can be present to the mind but an image or perception. We cannot prove that perceptions are caused by external objects entirely different from them, though perhaps resembling them in some way. Experience is silent here, for we have before the mind only perceptions. We observe a relation of cause and effect between two perceptions, but we can never observe it between perceptions and objects; hence we cannot proceed by causal inference from perceptions to objects. If we deprive matter of primary as well as of secondary qualities, what remains is only a certain unknown, inexplicable something as the cause of our impressions—an entity so devoid of meaning that no skeptic will think it worth his while to dispute its reality. The objects of all our knowledge are impressions and ideas derived from them. There is no evidence that these are caused by external objects, or an unknown substance, or by ourselves, or by God. Impressions and sensations simply appear and reappear in our experience. All we can do, then, is to limit ourselves to the world of experience, to our impressions and ideas. We can compare our ideas, note their relations, and reason about the relations, thus attaining a kind of demonstrative knowledge. We can also observe the order of our sensations; through habit or custom we come to regard one object as connected with another by a relation which we call cause and effect.

We must limit our inquiries to such subjects as are best adapted to the narrow capacities of the human understanding. Philosophical decisions are nothing but the reflections of common life, methodized and corrected. Philosophers will never be tempted to go beyond common life, so long as they consider the imperfection of those faculties which they employ, their narrow reach, and their inaccurate operations. We can never hope to attain any satisfactory knowledge with regard to the origin of our impressions or the ultimate constitution of a universe behind our impressions and ideas.

Denial of Soul-substance. Metaphysics, therefore, in the sense of knowledge of the ultimate origin and nature of the universe, is impossible: rational cosmology is out of the question. Nor can we have a rational psychology, a science of the essence of the soul; we know nothing of an immaterial, indivisible, imperishable soul-substance. The idea of substance is meaningless, whether applied to matter or to mind. The doctrine of the simplicity and indivisibility of a thinking substance can neither be confirmed nor refuted by empirical evidence. Nor have we, as some philosophers hold, any idea of a simple and identical self—there is no empirical evidence for the existence of such a simple and continuing principle in us. "When I enter intimately into what I call *myself*, I always stumble on some particular perception or other, of heat or cold, light or shade, love or hatred, pain or pleasure. I never catch *myself*, at any time, without a perception, and never can observe anything but the perception." The mind is "a bundle or collection of different perceptions, which succeed one another with an inconceivable rapidity, and are in a perpetual flux and movement. The mind is a kind of theater where several perceptions successively make their appearance, pass, re-pass, glide away, and mingle in an infinite variety of postures and situations. There is no *simplicity* in it at one time, nor *identity* in different [times]." [10] The comparison of the theater must not mislead us; the perceptions which constitute the mind succeed each other in kaleidoscopic succession; nor have we the vaguest notion of the place where these scenes are represented, or of the materials of which they are composed. Every distinct perception is a distinct existence, and is different, distinguishable and separable from every other perception, either contemporary or successive. Is this relation of identity something that really binds our several perceptions together, or does it only associate them in the imagination? In pronouncing concerning the identity of a person, do we observe some real bonds among his perceptions, or do we only feel one among the ideas we form of them? The understanding never observes any real connection among objects; even the union of cause and effect resolves itself into a customary association of ideas. Hence, self-identity is nothing really belonging to these different perceptions and uniting them together; it is merely a quality which we attribute to them because of the union of their ideas in the imagination, when we reflect on them. Mind is nothing but a heap or collection of different perceptions united together by certain relations, and supposed, though falsely, to be endowed with a perfect simplicity and identity.

Liberty and Necessity. The ideas of necessity and causation arise entirely from the uniformity observable in the operations of nature. Where similar objects are constantly conjoined, the mind is determined by custom to infer the one from the appearance of the other. Beyond the constant conjunction of similar objects and the consequent inference from one to the other, we have no notion of any necessity or connection. This idea of necessity is applied to the voluntary actions of men as well as to connections in nature. The doctrine of necessity, when applied to the human will, leads to

[10] *A Treatise of Human Nature,* Bk. I, Pt. IV, sec. 6.

a theory of extreme determinism, such as we encountered in the philosophy of Spinoza. Hume is of the opinion that the disputes about liberty and necessity are due to misunderstandings which a few intelligible definitions could end. There is, admittedly, great uniformity in the actions of men; mankind is much the same in all times and places. The conjunction between motives and voluntary actions is as regular and uniform as that between cause and effect in any part of nature, and has been universally acknowledged among mankind. It seems almost impossible to engage either in science or action of any kind without acknowledging the doctrine of necessity, in the sense of a uniformity or regularity of volitional action, and the possibility of inference from motives to voluntary actions, from characters to conduct. But why do men oppose this doctrine in words? It is because they have the false notion of absolute necessity. They believe that they perceive something like a necessary connection between cause and effect in nature, while they feel no such connection between the motive and the action when they reflect on the operations of their own minds. Necessity, properly understood, however, is not constraint, but uniformity of action, constant conjunction between motive and effect. Hume's position on the free will issue is a determinism which insists on the regularity and uniformity of volition, while refusing to go to the extreme of Spinoza's necessitarianism. Moreover, while he rejects freedom in the sense of causeless volition unconnected with antecedent motives and circumstances, he finds that there is a significant sense in which man has liberty of action; "liberty is a power of acting or not acting according to the determinations of the will; that is, if we choose to remain at rest, we may; if we choose to move, we also may." [11] The dispute about free will is, then, in Hume's opinion, purely verbal. Philosophers can achieve agreement among themselves and with other men, provided they adopt a set of consistent definitions of such terms as liberty and necessity, freedom and determinism.

The doctrines of liberty and necessity, thus explained, are not only consistent with morality, but absolutely essential to its support. Necessity is the constant conjunction of like objects, or the inference of the understanding from one object to the other. We draw inferences from human actions; they are based on the experienced union of like actions with like motives. If actions did not proceed from some cause in the character and disposition of the person who performed them, the person would not be answerable for them. But where liberty is wanting, human actions are not susceptible of

[11] *An Enquiry Concerning Human Understanding,* sec. VIII.

any moral qualities, nor can they be objects of approbation or dislike. To be called moral, acts must spring from the internal character, passions, and affections of the person; in that sense they are free; where they are derived altogether from external objects, they can give rise neither to praise nor blame: they are not free.

God. We cannot demonstrate the independent existence of a world, although we continue to believe in it: rational cosmology is impossible. Nor can we demonstrate the existence of a soul-substance and the immortality of the soul: rational psychology is impossible. Finally, we cannot demonstrate anything concerning the nature of God, his attributes, his decrees, his plan of providence. Human reason is too weak, too blind, and limited in its scope to solve such problems as these: rational theology is impossible. When the coherence of the parts of a stone, or even that composition of parts which renders it extended, is so inexplicable and contains circumstances so repugnant and contradictory, with what assurance can we decide the origin of worlds or trace their history from eternity to eternity? We are far beyond the reach of our faculties when we carry our speculations into two eternities, before and after the present state of things: into the creation and formation of the universe, the existence and properties of spirits, the powers and operations of one universal spirit existing without beginning and without end, omnipotent, omniscient, immutable, infinite, and incomprehensible.

The question is not concerning the being of God, but his nature. No truth is so certain as the being of God; it is the basis of all our hopes, the surest foundation of morality, the firmest support of society. Nothing exists without a cause, and the original cause of this universe—whatever it be—we call God, and piously ascribe to him every species of perfection. But we cannot comprehend the attributes of this divine being, nor suppose that his perfections have any analogy or likeness to the perfections of a human creature. Hume directs his attacks particularly against the *argument from design,* the so-called teleological proof, which attempts to infer the existence, wisdom and goodness of God from the order, beauty, and goodness of the universe. Unless the cases be exactly similar, we cannot repose perfect confidence in reasoning by analogy here. There is a wide difference between the universe and houses, ships, furniture, and machines, and we are not justified in inferring similar causes from a slight similarity in effects. Intelligence is indeed an active cause by which some particular parts of nature are found to produce alterations in other parts. But thought, design or intelligence, such as we discover in men and other animals, is no more than one of the springs and principles of the universe, like heat or cold, attraction or repulsion, and a hundred others which fall under daily observation. We cannot rightly conclude from the part to the whole. But even if we could, what peculiar privilege pertains to thought, that we must thus make it the model of the whole universe? Can we imagine that nature incessantly copies herself throughout so immense a universe? If we see a house, we conclude with the greatest certainty that it had an architect or builder—because this is precisely that species of effect which we have experienced from that species of cause. But the universe bears no such exact resemblance to a house that we can, with the same certainty, infer a similar cause, or that the analogy is here entire and perfect. The dissimilitude is so striking that the utmost we can here pretend to is a guess, a conjecture, a presumption concerning a similar cause.

We cannot represent the Deity as similar to the human mind: to do so would be to fall into anthropomorphism. The human mind is in constant change; but change is not compatible with the perfect immutability and simplicity ascribed to God. Besides, why not stop at the material world? To say that the different ideas which compose the reason of the Supreme Being fall into order of themselves and by their own nature is no more clarifying than to say that the parts of the material world fall into order of themselves and by their own nature. We have experience of matter doing this, and we also have experience of mind doing it.

The attempt to infer the nature of God from the nature of the universe must end in disaster. By this anthropomorphic method of reasoning, we cannot ascribe infinity to the divine Being, because the effect is not infinite; nor perfection, because the universe is not perfect. Even if it were perfect, it would still remain uncertain whether all the excellencies of the work can justly be ascribed to the workman. Many worlds might have been botched and bungled, throughout an eternity, ere this system was struck out, much labor lost, many fruitless trials made, and a slow but continued improvement carried on during infinite ages in the art of world-making. Besides, there is no proof, from this argument, of the unity of God; perhaps many gods united in making a world. Again, men are mortal and renew their species by generation; hence, if we reason by analogy, why, then, must we exclude this universal circumstance from these deities? And why not complete our anthropomorphism and ascribe bodies to the Deity or deities?

A more probable hypothesis than the anthropomorphic theory, according to Hume, is that which infers that the world is an animal and the Deity the soul of the world, actuating it and actuated by it. The world itself plainly resembles an animal or a vegetable more than it does a watch or a knitting-loom. It is more probable, therefore, that its cause resembles the cause of the former, which is generation or vegetation. Consequently, we may infer the cause of the world to be something similar to generation or vegetation.

These speculations are, it is true, world-fancies, we have no data to establish any system of cosmogony. Our experience is limited and imperfect, and can afford no possible basis for conjecture concerning the whole of things. But the hypothesis which compares the world to an animal is as probable as the one which compares it with a human contrivance; indeed, the analogy is more striking in the former case than in the latter.

Hume also points out that we cannot infer from the universe the existence of a being possessing moral attributes like those of men. The purpose and intention of nature seems to be the preservation and propagation of the species, and not their happiness. Misery exceeds happiness in the world. The fact of pain in the world would prove that God is either not benevolent, or not almighty. Physical and moral evil do not allow us to infer a good God. It may be said that human reason is too weak to understand the purpose of the universe; but this does not allow us to infer anything of God's goodness; a man must infer from what he knows, not from what he is ignorant of.

We cannot demonstrate a priori that the Deity is a necessarily existent being; there is no being whose non-existence implies a contradiction. We cannot prove his existence as a necessary consequence of his nature, because we do not know what that nature is. The material universe may, for all we know, have qualities which make its non-existence inconceivable.

As to the origin of religion, Hume holds that the belief in God is not the result of speculation, curiosity, or the pure love of truth, but rests on man's anxious concern for happiness, his dread of future misery, terror of death, thirst for revenge, appetite for food, and other necessaries. Polytheism or idolatry, and not theism, must have been the first and most ancient religion.

In spite of these skeptical reflections, Hume declares that it hardly seems possible that anyone of good understanding should reject the idea of God when once it is suggested to him. A purpose, an intention, and design, is evident in everything, and when our comprehension is so far enlarged as to contemplate the first rise of this visible system, we must adopt with the strongest conviction the idea of some intelligent cause or author. The universal propensity to believe in invisible, intelligent power, if not an original instinct, being at least a general attendant of human nature, may be considered as a kind of mark or stamp which the divine Workman has set upon his work. How seriously these remarks are to be taken in view of what has been said before, the reader is left to decide for himself.

Voluntarism and Anti-intellectualism. Theology is not a demonstrable science, we cannot prove the existence or the attributes of God. The teleological argument is imperfect; anthropomorphism is prejudice. Hume inclines to an *organic* conception of the universe, in this respect opposing the eighteenth-century ideal. His view of the origin of religion is also out of harmony with eighteenth-century notions, according to which religion owes its origin either to the rational faculties of primitive men, or is an invention of crafty priests. Hume rejects all such theories: the belief in God is not the result of speculative reasoning, but is based on man's emotional and impulsive nature. The intellectualistic or rationalistic explanation is replaced by the *voluntaristic* conception: religion is rooted in the will. Moreover, religions are not made, but *grow;* theism has developed from polytheism. The same views are introduced by Hume into his theory of the State; he rejects both the theological conceptions, and the contract theory which found such favor in the eighteenth century. No compact or agreement to general submission was expressly formed, for this idea is far beyond the comprehension of savages. Each exertion of authority in the chieftain must have been particular, and called forth by the present exigencies of the case; the sensible utility resulting from his interposition made these exertions become daily more frequent, and their frequency gradually produced an habitual, and, as it were, a voluntary and therefore precarious, acquiescence in the people. The people, if we are to trace government to its first origin in the woods and deserts, are the source of all power and jurisdiction, and voluntarily, for the sake of peace and order, abandoned their native liberty, and received laws from their equals and companions. The rationalistic conception here gives way to the *historical* or genetic point of view.

53. THE RATIONALISTIC REACTION IN ENGLAND

Cambridge Platonism. Although empiricism remained the dominant note in British thought from the days of Roger Bacon and William of Occam down to the present time, the opposition to this school never entirely disappeared. The rationalistic traditions of scholasticism were kept alive at the universities and among theologians, and spiritualistic systems of philosophy arose as a reaction against the radical speculations of Hobbes, Locke, and Hume. Ralph Cudworth (1617-1688), a professor at Cambridge, opposes the atheistic and materialistic teachings of Hobbes from the standpoint of Christian Platonism in his *True Intellectual System of the Universe* (1678). He accepts Descartes' rationalism, but rejects all mechanical explanation of nature as leading to atheism. All men have the same fundamental concepts or categories, and what is clearly and distinctly perceived is true. These a priori categories are the constant reflections of the universal reason, of God's mind, and likewise form the nature or essence of things. Among such innate truths are the moral laws, which are as binding on God as the axioms of mathematics. Cudworth's ethical philosophy is given in his posthumous works, *Treatise Concerning Eternal and Immutable Morality* (1731), and *A Treatise of Free Will* (1838).

Other members of the Cambridge school of Platonists and opponents of English empiricism are: Henry More (1614-1687; *Enchiridion metaphysicum, Enchiridion ethicum,* 1668); Theophilus Gale (1628-1677; *Philosophia universalis,* 1676); and John Norris (1657-1711; *An Essay towards the Theory of the Ideal or Intelligible World,* 1701, 1704).

W. R. Scott, *Introduction to Cudworth's Treatise,* 1891; F. I. MacKinnon, *Philosophy of John Norris,* 1910; E. Cassirer, *Die platonische Renaissance in England und die Schule von Cambridge,* 1932.

The rationalistic conception that there is universal and necessary truth, which is both speculative and ethical and not derived from experience, continues in the English thought of the eighteenth century. Samuel Clarke (1675-1729; *Discourse concerning the Unalterable Obligations of Natural Religion,* 1708) teaches that there are eternal and necessary differences and relations of things, and that divine and human reason perceives these as they are: no one can refuse to assent either to a correct mathematical proof, or to moral truth. William Wollaston (1659-1724; *The Religion of Nature Delineated,* 1722) and Richard Price (1723-1791; *Review of the Principal Questions in Morals,* 1758, and *Letters on Materialism and Philosophical Necessity,* 1778) agree with this view, which is later taken up by the Scottish philosophy of Reid and his school.

The Scottish Common-sense School. The Scottish school, led by Thomas Reid (1710-1796), represents a reaction against the idealism of Berkeley and the skepticism of Hume. Empiricism had ended in the denial of the very things which the common sense of mankind accepts as the most certain facts of knowledge—the existence of an external world and of an immortal soul; indeed, it had called in question the possibility of truth itself. If the categories of substance and causality are mere illusions, if objects are mere ideas in our minds, if there is no substantial soul and the existence of God is undemonstrable, then philosophy breaks down; for philosophy cannot contradict the common consciousness of mankind. Sensation carries with it an immediate belief in the reality of the object, and this immediate certainty supplies us with a criterion of truth. All proof rests on such direct knowledge, on self-evident principles which cannot be proved. The knowledge of these principles and of the criterion of truth is common sense: such principles, which we discover by observation, are either first principles of necessary truths or first principles of contingent truths. As belonging to the former class, Reid mentions the axioms of logic and mathematics, the principles of grammar, taste, morals, and metaphysics; among the latter he cites the existence of everything of which I am conscious. I am conscious of the thoughts of a being which I call my self, my mind, my person; I am also conscious of my own personal identity and continued existence. Things really exist which we distinctly perceive by our senses, and are what we perceive them to be. We may rely on our natural faculties to distinguish truth from error.

Writings of Reid: An Inquiry into the Human Mind on the Principles of Common Sense, 1764; *Essays on the Intellectual Powers of Man,* 1785. *Collected Works,* ed. by Sir William Hamilton, 7th ed., 1872. *Essays on the Intellectual Powers of Man,* ed. and abridged by A. D. Woozley, 1941.

Other members of the Scottish school are: James Beattie (1735-1803), James Oswald (d. 1793), and Dugald Stewart (1753-1828; *Collected Works,* edited by Hamilton, 1854-1858). Thomas Brown (1778-1820; *Inquiry into the Relation of Cause and Effect,* 1803) seeks to reconcile the teachings of Hume with the philosophy of common sense.

General Works on English Philosophy

L. Stephen, *History of English Thought in the Eighteenth Century,* 2 vols., 1876-1925; J. J. Rickaby, *Free Will and Four English Philosophers,* 1906; F. M. Forsyth, *English Philosophy,* 1910; C. W. Eliot, ed., *English Philosophers of the Seventeenth and Eighteenth Centuries,* 1910; J. W. Hudson, *The Treatment of Personality by Locke, Berkeley and Hume,* 1911; J. Seth, *English Philosophers and Schools of Philosophy,* 1912; W. R. Sorley, *A History of English Philosophy,* 1920.

G. Kennedy, *Bacon-Hobbes-Locke* (Selections), 1937; E. A. Burtt, *The English Philosophers from Bacon to Mill* (writings of the British Philosophers), Modern Library, 1939.

XIV
The Development
of Rationalism in Germany

54. GOTTFRIED WILHELM LEIBNIZ

Gottfried Wilhelm Leibniz (1646-1716) was born in Leipzig, and studied law, philosophy, and mathematics at the Universities of Jena, and Altdorf, receiving his doctorate in law from the last-named institution at the age of twenty. Among his teachers were Jacob Thomasius, the father of the celebrated Christian Thomasius, and E. Weigel. After a sojourn at Mayence (1670-1672), where he was engaged in the reform of the legal procedure of the Electorate, and a diplomatic mission to Paris (1672-1676), he was called to Hanover as court councilor and librarian, a post which he held until his death.

Among his writings, which consisted, for the most part, of shorter essays in Latin, French, and German—published in learned journals—and of private letters, are: *Meditationes de cognitione, veritate et ideis* (1684); *Lettres sur la question si l'essence du corps consiste dans l'étendue* (1691); *Ncuveau système de la nature* (1695); *Nouveaux essais sur l'entendement humain* (in reply to Locke's *Essay*, 1704; first published 1765); *De ipsa natura* (1698); *Essais de Theodicée* (1710); *La monadologie* (1714); *Principes de la nature et de la grâce* (1714).

Collections of philosophical writings ed. by J. E. Erdmann, 1840; by A. Foucher de Careil, 7 vols., 1859-75; by P. Janet, 2 vols., 1866; by C. I. Gerhardt, 7 vols., 1875-1890; German writings by G. E. Guhrauer, 2 vols., 1838-1840.

Translations: *Philosophical Works of Leibniz*, by G. M. Duncan, 2nd ed., 1908; *New Essays*, by A. G. Langley, 2nd ed., 1916; *Monadology and other Philosophical Writings*, by R. Latta, 1925; *Discourse on Metaphysics, Correspondence with Arnauld and Monadology*, by G. R. Montgomery, 1902, trans. revised, by A. R. Chandler, 1924; H. W. Carr, *The Monadology of Leibniz*, 1929; M. Morris, *The Philosophical Writings of Leibniz*, 1934; P. P. Wiener, *Leibniz: Selections*, 1951; an edition of Leibniz's works in 2 vols., ed. and trans. by L. E. Loemker is in course of publication by the University of Chicago Press.

J. T. Merz, *Leibniz*, 1884; J. Dewey, *Leibniz's New Essays*, 1888; B. Russell, *A Critical Exposition of the Philosophy of Leibniz*, 1900, 1937; L. Couturat, *La logique de Leibniz*,

1901; A. Foucher de Careil, *Leibniz, Descartes et Spinoza,* 1862; H. W. Carr, *Leibniz,* 1929; E. Cassirer, *Leibniz's System in seinen wissenschaftlichen Grundlagen,* 1902; H. W. B. Joseph, *Lectures on the Philosophy of Leibniz,* 1949; A. Foucher de Careil, *Mémoire sur la philosophie de Leibniz,* 1905; H. Schmalenbach, *Leibniz,* 1921; F. Thilly, *Leibniz's Streit gegen Locke* (Dissertation), 1891.

German Culture before Leibniz. Philosophy achieved little in Germany during the centuries preceding the eighteenth. The barren theological controversies following the Reformation and the Thirty Years' War (1618-1648), were not favorable to the development of science and philosophy. The period which produced Shakespeare, Bacon, Milton, and Locke in England, Montaigne, Corneille, Racine, Molière, Pascal, and Descartes in France, found culture at a low ebb in the land of Luther. The German language itself seemed to have perished as a literary instrument: the higher classes spoke French and the scholars still wrote in Latin—the common people alone used the mother-tongue. French culture was introduced through the countless courts which were patterned after the French paternalistic models and imitated French manners. With the division of Germany into independent territorial principalities, the spirit of nationalism declined, and Germans became ashamed of the German name. The universities, like those of England and France, took no part in disseminating modern ideas; the new science and philosophy grew up outside of the universities and were encouraged by educated society. The first great representatives of the new culture in Germany are Samuel Pufendorf (1632-1694), who advocated the theory of natural law, Christian Thomasius (1655-1728), who published the first periodical in the German language and was the first to lecture in German—at the University of Leipzig—and, greatest of all, Leibniz, who distinguished himself in mathematics, jurisprudence, and philosophy. Walter von Tschirnhausen (1651-1708), who corresponded with Spinoza and Leibniz, accepted the mathematical method, but held that all deductions must begin with the facts of experience and find their verification in experience. All these thinkers are pioneers of modernism in Germany and forerunners of the Enlightenment, which had already begun to sow its seed in England and France, and which was destined to reap a rich harvest in the land of Lessing, Goethe, and Kant.

The Problem. Descartes assumes two distinct principles of explanation, body and mind, the essential attributes of which are, respectively, extension and thought. Spinoza sets up one universal substance, which is conceived as both extended and thinking. Both philosophers regard the physical and mental realms as two absolutely closed systems, with the difference that Descartes permits interaction between the two at one single point in the human brain, while Spinoza permits no interaction whatever. Both agreed that everything physical is explained physically: the corporeal universe is a machine. The mechanical explanation was accepted by modern philosophers and modern natural scientists alike. It met with vigorous opposition, however, from the theological philosophies of scholastic origin which dominated most of the universities, and was condemned as a godless doctrine that failed to take account of the divine purpose in the world.

Like his predecessors, Leibniz became acquainted with the scholastic metaphysics at the university and in his youth subscribed to the traditional world-view of the Protestant schoolmen. But the study of modern philosophy and science and, especially, his discovery of the infinitesimal calculus, caused a significant advance in his thought, and suggested to him the necessity of a theory that would do justice to the achievements of modern science and philosophy as well as to the valuable elements in Christian-scholastic speculation—a system, in short, that would reconcile mechanism and teleology, natural science and theology, modern and ancient philosophy. The mathematician Weigel of Jena, his teacher, had convinced Leibniz of the truth of a conception that remained the basis and guiding principle of all his later efforts to construct a world-view: the Pythagorean-Platonic doctrine of the harmony of the universe. Leibniz never abandoned the idea that the universe is a harmonious whole, governed by mathematical and logical principles, that mathematics and metaphysics are, therefore, the fundamental sciences and the demonstrative method the true method of philosophy.

The Doctrine of Force. Leibniz examined the presuppositions of the new science and found them inadequate. Even the facts of physics, he felt, could not be satisfactorily explained by the hypothesis of merely extended bodies and motion. Descartes had taught that the quantity of motion is constant. But bodies come to rest and bodies begin to move: motion seems to be lost and gained. This would violate the principle of continuity, the principle that nature makes no leaps. There must be something that persists when motion ceases, a ground of motion: this is *force,* or the *conatus,* or the tendency of the body to move or to continue its motion; and force is constant in quantity. Hence, there is no substance that does not act, that is not the expression of force: what does not act does not exist; only what is active is real. Consequently, force, and not extension, is the essential attribute of body. Hence, also, the law of the conservation of motion must give way to the law of the conservation of force or energy. Another proof that extension cannot be the essential attribute of body is found in the composite nature of extension: that which is made up of parts cannot be a primary principle. Something simple is needed, and force is such a simple, indivisible reality.

The geometric or static conception of nature is replaced, in the philosophy of Leibniz, by the *dynamic* or *energetic* view. Bodies do not exist by virtue of extension, but extension exists by virtue of bodies or forces; there could be no extension without force, without dynamic bodies. According to Descartes, the existence of bodies presupposes extension; according to Leibniz, extension presupposes the existence of bodies or forces. Force is the source or "fountain of the mechanical world," the mechanical world is the sensible appearance of forces. "Extension presupposes in the body a property, attribute, or nature that extends itself, spreads itself out, and continues itself." There is a force in body that precedes all extension. It is owing to the force of resistance in the body that it appears as impenetrable and limited, or as matter. Every unit of force is an indivisible union of soul and matter, activity and passivity; it is an organizing, self-determining, purposive force that also limits itself or has the power of resistance.

Space, therefore, is conceived by Leibniz as the result of the harmonious coexistence of forces; hence it has no absolute existence—there is no absolute space in which things exist—but it is relative to the things and would disappear with them. Forces do not depend on space, but space depends on the forces. Hence, there can be no empty space between things and beyond them: where forces cease to act, the world comes to an end.

The Doctrine of Monads. Body, then, is a plurality of simple forces. Since many things exist, there is not one single force in nature, but an infinite number of forces, every one of which is a particular, individual substance. Force is indivisible or simple, hence it is immaterial and unextended. Simple substances or forces are called by Leibniz metaphysical points, formal atoms, essential forms, substantial forms, *monads* or units. They are not physical points, for these are nothing but compressed bodies; they are not mathematical points, for these, though "true" points, are not "real," but merely "points of view." Only metaphysical points are true and real; without them there would be nothing real, for without units there could be no manifoldness. Moreover, such centers of force must be eternal: they cannot be destroyed—only a miracle could destroy them—nor can they be created: monads can neither arise nor disappear. The original scholastic conception of individual active substantial forms, which Leibniz carried away with him from the university, is thus transformed into the doctrine of individual forces.

Leibniz established that the world of bodies is composed of an infinite number of dynamic units, or immaterial, unextended, simple units of force. What else can we say of the monadic unit, where can we study it? In ourselves. We discover such a simple immaterial substance in our own inner life—the soul. What is true of the soul, will be true, in a measure, of all monads. Reasoning by analogy, Leibniz interprets the monads as spiritual or psychic forces. There is in them something analogous both to our sensations and to our conations or tendencies to action; they have "perception" and "appetition." The same principle that expresses itself in the mind of man is active in inanimate matter, in plant, and animal. There is force everywhere; every part of matter is like a garden full of plants; all matter is animate, alive, even to its minutest parts.

But how can there be mind in the stone, or even in the plant? Mind, says Leibniz, is not absolutely the same in stone, plant, and man. For Descartes there is nothing unconscious in mind and nothing unextended in matter. The facts of physics, however, show that in nature force is essentially akin to mind, whereas the facts of psychology show that the mind may at times lapse into unconsciousness. Leibniz has overcome the Cartesian dualism by establishing a continuity between the physical and psychological realms. Body and extension are not identical terms; neither are mind and consciousness coextensive. Mind consists of perceptions and tendencies. Perceptions differ in clearness and distinctness in different monads; indeed, the human mind itself reveals perceptions of different degrees of clarity. When I attend carefully to an object, its elements stand out clearly and distinctly, whereas the surrounding parts become successively more and more obscure and indistinct, until they are scarcely discernible at all. The farther an object is removed from the focus of my attention, the smaller and fainter it is. There are, therefore, clear perceptions and obscure perceptions; the latter are called "small perceptions," *petites perceptions*. Sensation cannot distinguish in the roar of the ocean the different elements or the minute perceptions produced by the motion of each separate wave, and yet every one of these separate sounds is contained in the sensation. Just as there are different degrees of clearness within the individual monad, so monads differ among themselves in the clearness of their perceptions. In the very lowest monads, everything is obscure and confused, resembling sleep; they spend their entire existence in a comatose state. Such dormant life we find in the plant. In animals there is perception with memory, i.e., consciousness; in man, consciousness becomes still clearer; here it is called *apperception,* being a "reflexive knowledge of the inner state," or self-consciousness.

Every monad has the power of perception or representation; it perceives or represents and expresses the entire universe. In this sense it is a world in miniature, a microcosm; it is a "living mirror of the universe," a concentrated world, a world for itself. But each monad represents the universe in its own way, from its unique point of view, with its characteristic degree of clearness; it is limited, an individual, and has other individuals outside it. The higher the monad, the more clearly and distinctly it perceives, expresses or represents the world; the monads with which it is most closely associated constitute its own body, and these it represents most clearly. From this teaching it follows that "every body feels everything that occurs in the entire universe, so that anyone who sees all could read in each particular thing that which happens everywhere else and, besides, all that has happened and will happen, perceiving in the present that which is remote in time and space." [1]

The monads, moreover, form a graduated progressive series, from the lowest to the highest. The universe is composed of an infinite number of monads in a gradually ascending scale of clearness, no two monads being exactly alike. The law of the identity of indiscernibles, which is a cardinal principle of Leibniz's metaphysics, affirms that no two monads are exactly alike—if two monads were indistinguishable or indiscernible one from the other they would necessarily be identical, i.e., would really be one monad. Another fundamental principle of Leibniz's metaphysics is the law of continuity. There are no leaps in nature, no breaks in the line from the lowest to the highest; there is a continuous line of infinitesimal differences from the dullest piece of inorganic matter to God. God is the highest and perfect monad, pure activity (*actus purus*), the original monad, the monad of monads. The principle of continuity demands the existence of a supreme monad.

Leibniz's pluralism of monads may be profitably compared to earlier monistic and pluralistic philosophies. His pluralism contrasts most sharply with the monism of Spinoza. The latter accepts one absolute substance, Leibniz an infinite number of them. Descartes is a pluralist in one important respect: he asserts the existence of a plurality of individual things; but he considers them as modifications of one or the other of two substances

[1] *Monadology,* sec. 61.

diametrically opposed in essence—mind and matter. The monads of Leibniz, on the other hand, are essentially alike—although differing from one another in degree. The atomists were also pluralists, in that they asserted the existence of many homogeneous realities; but their atoms are material, whereas Leibniz's monads are spiritual.

Every monad is in process of evolution and realizes its nature with an inner necessity. It is not determined from without; it has no windows through which anything can enter; everything it is to be is potential or implicit in it. This follows necessarily from the principle of continuity: nothing can be in the monad which has not always been there, and nothing can ever come into it that is not in it now. It passes through a series of stages of evolution, unfolding what is preformed in it. The entire human race was preformed in the seed of Adam and in the ovaries of Eve. The developed individual existed in germ, preformed in miniature, in the embryo. Nothing in the monad can be lost, all is preserved in all its stages, and the future stages are predetermined in the earlier ones. Hence, every monad is "charged with the past" and "big with the future." This doctrine of preformation—sometimes called the incasement theory—was common among the biologists of Leibniz's time, such as Leeuwenhoek and Swammerdam. In opposition to the preformation theory, the theory of *epigenesis* asserted the "progressive formation and differentiation of organs from a germ primitively homogeneous." This latter conception, which was advanced by Caspar F. Wolff in 1759, did not, however, meet with general acceptance until after the appearance of Darwin's *Origin of Species* in 1859.

Leibniz described the difference between organic and inorganic bodies as follows: Both are composed of monads or centers of force, but the organism contains a central monad, a "queen monad" or soul, which represents, or has before it, a picture of the entire body, and which is the guiding principle of the monads surrounding it. Inorganic bodies are not centralized in this way, but consist of a mere mass or aggregation of monads. The higher the bodies, the more organized they are—the higher organism forming a well-ordered system of monads.

The problem of the relation of mind and body may be formulated thus: how, it may be asked, does the central monad influence the lower monads constituting its body? We might assume interaction between them, but Leibniz has already told us that monads have no windows, that they cannot be influenced or acted upon from without. The occasionalistic doctrine that God created both body and mind and regulates the actions of each to keep time with the other, as the watchmaker regulates his clocks, is also rejected.

Leibniz's explanation is that God, in creating minds and bodies has arranged it, from the very beginning, that the two shall go together: the relation between soul and body is a harmony pre-established by God. Causal interaction is out of the question. There is a parallelism, or *concomitance,* between the mental and physical states: in this sense the body is the material expression of the soul. It must not be forgotten, however, that the body itself consists of an infinitude of monads or psychic forces, every one of which is organic and acts in accordance with the preordained law of its nature. "Souls act according to the laws of final causes, by means of desire, ends, and means. Bodies act according to the laws of efficient causes or motions. And the two realms are in harmony with one another." [2] In other words, the organic body and its minutest parts are preformed by God: they are "divine automata" or "divine machines." [3]

This organismic conception is extended to embrace the universe as a whole. All monads act together like the parts of an organism, every one of which has its function to perform. Everything is causally related, but causation means no more than concomitant changes, a harmonious action of the parts, which has been predetermined by God. God, in other words, has arranged his universe in such a way that it works without interference from him: every state in every monad follows as the effect of the preceding state in that monad, and acts in unison with the states of all the other monads. There is complete harmony in the universe. Everything in nature can be explained *mechanically* in the sense that there is law, order, uniformity in the physical realm. But the plan of the whole points to a higher reason: God is the ultimate cause of all occurrence. "The source of mechanics lies in metaphysics," is the motto which Leibniz places at the head of his system.

We cannot demonstrate the necessity of the laws of nature, of motion; they are not necessary like the laws of logic, arithmetic, and geometry. Their existence depends on their utility, and this finds its ground in the wisdom of God. God has chosen them as ways of realizing his purpose, hence the world owes its existence to the purpose in the mind of God: God is the final cause, and uses secondary or efficient causes as means.

Here we have the promised reconciliation of mechanism and teleology. Nature can be explained without introducing the notion of purpose, but the mechanical philosophy leads us to God, for we cannot explain the universal principles of physics and mechanics without divine purpose

[2] *Op. cit.,* sec. 79.
[3] Cf. *op. cit.,* sec. 64.

Religion and reason are thus harmonized. There is also a harmony between the physical kingdom of nature and the moral kingdom of grace, which embraces all rational souls including God himself. The souls are copies of God, little divinities in their own spheres; man's reason is like God's reason in kind, though differing from it in degree. Man's purpose, too, agrees with that of God. Hence, we have a kingdom or union of spirits, a harmony of souls; a moral kingdom—a kingdom of grace, as Leibniz calls it—in contrast to the physical kingdom. But there is harmony between the two, between God the builder of the machine of the universe, and God the monarch of the divine spiritual kingdom.

Theology. Leibniz's theology is an integral part of his metaphysics. God is the highest monad, the monad of monads. His existence is proved in several ways. The principle of continuity demands a highest monad at the end of the series of forces. Moreover, in conformity with the principle of sufficient reason, a cause is needed to explain the monads themselves. The principle of sufficient reason is a generalized causal principle which asserts that, for everything which is real or true, there must be a sufficient reason why it is real or true. Finally, the order and harmony of nature call for a harmonizer; and here Leibniz advances the teleological or physico-theological proof. He thus employs a version of the causal argument for the existence of God, allied to but not identical with the cosmological argument. The cause of the world must be outside of it; it must also be one since the universe is one, and it must be rational because there is order in it. He presents another argument, which may be called an epistemological proof. There are eternal and necessary truths, the truths of logic and geometry, which presuppose an eternal intellect for their existence.

God and the monads are co-eternal. In his metaphysical discussions, as we have seen, Leibniz defines the monads as eternal substances, but adds that only a miracle could destroy a monad. In his theology, however, he declares that God created the monads and that God alone can destroy them. Sometimes he calls them "fulgurations" or manifestations of God, thus coming close to the pantheistic conception. But on the whole his theological position bears greater resemblance to theism than pantheism.

God as a monad is an individual, a person. But he transcends all monads, he is supernatural and superrational, the most perfect and most real being. Man cannot form a perfectly clear idea of God, because God is the highest monad and man is limited. Only a perfect mind could adequately know a perfect mind. Man, however, raises to the highest power the qualities which every monad possesses in a certain degree, and attributes to God omnipotence, omniscience, and absolute goodness. In this way we form a conception of God: he is superrational, but not contra-rational. Man also has obscure and confused ideas of God, a kind of longing or striving for God. There are, therefore, different stages of religion, corresponding to the different degrees of clearness with which the Deity is known.

God, being perfect, does not undergo change and development as do all other monads. He is complete in himself and his knowledge is complete; he sees all things whole and at a glance. He is reality fully realized. He created the world according to a plan, and chose this world as the best of all possible worlds. His choice was not groundless, but determined by the principle of goodness, that is, by moral necessity. He is also determined by logical necessity: the fundamental laws of thought are binding on him as well as on man.

But how shall we account for evil in the world according to this theory? The world is the best possible world, that is, the one in which there is at once the greatest possible variety and harmony. It is not perfect, however; God, in expressing his nature in finite forms could not avoid limitation and impediment. Such limitations are *metaphysical* evils; they result in pain and suffering, which Leibniz calls *physical* evil, and in sin or *moral* evil. Evil is a foil to goodness and beauty; like the dark shadows of a picture, it helps to bring out the good. Again, virtue gains strength in combating evil; evil is the spur that goads us to good action. All these arguments are traceable to the Stoics and the Neoplatonists, through whose influence they had become part of the Christian theology of the Middle Ages.

Ethics. Ethics is a rational science. There are certain moral principles native to the soul which cannot be demonstrated, but from which other moral truths necessarily follow. Moral principles operate unconsciously in us, as instincts, but we may become aware of them and express them as moral truths. Thus the truth that we ought to seek pleasure and avoid pain is based on the instinctive desire for happiness—a confused knowledge resting on inner experience. This principle can be enunciated as a moral truth, and from it other moral precepts can be deduced. Moral instincts guide men directly and without the need of deliberation, but not irresistibly, for they may be corrupted by the passions and by evil habits. The principle of justice is found even in savages and forms a part of their nature; it is so basic that even a band of robbers would have to obey it in order to preserve its unity. Although tradition, habit, and education help in developing the moral tendencies of the soul, they are ultimately rooted in human nature itself.

It is true that men do not always obey the inborn laws of morality; but this does not prove that they are ignorant of them. It is not an argument against the innateness of a moral principle to say that it is not recognized as such, nor is the public violation of such a law an argument against its validity; it is rather a proof of men's ignorance of the moral law. The fact is, these rules are not always clearly perceived, but need to be proved, just as the propositions of geometry require demonstration. Sustained attention and methodical reflection are necessary to bring them to the surface, and even scholars may not be fully conscious of them.

Mental life is, as we have found, essentially perception and appetite, that is, cognition and conation. The union of appetite and perception is called impulse or desire. Will is conscious impulse or striving, impulse guided by a clear idea. Hence, it is never an indifferent will, or caprice, but is always determined by an idea. Man is free in the sense that he is not determined from without—the monad has no windows by which anything can enter to compel it; he is, however, determined from within, by his own nature, impulses and ideas. Choice follows the strongest desire. To desire to be free to decide arbitrarily for one act but not another is to desire to be a fool. Leibniz is an ardent advocate of freedom of the will, but the freedom on which he so strongly insists is not the freedom of caprice or indeterminacy, but of the inner self-determination of the monad.

Logic and Theory of Knowledge. Leibniz's theory of knowledge rests on his metaphysical presuppositions. He accepts the rationalistic ideal of genuine knowledge as a system of universal and necessary truths based on principles, and not derived from experience. The universe is a mathematical-logical order which reason alone can decipher. Since the soul-monad is an independent being which no external cause can influence, knowledge cannot come to it from without, but must arise within the soul itself. The soul, therefore, cannot be an empty tablet upon which external nature writes its characters, as Locke had supposed. All our knowledge lies implicit in the mind—sensation and understanding alike; experience does not create it, but it is brought out, cleared up, made explicit by experience. Nothing can exist in the intellect that did not first exist in sensation—except, Leibniz adds, the intellect itself. But even if we disregard the monadic theory, he declares, it can be proved that knowledge does not come from the senses. If it did, universal knowledge would be impossible, for so-called empirical truths are without necessity, they are accidental propositions: we cannot assert that because something has happened, it must always happen in the same way. Universal and necessary propositions cannot be derived from the senses; they must have their seat and origin in the mind itself.

Locke had argued that there can be no such thing as innate or a priori knowledge, for, if there were, we would always have been conscious of it. Leibniz replies that this argument is valid only on the assumption that nothing could be native to the mind without the mind's being conscious of it. If the Cartesian identification of mental life with consciousness were legitimate, Locke's argument would no doubt be valid. But the mind is not always conscious of its ideas; Leibniz asserts the existence of "minute" perceptions—perceptions of which the mind is unconscious. May not innate ideas exist in the mind in this unconscious fashion? Leibniz finds other serious weaknesses in Locke's empirical theory of knowledge. The propositions derived from experience, or reached by induction, are wanting in universality and necessity; they do not yield certain knowledge: however numerous the examples of an occurrence may be, they do not prove that the event will always and necessarily take place. We possess knowledge which does not depend on the testimony of the senses: propositions that are universal and necessary, as, for example, the truths of mathematics. It is evident that the mind itself adds something in this case which the senses cannot furnish. Logic, metaphysics, ethics, theology, and jurisprudence abound in propositions which rest on principles having their origin nowhere but in the mind itself. To be sure, without sense experience we might never become conscious of such principles; our senses furnish the occasion for our perceiving them, but they do not produce or create them. Without basic principles there would be no science at all, but only a collection of factual details.

The final proof of necessary truths comes from the understanding alone, and the other truths are derived from experiences, or the observation of the senses. Our mind is capable of knowing both, but it is itself the source of the former. However numerous the particular experiences we have of a universal truth may be, we can never be absolutely sure of it by induction, unless we know its necessity through reason. . . . The senses can arouse, justify, and verify such truths, but not demonstrate their eternal and inevitable certitude.[4]

Such innate truths do not exist in the soul as conscious truths: "We cannot read off the eternal laws of reason as the edicts of the praetor are read off from the book, but we can discover them in ourselves by attending to them

---

[4] *New Essays on the Human Understanding,* Bk. I, ch. I, sec. 5.

when the senses offer us the occasion." Ideas and truths are innate as tendencies, predispositions, and natural potentialities, but not as actions, "although these potencies are always accompanied by certain, often insensible, actions, which respond to them." In this sense, arithmetic and geometry are potential in us; we can draw them out of ourselves without employing a single empirical truth. That such truths are discovered—as Locke had insisted—later than the ideas of which they consist, proves nothing against their originality; nor does the fact that we first learn the signs, then the ideas, and then the truths themselves. General principles—the principle of identity, for example—constitute the very life of our thinking; the mind depends on them every moment, although great attention may be required to become aware of them. We instinctively employ even the rules of logic in our natural reasoning, without being conscious of them. That there are also such innate principles in the field of ethics, we have already seen.

A bare faculty of receiving ideas is, therefore, a fiction. In the same way, the pure faculties or powers of the schoolmen are also fictions or abstractions. We never find a faculty anywhere that is shut up in itself, that does not do anything: the soul is always predisposed to act in one particular way rather than in another, i.e., it possesses definite tendencies. Experience is necessary to stir up the soul, but it cannot create ideas. The soul is not a piece of wax on which impressions are stamped; those who regard it thus, make a material entity of it. The empiricist objects that there is nothing in the intellect that did not previously exist in sensation. He is right, says Leibniz, only he should add—except the intellect itself. The soul contains within itself the categories of being, substance, unity, identity, cause, perception, reasoning, and quantity—concepts which the senses could never give us.

In this teaching, Leibniz aims to reconcile the differences between apriorism and empiricism, a task which was afterwards undertaken on a much larger scale by Kant. He also partly anticipates Kant in his conception of space as a form of the mind. Sense perception and intelligence are, as functions of the indivisible monad, identical in kind, but they differ in degree. Sensations are obscure and confused ideas, while the objects of the understanding are clear and distinct. Sense perception does not see things in their true reality, as they are in themselves, that is, as active spiritual substances or monads, but perceives them obscurely and confusedly as phenomena, as spatial. The coexistence of monads, which for clear conceptual thought is a harmonious order of spiritual substances, is perceived by sense perception as an extended phenomenal world. In other words, the perceiving subject sees and imagines the spiritual order in terms of space: "our ideas of space, figure, motion, rest," Leibniz tells us, "have their origin in the common sense, in the mind itself, for they are ideas of the pure understanding, which, however, have reference to the external world." [5] According to this view, the idea of space is native to the mind, as Kant later taught. Space is not real; it is a mere phenomenal appearance within a monad or system of monads.

Rational knowledge is possible only through innate principles, on which our valid reasonings are based. Among these are the principle of contradiction, which is the criterion of truth in the sphere of pure thought, and the principle of sufficient reason, which is the criterion of truth in the sphere of experience. The principle of sufficient reason has not merely a logical meaning for Leibniz—every judgment must have a ground or reason which proves its truth; it is a metaphysical principle as well—everything must have a sufficient reason for being. Reason denotes both logical grounds (*ratio cognoscendi*) and real ground (*ratio essendi*). On the principle of sufficient reason are based physics, ethics, metaphysics, and theology: "Unless we accept it, the proof of the existence of God and of many philosophical theories goes to pieces." The universe is a rational system in which nothing happens without a sufficient reason; it is conceived in analogy with a logical system in which the propositions are rationally related. The problem of philosophy is to discover the fundamental principles or presuppositions of knowledge, which are at the same time the fundamental principles of reality. There is the same necessity in the real universe as there is in a system of logic. Leibniz's logic influences his metaphysics. But his metaphysics in its turn influences his logic: we have already seen how his conception of knowledge as a development of principles immanent in the mind, rests on his idealistic monadology. His individualism does not follow as a necessary consequence from his logical conception of the universe; the existence of independent individuals cannot be justified to the logical reason. Leibniz, however, finds a teleological explanation for the existence of the individual: the production of individuals is a goal of the divine creative will, and finds its ultimate reason in the goodness and perfection of God. Moralistic value is here read into the logical ground of the universe; Leibniz

[5] Leibniz develops this point in "A Letter to Queen Charlotte of Prussia, 1702," trans. by Duncan in *Philosophical Works of Leibniz*, pp. 150 ff.

belongs to the great philosophical tradition which conceives of value as integral to reality.

Besides clear and distinct knowledge there is confused knowledge. Thus, for example, harmony and beauty are based on certain proportional relations. These may be clearly known by the scholar, but they need not be; they express themselves in a feeling of esthetic enjoyment, which is therefore an obscure perception of harmony or form. So, too, the soul may perceive the order of things, the harmony of the cosmos, without possessing a clear and distinct knowledge of it; in so doing, it has an obscure feeling of God, a confused knowledge which is capable of becoming clear.

55. SUCCESSORS OF LEIBNIZ

Christian Wolff. The Leibnizian philosophy is followed in Germany by a philosophy of common sense similar to that of the Scottish school of Reid. Leibniz was the first great German thinker of the modern period to attempt a metaphysical system, but nearly all of his writings consisted of letters and articles composed in French or Latin and published in various journals. It became the task of Christian Wolff (1679-1754), professor at Halle, to systematize the teachings of the master, to adapt them to common sense, and to present them in the German language. Wolff accepts the rationalism of Descartes, Spinoza, and Leibniz and identifies the method of philosophy with that of mathematics. At the same time, he holds that the facts of experience will agree with the deductions of reason: reason and sense perception are both legitimate faculties of knowledge. He adopts the Cartesian dualism of mind and matter, but like Leibniz, regards force as the essential attribute of body, and explains the apparent interaction between soul and body as a pre-established harmony. With Spinoza, he conceives the universe as an interrelated causal order, but at the same time retains the teleological interpretation of Leibniz. He likewise introduces the notion of development into his system.

Wolff divides the sciences into two groups, theoretical and practical, according to the two faculties of the soul, cognition and appetition; under the former he includes ontology, cosmology, psychology, and theology (all of which constitute metaphysics); under the latter, ethics, politics, and economics. The sciences are also classified as rational and empirical, according as their propositions are derived from reason or from experience (rational cosmology and empirical physics; rational psychology and empirical psychology, etc.). Logic forms the introduction to all the sciences.

Wolff wrote textbooks on all these subjects in German and Latin, which were used in the German universities for many years, and created many of the German philosophical terms in use today. Although he was lacking in originality and actually weakened Leibniz's philosophy, he gave an impetus to the study of philosophy in Germany, and contributed to the Enlightenment.

Among the followers of the Leibniz-Wolff school were A. Baumgarten (1714-1762), the founder of German esthetics and the first to use the term esthetics in its modern sense, and Kant during his early period. Wolff's philosophy developed into an eclectic movement, which sought to reconcile empiricism and rationalism and prepared the way for Kant's *Critique of Pure Reason.*

Mysticism and Romanticism. The rationalism of Leibniz and Wolff did not satisfy all thinkers; some who lacked faith in the competence of reason to arrive at truth were unwilling to join the ranks of the empiricists or skeptics. These men, the lineal descendants of the mystics, found the source of certainty in inner experience, in feeling and instinct; the highest truths cannot be demonstrated, but only felt. There was some suggestion in the teaching of Leibniz that feeling, craving, or impulse is but another stage of knowledge, an instinctive form of truth. Leibniz, however, regarded feeling as a lower, confused form of knowledge; the philosophers of faith or feeling discover in it a higher value: what the limited reason of man cannot fathom may be felt or divined in religious, esthetic, or moral feeling. Among those who display mystical or romantic tendencies we may mention J. G. Hamann (1730-1788), J. G. Herder (1744-1803), who criticizes Kant's *Critique of Pure Reason* in his *Metacritique,* and F. H. Jacobi (1743-1819), who opposes rationalistic metaphysics with a philosophy based on intuition.

XV

The Philosophy
of the Enlightenment

56. The Eighteenth Century

We have described the modern spirit as a spirit of revolt against medieval
society, its institutions and conceptions, and as the self-assertion of human
reason in the field of thought and action. The work begun by the Renaissance was continued in the sixteenth and seventeenth centuries; the Reformation, the Thirty Years' War, and the political and social revolutions in
England and in France were symptoms of the change. The great Continental systems of rationalism and English empiricism, with their various off-
shoots, added fuel to the flame which had produced them; and the spirit
of independent inquiry slowly but surely transformed the view of life. But
the new ideas had to be popularized and disseminated over larger areas,
and this task was performed during the eighteenth century, which has been
called the century of the Enlightenment: it represents the culmination of
the entire intellectual movement which we have been describing. It is an
age in possession of principles and world-views; full of confidence in the
power of the human mind to solve its problems, it seeks to understand and
to render intelligible human life—the State, religion, morality, language
—and the universe at large. It is an age of philosophical dogmas, an age
that has the courage to write books like Wolff's *Reasonable Thoughts on
God, the World, and the Soul of Man, also on All Things in General*. It is
the age of free and independent thought that speaks out its ideas boldly,
particularly in France, and fearlessly draws the consequences of its principles.

Philosophy in the eighteenth century not only mirrored the strivings of
the times, but influenced their action. It came out of the closet of the scholars,
and, as in the days of Socrates, mingled with the crowd in the market-place;

it no longer spoke a special language of its own—the language of the school-men—but expressed itself in the speech of the people and in terms intelligible to men of average intelligence. In France, owing to social, political, and ecclesiastical oppression, the Enlightenment found its most radical utterance, and here its influence was greatest: the Revolution was the result of the propagation of the new ideas. The respect for human reason and human rights which characterized nearly all the important modern philosophical doctrines, became universal in the eighteenth century, and the words humanity, good-will, natural rights, liberty, equality and brotherhood were on every tongue. Even the paternalistic governments regarded it as their function to contribute to the happiness and welfare of mankind. The revolt against medievalism culminated in the great social and political upheaval that marked the close of the century, and the old régime gave way to a new society. What the modern spirit had been demanding was in part achieved: liberty of conscience and worship, equal opportunity and economic freedom, representative government and equality of all individuals before the law.

Works on the Enlightenment

J. G. Hibben, *The Philosophy of the Enlightenment*, 1910; L. Lévy-Bruhl, *History of Modern Philosophy in France*, trans. by G. Coblence, 1899; F. Macdonald, *Studies in the France of Voltaire and Rousseau*, 1895; L. Stephen, *History of English Thought in the Eighteenth Century*, 1902; M. Whitcomb, *French Philosophers of the Eighteenth Century*, 1900; O. Ewald, *Die französische Aufklärungsphilosophie*, 1924; E. Cassirer, *Die Philosophie der Aufklärung*, 1932; I. O. Wade, *The Clandestine Organization and Diffusion of Philosophic Ideas in France from 1700-1750*, 1938; B. Willey, *The Eighteenth Century Background*, 1941.

Voltaire. Chief among those who helped to awaken the new spirit and to spread the new ideas in France, and indeed throughout Europe, were Voltaire (1694-1778) and Montesquieu (1685-1755), both of whom had visited England and were filled with admiration for English institutions. Voltaire, the brilliant and versatile propagandist of the Enlightenment, popularized and applied the Lockian ideas—which he had brought back with him from England together with Newton's natural philosophy and English deism—in his *Lettres sur les Anglais* (1728) a book which was burned by order of the censorship. He himself was a deist and never gave up his belief in God: "All nature cries out to us that he exists." In his earlier writings he also accepts the freedom of the will and the immortality of the soul, but later on he becomes skeptical with regard to life after death, and also inclines

to determinism: "When I can do what I will, I am free; but I will necessarily what I will." Throughout his life he ruthlessly attacked superstition
and ecclesiastical domination: revealed religion he regarded as the product
of ignorance and deceit, as the work of clever priests making use of human
stupidity and prejudice in order to rule over men. His own religion was
based on the immutable principles of morality, which, in his opinion, have
remained essentially the same in the teachings of philosophers. He com-
bated oppression of all kinds and fought for intellectual, political, and
religious liberty, for the freedom of the press, the freedom of elections, the
freedom of parliaments, and he demanded political rights for the third estate
or the *bourgeoisie,* which had grown prosperous in industry and trade.
And yet, in spite of all his liberalism, he was not an apostle of democracy;
he had no faith in the capacity of the lower classes for self-government:
"It seems necessary," he said, "that there should be an ignorant rabble;
when they begin to argue, everything is lost." The age of reason is not
intended to include "lackeys, cobblers, and hired girls" in its blessings.

Voltaire's thoughts, for the most part, express the spirit of Locke's philosophy—although the influence of Bayle's *Dictionary,* which affected nearly
all the intellectual leaders of France in the eighteenth century, must not
be overlooked. English ideas had a large share in liberalizing and revolution-
izing France. Among the men who assisted in developing and propagating
the English empirical philosophy were Condillac, Helvetius, Condorcet,
Cabanis, Volney, Bonnet, Destutt de Tracy, La Mettrie, Holbach, and,
especially, the Encyclopedists, led by Diderot and d'Alembert.

F. Macdonald, *Studies in the France of Voltaire and Rousseau,* 1895; J. Morley, *Voltaire,* 1923.

57. Progress of the Enlightenment

The Enlightenment in England. In England, the Enlightenment did not
reach its zenith within a comparatively short period, as it did in France;
nor did its influence express itself as spectacularly. The social conditions
were not the same, and there had been greater progress at an earlier period;
the new ideas and ideals had gradually found their way into the life of
the people. Nearly all the philosophers who based themselves on the Lockian
principles may be called illuminators. The deists, the moralists, Hume,
Hartley, Priestley, Erasmus Darwin, William Godwin, the author of *Political Justice* (1793), Thomas Paine, the author of *The Rights of Man*

(1791-92) and *The Age of Reason* (1794), all encouraged the progress of independent thought.

The German Enlightenment. In Germany the Leibniz-Wolffian metaphysics remained the dominant system until the middle of the eighteenth century, when English ideas began to exercise an influence through translations of the works of Locke, Hume, and the English moralists like Shaftesbury, Hutcheson, and Ferguson. The result was a combination of rationalism and empiricism, an eclecticism or common-sense philosophy that conceives the universe and human history as a rational, teleological order which can be made perfectly intelligible to reason because it is the expression of reason. Its task consists in "clearing up"—this is the literal meaning of *Aufklärung*— all mystery and banishing all superstition, in illuminating everything by the light of reason. It offers a natural or rational theology, undertaking to prove and make clear the fundamental doctrines common to all religions: the existence of God, the freedom of the will, and the immortality of the soul. We have already mentioned the leading figures of this movement in metaphysics. The same rationalistic method is applied to the study of history: language, law, the State, morality, religion owe their origin to human reason; language, for example, was invented by man to communicate his thoughts, the State was organized in order to insure his welfare. Since all these things are the work of reason, the ideal should be to make them more and more rational, to eliminate the irrational and accidental elements that have crept into them and corrupted them in the course of history. It was this rationalistic mode of thought that helped to transform the political theories in Germany and made popular the doctrines of equality and natural rights even in the courts of the rulers, teaching that social distinctions are contrary to nature and reason.

The *Aufklärung* even carries its standards of clearness and utility into the field of esthetics; poetry, sculpture, architecture and painting follow rationalistic models: Gellert's fables, as someone has said, are "moral philosophy in verse" and his religious hymns a "rational theology put into rhyme." Gottsched wrote a book on the *Art of Poetry* which shows how poetry must be written in order to serve as a means of enlightening and moralizing mankind.

This is the same movement which, a century before, had found its voice in England in the philosophy of Locke; now a reaction developed to it in the great leaders of literature and philosophy who made the last quarter of the eighteenth century the brightest period of German intellectual life.

Kant attacks the rational theology of the Enlightenment, Herder its rationalistic interpretations of history, Winckelmann and Lessing, Goethe and Schiller its rationalistic esthetics.

Materialism and Evolutionism. We have seen how the Cartesian philosophy led to an objective idealism in Malebranche, and how English empiricism became idealism in Berkeley. The same movements were also turned to materialistic account in the eighteenth century. Descartes had offered a mechanical explanation of the organic kingdom, conceiving the animal as a complete machine. This suggested the thought that man, too, is a machine, and that the soul is not a separate entity, but a function of the body. The attempt of Locke's successors—Condillac, Hartley, and others—to reduce all mental processes to sensations formed an easy transition to the view that such elementary states are merely effects of the brain. Leibniz reduced matter to force and conceived it as analogous to spiritual activity; others reversed the order and interpreted spiritual activity as physical force. And when the spiritual principles which filled the universe of the old Aristotelian metaphysics, were banished from nature by modern science and relegated to a separate world of their own by philosophy, is it at all surprising that some thinkers should have dispensed with them altogether and explained all phenomena as the results of matter in motion?

The materialistic world-view made headway in England and in France during the eighteenth century, and by the end of that period had become a popular doctrine in the enlightened circles of the latter country. According to John Toland (1670-1721), in one of his later writings (*Pantheisticon, 1720*), thought is a function of the brain, "a certain motion of the brain"; David Hartley (1704-1757) makes all mental processes depend on vibrations in the brain, which follow mechanical laws—psychological association being attended by physiological association—but does not reduce states of consciousness to motion. He is not sure whether the relation ought to be regarded as a causal one or not. Joseph Priestley, the discoverer of oxygen (1733-1804), however, identifies psychical processes with movements, thus boldly accepting the materialistic solution of the mind-body problem. Nevertheless, he does not deny the existence of God or the immortality of the soul; following Hobbes, he declares that there is nothing inconsistent with Christianity in the conception of the materiality of the human and the divine soul.

The Frenchman La Mettrie (1709-1751; *Histoire naturelle de l'âme, 1745, L'homme machine, 1748, L'homme plante, 1748*), who was influenced by both Descartes and Locke, bases his materialism on Descartes' mechanical explanation of the animal organism: if the animal is a machine, why not man? The materialistic theory is elaborated into a comprehensive system of metaphysics by the German Baron d'Holbach (d. 1789), in his *Système de la nature* (first published in London, 1770, under the pseudonym of Mirabaud). Everything is explained by matter and motion, as the effect of necessary laws. There is no soul; thought is a function of the brain; and matter alone is immortal. The human will is strictly determined; there is no design in nature or outside of nature, no teleology and no God.

Other advocates of materialism, though not always consistently and openly such, were: Denis Diderot (1713-1784, editor of the *Encyclopedia*) during the later period of his life; Cabanis (1757-1808), who is responsible for the crude materialistic analogy that thought is the function of the brain, as digestion is the function of the stomach, and the secretion of bile the function of the liver; and Destutt de Tracy (1754-1836). The French biologists Buffon (*Histoire naturelle,* 1749-1804) and Robinet (*De la nature,* 1761) accepted a modified form of materialism—hylozoism. Buffon assumes the existence of molecules endowed with life, and Robinet, who was influenced by Leibniz, gives sensation to every particle of matter. Evolutionary conceptions appear in the writings of many of the thinkers of the time, for example in La Mettrie's *L'homme plante* and *Le système d'Epicure,* 1748; in Diderot's *De la nature,* 1754, and Bonnet's *La palingénésie philosophique,* 1769. These men may be regarded as forerunners of Lamarck and Darwin.

However the thinkers of the French Enlightenment may differ in details, they agree that the phenomena of nature, be they physical or mental, are governed by law, that the mental and moral life of man is a necessary product of nature. From this standpoint, Helvetius (d. 1771) explains human morality, the economists Turgot and Condorcet (1743-1794) develop a philosophy of history, and Montesquieu (1689-1755; *Esprit des lois,* 1748) studies human laws and institutions.

D. Diderot, *Early Philosophical Works,* trans. by M. Jourdain, 1912; J. G. Hibben, *The Philosophy of the Enlightenment,* chap. V, 1910; L. Ducros, *Les Encyclopédistes,* 1900; H. Höffding, *History of Modern Philosophy,* Vol. I, Bk. V, 1900; J. B. Bury, *The Idea of Progress,* 1920; F. Lange, *History of Materialism,* 3rd ed., 1925; K. Martin, *French Liberal Thought in the Eighteenth Century,* 1929; J. Morley, *Diderot and the Encyclopedists,* 1914; C. Becker, *The Heavenly City of the Eighteenth-century Philosophers,* 1932; J. G. Frazer, *Condorcet on the Progress of the Human Mind,* 1933; E. Frankel, *The Faith of Reason,* 1948; M. Grossman, *The Philosophy of Helvetius,* 1926; G. V. Plekhanov, *Essays in the History of Materialism,* trans. by R. Fox, 1934.

Progress of the Sciences. The age of the Enlightenment did not confine itself, however, to the propagation of the general ideas which the preceding centuries had worked out; it devoted itself assiduously to the study of the sciences, both natural and mental. It has no reason to be ashamed of the men whom it produced in these fields: Euler, Lagrange, and Laplace in mathematics; Herschel and Laplace (*Mécanique céleste*) in astronomy; Galvani and Volta in physics; Lavoisier, Priestley, Davy, Haüy, and Berzelius in chemistry; Linné, Haller, Bichat, and C. F. Wolff in biology; Alexander von Humboldt, who was eminent in many sciences; Montesquieu in politics and jurisprudence; Quesnay, Turgot, and Adam Smith, the founders of the new economic theory; Baumgarten in esthetics; not to speak of the psychologists and moralists already enumerated.

Jean Jacques Rousseau. The Enlightenment glorified knowledge, the sciences and the arts, civilization and progress, and boasted of the achievements of the human race. Its pride and self-confidence were, however, rudely shaken by Jean Jacques Rousseau (1712-1778), who characterized the arts and sciences as fruits of luxury and indolence and the sources of moral decay. Man is by nature innocent and good; he possesses an impulse to preserve himself and to develop his capacities, but he is also prompted by sympathy for others and inspired by religious feeling, gratitude, and reverence. Morality and religion are not matters of reasoned thinking, but of natural feeling. Man's worth depends not on his intelligence, but on his moral nature, which consists essentially of feeling: the good will alone has absolute value. Rousseau emphasizes the importance of the sentiments in our mental life, and denies that the development of reason brings with it the perfection of man. Men are equal by nature; society, through the institution of property, has made them unequal, so that we now have masters and slaves, cultured and uncultured, rich and poor. Civilization, with its culture and the inequalities resulting from it, has corrupted our natural inclinations, producing the slavish and the lordly vices—servility, envy, hatred, on the one hand, contempt, arrogance, and cruelty on the other—and has made life artificial and mechanical. The origin of vices and virtues of mankind is sought in social and political institutions, and thus the only hope for the perfecting of man lies in the improvement of society.

Conception of Human Nature. Rousseau's romantic conception of human nature is perhaps his most distinctive, original, and influential achievement. In his two *Discourses* (*Discours sur les sciences et les arts,* 1750; *Discours sur l'origine et les fondements de l'inégalité parmi les hommes,* 1753) he portrayed in idyllic terms the original state of nature, and he pictured the life of the "noble savage" as one governed by free impulse, and one in which he displays pity and sympathy for his fellows. This representation of the state of nature contrasts strikingly with Hobbes' account of it as a "war of all against all." Rousseau presumably conceived of this state of nature too, not as an actual era in the history of mankind, but as a hypothetical state "which exists no longer, perhaps never existed, probably never will exist; and of which it is nevertheless necessary to have true ideas, in order to form a proper judgment of our present state."[1] It is a social and political fiction rather than an historical actuality, the function of which is to enable us to understand one aspect of human nature which is operative at all times. He departs from human nature as it is now constituted, analytically eliminates what is due to social intercourse and institutions, education, etc., and thereby isolates the natural and instinctive nature of man. The essential and distinctive feature of the state of nature is the dominant rôle played by immediate feeling; feeling is what men have in common beneath their diversities produced by intellectual activity, science, art, and the other artificialities of civilization. Emphasis on feeling, as opposed to intellect and its attendant cultural manifestations, is the core of Rousseau's romantic conception of human nature.

Rousseau's primitivism embodied in the injunction, "return to nature," is not a demand to return to nature in its naïveté and simplicity. Rousseau firmly believed that man cannot go back to nature in the sense of completely renouncing civilization with its attendant evils. It is rather an injunction to man, within the framework of civilized society, to remake himself by cultivating those feelings and sentiments which promote equality and social justice. His insistence that "man is naturally good, and only by institutions is he made bad," does not mean that man must abandon social institutions altogether—this he cannot do; he can, however, remold them in such a way as to realize a just and democratic society.

Political Philosophy. Rousseau substitutes for representative government direct government by the people. His political theory is the theory of the Swiss republican, as Locke's, which Voltaire followed, was that of the English constitutional monarchist. Among the people, Rousseau included not only the third estate, or the prosperous *bourgeoisie,* but the fourth estate, or the laboring and peasant class, to which he himself belonged and for which he demanded equal rights and deliverance from social bondage, as Voltaire had

[1] *Discourse on Inequality,* trans. by G. D. H. Cole, *The Social Contract and Discourses,* p. 155

demanded equal political rights and liberty of thought and conscience for the middle class. Rousseau takes the Lockian ideal of democracy seriously; if all men are created free and equal and have the same natural rights and capacities, there is no reason why they should be ruled or deprived of their inheritance by a privileged class, be it an aristocracy or an industrial *bourgeoisie*. It was Rousseau's ideas that found their way into the Declaration of the Rights of Man of 1789 and 1793.[2]

The return to nature can be accomplished only by the creation of natural social conditions and a natural method of education. (*Contrat social*, 1762, and *Emile*, 1762.) Natural society is based on a contract in which the individual surrenders his freedom for the liberty of citizenship, which is limited by the general will, or the moral will of the people. Freedom is obedience to self-imposed law. Sovereignty lies with the people; the general will—that is, the will of the people in so far as it aims at the common good—is the highest law. Rousseau's doctrine of the general will constitutes in large measure his solution to the problem of the corruption of man by society; his formula for amelioration of social evils requires the conformity of the individual will to the general will of society. The private interests of the individual frequently conflict with the common interest, but the individual finds his true freedom and satisfaction in obedience to that part of his will which he has as a citizen and which is conducive to the welfare of the society to which he belongs. In obeying that part of his will which is in conformity with the interests of society, the individual realizes his true freedom.

Educational philosophy. Rousseau's theory of education is a plea for natural education, for the free development of the child's natural and unspoiled impulses. Instruction should not begin until the desire for knowledge arises. Hence, education must be largely negative, consisting in the removal of unfavorable conditions, a task that requires the greatest care. The individuality of the child should be studied and nature assisted in distinguishing between good and bad impulses. It is wise, therefore, to isolate the child from its social environment in order that this development may follow its natural course under the guidance of private teachers. Rousseau's theory exercised great influence on modern education: Basedow, Pestalozzi, and Froebel are among those who have put it to the practical test.

[2] Article I of the Declaration of 1789 reads: "Men are born and remain free and equal in rights. Social distinctions can only be founded on social utility." Article VI: "The law is the expression of the general will. All citizens have a right to take part, personally or by their representatives, in its formation."

These educational ideas are compatible with Locke's empirical principles. If the soul is at birth an empty tablet, then men are by nature equal, and differences between them are the result of external influences, as Helvetius had already taught. Education and the social environment become the most important instruments for the perfection of the human race.

Rousseau, like Voltaire, combats materialism and atheism, accepting the tenets of natural religion; in this sense he is a deist. But with him religion is rooted in feeling, is a matter of the heart and not of the head, though its truths may be demonstrated by reason. The soul is immaterial, free, and immortal; a future life is made necessary by the triumph of evil in this life.

Rousseau's influence. Rousseau exercised a deep influence in Germany, on Kant, Herder, Goethe, and Schiller. Kant bears witness to the change produced in his thought by Rousseau's influence in the following passage: "I am myself an investigator by inclination, I feel the intensest craving for knowledge, and the eager impatience to advance in it, as well as satisfaction with every step of progress. There was a time when I believed that all this might redound to the glory of mankind; and I despised the ignorant rabble. Rousseau has set me right. The boasted superiority has vanished; I am learning to respect mankind, and I should regard myself as of much less use than the common laborer if I did not believe that this reflection could give value to all other occupations, that is, re-establish the rights of mankind."[3]

English translations of Rousseau's writings: *The Social Contract,* trans. by H. J. Tozer, 1924; *The Political Writings of Rousseau,* ed. by C. E. Vaughan, 1915; *Selections,* ed. by C. Gauss, 1920; *The Confessions,* ed. by E. Wilson, 1923.

F. Macdonald, *Jean Jacques Rousseau,* 1906; I. Babbitt, *Rousseau and Romanticism,* 1919; A. F. Amiel, *Jean Jacques Rousseau,* trans. by V. W. Brooks, 1922; J. Morley, *Rousseau and his Era,* 1923; E. H. Wright, *The Meaning of Rousseau,* 1929; H. Höffding, *Rousseau and His Philosophy,* 1930; J. Charpentier, *Rousseau, the Child of Nature,* 1931; M. Josephson, *Rousseau and his Philosophy,* 1931; A. Cobban, *Rousseau and the Modern State,* 1934; C. W. Hendel, *Jean Jacques Rousseau, Moralist,* 1934; R. Rolland, *The Living Thoughts of Rousseau,* 1939; A. O. Lovejoy, "The Supposed Primitivism of Rousseau" in *Essays in the History of Ideas,* 1948; E. Cassirer, *The Question of Jean-Jacques Rousseau,* trans. by P. Gay, 1954; J. W. Chapman, *Rousseau—Totalitarian or Liberal?,* 1956.

---

[3] G. Hartenstein, *Kant's Werke,* 2nd ed., Vol. VIII, p. 642.

XVI
The Critical Philosophy of Immanuel Kant

58. IMMANUEL KANT

Immanuel Kant was born in Königsberg, 1724, the son of a saddler, and was reared in religious surroundings, his parents being pietists. Nearly his entire life as student, teacher, and writer was spent within the boundaries of his native city. At the Collegium Fredericianum, where he prepared for the university (1732-1740), he was chiefly interested in the Roman classics; at the University of Königsberg he studied physics, mathematics, philosophy, and theology (1740-1746). From 1746 to 1755 he served as tutor in several families residing in the neighborhood of Königsberg; in 1755 he received an appointment as special lecturer (*privat docent*) at the University and lectured on mathematics, physics, logic, metaphysics, ethics, physical geography, anthropology, natural theology, and "philosophical encyclopedia." From 1766 to 1772 he combined with this position the post of assistant librarian of the Royal Library. In 1770 Kant became professor of logic and metaphysics, a position which he held until 1797, when his feeble physical condition made it necessary for him to retire. He died in 1804.

During his earlier years Kant followed the Leibniz-Wolffian philosophy, which dominated the German universities and had become popular even outside academic circles. From 1760 to 1770 he came under the influence of English empiricism; Locke and Shaftesbury, and then Hume, made a great impression on him; it was the latter who, as he himself said, "aroused him from his dogmatic slumbers." By the year 1770 he had reached the philosophical standpoint for which he is noted, and presented it in a Latin dissertation, *De mundi sensibilis atque intelligibilis forma et principiis;* the next ten years he spent in working it out. His master-work, *Kritik der reinen Vernunft,* appeared in 1781 (2nd revised edition, 1787) and was followed by *Prolegomena zu einer jeden zukünftigen Metaphysik* (1783), *Grundlegung zur Metaphysik der Sitten* (1785), *Metaphysische Anfangsgründe der Naturwissenschaft* (1786), *Kritik der praktischen Vernunft* (1788), *Kritik der Urtheilskraft* (1790), *Die Religion innerhalb der Grenzen der blossen Vernunft* (1793), *Metaphysik der Sitten* (containing his philosophy of law), 1797, and *Zum ewigen Frieden* (1795). *Über die Pedagogik* was published in 1803.

Works on Kant and German Idealism

Translations: *Critique of Pure Reason,* by M. Müller, 1881; by N. Kemp Smith, 1929; *Inaugural Dissertation of 1770,* by J. Handyside, 1929; *Prolegomena,* by E. B. Bax, 1891; by Mahaffy and Bernard, 1889; by P. Carus, 1933; *Foundations of Metaphysics of Morals, Critique of Practical Reason,* parts of *Metaphysics of Morals,* by T. K. Abbott in *Kant's Theory of Ethics,* 4th ed., 1889; *Critique of Practical Reason and Other Writings in Moral Philosophy,* by L. W. Beck, 1949; *Cosmogony,* by W. Hastie, 1900; *Critique of Judgment,* by J. H. Bernard, 1931, and by J. C. Meredith, 2 vols., 1911 and 1928; *Philosophy of Law, Principles of Politics,* and *Perpetual Peace,* by W. Hastie, 1887; *Perpetual Peace,* by H. C. Smith, 1915; *Religion within the Limits of Reason Alone,* by T. M. Greene and H. Hudson, 1934; *Dreams of Spirit-Seer,* by E. F. Goerwitz and ed. by F. Sewall, 1900; *On Philosophy in General,* 1935; J. Watson, *The Philosophy of Kant,* 1908 (selections from Kant's writings); *An Introducton to Kant's Critical Philosophy,* by G. T. Whitney and P. H. Fogel (contains a paraphrase of *The Critique of Pure Reason*), 1914; T. M. Greene, *Kant: Selections,* 1929. Quotations from the *Critique of Pure Reason* in our account are taken from either the Müller or the Kemp Smith translation.

F. Paulsen, *Immanuel Kant,* trans. by J. E. Creighton and A. Lefèvre, 1902; R. M. Wenley, *Kant and His Revolution,* 1911; W. Wallace, *Kant,* 1882; J. Watson, *Philosophy of Kant Explained,* 1902; E. Caird, *The Critical Philosophy of Kant,* 2 vols., 1889, 2nd ed., 1909; H. A. Prichard, *Kant's Theory of Knowledge,* 1909; H. Cohen, *Kants Theorie der Erfahrung,* 1871; H. Vaihinger, *Kommentar zu Kants Kritik der reinen Vernunft,* 2 vols., 1892; F. Adler, "Critique of Kant's Ethics," in *Essays in Honor of W. James,* 1908; J. G. Schurman, *Kantian Ethics and the Ethics of Evolution,* 1882; E. Pfleiderer, *Kantischer Kritizismus und englische Philosophie,* 1881; A. O. Lovejoy, "Kant and the English Platonists," in *Essays in Honor of W. James,* 1908; H. Cohen, *Kommentar zu Immanuel Kants Kritik der reinen Vernunft,* 1907; N. K. Smith, *A Commentary to Kant's Critique of Pure Reason,* 1918; J. Ward, *A Study of Kant,* 1922; K. Vorländer, *Immanuel Kant,* 1924; A. C. Ewing, *Kant's Treatment of Causality,* 1924; E. M. Miller, *The Basis of Freedom: A Study of Kant's Theory,* 1924; M. Wundt, *Kant als Metaphysiker,* 1924; J. W. Scott, *Kant on the Moral Life: an Exposition of Kant's "Grundlegung,"* 1924; E. Boutroux, *La philosophie de Kant,* 1926; J. H. W. Brindley, *A Comparison of Kant's Idealism with That of Berkeley,* 1929; N. Clark, *An Introduction to Kant's Philosophy,* 1925; F. E. England, *Kant's Conception of God,* 1929; C. B. Garnett, Jr., *The Kantian Philosophy of Space,* 1939; A. D. Lindsay, *Kant,* 1934; A. C. Ewing, *A Short Commentary on Kant's "Critique of Pure Reason,"* 1938; H. J. Paton, *Kant's Metaphysic of Experience,* 2 vols., 1936, and *The Categorical Imperative: A Study of Kant's Moral Philosophy,* 1948; G. T. Whitney and D. F. Bowers, *The Heritage of Kant,* 1939; I. D. Weldon, *Introduction to Kant's "Critique of Pure Reason,"* 1945.

Works on idealistic movement in Germany: J. Royce, *Spirit of Modern Philosophy,* 1892; E. Pfleiderer, *Development of Rational Theology in Germany Since Kant,* 1890; A. C. H. Drews, *Deutsche Spekulation seit Kant,* 1895; R. Kroner, *Von Kant bis Hegel,* 1921-24; A. S. Pringle-Pattison, *From Kant to Hegel,* 1924; E. Stabler, *George Berkeley's Auffassung und Wirkung in der deutschen Philosophie bis Hegel,* 1935; F. Holzheimer,

Der logische Gedanke von Kant bis Hegel, 1936; I. Knox, *Aesthetic Theories of Kant, Hegel, and Schopenhauer*, 1936.

Kant's Heritage from His Predecessors. Modern philosophy began with faith in the power of the human mind to attain knowledge; the only questions at issue were: by what method can it be attained and how far do its limits extend? Empiricists and rationalists alike conceived genuine knowledge as universal and necessary, and nearly all of them down to Hume declared that self-evident propositions were possible in some fields. Descartes, Hobbes, Spinoza, and Leibniz constructed systems of metaphysics which they deemed to be as valid logically as the Euclidean geometry. Bacon did not offer a universal theory, for that was an enterprise that could not be undertaken until the facts had been established by the new method; but he held that the existence of God could be demonstrated and the eternal essences of things or laws of nature discovered. Nevertheless, doubts began to arise concerning the competence of the human intelligence to solve ultimate problems, or even problems of lesser scope. At times, metaphysics and theology seemed to Bacon to transcend the powers of natural reason. Hobbes betrayed occasional misgivings with respect to the possibility of a genuine science of physics based on his recognition that sensation, which is the sole source of our knowledge, cannot yield certainty. Locke, too, saw the necessity of examining the problem of knowledge more thoroughly than had hitherto been attempted, and reached the conclusion that we possess certain knowledge of the agreement and disagreement of our ideas, certain knowledge of our own existence and of the existence of God, and that mathematics and ethics are secure. But we have no such knowledge, he held, of the existence of an external world and of the necessary connection of the qualities of things: true knowledge is out of the question in natural science. Berkeley declares that there is no external material world to know, but that we know ideas, spirits, and relations between ideas. Bayle plays havoc with theological and metaphysical doctrines, holding them to be not only beyond reason but contrary to reason. Hume draws what appear to him to be the consequences of the empirical view of knowledge: if we can know only what we experience in sensation and reflection, then rational theology, rational cosmology, and rational psychology are impossible, and knowledge of God, world, and soul is beyond our ken. Indeed, even our knowledge of matters of fact can yield nothing but probability; we have no knowledge of necessary connection, no knowledge of substance or of a self; we cannot even say that our ideas *necessarily* follow the order in which we experience them, and which we *believe* they will repeat. We can attain "a kind of demonstrative knowledge" by comparing our ideas, noting their relations, and reasoning about the relations; and nothing more.

The spirit of criticism which had undermined authority and tradition and enthroned reason was now bringing reason itself to the bar and denying reason's authority. It was not the empiricists alone, however, who were weighing rationalism in the balance and finding it wanting; protests against its supposed pretensions and results also came from the camp of the mystics and faith-philosophers, who distrusted the deliverances of the intellect and sought in other phases or functions of the human soul a means of stilling the longing for certainty. According to them, the discursive understanding can never pierce the covering of reality; truth has its source in feeling, faith, or mystical vision of some sort; the deepest realities cannot be conceived by reason, but only felt by the heart. What particularly provoked such anti-rationalistic outbursts as these in the modern era was the mechanistic and deterministic world-view to which scientific or rationalistic thinking seemed inevitably to lead and which degraded the individual to the rôle of a marionette. To many minds the unaided natural intelligence appeared to end either in a hopeless and cheerless skepticism, or in a tragic fatalism that mocked humanity's deepest yearnings and rendered fictitious its most precious values.

Kant's Problem. To the intellect's destructive criticism of its own competence and the will's demand for the recognition of its moral and religious values, philosophy was now compelled to make some answer. This task was assumed by Kant, who sought to do justice to the various currents of his age, to the Enlightenment, empiricism, skepticism, and mysticism; his problem was, as one of his contemporaries put it, "to limit Hume's skepticism on the one hand, and the old dogmatism on the other, and to refute and destroy materialism, fatalism, atheism, as well as sentimentalism and superstition." He himself had come from the rationalistic school of Wolff, but had also been attracted to English empiricism and Rousseau, and Hume had "aroused him from his dogmatic slumbers." He sees the pressing need of an examination or criticism of human reason, of a tribunal, as it were, that shall secure the just claims of reason and dismiss all its groundless claims—of a theory of knowledge, in other words, that shall investigate the possibility or impossibility of universal and necessary knowledge, its sources, extent, and boundaries. Philosophy, he thinks, has hitherto been dogmatic: it has proceeded without previous criticism of its own powers. It must now become critical, or enter upon an impartial examination of the faculty of reason in general; with this end in view Kant writes his three *Critiques:* the *Critique of Pure Reason,* an examination of theoretical reason or science; the *Critique of Practical Reason,* an examination of practical reason or morality; and the *Critique of Judgment,* an examination of our esthetic and teleological judgments, or purposiveness in art and in nature.

Genuine knowledge Kant defines as universal and necessary knowledge. He agrees with the rationalists that there is such knowledge, but only of the basic assumptions of the sciences of physics and mathematics; a speculative or rational metaphysics embracing cosmology, theology, and psychology is impossible. With the empiricists he agrees that we can know only what we can experience, that sensation provides the matter of our knowledge. He agrees with both the rationalists and the empiricists that universal and necessary truth cannot be derived from experience. Kant's view is that the senses furnish the materials of our knowledge, and the mind arranges them in ways made necessary by its own nature. Hence, we have universal and necessary knowledge of the order of ideas, though not of things-in-themselves. The contents of our knowledge are derived from experience (empiricism), but the mind *thinks* its experiences, *conceives* them according to its native a priori, that is, rational, ways (rationalism). Nevertheless, things-in-themselves exist; we can *think* them, but not *know* them as we know the facts of the empirical world. If it were not for the moral consciousness or practical reason, the questions concerning the existence of a world beyond the causal order in space and time, including questions concerning God, freedom, and immortality, would be left unanswered, indeed, could not even be meaningfully broached.

The Problem of Knowledge. The fundamental problem for Kant is the problem of knowledge: What is knowledge, and how is it possible? What are the boundaries of human reason? In order to answer these questions, we must examine human reason, or subject it to criticism. Knowledge always appears in the form of judgments in which something is affirmed or denied. But not every judgment is knowledge; in an analytical judgment the predicate merely elucidates what is already contained in the subject: e.g., Body is an extended thing. If it is to qualify as knowledge, a judgment must be synthetic; that is, we must add something to the predicate, extend our knowledge, not merely elucidate it: e.g., All bodies have specific gravity. Not all synthetic judgments, however, give us genuine knowledge; some are derived from experience. They inform us, for example, that an object has such and such properties or behaves thus or so, but not that it must have these qualities, or behave so. In other words, such judgments are lacking in *necessity:* reason does not compel their acceptance, as it compels the acceptance of a mathematical proposition. Again, they are lacking in *universality:* we cannot say because some objects of a class have certain qualities, that all have them. Judgments lacking in universality and necessity, or a posteriori judgments, are not scientific. To be knowledge, a synthetic judgment must be necessary, and it must be universal, i.e., admit of no exceptions. Universality and necessity have their source not in sensation or perception, but in reason, in the understanding itself; we know without experience—and in this sense prior to it—that the sum of the angles of a triangle must be equal to two right angles and that it will always be so.

Kant's claim, then, is that knowledge consists of synthetic a priori judgments. Analytic judgments are always a priori; we know without going to experience that all extended things are extended; such judgments are based on the principle of contradiction alone. But they do not add to our knowledge. Synthetic a posteriori judgments add to our knowledge, but are not sure; the knowledge they yield is uncertain and problematic. We demand apodictic certainty in our sciences, and such certainty is possessed only by synthetic a priori judgments.

That there are such judgments Kant never doubted for a moment: we find them in the basic principles of physics, and in mathematics; as regards the existence of such knowledge in metaphysics, Kant has serious reservations which we shall discuss later. He accepts the existence of universal and necessary knowledge as an established fact, hence he does not ask whether synthetic a priori judgments are possible, but only how they are possible. What are the conditions of such knowledge, what does the existence of such judgments logically presuppose or necessarily imply? Kant's critical method is, at least, in one of its phases dogmatic: the theory of knowledge is, as he says himself, a strictly demonstrable science, an a priori or pure science, one that bases its truths on necessary principles a priori. His method is not psychological, but logical or transcendental: he does not tell us to examine the conditions of knowledge in our own consciousness—how it arises psychologically—but to take real knowledge, such as the propositions of mathematics or the principles of physics, and to ask ourselves what the existence of such propositions logically presupposes. What, for example, follows necessarily from the fact that there can be judgments at all, or judgments concerning space relations, or judgments affirming causal relations? There can be no synthetic judgment without a synthetic mind, no spatial judgment

without a space-perceiving mind, no causal judgment without a mind thinking in terms of cause and effect. In employing this method Kant is, of course,
employing human reason with all its categories; he is taking for granted the
possibility and validity of knowledge—that is, he is a dogmatist; but this does
not disturb him, since it would be a "scandal," as he declares, if Hume were
right in denying the possibility of knowledge. We should simply never get
anywhere if the competence of reason to examine itself had to be established
before reason could undertake this task.

The problem, then, is: How are synthetic judgments a priori possible in
mathematics, in the foundations of physics, or, How are pure mathematics
and pure physics possible? The parallel question regarding metaphysical
knowledge cannot be asked in quite this same form because Kant holds
metaphysics suspect. His problem is to show how and why we can have
genuine knowledge in the scientific fields. In order to answer these questions,
we must examine the organ of knowledge; we must consider its powers, its
functions, its possibilities, its limitations. Knowledge presupposes a mind.
Moreover, we cannot think without having something to think about, and
we can have no object of thought unless it is given through the senses, unless the mind is receptive or has sensibility. Sensibility furnishes us with the
sense qualities which are constituents of perceptual objects. These perceptual
objects must also be thought, understood, or conceived by the understanding—the concepts of the understanding play their indispensable rôle in
knowledge. Knowledge would be impossible without the cooperation of
sensation and perception on the one hand, and thinking or understanding
on the other. These two preconditions of knowledge are fundamentally different, but supplement each other. "Percepts and concepts constitute the
elements of all our knowledge." Percepts without concepts are blind, concepts without percepts are empty. All that the intellect can do is to elaborate
what is given by sensibility.

The question, then, How is knowledge possible? divides into two questions: How is sense perception possible? and, How is understanding possible? The first question is answered in the *Transcendental Aesthetic* (doctrine of the faculty of perception), the second in the *Transcendental Analytic* (doctrine of concepts and judgments).

The Transcendental Method. Kant's formulation of the transcendental
method is perhaps the first attempt in modern philosophy to devise a distinctively philosophical method. Bacon, Hobbes, Descartes, and Leibniz before
him were enthusiastic methodologists, but they were satisfied to adapt to phi-

losophy methods already achieved by the special sciences, rather than to invent new and unique methods of philosophical inquiry. Thus Bacon espoused for philosophy the inductive method of the natural sciences; Hobbes and Descartes both advocated the mathematical method, although each conceived it very differently; and Leibniz's philosophy employs a combined inductive-mathematical method. Since Kant it has become the fashion among philosophers to invent new philosophical methods which shall be appropriate to the peculiar subject-matter of philosophy. Witness the antithetical method of Fichte, the intuitional method of Schelling and Bergson, the dialectical method of Hegel. Kant's claim to have devised a new technique of philosophical inquiry is usually implicit rather than explicit, but there can be no doubt about Kant's pretensions in the matter. In a characteristic passage, he makes it clear that the method of the transcendental philosophy is a "peculiar" method and not the mere revamping of the prevailing methods of the sciences.

The argument from experience to its necessary presuppositions is the crux of the transcendental method, and at this point Kant's procedure diverges widely from that of traditional empiricists. Empiricism proceeds *inductively* from experiential facts to hypotheses and generalizations grounded in those facts; whereas Kant argues demonstrably from the facts to the necessary conditions of their possibility. The empiricist appeals to the factuality of experience, Kant to its essential nature; the empiricist reasons inductively, Kant demonstrably. This is the full import of Kant's statement in the *Introduction* to the second edition, that ". . . although all our knowledge begins with experience it does not follow that it arises out of experience."

Kant's presuppositional argument concentrates attention upon the pervasive, formal features of experience, namely, space and time and the categories; for the transcendental method has no application whatsoever to the matter of experience, the *sense qualia*. The critical problem is: What are the necessary conditions of the very possibility of an experience, the formal features of which are space, time, and the categories? Kant's reply to this question is: Experience is possible only on the assumption that the formal features found *in* experience are a priori conditions *of* experience.

Preliminary Analysis of Experience. The starting-point of the critical investigation is experience. The opening sentence of the *Introduction* to the *Critique of Pure Reason* in the second edition reads: "There can be no doubt that all knowledge begins with experience." Experience is, to be sure, a notoriously ambiguous term for Kant and his idealistic successors, but in the present context its meaning is clear enough. It denotes any phenomenal object or system of such objects. The experience which is the point of departure of Kant's transcendental procedure is not a collection of atomistic impressions but rather a perceptual (or introspective) object, having relational and structural organization in addition to qualitative constituents. Kant's empiricism is a "radical empiricism," precisely in William James' sense, for it finds in experience relations as well as the bare sense qualia. The experience which is subjected to analysis is the system of physical objects—and presumably also individual minds—as cognitively apprehended.

The analysis of experience proceeds in accordance with the traditional distinction between matter and form. Kant here as elsewhere appropriates quite uncritically distinctions and classifications of traditional logic and metaphysics; nor does he trouble to state the general criteria by which the formal and material ingredients of experience are to be discriminated. Form apparently embraces everything structural and relational in experience; matter pertains to the qualia subsumed under the forms. Form is a principle of unity in experience; matter a principle of manifoldness or multiplicity. "That in the appearance which corresponds to sensation I term its *matter;* but that which so determines the manifold of appearance that it allows of being ordered in certain relations I term the form of appearance." The distinction, although not very precisely drawn at the outset, becomes progressively clear as the analysis proceeds.

Any object of experience may be analyzed into three constituents: (1) discrete qualia—the "impressions" of Hume's analysis, (2) the spatial and temporal continua—the so-called "forms of intuition," and (3) the pure concepts or categories. This analysis, which underlies the whole critical procedure is given in the "Transcendental Esthetic," where Kant indicates that his purpose is to "isolate" ingredient (2) from ingredients (1) and (3). "In the transcendental esthetic we shall, therefore, first *isolate* sensibility, by taking away from it everything which the understanding thinks through its concepts. . . . Secondly, we shall separate off from it everything which belongs to sensation, so that nothing may remain save pure intuition. . . . In the course of this investigation it will be found that there are two pure forms of sensible intuition . . . namely, space and time." Under item (1) are embraced all *material* ingredients of our experience—the external sense qualia such as colors, sounds, tastes, etc., as well as the qualia of the inner sense—emotional, volitional, and hedonic data. Items (2) and (3) together constitute the sole *formal* ingredients of experience, and it is with them that the transcendental method deals. The initial analysis of experience into its three component factors is purely *de facto,* that is to say, it involves nothing more than a direct scrutiny of the phenomenally given and the reporting of the several ingredients which it is found to contain. There is at this stage of the argument no pretension to an a priori or demonstrative proof of the correctness and exhaustiveness of the analysis. Kant's attitude seems to be: "I find these and no other ingredients in experience."

The foregoing analysis was devised primarily for perceptual or extrospective experience, but Kant unquestionably intended it to apply equally to introspective experience, and presumably also to the apprehension of other minds—a type of experience to which he gives scant attention. If I examine any perceived object or an imaginative reproduction of a perception, I can differentiate the following: the sense qualia, such as colors, sounds, tastes, etc., the spatio-temporal characteristics and relations, including shape, size, motion, etc., and the "categorial" features, including substance, causality, and the rest. A corresponding analysis may be given for the introspective experience of individual minds. On the side of matter there are the sense qualia which, as presentations, are members of the conscious series; moreover there are certain hedonic, emotional, and volitional items peculiar to the conscious series. On the formal side, time is the peculiar form of conscious processes and the categories are no less applicable to empirical consciousness than to physical objects. Kant's entire philosophical procedure could have departed either from the introspected self or from the perceived object; his preference for the latter is dictated solely by convenience.

The preliminary analysis of experience, like all intellectual analyses, is, of course, abstractive and not real. The "isolation" and "separation" of the components of experience, described in the passage quoted above, is only an ideal or imaginative separation. The three factors may—indeed, according to Kant, they do—differ in nature, origin, and function but, in the experience from which philosophical analysis departs, they are completely fused. The analysis, although ideal, is significant because it focuses attention upon real constituents of experience which are disparate both as regards origin and character.

Kant's initial analysis of experience—regardless of the success or failure of any subsequent constructions resting upon it—is a truly significant contribution to the empirical and phenomenological traditions in philosophy. Kant is as insistent as Locke or Hume that perceptual and introspective experience afford the only possible starting-point for philosophical construction and interpretation. He, too, is aware that rationalistic systems which profess to begin with self-evident principles derive whatever truth they possess from empirical generalizations, which are the more dangerous because they are hastily drawn and rest on concealed and inconclusive evidence. But Kant's empiricism is more radical and hence more adequate than even that of Hume: the latter dissolved experience into discrete and atomistic impressions; the former discerned the relational and structural features of every genuine experience. He saw that the atomistic impressions—though real constituents of experience—are mere abstractions when taken out of their structural context. Kant's analysis of experience thus has the virtues of comprehensiveness and completeness, not, as Kant claimed, an absolute and demonstrable completeness, but the completeness attainable by a remarkably discerning and circumspect analyst. Kant, at times, proceeds on the assumption that his initial analysis of experience is exhaustive; but this is, of course, a perfectly gratuitous assumption since no observer, however competent and circumspect, can be certain that some essential ingredient of experience may not have eluded him.[1]

The Theory of Sense Perception. Let us take up, first, the "Transcendental Esthetic." What are the logical preconditions of the faculty of sensibility or of sense perception? In order to perceive, we must have sensations—color, sound, hardness, etc. But mere sensation would not be knowledge; it would be a mere modification of consciousness, a mere change occurring in consciousness, a mere subjective state produced in us by something else. Every sensation must be referred to space and time; it must have a definite place in space and date in time in relation to other sensations, it must be apprehended in a definite spatial order and arrangement and come before or after or at the same time as other sensations. Perception can be analyzed into sensations, constituting the matter or content of experience, and space and time, constituting the form of experience. Sensations, including color, sound and weight, etc., furnish the raw material which is arranged within the framework provided by the forms of space and time. The formal and material elements together constitute percepts. The mind not only receives sensations, but by virtue of its faculty of intuition (from *intueri:* to look at, envisage) perceives them: it sees the color, hears the sound outside of itself in a spatio-temporal order. The mind possesses power to perceive space and time a priori; indeed, it is so constituted that it intuits pure space and time; it not

---

[1] The two above subsections and the one below entitled "The Unity of Self-consciousness" are largely excerpts from an essay by Ledger Wood, originally published in *The Heritage of Kant,* ed. by G. T. Whitney and D. F. Bowers, 1939. They are reproduced here with the permission of the Princeton University Press.

only perceives objects in space and time but space and time themselves. In this sense, we may speak of *pure* perception.

The functions or forms of arranging sensations in space and time cannot themselves be sensations. They are not empirical or a posteriori forms of intuition, but are inherent in the very nature of the mind—a priori. Time is the form of the inner sense: that is, our psychic states cannot be apprehended otherwise than as following one another in temporal succession; while space is the form of the outer sense: we must apprehend spatially that which affects our sense organs. But since everything given or presented to sense is a modification of consciousness and so belongs to the inner sense, time is a necessary condition of all our representations, whether of the inner or outer sense.

Space and time are not realities or things existing for themselves, nor are they qualities or relations belonging to things as such. They are ways our sensibility has of apprehending objects, they are forms or functions of the senses; if there were no beings in the world endowed with the intuition or perception of space and time, the world would cease to be spatial and temporal. "Take away the thinking subject and the entire corporeal world will vanish, for it is nothing but the appearance in the sensibility of our subject." We can never imagine that there is no space, although we can conceive that it contains no objects. That is, we are compelled to perceive and imagine in terms of space. Space is a necessary precondition of phenomena and hence a necessary a priori idea. This is an example of Kant's philosophical method —the transcendental method described above. We cannot think things without space, though we can think space without things; hence space is the necessary precondition of our perception of things, or of the phenomenal world. Whatever is a necessary precondition must be an a priori form of the mind. The same line of argument applies to time.

The question, then, How is pure mathematics possible? is answered: we have genuine knowledge, or synthetic judgments a priori in mathematics, because the mind has space and time forms, because it is by its nature compelled to perceive and imagine in spatial and temporal ways.

But it must be remembered that space and time are merely conditions of sensibility, forms of sense perception, ways we have of perceiving things; hence they have validity only when applied to perceived things, to appearances or phenomena, not when applied to things-in-themselves or to things independent of our perception of them. We cannot apply them beyond the world of our experience. But this restriction need not disturb us, since the certainty of our experiential knowledge is left untouched; knowledge is secure whether space and time inhere in things-in-themselves or are merely

the necessary forms of our perception of things. The things we perceive are
not things-in-themselves—though we commonly regard them as such—nor
are the relations we perceive the relations of things-in-themselves. If we
took away the subject, and its faculty of sensibility, all the spatio-temporal
properties and relations of things, and even space and time themselves would
disappear; they could no longer exist completely divorced from a perceiving
subject. What things-in-themselves are apart from our sensibility, what it
is that causes sensations in us, we simply do not know. Colors, sounds, tastes,
odors are all sensations in us; what the thing-in-itself (*das Ding an sich*) is
apart from the sensations produced in consciousness, we do not know. We
know only our peculiar way of perceiving things, a way that may not be
necessary for all creatures, though it is necessary for man. In this sense,
space and time are subjective or ideal. They are real or objective, however,
in the sense that all phenomena are arranged in a spatial and a temporal
order: no object can ever be given to us in experience that does not come
under the condition of time; and all objects as external phenomena will always be coexistent in space.

To sum up: Real knowledge, such as we human beings have, requires
sense qualities and the forms of space and time. The mind must have something presented to it, it must be capable of being affected, or of receiving
impressions. But if we merely received impressions or experienced modifications of consciousness, we should be shut up in our own subjectivity, we
should not perceive an objective world. Our sensations must be objectified,
referred outward, projected into space, ordered in time. It is only because
the human mind possesses these ways of perceiving, that there can be an
objective world at all.

The Theory of the Understanding. The spatio-temporal organization of our
experience is, however, not enough. Mere unrelated, disconnected percepts,
the mere perception of objects in space and time, would not yield knowledge.
The perception of the sun followed by the perception of a hot stone is not
the same as knowing that the sun heats the stone. Only by connecting these
two experiences in thought in a certain way, can I form the judgment that
the sun is the cause of heat in the stone. Objects must be connected, related,
conceived, or thought. Knowledge or judgment would be impossible without
a synthetic, thinking mind, that is, without understanding or intelligence.
Sensibility is receptive, but understanding is active, spontaneous. The
forms of sensibility are intuitional; the understanding, however, is conceptual: it thinks in concepts. We must make our percepts intelligible, or bring

them under concepts, as well as make our concepts sensible, or give them an object in perception. The understanding by itself cannot intuit or perceive anything; the senses by themselves cannot think anything. Knowledge is possible only in the union of the two. The science of the rules of sensibility is called "Transcendental Esthetic"; the science of the rules of the understanding is called "Transcendental Analytic."

The understanding has different forms of conceiving, relating or connecting percepts; they are called pure concepts or categories of the understanding, because they are a priori and not derived from experience. The understanding expresses itself in judgment; indeed, understanding is a faculty of judgment: to think is to judge. Hence, its ways of conceiving will be ways of judging, and to discover these ways of judgment we must analyze our judgments, examine the forms in which they appear. Since our common logic has already done this for us, we can seek help here. The logical table of judgments will serve as a guide to the discovery of the categories. There are as many pure concepts, or categories, of the mind as there are possible judgments in the table of judgments.

Kant finds that there are twelve kinds of judgment, arranged in four groups of three each: (1) the universal judgment—All metals are elements; (2) the particular judgment—Some plants are cryptogams; (3) the singular judgment—Napoleon was Emperor of France. (In these first three kinds of judgment we conceive things in terms of the categories of quantity: totality, plurality, unity.) (4) The affirmative judgment—Heat is a form of motion; (5) the negative judgment—Mind is not extended; (6) the infinite or unlimited judgment—Mind is unextended. (These forms of judgment express the categories of quality: reality, negation, limitation.) (7) The categorical judgment—The body is heavy; (8) the hypothetical judgment—If the air is warm, the thermometer rises; (9) the disjunctive judgment—The substance is either solid or fluid. (The judgments of this group express the categories of relation: inherence and subsistence or substance and accident, causality and dependence or cause and effect, and community or reciprocity between the active and the passive.) (10) The problematical judgment—This may be a poison; (11) the assertory judgment—This is a poison; (12) the apodictic judgment—Every effect must have a cause. (The judgments of this last group express the categories of modality: possibility and impossibility, existence and non-existence, necessity and contingency.)

The correlation of the forms of judgment and the categories is summarized in the table below, in which the twelve forms of judgment are listed in the left-hand column, and the corresponding categories appear opposite them in the right-hand column:

Judgments	*Categories*
I. QUANTITY	I. OF QUANTITY
(1) universal	(1) unity
(2) particular	(2) plurality
(3) singular	(3) totality
II. QUALITY	II. OF QUALITY
(4) affirmative	(4) reality
(5) negative	(5) negation
(6) infinite	(6) limitation
III. RELATION	III. OF RELATION
(7) categorical	(7) inherence and subsistence
(8) hypothetical	(8) causality and dependence
(9) disjunctive	(9) community
IV. MODALITY	IV. OF MODALITY
(10) problematic	(10) possibility—impossibility
(11) assertoric	(11) existence—nonexistence
(12) apodictic	(12) necessity—contingency

Validity of Judgment. The problem then arises, What right have we to apply these forms of the mind to things? What is the ground of their objective validity? They have a purely mental origin and yet they are employed in experience. We read the categories, which are independent of experience in the sense of not being derived from experience, *into* experience, into the world of objects. How is that possible, what right have we to do it? Jurists call the proof of rights and claims in a legal process the deduction. What we need here is a deduction or proof or justification, a transcendental deduction of the categories. Kant's proof consists in showing that without them intelligible experience would be impossible. There could be no knowledge, no connected world of experience, without such original a priori concepts of thought, without a unified and unifying consciousness or self-consciousness, or the synthetic unity of apperception, as Kant calls it, which operates with these categories. Understanding is judgment, the act of bringing together in one self-consciousness (unity of apperception) the many perceived objects. Without a rational mind that perceives in certain ways (space and time) and judges or thinks in certain ways (the categories), that is so constituted that it must perceive and judge as it does, there could be no universal and necessary knowledge of objects of experience. Knowledge is the application of pure concepts of the understanding, or categories, to objects furnished us by the senses and perceived as spatial and temporal. Categories serve to make experience possible; that is their sole justification.

So simple an act as the perception of the freezing of water, for example, would be impossible unless the mind apprehended two states (liquid and solid) as related in time and connected them in a single act of thought. The same synthetic unity of apperception which is necessary in order that we may have judgment is necessary in order that we may have perception, in order that we may apprehend. The same spontaneous acts of apprehension, reproduction, and recognition that operate in our thinking operate in sense experience; and the same categories are at work in them both. Our world of experience is made possible by the categories; the phenomenal order, or nature as we perceive it, depends on the forms of our intelligence, not vice versa, as the empiricists hold. This is what Kant means when he says that the understanding prescribes its laws to nature; this is the "Copernican revolution" which he effected in philosophy.

Since, then, the mind prescribes its laws to nature, it follows that we can know a priori the universal forms of nature. We can know that the perceived world will always be connected in certain intelligible ways, that our experiences will always be of things in fixed spatial and temporal order, of things related as substance and accident, cause and effect, and as reciprocally influencing one another. We cannot, therefore, go wrong in applying the categories to the world of sense. But let it not be forgotten that they can be legitimately employed only in the field of actual or possible experience, only in the phenomenal world; their use is not valid outside this sphere; we cannot transcend experience nor have conceptual knowledge of the supersensuous, of things-in-themselves. It also follows from this theory that we cannot know a priori the matter or contents of experience, what particular sensations—colors, sounds, weight, etc.—will be given; all we can say is that whatever they may be, the mind will organize them according to its necessary rules.

But how can categories, which are intellectual, be applied to percepts, to sensible phenomena? Pure concepts and sense percepts are absolutely dissimilar, or heterogeneous, according to Kant; how, then, can we get them together? There must be a third something, a mediating entity between the pure concepts and the sense perceptions, something that is pure, i.e., without anything empirical, and, at the same time, sensuous. This something Kant calls the *transcendental schema*. The employment of such a schema is the *schematism of the understanding*. The time-form fills the requirements laid down: it is both pure and sensuous. All our ideas are subject to the *time-form*—that is, all our experiences are ordered by us in time; they take place in time. Hence, if the intellect is to influence sensibility at all, if it is to relate sense experiences or connect them, it must make use of the time-form. It tries to image its concepts, its categories, its uniform ways of connecting and relating, by means of the pure time-form, that is, to imagine them in certain time-relations. For example, it successively adds one to one, or considers time as a series of homogeneous moments, thus getting number. This operation of numbering, adding one to one, is the schema of the category of quantity; the schema is the category expressed in the form of time. One moment of time expresses singularity; several moments express particularity; all, or the totality of moments, universality. The category of quantity is expressed in the schema of *time-series*. The intellect also imagines sensations occurring in time, a content in time, something in time, or it imagines nothing in time. This is its way of picturing to itself the category of quality: the concept of quality is expressed in the schema of *time-content*. The intellect looks upon the real in time, the content, as something that remains when everything else changes. This is the way it imagines the category of substance. It considers the real as something upon which something else invariably follows in time: this is its way of making perceivable the category of causality. Or it regards the qualities of one substance and the qualities of another as invariably appearing together in time: this is its way of imaging the category of reciprocal action. The categories of substance, causality, and reciprocal action are expressed in the schema of *time-order* (permanence, succession, simultaneity). Or it thinks of something as existing at any time (category of possibility), at a definite time (actuality), at all times (necessity). The categories of possibility, actuality, and necessity are expressed in the schema of *time-comprehension*.

The Unity of Self-consciousness. The culmination of Kant's transcendental procedure is his doctrine of the transcendental unity of apperception. This unity of self-consciousness is presupposed by the categories as the categories are presupposed by experience; or rather, it is directly presupposed by experience in so far as it is categorized. The deduction of the categories and the deduction of the transcendental unity of apperception are accomplished together; or rather, they constitute one and the same deduction. This is a consequence of the intimate relation obtaining between the categories and the unity of apperception. The latter is not something behind the categories which impresses them upon the manifold of experience, as a man with a set of rubber stamps imprints them successively on the sheet of paper before him; rather is it the unity in and of the categories. The transcendental unity of apperception is the functional unity which manifests itself identically— and yet with a difference—in each of the categories. The categories are all forms of a unitary synthesis—it is this which accounts for their interrelatedness—but each is an unique kind of synthesis. The synthesis of qualities in the unity of a substance is very different from the synthesis of events in the unity of a causal nexus, yet both belong to a single primitive synthesis which by differentiation becomes the several categorial syntheses.

The transcendental unity of apperception is a sine qua non of experience because it is presupposed by the categories, which in turn are presupposed by experience. Kant in his statement of the argument at times seems to proceed *directly* from experience to the transcendental unity of apperception as the condition of its possibility, rather than *indirectly* by way of the categories; but the deduction of the transcendental unity of apperception is mediated by the deduction of the categories which precedes it, and thus the retrogressive argument proceeds from experience to the categories and thence to the transcendental unity of apperception. The latter principle, because it is integral to the categories, is indispensable to the possibility of experience and is therefore like them a priori.

The transcendental unity of apperception occupies an unique position in the sphere of the transcendental, in that it is the final term in the retrogressive series; experience and the categories presuppose it, but it does not presuppose anything else. The transcendental unity of apperception accordingly occupies a position in Kant's system analogous to that of substance in systems which define substance as the ultimate subject of predication (Aristotle and Leibniz), or as the independent and self-sufficient (Descartes and Spinoza); it is the ultimate a priori, the last term in the transcendental regress. The backward movement from experience to its logical preconditions having been carried to its culmination, Kant, in the third and final step of the transcendental argument, reverses the direction of his thought and moves forward from the a priori forms to the a priori truths which they validate.

Knowledge of Things-in-themselves. As has been pointed out, we cannot transcend our experience or have a priori knowledge of the supersensible, of things-in-themselves, of things as they are apart from the way they affect consciousness. Knowledge involves perception, but things-in-themselves cannot be perceived by the senses: in sense perception we know only the way things appear to consciousness, not what they are in themselves. Nor can they be perceived or intuited by the intellect; we do not possess intellectual intuition, we cannot see things face to face, at one glance, in the mind's eye, as it were; the intellect is discursive, not intuitive. If we apply categories to such a thing-in-itself, we cannot justify their claim to validity: we cannot prove, for example, that behind every existing thing there is a substance in an intelligible world. We can, however, think such a thing-in-itself, speak of it as something to which none of the predicates of sense perception applies, say that it is not in space nor in time, that it does not change, and so on. Not a single category, however, can be applied to it, because we have no means of knowing whether anything corresponding to it exists. We should never know whether anything existed corresponding to the category of substance if perception did not furnish us with a case in which the category is applied. In the case of the thing-in-itself, however, perception can afford no evidence of the application of the category.

The thing-in-itself is essentially unknowable, but the concept of a thing-in-itself is not self-contradictory, for we surely cannot maintain that the phenomenal order is the only possible one. We can have sensible knowledge only of sensible things, not of things-in-themselves; the senses cannot presume to know everything the intellect thinks. The concept of the thing-in-itself, or *noumenon,* as something not knowable by the senses, but as something capable of being known by intellectual intuition, is at least thinkable. It is a limiting *concept;* it says to the knowing mind: here is your limit, you can go no further, here is where your jurisdiction ceases. You can know only phenomena; the non-phenomenal, the noumenal, the intelligible is beyond you.

I know things not as they are in themselves, but only as they appear to me. Similarly, I do not know myself as I am, but only as I appear to myself. I am conscious of my existence, of my activity, of my spontaneity. But consciousness of oneself is not knowledge of one's *self.* To know is to have percepts. I do not perceive my self, my ego, nor do I possess an intellectual intuition of my self; I see myself through the glasses of inner perception, that is, through the time-form, as a succession of states. But though I cannot know the ego in the sense of perceiving it, I can think it. Indeed, Kant's whole theory of knowledge is based on the supposition of such an ego: the synthetic unity of apperception is nothing but the self-conscious self. There can be no knowledge without a self-conscious, unifying self; but this self itself cannot be known in the sense of being perceived directly.

It is evident, therefore, that we cannot have universal and necessary or a priori knowledge of anything non-perceivable. Hence, we cannot have a metaphysics that transcends experience, a metaphysics of things-in-themselves, a metaphysics that can offer us genuine knowledge of a nonphenomenal world in which reside free will, immortality, and God. But we can have an a priori science of the phenomenal order, for the reasons already adduced. Mathematics owes its necessity to the forms of space and time—geometry being based on a priori space perception, arithmetic on the concept of number, which expresses a priori time perception. Natural science rests on the categories: we speak of substance and accident, cause and effect, interaction, etc. Hume and the empiricists are wrong in depriving substance and causality of their universality and necessity. We can have universal and necessary knowledge of mathematics and of the principles of physics, but it is knowledge of phenomena only, and knowledge only of the form and arrangement of phenomena. We cannot know things-in-themselves—in this Hume is right. Things-in-themselves, however, exist; indeed, exist they must, otherwise sensation is unexplainable. Corresponding to phenomena there must be something that appears, something *extra mentem,* something that affects our senses and supplies the matter of our knowledge. Kant does not for a moment doubt the existence of such a thing-in-itself. In the second edition of the *Critique,* in his "Refutation of Idealism," he even proceeds to prove its existence.

But after his strong insistence that it exists and that it is the ground of our sensations, he is compelled by the nature of his system to make it a very elusive and hazy factor. It becomes a limiting concept, a kind of check to the pretensions of our knowledge: we cannot know the supersensible by means of the senses. Then again, we are told that we cannot know it, for we are not entitled to apply the categories to it; if we attempt to do so, these categories have no objective validity. Yet we can think it in the sense of entertaining it as a possibility and as a limiting concept. The status of the thing-in-itself is anomalous and constitutes a problem which has to be worked out; and to this Kant himself gave further attention and to it his successors addressed themselves with zeal, if not always with success, as we shall see.

Impossibility of Metaphysics. The aim of Kant was to show, first, against the "skeptic" Hume, that we can have a priori knowledge in mathematics and physics; second, against the Leibniz-Wolffian "dogmatists," that we cannot have knowledge of the supersensible in metaphysics, that metaphysics in this sense is a pseudo-science. His rejection of metaphysics is not, however, absolute and unqualified. There are several senses in which he regards metaphysics as possible: (1) as a study of the theory of knowledge; (2) as absolute knowledge of the forms and laws of nature; (3) as absolute knowledge of the laws or forms of the will, i.e., as moral philosophy; (4) as knowledge of the spiritual world, based on the moral law; (5) as a hypothesis of the universe having a certain degree of probability. Let us consider, in some detail, the grounds on which he rejects "dogmatic" or speculative metaphysics of the kind advanced by his rationalistic predecessors. The understanding can know only what can be experienced; but reason strives to go beyond the confines of the understanding, and attempts to conceive the supersensible, that for which we have no objects in perception, that which is merely thought. The reason, when it enters the supersensible world, confuses percepts with mere thought, and in this way falls into all kinds of ambiguities, equivocations, false inferences, and contradictions. That is what happens in the metaphysics of the transcendent. Questions which have a meaning when asked with respect to our world of experience have none when we transcend phenomena. Categories like cause and effect, substance and accident, which are perfectly legitimate when applied to the phenomenal order, have no meaning when transferred to a noumenal world. Metaphysics too often forgets this, and, confusing phenomena with noumena, applies to the transcendent reality the concepts which are valid only in our world of sense. In this way it falls into error and illusion, which, as distinguished from ordinary sensory illusion, Kant calls transcendental illusion. He calls the principles which are applied within the confines of possible experience *immanent* principles, those which transcend these limits *transcendent* principles, or concepts of reason, or *Ideas*. It is an inevitable illusion of reason to mistake our subjective principles, which apply to sensations, for objective principles, and to apply them to things-in-themselves. It is the business of transcendental dialectic to discover the illusion of such transcendent judgments and to prevent such illusion from deceiving us. It cannot, however, destroy the illusion, for the illusion is natural and inevitable; we may see through it and avoid being deceived by it, but we cannot entirely rid ourselves of it.

A careful examination of the arguments of metaphysics will reveal many logical fallacies, equivocations, non sequiturs, and contradictions. As we have seen, the understanding is the name given to the faculty of the mind, or reason in general, which connects our experiences in uniform ways, according to rules or principles, thereby furnishing us with valid judgments. These judgments are validated by comprehensive a priori concepts—the categories.

Reason (*Vernunft*), as a faculty of subsuming the rules of the understanding under higher principles, is engaged in this speculative enterprise; it aims at a unification of the judgments of the understanding. But such higher principles are merely subjective laws of economy for the understanding, striving to reduce the use of concepts to the smallest possible number. This supreme Reason does not prescribe laws to objects, nor does it explain our knowledge of them; its function is solely to guide and direct our inquiries, to provide ideals of completeness which our knowledge never fully realizes. Thus, Reason strives to bring all mental processes under a general head, or Idea of a *soul*, in rational psychology; all physical events under the Idea of *nature* in rational cosmology; all occurrences in general under the Idea of a *God* in rational theology. The notion of God would, therefore, be the highest Idea, the highest unity, the one absolute Whole comprehending everything else. Such Ideas, however, are transcendent, beyond experience: they can never be empirically fulfilled or exemplified. Thus, we can never represent the Idea of an absolute Totality in the form of an image; it is a problem without a solution. Yet these Ideas have their value and use as guides to the understanding; they lead it onward in its pursuit of knowledge; they are, in Kant's language, regulative rather than constitutive.

Rational psychology. Thus, it is legitimate to conclude that there can be no knowledge unless there is a subject, self, or knower, unless thoughts come together in a single consciousness, unless the self that thinks the subject of a judgment is the same self that thinks the predicate. But we have no right to infer that this knower is a self-existent, simple, indecomposable self-identical soul-substance, one that remains the same in all change. In reasoning thus, rational psychology draws conclusions not warranted by the premises; it uses the terms self, subject and soul in different senses, and is guilty of a fallacy which Kant calls a paralogism. We cannot prove, theoretically, the existence of free will and an immortal soul. Still, although rational psychology does not add anything to our knowledge, it prevents us from adopting either a soulless materialism or a groundless spiritualism. Reason thus gives us a hint to turn from fruitless speculations and to put our self-knowledge to moral use. The moral law teaches man to esteem the mere consciousness of righteousness more than anything else in the world, and to render himself fit to become the citizen of a better world, which exists in his Idea only.

Rational cosmology. Reason also tries to reduce the objective conditions of all our phenomena to an ultimate and supreme condition, or an unconditioned. We form the Idea of nature as a whole, the Idea of a universe, and either conceive this as the principle on which all phenomena depend, or seek the unconditioned among the phenomena themselves. In either case we form cosmological Ideas, and involve ourselves in all kinds of antitheses, which Kant calls antinomies: sophistical propositions which can neither hope for confirmation nor need fear refutation from experience. The thesis is free from contradiction and is rooted in the necessity of reason, but, unfortunately, the antithesis can produce equally cogent and necessary grounds for its support.

There are four such antinomies in which both the thesis and the antithesis can be proved. It can be proved (1) that the world has a beginning in time, and that it has no beginning in time, or is eternal; that it is limited in space, and that it is unlimited in space; (2) that bodies are infinitely divisible, and that they are not infinitely divisible, that they are made of simple parts, or atoms, which cannot be further divided; (3) that there is freedom in the world, and that everything in the world takes place according to the laws of nature; (4) that there exists an absolutely necessary Being, either as part of the world or as cause of it; and that there is no such Being, either within the world or outside it as the cause of it. In preferring one side to the other, the disputants do not consult the logical test of truth, but only their own interest. Every right-thinking man has a certain practical preference for the thesis, or dogmatism, if he knows his true interests. That the world has a beginning, that my thinking self is simple and imperishable, that it is free and not subject to the compulsion of nature, that the whole order of things which constitutes the world, springs from an original Being whence everything receives its unity and purposeful connection—these are so many supports of ethics and religion. The antithesis, or empiricism, robs us, or seems to rob us, of all these supports. If there is no original Being, if the world is without a beginning and without a Creator, if our will is not free, and our soul is divisible and perishable like matter, our moral ideals and principles lose all validity and fall with the transcendental Ideas which form their theoretic support.

There is also a speculative interest involved. For if we assume the transcendental Ideas in the thesis, we can conceive a priori the whole chain of conditions and the derivation of the conditioned by beginning with the unconditioned. The antithesis does not accomplish this. Yet, if the empiricist were satisfied with merely suppressing intellectual presumption and rashness, his principle would be entirely legitimate, and would serve to teach moderation in claims to absolute knowledge. But the empiricist not only rejects the claims of the dogmatist; he also puts forward a counter-dogmatism of his own. He deprives the intellect of its legitimate aspirations, and, at the same time, destroys the theoretical basis of our practical interests. The real contribution of empiricism is to destroy the presumptuous claims and pompous titles of science and rational insight, and to reiterate that true speculative knowledge can never have any other object than experience. But empiricism itself becomes dogmatic in boldly denying what goes beyond the sphere of intuitive knowledge, and thereby does irreparable injury to the practical interests of reason.

Kant solves the difficulties involved in the antinomies by pointing out that the antithesis holds for the phenomenal world, and the thesis for the noumenal world. Our sense-perceived, spatial-temporal world has no first beginning in time and no extreme limit in space. We never experience absolute limits; we can never stop anywhere in the regressus of time or in the progressus of space. But there may be a non-spatial world in which absolutely simple beings exist, a world of spiritual entities. It does not follow that because a limit is impossible in the one world, it is also impossible in the other. For all we know, the true world may have had a beginning, it may have been created by God, and be limited. Still, we have no right to search for spiritual beings in space and for spatial things in the supersensible realm.

In the same way, the causal antinomy is solved. In the phenomenal series, everything is conditioned by something like it, every effect has a phenomenal cause; no breach is possible in the causal nexus. It is our business to go right on in the chain ad infinitum. Still, it is conceivable that a phenomenal condition has also an intelligible or noumenal condition, that there is something outside the phenomenal series on which the phenomenally conditioned depends. It is settled by the nature of our intelligence that we shall never find a free cause in the sense world, hence we cannot derive the Idea of freedom from experience. It is a transcendental Idea, because reason creates it independently of experience. It is easy to see, however, that if all causality in the world of sense were merely natural causality, every event would be necessarily determined by some other event, and every act would be a necessary natural effect of some phenomenon in nature. The denial of transcendental freedom, of spontaneity, would destroy practical or moral freedom. Practical freedom presupposes that although something did not happen, it ought to have happened; hence, that its phenomenal cause was not absolutely determining, that our will could have produced it independently of its natural causes and even contrary to their power and influence. If transcendental freedom is possible, practical freedom is possible: the will may be independent of the coercion of sensuous impulses, not necessitated as is the will of the brute.

In such a way freedom and natural necessity could be reconciled. We can regard the phenomena as caused by the thing-in-itself, the noumenal cause, which is not perceived, but whose phenomenal appearances are perceived and arranged in an unbroken causal series. One and the same phenomenon, looked at as part of the phenomenal world in space and time, would then be a link in a causal chain; looked at as the activity of the non-perceived thing-in-itself, it would be the act of a free cause, which, by itself, originates its effects in the world of sense. On the one side, the event would be an effect of nature only; on the other, an effect of freedom. In other words, this effect is a phenomenon and must have an empirical cause, but this empirical cause itself can be the effect of a non-empirical cause, or intelligible or free cause, without breaking in the least its connection with natural causes.

Applying this insight to man, we have the following interpretation of human action and conduct. Looked at through the spectacles of sense and understanding, man is a part of nature; in this aspect he has an empirical character, he is a link in a chain of causes and effects. But in reality man is an intelligible or spiritual being. To such a being the sense forms do not apply; such a being can originate acts. That man is cognizant of this power is attested by the fact that he holds himself responsible for his decisions and actions. Whenever we think of an act as a phenomenon, it must have a cause; as such it cannot be regarded as spontaneously initiated. This interpretation cannot, however, be extended to the reason; we cannot say that the state in which reason determined the will was preceded by another state, and so on, for reason is not a phenomenon, and is not subject to the conditions of sensibility, such as time, space, causality. We cannot interpret its causality in the natural way, that is, expect a cause for everything it does. Reason, or the intelligible, or man as he is in himself, is the permanent condition of all his voluntary acts. A man's character, considered in its empirical aspect, is only the sensuous schema of his character considered in its supersensuous aspect. The empirical is thus the way in which we image man or phenomenalize him.

Whether his position is tenable or not, Kant's meaning is quite clear. Every voluntary act is the direct expression of man's intelligible character, of pure reason; hence, man is a free agent, he is not a link in the chain of natural causes. Yet the act itself, when viewed as a phenomenon, is absolutely determined. Man in his intelligible aspect is a free agent, he originates acts; but when these acts are perceived by a mind they are woven into a web of causation and are the effects of particular impulses, ideas, education, natural disposition, and so on. But the real cause of the act is reason; the action is imputed to man's intelligible character, and as such is not affected at all by the influences of the world of the senses.

In the *Critique of Pure Reason,* however, Kant does not aim to establish the reality of freedom; he simply wishes to point out that reason creates the Idea, that it initiates, absolutely, a causal series and, at the same time, prescribes laws of causality to the understanding, and thereby involves itself in an antinomy. He thus seeks to prove that the determinism of nature does not altogether preclude the Idea of free causality.

The antinomy of necessary being and contingent being Kant solves in this way. The intellect refuses to regard anything within the phenomenal series as absolutely free and independent; everything is contingent, that is, depends on something else. But this is not to deny that the whole series may depend on some intelligible being, which is free, independent of all empirical conditions, and itself the ground of the possibility of all these phenomena. We can regard the whole world of sense as the expression of some intelligible being, which is the substance, the necessary being without which nothing can exist, and which itself needs nothing else in order to exist. The intellect is not entitled to say that because the intelligible is useless in explaining *phenomena,* it is, therefore, impossible. Perhaps there is no such being, but it does not follow from what we have found to be true of the understanding, that it is impossible. When we are speaking of phenomena, we must speak in terms of sense; but that is not necessarily the only way of looking at things. We can conceive of another order of existence, of an order of things-in-themselves, of non-sensuous things which, although they do not appear to the senses, are capable of being thought. We must assume transcendent objects on which phenomena depend, but we *know* nothing of such objects; all we can do is to form some kind of notion of them, conceive them by analogy with the ways in which we use the concepts of experience.

Rational theology. We form the Idea of an empirical whole, of a whole of experience, and we conceive this system of objects, this universe of things, or phenomena, as something existing apart from us. We forget that it is our Idea, and so make an entity of it. We represent it as an individual thing, containing in itself all reality: as the most real thing, as the highest reality, self-sufficient, eternal, and simple. This Idea Kant calls the ideal of a transcendental theology. The ideal of the most real being, however, is a mere Idea. First we make an object of it, that is, a phenomenal object, then we make an entity of it, and then we personify it.

There are only three proofs for the existence of God: the physico-theological, the cosmological, and the ontological, all of which are worthless. Kant rejects the ontological argument: the conception of a being that contains all reality does not imply existence. Existence does not follow from the bare concept of the most real being: we cannot spin out of an arbitrary Idea the existence of an object corresponding to it. In the cosmological proof, we conclude from the Idea of all possible experience (world or cosmos) the existence of a necessary being. God alone can be conceived as such a Being. We have no right, however, to conclude that because we think there must be an absolute Being, such a Being exists. This is really the ontological proof over again. Moreover, the argument proceeds from the contingent to a cause. Such an inference has no meaning outside of the phenomenal world, but in the cosmological proof it is used to transcend experience, which is forbidden. Kant points out that the argument contains a nest of dialectical assumptions. It may be permissible to assume the existence of God as the cause of all possible effects, in order to assist reason in the search for the unity of causes, but to say that such a Being necessarily exists is not the modest language of legitimate hypothesis, but the impudent assurance of apodictic certainty. The abyss between the contingency of the phenomenal world and the absolute necessity of God can never be bridged by the human reason. The physico-theological argument infers the existence of a Supreme Being from the nature and arrangement of the actual world. It, too, fails. The manifoldness, order, and beauty of the world, it tells us, entitle us to infer a cause of its origin and continuance. Such a cause must possess a higher degree of perfection than any possible experience of ours. What is to prevent us from conceiving all possible perfection as united in this Supreme Cause as in one single substance? The proof deserves respect; it is the oldest and clearest, and most in conformity with human reason. It discerns purposes and ends in nature, although our observation without its guidance would not have detected them. Nevertheless, we cannot approve of its pretension to apodictic certainty. It is an argument by analogy, inferring from the similarity between natural products and works of human art, such as houses, ships, clocks, that a similar causality, namely, understanding and will, lies at the bottom of nature. If we must name a cause, we cannot do better than to follow the analogy of such products of human design, in which alone we know completely both cause and effect. The argument is, at least, not guilty of surrendering a causality which is known, and having recourse to obscure and indemonstrable principles of explanation which are not known. It is, however, not conclusive; it can, at best, establish a world-architect, who would be much hampered by the resistance of the material with which he has to work; but it cannot establish a world-creator to which everything is subject. The physico-theological proof, in so far as it proceeds from the character of experience to its ultimate causes, is reducible to the cosmological proof, which, in turn, is merely the disguised ontological proof. The ontological proof would be the only legitimate proof—if, indeed, any proof were possible. The logical weaknesses of the ontological argument have been amply shown—and with the collapse of this argument the other two fall also.

Outside the field of experience, the principle of causality cannot be employed and has no meaning. All synthetic principles of the understanding are applicable immanently only, that is, in the phenomenal realm; to arrive at a knowledge of a Supreme Being, we must use them transcendentally, and for this our understanding is not prepared. Even if we should allow the causal leap beyond the limits of experience, we could not reach a concept of a Supreme Being, because we never *experience* the greatest of all possible effects from which to conclude the Supreme Cause. Transcendental theology has an important negative use, however; it acts as a constant censor of our reason and not only cuts the ground from under claims of deistic or anthropomorphic theology, but undermines atheism as well.

Use of Metaphysics in Experience. Though the transcendental Ideas produce an irresistible illusion, they are as natural to reason as are the categories to the understanding. The latter, however, convey truth, i.e., agreement of our concepts with their objects. Every faculty has its use, provided we can discover its right direction, and the reason with its Ideas is no exception. The transcendental Ideas have their immanent use in guiding inquiry, but when they are mistaken for concepts of real things, they are transcendent and deceptive in their application. They have no *constitutive* use, that is, they are not concepts productive of objects; they have a *regulative* use, that is, they direct the understanding in its inquiries: they unify the manifoldness of concepts, just as the categories bring unity into the manifoldness of objects. Through the Ideas reason aims to systematize our knowledge in conformity with a single principle. This systematic unity indicated by the Ideas is merely methodological; it urges the reason to keep on unifying its knowledge; but the systematic unity is subjectively necessary as a method, not objectively necessary as constituting transcendent realities. Many of the so-called scientific principles are Ideas, having hypothetical and methodological value, but not absolute truth. We can know a priori only the forms of reality, e.g., that it is spatial and temporal, that things are causally related. But that there are fundamental causes, powers, or substances, or even one such power, cause, or substance, is a mere hypothesis. We cannot assert that such unity exists, but we must always look for it, in the interest of reason, in order to introduce order into our knowledge.

Some students of nature—pre-eminently speculative—are more intent on the unity of nature, on discovering likeness in diversity; others—pre-eminently empirical—are constantly striving to divide nature into species. The latter tendency is based on a logical principle which aims at systematic completeness of classification. Every genus has different species; these, in turn, different sub-species, and so on. Reason demands that no species be regarded as the lowest and thereby exhorts the investigator to further inquiry. We have, therefore, two heuristic principles of method: the law of homogeneity and the law of specification, neither of which is derived from experience, but which are fruitful in promoting scientific inquiry. Moreover, there are always intervening species possible between the species and sub-species. This is the law of the continuity of species: there is no transition from one to another *per saltum* (by a leap), but only by ever smaller degrees of difference. This law presupposes a transcendental law of nature—the law of continuity in nature—which the understanding cannot afford to ignore, lest it be misled into following a path contrary to nature. But this continuity of forms is, likewise, a mere Idea; no object corresponding to it can be pointed out in experience; the actual species discoverable in nature constitute a discrete series. Yet the law guides the understanding in the general direction of its inquiry, although it has no reference to any particular objects. The two principles—of unity and difference—can easily be combined and perform an invaluable service in the pursuit of truth so long as we do not mistake them for objective knowledge. But if we interpret them as metaphysical truths, they cause discord and even put obstacles in the way of truth.

The Ideas have objective reality in a certain sense; not in the sense that we can find anywhere in experience an object corresponding to them—we cannot see anywhere a highest genus or a lowest species or the infinite number of intervening transition-species; but in the sense that they give rules to this understanding. They outline the procedure or method for understanding to follow; they say: keep on seeking for a highest genus for a lowest species, and for a continuous series of intermediate species. In this way they have an indirect effect on the objects of experience, by bringing consistency into the functions of the understanding.

The only purpose of the Idea of a Supreme Being is to preserve the greatest systematic unity in the empirical use of our reason. The Idea of a ground or cause of the objects of our experience helps us to organize our knowledge.

The psychological, cosmological, and theological Ideas are not referred directly to an object corresponding to them; yet by presupposing such an object in Idea we are led to organize and extend our knowledge without ever contradicting it. Hence, it is a necessary maxim of reason to proceed according to such Ideas. In psychology, we must connect all inner phenomena as if our soul were a simple substance existing permanently, and with personal identity—in this life, at least—in order that we may unify our facts. In cosmology, we must pursue the conditions of all natural phenomena in an investigation that can never be complete, as if the series were an infinite given totality. In theology, we must look at everything that may belong in the connection of possible experience, as if that experience formed an absolute unity of objects which are dependent upon and conditioned by one another. We must also approach experience as if the totality of all phenomena of the sense world had one supreme and self-sufficient ground outside of it, namely, an independent, original, and creative reason. This does not mean that we should seek to derive the inner phenomena of the self from a simple thinking substance, but merely that we should connect the inner phenomena according to the Idea of a simple being. In other words: treat the phenomena in the usual scientific way, but keep before your mind the idea of a unity in this body of phenomena. It does not mean that it is possible to derive from the Idea of God the world-order in its systematic unity, but only that we should use the Idea of a most wise Cause as a guide when we employ reason in connecting causes and effects in the world.

The Ideas of the reason, then, are not mere fictions of the mind but are highly useful, indeed necessary methodological ideals. We cannot think of a systematic unity without giving the Idea some object, without objectifying or entifying it. But no such object is ever experienced, it is assumed problematically—literally as a problem. We assume a God so that we may have some ground on which to fix the systematic unity, some focal point from which and to which to proceed. The same interpretation applies to the Idea of soul-substance. It is not to be regarded as a thing-in-itself, an entity which can be known, but a kind of focal point to which to refer all states of consciousness—an ideal unity of our inner experience. If we take the Idea for what it is, i.e., for a mere Idea, and not a metaphysical entity, we avoid all far-fetched hypotheses regarding the generation, extinction, and transmigration of souls.

Human knowledge begins with percepts, proceeds to concepts, and ends with Ideas. It has a priori sources of knowledge with respect to all three elements. A complete criticism shows that reason, in its speculative use, can never go beyond the field of possible experience with respect to these elements.

Use of Teleology in Nature. Among the Ideas which reason applies in the contemplation of nature is the Idea of purpose, or the teleological Idea. This Idea Kant subjects to careful criticism in a separate work called *The Critique of Judgment,* in which also the nature of esthetic judgment is discussed. The understanding conceives every existent whole of nature solely as the effect of the concurrent moving forces of its parts. In the case of organic bodies, however, the parts seem to depend on the whole, to be determined by the form or plan or Idea of the whole. Every part is both a means and an end and, in cooperating to make the whole possible, is determined by the Idea of the whole. Here, again, we have an antinomy and a dialectic, of which the thesis states: the creation of all material things is possible according to mechanical laws; the antithesis: the creation of some is not possible according to mechanical laws. The contradiction is removed when we take these propositions not as constitutive principles but as regulative principles. When so interpreted, the thesis invites us to seek for mechanical causes in material nature wherever possible; the antithesis, to search for final causes or purposes in certain cases—and even in nature as a whole—when the mechanical explanation does not seem to suffice. It does not follow from these principles, thus interpreted, that certain natural products cannot be explained mechanically, nor that they can be explained by mechanical causality alone. Human reason will never be able to discover a natural purpose by searching for mechanical causes. Yet it is not impossible that the physico-mechanical series and the teleological series may ultimately converge and be united in one principle which is, however, unknown to us. We are compelled by the constitution of our reason, by our *reflective* judgment, as Kant here calls it, to view the organic world as purposive; but sense experience never discovers such a purpose, nor do we possess any intellectual intuition that might reveal it to us. We cannot assume a blind unconscious purpose, for this would be a reversion to hylozoism, which is the death of all natural philosophy; besides, we never find such blind purposes in our experience; the only kind of purposes we know are the conscious purposes of man. Kant repudiates vitalism as a biological theory of unconscious purposiveness; we must either entirely abandon the effort to determine the cause of the unity of the organism, or we must be willing to invoke intelligent purpose. The value of the teleological Idea consists in guiding the investigator in the study of nature; it helps him to discover the purposes which the organs and the smaller structures of the body serve, and this purposive insight frequently promotes explanation in terms of efficient and mechanical causes. The teleological interpretation of nature is, therefore, an inevitable attitude of reason, aroused by the contemplation of certain phenomenal forms, but it has no legitimate use in experience except as a working-hypothesis or guiding principle.

Practical Use of Reason and Moral Theology. The whole interest of reason, whether speculative or practical, is centered about three questions: What can I know? What ought I to do? What may I hope for? We can never have knowledge, in the scientific sense, of the existence of God, freedom, and personal immortality. The purely speculative significance of these, however, is slight; even if all three of them were theoretically proved, the knowledge would not help to make any discoveries in the field of natural science. They are of no use to us in so far as knowledge is concerned; their real value is practical, ethical. Now, our reason commands moral laws, and these moral laws are necessary. The necessity of the moral law has certain implications for God, freedom and immortality. The law tells me to act so that I will be deserving of happiness; this is a necessary practical law. Since reason commands this, it follows that I may hope for happiness. Morality and happiness are inseparably connected, but they are connected in Idea only. Now, if God is the author of the natural order, it is legitimate to hope that this natural order is also a moral order, or rather, that in such a natural order happiness will accompany morality. Our reason compels us to regard ourselves as belonging to a moral world-order in which happiness and morality are connected. But in the world of sense which shows nothing but phenomena, a connection between morality and happiness is not revealed, and therefore we shall have to assume a future world in which the connection does exist. God, therefore, and a future life are two presuppositions which, according to the principles of pure reason, cannot be separated from the moral law which reason imposes upon us.

A morally grounded theology inevitably leads to the concept of a single, all-perfect, rational and original Being. This Being must be omnipotent, so that all nature in its relation to morality can be subject to him; omniscient, so that he may know the innermost moral disposition of man, and appraise its worth; omnipresent, in order that he may minister immediately to all the needs which the highest good of the world requires; eternal, that this harmony of nature and freedom may be eternally maintained. If the world is to harmonize with our practical reason, our reason, in its moral employment, demands that it must be regarded as derived from an idea, the idea of the highest good. It demands the union of virtue and happiness; there is no assurance of this union unless we ascribe a moral purpose to the world; a moral being must exist to realize the purpose. In other words, we are led to teleology and God through the moral law.

Pure reason, therefore, in its practical employment, that is, as moral reason, postulates for the sake of our highest moral or practical interests metaphysical principles which mere theoretical speculation can only conjecture, but cannot guarantee. It thereby makes these metaphysical and theological assumptions not demonstrated dogmas, but absolutely necessary presuppositions for the essential purposes of morality.

Ethics. Kant's moral philosophy, which he presents in his *Foundations of Metaphysics of Morals, Critique of Practical Reason,* and *Metaphysics of Morals,* may be regarded as an attempt to settle the quarrel between intuitionism and empiricism, idealism and hedonism. His fundamental problem is to discover the meaning of goodness, right and wrong, and duty, and the implications of our moral knowledge; how shall we define duty and what follows from man's moral nature?

Kant had learned from Rousseau that nothing is absolutely good in this world or out of it except a good will. To this, Kant added that a will is good when it is determined by respect for the moral law, or the consciousness of duty. An act that is done from inclination, say from self-love or even sympathy, is not moral; to be that, it must be done in the face of such impulses, from sheer respect for law. Moreover, the rightness or wrongness of an act does not depend on its effects or consequences; it is immaterial whether happiness or perfection results, so long as the motive of the agent is good. Pure respect for the law is the sole motive of genuine morality. The sentimental morality of "the volunteers of duty" was as distasteful to Kant as the ethics of utility. The moral law is a categorical imperative; it commands categorically, unconditionally; it does not say: Do this if you would be happy or successful or perfect, but: Do it because it is your duty to it. Kant's ethics, like its Stoic model, extols duty for duty's sake. It does not concern itself with particular acts or even with general rules, but lays down a fundamental principle: always act so that you can will the maxim or determining principle of your action to become universal law; act so that you can will that everybody shall follow the principle of your action. This law is the supreme test of what is right and wrong. For example, you cannot will that everybody should make lying promises, for if everybody did, nobody would believe anybody, and lying promises would defeat themselves. A rational being cannot really will a contradiction, and it would be a contradiction to will a lying promise. Nor can such a being will to disregard the welfare of others, for if such conduct became universal, he himself might some day be treated inhumanly. Thus no one can consistently and rationally will that inhumanity be universalized.

This law, or categorical imperative, is a universal, necessary law, a priori, inherent in reason itself. Its claim is recognized even by the common man; though he may not be clearly conscious of it, it governs his moral judgments; it is his standard or criterion of right and wrong. Implied in this law, or rather identical with it, is another law: Act so as to treat humanity, whether in your own person or in that of any other, in every case as an end in itself and never merely as a means. Every man conceives his own existence as an end in itself, as having worth, and must therefore regard the existence of every rational creature in the same way. Here we have the humanitarian ideal which was preached by the Stoics and primitive Christianity, and which played such an important rôle in the ethical and political theories of the eighteenth century.

The rational will imposes upon itself universal laws, laws that hold for all and are acceptable to all. If everybody obeyed the law of reason, a society of rational beings would result, a kingdom of ends, as Kant calls it, a society organized by rational purposes. The categorical imperative, in other words, implicitly commands a perfect society; it necessarily implies the ideal of a rational realm of spirits. Therefore, every rational being ought to act as if he were by his maxims, his universal principles, a legislating member of a universal kingdom of ends. He is both sovereign and subject: he both lays down and acknowledges the law. By virtue of his moral nature, he is a member of a spiritual kingdom; in recognizing the authority of the law over him, he recognizes the ideal world as the highest good.

A man who is governed by the moral law and not by his impulses, his selfish desires, his appetites, is free. The brute is the playball of its wants and instincts; through the knowledge of the moral law within him, man can resist his sensuous appetites, all of which aim at selfish pleasure. And because he can suppress his sensual nature he is free: he ought, therefore he can. The moral imperative is the expression of man's real self, of the very principle of his being. It is his innermost self that expresses itself in the moral law; the moral law is his command in so far as he is a rational being. He imposes the law upon himself, and this is his autonomy.

The moral imperative insures the freedom of the will. If it were not for our moral nature, or practical reason, a proof of free will would be out of the question. Our ordinary perceptual and scientific knowledge deals with appearances in the spatio-temporal order, where everything is arranged according to necessary laws: the occurrences in the phenomenal world are, as we have seen, absolutely determined. If this temporal, spatial, and causal order were the real world, freedom would be impossible. But Kant teaches that the world as it appears to our senses is not the real world; hence, freedom is possible. But whether it is actual or not, we should never know if it were not for the moral law which admits us to a timeless, spaceless universe, to the intelligible world of free beings. In other words, the moral consciousness of man, his knowledge of right and wrong, gives him an insight into a realm that is different from the world in space and time which is presented to the senses. The moral dimensions of human experience give man access to a world transcending the phenomenal.

Moral consciousness implies freedom of the will. It also implies the existence of God and the immortality of the soul, notions which the *Critique of Pure Reason* had shattered as scientifically demonstrable dogmas, but had left as possibilities. The moral proof for the existence of God runs as follows. The categorical imperative commands an absolutely good, virtuous and holy will. Reason tells us that such a will is deserving of happiness: a good man ought to be happy; hence, the highest good must consist in virtue *and* happiness, for virtue without happiness would not be a complete good. But virtue and happiness do not go together in this world; the virtuous man does not necessarily achieve happiness. Reason tells us there ought to be a being who apportions happiness according to desert. In order to do this, such a being must have absolute intelligence, or be omniscient: he must see our inner motives and dispositions; he must accept the highest moral ideals, that is, be all-good; and he must have absolute power to establish the apportionment of happiness to virtue, or be omnipotent. Such an all-wise, all-good, and all-powerful Being is God. The proof for immortality rests on the same premise: The moral law commands holiness or an absolutely good will. Since the moral law is a deliverance of reason, what it enjoins must be realizable. But we cannot reach holiness at any moment of existence; hence an endless time, an eternal progress towards this perfection is necessary. In other words, the soul must be immortal.

In the *Critique of Pure Reason* Kant rejects all the old arguments for the freedom of the will, the existence of God, and the immortality of the soul; the outcome of the first *Critique* is negative in this respect. In the *Critique of Practical Reason,* these three notions are reinstated on the basis of the moral law. Man is free, man is immortal, and there is a God: all these truths are necessary implications of the rational moral law within us. The moral law guarantees freedom, immortality, and God; religion is based on morality.

This teaching is closely connected with the Christian conception, as Kant himself tells us. (1) Morality demands holiness, perfection, an absolutely good will. (2) Man, however, cannot completely realize this ideal. Only God is perfect and holy; man has strong desires, hence a propensity to sin. All he can do is to respect the law—attain a dutiful disposition. (3) The highest good can be realized only in the life to come. (4) A character that is perfectly in accord with the moral law, a perfectly moral man, has infinite worth and deserves all possible happiness. (5) But the moral law does not promise happiness; we must do the right because it is right, whether we are happy or not. Obedience to morality does not guarantee happiness. (6) Our reason, however, tells us that a moral man is worthy of happiness. Hence, it is reasonable to suppose that there is a Being who will apportion happiness to the good according to their deserts. A world in which such apportionment is made is the kingdom of God. (7) But happiness can never be the motive to moral conduct. We must do right, not for the sake of eternal happiness, but for right's own sake. It is such doctrines as these that have won Kant the title, "the Philosopher of Protestantism."

59. SUCCESSORS OF KANT

Problems Raised by Kant. The philosophy of Kant suggested a number of problems. The first, and perhaps not the least difficult, task consisted in understanding the nature of Kant's "Copernican Revolution" in philosophy— his contention that mind prescribes laws to nature, and not vice versa. The literature of the age shows how unsuccessful were many of the initial efforts to grasp its meaning. Hamann labeled Kant a Prussian Hume, Garve identified his teaching with Berkeleyan idealism; some perceived in it a subtle artifice for destroying the historical foundations of religion and for proving naturalism, others suspected it of being a new support for the declining faith-philosophy. In order to bring about a clearer understanding of the subject, Kant wrote his *Prolegomena to Every Future Metaphysik* (1783), Johannes Schultz published his *Erläuterungen* (1784), Reinhold his *Letters on the Kantian Philosophy* (1786-1787), and Hufeland and Schütz established *Die Jenauer allgemeine Literaturzeitung* (1785) as the organ of the critical movement. Jena became the home of the new school, and through the efforts of Schiller, Reinhold, Fichte, Schelling, and Hegel, who taught there, philosophy became one of the most honored subjects of study in Germany.

Among the other tasks that confronted the successors of Kant were the development of his epistemology, the unification of its principles, the solution of the problems following from his dualism between the intelligible and phenomenal worlds, freedom and mechanism, form and matter, knowledge and faith, practical reason and theoretical reason; and the removal of the inconsistencies introduced by the notion of the thing-in-itself. Another work to be undertaken was the construction of a universal system on the critical foundation laid by Kant; this became the chief occupation of the most famous successors of the great reformer: Fichte, Schelling, and Hegel.

Idealism and the Thing-in-itself. Kant had examined the judgments of mathematics, natural science, and metaphysics, the moral, esthetic, and teleological judgments, and had pointed out the presuppositions, preconditions, or principles on which they all rest. The question suggested itself, indeed was frequently asked by Kant himself, whether there was not a common root in which these principles had their origin and from which they might, perhaps, be derived. The thought of an ideal system of judgments, or of an interrelated system of knowledge held together by a fundamental and absolutely certain principle, took possession of some of the thinkers of the age and led in time to the attempt to construct an all-embracing system of idealistic metaphysics. But before this stage was reached, a great deal of work had to be done in the way of clearing up the difficulties presented by the Kantian *Critique of Pure Reason.*

K. L. Reinhold (1758-1823) in his *Versuch einer neuen Theorie des menschlichen Vorstellungsvermögens* (1789), seeks to derive the faculties of sensibility and understanding as well as the categories from a single principle, the faculty of representation (*Vorstellung*), which is both receptive and active, or spontaneous: it receives matter and produces form. The object, as it exists independently of representation, is the thing-in-itself, which is unknowable. G. E. Schulze, in his *Aenesidemus* (1792), attacks the new critical philosophy as presented by Kant and Reinhold; instead of doing away with skepticism, he thinks, it restores it, leaving philosophy exactly where Hume had left it. The Kantian philosophy denies the possibility of knowledge of the thing-in-itself, and yet assumes its existence and applies categories to it, after having declared that these are valid only in the world of experience. The only way to overcome the skepticism and contradictions implied in the notion of the thing-in-itself, according to S. Maimon (*Versuch über die Transcendentalphilosophie,* 1790), is to abolish the thing-in-itself as inconceivable and impossible. The cause and origin of the given or a posteriori element in consciousness, is unknown to us, an irrational quantity, a surd, a problem that can never be entirely solved. Hence, we can have no complete knowledge of experience; we do not produce the objects of our experience, but we do produce the objects of our thought, which, therefore, are the only objects of our knowledge. S. Beck, influenced by the criticisms leveled against the *Critique,* interprets it idealistically: either the thing-in-itself must be rejected or the *Critique* contradicts itself (*Einzig möglicher Standpunkt aus welchem die kritische Philosophie beurteilt werden muss,* 1796). Kant, he thought, could not have been the author of such a self-contradictory philosophy. What Kant really meant to assert was that whatever is given in consciousness is the product of consciousness. Without idealism there can be no *Critique.*

Herder. The poet J. G. Herder (1744-1803) opposes the Kantian dualism of mental faculties and emphasizes the unity of soul-life; thought and will, understanding and sensation spring from a common ground. All of these factors cooperate in knowledge. The so-called "pure" or transcendental reason, divorced from sensibility, is an abstraction and a delusion; all our thinking originates in sensibility and retains, even after intellectual elaboration, traces of its sensuous origin. He holds that rationalism with its conceptual method cannot do justice to "living reality," and he accordingly interprets nature and mind organically and historically. In the spirit of pantheism he asserts that God reveals himself in nature and in man, particularly in the religion, art, and the life of peoples. The history of mankind is a process of evolution towards the ideal of humanity, that is, the harmonious development of all human capacities in relation to the environment. Our rational capacity should be educated and fashioned into a developed reason, our more refined senses into art, our impulses into genuine freedom and beauty, our motives into love of humanity.

Herder was deeply concerned with the problem of nationalism in relation to his broad humanitarianism and cosmopolitanism. He affirmed the brotherhood of man in conformity with his religious doctrines of the common ancestry of all men, and emphatically rejected racial distinctions based on biological differences. The inequalities and differentiation of races of men are attributed by him to climatic and geographical factors reflected in social and cultural patterns, and embedded in language and custom. All differences of national character are thus ultimately traceable to geography and climate. Herder's philosophy of history rests on the doctrine of progress; world history is a fulfillment of God's will on earth, in which each national group makes its unique contribution to the history of mankind. Herder's nationalism, set in a religious and humanitarian context, is a refutation of the later nationalism of the Nazis based on racial theories.

Metakritik, 1799; *Ideen zur Philosophie der Geschichte der Menschheit,* 1787-1791; R. R. Ergang, *Herder and the Foundations of German Nationalism,* 1931; C. J. H. Hayes, "Contributions of Herder to the Doctrine of Nationalism," in *The American Historical Review,* Vol. XXXII, No. 4, pp. 719-736, July 1927; F. McEachran, *The Life and Philosophy of J. G. Herder,* 1939.

Jacobi. F. H. Jacobi (1743-1819) declares that the *Critique* logically ends in subjective idealism, and, therefore, rejects its conclusions. Such a "system of absolute subjectivity," or nihilism, as he calls it, seems to him incapable of grasping the ultimate realities—God and freedom—upon which his heart is set. For the critical philosophy, objects are phenomena, ideas, dreams, "specters through and through": it can never escape from the web of ideas which it spins for itself. Dogmatic rationalism, on the other hand, of which the mathematical method of Spinoza furnishes the most consistent example, Jacobi thinks equally unable to reach truth. According to it, everything is determined, and what has no ground is inexplicable, irrational, and non-existent: it culminates in atheism and fatalism. It operates with universal abstractions and must of necessity miss the living, moving spontaneity of freedom and God. Rationalism exaggerates the claims of the universal over the individual, the claims of deductive inference against immediate certainty, of rationality against faith, and narrows the range of experience to include only sense experience. Jacobi escapes the alleged skepticism of idealism and the fatalism and atheism of rationalism by basing himself on feeling, belief, or faith, in which he finds an instinctive form of truth. We are immediately certain of the existence of things-in-themselves. This faith is made possible only by their direct revelation, it springs from our direct perception of the objects. We come face to face with the real, and not merely with ideas, as idealism holds; ideas are mere copies of originals which we immediately perceive. No existence of any kind can ever be demonstrated by reason with its abstract principles. Just as we immediately experience external objects, we experience our own being, the self, the beautiful, the true, and the good, free causality, and God. Kant and Jacobi both oppose naturalism with its atheism and fatalism, and strive to save God, freedom, and immortality. With this end in view, both discredit the discursive understanding as a source of ultimate truth; both are in this sense anti-intellectualists: we can have no "knowledge" of things-in-themselves. Yet, both seek to give naturalism its due, Kant by turning over to it the entire phenomenal world, Jacobi by setting up a world of real objects which, however, is not completely subject to determinism. But Kant remains a rationalist in his effort to derive God, freedom, and immortality as implications of a rational moral law, while Jacobi finds their reality directly guaranteed by the mind's inner experiences, which carry with them the feeling of immediate certainty or faith. Kant's faith is a rational faith grounded on practical or moral certainty, that is, on man's knowledge of right and wrong. Jacobi's faith rests on direct experience of the supersensible: the ultimate realities are immediately revealed to us in our consciousness; in such experience, we come face to face with spirit, freedom, and the divine Being: we believe in these things because we experience them directly. With Hamann and Herder, Jacobi broadens the scope of experience to include the vision of realities which the critical philosophy had placed beyond the reach of the human understanding.

In his *Neue oder psychologische Kritik der Vernunft* (1807), Jacob Fries (1773-1843) seeks to combine the teachings of Kant and Jacobi. He bases the critical philosophy on psychology, substituting self-observation for the transcendental method. The principles of reason, which Kant seeks to prove a priori, are, according to Fries, immediately known in consciousness: we become directly aware of their certainty in ourselves. Only that which is sense-perceived can be known; we cannot know the supersensible, or things-in-themselves; they are objects of faith which satisfy the demands of the heart.

XVII
The Development of
German Idealism

60. JOHANN GOTTLIEB FICHTE

Johann Gottlieb Fichte was born in Saxony in 1762, the son of a poor weaver. Through the generosity of a nobleman who was impressed with the child's talent, he obtained the means to attend the schools at Meissen and Schulpforta. He studied theology at Jena, Leipzig, and Wittenberg (1780-1784), and gave private lessons, often interrupting his university work for long periods of time, in order to gain his livelihood as a tutor (1784-1793). In 1790, at the request of some students who desired him to instruct them in the new critical philosophy, he began the study of Kant, which revolutionized his thought and determined the direction of his life. In 1794 he was called to a professorship at Jena, then the intellectual center of Germany, and became the leader of the new idealism, the aim of which was the reform of life no less than the reform of science and philosophy. During the Jena period (1794-1799) Fichte wrote *Science of Knowledge, Natural Right,* and *Ethics.* The publication of an essay, *On the Ground of Our Belief in a Divine World-Order* (1798), in which he seemed to identify God with the moral world-order, provoked the charge of atheism. He resigned his professorship and went to Berlin, where he developed his philosophy and presented it in popular form in lectures and in books. In 1807-1808 he delivered his celebrated *Addresses to the German Nation,* in which he appealed to the patriotism of his people while Napoleon's army was still occupying Berlin. He became professor of philosophy in the newly founded University of Berlin, in 1809, and served the institution ably and faithfully until his death in 1814.

Versuch einer Kritik aller Offenbarung, 1792; *Grundlage der gesammten Wissenschaftslehre,* 1794; *Grundlage des Naturrechts,* 1796; *Das System der Sittenlehre,* 1798; *Die Bestimmung des Menschen,* 1800; *Die Anweisung zum seligen Leben,* 1801; *Reden an die deutsche Nation,* 1808.

Complete works ed. by I. H. Fichte, 8 vols., 1845-46; also by F. Medicus, 6 vols., 1908-12; Translations: *Fichte's Popular Works* (*Nature of the Scholar; The Vocation of Man, Religion; Characteristics of Present Age*), by W. Smith, 2 vols., 4th ed., 1889; *The Vocation of Man* (published separately), 1925; *Science of Knowledge* and *Science of Ethics,* by A. E. Kroeger, 1889 and 1907; *Addresses to the German Nation,* by R. F. Jones, 1922. R. Adamson, *Fichte,* 1881; A. B. Thompson, *The Unity of Fichte's Doc-*

trine of Knowledge, 1896; E. B. Talbot, *Fundamental Principles of Fichte's Philosophy,* in *Cornell Studies in Philosophy,* No. 7, 1906; H. C. Engelbrecht, *J. G. Fichte,* 1933.

Post-Kantian Philosophy. The interest of the contemporaries and immediate successors of Kant was, as we have seen, focused on the following tasks: how to bring unity into the system of knowledge or to find a common basis for the principles of natural science, morals, esthetics, and teleology; what to do with the thing-in-itself; how to justify the ideas of God, freedom, and immortality. It now seemed desirable to comprehend in the unity of a system the various tendencies of the age: critical idealism, Spinozism, rationalism, the faith-philosophy, as well as the notion of development which occupied a prominent place in French thought and in the writings of Herder.

Kant had opposed the entire naturalistic world-view with its mechanism, fatalism, atheism, egoism, and hedonism, and had made room for a rational faith in human values by limiting the discursive understanding to the field of phenomena. In the world of sense experience, the subject matter of natural science, law reigns supreme: every event, human action included, is a link in the causal chain. There is no scientific knowledge possible outside of this domain: so far as the *Critique of Pure Reason* is concerned, the thing-in-itself is beyond the pale of the knowable. The perusal of the other *Critiques,* however, shows us that the notion of the thing-in-itself develops as we advance in our knowledge of the critical system. Conceived, at first, as a mere abstraction it becomes a necessary idea of reason, a regulative principle expressing the rational demand for unity by means of the ideas of the soul, the world, and God. The idea of freedom is found to be a possible or thinkable ground of all things; the moral law, moreover, demonstrates the reality of this idea and vouchsafes the existence of God, a spiritual kingdom, and immortality. The thing-in-itself which began as an abstraction is interpreted in the sequel as freedom, practical reason, will. There is, then, a higher kind of truth than that offered by scientific intelligence; the moral law within us is a sure guarantee of the existence of the supersensible world, which is inaccessible to the physico-mathematical methods of the understanding. But Kant was cautious in developing the speculative possibilities suggested by the categorical imperative; he hesitated to transcend the limits of experience and refused to lead his followers into the promised land. It could not be reached through the theoretical reason, and he saw no possibility of entering it through the gates of immediate experience: the closer we come to immediacy, according to him, the nearer we are to chaos and the farther from truth: percepts without concepts are blind. And we do not possess the power of intellectual intuition which would enable us to meet the thing-in-itself face to face. Nor was Kant, the sober-minded critic, ready to seek in sentimentalism or mysticism the clue to reality; indeed, he had nothing but contempt for extravagances of this sort in philosophy, for such they seemed to him. And yet, in spite of all his rationalism, there is an element of faith in his method: faith in the moral imperative saves us from agnosticism, materialism, and determinism; we know because we believe in the moral law. If it were not for the moral law, we should know nothing of freedom and the ideal order, and be helpless to free ourselves from the mechanism of nature; it is moral truth that both sets us free and proves our freedom. It was this phase of the new philosophy that particularly appealed to the new generation; it offered an escape from the causal universe without, apparently, sacrificing the legitimate claims of knowledge. Spinozism had become popular in Germany during the latter part of the eighteenth century and was regarded by many thinkers, even by those who rejected it, as the most consistent dogmatic system, indeed as the last word of speculative metaphysics: Lessing, Herder, and Goethe had been attracted to it, and Fichte had heroically accepted its rigid determinism as inevitable, before his acquaintance with the critical philosophy. It was the Kantian solution of the controversy between the head and the heart and the idealistic world-view which it vouchsafed that now became popular in German philosophy and formed the starting-point of what is called Post-Kantian idealism, the chief representatives of which are Fichte, Schelling, and Hegel.

Kant had reached his position by a laborious critical examination of scientific, moral, and metaphysical knowledge; his successors made the intelligible world, or freedom, to which the moral law points, the starting-point of their speculations: the ideal or supersensible world, the world of mind or spirit (*Geist*), is the real world. With this self-determining spiritual activity as the principle, they seek to solve all the problems of philosophy, to account for knowledge and experience, to explain nature, history and human institutions. The ideal principle, they tell us, brings unity into our knowledge, integrates the categories, unifies theoretical and practical reason, enables us to overcome the dualism between mechanism and teleology, and removes the inconsistencies in the Kantian thing-in-itself. We can understand reality only when we interpret it in the light of self-determining reason; reason understands the world only when it understands itself. Hence the importance of the science of knowledge, or *Wissenschaftslehre,* as Fichte called it, in the systems of the Post-Kantians: the discovery of the correct method of knowledge will solve the problems of metaphysics; indeed, philosophy is *Wissenschaftslehre*. Hence, also, philosophy is the absolute science, which explains everything and alone can explain everything: mere empirical knowledge of facts is not real knowledge, and the empirical sciences of nature and history are not true sciences. If to know means to comprehend the active, living, synthetic, spiritual process of reality, a method that limits itself to phenomena in a spatial-temporal-causal series cannot be knowledge: on this point Fichte, Schelling, Schleiermacher, and Hegel are agreed. They agree also in their conception of reality as a process of evolution, in the organic and historical view of things, which Lessing, Herder, Winckelmann, and Goethe taught; but they differ in their methods of reaching a knowledge of it.

Fichte's Principle. Fichte's basal insight, the one which he regards as the keystone of the critical philosophy, is the conception of freedom. He held that the will, or ego, is not a thing among things, a mere link in the causal chain, but free, self-determining activity. Only such activity is truly real, all else is dead passive existence: it is the principle of life and mind, of knowledge and conduct, indeed, of our entire world of experience, the moving power in all progress and civilization. It is the ground on which knowledge rests, the unifying principle of the theoretical understanding, at which Kant had hinted and which Reinhold sought, and the common root of theoretical and practical reason. The study of knowledge will, therefore, prove to be the most important subject of philosophical inquiry, and to this Fichte constantly addressed himself during his strenuous career. The *Wissenschaftslehre* is the key to all knowledge: in it he offers a comprehensive and detailed account of the conditions, principles, or presuppositions of both theoretical and practical reason.

Aim and Method of the Science of Knowledge. Kant, according to Fichte, had abstracted the categories from experience, but had not shown that they were necessary laws of intelligence: he had not demonstrated his principles. This can only be done, Fichte tells us, by deriving them from a common root, that is, only by means of a strictly scientific procedure. Every science, in order to be science, must possess a coherent body of propositions, held together by a first principle; it should be an interrelated system of propositions, an organic whole in which each proposition occupies a definite place and bears a definite relation to the whole. Thus, the concept of space is the central idea in geometry, that of causation in natural science. The different sciences call for an all-embracing science, a science of sciences, a *Wissen-*

schaftslehre, which shall establish or prove the basal principle on which every one of them rests. And this universal science or philosophy, the source of the certainty of all the others, must itself proceed from a self-evident or necessary proposition, from an absolute first principle that shall give its own judgments their scientific character, while, at the same time, validating those of all the other fields of research.

This central science, however, is not the lawgiver, but the historiographer of knowledge: it becomes conscious of the system of the necessary acts of the mind, observes or watches the mind in process of creation. And yet it is not a mere register of what happens, though Fichte sometimes declares it to be such; it seeks to understand the necessity of these acts, to discover the grounds or logical presuppositions of the various forms of knowing. "If but a single link in the long chain which idealism has to forge does not finally connect itself with the one next to it, our science does not claim to have proved anything at all." The assumption is that the mind itself is a rational system, that it acts as organic reason, that the different functions of intelligence are not disconnected and unmeaning acts, but all contribute to a common end; that if it were not for these rational functions, the purpose of reason—namely, the evolution of self-consciousness—could not be realized. The philosopher should, therefore, understand the purpose or meaning of all consciousness before undertaking the task of deduction. Just as in a clock, if we know the purpose of the whole, its structure, size, and so on, we can tell what the parts must be, so in the case of the system of consciousness, we can understand the parts if we understand the purposive whole—a clear, complete, and developed, self-consciousness. The method of the *Wissenschaftslehre* consists in showing that the various acts of intelligence contribute to the evolution of self-consciousness, that the mind could not become free and self-conscious if it were not for these particular acts of intelligence. In his earlier and more technical works Fichte develops the system of knowledge from the fundamental principle; in the more popular presentations he proceeds from the observation of knowledge to the principle; but his object is always the same—the illumination of the organic unity of knowledge. He sometimes calls his method a *genetic* method; it does not, however, aim to describe the *psychological* genesis of the principles of knowledge, but to show how they arise from their necessary presuppositions, or how reason itself evolves them.

In order to study the genesis of rational thinking, the philosopher must set his thought in motion by an act of will: philosophy, therefore, begins, not with a *fact,* but with an *act.* Knowledge is not a mere passive mirroring or opinion of the world, but a self-determining living process—not a possession, but an achievement. Genuine knowledge is possible only by an act of freedom. I understand only what I can create freely in thought; what I cannot create, I do not understand. Consciousness can be explained by nothing outside of itself; it cannot be produced by anything external to it, it is a spontaneous act or creation which becomes aware of itself in the act of creation. Knowledge, in other words, necessarily presupposes as its ground pure, self-determining activity, or rather, it is such activity. Knowledge, intelligence, thought, is free. There could be no world of sense, no experience, no thinking, without such activity; this activity of thought, therefore, is the fundamental principle which we have been seeking. The pure ego, the principle of egoity, or self-active reason, is the starting-point of the *Wissenschaftslehre,* the self-evident presupposition of all knowledge; it is also the end or goal of our science, for when the *Wissenschaftslehre* has reached complete self-consciousness, consciousness has grasped the meaning of all knowledge.

As we have seen, an act of will is needed to set the mind or the ego in motion, but, once at work, it will act in certain necessary ways. In this sense, necessity is a product of freedom. I am not compelled to think, but if I think, I must think according to laws—according to the forms of space and time, according to the principle of sufficient reason, and so on. But no consciousness would be possible without an active ego. Take, for example, the judgment $A = A;$ simple as it is, it would be impossible if it were not for a synthetic mind. If the ego did not spring into existence and act, or posit itself, as Fichte puts it, there could be no subject, no object, no world of experience. And since there can be no world of experience, no phenomenal world, without the ego as its condition, it is impossible to conceive the ego as a link in the chain of objects; that would be putting the cart before the horse. The ego is the ground or condition of the entire sequence of natural events and cannot, therefore, be included among such events.

Knowledge of the Ego. The question arises, How do we reach the ego-principle? We can infer it as the ground of experience and of the forms of thought, as the unity of theoretical and practical reason. But Schulze had warned against such reasoning as being contrary to the spirit of the *Critique,* and Fichte himself sometimes sees no more speculative warrant for assuming a spiritual ground than a material ground. He offers several other lines of argument in support of his idealism. One of them is inspired by the main insight of Kant's ethical philosophy, and finds its way to the basic principle through the moral law. Fichte shares Kant's view of the insufficiency of the intellect: we cannot grasp the living reality by the discursive under-standing with its spatial, temporal, causal ways of thinking; only when we have seen through the nature of ordinary knowing, detected its super-ficiality and relativity, can we grasp the living realities behind the surface: freedom, the moral world-order, and God. If we were limited to scientific intelligence, we could never rise above the notion of an inexorable causal order, and would ourselves be unable to escape the machinery of nature. But there is a way out. In an act of *intellectual intuition,* which is itself an act of free will, we become conscious of the law of duty, or the universal purpose, which commands us to be free persons, to free ourselves from the determinism of nature, to refuse to be mere links in a causal chain. Acceptance of the law of duty and of the freedom which it implies will give our life worth and meaning; it will enable us to understand the world as the instrument of a universal purpose—the realization of freedom —and thereby to transform ourselves from blind tools of this purpose into its willing helpers. Now it becomes clear that our ordinary knowledge gained by sense perception is a practical instrument for achieving freedom; it presents us with the resistance needed for the exercise of will: we cannot become free without putting forth effort, hence we need a world to struggle against and to overcome. The world would have no meaning, therefore, if the command of duty to achieve freedom were not realizable; but it is perfectly intelligible to us in the light of the deliverances of the moral consciousness.

These thoughts won for Fichte's philosophy the name of ethical idealism: it is a world-view based on moral faith. We cannot prove to theoretical reason the primacy of a free self-determining being—for theoretical reason never ceases to search after grounds—but we accept such a principle as ultimate, because it alone can satisfy the demands of our moral nature and give our life meaning and worth. An ethical decision is basic to philosophy and "the choice of one's philosophy depends on what kind of man one is." The man without the ethical ideal, the man who cannot free himself from the machinery of nature, cannot conceive of himself otherwise than as a thing or product, or take an interest in the free self: he cannot know and prize what he has not experienced—the freedom to be a person—and he cannot experience it because he has never achieved it. The man who has freed himself from the slavery of the senses, who is a self-determining agent, regards himself as a power superior to everything sensuous, and cannot will to conceive himself as a mere thing.

There is another line of thought in Fichte, according to which the ego is immediately conscious of its free activity in itself. Idealism has this advantage over dogmatism or materialism: the basic reality for idealism, the ego, appears in consciousness, not as an object of experience nor as a phenomenon or link in the causal series, but as an ego-in-itself, as something real, above all experience. There exists an immediate self-consciousness of free mental action. But such consciousness does not force itself upon us, we must produce it in ourselves by an act of freedom. If we cannot perform the act, we will not understand the idealistic philosophy, we will get no glimpse into the real world of mind. The dogmatist denies the postulate of the freedom and independence of the ego because he cannot discover it in his world; if he is consistent, he must be a fatalist and a materialist. We cannot prove conceptually that there is such an act of intellectual intuition, nor what it is. Everyone must find it directly in himself, or he will never know of it. As well might we attempt to explain to a man born blind what colors are, as try to demonstrate what this intellectual intuition is. But it can be pointed out to everyone that it occurs in every phase of his consciousness. Every person who ascribes activity to himself, tacitly appeals to such an intuition. Fichte holds that wherever there is spiritual activity, there is consciousness of it, even though it escapes the attention of the dogmatist.

Fichte also points out that the truth of idealism can be verified by experience. If the presupposition of idealism is correct and if the correct deductions have been made, the final result must be a system of necessary ideas, or the sum-total of experience. If the results of a philosophy do not agree with experience, the philosophy is certainly false, for it has not kept its promise to deduce the whole of experience and to explain it by the necessary action of intelligence. But idealism does not keep experience in view as a goal to be reached; it pays no attention whatever to experience. In its procedure, it evolves its propositions from the basal idea, regardless of what the results may be. That is what Fichte says, but, as a matter of fact, he does pay attention to experience; he asks us to observe the intelligence in its operations, to watch the mind at work. What he is suggesting is that mere observation of such acts would not be philosophy, that genuine philosophy demands an understanding of these acts, of their ground and purpose, and that such an understanding can only be reached by logical thought.

The External World. Fichte bases all reality on the ego; since ego is everything, there can be nothing outside, no thing-in-itself in the sense of an independent extra-mental object. The problem of idealism is, therefore, to explain how we happen to ascribe objective reality to what seems to be merely subjective, or, how we come to assume existence or being as opposed to life, action and mind. Fichte tells us that it belongs to the very nature of the self-active principle to limit itself: in springing into existence it at the same time limits itself, and limit itself it must if it is to be at all. I experience my limitation in my feelings of red, sweet, cold; the sense qualities force themselves on me and thereby limit me. Dogmatists attempt to explain such original feelings or sensations as the effects of something, of a thing-in-itself; but Fichte rejects all explanation of sensation by a transcendental object. The objective world is produced by the ego for itself, in the sense that the mind projects the purely subjective modifications of consciousness into space, or makes objects of them. If it were not for sensations and the necessary functions or acts of the ego, involving space, time, and causality, we should never produce the phenomenal world which we perceive. What arouses sensations, we do not know. This does not mean that our knowledge of the phenomenal world has no objective validity. Far from being an illusion, the world of phenomenal objects is the sole domain of truth. It would be illusory only if there were things-in-themselves existing independently of us. The thing-in-itself is a fictitious notion, the invention of a false philosophy; common sense knows nothing of it. Accept this world as you find it, seek to understand it and to act on it—this is the attitude of critical idealism. We cannot transcend consciousness by our theoretical reason. All that we can know is that the ego posits itself and limits itself by the non-ego; but why it does so cannot be explained *theoretically*. Fichte, however, solves the problem practically: we cannot explain to reason the origin and the limits of knowledge, but we can make their significance or ethical value perfectly clear and definite. The domain of knowledge with its well-defined limits has a definite function in the moral order of things. What we perceive through reason has reality, the only reality that concerns us or exists for us. Our world is "the sensualized material of our duty"; through things existing in the world as we know it we can and must realize our moral ideals. The world is a means of realizing moral purposes; since it affords a sphere for moral endeavor, what difference does it make whether it is real or apparent? The ego as a self-active being needs a world of opposition, one in which it can struggle, one in which it can become conscious of itself and its freedom, one in which it can achieve freedom. It demands a world ordered according to laws, a strictly determined world, in order that the free self may realize its purposes by relying on these laws. The ego must know what to expect, otherwise rational purposive action would be impossible.

Objective Idealism. There is much in this view that is suggestive of subjective idealism, and most of Fichte's contemporaries interpreted it as such. Fichte, however, means by the ego, on which he bases his philosophy, not the individual ego of common sense, but the pure ego, pure activity, universal reason, intelligence as such. Absolute ego (egoity, or *Ichheit*) and individuality are quite different concepts for him. The pure ego is logically prior to the personal ego, it is the condition, or logical ground, of the individual ego. We cannot think of individual selves without ascribing to them all the same reason, the same universal processes of thought. The logical *prius,* however, does not remain a mere logical *prius* with Fichte; as we saw before, the absolute ego turns out to be more than an abstraction. It is a reality, above all persons, over-individual; it is the universal active reason, the same in all persons; the individual ego can have a vision of it if it so wills. The highest degree of self-consciousness is that of the philosopher; his is an intellectual intuition in which the ego returns unto itself and is conscious of its activity. The ego, intuiting its own activity, rises above space and time perception; it no longer beholds a phenomenal causal order, but withdraws within itself, looks at itself, and knows itself. Intuitive self-knowledge is what gives Fichte's philosophy such certainty in his eyes; the ego not only infers a principle or reaches it by logical abstraction, but experiences it, in a way which was excluded by Kant's analysis. In his earlier writings Fichte speaks of this principle as the universal reason that acts in each of us; it is that dimension of the self that thinks in universal terms, knows universal truths and has universal purposes or ideals. He was interested in refuting naturalism, the mechanistic and deterministic conception of reality; and so emphasized the idealistic character of all experience. His failure to define his conception with precision, together with the fact that he called it ego, led to the misconception of his system as subjective idealism, against which he protested vigorously from the beginning. As his system developed, he expressed himself more definitely, and the principle which his opponents had misinterpreted as the personal subjective ego, he unequivocally described as an absolute ego, or God. But whether it be called reason, absolute ego, or God, the principle is conceived as a universal rationality that dominates every individual consciousness. There are other rational beings outside my personal ego, who both act on the phenomenal world and represent the absolute ego in much the same way as I do; the same universal principle of rationality is active in all egos. Nature is not the creation of the particular ego, but the phenomenal expression or reflection in an individual of the universal spiritual principle. The universal ego is the true reality of which the individual selves are the products or manifestations. Fichte is an absolute idealist and not a subjective idealist, since he assumes a universal principle of reality and not merely an individual consciousness; but he refuses to conceive this principle as a static substance, either material or spiritual: it is a living, flowing, self-determining spiritual process that expresses or manifests itself in individual selves, and that is the law of their nature, the common ground of their sensational or phenomenal life as well as of the necessary laws of thought. It is this universal life and reason that lives and thinks and acts in us: in it we live and move and have our being. Fichte does not deny the existence of an extra-mental world, in the sense of a reality outside of the individual personal consciousness; indeed, he tries to show that there could be no such consciousness, no individuals, if it were not for the universal life-process. In so far as he acknowledges extra-mental realities, his position may be described as realistic. His realism is, however, asserted within the framework of absolute idealism. The real world is not a world of dead things, arranged in a spatial-temporal-causal order; the latter is the revelation in human consciousness of the absolute principle, and could not exist if it were not for the universal ego. Fichte's subjective idealism is supplemented by an objective or metaphysical idealism; he himself called it real-idealism. We are the creatures, products or revelations of universal nature; in us the universal principle of rationality thinks and comes to consciousness; and, for that very reason, nature must be *Geist* (spirit or mind), and can be nothing else.

How the universal and unlimited life-principle comes to differentiate itself into the countless individual selves, Fichte tries to make clear by means of the analogy of light. As light is broken by an obstacle and reflected or turned back to its source, so the universal activity must be reflected, or turned back upon itself, by some obstacle. There could be no consciousness, no self-consciousness, no self-determining thought, no knowledge, unless the infinite activity met with some check: it can become conscious of itself only in finite form, in an ego limited by opposition to other finite egos. And since universal life is infinite, it cannot exhaust itself in finite form, but must go on, infinitely, producing egos, and become conscious of itself in this process of separation or individuation. Consciousness, it seems, arises through the self-limitation of the universal ego, through an act that precedes the birth of consciousness, and of which, therefore, we are not conscious as individuals. The absolute ego produces the selves unconsciously, and the selves are unconscious of their creation.

But why should there be life at all, and why should it express itself in countless forms of consciousness? We cannot conceive of the universal life process or pure activity as purposeless; it would be meaningless if it were not dedicated to an ethical goal. The purpose of nature, or the non-ego, is the same: it, too, is a means of realizing the ego. It is the same absolute ego that expresses itself in man and in nature, in the individual self and in the non-self. Events in the world of nature and acts of individual selves are the visible expressions of the ultimate moral purpose; we can understand them only as such; they have no reality except as instrumentalities of the moral purpose of the universe. The individual selves can, however, by acts of will raise themselves from the state of mere appearance to the knowledge of the supersensible, and in this way identify themselves with the universal moral purpose.

There is, then, a difference between the absolute, independent ego and the conscious, dependent, individual ego. The absolute ego is present in the individual ego as a pure impulse to action and as a moral purpose, as the consciousness of duty, which commands the self to overcome the opposition of the world of sense, to realize the ideal of freedom toward which the absolute ego strives. When we become aware of pure activity in ourselves, we know the essence of reality, and when we strive to realize our moral purpose, we are striving to realize the meaning of the universe, the purpose of the absolute ego. The purpose of which the individual ego becomes conscious in itself is the voice of the absolute, the purpose of the same absolute ego that expresses itself in the world of things. We can accomplish what our nature urges, or impels us to do, since the same universal will that prompts the act at the same time produces the appropriate changes in the external world.

The question arises: What freedom is left to the individual self in this scheme? The individual self is a manifestation of an absolute activity; it is determined, on its theoretical side, by necessary laws of sense perception and thought, and, on its practical side, by the universal purpose. The universal purpose is bound to realize itself in the world whether the individual wills it or not, and the sense world will follow its laws regardless of him. But the individual has the power to choose whether he shall think or not—thinking, in the real sense of the term, is only possible by an act of will—and he can decide, also, whether to make the universal purpose his own; that, too, will depend on his free choice. It lies in our power to decide whether we shall remain blind tools of the universal purpose or become its conscious and willing instruments in the service of the good. When once we have decided freely to do our duty, to realize the universal purpose, we are no longer free; we have made ourselves instruments of the absolute, and our moral life is there-after determined.

Freedom, in this connection, means a free and inexplicable choice, the freedom of indifference, a sudden leap of the will. Fichte concludes from this view that men are either good or bad, according to whether they have chosen the good or have remained mere cogs in the machinery of sense, and that the good alone win immortality. He also concludes that resistance and moral struggle are never eliminated; the universal moral purpose is never completely realized; moral life is in constant progress towards a good which is never reached, and world will be succeeded by world without end. The moral good does not consist in a static goal achieved once and for all, but in the perpetual struggle to realize the moral purpose of the universe.

Moral Philosophy. Fichte's entire system is tinged with ethical ideas: it begins with Kant's categorical imperative and ends with the universal moral purpose of God. We have seen how he deduces our world of experience from the moral law: the moral law commands freedom from the rule of sense. There can be no deliverance from sense unless there is something to be delivered from, a state of unfreedom, a natural ego limited by a world. The moral law implies freedom, freedom implies overcoming of obstacles, and this implies a sensible world. The moral law thus implies an indefinitely continued life of struggle, hence immortality; and it implies a universal purpose or a God. It also presupposes that what the individual aims at in his dutiful conduct is actually achieved and realized, that there is a moral order of the universe, an order that ought to result from the moral determination of man's will, something that lies beyond the sphere of his own individual moral will, but which must be assumed in order to give it purpose and meaning. In other words, the moral law implies a religious faith: it would have no meaning without religious faith, without the belief in a moral world-order and in a moral world-orderer. It is faith, then, that gives certainty and conviction to what might otherwise be mere illusion, and this faith is a decision of the will: I will to believe. The moral conscience is thus the touchstone of every truth and every conviction.

The ethical purpose realizes itself in the world; nature and man are instruments in the service of the good. Man's vocation is, therefore, to do his duty, to work consciously and voluntarily for the realization of the highest good, to turn his gaze toward the universal moral end. His conscience commands him to free himself from the slavery of sense, to be a person, not a thing. He cannot, however, escape the determinism of nature without knowledge, and he cannot act on nature without knowledge; hence he must seek knowledge for moral ends and not from mere curiosity. It is, therefore, man's duty to know what he is doing, and not to act unless he does know what he is doing. He should act from conviction always and never under the compulsion of authority. The command to be free carries with it the command to exercise one's reason, to understand the purpose established by conscience. Conscience commands duty for duty's sake; conscience tells me what my purpose ought to be. I do not act as I act because something is a purpose for me, but it becomes a purpose because I ought so to act. Hence conscience is infallible, it will always tell us, in every concrete situation, how to act—that is, if we stop to think the matter through.

For Fichte, morality does not consist merely in the good will—respect for the moral law is not enough; the good will must express itself in acts, it should seek to overcome the resistance of nature, inner and outer: morality is a struggle. The battle with nature, however, does not consist in its annihilation, but in adapting it to man's ethical purposes; it can and ought to be made an appropriate instrument for the purposes of reason. The ethical significance of natural goods, of property, the various callings and our entire industrial life, lies in the fact that all of them can be placed in the service of the universal moral purpose. And since the moral life is not an isolated individual existence but a community life, each individual should regard himself as a member of a working society and sacrifice his own earthly possessions for the common good, by which alone the ultimate purpose can be realized. Every man should freely choose his proper sphere of action in the world in accordance with the dictates of his conscience, but in order that he may choose properly education is needed. Indeed, it is necessary that the individual be educated in order that conscience may arise in him; without instruction the voice of duty would not speak, and its significance would not be understood.

Every individual has his particular place in society in which to labor for the whole. Similarly, every people has its peculiar place in civilization, its unique contribution to make in the battle of humanity for freedom. In his patriotic *Addresses to the German Nation,* Fichte held up before his people the ideal of German unity; it is Germany's mission, he said, to regain her national existence, to assume philosophical leadership in the interest of civilization, to establish a State rooted in personal liberty, a veritable kingdom of justice, such as has never appeared on earth, which shall realize freedom based on the equality of all who wear the human form; it is the vocation of the human race to incorporate itself in a single united body, a universal federation of states, in which the culture contributed by every age and people shall be distributed over the entire globe. Fichte's nationalistic ideals for the German nation were subservient to a higher humanitarianism.

But the earthly goal cannot be our highest goal: We promote the earthly human end merely as a means to the universal purpose—the realization of a spiritual kingdom which alone gives worth and meaning to the phenomenal order. Man is a citizen of both worlds: he cannot work for the other world without being willing to work for this. We work for the other world by making the will good; every act in accordance with the will affects God and through him other spirits. The voice of conscience is God's voice in me; through conscience the spiritual world reaches down to me, through the will I reach up to it and act on it. God is the mediator between the spiritual world and me. The only principle by which I recognize your work is the voice of conscience, which commands me to respect your work, and this voice is God's voice. Our belief in the truth of the sense world is nothing but the faith that a life promoting freedom and morality will evolve, world without end, from our disinterested and faithful performance of duty in this world of sense.

The state of universal peace among men and of their absolute dominion over the mechanism of nature is not something to be possessed for its own sake; the ideal is that men should produce it themselves, and that it should be produced by all men, as one great free moral community. The basal law of the great moral kingdom of which our present life is a part is that there can be nothing new or better for a particular individual except through his own moral will, nor for the community except through the social moral will.

I do not understand my complete vocation; what I ought to be and what I shall be transcends all my thinking. I know for certain at every moment of my life what I ought to do in it: I ought to develop my intelligence and acquire knowledge in order to extend the sphere of my duty. I ought to regard myself, body and soul, merely as a means to the end of duty.[1]

The New Idealism and Romanticism. Fichte's philosophy takes account of the diverse currents in the thought of his times, and seeks to direct them into a common stream. With the *Aufklärung,* he opposes authority and tradition, and seeks a rational explanation of the world. In exalting the free personality and the rights of man, as well as civilization and progress, and demanding the reform of science, philosophy, religion, education, and of human life in general, he simply expresses the spirit of the entire modern

[1] *Vocation of Man,* Bk. III. Cf. trans. by W. Smith, pp. 165-66.

age. His patriotic appeal for German national unity and his ideal of a State based on equality and justice voice the yearnings of a people oppressed by absolutism and humiliated by the Napoleonic wars. In making mind or spirit (*Geist*) the central principle of reality and in delivering man from the incubus of mechanism, he expresses the yearning for a universe that shall be intelligible to reason and in sympathy with human ideals. Consistent with the new idealism, as interpreted by him, and in agreement with the great leaders of German literature, Lessing, Herder, Goethe, he conceives existence as a dynamic process of evolution guided by a moral purpose. With both the classic and Romantic poets of his age and the faith-philosophers— and, indeed, with Kant himself—he agrees that the universal living whole cannot be grasped by the categories of science: with Goethe, that the universe must be conceived organically, as a unity in diversity; with Jacobi, that it can be known only in the inner living experience of the free agent, in intuition; in the act of freedom, in the sense of duty, and in the love of truth, spirit speaks to spirit. The anti-rationalistic and mystical element in Fichte's system—which accompanies his rigorous logic—attracted the Romantic poets—the two Schlegels, Tieck, and Novalis. Many other phases of the new idealism found favor in their eyes: its seeming subjectivism, its historical point of view, and its conception of the uniqueness of German culture. But they tended to exaggerate all these characteristic features of the Fichtean philosophy. They emphasized Fichte's sentimentalism but ignored his rationalism; Fichte's intuition became the divining, sympathetic insight of the poetic genius; the rational and ethical ego was transformed into a romantic, mystical, impulsive, even freakish, individualistic self. Nature was interpreted in analogy with such an ego and conceived as the abode of occult personified forces, while history was appealed to in support of tradition and the past given authority over the present.

Schelling brought all these tendencies to a focus, particularly the new idealism and the poetic romanticism. He was, likewise, interested in Spinozism and in the natural-scientific movement, which had made headway in Germany under the impetus given it by the critical philosophy. As a youth, while still at the Theological Seminary at Tübingen, Schelling gained fame as the best interpreter of Fichte; and, a few years later, supplemented Fichte's philosophy with a philosophy of nature that not only pleased the romanticists and Goethe, but even found friends among the natural scientists of his country.

61. FRIEDRICH WILHELM SCHELLING

Friedrich Wilhelm Joseph Schelling, born 1775, studied philosophy and theology at the Theological Seminary of the University of Tübingen from 1790 to 1795. After serving as private tutor to two young students at Leipzig for two years, during which he himself studied mathematics, physics, and medicine at the university, he accepted a professorship of philosophy at Jena (1798). Here he became attached to the Romantic circle presided over by August and Caroline von Schlegel, and produced his most brilliant works. After holding various positions, at Würzburg (1803-1806), at Munich as Director of the Academy of Fine Arts (1806-1820), at Erlangen (1820-1827), and at Munich, as professor of philosophy in the newly established university (1827-1841), he was called to Berlin to stem the tide of the popular Hegelian philosophy, but met with little success. He died in 1854.

During his earlier period, Schelling accepted the Fichtean philosophy and developed it in the spirit of the master; among his writings are: *Ideen zu einer Philosophie der Natur* (1797); *Von der Weltseele* (1798); *System des transcendentalen Idealismus* (1800). During the second period, which shows the influence of Bruno and Spinoza, he conceives both nature and mind as two aspects of a higher principle: this is his philosophy of identity, presented in *Bruno* (1802) and *Methode des akademischen Studiums* (1802). In his third period Schelling develops what he calls his positive philosophy, a philosophy of mystical revelation and mythology, which resembles that of Jacob Boehme. The universe is conceived as a fall from God. The meaning of universal history is sought in the obscure beginnings of mythology and revelation, from which, Schelling thinks, we may gain hints of the original fall of man. The works of this period, with the exception of one on human freedom, were not published until after his death.

Complete works ed. by his son, 1856-1861, 14 vols.; selected works ed. by O. Weiss, 1908. *Of Human Freedom,* trans. by J. Gutman, 1936; *Ages of the World,* trans. by F. Bolman, Jr., 1942.

Philosophy of Nature. Schelling was drawn to the new idealism, which explained the world of experience in terms of mind, and became an ardent exponent of the idealistic position. He was not, however, satisfied with Fichte's original conception of nature as a product of the absolute ego, which serves, in the individual consciousness, merely as an obstacle or incentive to the will. Schelling rejects the thesis: "Nature is the material of our duty," and advances to objective idealism and pantheism, as Fichte himself had done. The pure ego of epistemology becomes the absolute ego of metaphysics. If reality is, at bottom, a living self-determining process akin to the human spirit, nature cannot be conceived as a mere external impediment to the will or as a dead mechanical order. We can understand nature because it has kinship with us, because it is the expression of a dynamic mind, because there is life and reason and purpose in it. But reason is not necessarily *conscious* intelligence; with the romanticists and faith-philosophers, Schelling broadens the conception of spirit, mind, or reason, so as to include the unconscious, instinctive, purposive force that manifests itself in inorganic and organic nature, as well as in the highest self-consciousness of the philosopher. That which is common to unconscious nature and to self-conscious mind is pure activity, self-determining energy; reality consists of action, life, and will. The absolute ground, or source of all things, is creative energy, absolute will or ego, the one all-pervading world-spirit, in which everything dwells in potency and from which everything that is actual proceeds. The ideal and the real, thought and being, are identical in their root; the same creative energy that reveals itself in the self-conscious mind operates unconsciously in sense perception, in animal instinct, in organic growth, in chemical processes, in crystallization, in electrical phenomena, and in gravity: there is life and reason in them all. The principle, which, as blind unconscious impulse, forms and moves my body, becomes conscious of itself, and thereby separates itself from its blind, striving stage—while still continuing to exist at the unconscious level—and becomes pure spirit, pure self-consciousness. The universal ego expresses itself in me and in numberless other individual selves—only in conscious minds does it become aware of itself. We are real in so far as we are rooted in the universal ego; we are not real as independent, isolated individuals: absolute personal selfhood is an illusion. Schelling's insight that nature is visible spirit, and spirit invisible nature, gave an impetus to the Romantic imagination and encouraged the new poets to endow the world with life and mind, and to view it with a loving sympathy which they could not feel in the presence of a dead machine.

Nature and mind, being and thought, are not, however, as Spinoza held, two parallel aspects of the Absolute, but different steps, stages or epochs in the evolution of absolute mind. The Absolute unfolds itself, it has a history: it is an evolutionary process, the highest goal of which is self-consciousness. Just as in our own selves we rise from the unconscious or subconscious stage to clear self-consciousness and yet remain one and the same self, so the one universal ego rises from darkness to light. The graduated scale of organized objects, from inanimate nature to man, clearly betrays a creative power which only gradually evolves into complete freedom. The dead and unconscious products of nature are merely unsuccessful attempts of nature to express itself; so-called dead nature is an unripe intelligence, but its phenomena unconsciously exhibit the traces of reason. Nature reaches its highest goal, self-consciousness, in man; in human self-consciousness, the original identity of nature and mind is revealed to us. The most perfect theory of nature would, therefore, be one in which all the laws of nature could be reduced to laws of perception and thinking; in which the whole of nature would resolve itself into intelligence.

According to Schelling, it is immaterial whether we begin with nature or with mind, with the philosophy of nature or with the system of transcendental idealism; whether we ask: How does nature become conscious intelligence? or, How does intelligence become unconscious nature? The principles of knowledge and the principles of reality are the same; the questions, How is knowledge possible? and, How is a world possible? are answered by referring to the same conditions and laws. In tracing the different epochs in the history of self-consciousness, from primitive sensation to the higher intellectual processes, we are, at the same time, tracing the development of the absolute principle as it manifests itself in nature. "All qualities are sensations, all bodies are percepts of nature; nature itself, with all its sensations and percepts, is a congealed intelligence."

The same law pervades all things: the principle at the root of things acts in the same uniform ways, pulsates in the same rhythms everywhere. Its action is a process of expansion and contraction: the principle unfolds what is potential or implicit in it, objectifies itself, goes out of itself, so to speak, and then returns to itself enriched and enhanced: in self-consciousness nature expresses itself as subject and object, differentiates and becomes conscious of itself in the process. The different forces of nature are fundamentally the same; heat, light, magnetism, electricity are different stages of one and the same principle, as are also inorganic and organic nature. There is unity in the different organic forms; they constitute a graduated scale and are the products of the same principle of organization; they are all built on the same plan. All the products of nature are held together by one creative spirit; every part of nature subserves the whole. Man is the highest product of nature. In man, nature attains the realization of the goal of self-consciousness.

Schelling attempts to construct nature a priori, to reason out the necessary stages in the process of its evolution, as Fichte had tried to show the logical steps in the development of mind. Like Herder and Fichte before him and Hegel after him, he finds a dialectical process at work in the world, a process in which two opposing activities—thesis and antithesis—are united and harmonized or reconciled in a higher synthesis. This he calls the law of triplicity: action is followed by reaction; from the opposition a harmony or synthesis results, which, again, is dissolved in the never-ending movement of time. There can be neither dead, static substance nor complete flux in nature. Schelling applies the triadic law to the details of inorganic and organic nature; we find it expressed in the series: attraction, repulsion, gravitation; magnetism, electricity, chemism; sensibility, irritability, reproduction. We shall not follow him in his nature philosophy, in which poetry and science, fancy and logic intermingle; fantastic as it is in detail, Schelling's basal idea of nature as a dynamic evolution foreshadows the dynamic conception of matter of contemporary physics.

It is because nature is alive, because there is law, reason, and purpose in it, that we can understand it, that it can mean anything to us. It is bone of our bone and flesh of our flesh. With Fichte, Schelling rejects the old notion of the unchangeable static substance and substitutes for it the dynamic idea, the conception of universal life, of a living, creative, purposive principle of evolution, which develops from unconsciousness to consciousness, and whose ultimate end is the self-conscious reason of man. He opposes the mathematical-physical conception of nature and substitutes for it the teleological conception, or rather, reconciles mechanism with the older teleology by the doctrine of unconscious purpose. On the lower stages, the Absolute acts *as if* it had conscious purpose; it acts without intention, yet it is not pushed into action, mechanically, from the outside. If the observer, who sees only the outside of the thing—its changes in appearance, its different states and stages—could place himself on the inside; if he could himself be the impulse or the movement, and at the same time be conscious of it, he would find that the impulse is not compelled from without but directs itself from within.

Schelling's philosophy of nature contained much that was fantastic and frequently offered bold assertions, fanciful analogies, and brilliant figures of speech instead of proofs and facts. In attempting to force nature into its logical rubrics, it tended to withdraw the attention from the factual details of nature. It did, however, arouse an interest in nature and in the study of nature, counteracted the influence of a one-sided mechanism, kept alive the philosophical instinct or craving for unity, which has always marked German thought—even among its leading natural scientists—and emphasized the dynamic and evolutionary conception of reality, which has its adherents even at the present day.

Philosophy of Mind. We shall not attempt to offer a detailed account of Schelling's philosophy of mind, as given in the *System of Transcendental Idealism*, in which his dependence on Fichte is most marked. It traces the history of self-consciousness in its different epochs, from primary sensation

to creative imagination; from creative imagination to reflection; from reflection to the absolute act of will. Since there is the same principle at work
in all forms of life, we shall expect the activities of mind to correspond to
those found in nature; the forces of nature continue to operate in the consciousness of man. The method employed is the same as Fichte's: there
could be no finite ego unless the absolute ego or energy limited its infinite
activity and produced a phenomenal world; the ego could not achieve self-
consciousness and freedom were it not for such a phenomenal world. The
objective world is the product of absolute reason, which produces sense perception, the necessary categories of thought, and self-consciousness in the
individual. A further precondition of self-consciousness and freedom is life
in society and in an organized State. An isolated ego could have no thought
of a real world and hence no consciousness of freedom. In the State, which is
the expression of unconscious universal reason, the natural selfish impulses
are restrained by the universal will; individuals are unconsciously socialized
and prepared for a higher ethical stage, on which they do the right, not from
force, but consciously and willingly. The highest stage in the development of
self-consciousness is reached in art; the creative artist imitates the creative
action of nature and becomes conscious of it, becomes conscious of the activity of the Absolute; indeed, in artistic creation the Absolute becomes conscious of its own creative force. The view that art—and not morality, as
Fichte had thought—is the noblest function of man, was popular in the
golden age of German literature.

Logic and Intuition. Schelling's philosophy, in its most developed stage, is a
form of pantheism, in which the universe is conceived as a living, evolving
system, an organism, in which every part has its place and subserves the
whole. Subject and object, form and matter, the ideal and the real, are one,
together and inseparable; the one is the many, and the many are one. Just
as in an organism we cannot tear the part from the whole nor understand
it apart from the whole, nor understand the whole without its parts, so
reality is an organic whole of interrelated parts. The same unity in plurality,
or identity in diversity, which characterized nature, we find in mental life;
in the act of knowledge, the knower and the thing known are one.

But how can we be sure of the truth of this system, how can we prove
it? What guaranteee have we that action, or life, or will, is the principle of
things, and that it passes through the stages of evolution described by Schelling? His answer is not always the same. Sometimes he holds that since the
world is thoroughly rational, it is self-evident that reason can understand it,

and that we are able to reconstruct it in thought. Moreover, since there is a logic in its history, we can reproduce the necessary stages of its evolution in our thinking. His ideal is to produce an organic system of knowledge, in which every judgment has its proper place, depending on other judgments and on the whole system for its truth. In this mood he imitates Spinoza and employs the geometric method in order to make his philosophy logic-proof. However, in spite of his attempt at a rational deduction of the progressive stages of nature and mind from the notion and purpose of the Absolute, he was not always confident that his system could be made to rest on an a priori universal and necessary postulate. Philosophy, he held, cannot demonstrate idealism, any more than it can prove dogmatism or materialism; man's world-view is his free choice. The only way to prove freedom, or the reality of the creative principle, is to be a free self-determining being oneself. When we set up freedom as our ideal, we are tacitly assuming the reality of an absolute creative spirit; for, if the world were mere matter, it would be meaningless to strive to become free; belief in the ideal implies belief in a spiritual world. The will to be free must interpret the world in idealistic terms. There is another argument, which Fichte had used: a free being will know what freedom is, and understand idealism. We become aware of freedom, or the Absolute, only in the spontaneous activity of intelligence and in voluntary action: in an *intellectual intuition*, which is the unique endowment of the philosopher. The living, moving element in nature, the inner meaning of reality, cannot be grasped by the scientific understanding with its spatial, temporal, and causal categories. "What is described in concepts," Schelling tells us, "is at rest, hence there can be concepts only of things, of the finite and sense-perceived. The concept of movement is not movement itself, and without intuition we should never know what motion is. Freedom, however, can be comprehended only by freedom; activity only by activity." Natural science and common sense take a static view of things, comprehend only their *being;* philosophy knows them in their *becoming*, it is interested in the living, moving element in them. Natural science and common sense see them only from the outside; we must know them from the inside, as they are in themselves and for themselves, and that we can do only by knowing ourselves. Perhaps we can reconcile the rationalistic and intuitionistic tendencies in Schelling's thought by saying that intuition gives us our principle or fundamental postulate, on the basis of which we construct a rational theory of the world.

Under the influence of a great poetic era and of the artistic atmosphere

in which he lived, Schelling came to regard this intuition as an artistic intuition. At first he conceived self-consciousness, or pure self-reflection, as
the goal of the Absolute, as the highest achievement in the evolution of life
and mind, and held that such a state could be experienced only in the intuition of the philosopher. Afterwards he interpreted the universe as a work of
art: the Absolute realizes its purpose in the creation of a cosmos. Hence art,
and not philosophical knowledge, is the highest human function. In the
products of art, subject and object, the ideal and the real, form and matter,
mind and nature, freedom and necessity, fuse and interpenetrate: in art the
harmony sought by philosophy is achieved before our very eyes in a sensuous
medium; it is a unity to be seen, touched, and heard. Nature herself is a
great poem, and her secret is revealed by art. The creative artist, in realizing
his ideal, creates even as nature creates, and so knows how nature works;
hence artistic creation serves as model for the intuition of the world:
it is the true organ of philosophy. Like the artistic genius, the philosopher
must have the faculty of perceiving the harmony and identity in the universe: esthetic intuition is absolute knowing. Akin to the esthetic conception
is the organic conception, which Schelling sometimes describes as intellectual
intuition: it is the faculty of seeing things whole, the universal in the particular, unity in plurality, identity in diversity. He expressly declares that
there is nothing mysterious in this function, but that no one can hope to be
a philosopher who does not possess the power to transcend the disconnected,
isolated data of experience, and to pierce through the outer shell to the inner kernel of reality.

This type of thought is diametrically opposed to the logico-mathematical
method of science, against which German literature and German idealistic
philosophy both protest. Goethe's entire view of nature, art, and life rested
on the organic or teleological conception; he too regarded the ability to see
the whole in its parts, the idea or form in the concrete reality, as the poet's
and thinker's highest gift, as an *aperçu*, a revelation to consciousness that
gives man a hint of his likeness to God. It is this gift which Faust craves and
Mephisto sneers at as "the high intuition" (*die hohe Intuition*).[2]

In the last stage of his philosophical development, Schelling reaches a
religious mysticism: the world is conceived as a fall from God, and the goal
of man as a return to God, achieved in a mystical intuition in which the soul
strips off its selfhood and becomes absorbed in the Absolute. At every stage

[2] Cf. Thilly, "The World-View of a Poet: Goethe's philosophy," *Hibbert Journal,*
April 1908.

of his philosophy, however, Schelling defines the Absolute as a union or identity of spirit and nature, of the infinite and the finite, and adopts as the ideal for man the knowledge of the Absolute through some kind of intuition, be it the self-consciousness of the thinker, a free act of will, artistic creation, or religious feeling.

62. Friedrich Schleiermacher

Friedrich Daniel Ernst Schleiermacher was born in Breslau in 1768, and received part of his education in the schools of the Moravian brotherhood, a pietistic sect. Influenced by the new critical philosophy, he continued the study of theology and philosophy at the University of Halle (1787-1790), served as a tutor, and then entered the ministry (1794). In 1809 he became preacher of Trinity Church at Berlin, and in 1810 professor of theology at the new University of Berlin, positions which he filled until his death in 1834. In Berlin he came under the influence of the leaders of the Romantic school, but did not follow them in their extreme teachings. Although Schleiermacher achieved his greatest distinction as a theologian, he has gained substantial fame as an historian of philosophy by his painstaking study of the philosophical classics.

Works: *Reden über die Religion*, 1799 (trans. by Oman); *Monologen*, 1800; *Kritik der bisherigen Sittenlehre*, 1803; German trans. of Plato's *Dialogues*, with introductions and notes, 1804-1828; *Der christliche Glaube*, 1821-1822. Complete works, 1834-1864; R. B. Brandt, *The Philosophy of Schleiermacher*, 1941.

Philosophy of Religion. In Schleiermacher deep religious feeling is combined with marked intellectual capacity. Religion formed the core of his thought. The problem for such a personality was to develop a conception of reality that would satisfy the intellect as well as the heart. The great philosophical movements which confronted him, and with which as a thinker he had to reckon, were the theories of Kant, Jacobi, Fichte and Schelling, and the tendencies towards Spinozism which were so prominent in Germany at the time. He was also compelled to take account of romanticism, with many of whose representatives he came into friendly personal touch and whose mysticism appealed to his religious nature. His study of Greek philosophy, particularly of Plato, whose works he translated into German, also furnished his mind with material for a *Weltanschauung*. Schleiermacher was consciously influenced by each of these intellectual movements; he calls himself a dilettante in philosophy and was certainly an eclectic, a fact which accounts for many of his inconsistencies. But his eclecticism was of the independent, original type; he assimilated such elements in the culture of his age as satisfied his ethical and religious needs, and adapted them to his fundamental purpose: the construction of a great system of Protestant theology. It was owing to his understanding and appreciation of the intellectual life of his times that he came to exercise such a profound influence on religious thought and won for himself the title of the founder of the new theology.

Knowledge and Faith. Schleiermacher rejects the idealism of Fichte in so far as it seeks to derive all reality from the ego, and assumes the existence of a real world. We are compelled to infer a transcendent ground of all thought and being; all particular things have their source in a principle that is the absolute unity of both, the principle of identity, in which all differences and oppositions are resolved. We know the nature of things themselves and not, as Kant had taught, merely of phenomena. But owing to the perceptual nature of our thinking, we cannot reach an adequate knowledge of the original source of things; thought moves in opposites and can never realize absolute identity. The problem is to know the absolute principle, the identity of thought and being, God; but the very nature of this principle precludes all possibility of rational knowledge. It can never be realized, but only approximated: conceptual thinking can never free itself from differences and opposites, whereas the ultimate ground is without differentiation and opposition. Philosophy is not science, but *Wissenschaftslehre,* science of knowledge; it is the art of thinking, or dialectic; it is the product of social or cooperative thought and teaches us how to attain the goal of knowledge. Nor can we reach an adequate knowledge of God through practical reason, as Kant had taught. The fact is, Schleiermacher already possesses his touchstone of truth in his notion of God, and on this his conception of knowledge depends: human intelligence, with its habit of pulling things apart, cannot comprehend the unity of the divine nature.

We realize the ideal only in religious feeling or in divining intuition; in feeling we come into direct relation with God. The absolute unity or identity of thought and being, which we cannot define in conceptual terms, is immediately experienced in self-consciousness. Religion is the feeling of absolute dependence on an absolute world-ground; it is the immediate consciousness that everything finite is infinite and owes its existence to the infinite, that everything temporal is eternal and rests in the eternal. Schleiermacher opposes the shallow rationalism of the *Aufklärung* with its theological proofs, as well as the orthodox utilitarian conception of God as the dispenser of rewards and punishments, and, likewise, refuses to base religion on ethical conviction, as Kant and Fichte had done. According to him, religion does not consist in theoretical dogmas or rationalistic proofs, any more than in acts of worship and moral conduct. Since God cannot be known, theology must be a theory of religious feeling; its function is to formulate and to bring to clear consciousness the implications of religious feeling.

God, the World, and the Individual. This Schleiermacher proceeds to do in his theology, which represents a fusion of Spinozism and idealism that was quite common in Germany at the beginning of the nineteenth century. The Absolute is conceived organically, in analogy with the human mind, as unity in diversity, as the identity of thought and being. Schleiermacher did not consistently carry out the Spinozistic idea, but attempted to combine his pantheism with dualism. God and the world are one, it is true; but things are not mere accidents of God; the world has a relative independence. A legitimate theory of the universe must affirm the inseparableness of God and the world—God has never been without a world, nor the world apart from God—and yet it must distinguish between the idea of God and the idea of the world. God is a spaceless and timeless unity; the world, a spatial-temporal plurality.

We cannot ascribe personality to God, for that would make him finite. Nor can we attribute infinite thought and will to him, for these terms contradict each other; all thinking and willing are by their very nature necessarily finite. God is the universal creative force, the source of all life: so Herder, Goethe, Fichte, and Schelling had interpreted the Spinozistic substance.

The relation of the individual to the Absolute is conceived in a way to preserve some measure of freedom and independence for the individual. Individual egos are self-determining principles whose freedom consists, as it did for Leibniz, in the natural evolution of their individual capacity or endowment. Yet, they are imbedded in the universal substance; they are articulate members of the universe, and to it their individual nature must conform. Each particular ego, however, has its specific talent or gift; it occupies a place in the whole of things that is absolutely necessary, and must, therefore, give expression to its own individuality in order that the nature of the whole may be realized. The high value which Schleiermacher places on personality, and his insistence on self-development and self-expression, are characteristic of the romantic tendencies in German thought. It is this individualistic bent which, in spite of his doctrine of absolute dependence, prevented him from merging the human soul in the universal substance, and which gave rise to his individualistic ethics. He had little sympathy with Kant's rigoristic morality and Kant's dualism between reason and nature, a dualism which can never be bridged unless the subjective and the objective will are united in the original natural will.

Reason and will exist in nature as well as in man; morality is a higher development of something that already manifests itself in nature in a lower form. The reason immanent in nature is identical with that of the self-conscious subject: there is no irreconcilable conflict between the natural law and the moral law. The ideal is not the destruction of the lower impulses, but the unfolding of the individual's peculiar nature in harmony with the whole. The ethical value of the acts of each personality consists in their uniqueness. The moral maxim is: be a unique person and act in accordance with your own peculiar nature. Even in religion the individual should be left free to express himself in his own unique and intimate way. This teaching is not to be interpreted as a selfish individualism for, according to Schleiermacher, the consciousness of the value of one's own personality carries with it the appreciation of the worth of others. The sense of universality is the highest condition of one's own perfection; the ethical life is a life in society, in a society of unique individuals who respect humanity in its uniqueness, whether in themselves or in others. "The more each becomes like the universe, the more fully he communicates himself to others, the more perfect will be the unity of all; . . . rising above themselves and triumphing over themselves, they are on the way to true immortality and eternity." It is the religious feeling, however, that illuminates one's entire life and brings unity into it. In the feeling of piety man recognizes that his desire to be a unique personality is in harmony with the action of the universe; "Religion regards all events in the world as the acts of God." Personal immortality is out of the question; the immortality of religion consists in becoming one with the infinite; to be immortal is "to be eternal in every moment of time."

63. Georg Wilhelm Hegel

Georg Wilhelm Friedrich Hegel was born in Stuttgart in 1770, studied theology and philosophy at Tübingen (1788-1793), and held private tutorships in Switzerland and in Frankfort from 1794 to 1801. In 1801 he established himself at Jena, receiving a professorship in 1805, which he was compelled to relinquish after the battle of Jena, in 1806. After serving as the editor of a newspaper in Bamberg (1806-1808) and as director of the *Gymnasium* at Nüremberg (1808-1816), he was called to the professorship of philosophy at Heidelberg and then to Berlin, where he exercised a great influence and won many adherents. In 1831 he died of the cholera.

Bibliography

Works: *Phänomenologie des Geistes*, 1807; *Logik*, 1812-1816; *Encyclopedie der philosophischen Wissenschaften*, 1817; *Grundlinien der Philosophie des Rechts*, 1821. His lectures on the History of Philosophy, Esthetics, Philosophy of Religion, Philosophy of Right, and Philosophy of History were published by his pupils after his death in *Complete Works*, 19 vols., 1832. *Das Leben Jesu*, written in 1795, was published in 1906; *System der Sittlichkeit*, 1893. Translations: *The Logic of Hegel* (from *Encyclopedia of the Philosophical Sciences*), by W. Wallace, 1892; *Science of Logic* (the so-called "Greater Logic"), 2 vols., by Johnson and Struthers, 1929; *Phenomenology of Mind*, by J. B. Baillie, 2 vols., 1910; *The Philosophy of Mind*, by W. Wallace, 1894; *The Philosophy of Right*, by S. W. Dyde, 1896, and by T. M. Knox, 1942; *Ethics* (contains selections from *The Philosophy of Right*), by J. M. Sterrett, 1893; *History of Philosophy*, by E. S. Haldane and F. H. Simson, 1892-96; *Philosophy of History*, by J. Sibree, 1861; *Lectures on the Philosophy of Religion*, by E. B. Speirs and Sanderson, 1895; *The Philosophy of Fine Art*, by F. P. B. Osmaston, 1920; *Hegel's Logic of World and Idea*, by H. S. Macran, 1929; *Hegel's Doctrine of Formal Logic*, by H. S. Macran, 1917; *Hegel: Selections*, by J. Loewenberg, 1929.

E. Caird, *Hegel*, 1883; G. S. Morris, *Hegel's Philosophy of the State and of History*, 1887; J. H. Stirling, *The Secret of Hegel*, 2 vols., 1865; W. T. Harris, *Hegel's Logic*, 1890; A. Seth (or A. S. Pringle-Pattison), *Hegelianism and Personality*, 2nd ed., 1893; J. G. Hibben, *Hegel's Logic* (a paraphrase of the *Logic* of the *Encyclopedia*), 1902; W. Wallace, *Prolegomena to the Study of Hegel's Philosophy*, 1874; J. B. Baillie, *The Origin and Significance of Hegel's Logic*, 1901; J. M. E. McTaggart, *Commentary on Hegel's Logic*, 1910, *Studies in the Hegelian Dialectic*, 1896 and 1922, and *Studies in Hegelian Cosmology*, 1911 and 1918; G. W. Cunningham, *Thought and Reality in Hegel's System*, 1910; G. Noël, *La logique de Hegel*, 1897; B. Croce, *What is Living and What is Dead in the Philosophy of Hegel*, trans. by D. Ainslie, 1915; H. A. Reyburn, *The Ethical Theory of Hegel*, 1922; W. T. Stace, *The Philosophy of Hegel*, 1924; M. B. Foster, *The Political Philosophies of Plato and Hegel*, 1935; J. Maier, *On Hegel's Critique of Kant*, 1939; R. G. Mure, *An Introduction to Hegel*, 1940.

Hegel and His Predecessors. Both Fichte and Schelling had proceeded from Kantian presuppositions. Mind is the principle of knowledge; all philosophy is ultimately a philosophy of mind, in which forms and categories play a significant rôle. Both accepted the dynamic view of reality: for both the ideal principle is an active living process. Both thinkers, in spite of romantic tendencies, employed the logical method, seeking to explain the world of experience by exhibiting the conditions without which such experience would be impossible. We have seen how Schelling modified Fichte's earlier view, or at least elaborated it in several important respects. We may say that in Schelling philosophy again becomes metaphysics: nature and mind are conceived as progressive stages in the evolution of an absolute principle that expresses itself in the inorganic and organic realms, in individual and social life, in history, science, and art. The results of critical epistemology are applied in ontology; the necessary forms of thought are regarded also as necessary forms of being. Nature assumes an important place in his thinking: unconscious processes are at work, not only in the so-called inanimate sphere, but in history, society, and the human mind as well. The rigorous logical method followed by Schelling in some of his early writings is gradually supplemented or replaced. Esthetic intuition becomes the organ of knowledge and the esthetic ideal is set up as the goal of human development, in place of the Fichtean ethical ideal.

Hegel builds on the foundations laid by Fichte and Schelling. He agrees with the former in insisting on a logical method—indeed, he undertakes to put the world-view of his friend Schelling on a rational scientific basis; with the latter, in identifying logic with ontology or metaphysics; and with both in conceiving reality as a living developing process. For him, too, nature and mind, or reason, are one; yet he subordinates nature to reason. Indeed, for him all being and reason are identical; the same process that is at work in reason, is present everywhere; whatever is real is rational, and whatever is rational is real. There is a logic in nature as well as in history, and the universe is at bottom a logical system. The Absolute, then, is not an undifferentiated Absolute, as Schelling had taught. Hegel, in his criticism of Schelling, characterizes his Absolute as "the night in which all cows are black." Nor is the Absolute a substance—as Spinoza had taught; rather is it a subject, which means that it is life, process, evolution, as well as consciousness and knowledge. All motion and action, all life, are but an unconscious thinking; they follow the law of thought; hence, the more law there is in nature, the more rational is its activity. And, finally, the goal toward which the developing Absolute moves is self-consciousness; the meaning of the entire process lies in its highest development, in the realization of truth and goodness by a mind that knows the meaning and purpose of the universe and identifies itself with the universal purpose.

The Problem of Philosophy. It is the business of philosophy, according to Hegel, to know the world of nature and of human experience, to study and comprehend the reason in things—not their superficial, transitory, and accidental forms, but their eternal essence, harmony, and law. Things have a meaning, the processes in the world are rational: the planetary system is a rational order, the organism is rational, purposive, full of meaning. Since reality is at bottom rational, a necessary, logical process of thoughts or notions, it can be known only by thought; and the function of philosophy will be to understand the laws or necessary forms according to which reason operates. Logic and metaphysics are, therefore, one and the same. The world, however, is not static, it moves, it is dynamic; so is thought, or reason; the notion, or the true concept, is an active, moving process, a process of evolution. In evolution, something that is undeveloped, undifferentiated, homogeneous and, in Hegel's sense "abstract," develops, differentiates, splits up, assumes many different opposing or contradictory forms, until at last we have a unified, concrete, particularized object, a unity in diversity. The indefinite, abstract ground from which we have proceeded has become a definite concrete reality in which the opposites are reconciled or united in the whole. The higher stage in the process of evolution is the realization of the lower, it is really what the lower intends to be; in Hegel's language, it is the "truth" of the lower, its purpose, its meaning. What was implicit in the lower form becomes explicit or is made manifest in the higher. Every stage in the process contains all the preceding stages and foreshadows all the future ones: the world at every stage is both a product and a prophecy. The lower form is negated in the higher, that is, it is not what it was; but it is also preserved in the higher, it has been carried over and sublated. All these ideas Hegel expresses by the German word *aufgehoben;* and the process, in the thing, of passing over into its opposites he calls the *dialectical process.*

This is what Hegel means when he declares that contradiction is the root of all life and movement, that the principle of contradiction rules the world. Everything tends to change, to pass over into its opposite. The seed has in it the impulse to be something else: to contradict itself and to transcend itself. Without contradiction there would be no life, movement, growth, or development; everything would be dead existence, static externality. But contradiction is not the whole story; nature does not stop at contradiction, but strives to overcome it. The thing passes over into its opposite, true, but the movement goes on and oppositions are overcome and reconciled, that is, become parts of a unified whole. The opposites are opposites with respect to one another, but not with respect to the unity or whole of which they form the parts. Taken by themselves, they have no value or meaning, but considered as planfully articulated parts of a whole—of a process—they have value and meaning. They are expressions of the notion of the thing, of its reason or purpose. In realizing its purpose, its notion, or *Begriff,* the thing overcomes the contradiction between its being and its notion, between what it now is and what it has in it to be. Thus, for example, all nature strives to overcome its material being, to divest itself of its phenomenal encumbrances and to make manifest its true essence.

Again, the universe is a process of evolution, in which ends or purposes of universal reason are realized. This is an organic or teleological conception. The complete organism is the realization of the purpose, form, notion or concept of the organism, the truth of the organism, as Hegel would say. The important thing in evolution is not merely what existed at the beginning, but what happens or is made manifest at the end. The truth lies in the whole, but the whole is realized only in the completed process of evolution; being is at the end what it is in truth. And so we may say that the Absolute is essentially a result, a fulfillment, but the result of a process, and as such is not the complete whole; the result together with the entire process of development is the true whole; the thing is not exhausted in its purpose, but in its achievement.

Philosophy is accordingly interested in results; it has to show how one stage evolves from the other, how it necessarily emerges from the other. This movement proceeds unconsciously in nature and even in history—in this Hegel agrees with Schelling. But the thinker can become conscious of the process; he may describe it, rethink the concepts. He has reached the highest stage of knowledge when he has grasped the idea of the world, when he knows its meaning, when he can retrace the operations of the universal dynamic reason, its categories and notions. The concepts in his mind are of the same nature as the universal concepts; the dialectical evolution of the concepts in the mind of the philosopher coincides with the objective evolution of the world; the categories of subjective thought are likewise categories of the universe; thought and being are identical.

The Dialectical Method. Now, if the task of philosophy is to understand the nature of things, to tell us the what, the why, and the wherefore of reality, the existence, ground or essence, and purpose of things, its method must be suited to its end. The method must reproduce the rational process, or the course of evolving reason in the world. This goal cannot be attained by the artistic intuitions of genius or in a similar mysterious way, as Schelling and others supposed; there is no other way than that of hard thinking. Philosophy is conceptual knowledge, as Kant had declared. But, Hegel notes, we cannot exhaust reality by abstract concepts; reality is a moving dynamic process, a dialectical process, which abstract concepts cannot faithfully represent, for they tell only a small part of the story. Reality is now this, now that; in this sense it is full of negations, contradictions, and oppositions: the plant germinates, blooms, withers, and dies; man is young, mature, and old. To do a thing justice, we must tell the whole truth about it, predicate each of its contradictions, and show how they are reconciled and preserved in the articulated whole which we call the life of the thing. Ordinary abstract thought takes the existing things in isolation, it looks upon them as the true realities, and considers their special phases and oppositions by themselves.

The intellect can do nothing but distinguish, oppose, and relate; it cannot conceive the unity of opposites, the life and inner purposiveness of things; it can only wonder at animal instinct. The intellect is contemptuous of the speculative or dialectical method, but it can never grasp life itself. Conceived by themselves or torn from their relations, the contradictory aspects of things are meaningless appearances; they can be understood only as parts of an organic, articulated system; or, as Hegel puts it, all existence has truth only in the Idea, for the Idea is the only true reality. The Idea pervades the whole and all the parts of the whole; all particulars have their reality in this unity. The activity which sees things whole, or unifies the opposites, is a higher function of mind, which, however, let it be remembered, cannot dispense with the intellect. The two functions, speculative reason and abstract intellect, work hand in hand.

Thought will, therefore, proceed from the most simple, abstract, and empty concepts to the more complex, concrete, and richer ones, the "notions." Hegel calls this method, which we already find indicated in Kant and employed by Fichte and Schelling, the *dialectical* method, and, with them, distinguishes three moments or stages of it. We begin with an abstract universal concept (thesis); this concept gives rise to a contradiction (antithesis); the contradictory concepts are reconciled in a third concept which, therefore, is a union of the other two (synthesis). To illustrate: Parmenides held that being is permanent, Heraclitus that it is in constant change, the atomists that it is neither and both, that something is permanent and something changes. The new concept, however, suggests new problems and contradictions, which, in their turn, must be resolved in other concepts. And so the dialectical process, which seeks to follow the evolution of reality, continues until we reach an ultimate concept or notion in which all oppositions are resolved and preserved. But no single concept, not even the highest, represents the whole truth; all concepts are only partial truths; truth or knowledge is constituted by the entire system of concepts, every one of which has evolved from a basal concept. Truth, like rational reality itself, is a living logical process.

Or let us put it this way: one thought follows necessarily from the other, one thought provokes a contradictory thought with which it is united to form another thought. The dialectical movement is the logical self-unfolding of thought. Hegel speaks as though thoughts or notions think themselves: there is an inner necessity in them, they are like a growing organism that unfolds its capacities and becomes a concrete organized whole, a "concrete universal." Hence, all the thinker has to do is to let his thought follow its logical course in the manner described; since this process, if correctly carried on, is identical with the world-process, it will be a reproduction of the development immanent in things. In this way, we can think God's thoughts after him.

Thought and Being. Speculative or dialectical thinking, then, is a process that seeks to do justice to moving, living, organic existence, a process in which differences are reconciled, in which distinctions are not merely made, but comprehended. The philosophical notion is an organic unity of differences, a totality of parts, a unified and yet differentiated whole. When Hegel tells us that the concrete universal notion is the synthesis of opposites, he wishes to describe the nature of thought as well as the nature of reality. Being is what the romanticists were fond of calling it: a flowing reality, something akin to life and mind. The romanticists were also right in maintaining that being cannot be grasped by an abstracting intelligence which catches only abstract phases or partial aspects of being, cutting it into pieces, and ignoring its organic character. Hegel, however, emphatically rejects the romanticists' claim that being can be realized by mystical feeling, esthetic intuitions, or happy guesses. Being is a rational process, a process that has meaning and must be thought. It is not an irrational flux, an unorganized, absolutely meaningless happening, but an orderly evolution, a progress. By its fruits we shall know it; viewed in the light of the goal it achieves, all its seeming oppositions and contradictions are understood and reconciled. Our attempts to split up reality into essence and appearance, inner and outer, substance and attribute, force and its expression, the infinite and the finite, mind and matter, God and world, give us nothing but false distinctions and arbitrary abstractions. The world does not consist of an inner kernel and an outer shell; the essence *is* the appearance, the inner *is* the outer, the mind *is* the body, God *is* the universe.

Reality, then, is a process of logical evolution. It is a spiritual process, and we can understand it only in so far as we experience such a process within ourselves. But, let us not forget, it is not the particular ideas, the empirical or psychological content, which we find in ourselves, that give us such understanding. There is a rational necessity in the structure of absolute thought which is reproduced in our individual thinking. Thinking evolves or develops rationally; it moves logically or dialectically. In this sense, it is universal, trans-empirical, transcendental, or, as Hegel calls it, metaphysical. Nor is truth a product of the thought of this or that individual; it is the achievement of a cultural tradition, it grows out of the life and experience of the race. The divine mind or reason expresses itself in the evolution of the racial consciousness in human history. But only in so far as human history is rational, necessary, logical, can we speak of it as expressive of the divine reason.

Hegel calls God the Idea, meaning the potential universe, the timeless totality of all the possibilities of evolution. Spirit or mind (*Geist*) is this Idea realized. The Idea contains within itself, *in posse,* implicitly, ideally, the entire logico-dialectical process which unfolds in the actual world. The Idea is the creative logos or reason; its forms of action or categories are not empty husks or lifeless ideas, but objective thoughts, spiritual forces which constitute the very essence of things. The study of the creative logos, in its necessary evolution, is logic. Hegel did not mean by this teaching that God as pure thought or logical Idea existed before the creation of the world; for Hegel declares that the world was eternally created. The being of the divine mind consists in self-expression; God is the living, moving reason of the world, he reveals himself in the world, in nature and in history, which are necessary stages in the evolution of God toward self-consciousness. The evolution is a logical, not a temporal process. The Absolute is eternally that into which it develops: the categories are eternally potential in it, they have not evolved out of nothing. Nevertheless, the categories are developed successively, one after the other, each one being the logical condition of its successor in the dialectical series. God is not absorbed into the world nor the world into God; without the world God is not God, he cannot be without creating a world, without knowing himself in his other. There must be both unity and opposition in the Absolute. The finite world could not exist without the Idea, it is not an independent thing and has no real being without God: whatever truth it has it owes to God. Just as in our minds thoughts and feelings come and pass away without exhausting the mind, so the phenomena of nature come and go without exhausting the divine mind. Moreover, just as our mind is enriched and enlarged by its thoughts and experiences, and rises to ever fuller self-consciousness in and through them, so the divine Idea is enriched by its self-expressions in nature and history, and rises through them to self-consciousness. The Idea, apart from its expressions in nature and history, exists only "in itself"; considered in relation to its manifestations it exists also "for itself." In the rhythmical process of self-alienation and self-appropriation, the universal mind realizes its destiny; it thinks itself in thinking its object and so knows its own essence. The Absolute becomes conscious only in evolution, and above all in man. Hegel, therefore, does not mean that God, or the logical Idea, exists as a self-conscious logical process before the creation of the world; he cannot be conscious without a world, for he is a developing God and becomes fully self-conscious only in the minds of human beings who make explicit the logical-dialectical process that lies implicit in the universal reason. The characteristic Hegelian doctrine that the Absolute becomes self-conscious only through something other than itself—the world or finite human minds—is known as the doctrine of reflection.

Logic and Metaphysics. It is apparent that for Hegel logic is the fundamental science, since it reproduces the divine thought-process as it is in itself. Dialectical thought expresses the innermost essence of the universal mind; in such thinking the universal mind knows itself as it is. Here thought and being, subject and object, form and content are one. The forms or categories of thought which logic evolves are identical with the forms of reality: they have both logical and ontological, or metaphysical value. In the essence of things thought recognizes its own essence, seeing it as in a mirror. Reason is the same everywhere, and everywhere the divine reason is at work: the universe, in so far as it is real and eternal, is the expression of the thought of God. Hence it makes no difference where we begin. Whether we begin with logic and study the dialectical process in ourselves, or with metaphysics and investigate dialectic in the universe, we shall always reach the same results. In logical thinking, pure thought may be said to study itself, since thinker and thought are one; and in the process, the thinker evolves with his think-ing. Logic is the science of pure thought, and the other sciences are applications of logic. The philosophy of nature studies the Absolute, or universal reason, "in its otherness," in its self-objectification or self-alienation; the philosophy of mind shows how reason, after subjugating objective nature, returns to itself and thereby achieves self-consciousness.

In all instances of the revelation of reason, whether in nature or in mind, reason appears in an infinite variety of temporal and transitory forms. These accidental shapes showing on the surface are not the subject matter of philosophy. It is the business of philosophy to understand the reason in things, the essence or substance of nature and mind, the eternal harmony and order, the immanent law and essence of nature, the meaning of human institutions and of history, the eternal element shining through the temporal and accidental, the inner pulse beating in the external shapes. Moreover, this reason in things we can know only conceptually, through dialectical or logical thought, and the only knowledge worthy of the name is a priori or philosophical knowledge. The two fields of metaphysics or "applied logic" are philosophy of nature and philosophy of mind.

Philosophy of Nature and Philosophy of Mind. Logic deals with concepts, it shows how, in the necessary evolution of our thinking, one concept springs from another. If we think correctly, we are bound to pass from stage to stage until we reach the highest stage, the culmination and completion of the process, the epitome of all the others. When we think these concepts, we are in the world of true reality, the eternal, imperishable process of the universe. The system of concepts which we think in logic, forms an organic whole and represents the true essence of things. Logic is not merely a subjective process occurring in our minds. It is a relational structure exemplified in the world-process, in nature and in mind, in the individual mind and in the social mind, in the history of the world and in human institutions. In logic, we envisage reason in its purity, in its nakedness; pure logical thought is not as yet clothed in the garments of a universe. This is what Hegel means when he states that logic has no actual being, and that it only becomes actualized in the thinking processes of man. We are not concerned, in logic, with nature, history, or society, but with a system of truths, a world of ideas, as it is in itself. But we can also study thought in its manifestations; we can see how this skeleton or framework takes on flesh and blood. In nature reason reveals itself in its otherness, in its externality in space and in its succession in time.

We cannot truly say that the logical Idea passes over into nature: the logical Idea *is* nature, nature is a form of the logical Idea, it is the Idea in spatialized and temporalized form. Nature is reason, it is conceptual, it is the logical concept in its externality or "side-by-sideness." Hegel calls it petrified or unconscious intelligence. Nature is a stage of transition through which the logical Idea passes in its evolution into mind or spirit (*Geist*); the Idea, which embodies itself or is externalized in nature, returns into itself and becomes mind, or spirit: in mind, the Idea reveals itself to itself.

Mind, or spirit, passes through dialectical stages of evolution, revealing itself as subjective mind, objective mind, and absolute mind. Subjective mind expresses itself as soul (mind dependent on nature), consciousness (mind opposed to nature), and spirit (mind reconciled with nature in knowledge). Corresponding to these stages, Hegel has the sciences of anthropology, phenomenology, and psychology. The Idea, or universal reason, becomes soul in the animal organism. It embodies itself, creates a body for itself, becomes a particular, individual soul, the function and vocation of which is to exercise its peculiar individuality; it is an unconscious production. This soul, which has fashioned an organic body for itself, becomes conscious of itself, distinguishes itself from its body; consciousness is an evolution from the very principle of which the body is also an expression. The function of consciousness is knowing. It rises from a purely objective stage, in which it regards the sensible object as the most real and truest thing, to a stage in which reason is conceived as the innermost essence of both self-consciousness and objective reality. Mind or spirit in the highest sense unites both functions: it is productive knowing. We really know only what we create or produce. The objects of the spirit are its own products; hence, its essence, especially that of theoretical spirit, consists in knowing. Spirit or intelligence immersed in its object is perception. No one can speak or write illuminatingly of an object without living in it spiritually, i.e., without intuiting it in the true sense of the term. Knowledge in its highest form is the pure thinking of conceptual reason. Presentation—including memory, imagination, association— is intermediate between perception and reason. Reason evolves or unfolds concepts, i.e., conceives by pure thought the self-development of concepts. The understanding or intellect judges, i.e., separates the elements of the concept; reason concludes, i.e., binds together the elements of the concept. In the development of pure thought, theoretical intelligence reflects upon itself, knows itself; it becomes reason by recognizing and acknowledging its own rationality.

Intelligence or reason is the sole ground of its development; hence, the result of its self-knowledge is the knowledge that its essence is self-determination or will, or practical spirit. Will appears as a particular subject or natural individual, striving for the satisfaction of his needs or deliverance from his ills. The will immersed in its impulses is unfree; but when the will acts in accordance with rational and self-conscious purposes, it achieves the only freedom of which man is capable—the freedom of rational self-determination.

Philosophy of Right. The Idea, or universal reason, expresses itself not only in nature and in individuals, but in human institutions and in history, in right or law (property, contract, punishment), in morality or conscience, in custom or ethical observances (family, civic society, State). In these institutions and in history reason realizes itself or becomes actual, i.e., appears in external form; in this sense it is called objective reason. The reason which has produced human institutions is the same as that which seeks to understand them: the reason which has unconsciously evolved law, custom, and the State becomes conscious of the process in the philosophy of right. It is not the function of such a philosophy to tell us what the State ought to be, but to know it as it is, that is, to exhibit the reason immanent in it; and that can only be done by dialectical thinking. It is the function of philosophy to show how rational institutions follow from the very idea or nature of right or justice. In studying institutions, it is possible to explain them historically, to show to what conditions and circumstances—social, economic and political —they owe their existence. But such a causal explanation is not the true philosophical explanation; it is one thing to trace the historical evolution of institutions, to point out the circumstances, needs and events, which led to their establishment; another, to demonstrate the justice in them and their rational necessity. We can understand the reason of right, law, custom, State, only when we understand their respective concepts.

Objective reason is realized in a society of free individuals in which each wills the laws and customs of his people. In such a society the individual subordinates his subjective conscience to universal reason; in custom or the ethical observances of his people he finds his universal and true self expressed: he recognizes in the laws his own will and in himself a particularized expression of the laws. The evolution of the ethical spirit into a community of self-conscious individuals is the result of the evolution of active reason. After many experiences in society, the individual learns that in willing a universal cause he is willing his own will, and is thus free. The real and the ideal are one here: individual reason accepts universal reason as its own; the individual abandons his subjectivity and subordinates his individual reason to the universal reason, which expresses itself in the consciousness of a people, in the national mind—this is institutional morality. The perfect State, which realizes perfect freedom, is the goal and purpose of universal history: progress means the development of the consciousness of freedom. The various peoples and great historical personalities are the instruments by which the universal spirit realizes its ends: every great people has a mission to perform in the divine evolution and can be understood only in the light of the total development of world history. When it has accomplished the purpose of its existence, it is supplanted by more vigorous nations. The conquest of one nation by another is a confession that the idea for which the defeated nation stands is inferior to that of the victorious people: in this very special sense might makes right, physical power and rational justice coincide. War, in so far as it is a war of ideas, is justified by Hegel on the assumption that the stronger cause will defeat the weaker and that the progress of humanity is furthered by physical and moral conflict. World history represents an ideological struggle in which the dialectically superior nation triumphs. Providence, or universal reason, makes use of the passions and private interests of individuals to realize universal ends: this is the strategy of the Idea; great men are not decisive in history, they are the executives of the reason. In his *Philosophy of History* Hegel tries to show how the universal spirit realizes the purposes prescribed by the dialectical evolution of its essence.

Art, Religion, and Philosophy. In none of the preceding stages of the development of mind, however, does the universal mind come to know itself as it is, or reach the highest plane of self-consciousness and freedom. In none of them can it be said that thought and being, subject and object, are truly one, or that all the oppositions are fully reconciled. The supreme stage in the evolution of the logical Idea is the Absolute Mind, whose sole purpose and work consist in making manifest to itself its own nature, and which is, therefore, free and unlimited spirit. Every particular subject as a truly knowing subject is such an absolute subject. The Absolute Mind likewise passes through three stages, revealing itself in the art, the religion, and the philosophy of the human mind. The Absolute Mind expresses its essence or truth in the form of intuition in art; in the form of presentation or imagination in religion; in the form of conception or the pure logical concept in philosophy. The mind perceiving its inner essence in perfect freedom is art, the mind imaging it reverently is religion, the mind conceiving and knowing it in thought is philosophy. "Philosophy too has no other object than God and is, therefore, essentially rational theology, as well as an enduring worship of God in the service of truth." Each of the three forms realizes itself in the dialectical process of evolution and has its history: the history of art, the history of religion, and the history of philosophy.

In the history of philosophy every great system has its necessary place and represents a necessary stage of logical development. Each system provokes an opposing one; the contradiction is reconciled in a higher synthesis, which, in turn, gives rise to new conflicts, and the dialect continues until it reaches its culmination in Hegel himself. The Hegelian philosophy—so its author believes—represents the final synthesis in which the Absolute Mind becomes conscious of itself: it recognizes the content of its being in the historical development through which it has passed.

Hegelian Schools. From 1820 to 1840 Hegel's system was the reigning philosophy in Germany. It enjoyed the favor of the Prussian State, and had representatives in nearly every German university. What made it particularly attractive to many thinkers was its logical method, which seemed to avoid both the rigid abstractions of rationalism and the easy fancies of mysticism, its claim to absolute certainty, and its apparent success in overcoming difficulties and solving problems in nearly every field of human study. After the death of the master, the school divided into conservative and liberal groups. Differences arose with regard to theological questions—God, Christ, and immortality—upon which Hegel had not expressed himself definitely. The conservatives interpreted the system in the orthodox supernaturalistic terms, as teaching theism, personal immortality, and an incarnate God; while the liberals, the so-called Young Hegelians, held to a spiritualistic pantheism: God is the universal substance which becomes conscious in mankind. Mind as such—the universal mind, not the individual mind—is eternal. The incarnation of God in Christ is interpreted as the expression of the divine in humanity. To this liberal wing belonged Richter, Ruge and, for a time, B. Bauer, D. Strauss, and L. Feuerbach. The latter, however, eventually went over to naturalism.

The dialectical materialism of Marx, with its economic interpretation of history, is also indebted to Hegelian premises. What was once rational, Marx reasoned, becomes irrational in the process of evolution: private property, which was once right and rational, will be superseded and overcome as a result of the dialectical-logical process of history.

The impetus which Hegel gave to the study of the history of philosophy and the history of religion produced a school of great historians of philosophy including Trendelenburg, Ritter, Brandis, J. E. Erdmann, E. Zeller, Kuno Fischer, W. Windelband, and the historian of religion, O. Pfleiderer. Hegel likewise exercised a great influence on the philosophy of history, the study of jurisprudence, politics, and indeed on all the mental sciences.

For the period after Hegel, see: O. Siebert, *Geschichte der neueren deutschen Philosophie seit Hegel,* 1898; O. Külpe, *Philosophy of the Present in Germany,* trans. by G. Patrick, 1913; O. Gramzow, *Geschichte der Philosophie seit Kant,* 1906; F. Ueberweg, *Grundriss der Geschichte der Philosophie,* 1927; J. E. Erdmann, *Die Entwicklung der deutschen Spekulation seit Kant,* 1931.

XVIII
German Philosophy After Hegel

64. THE REALISM OF JOHANN FRIEDRICH HERBART

Opposition to Hegelianism. The Hegelian philosophy aroused great opposition in certain quarters and gave rise to reactionary movements, the most extreme of which rejected all metaphysics as a futile undertaking. Every phase of the new German movement was subjected to attack: its idealism, its pantheism, its rationalism, and its a priori methods. Some thinkers insisted on more exact scientific methods, and by their application reached results at variance with the new philosophy. Realism and pluralism represented the scientific reaction to idealism. Others refused to follow the view that the world was rational and pointed out the irrational elements in reality of which philosophy would have to take account. Thus voluntarism, mysticism, faith-philosophy, and intuitionism sought answers to the world-riddle in functions of the mind other than reason. The two greatest opponents of the so-called speculative philosophy are Herbart and Schopenhauer. Though they differ widely in their philosophical positions, they agree in that each regards himself as the true successor of Kant. Moreover, both are interested in the natural sciences, and seek a basis for their thought in the facts of experience. Finally, both offer systems of metaphysics: Herbart presents a pluralistic realism that harks back to Leibniz; Schopenhauer, an idealism that resembles Schelling's *Naturphilosophie,* and a voluntarism that is reminiscent of Fichte's philosophy and Schelling's later view.

Among the works of Herbart are: *Einleitung in die Philosophie,* 1813; *Psychologie als Wissenschaft,* 1824-1825; *Allgemeine Metaphysik,* 1828-1829; *Allgemeine Pädagogik,* 1806; *Allgemeine praktische Philosophie,* 1808. Complete works, by Hartenstein, 13 vols., 2nd ed., 1883-1893; by Kehrbach, 19 vols., 1887-1912.

Realistic Conception of Philosophy. In Johann Friedrich Herbart (1776-1841) we have an independent critical thinker who opposes the entire idealistic

490

movement as it had developed in Germany after Kant. He had already studied Kant and the pre-Kantian rationalists before he came to Jena in 1794, where he heard Fichte, and afterwards served as special lecturer and professor (1802-1809). He regarded the new philosophy as an aberration from the principles laid down by the great critical philosopher of Königsberg, to whose chair he was called in 1809, and once spoke of himself as a Kantian of the year 1828. He attacks its methods and results, and reaches conclusions directly opposed to those of the reigning school on nearly every important point. We cannot, in his opinion, deduce reality from a principle: such a principle comes at the end and not at the beginning of philosophy. We cannot reduce being to one single ground; monism and pantheism are philosophically untenable. Indeed, knowledge of the ultimate essence of things-in-themselves is impossible: metaphysics, in the Hegelian sense, is a dream. Yet things-in-themselves exist, not one, but many; and the world is not merely our idea. Herbart opposes the rationalistic method, apriorism, monism, pantheism, subjective idealism, and free will, and substitutes for these doctrines empiricism, pluralism, realism, and determinism.

Outside of experience, he tells us, there is no hope of progress in knowledge. It is the business of philosophy to begin with the general concepts of experience and of the sciences, with the thoughts which have been unconsciously evolved by the race. Such concepts we must examine with the help of formal logic, whose function it is to make their meaning clear and distinct, and to point out their inconsistencies, if such there be. Philosophy in general, therefore, consists in the elaboration of concepts: in analyzing them, comparing them, and attempting to harmonize them. Logic finds difficulties, inconsistencies, and contradictions in what seem to be our simplest, clearest, and most distinct concepts, such as *thing, change, becoming, matter, self-consciousness*: all of them contain nests of contradictions. A thing, for example, in ordinary thought, is a complex of qualities: gold is heavy, yet fusible; one thing is many things, a unity is a plurality. Herbart holds that nothing can be real that is contradictory—thereby restoring the old-time logical principle of contradiction to its former place of honor in philosophy. Reality can be conceived only as an absolutely self-consistent system. In this sense Herbart is, after all, a rigorous rationalist: genuine knowledge is a system of self-consistent concepts and hence, if our experience furnishes us with a world-view that is self-contradictory, it must be rejected. These inconsistencies in our knowledge and experience set the task of metaphysics; the contradictions must be removed and harmonized; we must modify and correct our ordinary and scientific concepts so that they will hang together, form a consistent picture of reality, render intelligible our world of experience.

Metaphysics. Herbart develops his metaphysics along realistic lines. He accepts the Kantian teaching that experience reveals only phenomena, but he insists that an appearance must always be the appearance of something; the very conception of appearance implies a reference to a reality beyond the appearance. Here, again, Herbart betrays his rationalism; ideas logically presuppose things-in-themselves as their ground. Our sensations cannot be explained, after the fashion of idealism, as mere products of the mind; subjective though they be, they suggest a being outside of them, a world of things-in-themselves. The question is, How is this world, the true reality, constituted?

Our seeming, appearing, phenomenal world is a world of contradictions, a world of many qualities and changes. We say, for example, a thing has many qualities, and a thing changes its qualities. How can one thing be many things? How can one thing be white and hard and sweet and fragrant, and how can it be now one thing, now another? It cannot be, for that would be contradictory. Every thing is what it is, identical with itself, absolutely one: to give it several qualities or to ascribe change to it, would be a contradiction in terms. Every sensation points to a single reality or being. A thing is simple, changeless, constant entity: absolute, indivisible, not extended in space or in time. It cannot be conceived as a continuum, otherwise it would not be simple and absolute. The principle of identity, in this sense, is for Herbart a basal law upon which he rears his theory of reality.

But if a thing is a simple, changeless substance, how do we account for the illusion of manifoldness and change? Why do the things we experience *appear* to have many qualities and to change? Metaphysics can explain this only on the assumption that there are many simple unchangeable entities, substances, or "reals"—as Herbart calls them. Each particular and apparently simple thing is really not a simple thing having many qualities, but a complex or aggregate of many simple things or reals, in more or less constant union. We must assume many reals, because the so-called thing has many qualities; when certain reals happen to form certain combinations with one another, enter into certain relations, then certain phenomena result. Change is explained as the coming and going of reals; to say a thing changes its quality means simply that a change occurs in the relation of the reals composing it; the reals themselves originally composing it are unchangeable, and every one of them remains unalterably what it is; only the relation has changed, reals have been added or taken away from a complex of reals. It is for this reason that we can call phenomena "the accidental viewpoints" of things. One and the same line can be a radius or a tangent; in the same way, a real may enter into different relations with other reals, without changing its essence. What we say of their mutual relations does not affect their being: it is merely an accidental viewpoint which we take.

The world of reals is absolute; there is no change, growth, or appearance in it, everything is what it is. But we relate the thing with another thing, with another real or reals; the semblance is in us, the contradictions of plurality and change are phenomena in us; all qualities are secondary qualities. This view would ascribe all variety and change to us; the real world would be an absolutely static world in which nothing would happen; all occurrence would be a phenomenon in consciousness.

Nevertheless, there appears to be change in the real itself and this Herbart explains as follows. Every real strives to preserve its identity against disturbances on the part of other reals. One and the same real will, therefore, behave differently in maintaining itself against others. There is no real change in the real; it asserts its quality, or preserves its essence, against all disturbance; but the way it preserves itself depends on the nature and degree of the disturbance threatening it. Even if there were no opposition, if it existed alone, it would preserve its quality. The real maintains itself at the same level always; it is constant, unchanging in the face it presents, but it seems to display varying degrees of effort to preserve its calm in the presence of different qualities and different degrees of opposition. But how is all this possible in view of the statement that reals do not influence one another? They do seem to influence one another; the presence of other reals does not change the nature or status of any real, but it does arouse different degrees of activity of self-preservation in it. Space, time, motion, and matter are interpreted in the same fashion: they are not reals, but objective appearances of reals.

Psychology. Herbart's psychology is a part of metaphysics, it is a rational psychology. Empirical psychology cannot be made the basis of philosophy; psychology presupposes metaphysics; without a metaphysical psychology the questions of a critique of reason cannot be answered, indeed, not even thoroughly discussed. Psychology rests on experience, metaphysics, and mathematics. The soul is a simple, absolute, timeless and spaceless real, the first substance science compels us to presuppose; hence, it cannot have the different faculties or powers, of which psychologists speak. Herbart's attack on the faculty-psychology results from his metaphysical presuppositions. Since the soul is a simple substance, there can be no action in it but self-preservation. It is related to the body, which is an aggregate of reals, the seat of the soul being in the brain. All souls are essentially alike; the differences in souls and in their development are due to external conditions, such as the organization of the body. The soul has originally no powers or capacities, neither ideas, nor feelings, nor impulses; it knows nothing of itself, has no forms, intuitions, or categories, no a priori laws of willing or acting. A sensation arises in the soul when the soul asserts itself against another real; sensation is the expression of its function of self-preservation. The entire content of the soul, as it exists in the developed state, is the result of the reproduction and association of sensations. Psychology is the science of the statics and mechanics of the mind. Herbart's aim is to create a science of psychology parallel to physical mechanics. The old physics explained everything by forces, the new physics reduces everything to motion; the old psychology explained everything by powers and faculties, the new psychology must explain everything by the movements of ideas: sensations and ideas tend to persist, but other psychic states contend with them for dominance, and thus there is action and reaction within the mind. Herbart seeks to formulate mathematically the relations existing between the sensations and ideas constituting the mind. Mental life, then, is explained as the complication, fusion, and opposition of ideas; feelings and strivings, or impulses, are modifications of ideas. Consciousness does not exhaust psychic life; processes occur beneath the threshold of consciousness, in the region of the unconscious. Everything in the mind follows fixed laws, and psychical processes are reducible to mathematical formulae. Hence there is no free will.

The permanent ground of mental life is the soul-substance, and not the so-called self-identical ego, the ego as knower, the self-conscious personality. Indeed, the very notion of such a self-conscious subject is contradictory. How can that which is a subject also be an object, how can the ego represent, or be conscious of, itself? It is contradictory to say the knower is the thing known, the subject the object. Besides, we can never become aware of the ego as subject, because it always shifts its base when we try to catch it, and leaves us with an object, the *me*. The eye cannot see itself; the ego can see only its picture; an ego that is seen or looked at is no longer the looking or perceiving ego: it eternally eludes our grasp. The self-conscious ego is not a principle, but a product; it is not the spontaneous ground or center of our mental life, but is itself the result of the mechanics of the soul. Self-consciousness is indeed possible, but comes later than the consciousness of objects, and is achieved by means of ego-ideas. Fichte's pure ego is an abstraction; the only kind of self-consciousness we know is our empirical self-consciousness, and this is always a consciousness of objects.

The main points of Herbart's psychology are his rejection of the faculty-theory, his theory of presentation as the sole and basal function of the soul, his doctrine of the unconscious, his theory of apperception, his associationism, his theory of interaction, his determinism, and his view that the ego is not a principle, but a product. Space, time, and the categories are not a priori forms of the mind, but products of the mechanics of the soul, the result of the interaction of psychic elements.

The Science of Values. Metaphysics has to do with reality. There is a science called esthetics, which deals not with realities, but with *values*—a science which pronounces judgments of taste. These two sciences are absolutely separate, and Herbart opposes all attempts that have been made to unite them. There are, besides theoretical judgments, judgments which express approval and disapproval: we call things beautiful and ugly, praiseworthy and blamable. The problem of esthetics is to examine the objects of these judgments and to discover what pleases or displeases us in them. Herbart finds that esthetic value does not reside in the content, but in the form of objects, that our feelings of approval and disapproval are aroused by certain simple relations existing between things.

Moral philosophy is a branch of esthetics and concerns itself with the morally beautiful. We approve and disapprove certain relations of will. Experience shows that there are five types of relations which give rise to ethical judgments, and which are called patterns or ideas. We approve (1) in accordance with the idea of inner freedom, the relation in which the individual's will agrees with his conviction; (2) in accordance with the idea of perfection, a harmonious relation between the different strivings of the will in the same subject; (3) in accordance with the idea of benevolence, a relation in which a will makes the satisfaction of another's will his object. (4) We disapprove a relation in which several wills impede one another by being in conflict and discord, but we approve a relation in which each will permits another will to impede its own. In these cases our approval and disapproval are guided by the idea of justice. (5) In accordance with the idea of retribution, we disapprove a relation in which the intended good or evil act is not recompensed. Corresponding to these five ideas in reverse order, are five systems of society: the legal system, the wage system, the system of administration, the system of culture; all of which are united in the realization of the idea of inner freedom as applied to society. The supreme ideal of society is the union of will and reason, one in which there is no discord between the members.

Herbart exercised his greatest influence through his theory of education. Pedagogy he regarded as applied psychology, directed by ends supplied by ethics. His mechanical conception of a mental life determined by the interplay of ideas accounts for the emphasis he places on instruction, the importance he ascribes to interest, and apperception in his philosophy of education.

F. H. Beneke (1798-1854; *Lehrbuch der Psychologie als Naturwissenschaft*, 1833, *System der praktischen Philosophie*, 1837) was influenced by Herbart, as well as by Fries and English empiricism. He agrees with Herbart that psychology must be based on experience, but rejects the view that makes it dependent on mathematics and metaphysics. It is the science of inner experience, the most certain of all our knowledge, and must serve as the foundation of metaphysics, epistemology, ethics, and pedagogy.

65. SCHOPENHAUER

Arthur Schopenhauer was born in 1788 in Danzig; his father was a wealthy banker and his mother a popular novelist of her day. The son entered business, but found commercial life distasteful and exchanged the counting-house for the university. At Göttingen (1809-1811) and Berlin (1811-1813), he devoted himself to the study of philosophy, natural science, and Sanscrit literature. His favorite philosophers were Plato and Kant; Fichte he heard at Berlin and was undoubtedly influenced by him, notwithstanding his contemptuous characterization of Fichte, along with Schelling, and Hegel as the "windbags of philosophy." Schopenhauer established himself as a *privat docent* at the University of Berlin and lectured there intermittently from 1820 to 1831, the period of Hegel's greatest popularity, but met with little success as a teacher. In 1831 he retired from the University, full of bitterness and hatred of all "philosophy professors," and settled at Frankfort on the Main, devoting himself to thinking and writing. His fame was slow in coming, but it sweetened the last few years of his life. He died in 1860.

Über die vierfache Wurzel des Satzes vom zureichenden Grunde, 1813; *Die Welt als Wille und Vorstellung*, 1819; *Über den Willen in der Natur*, 1836; *Die beiden Grundprobleme der Ethik*, 1841; *Parerga und Paralipomena*, 1851. Collected works, ed. by J. Frauenstädt, 6 vols., 1873-74, 2nd ed., 1877; by E. Grisebach, 5 vols., 1916; by R. Steiner, 13 vols., 1894; by P. Deussen, 14 vols., 1911-23.

Translations: *World as Will and Idea*, by R. B. Haldane and J. Kemp, 1923; *Fourfold Root of the Principle of Sufficient Reason*, by K. Hildebrand, 2nd ed., 1891; *The Basis of Morality*, by A. B. Bullock, 1903; *Selected Essays*, by T. B. Saunders, 5 vols., 3rd ed., 1892; *Selections*, ed. by D. H. Parker, 1928; *Works*, ed. by W. Durant, 1928.

R. A. Tsanoff, *Schopenhauer's Criticism of Kant's Theory of Experience*, in *Cornell Studies in Philosophy*, No. 9, 1911; J. Sully, *Pessimism*, 2nd ed., 1891; W. Caldwell,

Schopenhauer's System in Its Philosophical Significance, 1896; T. Whittaker, *Schopenhauer,* 1909; H. Hasse, *Schopenhauer,* 1926; H. Zimmern, *Schopenhauer, His Life and Philosophy,* 1876 and 1932.

The World as Will and Idea. Schopenhauer accepts the doctrine of Kant's *Critique of Pure Reason,* that the world of experience is a world of phenomena, conditioned by the nature of human intelligence. The mind has its forms of perceiving—space and time—and its categories of knowing; the latter Schopenhauer reduces to the single category of causality. What the world is apart from intelligence, Kant had declared, we do not know, and can never know, in the sense in which we know phenomena; it is the great unknown, the noumenon of which the perceived world is the phenomenon. We do not come face to face with the thing-in-itself in an intellectual intuition and can know nothing of it except that it exists; the forms of the mind, space, time, causality, and the rest are inapplicable to it.

At this point Schopenhauer's teaching diverges from that of his master. It is true, he says, that if I were merely an intellectual being, an outward-looking subject, I should perceive nothing but phenomena arranged in space and time, and in causal relation. In my own innermost consciousness, however, I come face to face with my true, real, basal self; in the consciousness of activity I become aware of the thing-in-itself. The thing-in-itself is *will;* it is the primary, timeless, spaceless, uncaused activity that expresses itself in me as impulse, instinct, striving, craving, yearning. I also become aware of myself as a phenomenon, as a part of nature; I image myself as an extended organic body. I know myself in two ways, as will and as body; but it is the one will which, in self-consciousness, appears as the consciousness of activity and, in perception, as my material body. The will is my real self, the body the expression of the will.

Will in Nature and in Man. This duality is the key to the solution of the whole question of metaphysics. All things are interpreted by Schopenhauer in analogy with his conception of the human being: the world is will and idea; idea to the intellect, but in reality will. We find this voluntaristic world-view corroborated by the facts. When I look inward, I come face to face with will; when I look outward, I perceive this will of mine as body. My will objectifies itself as body, expresses itself as a living organism. I am, therefore, justified in inferring by analogy that other bodies are, like mine, the outward manifestations of will. In the stone, will manifests itself as blind force; in man, it becomes conscious of itself. The magnetic needle always points to the north; bodies always fall in a vertical line; substances form crystals when acted on by other substances; and all such occurrences give evidence of the operation of forces in nature which are akin to the will in us. In the vegetable kingdom, too, we discover traces of unconscious striving or impulse. The tree desires light and strives upward; it also wants moisture and pushes its roots into the soil. Will or impulse guides the growth of the animal and directs all its activities. The wild beast desiring to devour its prey develops teeth and claws and muscles; the will creates for itself an organism suitable to its needs; function precedes organization: the desire to butt is the cause of the appearance of the horns. The will to live is the basal principle of life.

In man and the higher animals this primitive impulse becomes conscious; it creates intelligence as its organ or instrument; intelligence is the lamp that illuminates the will's way through the world. The will makes for itself a brain; the brain is the seat of intelligence; intelligence and consciousness are functions of the brain: in this respect Schopenhauer agrees with the materialists. On the lower stages of existence, the will is blind craving, it works blindly, without consciousness; in man it becomes conscious; intelligence is grafted on the will and becomes the greatest of all instruments of self-preservation. But it always remains in the service of the will; will is the master, intellect the servant.

Will controls perception, memory, imagination, judgment, and reasoning; we perceive, remember, imagine what we will to perceive, remember, and imagine; and our arguments are always pleas of the will. Schopenhauer foreshadowed the modern psychological theory of rationalization—reason's subservience to the will in devising reasons to justify conclusions accepted on volitional, emotional, and other non-rational grounds. As we pass down the scale of existence from man to the mineral, we observe intelligence falling into the background; the will, however, remains as the one, constant, persistent element. In the child and the savage, impulse predominates over intelligence; as we descend in the animal kingdom, instinct gradually becomes less and less conscious; in the plant, the will is unconscious; in the mineral, no trace of conscious intelligence remains.

This basal will, which manifests itself in mineral and in man, is not a person, not an intelligent God. It is a blind unconscious force that wills existence. It is neither spatial nor temporal, but expresses itself in individuals in space and time; that is, it acts in such a way that our mind perceives it in individual, i.e., temporal and spatial, form. It manifests itself in eternal, immutable types, which Plato calls Ideas. The different organic species, for example, are eternal immutable types. The species do not change; the individuals belonging to the species grow and die, but the will-type or the species endures. These types form an ascending scale, a graduated series or hierarchy, rising from the lowest stages of matter to man. Individuals may come and individuals may go, but will goes on forever. Hence, the fundamental part of us, the will, is immortal; the particular, individual form in which it expresses itself is mortal. Suicide, therefore, means the destruction of a particular expression of the will, but not of the will itself.

Pessimism. The will to be, the will to live, is the cause of all struggle, sorrow, and evil in the world. A world of ceaseless striving and battle, in which the different forms of the blind will to exist struggle with one another, a world in which the little fishes are devoured by the larger ones, is not a good world, but an evil one, indeed the worst of all possible worlds. The life of man is not worth living, because it is full of misery: it follows from the very nature of the human will that man's life is one of pain and misery. Life consists of blind craving, which is painful so long as it is not satisfied, and which when satisfied is followed by new painful desires, and so on *usque ad nauseam*. We are never permanently satisfied, there is a worm in every flower. We are like shipwrecked mariners who struggle and struggle to save their wearied bodies from the terrible waves, only to be engulfed at last.

Every breath we draw wards off the death that is constantly intruding upon us. In this way we fight with it every moment, and again, at longer intervals, through every meal we eat, every sleep we take, every time we warm ourselves, etc. In the end death must conquer, for we become subject to him through birth, and he only plays for a little while with his prey before he swallows it up. We pursue our life, however, with great interest and much solicitude as long as possible, as we blow out a soap-bubble as long and as large as possible, although we know perfectly well that it will burst. . . . Consequently, the nature of brutes and man is subject to pain originally, and through its very being. If, on the other hand, it lacks objects of desire, because it is at once deprived of them by a too easy satisfaction, a terrible void and ennui comes over it. . . . Thus its life swings like a pendulum backwards and forwards, between pain and ennui. This has also had to express itself very oddly in this way: after man had transferred all pain and torments to hell, there then remained nothing for heaven but ennui.[1]

Another reason why life is evil is because it is selfish and base; and it follows from the very nature of the will that it should be so. *L'homme est l'animal méchant,* a heartless and cowardly egoist, whom fear makes honest and vanity sociable, and the only way to succeed in the world is to be as

---

[1] *The World as Will and Idea,* Bk. IV, sec. 57; Haldane and Kemp translation.

grasping and dishonest as the rest. The progress of knowledge and civilization does not mend matters; it simply brings with it new needs and, with
them, new sufferings and new forms of selfishness and immorality. The
so-called virtues, love of labor, perseverance, temperance, frugality, are merely
a refined egoism. "In much wisdom is much grief; and he that increaseth
knowledge increaseth sorrow." "History is an interminable series of mur-
ders, robberies, intrigues, and lies; if you know one page of it, you know
them all."

Ethics of Pity and Self-denial. Schopenhauer teaches that sympathy, or pity,
is the basis and standard of morality, and that the race is wicked because it
is selfish. To be good, an act must be prompted by pure sympathy; if the
motive is my own welfare, the act has no moral worth at all; if the motive is the harm of others, it is wicked. The empirical character of man
is wholly determined, but the fact of remorse suggests that the will is free.
My will must therefore be ultimately responsible for my character: the intelligible ego has fashioned the empirical ego.

Since the selfish will is the root of all evil and the source of all sorrow,
man must negate the will and suppress his selfish desires, in order to enjoy
happiness or at least to be at peace. This is possible in several ways. The
artistic or philosophical genius may be delivered from the selfish will, forget
himself, lose himself in artistic contemplation or philosophical thought, a
method that affords only temporary relief though it offers a foretaste of deliverance. The individual can also free himself from his selfish will by contemplating the wickedness of the world, the futility of all desire, and the
illusoriness of individual existence. If he will think of these things and
remember that all individuals are one in essence, that they are all manifestations of the same primal will, he will feel sympathy or pity for all creation;
he will see himself in others and feel the sorrows of others as his own. This
is the moral way, but it likewise furnishes only temporary relief. The best
way is total negation of the will in an ascetic life, such as is practiced by
Christian ascetics and Buddhist saints. Resignation and will-lessness ensue,
the will is dead. The saint finds deliverance from his own will, from the
impulses which bind the natural man to the world; the will dies as soon as,
through the knowledge of life, it becomes aware of what it is.

Von Hartmann's Philosophy of the Unconscious. Influenced by Schelling,
Hegel, and Schopenhauer, E. von Hartmann (1842-1906) seeks to reconcile
Hegel's intellectualism with the voluntarism of Schopenhauer, basing his
philosophical speculations on the inductive-scientific method and offering a

philosophy of nature resembling Schelling's. Mechanism is inadequate as an explanation and must be supplemented by an idealistic conception of the world. We cannot account for the facts without assuming the operation of a will in nature, and this will is, according to von Hartmann, governed by a purpose of which, however, it is unconscious. Animal instinct, for example, is intelligent action towards an end without consciousness of that end. It is not determined by mechanical or psychical conditions, but adapts itself to the environment, transforming its organs to meet its needs. The directing principle in things, matter included, is an unconscious, impersonal, but intelligent, will—idea plus will—which becomes fully conscious only in the brain of man. Matter consists of centers of force, or unconscious will-impulses, which represent the activities of an absolute universal, unconscious spirit. This absolute spirit was originally in a state of inactivity, mere potential will or reason, but it was impelled to action by the groundless will. Since it contains the logical reason within it, the unconscious world-will is governed by rational purposes, and expresses itself in a rational process of evolution. But all willing is essentially evil and the cause of unhappiness. The final purpose of this process is the deliverance of the absolute will from itself and the return to the original state of rest, the *nirvana*. This end will be attained when the human race decides upon non-existence. Meanwhile, it is man's duty to affirm the will to live to the utmost, not to practice asceticism and world-flight.

Philosophie des Unbewussten, 1869 (trans. by Coupland); *Phänomenologie des sittlichen Bewusstseins*, 1879; *Grundproblem der Erkenntnistheorie*, 1890; *Religionsphilosophie*, 1881; *Kategorienlehre*, 1896; *System der Philosophie im Grundriss*, 1907.

J. Sully, *Pessimism*, 2nd ed., 1891; H. Vaihinger, *Hartmann, Dühring und Lange*, 1896.

66. NIETZSCHE

Friedrich Nietzsche was born in 1844, the son of a Protestant minister. He attended the universities of Bonn and Leipzig and, in 1869, was appointed professor of classical philology at the University of Basel, Switzerland. He became a Swiss subject, but during the Franco-Prussian War of 1870 he took leave from the university to serve with the Prussian armies as a medical orderly. After brief military service, he returned to Basel in a badly shattered state of health. He offered courses on such subjects as "The pre-Platonic Philosophers," "Introduction to the Study of the Platonic Dialogues," and the "History of Greek Literature." Richard Wagner, who then lived near Basel, became his close friend; but when the composer moved to Bayreuth, Nietzsche gradually grew very critical of him. The "Master"—as Wagner liked to be called—seemed to Nietzsche to stand in the way of his intellectual independence; moreover, Wagner was becoming a symbol of German chauvinism and racism, both of which Nietzsche had come to detest. The nearly simultaneous completion of Nietzsche's enlightened *Menschliches, Allzumenschliches* with a motto from Voltaire, and Wagner's *Parsifal*, which Nietzsche considered an essentially insincere obeisance to Christianity, confirmed the break. In 1879, Nietzsche resigned from the university, giving bad health as his reason, and spent the next ten years in great loneliness in various places in Switzerland and northern Italy. His books were largely ignored by the public until Brandes, in 1888, offered lectures on Nietzsche, in Copenhagen. After this, Nietzsche's fame spread like wildfire. But he did not know it for, early in 1889, he had suffered a complete mental breakdown, and he remained insane until his death in 1900.

   Die Geburt der Tragödie, 1872; *Unzeitgemässe Betrachtungen,* four parts, 1873-76; *Menschliches, Allzumenschliches,* three parts, 1878-80; *Morgenröte,* 1881; *Die fröhliche Wissenschaft,* 1882, 1887; *Also sprach Zarathustra,* four parts, 1883-92; *Jenseits von Gut und Böse,* 1886; *Zur Genealogie der Moral,* 1887; *Der Fall Wagner,* 1888; *Die Götzen-Dämmerung,* 1889; and, published by Nietzsche's executors: *Der Antichrist, Nietzsche Contra Wagner,* and *Ecce Homo.* Some of Nietzsche's notes of the years 1884-88 were published posthumously as *Der Wille zur Macht,* the arrangement not being his own. There are several German editions of the collected works. The most important are the *Grossoktavausgabe,* in 20 vols. and the more recent *Musarionausgabe,* in 23 vols., 1920-29, both including index volumes. Most of Nietzsche's letters are to be found in *Gesammelte Briefe,* 5 vols. in 6, 1900; but his correspondence with Wagner, Overbeck, and Strindberg was published later. The *Historisch-Kritische Gesamtausgabe* of Nietzsche's works and letters in chronological sequence, begun in 1933, has not yet reached his first book. Translations of all of Nietzsche's works in *Collected Works,* ed. O. Levy, 1909. Translations of five of his books in *The Philosophy of Nietzsche* (Modern Library).

   C. Andler, *Nietzsche: Sa vie et sa pensée,* 6 vols., 1920-31; A. Bäumler, *Nietzsche der Philosoph und Politiker,* 1931; E. Bertram, *Nietzsche: Versuch einer Mythologie,* 1918; C. Brinton, *Nietzsche,* 1941; E. Förster-Nietzsche, *Das Leben Friedrich Nietzsches,* 2 vols. in 3, 1895-1904; K. Jaspers, *Nietzsche,* 1936; L. Klages, *Die psychologischen Errungenschaften Nietzsches,* 1926; A. H. J. Knight, *Some Aspects of the Life and Work of Nietzsche,* 1933; K. Löwith, *Nietzsches Philosophie der ewigen Wiederkunft des Gleichen,* 1935; G. A. Morgan, *What Nietzsche Means,* 1941; H. A. Reyburn, *Nietzsche: The Story of a Human Philosopher,* 1948; G. Simmel, *Schopenhauer und Nietzsche,* 1907; H. Vaihinger, *Nietzsche als Philosoph,* 1902. The Nietzsche literature comprises well over a thousand volumes. The interpretation of Nietzsche advanced here is devoloped more fully in Walter A. Kaufmann, *Nietzsche: Philosopher, Psychologist, Antichrist,* Princeton University Press, 1950.

Nietzsche's Predecessors. The young Nietzsche greatly admired Schopenhauer, and under his influence found the clue to "the birth of tragedy" among the ancient Greeks in the distinction between the "Dionysian" and "Apollonian"—two conceptions which reflect the notion of the world as will and as idea respectively. The Dionysian is associated with music and refers more generally to the passionate aspect of human nature, which found an outlet in the Dionysian festivals; while the Apollonian is associated with the

Attack on Christianity. This is the background of Nietzsche's notorious attack against Christianity. Christian meekness, forgiveness, patience, and love are no more than the mimicry of impotent hatred which dares not be anything but meek and patient, or seem anything but loving, though it dreams of heaven and hell. This attitude is associated particularly with the slaves in the Roman Empire who early adopted Christianity, and Nietzsche thus speaks of a "slaves' revolt" in morals and of a "slave morality." He contrasts this with the "master morality" of other civilizations, but his own ethics is clearly distinguished from both types. It differs from "master morality" by vehemently condemning any such disregard for less favored human beings as one finds, for example, in the treatment of the outcasts in the Law of Manu. Nietzsche's critique of Christian morals, on the other hand, revolves around the state of mind which he associates with it, namely, *ressentiment.* By this he means the secret hatred and envy of all those more favored than oneself, and that kind of renunciation of revenge which is inseparable from the faith that "Vengeance is mine; I will repay, saith the Lord." (*Romans* 12:19) Nietzsche's "revaluation of all values" thus does not involve a new table of virtues. It consists in an internal criticism of what he considers Christian ethics, and he tries to show that what usually passes for Christian morals is immoral when judged by its own professed standards.

Some forms of pity and neighborly love are also condemned for other reasons. Instead of perfecting oneself, which would involve hardness against oneself, one "flees" to one's neighbor "and would fain make a virtue of that." And pity, in the sense in which Nietzsche opposes it, rests on the assumption that suffering is necessarily an evil. If what men desire most is "power," then some suffering is required both as a means to the requisite self-control and as an ingredient of the creative life. We should show our love of our fellows not by commiserating with them, but by aiding them to attain this richer state of being, by sometimes being hard with them to this end, and by vying with them in a competitive effort. Thus we should be educators and spurs to each other. Inasmuch as the end of morals is here found in a state which men are held to desire by virtue of their human nature, Nietzsche's ethics may be considered naturalistic.

The Function of Reason. Nietzsche is not an irrationalist in the usual sense of the word. Reason, to be sure, is an instrument of the will to power, but it is a unique instrument without which man cannot achieve ultimate power or happiness. Only reason can effect that sublimation and integration

of our impulses short of which we remain, essentially, beasts. Thus Nietzsche criticizes the Christian faith in the name of rationality; and he considers as interdependent the deprecation of reason and the advocacy of the extirpation of the passions, which he finds in some Christian writers. Those lacking in rational powers cannot harness their impulses to employ them creatively; they must either yield to them or try to stamp them out.

Metaphysics and Epistemology. Nietzsche's metaphysics and epistemology are sketched mostly in posthumously published notes and are not developed as consistently and emphatically as the views outlined above. The cosmos is taken to consist of a finite number of "power quanta," comparable to Leibniz's monads. The essence of each is inseparable from its relations to all the others, and thus Nietzsche adheres to the doctrine of internal relations. Each monad strives, no less than does man, for an increase of power; but there is no ultimate progress, only an eternal recurrence. Moreover, each monad construes all the others from its own point of view, which suggests a kind of "perspectivism." But the philosophers have made the mistake of regarding categories and formulae as criteria of truth and reality; they have naïvely made this human way of looking at things—this anthropocentric idiosyncrasy—the measure of things, the standard of the "real" and "unreal." And in this way the world has come to be divided into a real world and a seeming world, and the world of change, becoming, plurality, and opposition, was discredited and calumniated. The real world was called a world of semblance, a mere appearance, a false world; and the fictitious, supersensible world of permanence, the false world, was enthroned as the true world. What "works," however, and even what is required for survival, is not necessarily "true." More than even survival, we covet "power"; and the state so designated is incompatible with self-deception. Hence, though man's will to truth may indeed impede his survival, Nietzsche accepts its priority nonetheless.

Nietzsche's Influence. Nietzsche's influence has been tremendous, but frequently harmful. His style, which is usually either aphoristic or—notably in *Zarathustra*—highly symbolical, and his addiction to hyperbole and polemical antithesis have greatly facilitated, if not invited, misunderstanding; and the manner in which his sister, after his death, published his notes—especially those which she subsumed under the title, *The Will to Power*—was not only objectionable from a scholarly point of view, but misleading in the extreme. As a result, not only Nietzsche's critics, but also many of his admirers, including some of the Nazis, have ignored his crucial

insistence on sublimation and construed his conception of the will to power and his opposition to Christianity in terms of wantonness and brutality. It is this kind of "influence" which is frequently associated with Nietzsche's name, especially in the English-speaking world; but the impact of his thought on some of the best-known modern writers, theologians, psychologists, and philosophers is no less notable. Indeed, most recent German philosophers have felt Nietzsche's influence: Simmel's philosophy of culture, Vaihinger's version of pragmatism, Spengler's philosophy of history, Scheler's phenomenology, and the *Existenz* philosophies of Jaspers and Heidegger, are but a few examples. Men of widely different temperaments and interests have found inspiration in Nietzsche's writings, and it is no exaggeration to say that his philosophy, which first became "timely" in the eighteen-nineties, has remained timely ever since.

67. Natural Science and Materialism

Reaction against Speculative Philosophy. Kant had sought to establish the validity of mathematics and natural science against the skepticism of Hume, but had denied the possibility of metaphysics as an a priori science of things-in-themselves. Rational theology, cosmology, and psychology have no scientific value for him: we cannot prove the existence of God, the immortality of the soul, and the freedom of the will by theoretical reason; theoretical knowledge is out of the question here, because these things are not and cannot be objects of experience. We can form metaphysical hypotheses, it is true, having more or less probability, but universal and necessary knowledge cannot be attained by them. We may, however, rise to a higher kind of knowledge of freedom, immortality, and God, through moral intuition: practical reason assures us of the validity of such truths, though we cannot give them a sensuous content and thus know them in the scientific sense.

As we have seen, the great successors of Kant—Fichte, Schelling, Hegel—did not share his misgivings with respect to metaphysics. Hegel offered a logical explanation of the universe in all its various phases, and his philosophy remained the reigning one in Germany until 1840. The critical opposition to rationalistic metaphysics, however, persisted outside of the post-Kantian school; we find it expressed in the writings of Fries, Beneke, Herbart, Schopenhauer, and many others. Many scientifically minded thinkers also challenged the claim of philosophy to possess a special method of knowledge in the artistic intuition of Schelling or in the dialectical process of Hegel; and repudiated the idealistic claim that scientific research is a mere prepara-

tion for philosophy, or even a false method. Speculative philosophy was accused of ignoring the facts or of attempting to spin them out of its own inner consciousness, and fell into wide disrepute. The progress of natural science invited a closer study of experience, and fostered positivism and a growing contempt for the type of metaphysics identified with the speculations of the post-Kantian idealists. In 1842 Robert Mayer formulated the principle of the conservation of energy; in 1859 Darwin published his epoch-making work *The Origin of Species by Means of Natural Selection.* The eclipse of idealistic philosophy and the triumph of natural science encouraged the growth of materialism.

Materialism. In the fifties began the aggressively materialistic movement in Germany represented by Karl Vogt (1817-1895), H. Czolbe (1819-1873), J. Moleschott (1822-1893), and L. Büchner (1824-1899; *Force and Matter,* 1855) who led the forces against the idealistic systems. The movement was as much a protest against the theological reactionaries as against the extravagances of speculative philosophy, and, indeed, combined with its materialistic metaphysics a humanitarian and idealistic ethics. The theories advanced by the group were, as a rule, not consistent materialistic theories at all, but conglomerations of many views: mind or thought being conceived sometimes as motion, sometimes as the effect of motion, sometimes as the necessary concomitant of motion, sometimes as one of the aspects of an underlying unknown principle of which motion is a parallel expression. Büchner's book had a great vogue, from the fifties on, and passed through at least twenty editions. Its place was later taken by Ernst Haeckel's *Riddle of the Universe* (1899), a work that shows the same inconsistencies as its predecessor.[2]

The chemist Wilhelm Ostwald (1853-1932; *Die Uberwindung des wissenschaftlichen Materialismus,* 1895, *Naturphilosophie,* 1902) rejects materialism and mechanism in favor of a dynamic or "energetic" theory. The various properties of matter are special forms of energy—kinetic, thermal, chemical, magnetic, electric, etc.—which cannot be reduced to one another. Psychic energy is another form of energy; it is unconscious or conscious *nervous* energy. Interaction is explained as the transition from unconscious to conscious energy or the reverse.

[2] See Thilly, "The World-View of a Scientist: Ernst Haeckel's Philosophy," *Popular Science Monthly,* September 1902.

68. THE REVIVAL OF IDEALISM IN GERMANY

Neo-Kantianism. With the decline of Hegelianism came the reign of natural science and materialism, and the temporary eclipse of all philosophy. No one could hope to re-establish philosophy in a position of respect who did not understand and appreciate the methods and results of natural science as well as those of philosophy. A number of thinkers arose in Germany, some from the ranks of natural science itself, through whose efforts philosophy has regained a place of honor in the hierarchy of the sciences. Most prominent in this group are Lotze, Fechner, Hartmann, Wundt, and Paulsen. All these men profited by a study of the different movements of thought: positivism, materialism, criticism, and post-Kantian idealism. They regarded as futile any attempt to construct a metaphysics by means of the rationalistic methods of the old schools and independently of natural science. Though rejecting subjective idealism and the a priori and dialectical methods, they may all be called descendants of German idealism. With Kant's *Critique of Pure Reason,* they hold that there can be no knowledge in science and philosophy without experience; with positivism, that there can be no system of metaphysics possessing absolute certainty.

Revival of Criticism. Under these circumstances, it was natural that philosophers should again take up the problem of knowledge, to which Kant had given such careful and sober attention, and subject the various intellectual tendencies of the age to critical examination. The critical philosophy became the rallying-point for all those who opposed both the methods of the Hegelians and the progress of materialism, as well as for those who distrusted metaphysics altogether. In 1865 O. Liebmann (1840-1912) raised the cry, "Back to Kant" in *Kant und die Epigonen,* and F. A. Lange published his celebrated work, *History of Materialism,* in 1866. The Neo-Kantian movement grew to large proportions; all the members of this group emphasized the need of epistemological investigations, some even regarding the philological study of Kant's writings, especially of the *Critique of Pure Reason,* as of primary importance (Vaihinger, B. Erdmann, Reicke, Kehrbach, Adickes, E. Arnold). Certain Neo-Kantians limited knowledge to epistemology and accepted the positivistic contention that we know phenomena only, and consequently rejected all metaphysics, whether materialistic or idealistic, as beyond our ken. According to Lange (1828-1875), who has exerted a great influence in positivistic circles, materialism is justified as a method, but not as a world-view, since it fails to explain the basal

nature of physical objects and of our own inner self. For him, metaphysical and religious speculations are the products of a kind of "constructive instinct" in man and have no theoretical value: the existence of an ideal world cannot be proved, but such a conception has practical worth in human life. H. Cohen (1842-1918), the head of the Marburg school, develops the critical philosophy and offers a system of his own (*System der Philosophie*, 1902-1912), on the basis of Kant's method. Among his pupils are P. Natorp (1854-1924; *Sozialpädagogik*, 1899) and R. Stammler (*Lehre von dem richtigen Rechte*, 1902). A distinguished recent exponent of this Neo-Kantian movement is Ernst Cassirer (1874-1945) whose *Substanzbegriff und Funktionsbegriff* (1910) appeared in English translation, under the title *Substance and Function* (1923).

Lotze. A thinker well-fitted by training and temperament to undertake the task of re-establishing philosophy was Hermann Lotze, who offered a system which combined the monadology of Leibniz with the pantheism of Spinoza, and which sought to reconcile monism and pluralism, mechanism and teleology, realism and idealism, pantheism and theism. He called it teleo-logical idealism; his aim was to do justice to the claims of the ethical-religious idealism of Fichte, as well as to the sober scientific interpretation of natural phenomena.

Lotze (1817-1881) studied medicine and philosophy at Leipzig, became a teacher of physiology and philosophy in that university (1839), and professor of philosophy at Göttingen (1844), where he remained until 1881, when he was called to Berlin.

Works: *Metaphysik*, 1841; *Allgemeine Pathologie und Therapeutik als mechanische Naturwissenschaften*, 1842; *Logik*, 1843; *Physiologie*, 1851; *Medizinische Psychologie*, 1852; *Microcosmus*, 3 vols., 1856-1864; *System der Philosophie: Logik*, 1874, *Metaphysik*, 1879.

Microcosmus, trans. by E. Hamilton and E. C. Jones, 2 vols., 1888; *Logic*, trans. by B. Bosanquet, 2 vols., 1884; *Metaphysics*, trans. by B. Bosanquet, 2 vols., 1884; *Outlines of Logic*, trans. by G. T. Ladd, 1892. On Lotze, see H. Jones, *A Critical Account of the Philosophy of Lotze*, 1895; E. Hartman, *Lotzes Philosophie*, 1888; E. P. Robins, *Some Problems of Lotze's Theory of Knowledge*, 1900; V. F. Moore, *The Ethical Aspect of Lotze's Metaphysics*, in *Cornell Studies in Philosophy*, No. 4, 1901; E. E. Thomas, *Lotze's Theory of Reality*, 1921.

Mechanism and teleology. Man is not a mere mirror of facts; he cannot find satisfaction for his ethical and religious interests in a mechanized universe. And yet the physical world, life included, is to be explained by physical and chemical laws, on the basis of a mechanistic atomism. Organic matter differs from inorganic matter, not in the possession of vital force, but only

in the different arrangement of its parts; and this arrangement is a system of physical reactions that determines the direction, form, and evolution of every one of the parts. The living body is an automaton—more of a machine than any invention of man. This view seems to leave no place for man and his purposes and ideals; and yet an examination of the presuppositions on which the mechanistic theory rests will show that this is not the case. The external world, as presented to perception, is not a copy of reality, as naïve realism assumes, but a reaction of our own consciousness to external stimuli: a creation of the soul in the soul itself. The spatial-temporal sense world is a phenomenal world, a product of consciousness. Sensation, perception, and the logical laws by which we interpret the given sensations, are functions of the subject. What, then, is the essence of the real external things, of the things-in-themselves? This question we can answer only by analogical reasoning, and such reasoning will bring us to a metaphysical idealism. Things-in-themselves must have the capacity to act and to be acted on, or to suffer change, and yet remain the same in all change. A being of such nature we know immediately only in ourselves: it is the self-determining principle of unity called the soul. This unity of consciousness, the capacity of the mind to combine manifold phenomena in the unity of consciousness, is what compels us to assume the existence of an indivisible, supersensible soul, as a being distinct from the body. Only in the soul do we find unity in variety, persistence in change, and development: what has been experienced is not lost, but carried over into the present as part and parcel of our mental life. The real universe must, therefore, be interpreted in terms of mind, in terms of the only reality directly known to us. The atoms of which science speaks are immaterial essences, like Leibniz's monads, or centers of force, analogous to what we experience in our own inner life. Space is not a metaphysical reality, but a mere sensible appearance of the existence of these dynamic units, a constant product of perception. Even the lowest forms of matter are not dead, inert masses, but finely organized systems, full of life and action. There are various degrees of reality: the human mind represents the highest, self-conscious, stage in the scale of mental life, but mental life is equally present in less clearly conscious modes of existence, even in gross forms of matter.

Lotze also bases the acceptance of metaphysical idealism on practical or ethical grounds. It is an intolerable thought to suppose that a cold material atomic mechanism should exist for the sole purpose of picturing, in the feeling soul, a beautiful illusion of colors and sounds. Such a universe would have neither meaning nor ethical worth. We can interpret reality only as something which we can absolutely approve, as something absolutely good; hence the phenomenal world cannot be a meaningless illusion, but must be conceived as the manifestation of an ethically ordered spiritual world. Lotze's logic and metaphysics are thus rooted in ethics. We cannot think of anything existing that ought not to exist; our forms of thinking—the logical laws—are rooted in the demand for the good, and reality itself is rooted in the highest good.

The relation of soul and body is one of interaction. How it is possible for the body to cause changes in the soul, or vice versa, cannot be explained, but the difficulty is no greater here than anywhere else. All we can mean by any causal action, is that on the occasion of a change in one object, a change takes place in another: how it takes place we cannot tell. The argument that causal influence of mind on matter is a violation of the physical principle of the conservation of energy, is no valid argument against the interaction of mind and body. The causal interplay between mind and body is made possible by the fact that the body is not different in essence from the soul. The body is, for Lotze as for Leibniz, a system of monads or spiritual forces, the soul being situated in the brain and coming into relation with the body only in the brain. The soul dominates the body, so long as the body is alive; what becomes of it after the dissolution of the body is an insoluble problem, but Lotze holds as an act of faith that every being will receive his due at some time—if not in this life, then in a life after bodily death.

Pantheism. We see how the mechanistic theory is transformed in Lotze's thought into a system of spiritual realities in reciprocal relation with one another. Such a pluralistic world cannot be thought without a unifying, universal substance, of which all phenomena are the modes or expressions. Even the mechanistic world-view, assuming, as it does, the harmonious interrelation of the movement of the smallest atom with the motions of all the other atoms in the world, makes necessary the conception of such an infinite being; indeed, the mechanism of nature is the expression of the absolute will, the way in which the Absolute gives itself external finite form. We cannot understand a single case of interaction or even of causal efficacy within the mental or the physical domains, the possibility of the influence of one thing on another, unless we regard the manifold processes of nature as states of one and the same all-comprehending substance. Thus Lotze's philosophy develops into an idealistic pantheism, uniting Leibnizian and Spinozistic elements. The human soul is compelled to interpret the universal substance in terms of the highest reality that it knows—its own personality; and we must think of this divine personality as an absolutely good being, as a God of love.

Fechner. Gustav Theodor Fechner (1801-1887), professor of physics at Leipzig, and one of the founders of psychophysics—the science of the correlation between physical stimulus and resultant sensations—is a representative of the same movement.

Leben nach dem Tode, 1836; *Das höchste Gut,* 1846; *Nanna, oder Seelenleben der Pflanzen,* 1848; *Zend-Avesta,* 1851; *Über die Seelenfrage,* 1861; *Elemente der Psychophysik,* 1860; *Vorschule der Aesthetik,* 1876.

Fechner reasons by analogy from the existence of mental processes in ourselves and their manifestation in our bodies, to the existence of psychic life, in descending degrees of clearness, in animals, plants, and finally also in inorganic matter, the atoms of which are centers of force. In the spirit of panpsychism he maintains that the entire universe consists of minds. There are higher forms of psychic life than man's; the earth and the other planets have souls, and these, together with all psychic existences, are comprehended in a highest soul, a world-soul, the soul of God. The relation of God to the universe is analogous to that of the human soul to the human body; nature is the body of God, the objective expression of the world-soul, which is above nature, as the human soul is above the human body.

Friedrich Paulsen (1846-1908), in his *Introduction to Philosophy,* a book widely read in both Germany and America early in the present century, offers an idealistic world-view similar to that of Lotze and Fechner.[3]

Wundt. Wilhelm Wundt (1832-1920), whose writings show the influence of the teachings of Spinoza, German idealism, Herbart, Fechner, Lotze, and the modern theory of evolution, first held a professorship of physiology at Heidelberg (1864-1873). In 1873 he became professor of philosophy at Zurich, and was called to Leipzig in 1875. He is the father of modern experimental psychology.

Lehrbuch der Physiologie, 1864; *Lectures on Human and Animal Psychology,* 1863 (trans. by Creighton and Titchener), 5th ed., 1911; *Physiological Psychology,* 1874, 6th ed., 1908-1911; *Introduction to Psychology,* trans. by Pinter, 1912; *Logik,* 3 vols., 1880-1883; *Ethics,* trans. by Titchener, Washburn, and Gulliver, 3 vols., 1897-1901; *System der Philosophie,* 1889; *Einleitung in die Philosophie,* 1901.

Wundt defines philosophy as the universal science whose function it is to combine the general truths obtained in the special sciences into a self-consistent system. The facts of consciousness form the basis of all our knowl-

[3] Cf. Thilly, "Paulsen's Ethical Work," *International Journal of Ethics,* XIX, 2.

edge; so-called external experience, the perception of an external world, is a phase of inner experience; all our experiences are mental. But this cannot be interpreted, in the manner of subjective idealism, as meaning that the world is a mere reflection of consciousness; we are entitled to infer the existence of an external world; his position is thus one of critical realism. Space and time, causality and substance, are concepts which originate in the mind and would never arise in us without the cooperation of the objective world. A knowledge of nature would be impossible without both external causes and conceptual forms. If we make our external experiences the basis of our world-view, we are driven to an atomistic materialism; if we limit ourselves to the facts of our mental life, we shall end in idealism. We cannot, however, interpret the external world as devoid of inner life: the cosmic mechanism is the outer husk behind which lies concealed a spiritual creation, a striving and feeling reality resembling that which we experience in ourselves. The psychic element is given the priority, for, in accordance with the results of the theory of knowledge, inner experience must remain the original datum. Psychology shows that mental life is essentially activity, will—Wundt's psychology is voluntaristic; the will manifests itself in attention, apperception, association, in the emotions and in volitions, and constitutes the central factor of mind.

The soul is not to be regarded as substance—substance is a materialistic conception—but as pure spiritual activity, *actus purus*. Reality must be conceived as a totality of striving, willing beings, manifesting themselves in material form: it is composed of independent beings determined by inner purposes, thus Wundt's philosophy is teleological as well as metaphysical. We are led by ethical reasons to comprehend these individual wills in a universal absolute will, the nature of which we cannot further define. The world is the evolution of a mind, a progressive development of interrelated purposive forms.

The Philosophies of Value. Some of the Neo-Kantian systems consider value as an ultimate ontological category; they interpret reality in terms of a highest good: the world must be, at bottom, what the ethical, esthetic, or logical consciousness demands as the ideal. For Kant the universe is essentially what the moral consciousness implies—what ought to be: the noumenal world must be a spiritual realm, a kingdom of ends, a free rational community in which each person wills the union. Fichte's world-view is similar to this, and Lotze, too, is guided by the conception of the good: we cannot conceive the world otherwise than based on a good principle.

The introduction of such conceptions into metaphysics is said by many to rob it of its scientific character. Philosophy, they hold, is a work of the theoretical intellect; its business is to offer an explanation of reality free from the demands of man's moral, esthetic or religious nature. The universe should not be conceived in terms of what we desire or of what ought to be, but in terms of what is. Against this scientific and rationalistic view, it is pointed out by the value-philosophers that the desire for truth and rationality, the demand for logical consistency and unity, is itself a craving for what ought to be; that here, too, we are moved by an ideal: it offends our love of order and harmony, our ideal of perfection, or our longing for beauty to conceive reality as chaos. Hence, they argue, the logical impulse has not the primacy over the other demands of our nature, and no philosophical system can be adequate that fails to do justice to them all.

Windelband. Wilhelm Windelband (1848-1915; *Präludien,* 3rd ed., 1907, *Geschichte und Naturwissenschaft,* 3rd ed., 1904, *Willensfreiheit,* 2nd ed., 1905, *Wille zur Wahrheit,* 1909), who was influenced by Kant and Fichte, works out a system of philosophy in which value has a central rôle. According to him, philosophy is the science of universal values, the study of the principles of absolute value-judgments—logical, ethical, esthetic; all the other sciences, however, consist of theoretical judgments. There is a fundamental difference between the propositions: This thing is white, and, This thing is good. In the one case we predicate a quality belonging to the presented objective content; in the other, a relation pointing to a consciousness that sets up a purpose. The validity of logical axioms, moral laws, and esthetic rules cannot be proved; the truth of each rests upon a purpose that must be presupposed as the ideal of our thinking, feeling, or willing. That is, if you desire truth, you must recognize the validity of the principles of thought; if you are convinced that there is an absolute standard of right and wrong, you must recognize the validity of certain moral norms; if beauty is to be something more than subjective satisfaction, you must recognize a universal esthetic norm. All such axioms are norms whose validity is based on the presupposition that thought aims at truth, the will at goodness, and feeling at beauty—in a form which is universally acceptable. Faith in universal purposes is the presupposition of the critical method; without it, the critical philosophy can mean nothing.

Logical rules are, therefore, necessary instruments of the will for truth. This, however, is not to be understood in the pragmatic sense that their utility is their truth; truth is not derived from the will but from the things themselves, and is not an arbitrary affair. Windelband distinguishes between natural sciences and the historical sciences, or sciences of events: the former deal with the constant, the abstract, the universal, with law, and are "nomothetic"; the latter deal with the individual, the concrete, the unique, the novel, and are "idiographic."

Similar views are expressed in the writings of H. Rickert (*Grenzen der naturwissenschaftlichen Begriffsbildung,* 2nd ed., 1913; *Kulturwissenschaft und Naturwissenschaft,* 2nd ed., 1910), and H. Münsterberg (*Psychology and Life,* 1899, *Eternal Life,* 1905, *Science and Idealism,* 1906, *Eternal Values,* 1909). W. Dilthey (*Introduction to the Mental Sciences,* 1883) emphasizes the uniqueness of the "mental" sciences as distinguished from the "natural" sciences. We must study the relations, methods, and presuppositions of the mental sciences; in them we gain a knowledge of reality, values, norms, and purposes, by reflecting on the expressions of the mind in history and psychology. Metaphysics, however, as a logical system of reality, values, and purposes is impossible. The mental sciences are based on a teleological, analytical, and descriptive psychology, which includes general psychology, comparative psychology, and socio-historical psychology.

Eucken. Rudolf Eucken (1846-1926) offers a system of metaphysics that seeks to do justice to human values, as well as to the logical intellect, and which has succeeded in arousing an interest in ethical idealism outside of academic circles and in many lands.

> *Geistige Strömungen der Gegenwart,* 1909 (trans. by Booth, under the title *Main Currents of Modern Thought*), first appeared in 1878, under the title *Geschichte und Kritik der Grundbegriffe der Gegenwart; Die Lebensanschauungen der grossen Denker,* 1890, trans. by Hough and Gibson, under the title, *The Problem of Human Life; Der Kampf um einen geistigen Lebensinhalt,* 1896; *Der Sinn und Werth des Lebens,* 1907, trans. by Boyce Gibson, under the title: *Value and Meaning of Life; Grundlinien einer neuen Lebensanschauung,* 1907, trans. by Widgery, under the title: *Life's Basis and Life's Ideal; Einführung in eine Philosophie des Geisteslebens,* 1908, trans. by Pogson, under the title: *The Life of the Spirit; Ethics and Modern Thought,* 1913. On Eucken see Boyce Gibson, *Eucken's Philosophy of Life;* Booth, *Eucken: His Philosophy and Influence;* A. J. Jones, *Eucken: A Philosophy of Life.*

According to Eucken, neither naturalism nor intellectualism can fully interpret reality; the former always tacitly presupposes the mental world which its principles deny, while the latter can never make experience square with logical thought. The mind with its yearning for the infinite, revealing itself in ourselves and in history, points to a universal spiritual process, an independent and intelligible world beyond, as the source of all individual mental life. We experience such a free, self-active spirit in ourselves: it is an axiomatic fact or act which we cannot deduce, but only apprehend in its immediacy. In his essence man transcends history; he is a historical being only in so far as he is imperfect and strives for perfection. Either the spiritual life is an epiphenomenon of material nature or it is a self-existent totality, a universal whole, the source of all being. If human life is a mere incident in nature, then it is nugatory; all that is noblest and best in it is a mere illusion, and the universe irrational. What religion is struggling for, is not the happiness of man, but the preservation of a genuine spiritual life on a human basis. The sharp contrast between the spiritual endowment of man and his real situation inspires him with the deep conviction that a higher power is active in him. The yearning for truth and love, the longing to live a genuine life instead of drifting with the current of mere phenomena, we cannot uproot from the human heart. The ceaseless striving in man, the impulse for self-activity, immediacy, and infinity would be inconceivable without the operation in him of an infinite power. If there is no transcendent world, the spiritual life falls to pieces and loses its inner truth. An idealistic pantheism rises out of the desire for a higher world.

The universal life forms the ground of all being—of human history, of human consciousness, and of nature itself. The universal process evolves from the inorganic to the organic, from nature to mind, from mere natural soul-life to spiritual life; and in this process of evolution towards independence and self-realization the world becomes conscious of itself. Human personality is not, however, submerged in this universal mind; indeed, the development of individuality is possible only within, and as sharing in, the universal life.

XIX

French and British Philosophy of the Nineteenth Century

69. Positivism in France

Reaction against Sensationalism. In France the Enlightenment, which rested on a naturalistic philosophy, led to the great Revolution with its disturbing social and political changes. After the Revolution, the sensationalistic and materialistic theories of Condillac, the Encyclopedists, and Holbach, which had been so popular during the last half of the eighteenth century, lost their vogue, and new philosophies came to the front. It was not surprising that an excess of criticism and liberalism should have aroused a conservative reaction, and that the demand for free thought should have been opposed by a school of thinkers who emphasized the principle of authority and offered a supernaturalistic philosophy as a remedy to the troubled age. Thus, Joseph de Maistre (1754-1821) declared that human reason had shown itself impotent in governing man, and that faith, authority, tradition alone could hold him in check and bring about a stable order of society. Psychology, however, seemed to offer the best arguments against materialism and became the most promising field of study. Condillac's sensationalism had proved unsatisfactory even to members of his school. The materialist Cabanis called attention to vital feelings and instinctive reactions, elements of conscious life which it was difficult to explain as mere products of the external senses. Maine de Biran (1766-1824), who began as a follower of Condillac and Cabanis, finds in effort the central element of consciousness and the basal principle of knowledge: in this inner experience, he thinks, we become directly aware of the activity of the soul as well as of the existence of a material world. The feeling of effort is also the basis of such notions as force, causality, unity, and identity.

The most important opposition to materialism, however, came from Royer-Collard (1763-1845), Victor Cousin (1792-1867), and T. Jouffroy (1796-1842). Royer-Collard, an eloquent teacher of philosophy at the Sorbonne, accepted the common-sense philosophy of Thomas Reid. Cousin offered an eclectic system with a spiritualistic keynote, which showed the influence of Reid, Collard, Biran, Schelling, and Hegel, and became a leading force in French education.

On French philosophy of the first half of the nineteenth century, see L. Lévy-Bruhl, *History of Modern Philosophy in France,* trans. by G. Coblence, 1899; J. H. Merz, *History of European Thought in the Nineteenth Century,* 1904-14; G. Boas, *The Major Traditions of European Philosophy,* Ch. IX, 1929, and *French Philosophies of the Romantic Period,* 1925.

Saint-Simon. Not one of these movements, however, possessed sufficient vigor to satisfy the needs of an age that still felt an interest in the ideals of liberty, equality, and fraternity. The reform of human society remained the dream of many French thinkers, and practical questions appealed to them more strongly than the theories of eclectic philosophers. The political revolution had not brought universal happiness, it is true; the ignorance and misery of the lower classes had not been removed by the proclamation of universal human rights. But it was now held that the goal could be reached by social evolution, through the gradual reform of society by education and enlightenment. Claude Henri de Saint-Simon (1760-1825) conceived the idea of a new science of society which would do away with the unequal distribution of property, power, culture, and happiness. The main thing, according to him, was the economic and intellectual emancipation of the workers; the form of government he regarded as immaterial. A new Christianity is needed, he declared, which shall preach not self-denial, but love of the world, and emphasize the commandment of love, which for Saint-Simon meant love of the poor and lowly. The reform of society presupposes a knowledge of social laws and, therefore, implies a reform of the sciences as well as of our world-view. The present, he held, is a period of criticism, negation, and dissolution, an age of spiritual chaos, a critical and not an organic age. The Middle Ages were an age of construction, of spiritual and social organization, an organic age, and to such a period we must again return. We need a new system of thought, and this must be a *positive* philosophy: a system based on experience and science.

Comte. Saint-Simon, a sympathetic seer and enthusiast rather than a systematic thinker, was not the man to construct the positive philosophy. That task was undertaken by Auguste Comte, who had been commissioned by Saint-Simon to write for his *Catéchisme des industriels* (1823-1824) the part dealing with the scientific system of education; but the account did not seem to the master to do justice to the emotional and religious phase of education.

Comte was born in 1798, in Montpellier, the son of an orthodox Catholic family. He attended the Ecole Polytechnique at Paris (1814-1816), where he acquired a thorough knowledge of the exact and applied sciences and imbibed the principles of Saint-Simonism, which had an enthusiastic following in that institution. After leaving the Ecole, he studied biology and history and gave lessons in mathematics in order to gain his livelihood. He was associated with Saint-Simon for a number of years, but the two did not agree, and Comte began to work out his own ideas independently of the master, supporting himself, as best he could, by means of his pen and through private instruction. Although he made several attempts to obtain a professorship, he never succeeded. He died in 1857.

Plan des travaux scientifiques nécessaires pour réorganiser la société, 1822; *Politique positive*, 1824; *Cours de philosophie positive*, 6 vols., 1830-1842 (abridged trans. by H. Martineau, entitled, *Comte's Positive Philosophy*, 1896); *Système de la politique positive*, 4 vols., 1851-1854 (Eng. trans., 1875-1877); *Catéchisme positiviste*, trans. by R. Congreve, 1858; J. S. Mill, *Auguste Comte and Positivism*, 4th ed., 1891; J. Watson, *Comte, Mill, and Spencer*, 1895; L. Lévy-Bruhl, *The Philosophy of Auguste Comte*, trans. by K. de Blaumont-Klein, 1903; T. Whittaker, *Comte and Mill*, 1908; F. J. Gould, *Auguste Comte*, 1920; H. Gouhier, *Auguste Comte et Saint-Simon*, 1941; F. S. Marvin, *Comte: The Founder of Sociology*, 1937; R. L. Hawkins, *Auguste Comte and the United States*, 1936, and *Positivism in the United States*, 1938.

Reform of society and the sciences. As the titles of his books indicate, Comte's ideal is, like that of Saint-Simon, the reform of society. This end cannot be reached until we have a knowledge of the laws of society, a social science, which, in turn, presupposes all the other sciences and a philosophical point of view. The reform of society, therefore, calls for the reform of political and social science and of philosophy—a new philosophy, to the working out of which Comte devoted his entire life. The Middle Ages had their world-view—a common conception of the universe and of life—in their theology, which, however, represented a primitive stage of thought. The remarkable development of the natural sciences in modern times, especially in France, suggested the scientific method as the one to be followed in the new undertaking. The sole object of science is to discover natural laws or the constant relations existing between facts, and this can be done only by observation and experience. Knowledge thus acquired is *positive* knowledge; and only such knowledge as is verified by positive science can be successfully applied in the various fields of human practice. Wherever we have not yet reached such knowledge, it is our business to obtain it by imitating the methods employed in the advanced natural sciences. Comte sides with the thinkers of the empirical school; he belongs to the chain of philosophers in which Hume and Diderot are important links.

Evolution of knowledge. Positive knowledge, which is Comte's ideal, is the result of historical evolution. The human mind passes through three stages—the law of the three stages—or employs three methods of philosophizing: the theological, the metaphysical, and the positive, each of which has its practical value and its corresponding social institutions. In the theological stage, the age of childhood, man regards things anthropomorphically, as the expressions of supernatural beings, passing from fetichism through polytheism to monotheism. This is the age of monarchy and absolute authority, and its leaders are priests. In the metaphysical stage, the age of youth, abstract powers or entities are substituted for personal beings; such powers or essences are supposed to inhere in the different things and to be the necessary causes of the phenomena observed in them; from the knowledge of these causes, the knowledge of their effects is said to be deduced. At first, different powers are assumed to explain different groups of phenomena—such as chemical force, vital force, mental force—but the tendency is to reach a single primary force, as in the preceding stage. The metaphysical age is the age of nationalism and popular sovereignty; jurists are its leading spirits. Both theology and metaphysics believe in the possibility of absolute knowledge and of explaining the innermost essence of things. In the stage of positivism, the attempt to discover the inner essences of things is abandoned as futile and replaced by the effort to discover the uniform relations existing between phenomena. The question asked is not Why? but How? Laws of nature are substituted for absolute causes; the aim now is to ascertain invariable relations between facts by the method of observation. Galileo, Kepler, and Newton have established the positive sciences. We cannot know what heat, light, and electricity are in themselves, but we can know the conditions under which they occur, and the general laws governing them. To explain light is to bring it under the laws of motion. Such knowledge is sufficient for practical purposes; to see in order to foresee (*voir pour prévoir*) is the motto of the positivist.

The human mind seeks to reduce everything to unity, but this is a mere subjective bent. We cannot reduce the many different laws of nature to a single all-embracing law; experience reveals too many irreducible differences for that. The term positive, says Comte, means real, useful, certain and indubitable, exact, it means the opposite of negative: positive knowledge is not mere negation or criticism.

Classification of the sciences. Comte sets himself the task of constructing a positive philosophy, which shall collect and arrange the general laws yielded by the different sciences, give us the method common to them, and show how they are connected with one another—that is, provide us with a classification of the sciences. Such a synthesis is of value to education as well as a means of overcoming the evils of specialism. Comte arranges the sciences according to the order in which they enter upon the positivistic stage: mathematics (arithmetic, geometry, mechanics), astronomy, physics, chemistry, biology, and sociology (to which he later adds ethics as the culmination of them all). This classification also exhibits a gradual advance from simplicity to complexity: mathematics, which contains the simplest, most abstract and universal propositions, comes first and forms the basis of all the rest, while sociology, the most complex of all, presupposes the sciences preceding it. The reason for this is that the simpler and more general laws are, the wider will be their application. The truths of geometry hold for all phenomena in so far as they are regarded as extended—the static view; those of mechanics hold for all phenomena in so far as they are regarded as in motion—the dynamic view. Although every science in the ascending series presupposes its predecessors, Comte does not claim that the phenomena of a given level can be derived from those of a lower one—the phenomena of life, for example, from those of motion. Such a reductionistic view would be materialism, which Comte categorically rejects: we cannot explain organic phenomena mechanically or chemically. In each of the six fields of science, a new element is added which is distinct from those of the others. The same remarks apply to phenomena within a single science: heat is distinct from electricity, the plant from the animal, the various organic species from each other.

We miss, in Comte's list of sciences, logic, psychology, and ethics. Logic as the science of intellectual functions would seem to take precedence even over mathematics, but the French philosophers regarded it as a branch of psychology; and psychology was not a special science, according to Comte. Mind or soul is a metaphysical entity and does not exist for positivism: we cannot observe mental processes subjectively, introspection being impossible. All we can do is to study them objectively, that is, study the organic phenomena with which they are connected and the human institutions in which they are expressed. Psychology, therefore, belongs in part to biology, in part to sociology. The fact is, the insertion of psychology into the scheme would have given Comte a great deal of trouble; geometry and mechanics would not be applicable to unique processes like the mental, and his classification would break down. But if organic processes, though regarded as unique and not explainable mechanically, can have their place in the series, it is difficult to see why psychology should be excluded. Comte did not work out these ideas consistently; his interest in the phrenology of Gall and his aversion to all introspective psychology led him to regard psychic states as functions of the brain.

Social science. The last and most complex science in the scale, and the one about to enter upon the positivistic stage, is sociology, which depends upon the others, especially upon biology—for society is made up of organic individuals—and comprises economics, ethics, the philosophy of history, and a large part of psychology. Comte claimed the credit of being the founder of this science, and it was he who gave it its name. It is impossible to study psychology, ethics, and economics apart from the science of society and the philosophy of history: the phenomena with which they deal stand in reciprocal relation with society and social evolution. Social statics is a study of society as a fact, of the laws of its existence, of the social *order;* social dynamics, a study of society in its evolution: it is a philosophy of history and aims to trace the *progress* of society.

Social life owes its origin, not to self-interest, but to the social impulse. Man has egoistic impulses, and these, too, are indispensable to society. The nobler impulses, the altruistic feelings, supported by intelligence, gain mastery over the selfish instincts, which are stronger in the beginning than altruism—a term coined by Comte—and must be held in check in order to make society possible. The family is the social unit and the preparation for a larger social life. Intelligence is the leading principle in progress. Progress consists in the development of the human functions which distinguish man from the brute, in the advance of reason and the higher or nobler impulses. Society passes through three stages of evolution, corresponding to the stages of intelligence already enumerated. Militarism is characterized by order, discipline, force: organization is the primary condition of progress. It is followed by the revolutionary stage, the stage of political rights, a transition period of negation. The positivistic stage, "the definitive stage of humanity," is one of industrialism, in which the emphasis is placed on the social and economic rather than on the political problem activities of man. It is the era of experts whose function it will be to guide scientific research, to superintend public instruction, to inform public opinion on the one hand, and to regulate social production on the other. Comte is opposed to popular representation on the ground that it would make the experts dependent on the ignorant. Public opinion is the antidote to misgovernment. He believes that the social problem is, after all, a moral problem, that the positivistic society will be brought about only by a change in ideas and customs. Comte's main objective is the reform of society, and this necessarily rests on an ethical ideal. He interprets history in the light of his ideal: progress means the realization of the ideal of humanity, the perfection of man in society. History is moving toward this ideal; intellectual, social, and ethical evolution is making straight for positivism—the definitive stage of humanity. It is not difficult to see that positivism ends in dogmatism: it becomes a system of metaphysics.

Ethics and the religion of humanity. During his later period, Comte laid greater stress on the emotional and practical phases of life and brought the ethical ideal into bolder relief. In his earlier period, intelligence had been emphasized as the great factor in the reform of society; now, reason and science are subordinated to feeling and practice. The objective method is replaced by the subjective method, subjective in the sense that it connects knowledge with the satisfaction of subjective needs and with the desire for unity and simplicity in our world-view. Ethics is added to the sciences as the seventh and highest science, to which all the others are subservient. The great human problem is to subordinate, as far as possible, personality to sociability; everything must be related to humanity, love is the central impulse, to live for others the absolute demand. Humanity is the Great Being worthy of worship —this is the central tenet of the positivistic "religion of humanity."

70. Utilitarian Ethics of Bentham

Utilitarianism as an ethical theory was developed by Jeremy Bentham (1748-1832) within the psychological and philosophical framework of British empiricism. Bentham was greatly indebted to the classical British empiricists, especially to Hume, for his empirical method, for his psychological analysis of ethical motivation, and for the individualism and nominalism which pervade his ethical and legal theories.

Bentham's primary interest was the theory of the law, and he developed his utilitarianism to provide an ethical basis for legal theory and practices. He was essentially a reformer whose chief concern was the formulation of an ethical doctrine which would serve as a guide in the moral conduct of the individual, and as the basis for the legislative improvement of society. We must not expect of him a systematic ethical theory of the type expounded by the great moral philosophers. He had little interest in defining his own ethical position in relation to historical positions in ethics. What little criticism he does offer of earlier theories is very general and sweeping, and is directed mainly against asceticism and the ethics of sympathy. The ethics of asceticism he summarily dismisses as an inverted hedonism, "approving of actions inasfar as they tend to diminish happiness; disapproving of them inasfar as they tend to augment it." Under the caption of the principle of sympathy and antipathy, Bentham criticizes a variety of ethical doctrines ranging from the moral sense theory to the rationalism of "an eternal and unmistakable rule of right." The charge which he brings against all forms of intuitionist ethics is that they provide no more than a subjective feeling as the basis of ethical judgment and the standard of morality.

The Principle of Utility. In opposition to asceticism and intuitionism, Bentham offers his own principle of utility, "that principle which approves or disapproves of every action whatsoever according to the tendency which it appears to have to augment or diminish the happiness of the party whose interest is in question." [1] He hastens to explain that "by utility is meant the property of any object, whereby it tends to produce benefit, advantage, pleasure, good or happiness or to prevent the happening of mischief, pain, evil, unhappiness to the party whose interest is considered." [2] The principle of utility does not, according to Bentham, admit of direct proof; it is so fundamental as to be the basis of all proof in the moral and legal fields. The logical ground of all proof is, he contends, itself unprovable. The only proof of which it admits is of the indirect sort, which consists of showing that all other ethical principles—for example, the principle of asceticism and the principle of sympathy—unwittingly presuppose the principle of utility. The principle of utility equates the good with happiness or pleasure and evil with pain; hence Bentham's utilitarianism is a version of hedonism, closer, as we shall see, to the crass hedonism of Aristippus than to the more refined hedonism of Epicurus. He is not only an ethical hedonist by virtue of his employment of the pleasure principle as the standard for conduct as right or wrong, good or evil, but is also a psychological hedonist in that he acknowledges desire for pleasure and aversion to pain as the sole motives or springs of human action.

[1] *Principles of Morals and Legislation*, Ch. I.
[2] *Loc. cit.*

"Nature," he states at the beginning of his great work, "has placed mankind under the governance of two sovereign masters, *pain* and *pleasure*. It is for them alone to point out what we ought to do, as well as to determine what we shall do. On the one hand the standard of right and wrong, on the other the chain of causes and effects, are fastened to their throne."[3] Pain and pleasure govern us in everything we do, say or think, and any attempt to separate ourselves from their control will itself be prompted by them. In his further elaboration of the pleasure principle as it operates in ethics and in the system of law, Bentham enumerates four "sanctions" or sources of pleasure and pain: (1) the physical, (2) the political, (3) the social and (4) the religious. Of these four, the physical is the most important—indeed he suggests that the other three sanctions are resolvable into the physical. What, then, is the value of the enumeration? Apparently the classification of sanctions is of practical rather than theoretical significance; it affords Bentham a convenient guide in seeking out the kinds of motives or incentives which may be employed to lead man to act morally, and thus promotes the practical interest of inculcating moral action. The several sanctions are theoretically and psychologically one in that they all rely on pleasure and pain as the sole springs of action, but they represent four distinct ways of bringing this motivating force into play.

Hedonistic Calculus. No account of Bentham's utilitarianism would be complete without some reference to his hedonistic calculus, or system of quantitative measurement of pleasures and pains in determining the relative worth of alternative courses of action. The seven elements or dimensions of value which must be weighed in the appraisal of moral conduct are: (1) intensity, (2) duration, (3) certainty or uncertainty, (4) propinquity or remoteness, (5) fecundity ("or the chance it has of being followed by sensations of the *same* kind"), (6) purity ("or the chance of its *not* being followed by sensations of the opposite kind"), and (7) extent (the number of persons to whom it *extends* or who are affected by it).[4] All of these dimensions of pleasure and pain are measurable quantities, and it is thus possible in appraising the pleasure-pain consequences of a projected action to estimate their resultant hedonistic value. The quantitative method for measuring the total value of an intended action, or of comparing the worth of alternative courses of action, is Bentham's hedonist calculus. It is significant that Bentham includes "extent" among the elements to be considered in appraising the

[3] *Loc. cit.*
[4] *Op. cit.*, Ch. IV.

moral worth of an action; Bentham's hedonism, although individualistically oriented, does not ignore the happiness of others. The interest of society or the community of individuals must be taken into account by ethics and, of course, by legislation, which Bentham defines as "the art of directing men's actions to the production of the greatest possible quantity of happiness." The community is not, however, to be construed as a corporate entity over and above its component individuals. In strict adherence to his empirically grounded individualism, Bentham describes the community as "a fictitious body, composed of the individual persons who are considered as constituting as it were its members. The interest of the community then is, what?—the sum of the interests of the several members who compose it." [5] It is in terms of this nominalistic or fictionalistic conception of the community that Bentham formulates the utilitarian ideal of the "greatest good of the greatest number." Furthermore, he is convinced that "the conduct which is conducive to the general happiness always coincides with that which conduces to the happiness of the agent." [6] Hence it is to the interest of the individual to strive for the general happiness.

A Fragment of Government, 1776; *An Introduction to the Principles of Morals and Legislation*, 1789; *The Rationale of Punishment*, 1830; *Deontology or Science of Morality*, 1834.

C. M. Atkinson, *Jeremy Bentham*, 1905; J. McCann, *Six Radical Thinkers*, 1910; C. Phillipson, *Three Criminal Law Reformers*, 1923; D. Baumgardt, *Bentham and Ethics of Today*, 1952.

71. Scottish Rationalistic Philosophy

Although British philosophy since the days of William of Occam had shown a decided leaning toward nominalism and empiricism, and an indifference to metaphysics, the opposing rationalistic schools never entirely disappeared. We have already mentioned the Cambridge Platonists of the seventeenth century, and the reaction against Hume represented by Thomas Reid and his school in the eighteenth and early nineteenth century, when the commonsense philosophy dominated the Scottish universities. The value of the latter movement consisted not so much in its positive teachings as in its criticisms of empiricism and the impetus it gave, in England, to a more thorough re-examination of the presuppositions of empiricism. The Scottish philosophy later came under the influence of the critical philosophy of Kant, notably in the persons of William Whewell and Sir William Hamilton.

[5] *Op. cit.*, Ch. I.
[6] *Op. cit.*, Ch. XVII. Cf. F. Thilly, *Introduction to Ethics*, p. 169.

Whewell. William Whewell (1795-1866), who is the author of *History of the Inductive Sciences, Philosophy of the Inductive Sciences,* and *Elements of Moral Philosophy,* argues that empiricism has ignored an important feature of induction: the fact that the mind itself contributes to the knowledge of phenomena a number of ideas and principles, by virtue of which the content of experience is organized and unified. These basic concepts of the mind are employed when we interpret nature and translate its data into our own language, long before we become conscious of their operation. These ideas and principles involved in our unconscious inferences are necessary in the sense that their opposites are inconceivable. Such fundamental ideas and principles act in simple apprehension; indeed, we cannot conceive of any activity of mind in which they are not at work. They are acquired and developed through experience, though not derived from experience; they do not exist in the mind ready-made, but arise when the mind is set in motion by sensation; they are ways the mind acts on its material. Among such principles Whewell mentions space, time, cause, and purpose, as well as the moral axiom that we ought to do what is right. His works on the inductive sciences are valuable; indeed, without them, John Stuart Mill tells us, he could not have accomplished his own task in this field.

Hamilton. Sir William Hamilton (1788-1856) likewise advanced beyond the common-sense school, in the direction of Kantian criticism. Among his works are *Discussions on Philosophy and Literature,* 1852, and *Lectures on Metaphysics and Logic,* 1859. He was chiefly interested in moral and religious problems, and found in Kant's critical philosophy a basis for his theology.

Hamilton holds that there are necessary or a priori truths—simple self-evident truths which carry absolute conviction in themselves, and for which universality and necessity are the ultimate tests. The law of causality, the law of substance, and the logical laws of identity, contradiction, and excluded middle are necessary truths; it is unthinkable that they should not be true. Contingent truths,—e.g., the existence of an external world—while their falsity is not unthinkable, must be accepted as a basis for practical action.

Hamilton betrays the influence of the Scottish common-sense school in his doctrine of natural realism: we have a direct consciousness of the world as really existing, but we do not perceive the material or mental substance directly. We perceive directly only phenomena, a series, or aggregate, of appearances in coexistence. These phenomena or qualities must be appearances of something, of something that is extended, solid, figured, and so on. A law of thought compels us to think something absolute and unknown as the basis or condition of the relative and known. What applies to matter applies to mind. Mind and matter, as known or knowable, are only two different series of phenomena or qualities; as unknown and unknowable they are two substances in which these different qualities are supposed to inhere. We, therefore, directly perceive qualities, attributes, phenomena, and not substances.

J. S. Mill, *Examination of Sir William Hamilton's Philosophy,* 1865; On Hamilton and his school, see J. Seth, *English Philosophy and Schools of Philosophy,* 1912; H. Laurie, *Scottish Philosophy in Its Natural Development,* 1902.

72. THE EMPIRICISM OF JOHN STUART MILL

Empiricism and Positivism. Hume had drawn what seemed to him the ultimate consequences of the presuppositions of empiricism. If our knowledge is limited to impressions and their faint copies or ideas, and the self is a mere bundle of sensations, we have no universal and necessary knowledge: the notion of cause is reduced to the idea of temporal succession; and the consciousness of necessity accompanying it, to habit or belief; it is illusory to assume either a spiritual or a material substance as the cause of our sensations. Hume's reflections, ending as they did in partial skepticism, agnosticism, and phenomenalism, caused a violent reaction and led to the development of the common-sense philosophy of the Scottish school, as we have seen. Owing to the progress of the natural sciences, however, and the rise of positivism in France, the empirical conception again came to occupy the leading place in British thought near the middle of the nineteenth century. It developed from the doctrines of Hume and Hartley and attained its highest form in the *Logic* of John Stuart Mill. Though this thinker did not escape the influence of Auguste Comte, whom he greatly admired, he had as his intellectual ancestors the leaders of the traditional English school, among them his own father, James Mill (1773-1836), and Jeremy Bentham (1748-1832), and had taken his stand even before the appearance of Comte's writings. There is, indeed, much in common between French positivism and latter-day English empiricism, enough to have induced some historians to regard the latter as an offshoot of Comte's movement. The same attitude of mind characterizes both views: both emphasize the value of facts and of scientific method, and both are, in principle, opposed to metaphysics; both aim at social reform and make the happiness and development of humanity the ethical ideal. The positivists, however, turn their attention to the methods and results of the special sciences and seek a classification and systematization

of human knowledge, while John Stuart Mill, true to the traditions of his
school, makes psychology and logic, which Comte neglects, his starting-point
and finds in these the solution to his problems.

John Stuart Mill (1806-1873) was the son of James Mill, a secretary in the East India
Company and a writer on economic, political, sociological, and philosophical subjects.
The elder Mill began the intellectual training of his son during the latter's infancy, and
gave it his careful personal attention. He introduced him to the philosophy of the
eighteenth century, and Hartley's psychology and Bentham's ethics—all of which made
a great impression on the boy. Hartley's doctrine of the association of ideas became—
as it had been to his father—the guiding principle of Mill's psychology and kindred
studies; while Bentham's principle of utility, as he himself says, gave unity to his conception of things and a definite shape to his aspirations. In 1823, after a few years spent
in travel and in the study of law, Mill entered the service of the East India Company,
where he remained until its abolition by Parliament in 1858. In 1865 he was elected to
Parliament as a Liberal and served for three years, but his greatest influence on the political life of his country was exercised through his writings.

Logic, 1843; *Principles of Political Economy*, 1848; *Liberty*, 1859; *Thoughts on Par-
liamentary Reform*, 1859; *Representative Government*, 1860; *The Subjection of Women*,
1861; *Utilitarianism*, 1861; *Auguste Comte and Positivism*, 1865; *Examination of Sir William Hamilton's Philosophy*, 1865; edition of James Mill's *Analysis of the Human Mind*.
1869; *Dissertations and Discussions*, 1859-1874. His *Autobiography* and *Three Essays on
Religion: Nature, The Utility of Religion*, and *Theism* were published after his death.
Correspondence of Mill and Comte, ed. by Lévy-Bruhl; correspondence with d'Eichthal;
Letters, ed. by Elliot, 2 vols. Ed. of works in *New Universal Library*.

E. Albee, *Utilitarianism*, 1902; W. Davidson, *Utilitarians from Bentham to J. S. Mill*,
1915; F. Thilly, "The Individualism of J. S. Mill," in *Philosophical Review*, Vol. XXXII,
1923; O. A. Kubitz, *Development of J. S. Mill's System of Logic*, 1932; G. Morlan,
America's Heritage from J. S. Mill, 1936; D. Fosdick, *Introduction to J. S. Mill on Social
Freedom*, 1941.

Science and Social Reform. The ideal of social and political reform gave
direction to Mill's intellectual labors. He shared the eighteenth century's
enthusiasm for progress and enlightenment, and believed in the supreme
efficacy of education, holding that there is no natural impulse which it cannot transform or destroy, and that human character will change with men's
ideas. In order to bring about reforms, knowledge is necessary, knowledge
of the right ends and of the means of realizing them. But in order to reach
knowledge, correct methods must be employed, and to the study of these
Mill addressed himself in his *Logic*. The wonderful progress of the natural
sciences suggested an examination of scientific methods and their application
in the mental or moral sciences—psychology, ethics, economics, politics, and
history. The investigation of methods of knowledge, however, could not

be carried on successfully without a consideration of the general principles of the theory of knowledge, and such a study we have in the *Logic,* which has been called the most thoroughgoing exposition of the epistemology of empiricism ever written.

Logic. Hume had taught that we cannot reach universal and necessary knowledge: we do not experience any necessary connection among things; the necessity of judgments, on which intuitionists lay so much stress, is merely the result of habit. We know only our ideas, which follow one another in a certain temporal order, according to the laws of association by similarity, contiguity, and causality. Hartley worked out this theory of association, reducing Hume's three laws to the single law of contiguity: ideas call up other ideas with which they have been associated in consciousness before. He sought to explain all mental processes as cases of this law. On the basis of this theory, knowledge is nothing but a firm and coherent association of ideas, and the so-called necessity of thought nothing but an expression of the firmness of these associations. To know, therefore, means to study the sequence of our ideas, to eliminate the accidental, transitory associations, and to discover the permanent, enduring, invariably recurring ones, the correct and valid sequences; this is accomplished by the methods of induction, which Mill describes as they are employed by modern experimental research. Hence, all inference and proof, and all discovery of truths not self-evident, consist of inductions and the interpretation of inductions. All our knowledge that is not intuitive comes exclusively from this source.

Inductive Inference. Mill's entire logical theory is based on the laws of association. The child infers that the fire will burn because fire and the burn came together before; the inference, in this case, is from one particular to another, and not from the universal to the particular, nor from the particular to the universal. This is, indeed, the elementary form of all inference. It makes no difference whether I infer from the fact that Peter died the death of Paul or the death of all men: in the latter case I am simply extending the inference to an indefinite number of particular cases instead of only to one. I have passed from the known to the unknown in both cases, and the same process of inference is involved. The conclusion in an induction extends what is observed in certain particulars to one or more similar particulars and thus embraces more than is contained in the premises.

The syllogistic process—e.g., all men are mortal, Paul is a man, hence he is mortal—is not a process of inference, because it is not a progress from the known to the unknown. In every syllogism, considered as an argument to prove the conclusion, there is a begging of the question: the proposition, Paul is mortal, is already contained in the general proposition, all men are mortal. The major premise of a syllogism does not prove the conclusion. The inference is finished when we have asserted that all men are mortal; the major premise is established by the particular instances: it is a concise or compressed form of expression of the results of many observations and inferences. It tells us in effect what has already been found, registers what has been inferred, what events, or facts, have gone together and were, therefore, inferred to belong together, and gives directions for future inductive inferences.

Warrant of Induction. But what warrant have we for making such inferences? The assumption involved in every case of induction is that what happens once, will, under circumstances sufficiently similar, happen again, as often as the same circumstances recur. And what warrant have we for this assumption itself? The warrant of experience: it is a universal fact that the universe, as we know it, is so constituted that whatever is true in any one case is true in all cases of a certain description. This principle, that the course of nature is uniform, is the fundamental principle of induction. It is, however, itself an instance of induction, one of the latest to attain strict philosophical accuracy. If this is so, how can it be regarded as our warrant for all the others? Is not Mill here reasoning in a circle, proving the particular inductions on the assumption of the law of the uniformity of nature and then proving this law by these very inductions? No, says Mill, the principle of the uniformity of the course of nature stands in the same relation to all inductions as the major premise of a syllogism always stands to the conclusion: it does not constitute its proof, but is a necessary condition of its being proved—that is, the conclusion is not proved unless the law is true. The real proof that what is true of John, Peter, and others is true of all mankind, can only be that a different supposition would be inconsistent with the uniformity which we know to exist in the course of nature. Mill regards the law of nature as an abridgment or summation of our past experiences: it simply registers what has been observed. It does not prove the particular inductions, but merely increases their certitude. But though we may acquit Mill of the charge of circular reasoning, it is plain that he fails to find a logical basis for his theory of induction. He does not accomplish what he promises, and seems, moreover, to be unconscious of the skeptical consequences of his position.

The uniformity in question, Mill also points out, is not properly uniformity, but uniformities. A certain fact invariably occurs whenever certain circumstances are present, and does not occur when they are absent; the same is true of another fact, and so on. Such uniformities among natural phenomena are called laws of nature. The problem of inductive logic is to ascertain the laws of nature and to follow out their results. Its purpose is to ascertain what kinds of uniformities have been found perfectly invariable, pervading all nature, and what are those which have been found to vary with difference of time, place, or other changeable circumstances. Though no uniformities are absolutely certain, some uniformities—as far as any human purpose requires certainty—may be considered as in the highest degree certain and universal. By means of these uniformities we can raise multitudes of other inductions to the same point in the scale. For, if we can show with respect to any inductive inference that either it must be true or one of these highly certain and universal inductions must admit of an exception, the former generalization will attain the same degree of certainty, within the bounds assigned to it, as belongs to the latter.

The Law of Causation. We have uniformities of simultaneity and uniformities of succession. In the laws of number and those of space, we recognize, in the most unqualified manner, the rigorous universality of which we are in quest. But the most valuable to us of all truths relating to phenomena are those which relate to the order of their succession. Of these truths, one only has been found that has never been, in any instance whatever, defeated or suspended by any change of circumstances. This is the law of causation, which is universal also in the sense that it is coextensive with the entire field of successive phenomena, all instances whatever of succession being examples of it. The truth that every fact which has a beginning has a cause, is coextensive with human experience.

The concept of cause is the root of the whole theory of induction; it is, therefore, necessary to reach a clear and precise idea of it. The only conception of a cause which the theory of induction requires, is such as can be gained from experience. The law of causation is but the familiar truth that invariability of succession is found by observation to exist between every fact in nature and some other fact which has preceded it. To certain facts, other facts always do, and will continue to succeed. We do not mean by the cause a mysterious and powerful tie between things, or some essence that actually produces something else. The invariable antecedent is termed the cause; the invariable consequent, the effect. Philosophically speaking, the cause of a fact is the sum-total of its conditions, positive and negative.

The objection may be urged against this definition of cause that it leaves out of account an important element, the idea of necessity or necessary connection. If the invariable antecedent is the cause, then night must be the cause of day, and day the cause of night. To obviate this objection, Mill adds that causality implies not only that the antecedent always *has* been followed by the consequent, but that, as long as the present constitution of things endures, it always *will* be so. All that the term necessity can imply is unconditionality. That which is necessary, that which must be, means that which will be. Hence, the cause of a phenomenon is the antecedent, or the concurrence of antecedents, on which it is invariably and unconditionally consequent. The question, How do we know that a sequence is unconditional? is answered: By experience. In some cases we are not sure that a hitherto invariable antecedent *is* the invariable antecedent. But there are certain primeval or permanent causes of which all phenomena are the effects, and these invariable causes are truly unconditional. Anyone knowing all the agents which exist at the present moment, their collocation in space, and all their properties—in other words, the laws of their agency—could predict the whole subsequent history of the universe. Anyone acquainted with the original distribution of all natural agents, and the laws of their succession, would be able to construct inferentially the whole series of events in the history of the universe, past and future.

Mill's underlying assumption is that inexorable law and order reign in the universe, that there are invariable, unconditional sequences, and that these can be ascertained by induction, deduction, and verification, which constitute the scientific method. This doctrine, if consistently carried out (which it is not), would lead to a rationalistic science and make possible, in theory at least, an absolute body of knowledge. It does not, however, agree with his theory of induction, according to which the idea of causation can be nothing but a belief in the succession of phenomena, a belief that rests on the succession of ideas in consciousness. Mill wavers between the rationalistic and empiricist conceptions of causality: the view that causality implies necessary connection, and the view that it means merely invariable temporal succession. On the latter hypothesis, all we can say is that the belief in causation increases with our experiences of succession. And, indeed, this is the view generally taken by Mill when he examines our right to assume the universality of the law of causation, as we do in all the inductive methods. We cannot justify the assumption, he tells us, by the disposition of the human mind to believe it, for belief is not proof, and, besides, not one of the so-called instinctive beliefs is inevitable. Even now, many philosophers regard volitions as an exception to the law of causation. His position on this question agrees with his view of the uniformity of nature. Indeed, the universality of the causal law is merely a case of the uniformity of sequences in nature. We arrive at the universal law of causation by generalizing from many partial uniformities of sequence. Since the law of causation is reached by the loose and uncertain method of induction *per enumerationem simplicem,* it might seem, at first sight, that such a principle would prove a weak and precarious basis for scientific induction. But the precariousness of the method is in an inverse ratio to the largeness of the generalization, and the law of causation is the most extensive, in its subject-matter, of all generalizations which experience warrants, respecting the sequences and coexistences of phenomena. In point of certainty, it stands at the head of all observed uniformities, and adds to these as much proof as it receives from them. The criticism that it is a paradox to base induction on the law of causation, and then to explain this law itself as a case of induction, is answered by Mill in the same manner in which he answers a similar objection against the uniformity of nature. When we have ascertained that the particular conclusion is liable to no doubt except the doubt as to whether every event has a cause, we have done all that can be done. Mill has, however, forgotten his assumption of causation as an *unconditional* sequence, and that there are certain primeval and permanent causes in nature, which determine the whole series of events in the history of the universe. According to this view, the particular conclusion could be liable to no doubt whatever, for it assumes that *all* phenomena are the effects of these primeval and permanent causes of nature.

In matters of evidence, we neither require nor can attain the absolute. Whatever has been found true in innumerable instances, and has never been found to be false, can safely be accepted provisionally as universal, until an undoubted exception appears; provided that the nature of the case is such that an exception could scarcely have escaped notice. But we cannot affirm confidently that this general law prevails beyond the range of our experience in distant parts of the stellar region. It must be received not as a law of the universe, but of that portion of it only which is within the range of our means of observation, with a reasonable degree of extension to adjacent cases.

Rejection of a priori Truths. The law of the uniform course of nature and the law of universal causation are both the results of experience. They are not necessary or a priori truths; indeed, there are no such truths. Even the principles of logic and the generalizations of mathematics are generalizations from experience. The proposition that two straight lines cannot enclose a space is an induction from all the experiences we have ever made. Besides, mathematical propositions are only approximately true; there cannot be a line without breadth; the radii of perfect circles would be equal, but such circles do not exist. There are no real points, lines, or circles which conform to the definitions of geometry; mathematical entities are idealizations of the points, lines, etc., which we experience—they are abstractions, fictions. Mathematical propositions, therefore, have only hypothetical validity. The argument that a proposition, the opposite of which is inconceivable, must of necessity be true is also unavailing. The inconceivability proves nothing regarding the existence of a thing—this can only be decided by experiential evidence. The results of the so-called deductive sciences are necessary in the sense of necessarily following from first principles called definitions and axioms; that is, they are certainly true if these definitions and axioms are true. The definitions are experiential ideas which rest on abundant and obvious evidence, while the axioms are but the most universal class of inductions from experience, the simplest and easiest cases of generalization furnished to us by our senses and by our internal consciousness. The demonstrative sciences are all, without exception, inductive sciences, their evidence is that of experience; but they are also hypothetical sciences because their conclusions are only true on certain suppositions, which are, or ought to be, approximations to truth, but are seldom if ever exactly true.

The External World and the Self. With critical idealism, Mill holds that we can know phenomena only and not things-in-themselves. On the inmost nature of the thinking principle, as well as on the inmost nature of matter, we are and must always remain in the dark. As physical objects manifest themselves to me only through the sensations of which I regard the external objects as the causes, so the thinking principle, or mind, in my own nature makes itself known to me only by the feelings of which it is conscious. But if we know only sensations, the effects of an unknown external cause, how do we come to believe in things independent of us? Mill gives a psychological explanation of our belief, based on memory, expectation, and the laws of association. I see a piece of white paper on the table, I shut my eyes or go into another room; I no longer see the paper, but I remember it and expect or believe I shall see it again if the same conditions recur. I form the notion of something permanent, enduring; the so-called external thing is simply the possibility that certain sensations will recur in the same order in which they have occurred. The external world is "a permanent possibility of sensation." We come to believe that the permanent possibilities are the true realities, and the passing sensations merely the accidents or representations of the possibilities. The belief, then, in external objects is the belief that sensations may recur. This belief is not an original belief or innate notion, but the result of our experience, an acquired belief, the product of the association of ideas. Mill is not trying to prove that objects are external to us; he is simply trying to account for the fact that, although we experience nothing but a succession of ideas, we are yet able to form the picture of a persisting world of objects outside of consciousness.

We find also, in Mill's philosophy, a doctrine of the thing-in-itself—an unknown something or external cause to which we refer our sensations. In spite of his phenomenalism and idealism, Mill cannot entirely relinquish the transcendent substance, or cause of sensations. The world of knowledge is a phenomenal world, but there is, besides, a noumenal world, an unknown and unknowable world of things-in-themselves. This doctrine poses a problem which Mill does not seriously consider: the problem of the possibility of such a world on his own premises. He speaks of the thing-in-itself as substance and cause, without even inquiring into the possibility of such a view on his definition of substance and cause. If by substance we mean a complex of sensations, and by cause the invariable phenomenal antecedent, how can we speak of something outside of the sensation-series as substance and cause?

Mill's conception of mind, or the ego, is somewhat vacillating. With Hume and James Mill, he calls mind a series of feelings. He tries to explain our belief in the constancy or permanency of the self as he explained our belief in an external world: it is the belief in a permanent possibility of feelings, and this accompanies our actual feelings. But he sees difficulties in the associationistic conception of mind as a mere succession of feelings and is frank enough to confess them. Many inconsistencies in Mill's thought—such as those pertaining to the thing-in-itself and the ego—are due to his faithful adherence to the English association-psychology, which he inherited from his father, along with his tacit acceptance, or at least appreciation, of many of the doctrines of the rationalistic thinkers of his time. We shall encounter a similar vacillation in his utilitarian ethical theories.

Reform of the Mental and Moral Sciences. As was pointed out previously, Mill was deeply interested in the reform of society and the happiness of man. He believed that the progress of knowledge in the social and political fields would be attended by results equal to those of the natural sciences. But in order to attain such knowledge, he held it to be necessary to apply the methods which had been so successfully employed in physics, anatomy, and physiology. What is needed, he insists, is a reform of the mental and moral sciences.

Psychological Determinism. The scientific treatment of human nature, however, presupposes that there is order, uniformity, law, invariable sequence in the mental realm; and the question at once arises: Can there be science in this field, are human actions subject to law? The objection is raised that man is not subject to law, not determined, but free. Mill finds, with Hume, that the chief objection to the necessitarian doctrine rests on a misapprehension. Determinism, properly understood, means invariable, certain, and unconditional sequence, and not compulsion or restraint. Determinism, as applied to human action, means not that one phenomenon compels another, that a given motive compels a certain effect, but that, given certain motives, character, and circumstances, we can predict conduct. The act does not necessarily follow on a certain condition; other conditions may supervene to bring about a different result. Necessity means that a given cause will be followed by the effect, subject to all possibilities of counteraction by other causes; not that the cause is irresistible. The fatalistic error is the supposition that my character is molded for me by some outside agent and not by me. Actually, my desire to mold my character is among the causes of my action. I can change my character if I will; I can resist my habits and temptations if I wish. But my decision to do so is a result of inner causation. The sense of moral freedom consists in the consciousness that I can act in a certain way if I so wish. Another misapprehension regarding the will is the widespread belief that the motive of my action is always the anticipation of pleasure or pain. Mill does not deny that pleasure and pain can be motives to action, but he insists that we may at times act without reference to pleasure and pain. In conformity with the law of association, pleasure and pain may drop out as motives, we may form a habit of desiring or willing without being moved by the thought of pleasure or pain. Mill emphatically rejects the theory of motivation known as psychological hedonism—the theory that we are motivated exclusively by the desire for pleasure and the aversion to pain.

Mill's theory of volition and motivation may be summed up as follows: (1) All human actions are determined in the sense that action follows with causal uniformity from a man's circumstances and motives—there are no causeless actions. (2) Man is free in so far as his inner desires and wishes direct his actions; he is not a puppet fatalistically controlled by outside agents. (3) Human will, though frequently directed toward pleasure or pain, is not always hedonistically motivated.

Wherever, then, facts follow each other according to law, we can have science. These laws, however, may not have been discovered, and, indeed, may not be discoverable by our existing resources. We cannot predict in the science of human nature because we do not know all the circumstances and because we do not know the characters of the individuals. Yet, many of the effects are determined by general causes; they depend on circumstances and qualities common to all mankind. With regard to these, we can make predictions which will almost always be verified, and we can formulate general propositions which are almost always true. Such approximate generalizations must be connected deductively with the laws of nature from which they result; we must show that they are corollaries from the universal laws of nature. In other words, we need a deductive science of human nature, resting, however, on general laws which have an inductive basis. We do not ask, what is the nature of mind, but what are the laws of its various thoughts, emotions, volitions, and sensations. Moreover, psychology is not physiology; its subject-matter is not nerve-excitations but mental events. The simple and elementary laws of mind are found by the ordinary methods of experimental inquiry. Among such laws are the laws of reproduction and memory, and the laws of the association of ideas: these compose the basic assumptions of the philosophy of human nature. All the maxims of common experience— e.g., old men for counsel, young men for war—are the results or consequences of these laws. We have no assurance, however, in the case of such empirical laws, that they will hold true beyond the limits of our observation, because the consequent—in this case, wisdom—is not really the effect of the antecedent—old age—and because there is ground for believing that the sequence is resolvable into simpler sequences. The real scientific truths are the causal laws which explain these empirical maxims; the latter verify the general theory. Empirical laws are never entirely reliable except in the "simple" sciences, such as astronomy, where the causes or forces are few in number: few causes great regularity. The complexity of the phenomena of human nature is an obstacle—though not an insurmountable one—to a genuine science of human conduct.

Ethology. Psychology ascertains the simple laws of mind in general; it is a science of observation and experiment. Ethology, or the science of the formation of character, traces the operation of these simple laws in complex combinations of circumstances and is altogether deductive. It is a science which is still to be created; its great problem is to deduce the requisite middle principles from the simple or general laws of psychology; to determine from the general laws of mind, combined with the general position of our species in the universe, what actual or possible combinations of circumstances are capable of promoting or of preventing the production of those qualities of human nature or character which are interesting to us. Such a science will be the foundation of a corresponding art, the art of education. To be sure, verification a posteriori must go hand in hand with deduction a priori. The conclusions of theory cannot be trusted unless confirmed by observation; nor those of observation, unless they can be affiliated to theory by deducing them from the laws of human nature and from a close analysis of the circumstances of the particular situation to which the theory is applied.

Social Science. Next, after the science of individual man, comes the science of man in society—of the actions of collective masses of mankind and of the various phenomena which constitute social life. Can we make the study of politics and of the phenomena of society scientific? All phenomena of society are phenomena of human nature, generated by outward circumstances upon masses of human beings; hence the phenomena of society, too, must conform to fixed laws. Prediction is difficult, if not impossible here, because the data are innumerable and perpetually changing, and the multitude of causes is so great as to defy our limited powers of calculation. There are two erroneous methods of philosophizing on society and government, the exclusively experimental mode of investigation, and the restricted geometrical mode. The true method proceeds deductively, to be sure, but by deduction from many, not from a very few, original premises or axioms as in geometry; it considers each social effect to be an aggregate result of many causes, operating sometimes through the same, sometimes through different mental agencies or laws of human nature. The science of social phenomena is deductive, not after the model of geometry, but after that of the more complex physical sciences. It is difficult, to be sure, to calculate the result of the conflicting tendencies which are acting in a thousand different directions and promoting a thousand different changes at a given instant in a given society. But our remedy here consists in verification: the process of comparing our conclusions either with the concrete social phenomena themselves or of assimilating them to already well-established empirical laws of social behavior.

Sociology, however, as a system of deductions a priori, cannot be a science of positive predictions, but only of tendencies. All its general propositions are, therefore, hypothetical: they are grounded on some supposititious set of circumstances and declare how a given cause would operate in those circumstances, supposing that there are no other factors in the situation. Mill also points out that different species of social facts, being, in the main, dependent on different kinds of causes—e.g., the desire of wealth—must be studied apart, which gives us distinct and separate, though not independent, branches or departments of sociological speculation. Political economy (economics), for example, inquires into the laws which govern various operations, under the supposition that man is occupied solely in acquiring and consuming wealth. What are the actions which would be produced by the desire for wealth if it were unimpeded by other desires? The conclusions of each separate science must afterwards be corrected by the modifications supplied by the other separate sciences.

There can be no separate science of government, because political facts, as causes and effects, mingle with the qualities of the particular people or of the particular age. The science of government must be a part of the general science of society. In this general science of society, nothing of a really scientific character is possible except by the inverse deductive method, which asks not what will be the effect of a given cause in a certain state of society, but what are the causes which produce, and the phenomena which characterize, states of society in general. The fundamental problem is to find the laws according to which any state of society produces the state which succeeds it and takes its place. This opens up the question of the progressiveness of man and society. There is a progressive change both in the character of the human race and in its outward circumstances. History, when judiciously examined, illustrates empirical laws of society. Sociology must ascertain them and connect them with the laws of human nature, by deductions showing that they were the derivative laws naturally to be expected as the consequences of those ultimate ones. The only check or corrective on the empirical laws is constant verification by psychological and ethological laws. The empirical laws are uniformities of coexistence and succession, and we have, in consequence, social statics and social dynamics. Social dynamics is the study of society considered in a state of progressive movement; social statics is the study of the *consensus,* that is, of the mutual actions and reactions of contemporary social phenomena, the study of the existing order. One of the main problems of the science of social statics is to ascertain the requisites of stable political union. Mill himself includes among the conditions of a stable political order: a system of education, the feeling of allegiance or loyalty, and mutual sympathy.

It is necessary to supplement the static view of social phenomena with the dynamic, considering both the progressive changes of the different elements, and the contemporaneous condition of each; we thus obtain, empirically, the law of correspondence, not only between the simultaneous states, but also between the simultaneous changes, of those elements. This law of correspondence, if duly verified a priori, would become the real scientific derivative law of the development of humanity and human affairs. The evidence of history and of human nature affords ample testimony that the state of the speculative faculties of mankind, including the prevalent beliefs of men regarding themselves and the world in which they live are—however they may have been arrived at—decisive factors in social progress. Speculation is a determining cause of social progress; all the other dispositions of our nature which contribute to that progress are dependent on it for the means of accomplishing their share of the work. The order of human progression in all respects will depend largely on the order of progression in the intellectual convictions of mankind, that is, on the law of the successive transformations of human opinions. Mill adopts what would today be called a predominantly ideological interpretation of history. A closely parallel, though perhaps more extreme, interpretation was advanced by Thomas H. Buckle (1821-1862), who attempted, in his *History of Civilization in England,* 1857-1861, to show that progress depends solely upon intelligence. Mill next asks whether the law of historical progression can first be determined from history as an empirical law, then converted into a scientific theorem by deducing it a priori from the principles of human nature. To accomplish this, it is necessary to take into consideration the whole of the past, from the earliest recorded history down to the memorable phenomena of the present generation. This is an enormous task, but it cannot be avoided. It has become the aim of scientific thinkers to connect by theories the available facts of history. Only in this way is there any hope of fulfilling man's ideal of a comprehensive science of human nature and human society.

Ethics. In his ethical theories Mill follows, in the main, the traditional English hedonistic school, the most important representatives of which are Locke, Hutcheson, Hume, and J. Bentham (1748-1832). Mill regarded the reading of Dumont's *Traité de législation,* an exposition of Bentham's principal speculations, as an epoch in his life, one of the turning-points in his intellectual history. In his *Utilitarianism,* he agrees with Bentham that happiness, or the greatest good of the greatest number, is the *summum bonum* and the criterion of morality. He differs from his master, however, on several important points. According to Bentham, the value of pleasures is to be measured by their intensity, duration, certainty or uncertainty, propinquity or remoteness, fecundity, purity, and extent (the number of persons affected by them). No difference is to be made in quality; other things being equal, "push-pin is as good as poetry." Mill, on the other hand, teaches that pleasures also differ in quality, that those which go with the exercise of intellectual capacities are higher, better, than sensuous pleasures, and that persons who have experienced both prefer the higher pleasures. "No intelligent person would consent to be a fool; no instructed person would be an ignoramus"; no person of feeling or conscience would consent to be selfish or base. You would not exchange your lot for that of a fool, dunce, or rascal, even if you were convinced that a fool, dunce, or rascal is better satisfied with his lot than you are with yours. "It is better to be a human being dissatisfied than a pig satisfied; better to be Socrates dissatisfied than a fool satisfied." The fool and the pig may think otherwise, but that is because "they only know their side of the question," the fool's and the pig's. Bentham and Mill also agree that we ought to strive for the greatest happiness of the greatest number; but Bentham justifies this on the ground of self-interest, while Mill bases it on the social feelings of mankind, the desire for unity with our fellow-creatures. He tells us that utilitarianism requires a man to be as strictly impartial between his own happiness and that of others as if he were a disinterested and benevolent spectator. "In the golden rule of Jesus of Nazareth, we read the complete spirit of the ethics of utility. To do as one would be done by, and to love one's neighbor as oneself, constitute the ideal perfection of utilitarian morality." Indeed, the greatest happiness principle is a mere form of words without rational signification, unless one person's happiness—on the assumption that it is equal in degree and that proper allowance is made for kind—is of exactly as much importance as another's; Bentham's dictum, "Everybody to count for one, nobody for more than one," may be considered an explanatory commentary on the principle of utility.

Mill's utilitarianism, like many of his other theories, vacillates between opposing views; in addition to the empirical association-psychology with its hedonism, egoism, and determinism, we find leanings towards intuitionism, perfectionism, altruism, and free will. The very inconsistencies of the theory, however, made it attractive to many minds, and there is much in it with which the opposing schools may agree. As Green pointed out, Mill's version of utilitarianism was of the greatest significance in practice; it substituted a critical and intelligent conformity to conventional moral precepts for a blind and unquestioning one. The theory of the greatest happiness of the greatest number has tended to improve human conduct and character. It has helped men to expand their ideals in a manner beneficial to a wider range of persons; and it has done this, we may add, not because of its hedonistic elements, but because of the emphasis which it placed on universalism; for, after all, what the utilitarians were aiming at was the realization of a better social life, in which each man should count for one and no one for more than one. Mill in particular became the philosophical spokesman of liberalism in England, and fought the intellectual battles of democracy. In his works on *Liberty* and the *Subjection of Women* he insisted on the fullest possible individual rights, because he regarded social well-being as inevitably bound up with individual well-being. He pointed out "the importance, to man and society, of a large variety in types of character, and of giving full freedom to human nature to expand itself in innumerable and conflicting directions," and he regarded the repression of women as a greater loss to the community than to women themselves. In the first edition of his *Political Economy* (1848), he favored economic individualism, but in time his "ideal of ultimate improvement went far beyond Democracy" and brought him close to socialism.

While we repudiated with the greatest energy that tyranny of society over the individual which most Socialistic systems are supposed to involve, we yet looked forward to a time when society will no longer be divided into the idle and the industrious; when the rule that they who do not work shall not eat, will be applied not to paupers only, but impartially to all; when the division of the produce of labor, instead of depending, as in so great a degree it now does, on the accident of birth, will be made by concert, on an acknowledged principle of justice; and when it will no longer either be, or be thought to be, impossible for human beings to exert themselves strenuously in procuring benefits which are not to be exclusively their own, but to be shared with the society they belong to. The social problem of the future, we considered to be, how to unite the greatest individual liberty of action, with a common ownership in the raw material of the globe, and an equal participation of all in the benefits of combined labor.[7]

He had an abiding faith in the possibilities of human nature. "Education, habit, and the cultivation of the sentiments, will make a common man dig or weave for his country, as readily as fight for his country."

[7] Mill, *Autobiography.*

73. THE EVOLUTIONISM OF HERBERT SPENCER

Herbert Spencer was born in 1820 at Derby, England, the descendant of a family of teachers. He seems to have inherited his intellectual gifts from his father, who is described as a man of fine culture and independence of thought, and whose example in teaching his pupils to think instead of to memorize, influenced Spencer's views on education. Owing to the boy's delicate health, his father did not push him in his work, and we hear that he was inattentive and lazy, stubborn and disobedient in school. He made better progress outside the classroom, under the guidance of his father, who taught him to draw from nature, encouraged his desire to make collections, and introduced him to physical and chemical experiments. Spencer afterwards (1833-1836) received instruction from his uncle, Thomas Spencer, a clergyman of the Established Church, a man of public spirit and democratic ideals, who was to prepare him for Cambridge; but Spencer refused to go to a place where things were taught in which he was not interested. He could grasp principles and draw conclusions, and surpassed his fellow-students in mathematics and mechanics, but memorizing words and rules of grammar did not appeal to him. His works show the effects of the manner in which he was trained: he is independent, original, and natural. In 1837 he assisted his father in teaching, and then studied civil engineering. He followed this profession intermittently until 1846, when he devoted himself to journalism. His spare hours he devoted to the study of geology and other sciences. His first great work, which attracted the attention of a small though select circle of thinkers, was *Social Statics* (1848-1850). In 1852 Spencer relinquished his editorship of the *Economist* and devoted the rest of his life to working out his system of synthetic philosophy, a prospectus of which appeared in 1860. He suffered great financial losses in publishing his works, and his literary ventures did not prosper until American admirers arranged for the publication of his books in the United States. He died in 1903.

Proper Sphere of Government, 1842; *Social Statics,* 1850; *Principles of Psychology,* 1855; *Education,* 1858-1859; *First Principles,* 1860-1862; *Principles of Biology,* 1864-1867; *Principles of Sociology,* 1876-1896; *Principles of Ethics,* 1879-1893; *The Man versus the State; Essays,* 5th ed., 3 vols., 1891; *Facts and Comments,* 1902; *Autobiography,* 2 vols., 1904.

F. H. Collins, *An Epitome of the Synthetic Philosophy* (contains preface by Spencer, giving summary of his philosophy), 5th ed., 1905; W. H. Hudson, *Introduction to the Philosophy of Herbert Spencer,* 1900; D. Duncan, *The Life and Letters of Herbert Spencer,* 1912; J. Royce, *Herbert Spencer,* 1904; J. Rumsey, *Herbert Spencer's Sociology,* 1934; E. Asirvatham, *Herbert Spencer's Theory of Social Justice,* 1936.

The Ideal of Knowledge. Spencer's ideal of knowledge is that of a completely unified system of thought. The knowledge of the ordinary man is ununified, disconnected, inconsistent; the various parts do not hang together. Science furnishes us with partially unified knowledge. Philosophy, however, is completely unified knowledge, an organic system: its problem is to discover the highest truths from which the principles of mechanics, physics, biology, sociology, and ethics can be deduced. All these propositions must be in harmony with one another. In the *First Principles,* which forms the basis of the entire system, the fundamental axioms are set forth, and are later applied in the *Principles of Biology, Principles of Psychology, Principles of Sociology,* and *Principles of Ethics.* In the last-named book we have the restatement of all the generalizations reached in the preliminary works, so that the truths of ethics are grounded on the results of all the other fields of knowledge. These generalizations of the sciences may be empirically ascertained, but they can also be derived from first principles.

Spencer calls his philosophy synthetic philosophy, and considers it the function of such a universal science to combine into a consistent system the universal truths arrived at by the particular sciences. In this respect, he differs from Hamilton and Mill. Hamilton offered no system of philosophy at all and regarded it beyond human capacity to offer one, the absolute being unknowable. Mill criticized Comte for his relapse into philosophy in attempting to unify the sciences. Although Mill, too, envisaged the ideal of a system of truths held together by universal principles in his logic of the moral sciences, and also suggested the possibility of an a priori science of nature, he himself made no effort to systematize his thoughts; indeed it was impossible, from his general standpoint, to reach a universal synthesis, as his predecessor Hume had clearly seen.

Spencer also differs from the empiricists in his attempt to base knowledge on what Kant called a priori forms of the mind, and to reduce these functions to simple principles. In this respect he is influenced by the critical philosophy, with which he became acquainted largely through Hamilton's works. All our knowledge, he holds, rests on the primary act of thought; even the skeptic who seeks to deny the possibility of knowledge presupposes the basal functions of thinking. Knowledge would be impossible if it were not for the mind's capacity to discover likeness and difference, as well as for its demand for logical consistency. None of these functions is the result of individual experience. Applying the evolutionary hypothesis, Spencer attempts to explain them as products of racial experience, thus seeking a compromise between intuitionism and empiricism from the side of empiricism. Absolute uniformities of experience generate absolute uniformities of thought. External uniformities are repeated for countless generations, giving rise to fixed associations of ideas and necessary forms of thought. How it was possible for connections to be made at the dawn of knowledge, which are today impossible without an a priori synthetic mind, Spencer does not tell us. Nor does he establish the validity of knowledge on this basis of inheritance: the fact that principles, which epitomize the inherited experiences of countless generations of men are now felt to be necessary, does not in itself guarantee their absolute truth.

Relativity of Knowledge. Like Hamilton, Spencer calls attention to the relativity of knowledge, and shows that this may be inferred from an analysis of the product as well as by an examination of the process of thought. Explanation is a relative matter, and the basic principles of explanation are inexplicable. The most general cognition which we can attain cannot be subsumed under a more general one, and cannot, therefore, be understood, interpreted, or explained. Explanation must eventually bring us to the inexplicable; and the deepest truth which we can attain, must be unaccountable. Moreover, the process of thought itself involves *relation, difference,* and *likeness;* whatever does not possess these, is incapable of cognition. Thinking being a process of relating, no thought can ever express more than relations. The primary act of thought through which we discover likeness and difference underlies all our knowledge, both perception and inference. Without it there could be neither, hence the validity of this primary function of mind must be presupposed.

It is the business of philosophy to work out the system of ideas rooted in consciousness, to discover the implications of our basal intuitions, and to construct a body of related propositions. The criterion of the validity of thought is its necessity. The test of truth is, on the one hand, the inconceivability of the opposite and, on the other, the agreement of our results with actual experience. Spencer employs a rationalistic criterion of truth in conjunction with an empirical one.

If knowledge is relative in the sense indicated, it follows that we can know only the finite and the limited. The Absolute, the First Cause, the Infinite cannot be known, since it cannot be likened to, or differentiated from, anything else. We can, however, always relate things to an Absolute; indeed, we must have an Absolute to which to relate them. A relative is itself inconceivable except as related to a real non-relative—the relative presupposes an Absolute. Hence, we can know things in relation to one another and to an Absolute. If we could not relate them to an Absolute, they would not be known; indeed, they would themselves be absolutes. We reach the consciousness of a substance that underlies all phenomena. It is impossible to get rid of the consciousness of an actuality lying behind appearances; and from this impossibility results our indestructible belief in that actuality. Spencer is thus committed to realism. The Absolute itself, however, cannot be related to anything else: there is no head under which it can be brought, hence it is unknowable. The unknowableness of the Absolute is not only proved deductively, from the nature of our intelligence, but also inductively, by the facts of science: we cannot comprehend ultimate scientific ideas, such as space, time, matter, motion, force, the ego, and the origin of mind.

Nevertheless, the fact that we can form no notion of the Absolute is no reason for denying its existence. Science and religion can agree on this point: there is an Absolute Being behind all phenomena. Religion seeks to interpret this universal substance for us; it has given us all kinds of definitions of it, but the more advanced a religion is, the more it understands that the Absolute is a complete mystery. Thought continues to seek for some definition of it, to form some idea of it, and there is no objection to this, so long as it is remembered that the forms in which we endeavor to express it are merely symbols. We are compelled to conceive it, vaguely, as the objective correlate of our subjective feeling of activity, or muscular strain, that is, as power, or force. Noumenon and phenomenon are two sides of the same process, and the second is no less real than the first.

Persistence of Force. This objective power, which is the necessary correlate of the subjective feeling of force, must be thought of as persistent. It is inconceivable that something should become nothing; when we say that something becomes nothing, we are establishing a relation between two entities, one of which does not exist. By the persistence of power we mean the persistence of some cause that transcends our knowledge and conception. In asserting it, we assert an unconditional reality without beginning and end. The sole truth which transcends experience by underlying it, is the persistence of force. It is the basis of experience and must, therefore, be the scientific basis of any scientific organization of experiences. An ultimate analysis brings us to this power; on it our rational synthesis must be constructed.

By the indestructibility of matter we mean the indestructibility of the force with which matter affects us. This truth is made manifest by an analysis of a posteriori and of a priori cognition. Another general truth is the continuity of motion. It is inconceivable that something—in this case motion— should become nothing, and yet movements are constantly disappearing. The fact is, translation through space is not itself an existence, and hence the cessation of motion, considered simply as translation, is not the cessation of an existence, but of a certain *sign* of existence. In other words, the space element in motion is not in itself a thing. Change of position is not an existence, but the manifestation of an existence. This existence may cease to display itself as translation, but can do so only by displaying itself as strain. The principle of activity, now shown by translation, now by strain, and often by the two together, is not visible; the principle of activity which is manifested in motion is the objective correlate of our subjective sense of effort. The continuity of motion is really known to us in terms of force.

Force is of two kinds: force by which matter demonstrates itself to us as existing, and force by which it demonstrates itself to us as acting; the latter is called energy. Energy is the common name for the power shown alike in the movements of masses and in the movements of molecules. Each manifestation of force can be interpreted only as the effect of some antecedent force, no matter whether it be an inorganic action, an animal movement, a thought or a feeling. *Either* mental energies, as well as bodily ones, are quantitatively correlated to certain energies expended in their production and to certain other energies which they initiate; *or*, nothing must become something, and something must become nothing. We must either deny the persistence of force, or admit that every physical and psychical change is generated by certain antecedent forces, and that from given amounts of such forces neither more nor less of such physical and psychical changes can result.

The basal principle of science, then, is the principle of the conservation of energy: no energy can originate or be lost. This principle Spencer does not seek to prove experimentally; indeed, it is, according to him, presupposed in all experimentation. It is a necessity of thought, a postulate: we cannot conceive of something coming from nothing or going into nothing; the principle is implied in the notion of causality or is identical with it. We are compelled to assume something as persisting.

Mind and Matter. The Absolute or Unknowable manifests itself in two great groups of facts which are diametrically opposed: subjective and objective, ego and non-ego, mind and matter. But it is the one force or power that expresses itself in both; both what we think and our thinking itself are different kinds of force; and both the physical and the psychical are subject to the same laws of experience. If the mental and the material are conceived as two irreducible phases of the Absolute, then mind cannot be derived from matter; the material cannot pass into the psychical, as motion passes into heat. In the earlier editions of *First Principles* and in the *Psychology*, Spencer assumed that it could; afterwards he saw the impossibility of explaining consciousness by the principle of the conservation of energy interpreted physically. But he continued to apply to all phenomena, including those of life, mind, and society, the formula of evolution stated in terms of force, matter, and motion. This is what gives his system the appearance of materialism, and as such it is often attacked, although he himself warns us against interpreting it in this way. The Absolute is unknowable; we can interpret it in materialistic or in spiritualistic terms, in either case we are employing mere symbols. A power the nature of which ever remains unintelligible to us, and which we cannot think of as limited in space or in time, produces certain effects in us. We embrace the most general of these effects under the terms matter, motion, and force; among these effects of the Absolute, there exist certain similarities of connection of which the most constant are formulated as laws of the highest certainty.

The Law of Evolution. We are limited in our knowledge to the relative phenomena, to the inner and outer expressions of the Absolute. It is our business, as philosophers, to discover the traits common to all phenomena, or to find the universal law of things. Such a law we have in the law of evolution. The process of evolution consists of various phases: (1) concentration, as seen in the formation of a cloud, in the sand-heap, in the primitive nebula, in the organism, and in society; (2) differentiation, or the separation of the mass from its environment, and the formation of special masses within it; (3) determination, or the formation of the differentiated parts into a unified, organized whole, whose parts are different and yet in mutual relation with one another. This is what distinguishes evolution from dissolution, in which we have differentiation, but not organization. In determination, there is differentiation of parts and integration or concentration of parts into a whole. In this sense, evolution is the passage from a state of indefinite, incoherent homogeneity to a state of definite, coherent heterogeneity. This law is derived inductively, but it can also be reached by deduction from the primary principle of the persistence of force, which, as we have seen, Spencer identifies with the law of causation. From the law of causation also follow the indestructibility of matter, the continuity of motion—potential and actual—the persistence of relations among forces, the transformation and equivalence of forces—both mental and social—the law of the direction of motion, and the unceasing rhythm of motion. The law of universal synthesis is the law of the continuous redistribution of matter and motion. Evolution consists in the integration of matter and the dissipation of motion; dissolution, in the absorption of motion and the disintegration of matter. When both concentration and differentiation have reached a state of equilibrium, the climax of evolution has been reached. This state cannot endure, because external influences will tend to destroy it. In other words, dissolution is bound to result, and the whole process will begin over again. All this applies not to the universe as a whole, but only to its particular parts which appear in our experience.

The universal principles, obtained in *First Principles,* are applied by Spencer to the various forms of existence—life, mind, society, and conduct. They are postulated as true and are employed to prove the special truths of biology, psychology, sociology, and ethics: the latter are illustrations of universal truths; universal truths are explanations of the special truths. Thus, the law of evolution applies to all phenomena; the special laws discovered in the various fields of investigation will, therefore, be found to come under the universal law, or to be expressions of this law. Such empirical laws or truths are deductively proved when they are shown to be special cases of the universal law.

Biology. Life is a continuous adaptation of internal or physiological, to external or environmental relations. The organism not only receives impressions, but undergoes changes in consequence, which enable it to react upon subsequent changes of the external world in a specific way. That is, inner changes take place in the organism which adapt it to external relations: there is reciprocal action between internal and external events. The organism cannot maintain itself unless it evolves a system of inner relations corresponding to the external ones. The more intimate the correspondence between the inner and the outer relations, the more highly developed is the organism. The most perfect life would be that in which there is complete adaptation, or harmony, between internal and external relations.

Organic forms did not arise from inorganic matter, but from an original structureless organic mass, or homogeneous protoplasm, under the influence of external causes. Differences are produced in the organic tissue in accordance with the operation of the universal law of evolution; that is to say, the original heterogeneous mass differentiates. The species arise as a result of the interaction between the organism and the external world. Morphological and physiological differentiation is the direct result of the differentiation of external forces; astronomical, geological, and meteorological conditions change slowly, but the changes have been continuous for millions of years. Variations occur in the organism through external causes, and, if adaptive, are preserved by natural selection. Changes are produced in the relation of the physiological units composing the organism by the continuous functioning of the parts—the doctrine that function precedes structure—and are transmitted to progeny—the theory of the inheritance of acquired characters. Spencer is of the opinion that natural selection alone fails to explain the origin of species and that Darwin exaggerates the influence of this indirect mode of evolution. The organism adapts itself to an external impression, and such adaptation brings about a new state of equilibrium in the organism.

Psychology. Physics examines external phenomena as such; psychology, internal phenomena as such; physiology investigates the connection and relation between the internal and the external. Subjective psychology is introspective: it studies the feelings, ideas, emotions, and volitions which accompany the visible adaptations of inner to outer relations, and inquires into the origin and reciprocal relations of states of consciousness. Psychical occurrences and nerve-action are the inner and outer sides of one and the same change. What is, objectively considered, a nervous change, is, subjectively considered, a phenomenon of consciousness. Objective psychology does not study mental processes as such, but considers them in their relation to human and animal actions. As a part of biology, it examines mental phenomena as functions by means of which internal relations are adapted to external relations.

Consciousness arises when impressions become so numerous as to necessitate their arrangement in a series—when the organism cannot adapt itself to its environment without such a serial arrangement. Consciousness is, therefore, defined as a form of adaptation of serially arranged inner states to outer states. But it is not a mere sum of feelings and ideas; there is a substantial something or combining medium behind them, which, however, is unknowable, for the same reason that all ultimates are unknowable. But we can study the changing states or modifications in which this substance manifests itself. It is the business of psychology to discover the units of consciousness, the elements of which it is composed. An analysis of the phenomenal aspects of consciousness reveals ultimate units, which Spencer regards as "something of the same order as that which we call a nervous shock"—as the mental equivalent of a nervous shock. Just as the different sensations are made up of common units, so a perception is composed of units or atoms of feeling. The mental unit or atom is irreducible to the material unit or atom. We conceive the material atom as resistance, in analogy with our own feeling of effort; that is, we read into it our own consciousness of activity. In reverse fashion, we interpret our mental events in material terms. Spencer finds in conscious life the same features which are exhibited in all relative reality: concentration, differentiation, and determination; consciousness is an evolution and can be understood only as a process of development, as a continuous series of gradations, from reflex action to instinct, memory, and reason. These are merely different degrees or stages of intelligence, which pass into one another imperceptibly, corresponding to the gradually increasing complexity and differentiation of external conditions. Memory and reason, for example, arise from instinct. Primary inference is entirely instinctive. Volition appears when automatic action becomes impossible, owing to the growing complexity of the situation. We have already seen how Spencer derives the principles of knowledge from the experience of the race. In the same evolutionary way he explains the feelings; anger, justice, and sympathy, which are native to the individual, have been acquired by the race as a result of the constant struggle of our ancestors with their environment.

The External World. It is not true that we are originally conscious only of sensations, and that from them we infer the existence of external objects. Idealism is a disease of language; it lives only in our words, not in our thoughts. Reason, in so far as it undermines the assertions of perception, destroys its own authority. Realism is forced on us by the basal law of consciousness, the universal postulate of reason. It is inconceivable that there should be no object when I feel it and see it. We are compelled to think an extra-mental reality, and we are compelled to think it as force, as the objective correlate of the subjective feeling of force or feeling of muscular tension, which we experience in ourselves and which is the universal symbol of the unknowable objective existence or the persisting reality. This unknown reality is also symbolized in our ideas of space, time, matter, and motion.

This transfigured realism, as Spencer calls it, takes the place of crude realism. It holds that the things represented in our consciousness are not images, copies, or pictures, of the objective reality, but symbols which have as little in common with the realities they represent as letters have in common with the psychic states for which they stand. But that there is something beyond consciousness is an inevitable conclusion; to think otherwise is to think of change taking place without an antecedent. "There is some ontological order whence arises the phenomenal order we know as space; there is some ontological order whence arises the phenomenal order we know as time; and there is some ontological nexus whence arises the phenomenal relation we know as difference." Such knowledge of the external world is greatly limited, but it is the only knowledge which is of use to us.

We do not need to know the outer agencies themselves, but only their persistent relations, and this knowledge we have. An ever-present sense of real existence is the very basis of our intelligence. There ever remains with us a sense of that which exists persistently and independently of the special conditions of our knowledge. We cannot form a conception of this absolute existence; every notion which we frame of it is utterly inconsistent with itself. From the impossibility of getting rid of the consciousness of an actuality lying behind appearances results our indestructible belief in that actuality.

Ethics. In the preface to the *Data of Ethics,* Spencer declares all the preceding parts of his task as a synthetic philosopher to be subsidiary to his principles of morality. His purpose had been, ever since the appearance of his first work, *The Proper Sphere of Government* (1842), to find a scientific basis for the principles of right and wrong in conduct at large. In order to understand the meaning of moral conduct, he tells us, we must comprehend conduct as a whole, the conduct of all living creatures and the evolution of conduct, and we must examine it in its physical, biological, psychological, and social aspects; in other words, study it in the light of the results of the other sciences.

Such a study will lead us to define conduct either as acts adjusted to ends or the adjustment of acts to ends, and will show us that the most highly evolved and, therefore, ethically best conduct is such as makes life richer and longer for the individual, for his offspring, and for those among whom he lives. The limit of evolution is reached in a permanently peaceful society, in which every member achieves his ends without preventing others from achieving theirs (justice), and in which members give mutual help in the pursuit of ends (beneficence). Whatever facilitates the adjustments of each member of a society increases the totality of the adjustments made, and serves to render the lives of all more complete. We call acts good or bad which subserve or hinder life, on the supposition that life brings more happiness than misery (optimism). The good is universally the pleasurable (hedonism). Actions are completely right only when, besides being conducive to future happiness, they are immediately pleasurable. A large part of human conduct is not absolutely right, but only relatively right, because it entails some pain. The ideal code of absolute ethics formulates the behavior of the completely adapted man in the completely evolved society. Such an absolute code will enable us to interpret the phenomena of real societies which, in their transitional states, are full of miseries due to non-adaptation.

This code also provides the basis for approximately true conclusions respecting the nature of the abnormalities of actual societies, and the courses of action which tend most in the direction of the normal.

Spencer insists that the well-being of the units and the social groups, and not the welfare of society as such, is always the ultimate end of morality. The welfare of society as a whole is a means to the welfare of the units, hence whatever threatens this integrity will injure the units. In the early stages of social evolution, egoism is strong and altruism weak; this explains why the relative moral code emphasizes those restraints on conduct which are entailed by the presence of fellow-men. The moral code prohibits acts of aggression and imposes restraints on the individual in the interest of cooperation (justice), and enjoins spontaneous efforts to further welfare (beneficence). The root of both justice and beneficence is sympathy. Since the ideal is the greatest amount of individual perfection and happiness, egoism inevitably precedes altruism; each creature enjoys the benefits and must be prepared to endure the evils consequent upon his own nature, inherited or acquired. But altruism, too, is essential to the development of life and the increase of happiness, and self-sacrifice is no less primordial than self-preservation. The egoistic satisfactions of each unit in a society depend on such altruistic actions as being just, seeing justice done, upholding and improving the agencies for the administration of justice, and improving others physically, intellectually, and morally. Pure egoism and pure altruism are equally illegitimate. With increasing social discipline, sympathetic pleasures will come to be pursued spontaneously and will be found advantageous to each and all. Eventually, a utopian equilibrium will be achieved in which every member of society will be eager to surrender his egoistic claims, while others, by virtue of their altruism, will not permit him to do so.

Spencer offers an evolutional hedonism, which combines the hedonistic teachings of traditional English utilitarianism with the emphasis upon survival and adaptation of the new theory of evolution. This combined ethical theory is possible because, in his opinion, the most highly evolved conduct yields the greatest amount of happiness. He also distinguishes his rational utilitarianism from the empirical utilitarianism of his predecessors; his system of ethics is rational in that he deduces the rules of morality from the fundamental principles supplied by the various sciences.

Politics. The ethical ideal, then, is the production of perfect and happy individuals, the survival of the fittest individuals and the spread of the best adapted varieties. This end can only be realized when each individual receives the benefits and the evils of his own nature and of his consequent conduct. But since group-life is essential to the survival of the fittest, every individual has to subject his conduct to the restriction that it shall not in any large measure impede the like conduct of others. In the case of defensive war, individuals may be further restricted, even to the extent of having to sacrifice their lives. Justice, therefore, demands that each mature man be free to do what he will, provided he infringe not on the equal freedom of any other man. Rights, truly so-called, are corollaries of the law of equal freedom: every man has the right to act up to a certain limit, but not beyond it.

From these premises Spencer argues against the modern socialist State. All-embracing State functions, he holds, characterize a low social type; and progress to a higher social type is marked by the relinquishing of functions. The incorporated body of citizens has to maintain the conditions under which each may gain the fullest possible life compatible with the fullest lives of his fellow-citizens. The State must prevent internal aggression and protect its members from foreign invasion; when it goes beyond that, it transgresses justice. Extension of State functions has always proved disastrous, and only legislation which has been guided by considerations of equity has proved successful. Moreover, the various non-governmental agencies work best under the stress of competition. Competition impels them to make improvements, to utilize the best available techniques, and to secure the best men for public service. The social and economic needs of men are best served in this way. Finally, State interference has an evil effect on the moral character of the individual. The nature which we have inherited from an uncivilized past, and which is still very imperfectly fitted to the partially civilized present, will, if allowed to do so, slowly adjust itself to the requirements of a fully civilized future. The discipline of social life which has accomplished so much in these few thousand years, will, in the course of time, work without State control and interference. There is ample evidence to show that artificial molding is incapable of accomplishing as much as natural molding. Spencer is bitterly opposed to socialism in all its forms. He approves mutual cooperation; indeed, he believes that a voluntary cooperation characteristic of industrialism will in the end prevail. He is committed to the *laissez-faire* theory in the social, economic and political spheres, and believes that the general happiness can be realized only by letting individuals work out their own salvation, without undue interference by the State.

XX

Idealistic Tendencies in Recent Philosophy

74. ABSOLUTE IDEALISM IN ENGLAND AND THE UNITED STATES

The Influence of German Idealism. At the beginning of the nineteenth century, German idealistic thought, stemming from Kant, found its way into England through the great literary figures of Coleridge, Wordsworth, Carlyle, and Ruskin, and exerted an influence on both the empiricism of John Stuart Mill and the intuitionism of Whewell and Hamilton. A serious study of the new German philosophy was, however, not undertaken until after the appearance in 1865 of J. H. Stirling's *The Secret of Hegel.* During the remainder of the nineteenth and well into the present century, a group of vigorous thinkers, profoundly influenced by Kant and Hegel, and by the entire idealistic movement, assumed leadership of British thought. Among the influential figures of this movement were Thomas Hill Green, Edward Caird, John Caird, Francis H. Bradley, and Bernard Bosanquet.

The first great work of the British Neo-Hegelian school was Green's *Introduction to Hume* (1875), which was followed by E. Caird's *Critical Account of the Philosophy of Kant* (1877), the predecessor of his larger book, *The Critical Philosophy of Kant* (2 vols., 1889), and by a large number of expositions and translations of German philosophers.

The representatives of this school share a common emphasis on the organic conception of mind and knowledge in opposition to the atomistic treatment of English associationism; a repudiation of mechanism as a universal theory; and the conception of philosophy as the interpretation of experience in all its forms. The English philosophers did not adopt the a priori or dialectical methods of the classical German idealists, nor did they uncritically accept their conclusions; but, following Green's program, they "worked over" the entire material of German idealism in a fresh and independent manner, yet faithful to the fundamental principles of the movement inaugurated by Kant.

557

Works on English and American Idealism.—R. B. Perry, *Present Philosophical Tendencies,* 1912, and *Philosophy of the Recent Past,* 1927; A. K. Rogers, *English and American Philosophy Since 1800,* 1922; R. Metz, *A Hundred Years of British Philosophy,* ed. by J. H. Muirhead, 1938; *Contemporary British Philosophy—Personal Statements,* ed. by J. H. Muirhead, First Series, 1924, Second Series, 1926; H. Haldar, *Neo-Hegelianism,* 1927; G. W. Cunningham, *The Idealistic Argument in Recent British and American Philosophy,* 1933. Extensive bibliographies are contained in F. Ueberweg, *Grundriss der Geschichte der Philosophie,* Part V, 12th ed., by T. K. Oesterreich, 1928.

Thomas Hill Green.

Thomas Hill Green was born in Birkin, Yorkshire, in 1836, the son of the rector of the parish. From Rugby he went up to Balliol College, Oxford, where he spent the rest of his life as student, fellow, tutor, lecturer, and professor. He was chosen professor of moral philosophy in 1878, a position which he held until his death in 1882. In addition to his academic duties, Green devoted himself to educational, political, and social activities, and in these he always manifested a warm sympathy for the lower classes, and an abiding faith in democracy.

"Introduction to Hume's *Treatise on Human Nature,*" first published in 1874-75 in the Green and Grose edition of *Hume's Philosophical Works; Prolegomena to Ethics,* 1883; *Works of T. H. Green,* ed. by R. L. Nettleship, 3 vols., 1885-88, contains all Green's writings except the *Prolegomena; Lectures on the Principles of Political Obligation,* 1895.

A. Seth (or A. S. Pringle-Pattison), *Hegelianism and Personality,* 1887; W. H. Fairbrother, *The Philosophy of T. H. Green,* 1896; R. B. C. Johnson, *The Metaphysics of Knowledge, Being an Examination of T. H. Green's Theory of Reality,* 1900; H. G. Townsend, *The Principle of Individuality in the Philosophy of T. H. Green,* 1914.

The philosophical position of Thomas Hill Green (1836-1882) is a form of objective idealism, developed by him under the influence of the German idealists and in opposition to the traditional British conceptions of the world and of life. Accepting Kant's critical idealism and the idealistic metaphysics of Kant's successors, Green attacks the empiricism of Hume, the hedonism of Mill, and the evolutionism of Spencer. His philosophy attempts to reconcile the opposing tendencies of his time: rationalism and empiricism, religion and science, pantheism and theism, Greek culture and Christianity, idealistic ethics and utilitarianism, libertarianism and determinism, individualism and institutionalism. Man, for Green, is not merely a child of nature: how could a being who is merely a product of natural forces form a theory of those forces capable of explaining himself? Man is a spiritual being and as such not a member of the phenomenal series of natural events. There is in him a principle which is not natural, and the specific function of this principle is to render knowledge possible. The spiritual principle underlying knowledge also has an ethical function, the consciousness of a moral ideal, and the determination of human action thereby. Without the assumption of such a spiritual self, there can be neither knowledge nor morality.

Metaphysics. Natural science deals with the phenomenal, the temporal and spatial, with matters of fact which are ascertainable by observation and experience. Philosophy, or metaphysics, deals with the spiritual or noumenal, the principle of which these facts are the expression. The mistake of the empiricists and the evolutionists is that they consider the spiritual which produces the phenomenal order as the product of this order. There can be no knowledge of nature without a unifying, organizing spiritual principle; moreover, the order of nature itself is the product of the same principle. Nature is manifold, and yet there is unity in it. The source of the unity of nature is self-consciousness, and thus nature as a whole is a spiritual cosmos, a system of related facts rendered possible by an eternal intelligence. The existence of the world, as well as our knowledge of it, testifies to an all-uniting consciousness.

Man's place in nature. What is man's place in such a universe? As a knowing, self-conscious being, man exists as free activity—as activity that is not in time, not a link in the chain of natural events—which has no antecedents other than itself. Self-consciousness has no origin, it never began because there was never a time when it was not. All the processes of brain and nerve and tissue, all the functions of life and sense, including the successive phenomena of our mental history, are determined by the universal consciousness. Human consciousness is itself a replica of the universal mind, at least so far as it is synthetic and self-originative. The theory of evolution, Green thinks, does not conflict with this view. The human organism may have evolved from the animal; the animal organism may have been modified in countless generations in such a way that the eternal consciousness could manifest and reproduce itself through these natural organic functions. But this does not detract from the ultimacy of the original spiritual principle: the whole phenomenal order, including the entire sequence of biological evolution, which culminates in the mind and consciousness of man, is a manifestation of the eternal and universal self-consciousness.

Green shows that a mere succession of impressions or sensations is not knowledge; that knowledge is not possible without a unifying self which organizes these sensations. Nor does a mere succession of animal wants, or impulses, or appetites, constitute *human* action; it becomes such only when a subject consciously presents such wants to himself. An appetite or animal want is a natural event, and is not a genuine motive unless a self-conscious subject presents it to himself, unless he adopts it, identifies himself with it, and strives to bring into real existence his ideal self. Merely to be impelled to action by an animal appetite is not human action or conduct. When a man consciously identifies himself with one of his impulses or passions, he transforms natural desire into will. Volition is desire in which a man fulfills himself by realizing his ideal self. Undoubtedly the ideal good a person wills depends on the past history of his inner life and on external circumstances, emotions and actions: to this extent Green accepts determinism. But throughout his past experience he has been an ideal object for himself, and is thus the author of his acts. He is, therefore, entirely responsible for the ideal which guides his present conduct. Moreover, he can envisage a superior ideal for himself and seek to become in the future better than he is now. In this deeper sense a man possesses free will.

Ethics. Man's ability to conceive a better state of himself, and to realize this state, constitutes him a moral agent. He possesses this ability because he is a self-conscious subject, a reproduction of the eternal self-consciousness. The source of an individual's ideal of a better state of himself is an absolute ideal existing in God's mind. Man's participation in this ideal which is absolutely desirable, is the moralizing agency in human life.

What, then, is the content of the moral good? The true good is an end in which the effort of a moral agent can really find satisfaction, an end which his basal self, his real will, regards as an unconditional good, as something having absolute worth, as being absolutely desirable. Now, man has in himself the conception of something which is absolutely desirable. This self has many interests, including interests in other persons. Other men are included in the end for which I live in living for myself. I conceive as the highest good the realization of human personality,—whether in myself or in others— the perfection of the human self, the unfolding of its capacities. To achieve this goal, I must help other selves to achieve the same goal. The moral ideal is an absolute and common good, a good for me and for others. The absolute good embraces the ideal of personal morality, and the ideal of a society in which everyone shall treat everyone else as a neighbor. Every rational agent shall consider the well-being or perfection of every other agent to be included in his own perfection. Green resolves the conflict between egoism and altruism by defining the moral ideal of self-development so comprehensively as to embrace within it the fulfillment of others.

The source of morality is traced by many moralists to the law and authoritative custom of our ancestors. Green accepts this historical account, but insists that the law and custom were themselves originally the products of rational beings, of beings with ideals. Individuals, in submitting to prescribed law and custom, recognized the value of those forms of behavior which required them to restrain their inclination to pleasure. Green is prepared to accept a genetic and evolutionary theory of morality, but is most insistent that the evolution of morals itself presupposes a rational source of our moral ideals. Moral ideals are not the products of an historical process; they enter the historical series from a transcendent source.

The moral ideal is originally felt as an unconscious demand binding on the individual. It is a demand for a certain well-being shared by the individuals desiring it, and as such is responsible for such institutions as the family, the tribe, and the state, which in turn further determine the morality of the individual. Reflection on the natural development of institutions, and on the habits of action contributing to their maintenance, promotes the formation of a more adequate conception of the demand. There gradually emerges an ever-widening conception of the range of persons involved and, ultimately, the ideal of a universal society coextensive with all mankind.

We have no adequate idea of the perfect life, but the ideal embraces the perfection of the whole man and the perfection of man in society. Such a life must be the expression of one harmonious will, a will of all which is the will of each: a devoted will. A devoted will is not considered by Green to be something abstract, but a whole system of beneficent activities, sustained and coordinated by a comprehensive moral ideal. Moreover, he holds that the moral value of an action depends on the motives or the character which it reflects, and he assumes that a truly moral motive will always produce moral acts.

Green exalts the self-sacrificing, social type of goodness, the goodness of the reformer, and in this expresses the spirit of his times. However, he seems to have an even higher regard for the saintly or the religious type of goodness, for the medieval type of perfection. The ultimate form of moral endeavor, he tells us, is a spiritual act in which the heart is lifted up to God, in which the entire self aspires to an ideal of personal holiness. This endeavor has an intrinsic value, apart from any result beyond itself which it achieves. Both the good will—the social will—and this spiritual act have intrinsic value. The practical expressions of a good will have an additional value as means, because they result in amelioration of human society. However, the ultimate purpose and justification of all these ameliorations is a holy heart; the supreme value for man is man himself in his perfection. Goodness of the practical type and of the more self-questioning or consciously God-seeking type are both intrinsically valuable, both reside in the character, heart, and will of man. Neither type is barren of effects, though the effects in the case of the reformer are overt and transient, while in the case of the saint they are impalpable and immanent. In this way Green seeks to resolve the apparent incompatibility between the ethics of social amelioration and the ethics of saintliness.

Green's main ethical insights can be summed up as follows: the purpose of all social reform is, after all, the perfection of man on the spiritual side, the development of men of character and ideals. Green expresses his ideal in language that has a religious tinge: he speaks of holiness as a lasting mode of this perfection; of the spirit of self-abasement before the ideal of holiness as a state of mind having the highest value. The final purpose of all moral endeavor must be the realization of an attitude of the human soul, of some form of noble consciousness in human personalities. Social reform is a good thing, but social reform must have some end and justification beyond the promotion of mere physical comfort and material satisfaction. It is well enough to feed and house human bodies, but the paramount concern will always be: What kind of souls are to dwell in these bodies?

F. H. Bradley. The most subtle and best known of the English idealistic thinkers is F. H. Bradley (1846-1924), whose metaphysical system is presented in its maturest form in *Appearance and Reality*.

The Presuppositions of Critical History, 1874; *Ethical Studies*, 1876; *The Principles of Logic*, 2 vols., 1883; *Appearance and Reality*, 1893; *Essays on Truth and Reality*, 1914.
On Bradley, see H. Rashdall, *The Metaphysics of Bradley*, 1912; H. Höffding, *Modern Philosophers*, 1915; W. S. Gamertsfelder, *Thought, Existence and Reality as Viewed by Bradley and Bosanquet*, 1920; R. W. Church, *Bradley's Dialectic*, 1942; R. G. Ross, *Scepticism and Dogma, A Study in the Philosophy of F. H. Bradley*, 1943.

Bradley agrees with the German idealists that metaphysics is an attempt to know reality in contrast to mere appearance, or the study of first principles or ultimate truths, or the effort to comprehend the universe, not simply piecemeal or by fragments, but somehow as a whole. We have a knowledge of the Absolute which is certain and real, though incomplete. Man has an instinctive longing to reflect on ultimate truth, and to comprehend reality as adequately as his nature permits. With Fichte, Schelling, Hegel, and the romanticists he regards the discursive intellect as incompetent to understand the world.

The world of appearance. The first book of Bradley's *Appearance and Reality*, entitled "Appearance," is a devastating criticism of the intellect, and of the entire phenomenal world of objects in space and time with which the intellect is conversant. The subtlety of this criticism of the intellect and the world of experience and the paradoxical conclusions reached, earned for Bradley the title "the Zeno of modern philosophy." By a critical examination of a number of typical ways of interpreting reality—for example, in terms of primary and secondary qualities, substantive and adjective, relation and quality, space and time, motion and change, causation and activity, and the self—he reaches the negative result that they are all self-contradictory. Bradley's analysis of relation is typical of his paradoxical method. A relation without related terms is, of course, a meaningless nonentity; but a relation with its terms—for example, similarity between two sense qualities—is equally unintelligible, for new relations are required to link the relation with each of its terms: "The links are united by a link, and this bond of union is a link which also has two ends; and these require each a fresh link to connect them with the old." [1] An infinite chain of relations is required to link any two terms, and since this is unintelligible, Bradley concludes that "a relational way of thought—any one that moves by the machinery of terms and relations—must give appearance and not truth. It is a make-shift device, a mere practical compromise, most necessary but in the end most indefensible." [2] Phenomena, considered in these terms, are full of contradictions; they turn out to be mere appearance. Appearances, however, exist, that is absolutely certain. Though appearance is inconsistent with itself, and cannot, therefore, be truly real, yet it cannot be entirely divorced from reality. What, then, is the nature of this reality to which appearances belong? Can we say more of it than that it exists? Is it merely Kant's thing-in-itself or Spencer's Unknowable? Bradley conceives ultimate reality to be a self-consistent whole embracing all differences in an inclusive harmony; the bewildering mass of phenomenal diversity must be brought into unity and made self-consistent; and this can only be effected in reality. Moreover, the content of reality is nothing but sentient experience. Feeling, thought, and volition are the only materials of existence; there is no other material actual or possible. It is impossible for our finite minds to construct the life of the absolute in detail, to have the specific experience which constitutes the absolute; but we can gain an idea of its main features because these are exemplified in our own experience, and the idea of their combination is, therefore, in the abstract, quite intelligible to us.

Immediate feeling. At this point, Bradley joins the ranks of those philosophers who seek to solve the world-problem by the use of functions of the

[1] *Appearance and Reality,* p. 33.
[2] *Loc. cit.*

mind other than intellect. He does not, however, appeal to mystical intuition to bring him face to face with the Absolute, but finds in ordinary human experience a hint of the meaning of ultimate reality. We have the experience of a whole in mere feeling or immediate presentation. This whole contains diversity, and, at the same time, is a harmony. It serves to suggest to us the general idea of a total experience, where will, thought, and feeling fuse and interpenetrate. We can form the general idea of an absolute experience in which phenomenal distinctions are merged. Hence, Bradley concludes, we have real knowledge of the Absolute, positive knowledge founded on experience, and the conception of the Absolute as experience is inevitable if we are to think consistently.

Mere thinking, however, will not bring us into the promised land. Thought is relational and discursive: it yields a dissection of living experience and never reveals its inner life. If thought ceases to be discursive and analytical, it commits suicide; and yet if it remains discursive, how can it adequately represent immediate presentation? Thought strives for immediate, self-dependent, all-inclusive individuality; but if it were to attain its goal, it would lose its own character. Bradley seeks to escape this dilemma by showing that thought can envisage a mode of apprehension which is like feeling in its directness, but which also preserves the relational and structural features characteristic of discursive thought. "Sentient experience, in short, is reality, and what is not this is not real . . . there is no being or fact outside of that which is commonly called psychological existence. The Absolute . . . is one system and its contents are nothing but sentient experience." [3] This mode of cognition possesses the immediacy and strength of simple apprehension, yet it is not forced by its inconsistencies, as is discursive thought, to keep on relating and dissecting without ever seeing things whole. Volition, as well as feeling, enters into our apprehension of the Absolute; volition in achieving its goal becomes one with the Absolute. Again, we reach the identity of idea and reality, of unity and diversity. Bradley concedes that we cannot imagine how such immediate experience is filled out in detail, but we can say that it is real and that it unites diversity of experience within the living system of one undivided apprehension.

The Absolute. The Absolute, then, is knowable in the way described. It is a harmonious system, not the sum of things; it is the unity in which all things coming together are transmuted and changed in the same manner, though not changed equally. In this unity, relations of isolation and hostility

---

[3] *Appearance and Reality*, pp. 144, 146 f.

are affirmed and yet absorbed. Error, ugliness, and evil are transmuted and absorbed in it; they are all owned by and all contribute essentially to the wealth of the Absolute. There is no one mode of reality to which the others belong as its adjectives, or into which they can be resolved. Nature, taken in the sense of a bare skeleton of primary qualities, is dead, and cannot be called either beautiful or admirable. So understood, it has but little reality, it is an ideal construction required by science, and is a necessary working fiction. We must add to our conception of nature the secondary qualities, and even the joys and sorrows, affections and emotions excited by it. All the special sciences, psychological as well as physical, deal with fictions only: soul and body are both abstractions, appearances or special aspects of reality; and thus mentalism and materialism are half-truths.

Reality is one experience. We can discover nothing in it that is not either feeling, thought, will, emotion, or something else of the kind. Does not solipsism follow from this? No, says Bradley, finite experience is never, in any of its forms, shut in by a wall. In our first immediate experience the whole reality is present; the whole, as a substantive, is present in each of its adjectives. A finite experience already partially *is* the universe. The total universe, present imperfectly in finite experience, is merely the completion of finite experience. What I experience is in one aspect the state of my self or my soul. But it cannot be the mere adjective of my self. The self is an outgrowth of reality, a phenomenon; how then can experience be its product?

Reality, then, is not merely my experience; nor does it consist of souls or selves. The Absolute is not personal because it is more; it is superpersonal. We may speak of it as personal, but only in the sense that it is nothing but experience, that it contains all the highest that we can possibly know and feel, and it is a unity which completely pervades and embraces its details. But the term "personal" as applied to the Absolute is misleading; the Absolute stands above, and not below, its internal distinctions; it includes them as elements of its fullness.

The Absolute has no history of its own, though it contains histories without number. These are but its partial aspects in the region of temporal appearance. Progress has no meaning as applied to the universe, but this fact does not, according to Bradley, undermine morality. As to immortality, a personal continuance is possible, but it is little more than that. Still, if anyone can believe in it and find himself sustained by that belief it is, after all, a possibility. Bradley, however, is convinced that it is better to be rid of both fear and hope than to lapse into any form of degrading superstition regarding personal immortality.

Logic, truth and reality. Truth is one aspect of experience and, so far as it is absolute, it exemplifies an essential aspect of the real. The universe in its general character is known adequately, but it is not known, and never can be known, in all its details. Truth is the whole world in one aspect, an aspect supreme in philosophy; and yet even philosophy is conscious of its own incompleteness. In the *Principles of Logic*, Bradley elaborates an idealistic logic which endeavors to describe the modes of judgment and inference requisite to truth-seeking in philosophy. It is a philosophical logic in the tradition of Hegel, yet it departs significantly from the Hegelian model. Bradley, unlike Hegel, considers the judgment, and not the concept or category, basic to logic, and in his logical method he has liberated himself from the rigidity and formalism of the Hegelian dialectic with its triad of thesis, antithesis and synthesis. Yet his basic conception of the scope and function of logic is clearly Hegelian: logic is an investigation of the forms of thought in so far as thought is conversant with and reflects the structure of reality. It is truly a philosophical logic.

In considering the judgment rather than the term, concept, or category as the basic unit of logic—the term being merely an analytically distinguishable constituent of the judgment—Bradley achieved an important advance beyond Hegel, and also beyond the associationist logic of the British school of Hume and Mill, which subordinated judgments to ideas. Judgment is the unit of thought and knowledge, and in Bradley's theory, judgment, although a reflection of reality and the sole vehicle of truth concerning reality, is itself a symbol, a conveyor of meaning and truth concerning reality. A symbol is "a fact which stands for something else. In anything that is a symbol we have also . . . its signification or what it means." [4] A judgment is the reference of an ideal content or "logical idea" to a reality beyond the act of judgment; every judgment is conversant with reality. To use Bradley's own example, if I judge that the sea-serpent exists, I "qualify the real world by the adjective of the sea-serpent." By the truth of the judgment, then, I mean that its suggestion is more than an idea, that it is fact. In this sense, the ultimate subject of every judgment is reality. Judgment and inference are intimately interrelated logical activities: inference is a judgment made in a context of a system of judgments, and every judgment involves at least some rudimentary and perhaps unconscious inference. "Every inference," says Bradley, "is the ideal self-development of a given object taken as real." [5] Logical implication, the basis of all inference, "exists

[4] *The Principles of Logic*, Vol. I, p. 3.
[5] *Op. cit.*, Vol. II, p. 598.

and where genuine is also real." Implication "assumes the reality of an ideal universe, and of subordinate wholes and systems within this universe." [6]

Ethical Theory. Bradley's ethical position is, like that of Green, an ethics of self-realization, formulated in the metaphysical context of absolute idealism. The ethical end is not only the realization of the self, but of the self as a whole. The individual can only fulfill himself by relating his finite ends to ever wider and more inclusive ends which ultimately are embraced in the infinite absolute whole. The ultimate end of morality coincides with the ultimate reality, the Absolute, and thus ethics and metaphysics are convergent. The Absolute which Bradley posited in his metaphysics as the presupposition of his epistemological and metaphysical analysis functions in his ethics as the moral ideal. To be sure, the finite self can never become actually infinite, but it can constantly strive for ever wider and more inclusive ends, and this striving constitutes moral progress. "Realize yourself as an infinite whole" means, says Bradley, "realize yourself as the self-conscious member of an infinite whole, by realizing that whole in yourself." [7]

Although the infinite whole or the Absolute is the ideal toward which our moral endeavors are directed, there are intermediate wholes, short of the Absolute, identification with which promotes the moral development of the individual self; the intermediate wholes are the various communities, institutions, and social groups of which the individual is a member. Every individual is a part of many human communities, such as the family, society, and the state, which are held together by force, illusion, or contract. Every individual finds he can voluntarily and consciously pursue ends for himself which also promote the interests and well-being of the groups to which he already belongs. In so doing, he realizes a larger self than the self of his own personal and private interests, and at the same time promotes the welfare of the communal group. These social wholes, of which the self is a part, prescribe norms of conduct for the individual; they embody a system of duties and concomitant rights, which Bradley describes in some detail in the central essay of his *Ethical Studies,* entitled "My Station and Its Duties." In his account of social and institutional morality, Bradley repudiates the individualism, which is traditional in British ethics, and defends an aristocratic, caste-type system of morality which is reminiscent of the institutionalism and political absolutism of Hegel's *Philosophy of Right.* He describes the impact of these social forces in his example of an English child, born

[6] *Op. cit.,* Vol. II, p. 600.
[7] *Ethical Studies,* p. 80.

of certain parents who come of certain families. Such a child is not merely the member of a family, but he is born into other spheres, including the political; he is born a member of the English nation. Thus "a man's life with its moral duties is in the main filled up by his station in that system of wholes which the state is, and this, partly by its laws and institutions, and still more by its spirit, gives him the life which he does live and ought to live." [8]

Bosanquet. Bernard Bosanquet (1848-1923) is the third of the triumvirate of exponents of British absolute idealism. His position closely resembles that of Bradley, but displays stronger Hegelian tendencies. The parallel between the development of German idealism in Fichte, Schelling, and Hegel, and the British movement of Green, Bradley, and Bosanquet is striking. Green and Fichte are the voluntarists of their respective traditions; they both emphasize the primacy of the practical reason and give prominence to the self and its ethical fulfillment. They may accordingly be described as ethical or voluntaristic idealists. Bradley, like his German prototype Schelling, displays romantic and anti-intellectualistic tendencies in the rôle he assigns to feeling in the apprehension of the absolute. Bosanquet is the one of the British group who was perhaps closest to Hegel; his idealism, while not employing the Hegelian dialectic, is more intellectualistic and rationalistic than that of his British predecessors.

Logic, 1888; *History of Aesthetics*, 1892; *The Philosophical Theory of the State*, 1899; *Principle of Individuality and Value*, 1912; *Value and Destiny of the Individual*, 1913; *Meeting of Extremes in Contemporary Philosophy*, 1920.

The doctrine of the "concrete universal," originally expounded by Hegel, became the key concept in Bosanquet's Neo-Hegelian system. The concrete universal is not an abstract generality, but an individual which possesses its internal structurization and strives toward unity and fulfillment; "the concrete universal embodies the *nisus* of thought to individuality." [9] The striving toward completion and fulfillment which constitutes individuality, whether the individual be a logical system, the moral self, a social organism or institution, or a work of art, affords the clue for the understanding of reality. Since an individual cannot achieve its completion short of the whole, the absolute is the goal of knowledge, of moral conduct, and of artistic creation. In the sphere of knowledge, truth is the ideal totality or completion of the system of knowledge. Bosanquet advocates the coherence theory of

[8] *Ethical Studies,* p. 174.
[9] *The Principle of Individuality and Value,* p. 54.

truth: "the test of truth is more truth." In the sphere of ethics, the moral quality of any act is judged by its coherence with a wider and more inclusive scheme, and thus the ultimate moral goal is the absolute itself. The unity and harmony of reality is envisaged by Bosanquet dramatically, as well as logically and ethically, but this does not mean that esthetic and dramatic values are allowed to take precedence over the logical and ethical. All the domains of value manifest the same principle of individuality in the form of a striving toward unity, harmony, coherence, and completion. This urge toward unity is the characteristic feature of reality *and* value. The inseparability of reality and value, the assignment of ontological status to value, is expressed in the title of his most important work: *The Principle of Individuality and Value.* Values are not subjective, tertiary qualities projected into reality by the finite consciousness; "values are organic to reality." Likewise, in artistic creation, the esthetic ideal of beauty is the harmony of the completed whole, the supreme esthetic value; Bosanquet likens the absolute, in one of its aspects, to the great playwright before whom the drama of existence is portrayed.

McTaggart. John Ellis McTaggart (1866-1925; *Studies in the Hegelian Dialectic,* 1896; *A Commentary on Hegel's Logic,* 1910; *The Nature of Existence,* Vol. I, 1921, Vol. II, 1927) adhered more rigorously to Hegelian logic and dialectic than did the other representatives of British Neo-Hegelianism, but his own metaphysical position, which he elaborated in *The Nature of Existence,* departs from Hegelian absolutism and moves in the direction of a pluralistic and personalistic idealism which is closer to Leibniz and Lotze than to Hegel. All reality is spiritual, and the composite parts of this spiritual reality are integrated selves. If God exists, He also has personality and is a self; such a God, though, would not be perfect, and hence would not be an absolute of the sort postulated by Green, Bradley and Bosanquet.

Josiah Royce. The idealistic philosophy, partly through the influence of English Neo-Hegelianism, and partly through a direct influence of German thought, won a large following in the United States, counting many of the professors in the universities among its adherents. Josiah Royce (1855-1916), professor at Harvard University, a man of broad scholarship, speculative grasp, and literary taste was the leading figure of the idealistic school in the United States.

Works: *The Religious Aspects of Philosophy,* 1885; *The Spirit of Modern Philosophy,* 1892; *The Conception of God,* 1897; *Studies of Good and Evil,* 1898; *The World and the Individual,* 2 vols., 1900-1902; *Outlines of Psychology,* 1902; *Herbert Spencer,* 1904;

The Philosophy of Loyalty, 1908; *W. James and Other Essays,* 1911; *The Sources of Religious Insight,* 1912; *The Problem of Christianity,* 2 vols., 1913; *Lectures on Modern Idealism,* 1916. A Royce bibliography appeared in *Philosophical Review,* vol. XXV, 1916.

On Royce, see: G. Santayana, *Character and Opinion in the United States,* 1920; C. Barrett, ed., *Contemporary Idealism in America,* 1930; J. H. Cotton, *The Finite Self in the Philosophy of Josiah Royce,* 1930; *Royce on the Human Self,* 1954; J. E. Smith, *Royce's Social Infinite: The Community of Interpretation,* 1950; *The Social Philosophy of Josiah Royce,* ed. by S. G. Brown, 1950; *The Religious Philosophy of Josiah Royce,* ed. by S. G. Brown, 1952.

The world of ordinary experience, according to Royce's teaching, contains no fact which we cannot interpret in terms of ideas; this world is throughout of such stuff as ideas are made of. All the reality that we can attribute to the world, in so far as we know and can tell what we mean thereby, becomes an ideal. There is, in fact, a certain system of ideas forced upon us by experience, which affords us a guide for our conduct. We call it the world of matter. But is there not something beyond that corresponds in reality to this series of experiences in us? Yes, but it is itself a system of ideas outside of our minds but not outside of every mind. If my world out there can be known at all, it must be in and for itself essentially a mental world. It exists in and for a standard or universal mind, whose system of ideas simply constitutes the world. Minds I can understand because I am myself a mind. An existence that has no mental attribute is to me wholly opaque. Either a transcendent mind or else the unknowable, that is our choice. But nothing absolutely unknowable can exist; the very concept of it is nonsense. Everything knowable is an idea, the content of some mind. If it can be known by a mind, reality is essentially ideal and mental. The real world must be a mind or a group of minds.

How do I reach those ideas of the minds beyond me? In one sense I can never get beyond my own ideas, nor ought I to wish to do so, because all those other minds that constitute my outer and real world are in essence one with my own self. The whole world is essentially one world, and so it is essentially the world of one self. That external reality which one knows as an object is identical with one's self—*That Art Thou.* The self that "means" the object is identical with the larger self that possesses the object, just as, when one recovers a lost or forgotten idea, one finds it in the very same self which seeks it. This deeper self is the self which, in its unity, knows all truth. There is then but one self, organically, reflectively, consciously inclusive of all selves, and so of all truth. It is the Logos, the problem-solver, the all-knower. The only thing absolutely certain about this world is that it is intelligent, rational, orderly and in essence comprehensible. Consequently, all its problems are somehow solved, all its darkest mysteries are known to the supreme self. This self infinitely and reflectively transcends the consciousness of the individual; since it includes all finite selves, it is at the very least a person, and more definitely conscious than is the individual self; for it possesses self-reflecting knowledge, and what is self-awareness but a form of consciousness? The natural and spiritual orders, the physical and the moral orders, the divine and the human, the fatal and the free, may, according to Royce, be reconciled by Kant's doctrine of the compatibility of transcendental or extra-temporal freedom and the temporal necessity of all our actions.

The above account of Royce's philosophy is derived largely from his *Spirit of Modern Philosophy,* an historical work in which his own views emerge in the course of his examination of the great systems of modern philosophy. In his large systematic work, *The World and the Individual,* the theory is worked out with great detail and applied to the interpretation of the facts of nature and of man. Partly owing to the nature of the problems with which he is dealing, and partly, perhaps, in order to ward off the criticism that he exaggerates the intellectualistic element, Royce places greater emphasis upon the volitional and purposive side of experience in these later volumes than in the earlier presentations of his views. "To be means simply to express, to embody the complete internal meaning of a certain absolute system of ideas—a system, moreover, which is genuinely implied in the true internal meaning or purpose of every finite form of the idea, however fragmentary." [10] The final form of the idea, the "final object sought when we seek Being, is (1) a complete expression of the internal meaning of the finite idea with which, in any case, we start our quest; (2) a complete fulfillment of the will or purpose partially embodied in this idea; (3) an individual life for which no other can be substituted." [11] Royce seeks to escape the charge of intellectualism by emphasizing the active aspect of ideas, and the charge of mysticism, by emphasizing the significant rôle of the individual self despite its dependence on the absolute self.

In his *Philosophy of Loyalty,* an eloquent presentation of his ethical theory, Royce deduces the idealistic world-view from the basal moral principle, which enjoins loyalty to loyalty, that is, loyalty to a cause which shall make possible the greatest amount of loyalty. My causes must form a system, they must constitute a single cause, a life of loyalty; they must make universal loyalty possible. Loyalty, therefore, implies faith in a universal cause, in a highest good, in a highest spiritual value. The principle of loyalty for

[10] *The World and the Individual,* First Series, p. 36.
[11] *Op. cit.,* pp. 341 f.

loyalty's sake is a meaningless illusion unless there exists spiritual unity, a unity in which all values are preserved. The principle of loyalty is not only a guide of life, it is also the revelation of an eternal all-embracing spiritual unity that preserves and upholds truth and goodness. Royce thus advances a moral argument for the existence of God, similar to that presented in Kant's *Critique of Practical Reason.*

75. IDEALISM IN FRANCE AND ITALY

Sources of French Idealism. The idealistic movement in France was not derived so directly from the German movement as was the British school of Green, Bradley, and Bosanquet. It was a development of voluntaristic and dynamic ideas which were already present in the main stream of French thought, and it represented a reaction against the positivism of Comte and his followers. French idealism, to be sure, derived much inspiration from Kant's critical idealism, and reflected the post-Kantian idealism of Fichte, Schelling and Schopenhauer, but the influence of Hegel on the French school was notably less significant than in the case of the British school. The chief native source of French idealism was the psychologically-oriented dynamism of Maine de Biran (1766-1824), who has already been mentioned among the chief opponents of positivism. The key concept of Biran's philosophy was "effort," or "active force," of which the mind is conscious in overcoming obstacles—a concept reminiscent of Fichte's conception of the active ego which realizes itself only when confronted with obstacles expressive of the non-ego. Biran's activism was one of the elements incorporated into Victor Cousin's eclectic philosophy, and this fact both enhanced its prestige and prepared the way for its influence on the French spiritualism and idealism of the late nineteenth and early twentieth century, the chief representatives of which are Ravaisson (Félix Ravaisson-Mollien, 1813-1900), Renouvier, Fouillée, and Boutroux.

L. Lévy-Bruhl, *History of Modern Philosophy in France,* trans. by G. Coblence, 1899; N. E. Truman, *Maine de Biran's Philosophy of Will* (Cornell Studies in Philosophy, No. 5), 1904; L. S. Stebbing, *Pragmatism and French Voluntarism,* 1914; H. Höffding, *Modern Philosophers,* 1915; J. A. Gunn, *Modern French Philosophy,* 1922; G. Boas, *French Philosophies of the Romantic Period,* 1925; I. Benrubi, *Contemporary Thought in France,* trans. by E. Dicker, 1926.

Renouvier. C. Renouvier (1815-1903) calls his system neocriticism, to indicate his allegiance to the critical philosophy of Kant. It does not, however, remain consistently faithful to the critical spirit, since it develops into an idealistic metaphysics—reminiscent of the monadology of Leibniz—of which pluralism and personalism are the characteristic features. There is no noumenal world, no thing-in-itself; things, so far as they are presented, are phenomena, and nothing exists for us but ideas. The notion of reality as an actual infinitude is a logical contradiction, as well as a contradiction of experience. The universe is a finite sum of finite beings. There can be no infinite transitions in phenomena, and from this follows the necessity of the notion of discontinuity. The idea of discontinuity implies the possibility of uncaused beginnings and free will. Knowledge is relative, and limited to the discovery of the relations between things. Many of Renouvier's leading ideas had been anticipated by Antoine Cournot (1807-1877), who found chance and contingency in nature and in history, and considered the laws of nature as only approximations to truth.

Fouillée. A. Fouillée (1838-1912) attempts to reconcile idealism and materialism in his voluntaristic and evolutionistic philosophy of *idées-forces*. Materialism is one-sided when it emphasizes motion to the exclusion of other factors; idealism is one-sided when it exaggerates thought at the expense of matter. Mind and matter, consciousness and life, operate in nature as a single principle. They are two abstractions from one unique and total reality, two ways of conceiving one and the same thing. All psychic phenomena are expressions of impulse or *appétition*. Psychic existence is the only reality which is directly given to us, hence we must interpret the world in analogy with active mind and its *idées-forces*.

Boutroux. Emile Boutroux (1845-1922) represents the culmination of the movement which emphasizes the element of contingency in science. Cournot (1801-1877), on the basis of his study of the mathematical theory of probability, had challenged the traditional view that scientific laws are certain and absolute truths expressive of objective uniformities of nature, and maintained that scientific law is problematic—not merely because of the limitation of human knowledge but also because of objective chance or contingency in nature. Boutroux, in his chief work, *The Contingency of the Laws of Nature*, adopted Cournot's theory of objective chance or indeterminacy underlying scientific law. It is elevated by Boutroux into a philosophical theory, and is alleged to support freedom of the will. His employment of causal indeterminacy in nature as the basis of human freedom is a modern version of the Epicurean theory that the "swerve" of the atom conditions free will in man. Thus Boutroux' theory is subject to much the same difficulty as its

Epicurean prototype: what ethical worth is possessed by a freedom of will which is mere causal indeterminancy? Contingency in Boutroux' system does not preclude some degree of mechanism and determinism in the world: he envisaged the world as a hierarchy of levels of existence, the lowest of which, inert matter, contains a maximum of determinancy and a minimum of indeterminancy, and proceeds upward through stages of greater and greater indeterminancy. The series culminates in God, who embodies the highest degree of indeterminancy and freedom.

Fouillée's views are presented in *La liberté et le déterminisme*, 1872; *L'Evolutionisme des idées-forces* (his main work), 1890; *La psychologie des idées-forces*, 1893; *La morale des idées-forces*, 1908; *La pensée*, 1912; *Esquisse d'une interprétation du monde*, 1913.

Works of Renouvier: *Essais de critique générale*, 4 vols., 1875-1896; *La nouvelle monadologie* (with L. Prat), 1899; *Le personnalisme*, 1902; *Derniers entretiens*, 1905. See O. Hamelin, *Le système de Renouvier*, 1927; R. Verneaux, *Renouvier, disciple et critique de Kant*, 1945, and *L'idéalisme de Renouvier*, 1945.

Works of Boutroux: *De la contingence des lois de la nature*, 1874, 4th ed., 1902, trans. by F. Rothwell, 1916; *Science and Religion in Contemporary Philosophy*, trans. by J. Nield, 1909; *The Beyond That Is Within*, trans. by J. Nield, 1912. See L. S. Crawford, *The Philosophy of Emile Boutroux*, in *Cornell Studies in Philosophy*, No. 16, 1914; *The Idea of Natural Law in Contemporary Science and Philosophy*, trans. by F. Rothwell, 1914.

Sources of Italian Idealism. The idealistic movement in Italy departs from Hegel, but instead of stressing the Hegelian logic and the doctrine of the absolute, it draws its chief inspiration from Hegel's philosophy of mind or spirit, and more particularly from the evolutionary and historical aspects of the Hegelian doctrine. Hegel's dictum: "philosophy is history" becomes the main theme of the systems of Croce and Gentile. These thinkers identify the real with the historical process interpreted in terms of the Hegelian concepts of evolution, freedom and creativity.

On its negative side, Italian idealism is a criticism of the absolutism of Bradley and Bosanquet—an absolutism which had its main source in Hegel's logical writings and which ignores or depreciates that aspect of Hegel's philosophy contained in his *Phenomenology of Mind* and *Philosophy of Mind,* which emphasizes the progressive achievement of the human spirit in history, art, religion, and in philosophy itself. The chief objection of Croce and his school to the absolutism of the British Hegelians is that it conceives reality as an eternal, static and perfected whole, and thus tends to ignore or at least to de-emphasize the temporal, progressive, and creative achievements of the human spirit. The positive thesis of Hegel, adopted by the Italian idealists, is that reality is thought, conceived as an active, creative, and progressive development. This is the substance of Croce's reply to the question posed by the title of his book: *What is Living and What Is Dead in the Philosophy of Hegel?*

Croce. Benedetto Croce (1866-1952) accepts the central thesis of idealism that spirit, as manifested in thought and experience, is the basic reality. What is distinctive of his version of idealism is the way in which he characterizes thought and experience. The experience which he equates to reality is human experience, not transcendent or absolute experience. Furthermore, experience is temporal, and is limited to the living present experience; the past is real only in so far as it conditions the present, and the future in so far as it unfolds from the present. The two main forms or aspects of present experience are: (1) its theoretical aspect, which includes all knowing either by the intuitive or conceptual activity of the mind and (2) its practical aspect, which embraces willing and the activities of the mind resulting from the exercise of the will.

Theoretical activity provides the mind with both the material and form of knowledge: intuition is the process of mind which creates the material of all our experience; esthetic is the branch of theoretical philosophy concerned with intuition. Conceptual thinking is that phase of the theoretical activity of the mind which provides the structure and organization of experience; logic, which Croce describes as the science of the pure concept, is devoted to the conceptual side of theoretic philosophy. Esthetic, the general science of the intuitive, is concerned both with the theory of perception and theory of beauty. Croce's employment of the term "aesthetic" in this dual sense combines the original epistemological meaning of "aesthetic" found in the first part of Kant's *The Critique of Pure Reason* with the restricted sense in which Baumgarten employed the term "aesthetic" to designate the philosophical theory of beauty. The dual use of this term is doctrinally significant for Croce's philosophy; it suggests that the intuition involved in sense perception ("aesthetic" in Kant's sense) is essentially the same as esthetic intuition ("aesthetic" in Baumgarten's sense). A theory of perception, if adequate, is at the same time an account of the activity of the creative artist or poet: ordinary perception has an esthetic quality, and esthetic creation and appreciation are refinements of perceptual experience. Sense perception is not a process in which the mind is passively aware of an external object; it is a cognitive process in which the data of thought are created by intuition. The difference between perception and artistic creation is not a difference of kind but of degree: they are both manifestations of the same expressive function of the mind. The esthetic intuition of sense perception requires expression in the medium of images, and this is the primary function of the creative artist. The artist's images, which are expressive of his perceptual intuitions, are not separate from the original intuition, but are rather a return to that intuition. In this way art frees the mind from the limitations of the reflective level of thought by reinstating the immediacy of perception.

Logic is concerned with the level of conceptual or reflective thinking which organizes and classifies the material of intuition. Croce defines logic as the science of the pure concept and his account of the pure concept is a theory of the philosophical categories in the idealistic tradition of Kant and Hegel. The pure concepts of logic as enumerated by Croce are: quality, evolution, shape and beauty. Croce contrasts the pure concepts of philosophy with the concepts of common sense and science, such as house, triangle, man, and he labels the latter "pseudo-concepts." The pure concept possesses the characteristics of (1) universality, (2) expressiveness and (3) concreteness. It is universal in that it is a pervasive feature of the whole of our experience. Every category is immanent in every experience, however fragmentary, but the pure concept is also transcendent in that it is not exhausted by the sum of its empirical instances. The concept is expressive of the logical activity of the mind, just as the perception or image is expressive of its esthetic activity. The concept is concrete in that it is constitutive of concrete experience: it is, to use Hegelian language, a concrete, rather than an abstract universal. By virtue of their concreteness and their immanence in experience, the pure concepts of philosophy contrast with the abstract or pseudo-concepts of science. The contrast between the concrete and the abstract underlies Croce's criticism of the sciences: the conclusions of science, since they utilize abstract concepts, possess only a relative validity. Although the special sciences study such abstractions from experience as matter, electrons, triangles as if they were true constituents of the world of experience, they are, in fact, artificial products of abstract intelligence, which, however useful in science, distort and misrepresent the true nature of reality. The real is accessible only to the pure concepts of philosophy.

The practical activity of the mind is analyzable into two distinguishable but inseparable phases: willing and action. Willing and action are identical; there can be no action which is not an expression of the will. Action which is not expressive of the will is not genuine action, but mere mechanical movement, and as such is a pseudo-concept of science. Action is expressive of willing, which in turn is always expressive of knowledge. The dependence of the practical on the theoretical is not, however, reciprocal. While it is impossible to will without knowing, it is quite possible to know without willing. The practical sphere is divided from another point of view into the economic, concerned with the merely useful, and the ethical, which is concerned with the good. The economic sphere is governed solely by egoism, whereas the ethical introduces altruism, a universalized egoism.

History is interpreted by Croce as the present creative process of historical understanding and interpretation occurring in the mind of the philosophical historian. History is not the mere factual reconstruction of a dead past, but is historigraphy in the sense of creative and imaginative interpretation of the historical process.

Gentile. The philosophy of Giovanni Gentile (1875-1944), although deeply indebted to the dynamic and individualistic idealism of Croce, reverts to some extent to the more absolutistic version of idealism of the classical German movement. He discovers a conflict in Croce's philosophy between the alleged unity of experience and the multiplicity of its expression in the esthetic, logical, economic and ethical spheres. Gentile resolves the incompatibility between the unity of experience and its four-fold expression by emphasis on the side of unity, but he is then confronted with the inevitable problem of the monist or absolutist, that of accounting for the apparent multiplicity of experience. He finds the clue for the solution of this difficulty in the conception of self-consciousness, which is a perfect synthesis of subject and object; in self-knowledge, the subject and object, knower and known, coalesce. Individual self-consciousness achieves a perfect unity of subject and object which renders intelligible the unity of universal experience. Art, which according to Gentile is always subjective in character, is correlated with the subject term in universal self-consciousness, whereas religion is exclusively preoccupied with the object term. But since subject divorced from object is an unreality, art and religion are one-sided and incomplete expressions of universal self-consciousness. Philosophy, which alone achieves the ideal unity of subject and object in its self-conscious experience, is a synthesis of art and religion. Since philosophy is the highest manifestation of self-consciousness in the world, philosophy is not merely knowledge of reality: philosophy *is* reality. The identification of reality and self-consciousness led Gentile to embrace the paradoxical position that the philosopher in his philosophical activity literally makes reality. Reality is self-consciousness, and the real can become conscious of itself only in and through the philosopher when he engages in reflectively self-conscious speculation. The philosopher in his theoretical activity does not merely contemplate reality, he makes reality. Since this self-revelation of the absolute through philosophical reflection is a temporal and historical process, philosophy is identical with history. History, art, and philosophy are three interdependent creative activities of the human spirit in which absolute reality achieves self-conscious fulfillment.

76. Romantic Reaction against Intellectualism [12]

Opponents of Intellectualism. One of the principal sources of the revolt against intellectualism in recent and contemporary philosophy is classical German idealism, which although itself strongly intellectualistic, especially among the followers of Hegel, was aware of the limitations of the intellect. A distinction is drawn by idealists between intellect, the function of thought which mechanizes experience, and rational insight or intuition, the function of mind which interprets experience dynamically. In German idealism this basic distinction is expressed by the opposition between understanding (*Verstand*) and reason (*Vernunft*), the former being a method of abstract or conceptional thought, the latter the source of metaphysical knowledge.

The opposition to extreme intellectualism is, however, not confined to idealists, intuitionists, and other romantic philosophers, but exists even in the ranks of natural scientists, among thinkers influenced in their theory of knowledge by Hume and the positivists. The twentieth-century reaction against intellectualism includes philosophers of widely different temperaments—idealists, skeptics, voluntarists, intuitionists, positivists, pragmatists, and fictionalists. We may distinguish two main groups of opponents of intellectualism. One group includes pragmatists, positivists, fictionalists, conventionalists, and other scientifically-oriented philosophers who believe that the human intellect, although adequate in its own sphere, is unable to solve the world-riddle; hence metaphysics is impossible. They hold either that knowledge is limited to the study and description of the facts of experience, or that it is a mere instrument in the service of the will, or that its conclusions—even in the field of natural science—are mere conventions, symbols, or approximations to the truth. Another group of thinkers, which includes intuitionists, idealists, and romanticists, agrees that the intellect or the discursive understanding cannot comprehend the meaning of reality, and discovers a surer source of knowledge in other phases or functions of the human mind—in feeling, belief, immediate or pure experience, will, or intuition. Strong anti-intellectualistic or anti-rationalistic tendencies are also discussible within the ranks of the idealistic school, for example, in Lotze, Eucken, Bradley, and Royce.

Significance of Romanticism. These recent romantic and anti-intellectualistic tendencies have much to commend them. They put the older classical sys-

---

[12] This section is a condensation and revision of the concluding section of the original edition, which was taken, with minor modifications, from Professor Thilly's article, "Romanticism and Rationalism," *Philosophical Review*, March, 1913.

tems on their mettle, and force them to justify their existence. Without antagonisms, without battles to fight, philosophy easily falls into lethargy, sinks into "the deep slumber of a decided opinion." Conflict is preferable to complacency or indifference. These tendencies, in addition to contributing to the rejuvenation of philosophy, succeeded in focusing attention on important issues. They have again pushed to the fore the question of the relation of natural science and philosophy, and have re-emphasized the significance of human values in the scheme of things. They have warned us against accepting the conceptual framework of reality as a substitute for reality itself, and have insisted on our keeping close to concrete experience. They protested against a one-sided metaphysics, a metaphysics that fails to do justice to all the varied experiences of mankind. They refused to accept as adequate and complete the account of reality given by the outward-looking intellect which pictures reality solely in terms of abstract cognition. They accentuated the dynamic character of reality, the Heraclitean world-view as against the static Absolute of the Eleatics. They all plead for a more elastic universe, for a world in which human life is more than a mere puppet show or drama the characters of which simply play the parts cast for them; they find a place for freedom, initiative, individual responsibility, novelty, adventure, risk, chance, romance. Interest is shifted from the universal to the particular, from the machine-like to the organic, from the intellect to feeling and will, from logic to intuition, from the theoretical to the practical. Romanticism demands a world in which the human being shall have a fighting chance—a world which, with effort, he can fashion to his purposes and ideals.

77. THE INTUITIONISM OF HENRI BERGSON

Intellect and Intuition. The most interesting and popular figure in the anti-rationalistic movement of the present century is Henri Bergson (1859-1941), whose writings, like those of William James, have found a large number of sympathetic readers outside academic circles. With the romanticists, pragmatists, and mystics Bergson proclaims the incapacity of science and logic to penetrate ultimate reality; in the presence of life and movement conceptual thinking stands helpless. Science can apprehend only what is crystallized in death, the waste product of creation, that which stands still, the inert residue that escapes time or becoming, that about which we can make predictions. And yet, the work of the intellect is not without its purpose; it is, as the pragmatists declare, an instrument in the service of the will to live. But it is also more than that, according to Bergson, and pragmatism is only a half-truth. Conceptual thought is well adapted for employment in a dead, static world, the world of inert matter where mechanism reigns, and here it has won its greatest victories. Where there is no individuality, no inwardness, nothing but dead surface, science and logic have both practical and theoretical worth. When, however, they extend their operations to the world in which everything is moving, growing, becoming, living, they mutilate and falsify the real. Baffled by the infinite variety and change of forms, and taking the whirling flux for illusion, the intellect proceeds to construct a bony skeleton, a rigid framework, and offers this as the true reality in place of the disturbing and unpleasant temporal succession. Intellect is forever reading static elements, eternal substances and causes, into the flux, and omitting, as mere appearance, what does not fit into the logical scheme. The ideal of science is a static world; the scientific intellect translates the flowing time into space relations: for it duration, movement, life, and evolution are mere illusions; it mechanizes them all. Life and consciousness cannot, according to Bergson, be treated mathematically, scientifically, logically; the scientist who studies and analyzes them in the ordinary mathematical and physical ways destroys them, and misses their meaning. The metaphysician cannot give us scientific knowledge of them; philosophy is and must remain a direct vision of reality, a *Weltanschauung* in the literal sense of the term, a world-intuition. Intuition is life, real and immediate--life envisaging itself. There is something in the universe analogous to the creative spirit of the poet, a living, pushing force, an *élan vital*, which eludes the mathematical intelligence and which can be appreciated only by a kind of divining sympathy, a feeling which approaches nearer to the essence of things than does reason. Philosophy is the art of comprehending or seizing the universe in its process, in its vital impetus. Intuition is something like instinct—a conscious, refined, spiritualized instinct—and instinct is nearer to life than are intellect and science. The real, the "becoming," the inward *"durée,"* life and consciousness, we can apprehend only through the faculty of intuition. Only by observing for the sake of observing and not for the sake of acting, will duration reveal itself. Its essence is psychological, not mathematical or logical. An adequate philosophy must do justice to both intelligence and intuition, for only by a union of these two faculties will the philosopher succeed in attaining truth.

Metaphysics. The sharp distinction which Bergson draws between intelligence and intuition, science and philosophy, is based on his dualistically tinged metaphysics. Matter is a kind of immense machine without memory; mind or consciousness is a force essentially free and essentially memory, a creative force whose function is to pile up the past on the past, like a rolling snowball, and at every moment of duration to draw on this past to organize something new—this is real creation. Consciousness is not a mere arrangement of parts succeeding each other, but an indivisible process in which there is no repetition; it is free, creative action. Consciousness is, in principle, present in all living matter; indeed, life is nothing but consciousness using matter for its purposes. A living being is a reservoir of indetermination and unforeseeability, a reservoir of possible actions, or of choice. Life avails itself of a certain elasticity in matter, and turns it to the profit of liberty by stealing into whatever infinitesimal fraction of indetermination inert matter may present. The animal performs voluntary movements by generating the infinitesimal spark which sets off the potential energy stored up in the physiological system.

Consciousness is action that continually creates and multiplies, while matter is action that continually unmakes itself and wears out. Neither the matter constituting the world nor the consciousness which utilizes this matter can be explained by itself; there is a common source of both this matter and this consciousness. The whole evolution of life on our planet is an effort of this essentially creative force to attain, by traversing matter, something which is only realized in man and which, even in man, is realized only imperfectly. In seeking to organize matter and to make it an instrument of liberty, consciousness has itself been ensnared: liberty is dogged by automatism and necessity, and in the long run is stifled by it. With man alone the chain has been broken; the human brain can oppose to every contracted habit another habit; it sets necessity to fight against necessity. We are free when our acts spring from our whole personality, when they are the expression of that personality; hence, real acts of freedom are rare in our lives.

Matter plays the rôle both of obstacle and stimulus, causes us to feel our force and also enables us to intensify it. Joy—not pleasure—is a sign which apprises us that our activity is in full expansion, an emphatic signal of the triumph of life; wherever joy is, creation has been. The ultimate justification of human life is a creation which can be pursued at every moment and by all men alike, the creation of self by self, the continual enrichment of personality by elements which it does not draw from outside, but which it causes to spring forth from itself. The passage of consciousness through matter is destined to bring to precision—in the form of distinct personalities —tendencies or potentialities which at first were confused, and also to permit these personalities to test their force while at the same time increasing it by an effort of self-creation. But consciousness is also memory, and one of its essential functions is to accumulate and preserve the past; in *pure* consciousness nothing of the past is lost, the whole life of the conscious personality is an indivisible continuity. This leads us to suppose that the effort continues beyond this life. Perhaps in man alone is consciousness immortal.

Morality and Religion. The moral and religious nature of man is described with penetrating insight in Bergson's last important work: *The Two Sources of Morality and Religion.* The opposition between the static and the dynamic, which appeared in Bergson's theory of knowledge as the antithesis between the intellect and intuition, and in his metaphysics as the contrast between the mechanical and the vital, likewise pervades his treatment of morality and religion. The first type of morality rests on obligations resulting from the structure of society and the pressures which the elements of society exert on one another; the second type of morality is a creative morality, the expression of men's moral genius and insight. "Between the first morality and the second lies the whole distance between repose and movement." [13] Finally, in religion, Bergson draws a parallel distinction between a static religion which is a product of the myth-making activities of the human mind, and a dynamic religion associated with genuine mystical insight. A fundamental antithesis between the static and the dynamic pervades Bergson's philosophy in all its phases.

Time and Free Will, 1888, trans. by F. L. Pogson, 1910; *Matter and Memory,* 1896, trans. by N. M. Paul and W. S. Palmer; *Laughter,* 1900, trans. by F. Rothwell; *An Introduction to Metaphysics,* 1903, trans. by T. E. Hulme, 1912; *Creative Evolution,* 1907, trans. by A. Mitchell, 1911; *Mind-Energy,* 1919, trans. by H. W. Carr, 1920; *The Two Sources of Morality and Religion,* 1932, trans. by R. A. Audra and C. Brereton, 1935; *The Creative Mind,* 1946 (contains translations of essays and articles).

A. D. Lindsay, *The Philosophy of Bergson,* 1911; J. Stewart, *Critical Exposition of Bergson's Philosophy,* 1911; U. M. Sait, *Ethical Implications of Bergson's Philosophy,* 1911; H. W. Carr, *Henri Bergson,* 1912; G. R. Dodson, *Bergson and the Modern Spirit,* 1913; E. Le Roy, *The New Philosophy of Henri Bergson,* trans. by V. Benson, 1913; H. M. Kallen, *William James and Henri Bergson,* 1914; H. W. Carr, *The Philosophy of Change,* 1914; G. W. Cunningham, *A Study in the Philosophy of Bergson,* 1916; G. W. Peckham, *Logic of Bergson's Philosophy,* 1917; J. A. Gunn, *Bergson and His Philosophy,* 1920; G. R. Hamilton, *Bergson and Future Philosophy,* 1921; J. Solomon, *Bergson,* 1922; K. Stephen, *The Misuse of Mind,* 1922; O. Wheeler, *Bergson and Education,* 1922; C. Nordmann, *The Tyranny of Time, Einstein or Bergson?,* 1925; J. Chevalier, *Henri Bergson,* 1928; J. A. MacWilliam, *Criticism of the Philosophy of Bergson,* 1928; N. P. Stallknecht, *Studies in the Philosophy of Creation,* 1934; A. Szathmary, *The Aesthetic Theory of Bergson,* 1937; S. E. Dollard, *Bergsonian Metaphysics and God,* 1940; B. A. Scharfstein, *Roots of Bergson's Philosophy,* 1943.

[13] *The Two Sources of Religion and Morality,* p. 47.

78. Existentialism in Germany and France

The Revival of Kierkegaard. The early nineteenth century Danish philosopher, Sören Kierkegaard (1813-1855), after a long period of relative obscurity, began to exert a profound influence on German philosophy just before the first World War. This influence, which rapidly increased during the years between the two wars, has spread beyond the boundaries of Germany and helped to mold the philosophy of existentialism in France, Latin-America, and the United States. Kierkegaard's philosophy is theological in its motivation, esthetic in its literary and poetic form, and ethical in its import. At an early age he studied theology and was deeply impressed by what he considered the great insight of Protestant Christianity—the freedom and value of the human individual. His entire later philosophy is an elaboration of the Christian conception of man as an individual, confronted with basic choices who, in his commitments, is aware of himself and his inner freedom. Kierkegaard's radically individualistic Protestantism, although it brought him late in his life into open conflict with the established Danish church, exerted—principally through Karl Barth—a far-reaching influence on later Protestant theology. The predominantly religious and theological orientation of Kierkegaard's philosophy is combined with—and indeed frequently in conflict with—a literary and artistic sensitivity which is manifest both in the poetic and imaginative form of his writings and in an essentially romantic interpretation of human nature. Kierkegaard thought of himself as a poet, and he has been characterized by one of his biographers as "the poet of religion." Kierkegaard does not, however, allow his estheticism and romanticism to distract him from his deep concern with man's ethical nature. Though he propounds no system of ethics, a spirit of moral earnestness pervades his entire philosophy. His ethical philosophy is individualistic in its insistence that each individual is confronted with ethical choices which he alone can make and for which he assumes sole responsibility. Every decision an individual makes is irrevocable and presents him with the necessity for subsequent decisions.

Kierkegaard was not a philosopher in the technical and systematic sense, and any attempt to formalize his philosophy would inevitably falsify his position and do violence to the spirit of his thought. Yet we can bring together the main philosophical themes of his existentialist thinking, by virtue of which he is the fountain-head of contemporary existentialism. The three principal conceptions of Kierkegaard's philosophy are truth, choice, and God.

(1) Kierkegaard's conception of the nature of philosophical truth is

essentially Socratic. "Truth is not introduced into the individual from without, but was within him all the time." Kierkegaard sharply contrasts existentialist thinking with abstract speculation: whereas abstract thinking explores the realm of possibilities by means of logical techniques and achieves only hypothetical knowledge, existentialist thinking achieves truth about the actual, concrete individual. Existentialist truth is a passionate, inner commitment to something which is objectively and theoretically uncertain, and is the highest truth attainable by an existing individual. Kierkegaard is well aware that truth, according to his definition, is equivalent to faith. (2) The central concept of Kierkegaard's philosophy is choice—a concept which is expounded in an early work, *"Either/Or,"* and persists through his entire later philosophy. In *"Either/Or"* choice is presented as a decision between two ways of life: (a) the esthetic life, devoted to art, music, the drama, and (b) the ethical life, which seeks happiness in marriage, business or a profession. According to Kierkegaard, no adequate psychological description of the phenomenon of choice is possible; it must be experienced in order to be understood. The character of the choice can only be adumbrated by such epithets as individual, subjective, momentary, absolute, free, irrevocable. The choice by an individual of a way of life is a "leap over the abyss." (3) The culmination of existentialist thinking is the knowledge of God. The individual in his inner experience of choice, may achieve, at least momentarily, knowledge of the eternal God. "The eternal," says Kierkegaard, "aims from above at the existing individual, who by existing is in process of movement. . . ." The coincidence of the individual's momentary existence and God's eternal reality is admittedly paradoxical, but it is a paradox which exists only for the speculative intellect and which can be embraced without difficulty as a truth of faith. Kierkegaard's account of the individual's contact with God is in the tradition of the great Christian mystics. Kierkegaard is in the precise and literal sense of the term a mystic— he believed in the possibility of the individual's union with God, a union which does not obliterate the individual. The individual, even when he establishes *rapport* with God, preserves his individuality and God remains an "Absolute Other." Kierkegaard was a *Christian* mystic in his conviction that Christ mediates man's self-transcendence; Christ is described as the "Invitor" who draws the individual man to God.

Kierkegaard was an existentialist thinker from whom the German existentialist philosophers derived much of their inspiration, but he cannot properly be described as the founder of existentialism as a philosophy, for the existentialist point of view of his writings did not crystallize into a fixed doctrine. Kierkegaard gave to the term "existence" (*Existenz*) the peculiar meaning which it has in contemporary existentialist philosophy in Germany and France—a meaning which was described in the previous paragraph and which is quite distinct from the neutral sense of existence (*Dasein*). Kierkegaard and later existentialist philosophers are not asserting that the individual man exists merely in the neutral sense in which individual horses and dogs exist, while centaurs do not; the individual man exists in the sense of having a unique dimension, of being characterized by choice. Kierkegaardian "existence" became in the existentialist philosophers Heidegger and Jaspers the central concept of *philosophical* existentialism.

Kierkegaard's Writings in English Translation. Philosophical Fragments, trans. by D. F. Swenson, 1936; *Stages of Life's Way,* trans. by W. Lowrie, 1940; *Christian Discourses,* trans. by W. Lowrie, 1940; *Concluding Unscientific Postscript,* trans. by D. F. Swenson and W. Lowrie, 1941; *Fear and Trembling,* trans. by W. Lowrie, 1941; *Either/Or,* 2 vols., trans. by D. F. Swenson, L. M. Swenson and W. Lowrie, 1944; *The Concept of Dread,* trans. by W. Lowrie, 1944; R. Bretall, ed., *A Kierkegaard Anthology,* 1946; *Works of Love,* trans. by D. F. Swenson and L. M. Swenson, 1946.

Works on Kierkegaard. W. Lowrie, *Kierkegaard,* 1938; D. F. Swenson, *Something about Kierkegaard,* 1941; J. Collins, *The Mind of Kierkegaard,* 1953; M. Wyschograd, *Kierkegaard and Heidegger: the Ontology of Existence,* 1954.

Existentialism and Contemporary Culture. The philosophy of existence in Germany is the latest phase of the reaction against the extreme rationalism of Hegel and the Hegelians. Existentialism is a philosophy of irrationalism which, because of the prominence it gives to man's passionate and esthetic nature and to his feelings of anguish, love, guilt, and sense of inner freedom, is in the tradition of romanticism. It conceives of truth as a free commitment on the part of the individual, the product of a "resolute decision" as Heidegger expresses it. Existentialism is thus a form of "faith-philosophy." It is, however, not a commitment to voluntarism, since the decision is not the function of the will as a specific faculty of the self, but is the choice of the individual as a total being. Thus existentialism, despite its exaggerated emphasis on the freedom of the individual, is not committed to a theory of free will. It is, rather, a form of individualism which recognizes the crucial importance of the decisions of the individual man, but does not ignore the individual's relation to others; the individual, through his self-transcendence, communes with other individuals and ultimately with an all-embracing Being. Although German existentialism owes many of its insights to traditional idealism, both Heidegger and Jaspers would reject the idealistic label; they refuse to identify being with consciousness, mind, thought, spirit, or any other idealistic principle. Existentialism eludes the usual philosophical classifications, for it claims to have transcended the oppositions between naturalism and spiritualism, realism and idealism, pluralism and monism.

The significance of existentialism lies not in its contribution to technical philosophy, for as such it has little to say that has not been said more lucidly, articulately and systematically by earlier philosophical systems, but rather, in its having given philosophical utterance to a pervasive mood of contemporary culture. Existentialism is pre-eminently the philosophy of crisis; it has interpreted the whole of human, and likewise of cosmic existence, as a succession of critical situations, each fraught with danger and demanding for its resolution all the inner resources of the individual; each crisis gives rise to a new crisis requiring similar resolution, and the entire series leads to ultimate "shipwreck." Existentialism is a philosophy of disillusion and despair. It is not, however, properly speaking, philosophical pessimism, since it does not impute evil to ultimate being; ultimate being transcends both good and evil. Existentialism is a philosophy of nihilism which literally reduces all human endeavor to naught; but the existentialist derives a perverse consolation from the succession of crises and the ultimate confrontation with nothingness. Historically considered, existentialist philosophy is a basic response to the present cultural crisis.

General Books on Existentialism. G. de Ruggiero, *Existentialism,* trans. by E. M. Cocks, 1946; R. Harper, *Existentialism, A Theory of Man,* 1948; M. Grene, *Dreadful Freedom,* 1948; J. A. Wahl, *A Short History of Existentialism,* trans. by F. Williams and S. Maron, 1949; H. Kuhn, *Encounter with Nothingness,* 1949; E. Mounier, *Existentialist Philosophers,* trans. by E. Blow, 1949; H. J. Blackham, *Six Existentialist Thinkers,* 1951; J. Collins, *The Existentialists: A Critical Study,* 1952.

The Existentialism of Heidegger and Jaspers. A philosophical system of existentialism was elaborated by Martin Heidegger (1889-   ) in his *Being and Time (Sein und Zeit),* 1927. The central problem of Heidegger's philosophy is the problem of being, considered in its temporal and historical character as focused in the life and existence of man. He analyzes the individual man in his relation to himself, to his environment, and to other men. The existence of the individual is finite and temporal and it is man's sense of his finitude and transience which gives his existence its peculiar character. The whole of human existence is permeated by a tragic anxiety or anguish (*Angst*), induced by the sense of the inevitability of death. The individual, in envisaging his own death, is confronted by absolute nothingness—a nothingness which is not the mere absence of existence, but a primordial reality. In associating death with nothingness, Heidegger is ascribing to death a status beyond the mere non-existence of the individual. This is the import of his assertion that man's existence is a "being for death." Heidegger—again in the spirit of Kierkegaard—emphasizes the element of risk in all human decision and action; every decision, including commitment to a philosophical position, endangers not only the individual who makes the decision, but in some degree others also; it is in this context that Heidegger defines philosophy as the endangering of being by a being. The acceptance or rejection of a philosophical position is not to be made lightly or irresponsibly, since it endangers not only the philosopher himself but others and, since the individual is embedded in the world, all being is implicated or affected by his philosophical commitments.

The individual is not immured within himself; he achieves through resolute decision a self-transcendence—which is not, however, an access to God. The idea of transcendence is deprived by Heidegger of the religious and theological connotation which it had for Kierkegaard. The first of the transcendences enumerated by Heidegger is transcendence with reference to the world. The relation of the individual to the world is not primarily of the cognitive sort envisaged by traditional philosophers in the Descartes-Locke tradition and preserved even in Kant and post-Kantian idealism; the individual's relation to his world is not a subject-object relation, but one of direct, active participation. The egocentric predicament of Descartes and the epistemological problem of transcendence simply do not exist for Heidegger. The second mode of transcendence is the individual's *rapport* with other individuals, and this also is a relation of direct intercourse rather than mere communication. Finally, the individual achieves time-transcendence of his present momentary existence in his anxiety and care for the future, and particularly in his preoccupation with death; he not only anticipates the future cognitively, but in a sense lives ahead of himself. The doctrine of the essential temporality of being as suggested in the title of his work (*Being and Time*) is systematically elaborated by Heidegger, and is at times reminiscent of Bergson in its subtlety and penetration.

The philosophy of Karl Jaspers (1883-), whose name is commonly paired with Heidegger's, is another secularized version of the existentialist theme. At the hands of Jaspers, existentialism received its most lucid, articulate and methodical formulation. Jaspers' earliest writing was in the field of psychopathology, and he carried over into his philosophy something of the clarity and descriptive accuracy which characterized his work as a scientist. In his *Psychology of World-Views* (*Psychologie der Weltanschauungen*), 1919, he foreshadowed his later existentialism by considering the various possible world-theories as so many basic human responses or decisions of the individual man in the presence of such inevitabilities as chance, evil, and death. Existentialism itself may be considered as one of these basic world-theories, responsive to the present crisis in culture.

Jaspers' three-volume work, *Philosophy* (*Philosophie*), 1932, is a systematic formulation of his existential philosophy. In addressing himself to the methodological problem, Jaspers distinguishes three methods which have evolved in the course of the history of philosophy. These methods are by no means mutually exclusive, and each method makes its distinctive contribution to philosophical inquiry. (1) The method of philosophical world-orientation (*philosophische Weltorientierung*) is the utilization of scientific knowledge in the search for a philosophical understanding of man and the world. The physical and psychological sciences promote man's orientation in the world, provided—and this is for Jaspers an important proviso—the philosopher never loses sight of the essential limitations of scientific inquiry. The chief limitation of science is its incompleteness; neither in the formal sciences of logic and mathematics, nor in the empirical sciences of nature and of man is it possible to attain a complete system of truth. Certain scientifically rooted philosophies, such as positivism and idealism, have, indeed, achieved a spurious and artificial completeness; but a truly critical philosophy recognizes the essential incompleteness of science. This is one of the chief insights of Kant's philosophy, which regards completeness as a regulative idea of science which is incapable of fulfillment. (2) The second method Jaspers calls "the elucidation of existence" (*Existenzerhellung*); this is the method of existentialist thinking, the characteristics of which have already been noted in connection with Kierkegaard and Heidegger. The freedom of the individual in all his choices and his resultant absolute responsibility are the chief deliverances of existential elucidation. Jaspers' existentialism emphasizes the intercourse among free individuals, which he calls "communication." There is no such thing as a completely isolated personality; there is always an interplay between persons, which occurs not only in contemporary society but also within the structure of history. In the historical process, Jaspers discerns that reciprocal interplay between persons of different eras, by which individuals realize their freedom. (3) The third mode is that of metaphysics (*Metaphysik*). Metaphysics, in Jaspers' sense, is the philosopher's quest for "the one being," the all-enveloping (*umgreifend*) absolute which is the philosopher's equivalent of God. The philosophical absolute, which is the goal of speculative philosophy, cannot be reached by science, nor even solely by existentialist thinking. Metaphysical speculation employs, besides existentialist thinking, various dialectical, imaginative, speculative and symbolic techniques for adumbrating the ultimate reality.

Jaspers' philosophical method is more broadly conceived than Heidegger's, yet, despite its greater catholicity, his philosophy sounds the same notes of anguish and despair so characteristic of existentialism in all its forms. The same preoccupation with death expressed in Kierkegaard's "sickness unto death" and Heidegger's "being for death" is evident in Jaspers' contention that man by virtue of his very freedom and self-transcendence is doomed to ultimate shipwreck (*naufrage*), a destiny which he will accept freely and lovingly as the fulfillment of his being.

Heidegger's writings: *Sein und Zeit*, 1927; *Vom Wesen des Grundes*, 1929; *Was ist Metaphysik?*, 1929.

Jaspers' writings: *Psychologie der Weltanschauungen*, 1919; *Die geistige Situation der Zeit*, 1931; *Philosophie*, 3 vols., 1932; *Way to Wisdom*, trans. by R. Manheim, 1951; *Reason and Existence*, trans. by W. Earle, 1955; *Reason and Anti-Reason in Our Times*, trans. by S. Godman, 1952.

Existentialism of Sartre. Jean-Paul Sartre (1905-), the leading figure of the existentialist movement in France, came under the influence of German existentialism as a student of Heidegger. He developed existentialism as a philosophical position in *Being and Nothingness* (*L'Etre et le Néant*), published in 1943, and gave literary expression to his existentialism in his poetry, fiction, and plays. His version of existentialism is, like that of his teacher, Heidegger, secular and atheistic rather than theological. To Nietzsche, he was indebted for the atheistic formula: "God is dead," and his anti-intellectualism reflects the influence of Nietzsche both in form and substance. Like Heidegger, he combines existentialism with phenomenology, derived from Husserl: the subtitle of his main work is: *Essay in Phenomenological Ontology* (*Essai d'ontologie phénoménologique*). He owes little to the main tradition of French thought, save his subjectivist conception of consciousness, which is Cartesian in origin.

The basic ontological premise of Sartre's existentialism is negative and atheistic: "existentialism is nothing but an attempt to draw all the consequences from a consistent atheistic position." [14] He holds that the very notion of God is self-contradictory, and relegates religious beliefs and theological dogmas to a limbo of pure mythology. He draws many consequences from his initial atheistic assumption, including the thesis that existence is prior to essence—from which existentialism derives its name. The theistic position, according to Sartre, infers the existence of God and the world from the essence or nature of God, a procedure which in its purest form constitutes the ontological argument for the existence of God. Sartre's atheistic ontology, by repudiating God, reverses the theistic doctrine of the priority of essence over existence, or rather it rejects essence entirely in favor of existence.

[14] *Existentialism*, trans. by B. Frechtman, p. 60.

Theistic essentialism is replaced by atheistic existentialism. The ontological revolution effected thereby is a drastic one: essence, which is the realm of all rational and intellectual inquiry, is displaced by existence, which is opaque to reason. The substitution of existence for essence at the ontological level entails the rejection of rationalism in favor of irrationalism and anti-intellectualism. Atheistic existentialism states that "if God does not exist there is at least one being in whom existence precedes essence, a being who exists before he can be defined by any concept, and this being is man." [15] Sartre readily effects a transition from the ontological to the humanistic levels of his philosophy: his theory that existence rather than essence is at the core of being leads inevitably to an existentialist account of man. Sartre's interpretation of man, though derivative from his ontology, is perhaps the more significant and influential level of his philosophy. Central to his conception of man are the notions of conscious subjectivity, freedom, nothingness—all of which have their ontological basis in existential reality.

Sartre's existentialist theory of man departs from an examination of consciousness. Consciousness is always *of* something, and in being conscious of anything I am at the same time aware of my own consciousness. The object of consciousness is, however, not constituted by the awareness of it, and thus Sartre's emphasis on subjectivity does not commit him to idealism. Self-consciousness is simply the universal concomitant of the apprehension of objects. Knowledge is described by Sartre in terms of a distinction between the conscious subject, with its attendant self-consciousness, and the object of consciousness, considered as a phenomenal appearance and not as a transcendent object behind appearances. In this context the conscious subject is referred to as the *pour-soi* (the for-itself); it is so designated because it exists for itself in every act of reflective self-consciousness. The object, if we strip from it all meaning and interpretation contributed by the subject, is designated the *en-soi* (the in-itself). The basic polarity between the *poir-soi* and the *en-soi* is the factor of negation, which is responsible for the feelings of tension, isolation, and frustration which characterize human existence; it is also responsible for man's freedom. The life of man is a perpetual striving for a unity of the *pour-soi* and the *en-soi,* a unity which, though inherently unattainable, prescribes the inescapable condition of human knowledge, choice and action. The freedom of man consists in his conscious separation from the *en-soi,* his choice of an ideal for himself and his self-projection into the future. The self is free in that man generates ideals for himself and thereby projects himself into the future. In so doing he aims at the union of the *pour-soi* and the *en-soi,* an attempt which is foredoomed

[15] *Op. cit.,* p. 18.

to failure. Man's exercise of liberty is inescapable: "man is condemned to be free," for freedom is inherent in the very constitution of human existence; it persists until death supervenes and annihilates all future possibility of action A man's liberty is, while it lasts, unrestricted; it involves no subjection to a universally binding moral law, no coercive moral ideal or system of obligations other than that projected by the freely acting agent himself. This fact does not, however, deprive man of responsibility; he is responsible for his freely chosen ideals and for the influence which their adoption by him exerts on the ideals and actions of others. Man's awareness of his responsibility for his unrestricted and crucial decisions underlies the feeling of dread or anguish (*angoisse*), which accompanies all choice and ensuing action. "I am responsible for myself and for everyone else. I am creating a certain image of man of my own choosing . . . This helps us to understand what the content is of such rather grandiloquent words as anguish, forelorn-ness, despair." [16]

Sartre's works in English translation. *Existentialism* (*L'Extentialisme est un Humanisme*), trans. by B. Frechtman, 1947; *The Psychology of Imagination* (*L'Imaginaire*), 1948; *The Emotions: Outline of a Theory* (*Esquisses d'une théorie des émotions*), trans. by B. Frechtman, 1948; *The Age of Reason* (*L'Age de Raison*), trans. by E. Sutton, 1951; *Being and Nothingness* (*L'Etre et le Néant*), trans. by H. E. Barnes, 1956.

Gabriel Marcel. The existentialism of Gabriel Marcel (1889-   ) possesses religious overtones which contrast with the atheistic existentialism of Sartre. Marcel in his earliest philosophical publications shows the influence of the absolute idealism of Hegel and of such contemporary idealists as Bradley and Royce but he turned away from idealism in an existentialist direction. Marcel's existentialist philosophy has much in common with Kierkegaard's, though he did not become acquainted with Kierkegaard's writings until his own thought had crystallized; he shares with Kierkegaard a rejection of the Hegelian absolute idealism, an emphasis on the freedom of the human individual, and the incidence in man of a transcendent God.

Marcel's philosophy does not lend itself to systematization or schematic exposition, for his insights assume a highly personal form and indeed his principal work, *Metaphysical Journals,* is cast in the literary form of reflec-tions or meditations. One of the central themes of his existentialist ontology is the necessity of overcoming the radical dualisms and antitheses which infect traditional philosophy, notably the dualisms between subject and ob-ject, thought and being, intellect and will, soul and body, the "I" and the "You," the self and God. The epistemological dualism between subject and object, between thought and being, has generated the artificial and inherently

[16] *Existentialism,* trans. by B. Frechtman, p. 21.

insoluble problems which have baffled modern philosophers from Descartes to Russell. The philosophical ontology espoused by Marcel transcends the opposition between the subject who asserts the existence of being, and being as asserted by that subject.[17] From the ontological standpoint, in contrast to the epistemological, "knowledge is seen to be contingent on a participation in being for which no epistemology can account because it continually presupposes it."[18] Similarly, the problem of the relation between the soul and the body, with which successive generations of philosophers have grappled, dissolves in the presence of the existentialist's confrontation with being. The conception of the body as the property or instrument of the soul, which underlies the Cartesian formulation of the problem, misrepresents the ontological situation in which man confronts the world and his body. Instead of saying, "I have a body" or "I make use of my body," I ought more properly to say "I am my body," or "I participate through my body in the being which is the global world about me." For Marcel, the existential union of my mind and my body remains, no doubt, a "mystery" which must be accepted, but it ceases to be a "problem" for which an intellectual solution can be given. The supreme ontological mystery for Marcel's version of existentialism is that of the union of the self with the transcendent Being which is God. Man achieves this transcendence through his renunciation of his own self-sufficiency and his unqualified acceptance and affirmation of God's transcendent existence. Marcel's religious existentialism has sometimes been designated "Christian, or Catholic existentialism," but he himself disavows this label because he considers existential participation in Being valid prior to its formulation in terms of Christian or any other religious dogma. The central insight of his religious version of existentialism, namely the union of the being of man and the Being of God, is no doubt in the present historical situation, most readily expressed in terms of the symbols of the Christian religion, but he claims that the ontological mystery may be recognized and accepted by those "who are strangers to all positive religion of whatever kind" and "that this recognition, which takes place through certain higher modes of human experience in no way involves the adherence to any given religion."[19]

Journal métaphysique, 1913-1923, 1927; *Etre et avoir*, 1935; *Le Mystère de l'être*, 2 vols., 1951; *The Philosophy of Existence*, trans. by M. Harari, 1948; *The Mystery of Being*, Part I: *Reflection and Mystery* (The Gifford Lectures), trans. by R. Hague, 1951; *Being and Having*, trans. by K. Farrer, 1950. E. Gilson, ed., *Existentialisme Chrétien: Gabriel Marcel*, 1947.

[17] Cf. "On the Ontological Mystery" in *The Philosophy of Existence*, trans. by M. Harari, p. 8.

[18] *Loc. cit.*   [19] *Op. cit.*, p. 31.

XXI

Realistic Tendencies
in Recent Philosophy

79. THE REALISTIC TRADITION

Reaction against Idealism. The resurgence of realism in the twentieth century is among the most significant phenomena of recent and contemporary philosophy. From the very beginning of modern philosophy there have been recurrent and frequently violent outbreaks of realism, but realism has not maintained itself as a continuous and ascendant tradition comparable to idealism, empiricism, and rationalism. Realistic tendencies have usually appeared as reactions to the excesses of prevailing idealisms, rather than manifestations of a dominant independent tradition. The central thesis of realism is that there exists a reality external to and independent of consciousness, mind, or experience; it is a protest against the idealistic theory that reality is constituted by and exists only for mind, whether it be an individual mind or an absolute experience.

The central theme of realism has received varying expressions, depending on the peculiarities of the idealism against which it raises its voice of protest and on the cultural complexion of each period in which it emerges. In the eighteenth century, opposition to the excesses of Berkeley's subjectivistic idealism produced the common-sense realism of Thomas Reid and the other representatives of the Scottish school; this type of realism continued into the nineteenth century in the natural realism of Sir William Hamilton. The pluralistic realism of Herbart was the nineteenth-century German reaction to Hegelian absolute idealism. The twentieth-century phase of the realistic movement in Germany, England and the United States is perhaps a more vigorous, original and constructive expression of realism than any of its earlier manifestations in modern philosophy. It arose largely as a reaction against the prevailing idealisms, and it reflects the maturity of the nineteenth

593

and twentieth-century idealistic movements against which it protests; its attack is directed not only against idealistic arguments embodying Berkeley's *"esse est percipi,"* but it is forced also to cope with the critical idealism of Kant, the absolute idealism of Hegel and Bradley, and the psychological and epistemological theories of idealists of the type of Lotze, Royce and the German Neo-Kantians. The recent realistic revolt against idealism has been enriched by the maturity and subtlety of its adversaries.

The Influence of Hume. In the development of recent realism, the influence of Hume can scarcely by over-emphasized for, though Hume's theory of external perception is idealistic, his analytical and empirical method and his psychological atomism of impressions have exerted an incalculable influence on British and American realism.

Hume's psychological atomism was apparent in his analysis of experience into discrete impressions, by which he meant "our more lively perceptions, when we hear, or see, or feel, or love, or hate, or desire, or will." Impressions are considered by Hume to be analytically distinguishable, and hence separable components of our experience. The atomistic impressions into which experience is resolved by Hume's analysis are the building blocks of all our knowledge, including the perception of external objects and of our own mental states. The "impressions" of Hume's terminology are the "sense data" of the British and American realists. Sense data, like "impressions," provide the point of departure for all our knowledge; they are immediately apprehended by the mind in perception and are actual components of our percepts. The images of memory and imagination are, like Hume's "ideas," reproductions of data originally given in sense.

Abstract, conceptual, and scientific knowledge is, according to most realists, likewise traceable to sense perception; it is attained by processes of abstraction, inference, and construction applied to the empirical data of sense. A meaningful idea or concept, as defined in terms of Hume's empirical theory of meaning, is one which is traceable to original impressions; a meaningless idea is defined as one which is not so traceable. British realism adheres to essentially the same empirical criterion of meaning: a concept qualifies as meaningful only if it is analyzable into sense data originating in experience.

The Realistic Thesis. On its positive and constructive side, recent realism has availed itself of powerful analytical tools provided by the spectacular advances in logic and mathematics during the present century. The natural sciences also have made their contributions to the epistemology of realism: developments in physics have clarified and drastically modified the older interpretations of the nature of scientific objects, while physiology and psychology have enriched the realists' understanding of the processes involved in perception, memory, and the higher cognitive processes.

The central thesis shared by all types of realism is that the object of knowledge in perception, memory, abstract logical and mathematical thought and scientific theory is a reality which exists and possesses properties which are independent of the knowing mind. This thesis of "epistemological realism" is the realists' counter-proposal to "epistemological idealism," the assertion that the object of knowledge owes its existence as well as its properties to the creative activity of the knowing mind. Although realists agree on the central thesis of the independent existence of the object of knowledge, they differ among themselves in their theories concerning the nature and status of the knowing mind, the function of sense data in knowledge, and even on the nature of the object of knowledge.

In the present chapter, several types of realism will be surveyed, including: phenomenology, presentational realism, perspectivism, and representational realism. (1) German phenomenology stresses the mind's cognitive transcendence in the "intentional" act of reference to "objectives" beyond itself. In assigning so important a rôle to the mind in the projection of "objectives," phenomenology, as formulated by Brentano, retains a vestige of idealism, but the realism latent in his theory emerges with clarity and vigor in his followers, Meinong and Husserl, who reify and hypostatize the "objectives." (2) The direct, "naïve," or presentational realism of G. E. Moore ascribes to perceived objects, constituted by sense data, a status completely independent of mental activity; its only concession to idealism is the retention of mind as a pure act of awareness. (3) "Objective relativism," perspectivism, and neutral monism (including the so-called "New Realism") are the most radical versions of realism: they reduce the object of knowledge to a collection of subsistent entities or perspectives, and dispense entirely with the knowing mind regarded either as substance, subject or act. (4) Representational, dualistic realism (including American "Critical Realism") is a compromise theory which is idealistic in its retention of mind with its subjective data, but realistic in its acceptance of extra-mental physical objects.

80. The Development of German Phenomenology

The historical antecedents of modern phenomenology are for the most part idealistic. The theory derived much of its inspiration from Descartes' subjectivism and his analysis of the self and its activities; from Kant's analysis of the phenomenal world, and from Hegel's phenomenology of mind. Despite its indebtedness to idealism for its method and analysis of experience, phenomenology, in its epistemological and metaphysical doctrines, displays thoroughly realistic tendencies which are derived from Platonism. German phenomenology combines phenomenalistic analysis and description of experience with a theory of logical essences.

Brentano's "Intentional" Psychology. The most immediate source of the central insights of phenomenology is to be found in the psychology of Franz Brentano (1838-1917). Brentano's work, *Psychology from an Empirical Standpoint* (*Psychologie vom empirischen Standpunkte,* 1874) prepared the way for later phenomenology by its rigorous distinction between the psychological genesis of a thought and its logical or epistemological import and validity. An exclusive concern with the psycho-genetic problem—characteristic of most British empirical psychology stemming from Hume—is guilty of the fallacy of "psychologism." A truly "empirical" psychology, according to Brentano's usage, will concern itself not with the origin of the contents of consciousness, but with the analysis and description of mental acts whereby the mind envisages objects. The central concept of Brentano's psychology, derived from scholastic sources, is that of intentional reference; the essential and defining trait of mind, according to his psychology, is the ability of a mental act to refer to something beyond itself. Our thoughts are always thoughts *of* something. The capacity of the mind to refer beyond itself is one of its intrinsic and essential functions. Brentano's psychology is largely restricted to an account of the referential function of the mind; he did not undertake the more ambitious task of examining the "objects" of intentional reference. The development of an extended theory of phenomenological objectivity was the achievement of Meinong and Husserl.

Besides his influential *Psychologie vom empirischen Standpunkte* (1874), Brentano's works include *Vom Ursprung sittlicher Erkenntnis* (1884); *Ueber die Zukunft der Philosophie* (1893); *Die vier Phasen der Philosophie* (1895).

Meinong's Theory of Objects. Alexius Meinong (1853-1921), a student of Brentano, formulated in the context of a modified version of Brentano's theory of intentionality, a "general theory of objects" (*Gegenstandstheorie*). An object, in Meinong's inclusive sense, is anything that can be intended or thought *of* and, in his theory of objects, he set himself the task of investigating and differentiating the several kinds of objects. Particular existing things—trees, tables, chairs, books and the like—constitute one class of objects. Because these are the objects of our practical everyday concern, we tend to treat them as alone real and to relegate all other objects of thought and imagination to a limbo of unreality. Meinong deplores this "prejudice in favor of the actual," which has led many philosophers to equate reality and existence. According to his theory, there is a significant sense in which non-existent objects are real. An important group of non-existent objects are ideal objects, such as relations, numbers, etc., which are investigated in logic and mathematics. "That 3 is an integer between 2 and 4," is a subsistent object, as also are the numbers "3," "2" and "4." Besides ideal or subsistent entities, there is another group of non-existent objects—objects of the imagination such as "golden mountains" and even "square circles." Not only do such objects have being of a sort, but we can investigate their properties and even formulate true statements concerning them.

Meinong used the technical term "objective" to designate a special type of object, namely, those which are present to the mind in judgment and supposition. "That the sun will rise tomorrow," "That 4 is greater than 3" are "objectives," whereas "the sun," "4" and "3" are objects but not objectives. Objectives differ from other objects principally in the capacity of the former for truth and falsity. According to Meinong's theory, an objective may be affirmed or denied with varying degrees of assurance, or it may merely be assumed or supposed without any commitment as to its truth or falsity. The theory that our statements and judgments refer to objectives has exerted a considerable influence on British and American philosophy through G. E. Moore and Bertrand Russell. Meinong's objective is, with certain qualifications, what Russell calls a proposition.

Meinong's theory of objects and objectives is in the tradition of the Platonic theory of forms and the medieval doctrine of universals. By ascribing reality to subsistent and other non-existent objects, Meinong places himself in the camp of the realists. His version of realism, however, differs significantly from typical Platonism. Unlike Plato, he does not sharply separate the perceptual and intellectual, but rather tends to assimilate the two to the same pattern. His theory of objects is not an ontology; his primary concern is not to ascribe to subsistent objects an unique ontological status; but rather, to describe the different kinds and orders of objectivity. The whole temper of his philosophy is thus phenomenological rather than ontological.

Meinong's writings include *Psychologisch-ethiche Untersuchungen zur Werttheorie,* 1894; *Über Annahmen,* 1902; *Untersuchungen zur Gegenstands-theorie und Psychologie,* 1904; *Gesammelte Abhandlungen,* 3 vols., 1914.

J. N. Findlay, *Meinong's Theory of Objects,* 1933, is an excellent and comprehensive account of Meinong's philosophy, with special emphasis on the theories which influenced the realism of Bertrand Russell and G. E. Moore.

Husserl's Phenomenology. The true founder of modern phenomenology, of which Brentano and Meinong were the forerunners, was Edmund Husserl (1859-1938). Husserl set himself the task of describing in general terms the method and subject matter of a new science of pure phenomenology; he also executed numerous detailed and penetrating phenomenological investigations. Phenomenology is an investigation of phenomena—i.e., items displayed or found in experience. A phenomenon is anything with which the subject is confronted, without any suggestions that the phenomenon is, as Kant supposed, a mere appearance of a basic reality. Phenomenology is thus not to be confused with phenomenalism—the theory which restricts our knowledge to phenomenal appearances of an inaccessible reality. In the first edition of his *Logical Investigations* (*Logische Untersuchungen,* 1900-01), Husserl defined the science of phenomenology as the description of subjective processes, and thereby made phenomenology coextensive with psychology as regards subject matter; the two sciences differ solely in that psychology seeks to explain phenomena in causal and genetic terms, whereas phenomenology merely analyzes and describes phenomena as they are presented. Phenomenology as the descriptive analysis of subjective phenomena, independently of any philosophical or epistemological presuppositions or commitments, is advocated by Husserl as an indispensable preliminary to all other sciences. Husserl conceived pure phenomenology as a necessary preparatory science much as Aristotle considered logic as a propaedeutic science.

Phenomenology is subjectivistic in that its investigations are initially directed, in Cartesian fashion, toward the ego and its presentations. Indeed, Husserl discerns in Descartes' *Meditations* the first halting steps in the direction of pure phenomenological inquiry. Phenomenology, however, is not subjectivistic in a psychological or mentalistic sense. The subject matter of phenomenology is not the realm of psychological ideas affirmed by Locke or Berkeley, but rather the ideal meanings and universal relations with which the ego is confronted in its experience. Husserl vigorously attacked the "psychologism" prevalent among many of his contemporaries, including Stumpf and Lipps; he opposed the attempted reduction of logic to psychology. Husserl insists on the autonomy of rational inquiry into the ideal relational factors in experience. Phenomenology is philosophical science prior to and independent of psychology, yet it does not preclude legitimate psychological investigation. Husserl's polemic against psychologism is directed only against the presumptuous claims of psychology to supersede logical and phenomenological inquiries—not against psychology as a special, factual science.

An essential feature of the phenomenological method is its technique of "bracketing" or "elimination" of the factual dimension of our experience, in order to focus attention on its essential, ideal aspect—the proper subject matter of philosophical inquiry. The phenomenologist is not concerned with particular facts as such, but with the ideal essences which shine through the particulars. Husserl frequently uses the expression *Epoche* (suspension of judgment) to refer to the purification of experience of its factuality; the characteristic phenomenological attitude involves an initial suspension of judgment regarding the existence—whether physical or psychical—of the presentations of consciousness. The phenomenological bracketing or elimination of existence is a methodological attitude which must be preserved throughout to insure investigation of the essential constitution of experience. Mathematics affords a typical example of the sustained employment of the phenomenological technique; pure mathematics systematically "brackets" the factual and existential aspects of our experience of space and quantity and focuses attention exclusively on ideal relations. Phenomenology, like mathematics, says Husserl, is "the science of pure possibilities [which] must everywhere precede the science of real facts." [1]

Phenomenological analysis and description is conversant with the ideal entities with which we are confronted after we have bracketed or eliminated factuality. The question suggests itself whether these ideal objects of phenomenological inquiry are Platonic universals. Husserl's reply is in the negative: he refuses to commit himself to Platonic realism by entifying or hypostatizing these idealities. Instead, like Meinong, he invokes the theory of intentional reference in his interpretation of the objects of phenomenological study. Intentionality (*Intentionalität*) is an intrinsic trait of the subjective processes of consciousness whereby they refer to objects; the objects of phenomenological inquiry are intentional objects. The phenomenologist is not committed to assigning to these objects any ontological status beyond the mere fact that they are envisaged. From the point of view of phenomenology, the important thing is not the status of ideal objects but the fact that such objects may be investigated in their interrelations; and that the results of such descriptive analysis are coercive and communicable. They then possess the only kind of objectivity which is necessary or desirable for the purposes of genuine knowledge. Husserl and his followers carried through

---

[1] Author's Preface to *Ideas: General Introduction to Pure Phenomenology*, p. 13.

many detailed and significant phenomenological investigations, most of which are too technical to be reproduced here. The vitality of the phenomenological movement is attested by its development in Germany by Scheler, Geiger, Heidegger and others, and its ability to survive transplantation to English and American soil.

Philosophie der Arithmetic, 1891; *Logische Untersuchungen,* 1900-01, revised edition, 1913-21; *Ideen zu einer reinen Phänomenologie,* 1913 (English trans. by W. R. Boyce Gibson, entitled *Ideas,* 1931, contains a preface by Husserl); *Formale und Transzendentale Logik,* 1929; *Meditations Cartésiennes,* 1932; *Erfahrung und Urteil,* 1939. "Phenomenology" in *Encyclopaedia Britannica,* 14th ed., 1927.

See E. P. Welch, *The Philosophy of Edmund Husserl,* 1941, which contains a good bibliography; Marvin Farber, article on "Phenomenology" in *Twentieth Century Philosophy* (ed. by D. D. Runes), 1943; article on "Phenomenology" in *The Dictionary of Philosophy* (ed. by D. D. Runes), 1942; Marvin Farber, *The Foundations of Phenomenology,* 1943; *Philosophical Essays in Memory of E. Husserl* (ed. by Marvin Farber), 1943; and the journal, *Philosophy and Phenomenological Research.*

81. Recent British Realism

G. E. Moore. English realism owes its inception largely to a vigorous and highly original article by the Cambridge philosopher G. E. Moore (1873-   ) entitled "Refutation of Idealism," which appeared in 1903 in the British philosophical journal, *Mind.* (The article is included in Moore's *Philosophical Studies.*) In this paper Moore, following the German phenomenologist Meinong, distinguishes between the *act* of awareness and the *object* of which we are aware, and in terms of this distinction formulates a penetrating refutation of idealism of the Berkeleian type, and also outlines his own realistic epistemology. He claims that Berkeley, in failing to distinguish sharply between the act of knowing and the object known, erroneously concludes that objects exist only in so far as they are known. In arguing that any object of knowledge, for example the sensation of blue, exists only in being perceived, Berkeley is guilty of a confusion between the sensation as a conscious act of sensing and sensation as the object sensed. The sensing of blue is, to be sure, a conscious or mental act which exists only when we are conscious, but the blue which is sensed is an "object" of sensation which may very well exist unsensed and unperceived. "We have then in every sensation," says Moore, "two distinct elements, one which I call consciousness, and the other which I call the object of consciousness." [2] The plausibility

[2] *Philosophical Studies,* p. 17.

of Berkeley's identification of *esse* and *percipi* as applied to sensations arises from the ambiguity of the term sensation, which refers both to the act of sensing and to the object sensed. The act of sensing is often overlooked in introspection because it is "diaphanous" or transparent; it is easy to inspect the blue but difficult to introspect the sensing of blue. If we consider the existence of blue to be something distinct from the existence of the sensation or consciousness of blue, "we can and must conceive that blue might exist and yet the sensation of blue not exist." [3] Blue as an object of sensation may exist unsensed; its *esse* is not *percipi*. Moore readily admits that in refuting the essential and necessary argument for Berkeley's and other forms of idealism by differentiating between the conscious sensation and its object, he has not refuted idealism; the idealistic position may quite possibly be correct even though its basic argument is fallacious. But Moore's refutation of the *esse est percipi* argument demolishes the chief underpinnings of the idealistic position advanced by Berkeley and repeated with variations by Fichte, Schopenhauer, Bradley, Royce and others in the idealistic tradition. This negative achievement of Moore's refutation cleared the way for his own constructive realism and gave impetus to the entire movement of British and American Realism.

Realism as a constructive epistemological position asserts that the object of knowledge is distinct from and independent of the act of awareness; the object of awareness, "when we are aware of it, is precisely what it would be, if we were not aware." [4] Moore's constructive realism as applied to sense perception is clearly formulated in a paper on the "Status of Sense-data" which appeared in 1914. In this essay he raises the question as to whether sense data—or, as he prefers to call them, "sensibles"—"ever exist at times when they are not being experienced at all." [5] He replies that there is reason to believe that a certain class of sensibles—namely, those which would be experienced in an ordinary waking experience, in contrast to after-images, memory and imagination of a sensory kind, dreams and hallucinations, etc. —may in fact exist under conditions in which they are not present to any percipient.[6] "A vast number of sensibles exist at any moment, which are not being experienced at all, but [they are] only sensibles of a strictly limited class, namely, sensibles which would be experienced *in a sensation proper*, if a body, having a certain constitution, were in a position in which it is not,

---

[3] *Ibid.*, p. 19.
[4] *Ibid.*, p. 29.
[5] *Ibid.*, p. 180.
[6] *Ibid.*, p. 181.

under the given physical condition." [7] This is a clear and explicit statement of the realistic thesis as applied to an important though restricted class of objects—namely, the colors, sounds, tastes, odors and other data of ordinary sense perception.

Moore proceeds next to the puzzling question as to how sensibles or sense data are related to physical objects. By physical object he means such a thing as a coin, which is seen as circular when viewed from above and as elliptical in other perspectives, and is considered to have an interior and an outer side. Moore takes the position that whereas the sensibles or sense data by means of which the coin is perceived, are capable of existing unsensed, the physical object has no such independent status. The coin as a physical object exists unperceived only in the sense that *"if* certain conditions are fulfilled, I or any other person, *should* directly apprehend certain other sensibles." [8] "It is obvious that, on this view, though we shall still be allowed to say that the coins *existed* before I saw them, are circular, etc., all these expressions, if they are to be true, will have to be understood in a Pickwickian sense." [9] In interpreting propositions about physical objects in this hypothetical, "Pickwickian" fashion, Moore has considerably weakened his initial realism as applied to sense data. His realism is, indeed, almost the exact reverse of Locke's position, which combined a realism of physical objects with a subjectivism of sense qualities. Moore's realism of physical objects is, as he suggests in another essay, a reaffirmation of the type of view held by Mill when he describes matter as "a permanent possibility of perception." [10]

Principia Ethica, 2nd ed., 1922; *Ethics*, 1912; *Philosophical Studies*, 1922 (includes "The Refutation of Idealism").

Bertrand Russell. The neorealism of Bertrand Russell (1872-   ) shows the influence of G. E. Moore's realistic theories of sense data and physical objects, and also of the logical realism of Meinong's theory of objects. In the course of his long philosophical career Russell's position has undergone many changes, but realism of some sort is a persistent theme of all his writings, from *The Problems of Philosophy* (1911), to *Human Knowledge* (1948). In the theory of perception advanced in *The Problems of Philosophy*, he distinguishes, as did Moore, between the "sensation" as a conscious experience and the sense data of which we are aware: "Thus, whenever we see a

[7] *Ibid.*, p. 182.
[8] *Ibid.*, p. 189.
[9] *Ibid.*, p. 190.
[10] *Ibid.*, p. 224.

colour, we have a sensation *of* the colour, but the colour itself is a sense-datum, not a sensation." But whereas Moore interpreted sense data as public objects capable of existing unsensed, Russell describes them as private, since there is only one person to whom they can be immediately present,[11] and he regarded them as capable of existing only when sensed. "The colour," says Russell, "ceases to exist if I shut my eyes, the sensation of hardness ceases to exist if I remove my hand from contact with the table . . ."[12] Russell, unlike Moore, accepts the idealistic argument as regards the sense data; their *esse* is *percipi.* "Berkeley was right in treating the sense-data which constitute our perception of the tree as more or less subjective, in the sense that they depend upon us as much as upon the tree, and would not exist if the tree were not being perceived."[13] But here his agreement with Berkeley ends, for the subjective sense data mediate our knowledge of the physical object, which enjoys a realistic status independent of the act of perception. What, then, is the ground for accepting physical objects in addition to the sense data? Russell admits that we can never prove the existence of a physical object behind our sense data, yet he accepts physical realism as the simplest hypothesis to account for the facts of ordinary sense perception. "Every principle of simplicity urges us to adopt the natural view, that there really are objects other than ourselves and our sense-data which have an existence not dependent on our perceiving them."[14]

In *The Problems of Philosophy*, Russell extends his realism beyond physical objects to universals, thus combining physical and logical realism. He advances a theory of universals akin to Plato's theory of forms or ideas, by asserting the extramental reality of qualitative universals like whiteness and relational universals like equality to account for our a priori knowledge. Universals are real entities which exist neither in the mental nor in the physical worlds, and yet have a subsistent or logical status. Russell claimed that the mind has a direct acquaintance with or intuition of universals, and that such intuition affords the basis of our rational knowledge of a priori truths. "All a priori knowledge deals exclusively with the relations of universals."[15] For example, the arithmetical proposition "two and two are four" is a truth regarding the relation of equality between the universal "4" and the complex of universals, "the sum of two and two." Russell's logical realism

[11] *The Problems of Philosophy*, pp. 32, 213.
[12] *Ibid.*, p. 42.
[13] *Ibid.*, p. 64.
[14] *Ibid.*, p. 37.
[15] *Ibid.*, p. 162.

rests, in his opinion, on an intuitive basis, and hence is more firmly grounded than his physical realism, which he advanced solely as an hypothesis.

In *Our Knowledge of the External World,* published in 1914, which also appears under the title, *Scientific Method in Philosophy,* Russell modifies in several important respects the epistemological realism of *The Problems of Philosophy.* He retains his earlier analysis of perceptual knowledge into three factors: (1) "consciousness" or the act of mental awareness, (2) the "sense-data" or "sensible objects" of which we are aware, and (3) the perceptual object known through the mediation of the sense data. The "sensible object" is not a *thing* such as a table, but the color patch or feeling of which I am momentarily aware when I look at or touch the table. Russell is no longer as confident as he was in his earlier work that the hypothesis of an independent physical object is the simplest and consequently the true and correct view; he now regards the perceptual object, e.g., the perceived table, as nothing but a "logical construction" based on the different appearances of the table to a given observer or to different observers at the same or different times: "all the aspects of a thing are real, whereas the thing is a mere logical construction." The only claim he makes for his hypothetical construction is that "there are no grounds *against* the truth of this belief, but we have not derived any positive grounds in its favor."[16] Russell's theory that the physical object is a logical construction has obvious affinities with Poincaré's conventionalism.

In *The Analysis of Mind,* published in 1921, Russell develops, under the influence of American new realism, an epistemological position in which the pure act of consciousness of his two earlier works is entirely eliminated and the "sense-data" or "sensible objects"—now frequently referred to as "sensations"—are treated as real aspects or perspectives, constituting both mental and physical objects. The "sensations" are neutral entities—i.e., they are neither physical nor mental—which, as part of one class or collection, constitute physical objects and as belonging to another collection constitute minds. "Sensations," he says, "are what is common to the mental and the physical worlds; they may be defined as the point of intersection of mind and matter."[17] The theory summarized in the above quotation may be described as neutral monism; the ultimate constituents of reality are all of one kind (monism) and are neither mental nor physical (neutralism). Individual minds are certain selections of neutral entities; material objects are other selections. Knowledge occurs when there is an overlapping or

[16] *Our Knowledge of the External World,* p. 99.
[17] *The Analysis of Mind,* p. 144.

partial identity of a mind and a material object. Thus in perception, certain neutral perspectives constituent of the physical object are also constituents of my biography; in the one context they may be called "mental" and in the other "physical." There are "two ways of grouping particulars, one into 'things' or 'pieces of matter,' the other into series of 'perspectives,' each series being what may be called a 'biography.'"[18] For example, "when I look at a star, my sensation is: (1) A member of the group of particulars which is the star, and which is associated with the place where the star is; (2) A member of the group of particulars which is my biography and which is associated with the place where I am."[19] The epistemological position associated with Russell's neutral monism is completely realistic, in that a given perspective which is now part of my biography continues to exist as a perspective of a physical object, even when unexperienced by me or by any other observer.

The version of realism presented by Russell in *An Inquiry into Meaning and Truth* (1940), contains scarcely a trace of the perspective realism of *The Analysis of Mind;* it is much closer to the representational realism of his earliest epistemological writings. His discussion still focuses attention on the problem concerning the relation between our "perceptive experience," for example, "seeing the sun" or "seeing a cat," and the correlative physical objects. "We have a number of experiences which we call 'seeing the sun'; there is also, according to astronomy, a large lump of hot matter which *is* the sun. What is the relation of this lump to one of the occurrences called 'seeing the sun'?"[20] There is a causal relation between the sun and "seeing the sun," and there is presumably also a degree of resemblance between the two: "The sun *looks* round in my visual space and *is* round in physical space."[21] The existence of a physical object causing and perhaps resembling my perceptive experience, is grounded in inductive inference. "We have therefore grounds for holding . . . that when I 'see a cat' there probably is a cat. We cannot go beyond 'probably,' since we know that people sometimes see cats that are not there, for instance in dreams."[22] In his recent discussion of perceptual knowledge in *Human Knowledge* (1948), Russell again addresses himself to the problem: How and to what extent can percepts be a source of our knowledge of physical objects? And again he replies that it is by probable causal inference in accordance with the laws of physics

---

[18] *Ibid.,* p. 124.
[19] *Ibid.,* pp. 129-30.
[20] *An Inquiry into Meaning and Truth,* p. 146.
[21] *Ibid.,* p. 147.
[22] *Ibid.,* p. 151.

that it is possible to proceed from the percept as effect to the physical object as cause; but he concedes that "the relation of a percept to the physical object which is supposed to be perceived is vague, approximate, and somewhat indefinite." [23] "There is no *precise* sense in which we can be said to perceive physical objects." [24] Throughout the long course of his philosophical development, Russell has been absorbed in the problem of the relation of perceptual experience to the physical object, and despite radical shifts in his epistemological position, he has at no time abandoned his fundamental physical realism; in all his writings, he emphatically claims that the physical object, however it may be conceived, continues to exist when unperceived.

The Principles of Mathematics, 1903, 1938; Principia Mathematica, 1910-13; Philosophical Essays, 1910; The Problems of Philosophy, 1911; Scientific Method in Philosophy, 1914 (also published under the title, Our Knowledge of the External World, 1914); Mysticism and Logic, 1918; Introduction to Mathematical Philosophy, 1919; The Analysis of Mind, 1921; The Analysis of Matter, 1927; Philosophy, 1927; Sceptical Essays, 1928; What I Believe, 1929; The Scientific Outlook, 1931; Religion and Science, 1935; An Inquiry into Meaning and Truth, 1940; Philosophy and Politics, 1947; Human Knowledge, 1948; Authority and the Individual, 1949.

P. A. Schilpp, ed., The Philosophy of Bertrand Russell, Vol. V, in The Library of Living Philosophers, 1941.

Samuel Alexander. British realism attained its most systematic expression in the writings of Samuel Alexander and Alfred North Whitehead, both of whom formulated epistemological realism in the context of a naturalistic metaphysics—a naturalism which, however, revolts against the mechanism of traditional materialism. Alexander's realistic and naturalistic philosophy is contained in a single work of two volumes, *Space, Time and Deity*, published in 1920. In this work Alexander achieved a remarkable philosophical synthesis, the main components of which are: (1) a metaphysical theory of space and time which has close affinities with the physical theory of relativity; (2) a doctrine of emergent evolution, allied to Bergson's creative evolutionism; (3) a perspectivism, akin to the direct realism of Moore, Russell, and the American New Realists; (4) an empirical theory of knowledge in the British tradition, which yet finds a place for the non-empirical or a priori; and (5) a theory of value, of human freedom and of Deity which has much in common with the main insights of the British school of absolute idealism represented by Bradley and Bosanquet.

We may conveniently deal with Alexander's theory of knowledge at the

[23] *Ibid.*, p. 207.
[24] *Loc. cit.*

beginning of our account of his philosophy, although he repudiates the primacy of epistemology in these words: "The problem of knowledge, the subject-matter of epistemology, is nothing but a chapter, though an important one, in the wider science of metaphysics, and not its indispensable foundation." [25] Though epistemology is not the indispensable preliminary to metaphysics, it is an important part of it and Alexander tells us that in the course of his own mental history epistemology came first.

Alexander distinguishes between two forms of knowledge which he calls "enjoyment" and "contemplation": "enjoyment" is the mind's direct awareness of itself, the mind's living through its own activity; "contemplation" is the mind's apprehension of an object other than itself. "The mind enjoys itself and contemplates its objects." [26] The enjoyment and the contemplation are distinguishable but inseparable aspects of the mind's knowledge of objects; the mind "enjoys" itself in the process of contemplating a foreign object. Alexander presumably accepts "enjoyment" as an ultimate and irreducible mode of self-apprehension; the mind is capable of enjoying itself because it *is* itself. Contemplation is a relation of togetherness between the act of enjoyment and the contemplated object. This togetherness, or "compresence," as Alexander calls it, is not a unique cognitive relation, but is merely an instance of the pervasive spatio-temporal relation of togetherness. Mind occupies for Alexander no privileged position in the universe; it has no special dignity or pre-eminence. "Minds are but the most gifted members known to us in a democracy of things. In respect of being or reality all existences are on an equal footing." [27]

Sense perception is basic for Alexander's theory of knowledge, since "all our experience whether enjoyed or contemplated is provoked through the sense-organs." [28] Sense perception is more complex than it appears on the surface. The primary qualities of matter are determinations of the real objects in their spatio-temporal character and are directly apprehended by intuition. The secondary qualities are apprehended by a sensuous act which discloses "the quality of the sensum, blue or hot or sweet or hard." [29] The intuition of the primary qualities and the sensing of the secondary qualities are fused in a unitary act of perception.

Alexander's metaphysics is naturalistic but not materialistic, since the ultimate metaphysical reality, the universal matrix which comprehends all

[25] *Space, Time and Deity*, Vol. I, p. 7.
[26] *Ibid.*, Vol. I, p. 12.
[27] *Ibid.*, Vol. I, p. 6.
[28] *Ibid.*, Vol. II, p. 143.
[29] *Ibid.*, Vol. II, p. 160.

things, is not matter but an infinite and continuous Space-Time. Alexander insists on the interdependence, or rather the inseparability, of space and time, and attempts to demonstrate that the features of one are dependent upon the character of the other: he argues that "the reason Space has three dimensions is that Time is successive, irreversible and uniform in direction." [30] He claims that by metaphysical argument he has reached the same conception of a four-dimensional space-time continuum attained mathematically by Minkowski in 1908 and incorporated by Einstein in the theory of relativity. In terms of his conception of Space-Time as "an infinite continuum of pure events or point-instants," he elaborates a theory of perspectives. A perspective is described as "a section of Space-Time considered with reference to the point-instant which is taken as the center of reference." [31] "The perspectives of Space-Time are analogous to the ordinary perspectives of a solid body." The system of perspectives of space-time underlies and conditions knowledge. When a mind "enjoys" a certain region of space-time, it is enabled to "contemplate" other regions spatially and temporally remote because of the perspectives existing at every center of reference. Thus perception, memory, and the other cognitive processes of mind have their basis in the original perspectival structure of reality. Alexander's metaphysical naturalism provides the foundation for his realistic epistemology, in accordance with which knowledge is construed as a natural event in space-time, differing solely from non-cognitive events in the presence of a mind.

Space-time is an infinite, continuous matrix, the elements of which are point-instants or bare events. The whole of space-time and every part or region of it are characterized by pervasive features or categories. The categories of identity, diversity, existence, relation, substance, causality, quantity, intensity, and motion are fundamental properties of space-time and do not, as Kant had supposed, owe their necessity and universality to mind. They are empirically discoverable. Nevertheless, since they are universal and essential constituents of whatever may be experienced, they may also be considered a priori or non-empirical characters of things. Alexander accordingly believes that he has achieved a validation of the philosophical categories in terms of a realistic and naturalistic theory of reality, without resorting to the idealistic and transcendental paraphernalia of Kant's deduction of the categories. Alexander has reversed the Kantian revolution in philosophy by rejecting Kant's claim that the mind, utilizing the categories, prescribes laws

[30] *Ibid.*, Vol. I, p. 57.
[31] *Ibid.*, Vol. I, p. 68.

to nature. On the contrary, the categories are applicable to the mind because they are primarily features of nature, and mind is a natural occurrence.

The doctrine of emergent evolution is incorporated into Alexander's naturalism; space-time is the universal matrix within which the higher qualitative levels of reality emerge. Following the example of Lloyd Morgan, Alexander considers mind "an 'emergent' from life, and life an emergent from a lower physico-chemical level of existence." [32] The term "emergent" as applied to mind serves to designate the novelty possessed by mind when considered in relation to underlying neural and physico-chemical processes. When physico-chemical processes attain a certain degree of complexity of organization, the quality of life emerges and when, in turn, neural processes in living organisms attain a certain level of complexity, consciousness or mind appears as a novel emergent. Values, likewise, are emergents; they arise from the amalgamation of objects and the mind's appreciation of them. "The tertiary qualities, truth and goodness and beauty, though they differ from the secondary and primary ones in being creations of the mind, are not the less real. They belong strictly to an amalgamation or union of the object with the mind." [33] Deity is the emergent quality one degree higher than mind: "What that quality is we cannot know; for we can neither enjoy nor still less contemplate it. That the universe is pregnant with such a quality we are speculatively assured." [34] God is not, as traditionally conceived, the first-cause and creator, but the last emergent in the series of emergents.

Moral Order and Progress, 1891; *The Basis of Realism*, 1919; *Space, Time and Deity*, 2 vols., 1920; *Artistic Creation and Cosmic Creation*, 1927; *Spinoza and Time*, 1927; *Spinoza*, 1933; *Philosophical and Literary Pieces*, 1939.

A. F. Liddell, *Alexander's Space, Time and Deity*, 1925; P. Devaux, *Le système d'Alexander*, 1929.

A. N. Whitehead. The philosophy of Alfred North Whitehead (1861-1947) resembles that of Alexander in several important respects: both were inspired by modern developments in relativity physics; both incorporated organic and evolutionary conceptions derived from biology; both, on their epistemological side, are forms of perspective realism, and on their metaphysical side are naturalistic without being materialistic, thus belonging to the contemporary revolt against dualism; finally, both adopt objectivistic interpretations of value and seek to find a place for God in a naturalistic universe.

In Whitehead's theory of knowledge, perception is treated as the basic and typical form of knowledge, and the pattern of knowledge exemplified

[32] *Ibid.*, Vol. II, p. 14.
[33] *Ibid.*, Vol. I, p. 244.
[34] *Ibid.*, Vol. II, p. 347.

in perception recurs at all levels from the most rudimentary sense experience to the most elaborate scientific and cosmological theories. The term perception in ordinary usage designates conscious, cognitive apprehension of objects. Whitehead feels the need of a term more general than the terms perception and apprehension to designate a process of *taking account of* the essential character of an object, and suggests the term "prehension," which omits the prefix from "apprehension." "I will use the word *prehension* for *incognitive* apprehension: by that I mean apprehension which may or may not be cognitive." [35] Whitehead's use of the term prehension corresponds closely to Alexander's "compresence" or "togetherness" which underlies the cognitive process of "contemplation." Cognition for both Whitehead and Alexander has lost the pre-eminence assigned to it by the idealists, and is interpreted as a specification of a more general non-cognitive relation which pervades the whole of nature. "The actual world," says Whitehead, "is a manifold of prehensions. . . . Perception is simply the cognition of prehensive unification; or more shortly perception is cognition of prehension." [36] The historical prototype of Whitehead's theory of prehensions is Leibniz's theory of the mirroring, by each monad of the universe from its unique perspective; indeed, Leibniz's theory of small, unconscious perceptions (*petites perceptions*), is clearly a foreshadowing of Whitehead's non-cognitive, or rather pre-cognitive, prehensions.

The prehensive situation which underlies cognitive perception is highly complex, and in his principal work, *Process and Reality,* 1929, Whitehead analyzes its constitution into factors of which the following are the most important: (1) "subject," (2) the "initial data," and (3) the "objective datum." [37] This analysis may be illustrated at the cognitive level by the audition of a sound; and "to avoid unnecessary complexity, let the sound be one definite note." [38] The auditor is the subject which "feels," or hears the sound; the sound as immediately heard is the initial datum which is felt; the sound considered as part of the complex ordered environment composed of this and other actual entities, is the objective datum. This triadic analysis is not to be construed as a theory of representational perception, for the "initial datum" and the "objective datum" are not numerically distinct entities, but coalesce completely. "The actual entity which is the initial datum is the actual entity perceived, the objective datum is the 'perspective'

[35] *Science and the Modern World,* 1925, p. 101.
[36] *Ibid.,* p. 104.
[37] Cf. *Process and Reality,* pp. 337 ff.
[38] *Ibid.,* p. 357.

under which that actual entity is perceived, and the subject of the simple physical feeling is the perceiver." [39]

Though perception was central in his theory of knowledge, Whitehead was acutely aware of the limitations inherent in the scope of sense perception, and of the dangers to epistemology and to systematic metaphysics resulting from "the tacit identification of perception with sense perception." [40] He eloquently attacks the preoccupation with bare sense data which characterizes the British epistemology which derives from Hume. "Gaze at a patch of red. In itself as an object, and apart from other factors of concern, this patch of red, as the mere object of that present act of perception, is silent as to the past or future . . . No material for the interpretation of sensa is provided by the sensa themselves, as they stand starkly, barely present and immediate." [41] This indictment of sensationalism in all its forms—and in particular of the British and American sense datum epistemologies stemming from Hume, is one of Whitehead's most significant contributions to epistemology; it marks a radical reversal of trend within the British empirical tradition. To be sure, the British idealists, Green, Bradley and Bosanquet had attacked the atomicity of the prevailing British tradition in epistemology, but their attack largely failed to demolish psychological atomism because it was supported by an absolutistic metaphysics uncongenial to the British mind. In both Whitehead and Alexander, the criticism of atomistic sensationalism proceeds from an empirical, naturalistic, and realistic philosophy and therefore carries greater conviction for the British mind. Whitehead's criticism of the sense-datum theory rests on a principle of empirical concreteness which repudiates false abstractions. The sense-datum theory is guilty of excessive abstraction; it commits what he calls "the fallacy of misplaced concreteness." This fallacy consists in treating an abstraction from a concrete experience as if it were a concrete thing—it thus "misplaces" concreteness. Whitehead is far from asserting that abstractions as such are illegitimate— indeed, he devotes much attention to the legitimate rôle of abstraction in logic, mathematics and in the physical sciences:

The advantage of confining attention to a definite group of abstractions, is that you confine your thoughts to clear-cut definite things, with clear-cut definite relations. . . . Furthermore if the abstractions are well-founded, that is to say, if they do not abstract from everything that is important in experience, the scientific thought which confines itself to these abstractions will arrive at a variety of important truths relating to our experience of nature. . . . The disadvantage of exclusive attention to a group of abstrac-

---

[39] *Ibid.*, p. 361.
[40] *Adventures in Ideas*, p. 231.
[41] *Ibid.*, p. 232.

tions, however well-founded, is that, by the nature of the case, you have abstracted from the remainder of things.[42]

British empiricism from Hume to Moore and Russell has frequently treated sense data—isolated and abstracted from concrete perceptual experience— as real constituents of perceptual cognition; Whitehead's prehensions, which bring the remote in space and time into the unity of the present experience, avoid this false abstractionism.

Whitehead's theory of prehensions is not restricted to perception; he readily assimilates to the theory of prehensions our primary memories of the immediate past: "In human experience, the most compelling example of non-sensuous perception is our knowledge of our own immediate past . . . Roughly speaking, it is that portion of our past lying between a tenth of a second and a half a second ago . . . It is gone and yet it is here . . ."[43] The future is also, according to Whitehead, "immanent in the present" in so far as the present stands in essential relationship to what is to come. The influence of Bergson is apparent in Whitehead's contention that the present prehends both past and future.

Whitehead's metaphysics, which he has described as "organic mechanism" or "philosophy of organism," is a form of naturalism, but it contrasts with traditional materialistic naturalism. Traditional naturalism or "scientific materialism," as Whitehead prefers to call it, describes nature as mechanical interaction of mass particles having definite locations in space and time. Scientific materialism, says Whitehead, "presupposes the ultimate fact of an irreducible brute matter, or material, spread through space . . ."[44] The essential property ascribed to matter by scientific materialism is its "simple location" in space and time; every material object is assumed to occupy a determinate bounded space and to persist through a well-defined time interval. The postulation of simply located material substances is, according to Whitehead, the result of a false and misleading intellectual abstraction; it is an instance of what he calls "the fallacy of misplaced concreteness," the mistaking of an abstraction for a concrete reality. Whitehead challenges the basic assumptions of scientific materialism, and in so doing offers a drastic criticism of the modern cosmological scheme which has dominated modern thought since the time of Galileo, Descartes, and Newton. Whitehead proposes, as an alternative to the traditional cosmology, a theory which conceives nature as an organic, structured system of interpenetrating "events," "occasions,"

[42] *Science and the Modern World*, p. 85.
[43] *Adventures in Ideas*, pp. 232 ff.
[44] *Science and the Modern World*, p. 25.

or "actual entities." An event is a spatio-temporal occurrence which enters into transactions with other events. The real world is a process consisting of the totality of such actual entities or patterned events; "the actual world is in process and the process . . . is the becoming of actual entities." [45] All actual entities interpenetrate, and in their "togetherness" constitute reality as process. The events constitutive of reality are bound together by internal relations, whereby the events "prehend" one another. The prehensive relations which obtain among all actual events provide the metaphysical substructure of Whitehead's realistic epistemology. Prehension is a fundamental relation binding all events together, and, when one of the terms of this prehensive relation is a conscious mind, prehension rises to the level of cognitive apprehension. Cognitive apprehension is, for Whitehead, a special instance of the prehensive relation which binds all actual events together. Whitehead's metaphysics deprives the cognitive relation of the pre-eminence assigned it by idealistic philosophies; mind, with its cognitive acts, far from being constitutive of reality, is for Whitehead merely one among other events, and the cognitive relation is an instance of the prehensive relation which pervades all reality. Whitehead's position is a complete reversal of the Kantian thesis that knowledge is constitutive of reality: "for Kant the process whereby there is experience is a process from subjectivity to apparent objectivity. The philosophy of organism inverts this analysis, and explains the process as proceeding from objectivity to subjectivity. . . ." [46] Kant's "Copernican revolution" has been superseded by Whitehead's counter revolution: Kant's critical idealism inverted the realism of Locke and Descartes, and Whitehead's naturalistic realism has, in turn, inverted Kantian idealism.

Whitehead's theory of the real world as a system of actual entities does not exhaust his metaphysics; his metaphysical scheme also embraces a theory of "essences" or "eternal objects." "Every scheme for the analysis of nature has to face these two facts, *change* and *endurance*. There is yet a third fact to be faced by it, *eternality*." [47] The theory of actual entities suffices for the explanation of the phenomena of change and endurance, but for the explanation of eternality, Whitehead finds it necessary to broaden the base of his metaphysical scheme by introducing "eternal objects." Eternal objects are identically recurrent entities such as colors. "A colour is eternal. It haunts time like a spirit. It comes and it goes. But when it comes it is the same colour." [48] A mountain, in contrast, is an actual entity; it persists and endures;

[45] *Process and Reality*, p. 33.
[46] *Process and Reality*, p. 236.
[47] *Science and the Modern World*, p. 126.
[48] *Loc. cit.*

or if it is worn away, it is gone—perhaps to be replaced by a new mountain. Whitehead's distinction between eternal objects and actual entities closely parallels the traditional realistic distinction between universals and particulars. Eternal objects, as Whitehead recognized, are akin to Platonic forms; like Platonic forms, they enter into actual entities or particulars. Eternal objects possess the potentiality of "ingression" into the becoming of actual entities. The term "ingression" refers to the peculiar mode in which an eternal object is realized in a particular actual entity, whereby it contributes to the definiteness of that actual entity.[49]

In addition to the reality of actual entities and eternal objects, Whitehead's cosmological scheme posits God as the rational principle responsible for the selection of eternal objects for ingression in the world of actual entities. According to this conception, "God . . . is considered as the outcome of creativity, as the foundation of order, and as the goal towards novelty."[50] Although God functions as a principle of order and rationality in the universe, "His existence is the ultimate irrationality . . . No reason can be given for the nature of God, because that nature is the ground of rationality."[51]

Principles of Natural Knowledge, 1919; *The Concept of Nature*, 1920; *Process and Reality*, 1929; *Science and the Modern World*, 1925; *Adventures in Ideas*, 1933; *Dialogues*, as recorded by L. Price, 1954.

D. N. Emmet, *Whitehead's Philosophy of Organism*, 1932; N. P. Stallknecht, ed., *Studies in the Philosophy of Creation*, 1934; P. A. Schilpp, ed., *The Philosophy of Alfred North Whitehead*, 1941; F. Casselin, *La philosophie organique de Whitehead*, 1950; F. S. C. Northrup, *Alfred North Whitehead: An Anthology*, 1953.

82. RECENT AMERICAN REALISM

"New" Realism. A realistic reaction against idealism has arisen in the United States which regards science as the most certain body of knowledge and looks upon the divorce of philosophy from science as disastrous for philosophy. In accordance with what it believes to be the spirit of the scientific method, this school rejects the idealistic theory that relations are internal or organic, and instead conceives them as not affecting the nature of the things or terms related, that is, as external. The school, therefore, emphasizes analysis —the very method of knowledge which Hegel and his followers, no less than the pragmatists and intuitionists, had repudiated as an inadequate

---

[49] Cf. *Process and Reality*, p. 34.
[50] *Process and Reality*, p. 135.
[51] *Science and the Modern World*, p. 257.

instrument of truth—and finds itself driven to pluralism rather than to monism.

American new realism is a school which had its beginning in "The Program and First Platform of Six Realists," which appeared in *The Journal of Philosophy* in 1910, and in a cooperative volume, *The New Realism,* by the same authors, E. B. Holt, W. T. Marvin, W. P. Montague, R. B. Perry, W. B. Pitkin and E. G. Spaulding. The new realism, on its negative side, attacks the Berkeleian argument along lines similar to Moore's refutation of idealism. W. P. Montague casts the principal Berkeleian argument in syllogistic form as follows: *"Ideas are incapable of existing apart from a mind. Physical objects in so far as they are perceived or known at all are certainly 'ideas.' All physical objects are, therefore, incapable of existing apart from a mind,"* and then diagnoses the Berkeleian fallacy as an ambiguous use of the term "idea," which "is used in the major premise to denote an act or process of perceiving, while in the minor premise it is used to denote the object of that act, i.e., the thing or content that is perceived." [52] Montague imputes a similar fallacy to the absolute idealism of Bradley, which is guilty of an ambiguous use of the term experience: "The constant use of the one word *experience* to denote an *experiencing* and an *experienced,*" says Montague, "has produced in the mind of the idealist the curious delusion . . . that the objects that we experience can only exist at the moments when they are experienced." [53]

The epistemology of the new realism, on its constructive side, offers an analysis of the knowledge-situation which closely resembles the realism of G. E. Moore. The new realists formulate their main realistic theory in terms of the theory of independence, which is defined by R. B. Perry in his essay entitled "A Realistic Theory of Independence" as non-dependence or absence of dependence with respect to a specified relation. When the notion of independence is applied to the knowledge relation, Perry finds that at least some physical things, logical and mathematical entities and other minds are independent of a knowing consciousness and that they may become objects of consciousness without sacrificing their independence. "Realism," says Montague, "holds that things known may continue to exist unaltered when they are not known, or that things may pass in and out of the cognitive relation without prejudice to their reality, or that the experience of a thing is not correlated with or dependent upon the fact that anybody experiences it, perceives it, conceives it, or is in any way aware of it." [54]

[52] *The New Realism,* p. 258.
[53] *Ibid.,* p. 260.
[54] *Ibid.,* p. 476.

A second characteristic thesis of new realism is epistemological monism—the doctrine that knowledge is presentational, that the object of knowledge is directly given to consciousness. The issue here is between epistemological monism and epistemological dualism—between presentationalism and representationalism. Epistemological dualism is the doctrine that the "object" of knowledge is known only through the mediation of "ideas" or "contents" of knowledge; that content and object of knowledge are two numerically distinct elements in the knowledge situation. Perhaps the most typical historical exponent of dualistic realism is Locke; the world of ideas, according to Locke, contains images, copies, or representations of the real world outside the mind. The new realism in its monistic aspect is a revolt against Locke's dualistic epistemology.

Epistemological monism [says R. B. Perry] means that when things are known they are identical element for element, with the idea or content of the knowing state . . . That which is commonly called the "object" of knowledge merges, according to this view, with the idea, or is the whole thing of which the idea is a part. Thus when one perceives a tulip the idea of the tulip and the real tulip coincide, element for element; they are one in color, shape, size, distance, etc.[55]

Error, illusion and hallucination are crucial phenomena for monistic realism: if all knowledge is immediate and presentational, it is difficult to see how any distinction can be drawn between veridical and non-veridical forms of knowledge, and yet such a distinction is unavoidable. The new realists have not tried to evade the epistemological difficulties raised by the fact of delusive knowledge. E. B. Holt in his essay in *The New Realism*, entitled "The Place of Illusory Experience in a Realistic World," and in his chapter on "Error," in *The Concept of Consciousness* (1914), comes to grips with this problem. We cannot here consider the ingenious devices by which Holt and other monistic realists assimilate delusive cognition to their theory; we observe merely that, for the most part, they have the courage and consistency to ascribe reality of a sort to illusory and hallucinatory objects.

Critical Realism. The theory of representative perception is epistemologically dualistic in that it insists on the numerical duplicity of the sense data directly present to the mind and the real external object. The theory had its historical origin early in the modern period in the causal theories of perception of Descartes and Locke. In both Descartes and Locke the epistemological dualism of representative ideas and of external object was associated with and fostered by a metaphysical dualism of the mental and physical orders; but

[55] *Present Philosophical Tendencies*, p. 126.

this association is not logically necessary and in the present section we shall ignore psycho-physical dualism and be concerned solely with epistemological dualism. Epistemological dualism was advanced in America by a group of critical realists composed of G. Santayana, C. A. Strong, A. K. Rogers, A. O. Lovejoy, R. W. Sellars, J. B. Pratt and Durant Drake. These thinkers differed greatly among themselves in general philosophical orientation and metaphysical allegiance, but in their cooperative volume, *Essays in Critical Realism* (1920), they attacked the monistic tenets of the new realism and agreed on the bare essentials of a dualistic epistemology, which may be summarized as follows: (1) the mind is directly confronted with sense data which constitute the content or vehicle of knowledge; (2) physical objects exist independently of the mind and are known through the mediation of the sense data; (3) material objects are numerically distinct from the data by which they are known.

As in the case of new realism, the several critical realists, instead of continuing their cooperative epistemological inquiries, developed their individual theories frequently along diverging lines. A. O. Lovejoy's (1873-   ) *The Revolt Against Dualism* (1930), and G. Santayana's *Scepticism and Animal Faith* (1923), represent two such divergent developments of the critical realistic epistemology. Lovejoy's work is critical rather than constructive: the early lectures of the volume contain a detailed exposition and criticism of the "objective relativism" of Whitehead and Russell; only in the two concluding lectures does Lovejoy formulate his own epistemology in positive terms. The main tenets of his version of dualistic realism are: (1) The mind is directly aware of "ideas." By "ideas" Lovejoy means "non-physical experienced particulars"; he used the term "idea" in essentially the same sense as did Descartes and Locke. (2) The ideas afford evidence for inference to "an order of existences or events which persist when unperceived" and which are "causally related to our sensa." The external object "cannot be identical with our sensa." [56] "Whatever knowledge we have of real objects is indirect or representative; the datum whereby you know any such object is not identical with the object known." [57] (3) Memory and anticipation are, like perception, indirect or representative modes of apprehension: "In memory and other retrospection there is a conscious and intrinsic reference to a reality other than the content given . . ." [58] "Of the other form of intertemporal cognition, actual or supposed—that is, foreknowledge or expecta-

[56] *The Revolt Against Dualism*, p. 298.
[57] *Op. cit.*, p. 303.
[58] *Op. cit.*, p. 305.

tion—the dualistic implications are, if possible, even more manifest . . ."[59] Lovejoy assimilates all forms of cognition: perception, memory, expectation, and knowledge of other minds to the same representational and realistic pattern.[60]

Writings of New Realists

E. B. Holt and others, *The New Realism*, 1912; E. B. Holt, *The Concept of Consciousness*, 1914; R. B. Perry, *Present Philosophical Tendencies*, 1912; E. G. Spaulding, *The New Rationalism*, 1918; W. P. Montague, *The Ways of Knowing*, 1925.

Writings of Critical Realists

D. Drake and others, *Essays in Critical Realism*, 1925; G. Santayana, *Scepticism and Animal Faith*, 1923; A. O. Lovejoy, *The Revolt Against Dualism*, 1930.

Santayana. George Santayana (1863-1952), poet, novelist and literary critic as well as philosopher, was born in Madrid of Spanish parents and came to the United States in 1872. He was educated at Harvard and taught there until 1912, when he resigned his Harvard professorship and returned to Europe to devote the remainder of his life to study and writing.

Santayana's European ancestry and American upbringing and education are reflected in the dual allegiance of his philosophy to continental European culture and its philosophical traditions and to the typically American movements of thought which prevailed at Harvard. His many-sided philosophical system betrays the European influence of the classical systems of Democritus, Plato, Aristotle, and Lucretius, and the modern systems of Spinoza, Hegel, and Schopenhauer; it also reflects his profound indebtedness to his teachers and colleagues at Harvard, William James and Josiah Royce.

Santayana's philosophical position defies assimilation to a single school, movement or type of philosophy, or reduction to any simple philosophical formula; it is a many-sided system in which may be discerned such diverse philosophical themes as naturalism, realism, essentialism (theory of essences or universals), idealism, and romanticism. Naturalism, which he describes as "that vulgar belief in material things about us" is, however, the most basic and pervasive theme of his philosophy.

The Sense of Beauty (1896); *The Life of Reason, or the Phases of Human Progress* (1905-06); *Three Philosophical Poets: Lucretius, Dante, and Goethe* (1910); *Winds of*

---

[59] *Op. cit.*, p. 308.

[60] The foregoing account of new and critical realism incorporates portions of the chapter entitled "Recent Epistemological Schools," contributed by Ledger Wood to *A History of Philosophical Systems*, 1950, edited by Vergilius Ferm. It is included here with the kind permission of Dr. D. D. Runes, President of the Philosophical Library.

Doctrine (1913); *Egotism in German Philosophy* (1916; rev. ed., 1940); *Character and Opinion in the United States* (1920); *Soliloquies in England* (1922); *Scepticism and Animal Faith* (1923); *Dialogues in Limbo* (1926); *Platonism and the Spiritual Life* (1927); *Realms of Being,* 4 vol. (1927-40); *Obiter Scripta* (1936); *Dominations and Powers* (1951).

G. W. Howgate, *George Santayana,* 1938; P. A. Schilpp, ed., *The Philosophy of George Santayana,* 1940; R. Butler, *The Mind of Santayana,* 1955; W. E. Arnett, *Santayana and the Sense of Beauty,* 1956; L. Wood, article on "George Santayana," *Encyclopædia Britannica,* 14th edition, 1956.

The life of reason. The earliest version of Santayana's many-sided philosophy is presented in his work, *The Life of Reason,* consisting of five volumes: *Reason in Common Sense, Reason in Society, Reason in Religion, Reason in Art,* and *Reason in Science.* This work, which Santayana describes as "a presumptive biography of the human intellect," discusses the rôle of reason in the manifold activities of the human spirit, including the social, religious, artistic, and scientific. The project resembles in its conception, though not in its detailed execution, Hegel's phenomenology; indeed, the first suggestion of such a work occurred to Santayana after reading Hegel's *Phenomenology of Spirit.* Santayana's "life of reason," like Hegel's "phenomenology of spirit," is not confined to the rational in the sense of the purely intellectual pursuits of man—though these are, of course, included in the life of reason broadly conceived. It embraces all the reflective activities of the human spirit which are governed and directed by ideals and values, whether artistic, religious, scientific, or philosophical. "The *Life of Reason* will then be a name for that part of experience which perceives and pursues ideals. Man's rational life consists in those moments in which reflection not only occurs but proves efficacious." [61] The recurrent theme of *The Life of Reason* is that the reason in all its manifestations is a union of instinct and ideation; it is instinct which has become reflective and enlightened through the incidence of ideals. "The life of reason is the happy marriage of two elements—impulse and ideation—which if wholly divorced would reduce man to a brute or a maniac." [62]

No brief summary of the five volumes of *The Life of Reason* can convey the sublety and freshness of insight and richness of illustration with which Santayana develops his central theme of the union of the instinctive and the ideal ingredients in the creative activities of man. In the following passage from *Reason in Common Sense,* which conveys the main theme as

[61] *The Philosophy of George Santayana: Selections,* ed. by I. Edman, p. 47.
[62] *Op. cit.,* p. 50.

well as the literary flavor of his great work, Santayana eloquently describes the union of the natural and ideal components of man in the life of reason: "Every phase of the ideal world emanates from the natural and loudly proclaims its origin by the interest it takes in natural existence, of which it gives a rational interpretation. Sense, art, religion, society, express nature exuberantly and in symbols long before science is added to represent, by a different abstraction, the mechanism which nature contains." [63] The same philosophical theme recurs in *Reason in Society* where Santayana offers a philosophical interpretation of love, the emotion which underlies the societal existence of man. Human love, in contrast to mere animal passion, is at once natural and ideal: "Two things need to be admitted by anyone who would not go astray in such speculation; one, that love has an animal basis; the other that it has an ideal object." [64] The same duality of the natural and the ideal components of human life manifests itself in religion: "Religion also," he insists in *Reason in Religion,* "has an instinctive and blind side, and bubbles up in all manner of chance practices and intuitions; soon however, it feels its way toward the heart of things, and, from whatever quarter it may come, veers in the direction of the ultimate." [65] In dealing with the question of human immortality, Santayana claims that man, as part of the natural order, is mortal, yet in his creative activities he achieves a certain ideal or rational immortality.

Theory of knowledge. Santayana's theory of knowledge is a novel combination of skepticism, intuitionism, and critical realism. His skepticism is ultimate and radical—even more radical than the skepticism of Descartes. "Belief in the existence of anything, including myself, is something radically incapable of proof, and resting, like all belief, on some irrational persuasion or prompting of life." [66]

Santayana's skepticism prepares the way for the discovery of essence, the realm of indubitable truth; certain and positive knowledge of a sort that does not invoke animal faith is confined to the realm of essences. Essences are universals which possess, like Plato's forms, being or reality, though they do not *exist*. They are known by direct or intuitive apprehension, and our knowledge of them possesses the highest degree of certitude. The realm of matter, though it is the basic reality of Santayana's metaphysical scheme, cannot be known with that degree of certitude which is the prerogative of essences. "That vulgar belief in things about us," [67] which is the central thesis of Santayana's naturalism, cannot be justified by direct intuition nor by

[63] *Op. cit.,* p. 74.
[64] *Op. cit.,* p. 88.
[65] *Op. cit.,* p. 144.

[66] *Op. cit.,* p. 375.
[67] *Op. cit.,* p. 42.

demonstration and inference; belief in matter rests, like all belief in existence, on "animal faith." Santayana's epistemological realism consists in his insistent claim that human knowledge is conversant with objects possessing an existence and a reality independent of the mind which knows them. "Knowledge . . . is not intra mental or internal to experience . . . Knowledge is knowledge because it has compulsory objects that pre-exist." [68] The objects of knowledge belong to the mechanistic order of nature—indeed, in their totality they constitute that order. They cannot be known directly or by intuition, but only through the mediation of data of sense which alone are directly present to the spirit or mind of man; their apprehension involves an act of "animal faith" on the part of the knowing mind. "An object of faith—and knowledge is one species of faith—can never, even in the most direct perception, come within the circle of intuition." [69] "Knowledge, accordingly, is belief; belief in a world of events, and especially of those parts of it which are near the self, tempting or threatening it." [70] The realm of spirit, consisting of myself and other selves, is, like the realm of matter, inaccessible to direct knowledge; it is an existential realm, and as such can be apprehended only with the assistance of animal faith. Santayana disputes the contention of Descartes and of the entire idealistic tradition in modern philosophy that self-knowledge is direct, certain, and intuitive.

Santayana, who associated himself with the critical realists and contributed to their cooperative volume, *Essays in Critical Realism,* opposed as vehemently as the other critical realists any form of presentational realism; he speaks of "the absurdity of wishing to have intuitions of things." His realism is representational, but is not the less confident. The objects are not inferred from the data, for no causal inference from the essences to existent things is possible; the existence of physical objects is accepted and believed on the basis of animal faith. "Knowledge accordingly is belief: belief in a world of events . . . This belief is native to animals and precedes all deliberate use of intuitions as signs or descriptions of things. . . ." [71] Santayana considers memory a crucial instance of representational knowledge; in examining the cognitive claims of memory, he insists that "memory itself must report facts or events in the natural world, if it is to be knowledge and to deserve the name of memory." [72]

Santayana's epistemological position as formulated in *Scepticism and Animal Faith* has little in common with Lovejoy's more typical version of the epistemology of critical realism, save its advocacy of dualistic or repre-

[68] *Op. cit.*, p. 410 f.
[69] *Op. cit.*, p. 407.
[70] *Op. cit.*, p. 417.
[71] *Op. cit.*, p. 417.
[72] *Scepticism and Animal Faith*, p. 150.

sentative realism. Santayana's theory contrasts with Lovejoy's in its characterization of the immediate data of knowledge: whereas Lovejoy considered the data existent and psychical, Santayana rejects existential data entirely. "The notion that the datum exists," says Santayana, "is unmeaning, and if insisted upon is false." The only immediate and indubitable data of knowledge are, according to Santayana, essences.

The realms of being. Santayana's metaphysical position, the outlines of which are clearly delineated in *Scepticism and Animal Faith* in the course of his examination of the epistemological problems, receives its mature and systematic elaboration in *The Realms of Being*. The three principal realms of being are the realms of matter, essence, and spirit; he thus combines naturalism with essentialism and idealism.

Santayana's naturalistic metaphysics equates the whole of existence to nature conceived as a mechanistic order in which everything is subject to constant and uniform scientific law. "Anyone," he says, "who can at all catch the drift of experience—moral no less than physical—must feel that mechanism rules the whole world." [73] Man is a part of nature and subject to its control even in his scientific, religious, moral, social, and artistic pursuits.

Santayana's essentialism or realism of essences consists in his commitment to a realm of essence in addition to the realm of material existence. Essences are universals which, though they do not *exist,* possess being or reality. Santayana assigns to the realm of essence, colors, tastes, odors, and other data of sense, as well as the ideal objects of thought and imagination. "All possible terms in mental discourse are essences existing nowhere: visionary equally, whether the faculty that discovers them be sense or thought or the most fantastic fancy." [74] Essences, "although (they) have the texture and ontological status of platonic 'ideas,' . . . are infinite in number and neutral in value." [75] The essences function in Santayana's epistemology as the vehicles of knowledge; "essences," he says, "are indispensable terms in the perception of matters of fact, and render transitive knowledge possible." [76]

Idealism appears as an ingredient of Santayana's system in so far as he posits a realm of spirit complementary to the realms of matter and of essence. The realm of spirit is the world of subjective experience which Santayana characterizes as "this world of free expression, this drift of sensations, passions and ideas, perpetually kindled and fading in the light of consciousness." [77] Spirit, though it is the realm of fulfillment—or frustration—of our highest human aspirations in art, religion, morals, science, and philosophy,

[73] *Reason in Science*, p. 76.
[74] *The Realm of Essence*, p. vii.
[75] *Scepticism and Animal Faith*, pp. 77 f.
[76] *Op. cit.,* p. 80.
[77] *The Realm of Essence*, pp. x f.

is subordinate to the other two realms of matter and essence; thus Santayana's idealism is overshadowed by his naturalism and essentialism. Indeed, naturalism is the dominant theme of Santayana's philosophy, for though the knowledge of essence surpasses belief in matter in respect to certitude, and although spirit is the domain of man's virtues, his creative activities and noblest pursuits, matter, with its attendant mechanism, is the substratum of all existence.

Theory of beauty. Santayana's theory of beauty is prominent at all stages of his philosophical development and preserves a remarkable continuity of expression throughout the varying contexts in which it appears. His first published essay in philosophy, *The Sense of Beauty,* (1896), was a major contribution to esthetics—perhaps the most important American work in this field. The essay is concerned with "the nature and elements of our esthetic judgments," and "it is," he adds, "a theoretical inquiry and has no directly hortatory quality." [78] The main contention of the essay is that esthetic judgments are expressive of artistic taste, and hence that "to make a judgment is virtually to establish an ideal." [79] An esthetic judgment is absolute, since "all ideals are absolute and eternal for the judgment that involves them . . . ," [80] but an ideal invoked at one moment may be replaced at the next by a new ideal no less absolute than its predecessor. Santayana's esthetic theory, while it emphasizes the ideal or formal aspects of esthetic judgment, does not ignore or depreciate the material or sensuous aspect. "Form cannot be the form of nothing. If, then, in finding or creating beauty we ignore the materials of things . . . we miss an ever-present opportunity to heighten our effects." [81]

Santayana's reputation as a philosopher rests on the range and richness of human experience on which he has drawn his materials for philosophical interpretation, and the diversity of philosophical themes which he has woven into the texture of his system. *The Life of Reason* unfolds the social, religious, artistic, and scientific ingredients of human existence and betrays the author's distinctive personal and philosophical predilections in the interpretation of these variegated experiences. His *Realms of Being* combines themes as diverse as naturalism, Platonic realism, and idealism into a comprehensive and penetrating system. His greatness resided in his ability to assimilate diverse philosophical trends of the past to his own system, and to confer on them the distinctive color and flavor of his own philosophical preferences and predilections. His philosophy, however, lacks the constructive power and speculative originality requisite to a truly great system of philosophy.

[78] *The Sense of Beauty,* p. 6.   [80] *Loc. cit.*
[79] *Op. cit.,* p. 12.   [81] *Op. cit.,* p. 77.

XXII

Pragmatism, Positivism, and Analytical Philosophy

83. SCIENTIFIC CONVENTIONALISM AND FICTIONALISM

Anti-realistic Tendencies. The influence of science on the development of recent philosophy has led philosophy in two widely divergent directions. On the one hand, the realists, taking scientific concepts and theories quite literally, affirm the existence of a real world of perceptual and physical objects and combine a realistic epistemology with a naturalistic metaphysics, which in such realists as Alexander and Whitehead assumed a bold and speculative form. On the other hand, positivistic and phenomenalistic philosophers, like Mach, Poincairé, and Vaihinger, have insisted that scientific concepts and theories are conventions, constructions or fictions which, though indispensable in the formulation of scientific systems, cannot justify any pretension to objectivity. The conventionalists and fictionalists, in questioning the literal objectivity of scientific concepts and theories, inevitably adopted a skeptical attitude toward metaphysics and its claims to a knowledge of the nature of ultimate reality.

Recent phenomenalistic, conventionalistic, and fictionalistic interpretations of science refuse to accept at their face value the truth-claims of science and metaphysics. They consider scientific and philosophical concepts and theories not as descriptive of reality, but as shorthand summaries of phenomenal facts or useful devices for the interpretation and explanation of the observed data of experience. Science and philosophy, though they can never attain objective knowledge of an extra-mental reality, afford the human mind its only available conceptual schemes for ordering and interpreting the facts of observation and experience.

The anti-realistic tendencies of recent and contemporary philosophy represent many different shades of doctrine, all of which agree in rejecting the realistic pretensions of science and philosophy, but differ appreciably in their several accounts of the logical and epistemological status of scientific and philosophical concepts and theories. These views range from the radical fictionalism of Vaihinger, which treats all theories as false and fictitious and is even tolerant of mutually inconsistent theoretical constructions, to the more moderate positions of conventionalism, pragmatism, and operationalism, which employ such criteria as simplicity, convenience, and utility in choosing among rival conceptual schemes.

Mach. Ernst Mach (1838-1916; professor of physics and later of philosophy) offers a theory of knowledge based on the phenomenalism of Hume and the French positivists: the world consists solely of our sensations, and the thing-in-itself is an illusion. Immediate "pure experience" constitutes the basis of his theory of knowledge. The aim of science is the complete description of facts, the contents of our consciousness; its sole function is to discover the connections among the not-further-analyzable elements of sensation—to recognize these connections instead of seeking to explain them by metaphysical assumptions. Science begins with hypotheses, but these are mere temporary expedients, methods of indirect description to enable us to understand the facts. Hypotheses are gradually replaced by direct observations, that is, verified by experience consisting of sensations. All science consists in a schematic reproduction of facts, in thought. It would be futile to mirror the world in thought if it were not possible to find something relatively constant in manifold change. In every scientific judgment a great number of observations are embraced or compressed: our concepts and judgments are abbreviated thought-symbols for groups of sensations, a kind of shorthand method of expressing the facts. This is the principle of the economy of thought. A law is nothing more than a comprehensive and condensed statement of facts, a statement of only that phase of the facts which is important to us. Matter is merely a relatively fixed and constant sensation-complex;[1] language strengthens and reinforces the grouping of sensations into complexes which we call physical objects. The self, likewise, is a group of sensations. The complex of memories, moods, feelings connected with a particular body is called the ego. Sensations considered as dependent on the body constitute the subject-matter of psychology; the same sensations considered as dependent on other material objects form the subject-matter of physics. Physics and psychology are both concerned with our sensations, but the two

[1] Cf. *Analysis of the Sensations,* 1910, trans. by C. M. Williams, pp. 24 f.

sciences relate the sensations to different contexts or conceptual schemes. Bodies do not produce sensations; on the contrary, complexes of sensations literally constitute bodies. The world does not consist of mysterious things-in-themselves that produce, in interaction with the ego, other mysterious things called sensations; sensations themselves as directly observed are the sole realities. The aim of science is to connect the less constant, and not yet sufficiently established complexes of sensations with the most constant and firmly established ones.

Although Mach restricts our knowledge to the field of our sensations and is, therefore, opposed to metaphysics—a futile undertaking that merely disturbs the economy of science, he, perhaps inconsistently, seeks in voluntarism a basis for his theory of knowledge. Knowledge is an instrument of the will, the result of the needs of practical life. This voluntaristic phase of Mach's philosophy is an anticipation of later pragmatism. Thoughts are not the whole of life; they are, as it were, fugitive flashes of light, intended to illuminate the path of the will. We need a world-view that will bring us into some sort of relation with the environment; and in order to achieve it in an economic manner, we create science. Science, which seeks the agreement of thought with observation, is an instrument of adaptation and a basis of biological selection. The conceptions of body and ego are mere temporary makeshifts for practical orientation in the world, and may be abandoned if they fail to achieve their end; likewise the notions of atoms, forces, and laws are conceptual constructions whose sole justifications are convenience and intellectual economy.

Every practical and intellectual need is satisfied as soon as our thoughts succeed in reproducing the sensible facts. We are satisfied when our conceptual thought brings before us the totality of the sense data which belong together, and these conceptual schemes almost seem to be a substitute for the data themselves. Mach speaks of an impulse to idealize, schematize, and complete facts.

Die Mechanik in ihrer Entwickelung, 1883, trans. by T. S. McCormack under the title, *The Science of Mechanics,* 4th ed., 1919; *Beiträge zur Analyse der Empfindungen,* 1886, trans. by C. M. Williams under the title, *Analysis of Sensations,* 1910.

Avenarius. The empirio-critical school, of which R. Avenarius (1843-1896; *Kritik der reinen Erfahrung,* 1888, *Der menschliche Weltbegriff,* 1891) is the founder, develops a scientific empiricism similar to Mach's. The method of knowledge is description based on exact perception. Scientific philosophy is the descriptive determination of the form and content of the universal and *pure* experience. Pure experience is the experience common to all possible individual experiences, and it is the business of knowledge to eliminate the variable individual elements of experience. Avenarius' theory of pure experience is one of the sources of the radical empiricism of William James, of the neutral monism of Russell and of the American neo-realists. Avenarius is well aware of the difficulty of achieving pure experience, but believes that philosophy is gradually approximating such a pure empirical conception of the universe. Originally, all men shared a common conception of the world; but by "introjecting" into experience thought, feeling, and will, by splitting it up into outer and inner experience, into subject and object, reality has been falsified. By eliminating "introjection," we can restore the original *natural* view of the world, the attitude of pure experience.

Views similar to those of Mach are expressed by James Clerk Maxwell (1831-1879; *Scientific Papers*), William Clifford (1845-1879; *Seeing and Thinking*, 1879, *Common Sense of the Exact Sciences,* 1885) and Karl Pearson (1857-1936; *Grammar of Science,* 1892, 2nd ed. 1900).

Vaihinger's Fictionalism. Hans Vaihinger (1852-1933), in his *Philosophy of the "As If"* (*Philosophie des Als Ob*), 1911, advanced a positivistic and fictionalistic theory of knowledge, which has many similarities to American pragmatism. Vaihinger's main insight, as well as his adoption of the expression "as if" to describe his position, was suggested by his study of Kant's *Critique of Pure Reason,* on which he wrote a celebrated commentary. The central contention of the philosophy of the "as if" is that the concepts and theories achieved by mathematics and the natural sciences, by economic and political theory and jurisprudence, by ethics, esthetics and philosophy, are convenient fictions, devised by the human mind. Vaihinger's fictionalism is of an extreme sort: he maintains that fictional constructions of the mind "contradict" reality and, in the case of the boldest and most successful fictions, are even "self-contradictory." Fictions are not, however, entirely divorced from experience—they are not invented *in vacuo.* Sensations, he insists, are "the starting-point of all logical activity and at the same time the terminus to which they must run." [2] This, of course, does not mean that fictions are verified by sensory experience—their fictional character precludes all verification—but merely that sensory experience provides the occasion, the stimulus and the clue for the mind's exercise of its inventive activities, as well as the sphere for the employment and application of its fictional constructs.

[2] All quotations are taken from the English translation by C. K. Ogden, 1924.

Vaihinger's position may be characterized as empiricism in so far as he assigns to experience an indispensable rôle in the initiation and application of thought; but the function he ascribes to experience is clearly different from that asserted by historical British empiricism. The material of sensation is, according to Vaihinger, radically transformed by thought; it is "re-modelled, re-coined, compressed, . . . purged of dross and mixed with alloys by the psyche itself. . . ."

Vaihinger's fictionalism stresses the free, creative and inventive activity of the mind or "psyche" in the constitution of concepts and theories; the psyche is not a substance but the sum-total of the so-called mental actions and reactions of the organisms. Many of the creative activities of the mind are originally unconsciously performed and only later enter into consciousness; others are deliberately and consciously performed. But whether consciously or unconsciously devised, the resultant fictions are mental in structure. By virtue of his insistence on the creativity of mind in fiction-making, Vaihinger's theory is idealistic; indeed, his position has been described as "positivistic idealism" or "idealistic positivism."

The context in which Vaihinger develops his theory of fictions is biological and purposive. Like James' pragmatism and Dewey's instrumentalism, Vaihinger's fictionalism interprets logical thought as an activity which fulfills the biological function of assisting the organism to adapt and accommodate itself to its physical and social environment. Vaihinger repeatedly calls attention to the purposiveness and practical value of thought; in language reminiscent of James and Dewey, he says: "We lay most stress on the practical corroboration, on the experimental test of the utility of the logical structures that are the product of the organic function of thought." Despite his agreement with the exponents of American pragmatism, in emphasizing the biological utility and practical value of thought, Vaihinger remains at variance with pragmatism in maintaining that his thought-constructs "contradict" reality and may even be self-contradictory. The typical pragmatist ascribes "truth" to his conceptual schemes—a truth which is attested by their practical consequences. Vaihinger's fictional constructs, although they are in contradiction to reality, have a predictive function: by their help we are enabled "to calculate events that occur"; in themselves fictitious, they lead to "correct" predictions regarding the future appearance of sensations. Vaihinger mitigates his fictionalism in another important respect: he admits that thought, besides inventing *fictions,* also devises *hypotheses,* which are "directed toward reality." An hypothesis is an ideational construct which "claims or hopes to coincide with some perception in the future. It submits its reality to the test and demands *verification*, i.e., it wants to be proved true, real, and an expression of reality." Vaihinger regards the distinction between fiction and hypothesis, between fictive and problematical judgments, of paramount importance to logic and philosophy and attributes many of the absurdities of past philosophy to a confusion between the two kinds of ideational constructs.

Vaihinger's *Philosophy of the "As If"* contains a wealth of illustrations of his theory of fictions drawn from such diverse fields as mathematics, physics, psychology, economics, politics, jurisprudence, ethics, esthetics and metaphysics. In mathematics particularly, the fictional method has been successfully employed and consciously acknowledged by the mathematicians themselves. Vaihinger points out that all the fundamental concepts of mathematics—space, point, line, surface—are ideal, imaginary, "contradictory," and thus fictitious. The paradoxes of Zeno result, according to Vaihinger, from taking seriously such spatio-temporal fictions as point and instant: "the fiction became an hypothesis and the crudest contradiction followed." As another illustration of a mathematical fiction, Vaihinger cites certain geometrical proofs in which a curved line is considered to be made up of innumerable straight-line segments; in this instance the mathematician is fully aware that a curve is not an infinite number of straight lines. The basic concept of differential calculus, the derivative, is defined by the method of limits and is a strictly fictional concept—thus the entire calculus has a fictional foundation. In physics, such basic concepts as matter and force are fictions of a sort. Vaihinger accepts as essentially cogent Berkeley's arguments for the inexistence of matter. Berkeley brought to light the contradictions inherent in the concept of matter, but unfortunately failed to give due recognition to the scientific utility of the fiction of matter. Like matter itself, the atom, as a constituent of material objects, is pure fiction—a fiction which is none the less necessary for physical science.

Condillac's hypothetical statue, endowed with the sense of smell alone, is mentioned by Vaihinger as a remarkable example of the fictional method in psychology. By the employment of this avowed fiction, Condillac was able to abstract from certain complications of the total sensory life of man, and thereby to contribute to the psychological understanding of consciousness, attention, memory, judgment, imagination, abstraction, reflection, etc. The fiction of the exclusively olfactory man thus contributes to the understanding of man in his totality. The history of the social sciences affords innumerable striking instances of the fruitful and productive employment of similar fictions. Vaihinger mentions Adam Smith's and Bentham's fictive assump-

tions, that man's economic and commercial behavior is motivated solely
by egoism; the fictive concepts of freedom and responsibility in relation
to punishment, which underlie the whole system of criminal law; the
legalistic conception of the State as in certain respects a person; the monetary
and credit system of a modern economy, which rests on the "fictional value"
of paper money. The central concept of Vaihinger's ethics, the moral ideal,
is *a practical fiction:* "The ideal," he says, "is an ideational construct contradictory in itself and in contradiction with reality, but it has irresistible
power." Moral ideals are the products of the creative imagination of the
noblest minds of history to which mankind cling, and in accordance with
which they guide their conduct. Vaihinger traces his view of ethics to Kant's
Metaphysic of Ethics, in which Kant advances the moral conceptions of
"the dignity of man," "the realm of ends" as "mere ideas," i.e., "heuristic
fictions" for the guidance of conduct. Though Vaihinger offers no fully
elaborated fictional esthetics, he interprets as esthetic fictions all poetic and
literary similes, metaphors, personifications, and allegories. Whereas scientific fictions are instruments of adaptation, esthetic fictions serve to arouse
"certain uplifting or otherwise important feelings"; Vaihinger insists that
the ultimate criterion of fictions in both fields is practical value. Speculative
metaphysics, too, is the elaboration of analogical and metaphysical fictions.
Vaihinger shows in considerable detail how the categories of metaphysics,
namely, substance and attribute, whole and part, cause and effect, purpose,
etc., may be viewed as ideational constructs—"convenient aids for bringing
the mass of sensations into subjection." They lead to error only if they are
taken to be literal and theoretical descriptions of an independent reality.
Philosophical systems and the categories which they employ "have value
only in practice and not in theory—namely, for purposes of order, communication and action; theoretically they are valueless but practically they
are important." Fictionalism itself, the theory which distinguishes between
fiction and hypothesis and describes the rôle of fictions in knowledge, is
an hypothesis and not a fiction.

Poincaré's Conventionalism. The French mathematician and physicist, Henri
Poincaré (1854-1912), developed a positivistic and conventionalistic interpretation of science closely paralleling the positivistic theory of Mach.
Poincaré held that the basic assumptions of the sciences are convenient
definitions or conventions, which cannot be validated either by a priori
methods or by inductive generalization from experience; our choice among
the possible conventions, though suggested and guided by experimental

facts, is, in the last analysis, governed by considerations of simplicity and convenience. Poincaré draws a sharp distinction between two principal types of scientific hypothesis: (1) hypotheses of the first type are essentially un-verifiable; they are the products of the free activity of the mind which are imposed by the scientific mind on our scientific schemes. Such hypotheses are indispensable to any broadly conceived scientific theory, even though they can neither be confirmed nor refuted by experience. (2) Hypotheses of the second type are ordinary inductive generalizations, which are valuable just because they can be verified or falsified by experimental procedures. A scientific theory will include hypotheses of both types. Poincaré gives more attention to the first type, the intrinsically unverifiable, because he believes that they have been largely neglected by students of scientific methodology; whereas the second type, the verifiable, have already been extensively treated by empirical logicians and methodologists from Bacon to J. S. Mill. Poincaré has given a comprehensive and illuminating account of the nature of un-verifiable hypotheses and their function in the system of scientific knowl-edge. He insists that an hypothesis of this type, although not verifiable by experience, is suggested by experience, and derives its value from its fruit-fulness in the scientific interpretation of experience. The facts given in experience may be assimilated to any one of an "infinite" number of al-ternative hypothetical constructions; each of these constructions is a product of the free activity of the mind, and the choice among them is made in accordance with considerations of convenience. Thus unverifiable hypotheses are indeed conventional, but they are not arbitrary: "Experience leaves us our freedom of choice but it guides us by aiding us to discern the easiest way." [3] Poincaré's conventionalism is far less radical than Vaihinger's fic-tionalism. Whereas Vaihinger's fictive constructs are self-contradictory and "contradictory" to the facts, Poincaré's conventional hypotheses are each internally consistent and are not inconsistent with the facts, for the facts can neither refute nor confirm them.

What criterion governs our selection of one among the infinity of alterna-tive hypotheses to which the observed facts may be assimilated? To this question, which is crucial for conventionalism, Poincaré replies unequivocally —simplicity. "Among all the generalizations possible, we must choose, and we can only choose the simplest. We are therefore led to act as if a simple law were, other things being equal, more probable than a complicated law." We choose the simplest law not because nature loves simplicity and thus

---

[3] This and the following quotations have been taken from Halsted's translations of three of Poincaré's works, published together under the title, *The Foundations of Science*.

the simplest is the objectively true, but solely in the interest of economy of thought. A perverse preference for complicated over simple explanatory hypotheses would defeat the scientific enterprise. "In formulating a general, simple and precise law on the basis of relatively few experiments . . . , we have therefore only obeyed a necessity from which the human mind cannot free itself."

Poincaré applies his conventionalism to the two sciences of his own special competence: mathematics and physics. In his interpretation of the foundations of mathematics, Poincaré rejects rationalism and empiricism alike. The various historical forms of apriorism are all unsatisfactory: the axioms of geometry are not, as Descartes claimed, a priori intuitions; neither can mathematics be derived analytically from the principle of contradiction alone in the way attempted by Leibniz; and Kant's attempted validation of mathematics as a system of synthetic a priori truths resting on the pure intuitions of space and time is unsuccessful. Poincaré finds Mill's empirical account of mathematics equally unacceptable: geometrical axioms are not inductive generalizations regarding the properties of perceptual space. Experience, to be sure, "plays an indispensable rôle in the genesis of geometry; but it would be an error to conclude that geometry is, even in part, an experimental science." "If it were experimental it would be only approximative and provisional." Poincaré finds in conventionalism a genuine alternative to both rationalism and empiricism: the so-called axioms of geometry are postulates, i.e., assumptions adopted not because they are true but because they are convenient. Experience "tells us not which is the truest geometry, but which is the most convenient"; thus, while geometry is not an experimental science, it is a science "born apropos of experience." Poincaré finds confirmation of his postulational interpretation of mathematics in the very possibility of non-Euclidean systems of geometry: observed phenomena are assimilable to either the Euclidean or to one of the non-Euclidean systems of geometry; it is, he says, impossible to imagine a concrete experiment which can be interpreted in the Euclidean system and not in the Labachevskian system—one of the non-Euclidean systems. No experience can ever be in contradiction to Euclid's postulate; nor, on the other hand, will any experience ever contradict the postulate of Labachevski. The postulates of any geometry, Euclidean or non-Euclidean, are thus irrefutable and unconfirmable; they are to be construed as hypotheses of the unverifiable (and unfalsifiable) type, adopted for reasons of simplicity and convenience.

In his brilliant and suggestive essay, *The Value of Science,* Poincaré writes: "Mathematics has a triple aim. It must furnish an instrument for the study of nature. But that is not all: it has a philosophic aim and, I dare maintain, an esthetic aim. . . . Its scientific function is to provide a simple, precise and economical language for the expression of our knowledge of nature; ordinary language is too poor, it is besides too vague, to express relations so delicate, so rich and so precise." The philosophic function of mathematics consists in promoting the philosopher's investigations of number, space, time, quantity, and related categories. But above all, Poincaré extols the esthetic values inherent in mathematics. "Its adepts find therein delights analogous to those given by painting and music. They admire the delicate harmony of numbers and forms; they marvel when a new discovery opens to them an unexpected perspective; and has not the joy they thus feel the esthetic character, even though the senses take no part therein?" Poincaré displayed penetrating insight into the nature of the creative processes of the mathematical mind in a remarkable chapter on "Mathematical Creation" in *Science and Method*. He describes with great psychological subtlety one of his own mathematical discoveries; the account illustrates the long preparatory period requisite to mathematical creativity, the rôle of unconscious processes in the achievement of the final insight, the importance of analogy, intuition and free play of the imagination, and finally the esthetic satisfaction and almost mystical exaltation which accompany the final achievement.

Physics, and in particular mechanics, is the second science in which, according to Poincaré, conventional hypotheses play an indispensable rôle. He subjects to critical scrutiny the basic concepts and underlying assumptions of the classic mechanics of Galileo and Newton, and concludes that they are to a considerable extent conventional. The basic assumptions regarding force, inertia, absolute space, and absolute time are conventional in the sense that they are neither verifiable nor falsifiable. Poincaré's conventionalism in physics as in mathematics proposes a significant third possibility in the traditional controversy between rationalism and empiricism. Conventionalism offers a plausible account of the epistemological character of the basic axioms of mathematics and the fundamental assumptions of natural science, and avoids both the dogmatic pretentiousness of the theory of a priori truth and the probabilism of the a posteriori theory. Conventionalism seeks to combine the precision and rigor of rationalism with the experimental fertility of empiricism.

La science et l'hypothèse, 1902, Engl. trans., *Science and Hypothesis*, 1914; *La valeur de la science*, 1905, Engl. trans., *The Value of Science*, 1907; *Science et méthode*, 1909, Engl. trans., *Science and Method*, 1914. The English translations of the above works by G. B. Halsted are contained in a single volume, *The Foundations of Science*, 1946.

84. Pragmatism

Pragmatism and Empiricism. Pragmatism is characterized by William James as "a new name for some old ways of thinking." This subtitle of his work, *Pragmatism,* is James' perhaps over-modest recognition of the indebtedness of pragmatism to earlier empirical movements, particularly the classical British Empiricism from Locke to Mill and the Continental Positivism of such thinkers as Mach, Poincairé, Oswald, and Duhem. Pragmatism is, however, no mere eclectical summation of earlier empirical and positivistic philosophies; it is a method of inquiry and a theory of meaning and truth derived from the natural sciences and applicable to philosophy. Pragmatism is not and does not profess to be a speculative philosophical system on the grand scale of the seventeenth- and eighteenth-century idealisms. Whatever unity it achieves in its re-examination of the traditional problems of philosophy derives from its empirico-pragmatic method and its appeal to the pragmatic principle of verification and meaning, which was enunciated with remarkable theoretical precision by C. S. Peirce and developed and applied by James, Dewey, and C. I. Lewis.

C. S. Peirce. The beginnings of American pragmatism can be traced to Charles S. Peirce (1839-1914), who enunciated the pragmatic principle in an epoch-making article entitled "How to Make Our Ideas Clear" which appeared in the *Popular Science Monthly* in January, 1878. Peirce's pragmatic principle, as the title of his article indicates, was a maxim designed to promote the clarification of the meaning of conceptions and propositions. The meaning of an intellectual conception or idea, as prescribed by the pragmatic maxim, is the envisaged practical consequences of the conception: "In order to ascertain the meaning of an intellectual conception one should consider what practical consequences might conceivably result by necessity from the truth of that conception; and the sum of these consequences will constitute the entire meaning of the conception." [4] (5.9) An alternative formulation of the pragmatic maxim—the one most frequently quoted—is the following from the *Popular Science* article: "Consider what effects, that might conceivably have practical bearings, we conceive the object of our conception to have. Then, our conception of these effects is the whole of our conception of the object." (5.2) We should guard against reading into Peirce's initial formulation of the pragmatic maxim, doctrines evolved by Peirce's sometimes over-enthusiastic disciples and later imputed to him. As Peirce himself

---

[4] An explanation of references to Peirce is given in the bibliography on p. 638.

recognized, "pragmatism is not a *Weltanschauung* but is a method of reflection having for its purpose to render ideas clear"; (5.13n.) it is not even a theory of truth, but merely a technique for ascertaining the meaning of conceptions. Peirce's own illustrations clearly indicated the limited pretensions of the pragmatic principle as he envisaged it. He employs the two illustrations of hardness and weight: ". . . let us ask what we mean by calling a thing *hard*. Evidently that it will not be scratched by many other substances. The whole conception of this quality, as of every other, lies in its conceived effects . . . Let us seek next a clear idea of weight . . . To say that a body is heavy means simply that, in the absence of opposing force, it will fall." (5.40) The meaning of ideas is constituted by their conceived or anticipated effects; the determination of the meaning of a concept is thus an ideal, intellectual activity, and does not require the actual performance of contemplated actions. Peirce warns us that if pragmatism "really made Doing to be the Be-all and the End-all of life, that would be its death. For to say that we live for the mere sake of action, as action, regardless of the thought it carries out, would be to say that there is no such thing as rational purpose." (5.429)

The methodological insights of Peirce, important as they are, have, because of his position as founder of the pragmatic movement, at times been accentuated to the neglect of other sides of his system. Peirce was a philosophical and scientific genius of breadth and originality, comparable, according to his admirers, to Leibniz. As in the case of Leibniz, the difficulties of expounding his system are enormous, because of the fragmentariness of his philosophical writings and his failure to produce any single magnum opus. We can, however, discern in his writings the outlines of a system.

Semiotic and epistemology. Central to Peirce's account of cognition is "semiotic" or theory of signs. A sign is anything used to refer to an object independent of itself. Thus the word "triangle" is a sign which stands for and refers to the geometrical figure. In describing the situation in which a sign is used, Peirce distinguishes (1) the sign itself (the word "triangle" as spoken or written), (2) the object of the sign (the triangle as a designated object), (3) the "interpretant" of the sign, which is another sign functioning as the interpretation or translation of the original sign (an interpretant of "triangle" would be "three-sided-plane figure"). Since the employment of signs is, according to Peirce, a prerogative of mind, the interpreter, a mind which uses and interprets signs, should perhaps be listed as a fourth distinguishable factor in the sign-situation. Peirce's theory of signs underlies his entire theory of cognition; in perceptual cognition the percept is the sign of the perceived object. His theory of perception is predominantly realistic. "There is nothing to prevent our knowing outward things as they really are, and it is most likely that we do thus know them in numberless cases . . ." (5.311) In the context of his theory of signs, Peirce advocated a correspondence theory of truth: a proposition is true in so far as there is a correspondence between the proposition, considered as a sign, and the object to which the proposition refers. The pursuit of truth is one of progressive approximation to an ideal truth—an ideal which is never perfectly realized. Peirce's denial of the attainability of absolutely certain, intuitive truth—his doctrine of fallibilism—is a characteristic feature of his theory of cognition. The principle of fallibilism means in effect that no synthetic statement can be finally and completely verified. "There are three things which we can never hope to attain, namely, absolute certainty, absolute exactitude, absolute universality." (1.141) Fallibilism is not, however, to be confused with agnosticism or skepticism. Everything is knowable in the sense that any question, which has a clear meaning, is answerable, if only our investigations are carried far enough. Everything is knowable even though it is impossible to know everything. As knowledge progresses, we come to know more and more with ever-increasing certitude, though we can never know anything with absolute certainty, nor aspire to a knowledge of everything. No number is large enough "to express the relation between the amount of what rests unknown and the amount of the known." (5.409)

Phenomenology and ontology. Metaphysics, which includes both epistemology (science of knowledge) and ontology (science of being or reality) is for Peirce an observational science: "Metaphysics, even bad metaphysics, rests on observation, whether consciously or not . . ." (6.2) The strict application of Peirce's pragmatic principle deprives a large part of traditional metaphysics of all meaning; yet Peirce is confident that, after the elimination from philosophy of pseudo-problems, "what will remain of philosophy will be a series of problems capable of investigation by the observational methods of the true sciences." (5.423) Metaphysics of a legitimate sort is rooted in phenomenology, "a science that . . . just contemplates phenomena as they are, simply opens its eyes and describes what it sees . . ." (5.37) Peirce's phenomenology has many affinities with the phenomenology of Husserl: both are attempts to describe phenomena as given, both focus attention on the universal or essential ingredients of phenomena. But

Peirce's phenomenology is in some respects even more radical than Husserl's; in a discussion of Husserl in 1898, Peirce deplores what he considers the hopelessly psychological complexion of Husserl's foundation of phenomenology. (Cf. 4.7)

Phenomenological inquiry is directed toward the universal and pervasive aspects of phenomenal experience—it is a doctrine of the categories. The categories are general and universal in that every category belongs to every phenomenon, although one category may be more prominent than the others in a given phenomenon. Peirce finds only three categories which are both necessary and sufficient for the interpretation of phenomena; they are, for certain logical reasons which we shall not undertake to explain, designated as firstness, secondness and thirdness. The first category, the category of firstness, "comprises the qualities of phenomena, such as red, bitter, tedious, hard, heartrending, noble . . ." (1.418) Qualities are not bare particulars, but are rather of the nature of qualitative essences; moreover they merge into one another and, in the case of visual and auditory qualities, constitute ordered series or systems. Peirce makes the interesting suggestion that, were it not for the fragmentariness of our experience, all qualities would fit into a continuous system without any abrupt demarcations. (Cf. 1.418) Peirce's phenomenological description of quality provides, within the framework of a radical empiricism, a significant alternative to the qualitative atomism of Hume and his followers in the British tradition: whereas Hume's impressions are particular, discrete and qualitatively discontinuous, Peirce's qualities are general, interpenetrating, and probably continuous. Peirce in his realistic interpretation of phenomenal quality avoided the mentalism and psychologism of Hume's theory. The second category, the category of secondness, comprises the brute factuality of phenomenal experience; whereas qualities, as such, are general, somewhat vague and potential, facts are particular, definite and actual. Peirce speaks of the "brutality" of facts, by which he means the resistance they offer to our wills. Matter as directly apprehended through sensation, exemplifies this aspect of brute factuality. Secondness is thus the factor of brute factuality which confronts us in the recalcitrancy of our sensations and in the contingencies and coincidences of things and events. (Cf. 1.419, 1.431) The third category, the category of thirdness, designates the law of things, which is to be distinguished from their qualitativeness and factuality. The law of phenomena is general in that it refers not merely to all actual but to all possible things. "No collection of facts can constitute a law; for the law goes beyond the accomplished facts and determines how facts that *may be*, but *all* of which never can have happened, shall be characterized." (1.420) The metaphysical categories of quality, fact and law, exhaust the essential categories of the phenomenal; no others are required for the interpretation of the phenomenal world.

Peirce is to be ranked among germinal thinkers—like Socrates, St. Augustine, and Leibniz—whose fertile minds reached out in many directions and provided the leading ideas for later more systematic philosophers. Among the leading ideas in his philosophy, we have called attention to his pragmatism, experimentalism, phenomenology, realism, fallibilism; these and other tendencies of his fertile thinking have already exerted their influence, and it is safe to predict that during the second half of the twentieth century Peirce will continue to influence not only pragmatists, instrumentalists, operationalists and positivists, but realists and idealists as well.

Collected Papers of Charles Sanders Peirce, edited by Charles Hartshorne and Paul Weiss was published by the Harvard University Press, 1931-1935, in six volumes as follows: I. *Principles of Philosophy;* II. *Elements of Logic;* III. *Exact Logic;* IV. *The Simplest Mathematics;* V. *Pragmatism and Pragmaticism;* VI. *Scientific Metaphysics.* All citations in the above account are to the volume and paragraph number in the *Collected Papers;* thus 5.9 refers to Volume V, paragraph 9. J. Buchler's *Charles Peirce's Empiricism,* 1939, contains an interpretation of the logical and epistemological doctrines of Peirce and clarifies the relevance of Peirce's empiricism to the doctrines of recent logical positivism. J. Feibleman's *An Introduction to Peirce's Philosophy,* 1946, is an exposition of Peirce's entire system and includes an account of the intellectual development of Peirce, his relation to Kant, Duns Scotus, Darwin and Descartes and considers Peirce's influence on James, Royce, Dewey and on recent positivism and realism.

James' Pragmatism. William James (1842-1910), in an address delivered before the Philosophical Union of the University of California in September 1898, recast Peirce's pragmatic formula in these words:

To attain perfect clearness in our thoughts of an object, then, we need only consider what effects of a conceivably practical kind the object may involve— what sensations we may expect from it, and what reactions we must prepare. Our conception of these effects, then, is for us the whole of our conception of the object, so far as that conception has positive significance at all.[5]

As thus enunciated, the pragmatic maxim is for James, as it had been for Peirce, a method of making our ideas clear—a test of the meaningfulness of our concepts and propositions—and James proposes the pragmatic test of meaning as "a method of settling metaphysical disputes that otherwise might be interminable." [6] He contends that if the issue between meta-

[5] *Collected Essays,* p. 411.
[6] *Pragmatism,* p. 45.

physical alternatives, say between materialism and spiritualism, makes no practical difference, then "the alternatives mean practically the same thing, and all dispute is idle." Pragmatism as developed by James embraces not only a theory of meaning but likewise a theory of truth, and in thus extending the scope and function of pragmatism, James goes far beyond Peirce's more modest and restricted formulation. As a theory of truth, pragmatism asserts that "any idea that will carry us prosperously from any one part of our experience to any other part, linking things satisfactorily, working securely, saving labor, is true for just so much, true in so far forth, true *instrumentally*."[7] "*The true . . . is only the expedient in the way of thinking, just as the right is the expedient in the way of our behaving.*"

Pragmatism is a method of determining the truth or falsity of propositions according as they do or do not fulfill our purposes and satisfy our biological and emotional needs; a true proposition is one the acceptance of which leads to success, a false proposition is one which produces failure and frustration. In introducing a reference to satisfactoriness, expediency, practicality and instrumentality in his definition of truth, James drastically alters the complexion of the pragmatism of Peirce's more intellectualistic formulation.

The test, then, of a theory, a belief, a doctrine, must be its effects on us, its practical consequences. This is the *pragmatic* test. Always ask yourself what difference it will make in your experience whether you accept materialism or idealism, determinism or free will, monism or pluralism, atheism or theism. On the one side, it is a doctrine of despair, on the other a doctrine of hope. "On pragmatic principles, if the hypothesis of God works satisfactorily, in the widest sense of the word, it is true." The test of truth, then, is its practical consequences; the possession of truth is not an end in itself, but only a preliminary means to other vital satisfactions. Knowledge is an instrument; it exists for the sake of life, not life for the sake of knowledge. James enlarges this pragmatic or instrumental conception so as to include in the idea of practical utility logical consistency and verification. True ideas are those that we can assimilate, validate, corroborate, and verify. Ideas that tell us which of the realities to expect count as true ideas. We can, therefore, say of truth that it is useful because it is true, or that it is true because it is useful. "Truth in science is what gives us the maximum possible sum of satisfactions, taste included, but consistency both with previous truth and novel fact is always the most imperious claimant." Even

[7] *Pragmatism*, p. 58.

with these important additions to the pragmatic formula, it is anti-intellectualistic in the sense that, in order to be true, a philosophy must satisfy other than logical demands.

The pluralistic universe. Pragmatism is a method of ascertaining truth in all areas, including philosophy; we can best understand the nature of the pragmatic method by an examination of James' own employment of it in the solution of an actual philosophical problem, such as the issue between monism and pluralism. James finds pluralism pragmatically preferable to monism. It was Renouvier's masterly advocacy of pluralism, he tells us, that freed him from the monistic superstition under which he had grown up. The "block-universe," the rigoristic, deterministic systems of both materialistic and idealistic monism, did not satisfy him: "If everything, man included, is the mere effect of the primitive nebula or the infinite substance, what becomes of moral responsibility, freedom of action, individual effort, and aspiration; what, indeed, of need, uncertainty, choice, novelty, and strife?" Does not the individual become a mere puppet in the hands of the absolute substance, whether conceived as universal matter or as universal mind? Such a system cannot satisfy all the demands of our nature, and hence cannot be true. Successful action, then, presupposes the recognition of variety and diversity in the world about us; the will would be paralyzed in the presence of a completely unified and undifferentiated absolute. And the practical moral and religious demands favor pluralism, freedom and individualism, idealism and theism, according to James. These are the conceptions in which the will believes and to save which James repudiates the intellect as the absolute judge of truth. Still, consistency is always the most imperious claimant.

Although the absolutistic hypothesis that perfection is eternal, aboriginal, and most real, has a perfectly definite meaning and works in the realm of religion, the pluralistic way is most consonant with the pragmatic temper, for it sets definite activities at work. A pluralistic world can only be saved piecemeal and *de facto* as the result of the behavior of a lot of "eaches." We may believe, also, that there is a form of experience higher than our human experience extant in the universe; on the evidence of religious experience we may well believe that higher powers exist and are at work to save the world and that they operate along lines similar to human minds in the pursuit of ideal ends.

James reaches the same results from another side, from the side of radical or pure empiricism, which opposes both the classical rationalism and the classical English empiricism. It is not true that whatever is rational is real; rather, *whatever is experienced is real*. We must take experience as it exists before it has been manipulated by conceptual thinking—experience in its purity and pristine innocence—if we would reach reality. We must go behind the conceptual function altogether and look to the more primitive flux of the sensational life for reality's true shape. Philosophy should seek this kind of living understanding of the movement of reality and not follow science in vainly patching together fragments of its dead results. Philosophy is more a matter of passionate vision than of logic; logic only finds reasons for the vision afterwards.

With German idealism James agrees that the scientific understanding mutilates reality, and that our ordinary sense experience does not reveal reality in its true colors. But, not unlike Bradley, he puts his faith in a living unsophisticated human experience. Reality is *pure* experience independent of human thinking; it is something very hard to find; it is what is just entering into experience and yet to be named, or else it is some imagined aboriginal presence in experience, before any belief about the presence has arisen, before any human conception has been applied. It is what is absolutely dumb and evanescent, the merely ideal limit of our minds. We may glimpse it, but we can never grasp it; what we grasp is always some substitute for it which previous human thinking has peptonized and cooked for our consumption. Yet, this immediate experience is a unity in diversity; the unity is as original as the diversity. Empiricism is, therefore, wrong in saying that our psychic life consists of a multiplicity of independent sensations, and rationalism is wrong in saying that these are combined by categories resident in the soul. The belief in a combining medium called soul is superfluous, because there are no independent elements to combine. Both conceptions are abstractions. Reality is, in part, the flux of our sensations, coming we know not whence; partly, the relations that obtain between our sensations; and, partly, previous truths. Some of these relations are mutable and accidental, others are fixed and essential, but both are matters of immediate perception. Relations and categories are objects of direct experience, not different from the things or phenomena; ideas and things are "consubstantial," made of the same neutral stuff.

James seems to vacillate between two views: reality is pure experience, experience independent of all thought, to which the life of the infant or semi-comatose person approximates; and reality is the entire field of the adult consciousness, experience permeated with thought. Perhaps his meaning is that the latter form grows out of the former. There *is* a sensible flux, he tells us, but what is true of it seems from first to last largely a matter of our own creation. The world stands malleable and waiting to receive its final touches at our hands. Reality is not ready-made and complete from all eternity, but still in the making, unfinished, growing in all sort of places where thinking beings are at work. Truth grows up inside all the finite centers of experience; minds lean on each other, but the totality of them, if such there be, leans on nothing. Nothing outside of the flux secures the issue of it; it can hope for salvation only from its own intrinsic promises and potencies. Behind the bare phenomenal facts there is nothing, no thing-in-itself, no absolute, no unknowable; it is absurd to attempt to explain the given concrete reality by an assumed reality of which we can form no idea except through symbols drawn from our experience itself. This sounds like subjective idealism, but it is not intended as such by James, who never doubted the existence of an extra-mental world; the pure original experience is not subjective, but objective; it is the primordial stuff from which consciousness emerges.

Radical empiricism makes for pluralism: experience shows us multiplicity, diversity, opposition, and not a block-universe, not the completely organized harmonious system of the absolutists or monists, in which all differences and oppositions are reconciled. Besides, the pluralistic universe satisfies the demands of our moral nature, which the absolutistic universe does not; pluralism is justified by the pragmatic method. Indeed, monism, too, is not a mere doctrine of the intellect; its acceptance depends on its consequences, it satisfies the esthetic and mystical impulses of some men. But it does not account for our finite consciousness; it creates a problem of evil; it does not account for change; and it is fatalistic. Pluralism takes perceptual experience at its face value, and the concrete perceptual flux, taken just as it comes, offers in our own activity-situations perfectly comprehensible instances of causal agency or free will. There is room for change, for novelty, for the unconditioned and the fortuitous in the world; this is the doctrine known as tychism or fortuitism. James' pluralism is melioristic; meliorism seeks a compromise between both optimism and pessimism: the world is neither good nor evil, but can be improved on the condition that its parts do their best to improve it. The melioristic universe is conceived after a social analogy, as a pluralism of independent powers. It will succeed just in the proportion in which more of these work for its success. If none work, it will fail; if each does his best, it will not fail. And in such a world man is free to take risks in realizing his ideal.

Theism is the only conception of God that will satisfy our emotional and volitional nature. God is a part of the universe, a sympathetic and powerful helper, the great Companion, a conscious, personal, and moral being of the same nature as ourselves, with whom we can come into communion, as certain experiences, such as sudden conversions, show. This conception of God harmonizes with James' meliorism. God is not, as the optimist supposes, the guarantor of the goodness of the world, but is a powerful ally in our efforts to combat evil. Thus God is good but not all-powerful; James subscribes to the finitist theory of God. To be sure, this theistic hypothesis cannot be completely proved, but neither can any system of philosophy be proved; each one is rooted in the will to believe. The essence of faith is not feeling or intelligence, but will, the will to believe what cannot be scientifically demonstrated or refuted.

Philosophical Psychology. James' great work, *The Principles of Psychology,* is not merely a treatise on psychology in the narrowly scientific sense, but is likewise a significant contribution to the broader philosophical issues regarding the nature and function of mind. His psychology is, indeed, a philosophical psychology or a philosophy of mind which, in the course of its analysis of the facts of the mental life, raises and offers at least tentative solutions to the major issues regarding the mind, consciousness, the self, and the freedom of the will. James was firmly convinced that introspection, i.e., the reflective and retrospective examination by the mind of its contents and operations, while not the sole method of psychological investigation, is an indispensable technique in psychology. It is the mind's scrutiny of its own processes and activities. James believed that self-observation, difficult though it be, is possible and will yield scientifically valid results and James himself was an introspectionist of incomparable subtlety and accuracy. But the introspective method was not intended by James to supersede the physiological and experimental methods in psychology. His medical training had impressed upon him the functional dependence of the consciousness upon bodily, and more particularly brain, conditions. The basic postulate of his psychology is that "no mental modification ever occurs which is not accompanied or followed by bodily change." [8] Introspection, then, is a supplement to but not a substitute for laboratory measurement of bodily responses. This explains the apparent anomaly that James, the champion of the introspective method in psychology, paved the way for the behavioristic school of John B. Watson, which repudiated introspection as delusive and unscientific, and relied solely on an observational technique restricted to behavior.

[8] *The Principles of Psychology,* Vol. I, p. 5.

James' introspective discoveries were truly remarkable; he discriminated conscious phenomena which had either entirely eluded earlier psychologists or had only been vaguely adumbrated by them. Many of his introspective insights are not only psychologically important, but are of far-reaching philosophical significance. James' conception of the "stream of consciousness," one of his most characteristic insights, contrasts with the traditional psychological and philosophical accounts of the nature of the mind, viz., sensationalism and spiritualism. Sensationalism or associationism treated the mind as a mere collection of discrete ideas which combine and recombine in varying ways. The mind is, according to the formula of David Hume, a mere "bundle" of impressions and ideas. James rejects this interpretation because of its failure to do justice to the unity of the conscious life of the mind. Spiritualism, the opposing theory, posits a substantial soul behind the conscious processes. This theory is in James' opinion the victim of obscurantism: there is no empirical, or introspective evidence, for such a principle. As an alternative to both these views he proposed his doctrine of the stream of consciousness, which considers the mind a unity in and of the conscious processes themselves.

In his famous essay "Does Consciousness Exist?", James replied with an emphatic "No" to the question posed in the title—that is, if by consciousness one means some sort of an entity or mind-stuff. But if by consciousness one means a functional unity, then it does unquestionably exist. Whitehead, in appraising this essay, has suggested that James' new functional concept of consciousness effected a revolution in psychology and philosophy comparable to Descartes' *cogito,* which inaugurated the modern era in philosophy.[9]

James' contribution to the psychology of volition is no less revolutionary than his new conception of consciousness. The will had been traditionally regarded as a mysterious faculty concealed in the depths of the soul, whose decisions are arbitrary and inscrutable. James is distrustful of the obscurantism of the faculty psychology; he brings the will out into the light of day by describing the processes of deliberation and by relating them to other phases of the conscious life. Volition is not an isolated phenomenon, unrelated to the rest of consciousness; it is, rather, a specification of a general trait of consciousness, namely, the tendency of all ideas to eventuate in action unless they are prevented from so doing by rival and conflicting ideas. James gave the name "ideo-motor action" to the inherent tendency of ideas to produce movement; every act of will is an instance of ideo-motor action.

[9] Cf. Whitehead, *Science and the Modern World,* pp. 205 ff.

The essence of volition lies in the ability of the mind to focus its attention on one idea to the exclusion of all others. When this has been accomplished, overt action automatically ensues. Thus the freedom of the will is the ability of the mind to control its effort of attention. James believes, for reasons into which we need not enter, that the human will is free. But whether or not we accept this final conclusion, we must regard his analysis of the volitional act as psychologically illuminating and as affording a context for the consideration of the free-will problem. James' psychological account of the will is also important because it gives us a clue to his later pragmatism. It is beyond dispute that James was led to pragmatism by the essential voluntarism of his psychological theories. In his famous chapter on reasoning in the second volume of *The Principles of Psychology,* in place of the barren formalism and intellectualism of a strictly logical interpretation of reasoning, he offers a psychological description of the reasoning processes in terms of sagacity. Reasoning is a form of problem-solving, the aim of which is the adaptation of man to his environment. There is latent in his psychology of reasoning James' own pragmatic conception of knowledge, and Dewey's instrumentalist theory of inquiry.

The Principles of Psychology, 2 vols., 1890; *The Will to Believe,* 1897; *Human Immortality,* 1898; *Talks to Teachers,* 1899; *Varieties of Religious Experience,* 1902; *Pragmatism,* 1907; *The Meaning of Truth,* 1909; *A Pluralistic Universe,* 1909; *Some Problems of Philosophy,* 1911; *Memories and Studies,* 1911; *Essays in Radical Empiricism,* 1912; *Collected Essays and Reviews,* 1920; (with C. G. Lange) *The Emotions,* 1922; *Selected Papers on Philosophy,* 1929.

The Philosophy of William James, ed. by Horace M. Kallen (*Modern Library*) contains selections from James' writings; *The Varieties of Religious Experience* is available in the *Modern Library,* and *The Principles of Psychology* is now available in a single volume edition. See *The Letters of William James,* ed. by Henry James, 1920; R. B. Perry's distinguished work, *The Thought and Character of William James,* 1935; R. B. Perry, *Annotated Bibliography of the Writings of William James,* 1920.

A. Menard, *Analyse et critique des "Principes de la Psychologie" de W. James,* 1911; J. Royce, *William James,* 1912; H. V. Knox, *The Philosophy of William James,* 1914; J. S. Bixler, *Religion in the Philosophy of William James,* 1926; R. B. Perry, *In the Spirit of William James,* 1938; J. M. Moore, *Theories of Religious Experience,* 1938; A. A. Roback, *William James, His Marginalia, Personality and Contribution,* 1942.

Dewey's Instrumentalism and Experimentalism. John Dewey (1859-1952) labels his version of pragmatism "instrumentalism" or "experimentalism," and describes its basic aim and method in these words: *"Instrumentalism is an attempt to constitute a precise logical theory of concepts, of judgments and inferences in their various forms, by considering primarily how thought* *functions in the experimental determination of future consequences."* [10] The essential feature of pragmatism in its instrumentalist version is its reference to consequences. "The term 'pragmatic' means only the rule of referring all thinking, all reflective considerations, to *consequences* for final meaning and test." [11] The meaning of a judgment consists of its anticipated consequences and its truth is established by the actual verification of these. Thus a judgment of any type—including a categorical judgment of fact— is to be construed as a set of hypothetical judgments embodying anticipated consequences of the judgment in question: "All propositions which state discoveries or ascertainments, all categorical propositions, would be hypothetical, and their truth would coincide with their tested consequences . . ." [12] The consequences by which the meaning and truth of a judgment is tested are not, according to Dewey, restricted to those yielding an emotional or esthetic satisfaction; his version of pragmatism "is not complicated by reference to emotional satisfactions or the play of desires." [13] A proposition may be instrumentally or experimentally true even though emotionally uncongenial to the individual investigator.

The instrumentalist theory advanced in Dewey's early logical essays persists in *The Quest for Certainty*, 1929, and receives its most systematic formulation in *Logic: The Theory of Inquiry*, published in 1938. In the first of these works, the instrumentalist position is cast in the language of the operational theory of the meaning of scientific concepts advanced by P. W. Bridgman. Dewey quotes with approval Bridgman's contention that "we mean by any concept nothing more than a set of operations; *the concept is synonymous with the corresponding set of operations.*" [14] Combining the operational technique of conceptual definition with the pragmatic emphasis on consequences, Dewey proposes a "definition of the nature of ideas in terms of operations to be performed and the test of the validity of ideas by the *consequences* of these operations . . ." [15] Thus operationalism complements and reinforces the instrumentalism and experimentalism of Dewey's earlier pragmatic theory. Dewey credits the operational theory with having

[10] *Studies in the History of Ideas*, Vol. II, pp. 353-371; reprinted in D. S. Robinson, *Anthology of Recent Philosophy*, pp. 431-445, and D. D. Runes, *Twentieth Century Philosophy*, pp. 451-468.

[11] *Essays in Experimental Logic*, p. 330.

[12] *Op. cit.*, p. 347.

[13] *Loc. cit.*

[14] Quoted by Dewey in *The Quest for Certainty*, p. 111, from Bridgman, *The Logic of Modern Physics*, p. 5.

[15] *Op. cit.*, p. 114.

achieved for the first time "an empirical theory of ideas free from the burdens imposed alike by sensationalism and *a priori* rationalism" [16] and believes that, historically considered, operationalism has successfully effected the reconciliation of rationalism and empiricism which Kant so boldly but unsuccessfully attempted. Dewey glowingly describes the achievement of operationalism and allied theories of scientific inquiry as "one of three or four outstanding feats of intellectual history." [17]

In his impressive work, *Logic: The Theory of Inquiry,* Dewey brings to fruition the research in logic which he first presented over forty years ago in his early essays on logical theory. In this work he avoids the word pragmatism because of the many misconceptions associated with this label, but observes in his "Preface" that "in the proper interpretation of 'pragmatic,' namely the function of consequences as necessary tests of the validity of propositions, *provided* these consequences are operationally initiated and are such as to resolve the specific problem evoking the operations, the text that follows is thoroughly pragmatic." Here again we see that Dewey has grafted the operational theory of conceptual and propositional meaning onto his basic instrumentalism, and that the result is a healthy logical organism. The basic forms, laws and principles of logic are interpreted in this operational context as postulates or stipulations. Dewey repudiates the rationalists' claim that the basic laws of logic are a priori principles, and holds that "they are intrinsically postulates of and for inquiry, being formulations of conditions, discovered in the course of inquiry itself, which further inquiries must satisfy if they are to yield warranted assertibility as a consequence." [18] As postulates or stipulations, the laws of logic are no more arbitrary than the law of contracts "regulating in advance the making of certain kinds of business engagements." [19] The postulational interpretation of logical principles thus places logical form in the context of concrete, empirical situations and, at the same time, accounts for their regulative function emphasized by rationalistic theories.

Dewey's instumentalism is no less radical than James' pragmatism in forcing a drastic revision of the older philosophical conceptions. Dewey does not tire of flouting the methods and conclusions of traditional metaphysics and epistemology, which he conceives as aiming at realities lying behind and beyond the process of nature, and as carrying on the search for these realities by means of rational forms transcending ordinary modes of perception and inference. Such problems, he thinks, have no real meaning,

[16] *Loc. cit.*
[17] *Loc. cit.*
[18] *Op. cit.,* p. 16.
[19] *Op. cit.,* p. 17.

and cannot, therefore, be solved; they vanish under critical examination. He protests against setting up a universe, in analogy with the cognitive side of human nature, as a system of fixed elements in fixed relations, be they mechanical, sensational, or conceptual, and making all the other phases of man's nature—beliefs, aversions, affections—mere epiphenomena, appearances, subjective impressions or effects in consciousness; he also protests against a purely phenomenalistic account of concrete selves, specific feeling and willing beings and the beliefs to which they give their allegiance; and against a world-view in which man's strivings are already eternally fulfilled, his errors already eternally transcended, his partial beliefs already eternally comprehended, in which need, uncertainty, choice, novelty, strife have no place. Reality is for him, the evolutionist, not a completely given, ready-made, fixed system, not a system at all, but changing, growing, developing things. Philosophy must renounce inquiry into absolute origins and absolute finalities in order to explore specific values and specific conditions that generate them. The sole verifiable and fruitful object of knowledge is the particular set of changes that generate the object of inquiry, together with the consequences that flow from it. No intelligible question can be asked about what is assumed to lie outside—about the whole essence behind specific changes, about an intelligence that shaped things once for all, or about the good as an ultimate goal. The questions of interest to the evolutionistic philosopher are not the old questions of ontology, but practical, living, moral, and social questions: how specific changes serve or defeat concrete purposes, how things are even now shaping particular intelligences, how to realize the direct increments of justice and happiness that intelligent administration of existent conditions may beget and that present carelessness or stupidity will destroy or reduce. To idealize and rationalize the universe at large is to shift upon the shoulders of the transcendent a burden of responsibility which should be borne by the intelligence of man.

This does not mean that instrumentalism is committed to metaphysical skepticism, and we find in Dewey's later writings, particularly in *Experience and Nature* (1925), and *The Quest for Certainty* (1929), an acknowledgment of the validity of certain metaphysical and ontological speculations, and even a willingness, though with many reservations, to engage in epistemological conjecture. "The naturalistic method, when consistently followed, destroys things once cherished . . . But its main purport is not destructive; empirical naturalism is rather a winnowing fan." [20] By pursuing

[20] *Experience and Nature*, p. iii.

the method of empirical naturalism, Dewey finds that experience and nature are not alien, as the modern philosophical tradition, stemming from Descartes, had insisted, but rather that experience, when intelligently used and properly understood, affords a means of discovering the realities of nature. The dualistic isolation of experience and nature rendered the body-mind question "an insoluble mystery"; in its Cartesian formulation the body-mind problem is indeed a pseudo-problem. When the essential continuity of experience and nature, of the individual self and the external world is acknowledged, the body-mind problem is resolved. The human organism is now viewed in its dynamic connection with nature, and the linkage between mind and nature, in both thought and action, becomes quite understandable. The continuity of mind and nature does not preclude a separation of psychological and physical inquiries; it does, however, assist us in unifying the results of psychology on the one hand, and of physics and biology on the other.

According to Dewey, philosophy must become a method of moral and political diagnosis and prognosis—the world is in the making, and we must help in the process. Such a new philosophy calls for a revision of the theory of thinking, for a new evolutionary logic which frankly starts out from the conception of thinking *as inquiring* and purely external existences as terms in inquiries. The revised theory of thinking will construe validity, objectivity, truth—both the test and the system of truth—in terms of what they actually mean and do within the inquiry-activity. Dewey sees in thinking an instrument for the removal of collisions between what is given and what is wanted—a means of realizing human desire, of securing an arrangement of things which means satisfaction, fulfillment, happiness. Such a harmony is the end and test of thinking: success in this sense is the goal of thought. When the ideas, views, conceptions, hypotheses, and beliefs which we frame succeed, secure harmony and adjustment, we call them true. Successful ideas are true. We keep on transforming, changing our ideas until they work, that is, we make them true, *verify* them. The effective working of an idea, its success, is its truth. When one says the idea works, it is the same as saying it is true. Successful working is the essential characteristic of a true idea, and the success of the idea is not the cause nor the evidence of its truth, but is truth itself: the successful idea is a true idea. The test or criterion of truth lies in the harmonized reality effected by the idea. Whenever, by a process of inquiry, an idea has been tested and has made good, there results a change in concrete existence, a completed or harmonized situation. We must not, however, separate the achieved existence from its process. When an idea is taken just as given, separated from its process, it is neither a truth nor a criterion of truth, but merely a state of facts like any other.

Thinking serves human purposes, is useful, removes collision, satisfies desire; and its utility, its teleology, is its truth. The human will, in other words, instigates thinking, which is an instrument for realizing human aims. The so-called fixities such as atoms or God—have existence and import only in the problems, needs, struggles, and instrumentalities of conscious agents and patients. We have a universe in which uncertainty, doubt, and other personal attitudes really inhere.

The revision of the theory of thinking also brings the principle of belief into its own. Belief—sheer, direct, unmitigated personal belief—reappears in science as working-hypothesis. Beliefs are the most natural and most metaphysical of all things; knowledge is the human and practical outgrowth of belief, an organized technique for working out the implications and interrelations of beliefs, and for directing their formation and employment. Beliefs, therefore, modify and shape reality; and empirical conscious beings genuinely determine existences. If this is so, there is no need to fear that natural sciences are going to encroach upon and destroy our spiritual values, because we can always translate values into existences—social and political institutions. The world in which Dewey is interested is the practical, social world of living, working individuals.

The instrumentalist theory of inquiry renders meaningless most of the focal issues of epistemology which divide contemporary epistemologists into the rival ranks of realists and idealists. In very much the same way in which Dewey's rejection of Cartesian dualism and his insistence on the continuity of experience and nature destroyed a whole nest of metaphysical problems—especially those concerned with the body-mind relation—so refusal to separate sharply the knowing subject and the object known circumvents the issues between the idealists and realists, between the immediatists and the representationists in epistemology. As early as 1917, in his contribution to *Creative Intelligence,* the cooperative volume issued by the American pragmatists, Dewey regarded the issues which divide the epistemologists as pseudo-problems arising from their initial separation of subject and object in knowledge. In Dewey's opinion "the chief divisions of modern philosophy, idealism in its different kinds, realism of various brands, so called commonsense dualism, agnosticism, relativism, phenomenalism, have grown around the general relation of subject and object." And, he asks, "Is it not time that philosophers turned from the attempt to determine the comparative merits of various replies to the questions to a consideration of the claims of the questions?" [21] Epistemological questions regarding the subjectivity or objectivity of sense data, the direct or representational character of perception, arise from the false assumption that consciousness is something outside nature, watching it as a detached spectator. Dewey also vehemently attacks the doctrine of the atomicity of sense data shared by sensationalism and many forms of new realism. The analysis of sense data may be legitimate for certain purposes, but theories which depart from atomistic sense data rather than ordinary perception of things thereby generate artificial and insoluble problems. Instrumentalism does not altogether preclude significant epistemological inquiry, provided the point of departure for such inquiry is "the objects of everyday experience, the concrete things of the world in which we live and which, from the standpoint of our practical affairs, our enjoyments and sufferings, form the world we live in." [22] Departing from the objects of everyday experience, Dewey describes the inferences whereby we proceed to scientific objects, such as atoms and electrons; to ascribe existence and properties to such scientific objects is merely to make predictions regarding perceptions to be had under specified conditions. Dewey adopts an operational interpretation of statements about physical objects and thereby circumvents the perplexing epistemological problem regarding the relation between perceptual objects and physical or scientific objects.

The world is in the making and will always be in the making, we shape it to our ends, and in this process the thinking and belief of conscious personal beings play an active part. It is to be remembered that, for Dewey, knowing is not the sole and genuine mode of experiencing. All things are what they are experienced as being, and every experience is something. Things are experienced as known, but they are also experienced esthetically, morally, economically, and technologically; hence, to give a just account of anything is to tell what that particular thing is experienced as. This is the fundamental postulate of immediate empiricism—Dewey's equivalent of James' radical empiricism. If we want to find out what any philosophical term—subjective, objective, physical, mental, cosmic, cause, substance, purpose, activity, evil, being, quantity—means, we must go to experience and see what it is experienced as. The individual is not merely a knower, but an emotional, impulsive, willing being; the reflective attitude is evoked by the will, the basal or primal side of the self.

[21] *Creative Intelligence,* p. 34.
[22] *The Quest for Certainty,* p. 195.

Psychology, 1887; *Leibniz's "New Essays,"* 1902; (with J. H. Tufts) *Ethics,* 1908; *The Influence of Darwin on Philosophy,* 1910; *How We Think,* 1910; *German Philosophy and Politics,* 1915; *Essays in Experimental Logic,* 1916; *Democracy and Education,* 1916; (with other pragmatists) *Creative Intelligence,* 1917; *Reconstruction in Philosophy,* 1920; *Human Nature and Conduct,* 1922; *Experience and Nature,* 1925; *The Public and Its Problems,* 1927; *The Quest for Certainty,* 1929; *Philosophy and Civilization,* 1931; *Art as Experience,* 1934; *Logic: The Theory of Inquiry,* 1938.

Intelligence in the Modern World: John Dewey's Philosophy, ed. with an Introduction by J. Ratner, 1928 (contains selections from Dewey's writings); M. H. Thomas, *A Bibliography of John Dewey,* 1882-1939; A. W. Moore, *Pragmatism and Its Critics,* 1910; D. T. Howard, *John Dewey's Logical Theory,* 1918; W. T. Feldman, *The Philosophy of John Dewey,* 1934; S. Hook, *John Dewey,* 1939; "A Symposium of Reviews of John Dewey's *Logic: The Theory of Inquiry,*" *The Journal of Philosophy,* Vol. XXXVI, No. 21 (Oct. 12, 1939); P. A. Schilpp (ed.), *The Philosophy of John Dewey* (Library of Living Philosophers), 1939; S. S. White, *A Comparison of the Philosophies of F. C. S. Schiller and John Dewey,* 1940; M. G. White, *The Origin of Dewey's Instrumentalism,* 1943; H. S. Thayer, *The Logic of Pragmatism: an Examination of John Dewey's Logic,* 1952; J. L. Childs, *American Pragmatism and Education,* 1956.

Conceptual Pragmatism and Contextualism. Clarence Irving Lewis (1883- ; Professor of Philosophy at Harvard University from 1930 until his retirement in 1953) has formulated a version of the pragmatic theory of meaning, knowledge, and verification, which greatly strengthens the theoretical foundations of the pragmatic philosophy. His position, which he calls conceptual pragmatism, avails itself of the techniques of modern symbolic logic, and may very well prove to be the definitive formulation of the pragmatic theory of knowledge. In his earlier work, *Mind and the World Order,* published in 1929, Lewis formulates the principal thesis of conceptual pragmatism as follows: "There are in our cognitive experience, two elements, the immediate data, such as those of sense, which are presented or given to the mind, and a form, construction or interpretation, which represents the activity of thought." [23] The pragmatic factor in knowledge resides in its formal or a priori aspect, not in its empirical or factual aspect; it consists in the interpretation of experience in terms of categories and concepts which the mind itself determines in respect to human needs. Such concepts and principles are a priori in that they are determinative of experience, though not derivative from it. The pragmatic a priori of Lewis' theory shows the influence of the Kantian theory but is less rigid and absolute than Kant's a priori. Whereas Kant insisted on the validity of a single necessary categorial scheme, Lewis' a priori allows for alternative conceptual systems for the description of experience. "Concepts and principles of interpretation are subject to historical alteration and in terms of them there may be

[23] *Mind and the World Order,* p. 38.

'new truth.' " [24] Lewis' pragmatic theory is further developed in his more recent *Analysis of Knowledge and Valuation,* which proceeds from a theory of meaning to a theory of knowledge and thence to a theory of value. The main contentions of this book are: (1) there are no synthetic a priori statements; a priori statements are without exception obtainable by analysis of their meaning; (2) empirical statements of the "expressive" type formulate directly presented contents of experience, whereas non-expressive empirical statements are to be interpreted, in pragmatic fashion, as predictions of the results of acts; and (3) value judgments are not fundamentally different in their mode of confirmation from other kinds of empirical statements. His pragmatism comes out most clearly in his account of "non-terminating" empirical judgments: the meaning of such a judgment is a set of predictions which involve a never-ending series of consequences. This conception of meaning is a further refinement of Peirce's pragmatic principle.

A Survey of Symbolic Logic, 1918; *Mind and the World-Order,* 1929; *An Analysis of Knowledge and Valuation* (The Paul Carus Lectures, 7th Series), 1946; *The Ground and Nature of the Right,* 1955.

A theory of knowledge which, like Lewis' theory, emphasizes the rôle of postulational systems in the constitution of knowledge has been advanced by F. S. C. Northrop. Northrop (1893-   ) draws a basic distinction between "a concept of intuition," "the complete meaning of which is immediately apprehended" (for example, the sensory concept of "blue" or the introspective concept of "want") and a "concept of postulation," one meaning of which is in whole or in part designated by the postulates of the deductive system in which it occurs" (for example the concept of "electron").[25] The two types of concepts belong to two different universes of discourse, and only confusion and nonsense result from their combination in a single proposition, such as "electrons are blue." Concepts of intuition relate to the "esthetic component" of human knowledge whereas concepts of the postulation pertain to its "theoretic component." Although the two components are quite distinct the assimilation of the esthetic component to the theoretic component is one of the principal tasks of all knowledge, scientific and philosophical. This assimilation is achieved by what Northrop calls an "epistemic" correlation between the intuitional or esthetic component of a thing on the one hand, and its postulational or theoretic component on the other. Despite his reliance on postulational techniques in the formulation of hypotheses,

[24] *Op. cit.,* p. 267.
[25] *The Logic of the Sciences and the Humanities,* p. 128.

Northrop's theory does not, as does Lewis', stress the pragmatic factor involved in the choice among alternative postulational systems, but instead proposes a theory of knowledge and a metaphysics akin to the realistic naturalism of Whitehead. "By the method of hypothesis and its indirect mode of verification we are able to learn of structures and orders of entities in ourselves and nature which have a character other than, and different from, the relatedness and ordering of the immediately sensed qualities in the immediately sensed aesthetic continuum." [26]

Science and First Principles, 1931; *The Meeting of East and West: An Enquiry concerning World Understanding,* 1947; *The Logic of the Sciences and the Humanities,* 1947.

Contextualism. Contextualism is an offspring of pragmatism which, like its parent pragmatism, propounds a relativistic epistemology and emphasizes the conventionalistic and postulational features of knowledge, the rôle of consequences in knowledge, and the fusion of knowledge and action. The view that philosophical systems are alternative hypotheses for the interpretation of all domains of experience—including common sense, science, and value-experience—is advanced by Stephen Pepper in his book, *World-Hypotheses.* He contends that there are four relatively adequate world-hypotheses: (1) formism (the theory of essences or universals); (2) mechanism (as represented by mechanistic and materialistic philosophies); (3) contextualism (a theory of a "textured" reality which is implicit in pragmatism); and (4) organicism (the interpretation of reality as an organically structured whole). Each of these world-hypotheses has its "root-metaphor" or basic analogy, its methodological and epistemological assumptions, and its metaphysical ramification. These four competing world-hypotheses are equal in relative adequacy, for all facts are assimilable to the context of each of the four theories, and no factual evidence is decisive against any one of them. Pepper rejects the conventionalistic view that the rival philosophical hypotheses are mere arbitrary conventions, or postulates, yet his theory of alternative philosophies, in terms of which all facts may be interpreted, seems to betray a postulational or conventionalistic bias. Moreover, despite his emphatic and repeated insistence that all four world-hypotheses are equal in relative adequacy, Pepper displays a strong predilection for contextualism. Contextualism, with its associated pragmatic and conventionalistic theory of knowledge, is the one among the four world-hypotheses most consonant with Pepper's own view that there are alternative philosophical theories.

[26] *The Meeting of East and West,* pp. 451 f.

85. RECENT POSITIVISTIC TENDENCIES

The Attack on Metaphysics. One of the most influential movements in recent philosophy is logical positivism, which originated in "the Vienna Circle" in the early twenties and which has historical affinities with the skeptical empiricism of David Hume and the scientific conventionalism of Mach and Poincaré. The original members of the Vienna Circle were for the most part specialists in fields other than philosophy: Moritz Schlick (1882-1936), the central figure of the school at its inception, had been a physicist, and the original group included specialists in mathematics, history, and sociology, as well as physics.

Logical positivism has, in the course of its brief development, undergone many radical transformations. There is a great diversity among the different representatives of the movement, yet the main outlines of the positivistic position stand out clearly. The central core of positivism is the employment of verifiability as the criterion of meaning: an empirical statement is significant or meaningful, if and only if it is verifiable by appeal to experience. The verifiability principle in its "strongest" form requires that a statement, if it is to be meaningful, should admit of verification or falsification by direct confrontation with experience. Thus the statement: "There is a red patch in my field of vision" is meaningful in this "strong" sense. Schlick and other members of the Vienna Circle insisted on this narrow sense of meaningful; but it proved to be much too restrictive, and positivists now generally accept a wider criterion, which would include indirect as well as direct verifiability, verifiability in principle as well as in practice. General statements such as "unsupported bodies tend to fall," historical statements about an inaccessible past, and statements which are not practically verifiable, such as "there are mountains on the other side of the moon," are yet meaningful in terms of this modified test.

Logical positivism has investigated the formal or a priori aspects of knowledge as well as the empirical or a posteriori ones. On the formal side, it has drawn on the achievements of modern mathematical logic as well as on the techniques of linguistic analysis to support its contention that the a priori in knowledge is analytical or tautological. Positivism, rejecting Kant's claim of the validity of synthetic a priori knowledge, insists with Leibniz that the a priori is always analytic. The only type of legitimate a priori statement is one which expresses a tautology: the whole of formal logic and pure mathematics consists of such tautologies. All cognitively significant statements for the logical positivist are, then, either empirically verifiable statements of fact or tautological statements, depending on the structure of language or other symbolic systems. The most striking philosophical consequence of the positivistic analysis of knowledge is that it rules out as meaningless—literally nonsensical—almost the whole of metaphysics. The works of traditional philosophy are filled with statements which are neither empirical statements of fact nor analytic tautologies, and the positivist is prepared to select almost at random statements from the classical philosophers to illustrate his contention that metaphysics is largely nonsense.

If all or most metaphysical utterances are relegated by the positivistic criterion to a limbo of nonsense, what is the function of philosophy? There are several legitimate tasks for philosophy within a positivistic framework. A philosopher may formulate speculative generalizations of a cosmological sort which derive from the factual evidence of the sciences of physics, astronomy and biology. Conjectures regarding the past history of the physical universe, the origin of life, may be meaningful factual hypotheses, verifiable at least in principle. The positivist is extremely dubious about the validity of cosmological theories, but does not reject them as metaphysical nonsense. There remains for philosophy also the perfectly legitimate task of analysis of philosophical concepts and resultant clarification of philosophical meanings. The positivist could, for example, concede some philosophical significance to the elucidation of the philosophical categories such as possibility, existence, probability, causality, etc. He will, however, construe as purely analytical and tautological the results of such conceptual and "categorial" investigations—they cannot, as Kant supposed, provide a basis and foundation for synthetic a priori knowledge. Philosophical analysis of the linguistic type may be significant and fruitful even though it cannot be expected to yield synthetic truth.

Rudolf Carnap (1891-   ; *Der Logische Aufbau der Welt*, 1928; *Philosophy and Logical Syntax*, 1935; *The Logical Syntax of Language*, 1937) is, at present, the leading figure in the positivistic movement originating in Vienna. He joined the Vienna Circle in 1926, came to the University of Chicago in 1936, and is now at the University of California in Los Angeles. Carnap is largely responsible for the transplantation of neo-positivism to America, where it continues to exert a profound influence on American philosophical thought. Positivism's astonishingly successful adaptation to the American scene is due in part to its inherent vitality and flexibility, and also to its congeniality with such American philosophical tendencies as pragmatism and operationalism. Carnap has given the positivistic position its most vigorous and precise formulation and it is he who is largely responsible for the transformation of the earlier restricted logical positivism into the more flexible and philosophically tolerant logical empiricism of the present day. Logical positivism in its anti-metaphysical phase held that scientific knowledge, consisting of the analytic truths of the formal sciences of logic and mathematics and the factual truths of the empirical sciences, exhausts all possible knowledge; consequently traditional metaphysics, which is neither a formal nor a factual science, is impossible. The problems of metaphysics and epistemology are all pseudo-problems and the solutions proposed by traditional philosophy are meaningless nonsense. Carnap's logical empiricism in its present linguistic form retains the anti-metaphysical claims of the earlier positivism, but differs from it in assigning to philosophy the important task of investigating the structure and function of language. The task of clarifying language and its meaning is carried out in three disciplines: (1) syntax, which is concerned with the formal interconnections of linguistic signs, systematizes the structural rules for the formation of sentences and the rules governing their logical derivation from one another; (2) semantics, which is concerned with the analysis of the meanings of terms and expressions by reference to extra-linguistic facts, and investigates questions pertaining to the empirical meaning and truth of terms and expressions; and (3) pragmatics, which investigates the functions of language in its psychological and sociological contexts.

Positivism has also flourished in England where Ludwig Wittgenstein (1889-1951), author of *Tractatus Logico-Philosophicus* (1921), and *Philosophical Investigations* (1953), has been the dominant figure. The favorable reception of positivism in England as in America is to be accounted for principally by its closeness to Anglo-American empiricism deriving from Hume. In England the analytic and empirical philosophies of G. E. Moore and Bertrand Russell provided a philosophical temper favorable to the reception of positivism in much the same way as, in America, the native pragmatism had prepared the way for the reception of positivism. In the *Tractatus*, the negative and anti-metaphysical theme of positivism receives striking formulation: "Most propositions and questions that have been written about philosophical matters are not false, but nonsensical. We cannot therefore answer questions of this kind at all, but only state their senselessness." [27] Although philosophy considered as a science of true propositions about reality is impossible, since truth of this sort is exhausted by the natural sciences which embrace the totality of all true propositions, philosophy serves the invaluable function of clarifying the meanings conveyed by language: "All philosophy

[27] *Tractatus Logico-Philosophicus*, 4.003.

is a 'critique of language.'" "The object of philosophy is the logical clarification of thoughts . . . A philosophical work consists entirely of elucidations. The result of philosophy is not a number of philosophical propositions, but to make our propositions clear." [28]

Positivism and Ethics. Positivistic analysis has been extended to the fields of ethics and value-theory. There are two ways in which the positivist may assimilate ethical and other valuations to his theory: On the one hand, he may consider ethics as empirical statements about valuations considered as facts; or he may treat ethical statements as non-cognitive. Schlick adopted the first approach in his *Problems of Ethics:* "Value, the good, are mere abstractions, but valuation, approbation, are actual psychic occurrences . . . The problem which we must put at the center of ethics is a purely psychological one." [29] A similar factual, psychological approach to ethics has been offered by J. A. Irving: "Our analysis suggests that the proper method of Ethics would be to study the undeniable moral consciousness as a *fact* . . . Ethics, then must become the science of the moral consciousness." [30] According to this version of positivism, ethics consists of factual, psychological statements about valuations and their moral efficacy in moral and social conduct.

There is another approach to the problem of ethics compatible with the positivistic position, according to which ethical and other valuational statements are viewed as non-cognitive. Thus Ayer asserts that one class of ethical statements—exhortations to moral virtue—"are not propositions at all, but ejaculations or commands which are designed to provoke the reader to action of a certain sort." [31] The statement, "Stealing is wrong," expresses nothing but my disapproval of theft; the sentence, "You ought to tell the truth," is tantamount to a command, "Tell the truth." The function of the ethical words in these cases is purely "emotive." A highly suggestive and original version of the emotive theory of ethics is contained in C. L. Stevenson's *Ethics and Language.* Stevenson's linguistic analysis of ethical statements testifies to the versatility of the positivistic theory and the fruitfulness of positivistic analysis in clarifying non-cognitive as well as cognitive statements.

---

[28] *Op. cit.,* 4.112.

[29] Engl. trans. by D. Rynin, pp. 21 ff.

[30] "Towards Radical Empiricism in Ethics," in *American Philosophy Today and Tomorrow,* ed. by H. M. Kallen and S. Hook, p. 243.

[31] *Language, Truth and Logic,* p. 103.

M. Schlick, "The Future of Philosophy," in *College of Pacific Publications in Philosophy*, 1932; R. Carnap, *Philosophy and Logical Syntax*, 1935, and "Testability and Meaning," in *Philosophy of Science*, 1935-36; M. Schlick, *Fragen der Ethik,* 1930, trans. by D. Rynin under the title of *Problems of Ethics,* 1939, and "Meaning and Verification," in *Philosophical Review,* 1936; A. J. Ayer, *The Foundations of Empirical Knowledge,* 1940; H. Feigl, "Logical Empiricism," in *Twentieth Century Philosophy,* ed. by D. D. Runes, 1943; C. L. Stevenson, *Ethics and Language,* 1944; H. Feigl and W. Sellars, *Readings in Philosophical Analysis,* 1949; G. Bergmann, "Logical Positivism" and "Semantics," in *A History of Philosophical Systems,* ed. by V. Ferm, 1950; J. Joergensen, *The Development of Logical Empiricism,* 1951; R. Von Mises, *Positivism. A Study in Human Understanding,* 1951.

Index